Karin Rohlfs

Import/Export

A Guide to Growth, Profits, and Market Share

HOWARD R. GOLDSMITH

PRENTICE HALL PTR
Englewood Cliffs, New Jersey 07632

Library of Congress Cataloging-in-Publication Data
Goldsmith, Howard R. (Date)
    Import/export : a guide to growth, profits, and market share /
  Howard R. Goldsmith.
        p.   cm.
    Bibliography: p.
    Includes index.
    ISBN 0-13-451865-9
    1. Export marketing—United States. 2. Imports—United States.
3. Foreign trade regulation—United States. I. Title.
HF1416.5.G65 1989
658.8'48'0973—dc 19   88–18021
                                                              CIP

Cover design: Lundgren Graphics, Ltd.
Manufacturing buyer: Mary Ann Gloriande

To Sherri—for all her understanding

Portions of this book have been taken from *How to Make a
Fortune in Import/Export* by Howard R. Goldsmith
(Englewood Cliffs, NJ: Prentice-Hall, 1980)

The publisher offers discounts on this book when ordered
in bulk quantities. For more information, write:
  Special Sales/College Marketing
  Prentice Hall
  College Technical and Reference Division
  Englewood Cliffs, NJ 07632

Printed in the United States of America

20 19 18 17 16 15 14 13

ISBN 0-13-451865-9

PRENTICE-HALL INTERNATIONAL (UK) LIMITED, *London*
PRENTICE-HALL OF AUSTRALIA PTY. LIMITED, *Sydney*
PRENTICE-HALL CANADA INC., *Toronto*
PRENTICE-HALL HISPANOAMERICANA, S.A., *Mexico*
PRENTICE-HALL OF INDIA PRIVATE LIMITED, *New Delhi*
PRENTICE-HALL OF JAPAN, INC., *Tokyo*
SIMON & SCHUSTER ASIA PTE. LTD., *Singapore*
EDITORA PRENTICE-HALL DO BRASIL, LTDA., *Rio de Janeiro*

Contents

Foreword

The attention being focused on the trade deficit of the United States (and the surpluses of its trading partners) is not unwarranted. Many reasons are attributed to the enormity of the imbalance. Internally, in the United States, local, state, and federal governments point their fingers at unfair trading practices of other nations. Externally, other nations point their fingers at the value of the U.S. dollar, complacency of U.S. manufacturers with their own marketplace, and laziness in marketing internationally. Everybody points to some of the "inequities" of the levels of natural resources, attitudes in enterprise, customs, and so on. The list of "reasons" goes on.

From my vantage point, it appears that a lot of rhetoric is being bandied about, yet very little is done about the actual condition. The change in the value of the U.S. dollar against other major world currencies has stimulated a reversal of the trend toward a larger U.S. annual trade deficit. But the largest portion of the grains from the reduction of that deficit has been accrued to the large U.S. companies already established in the international arena.

Small- and medium-size companies are intimidated by the complexities of international trade. Actual trade barriers are one thing. Financing is a significant deterrent, but not insurmountable. But the perceived barriers of eternal bureaucratic bumbling (ours and theirs), paperwork (ours and theirs), long distance trade and relationships (including phone calls), shipping, delivery, order minimums, and political instability do more to prevent the United States from recovering at a more rapid and secure rate than many of the actual barriers. The unfortunate reality of this is that many companies just do not want to bother if it is so difficult to accomplish, regardless of how much money can be made at it.

Many people knowledgeable in international trade are trying to help. There are hundreds of books on virtually every aspect of importing and exporting. Many are get-rich-quick schemes, or "How I" books to teach you "How You" can do the same thing. Others are tomes that serve as great reference guides. But publications that are useful tools in getting from A to Z with all the maps provided are gold nuggets in a field of limestone.

Such is the case with *Import/Export: A Guide to Growth, Profits, and Market Share.* It is truly a guide in that Mr. Goldsmith provides for the small- and medium-size companies that are relatively or completely new to the international trade arena, a step-by-step directive to simplify procedures that otherwise intimidate prospective importers and exporters.

In everyday language, Mr. Goldsmith offers suggestions for the obvious and not so obvious. Someone with no knowledge of importing or exporting can open this book and in a few minutes determine whether the international arena is suitable for his or her company. A questionnaire provided by the author on pages 3–5 will help the prospective trader make an important decision about importing and exporting. Once the decision to go on is made, Mr. Goldsmith takes the reader "by the hand," providing names and places, shipping and customs hints, sample letters-of-credit, trade data (statistics and sources), and many practical suggestions.

Pricing of a product, a large stumbling block for many exporters, and normally not discussed at length in other publications, is detailed for the reader, complete with forms for pricing determination. Government, customs, and shipping forms, which in other publications often are not filled out (or if they are, are not explained), are also discussed in detail. The Appendices at the back of the book serve as a directory for the reader, to aid in the search for any additional information or help.

Mr. Goldsmith has given the business community a timely road map for international traders. Although no author could provide a complete "atlas" for trading every product with every country in the world, Mr. Goldsmith has given us a tool that can facilitate any company's entry into international trading and take away the fears of doing so.

This text will occupy a space in my library and will be highly recommended to my clients. *Import/Export: A Guide to Growth, Profits, and Market Share* is a "must" compendium for anyone seriously contemplating international trade.

Paul T. Snapp
Associate Publisher
Editor
Showcase USA
Sell Overseas America

Preface

My purpose in writing this book is to give those people interested in international trade a practical guide—not just the operational aspects of the business, but what steps are necessary to become successful in a very competitive environment.

My reasoning is based on the belief that corporate America cannot nor will not become world traders. This is evidenced by the large volume of exports handled by Japanese and European companies with U.S. operations. It is your small- and medium-size U.S. companies or individuals with an entrepreneurial flair that have the momentum and drive to meet today's international challenges.

In this book I have outlined a basic map for both the importer and exporter. Those without fear of failure and the unknown can follow the signposts to their goals.

ACKNOWLEDGMENTS

I offer my thanks to Lori Adams (A & W International Customs Brokers), Ed Koblentz and Dan Young (U.S. Department of Commerce), Emilia Tomaszewski (American Export Register), Helga Weschke (Trade INFLO), Jim Gibbs (Excel International Forwarders), and Ted Johnson (Metrobank). Their help in completing this book is truly appreciated.

Howard R. Goldsmith

Chapter One

Is International Trade for You?

The purpose of this book is to discuss the most important points of international trading, to supply information that will enable you to decide if import-export is "right" for you, and to learn how to access the information necessary to start this type of business.

As you know from reading the newspapers, changes in trade situations can happen at anytime, such as President Reagan's not allowing goods from Iran into the United States. Although these situations happen on occasion, the long-range potential for making money in import/export is growing year by year. The world is getting smaller (time-wise); products and services that were never available in some parts of the world are now reaching more and more markets.

In 1987 alone, the United States exported $253 billion worth of goods, while importing, unfortunately, a great deal more. Products generally thought impossible to export from the United States are currently making their way to foreign markets. For example, American Honda is exporting cars from their Ohio manufacturing facility to the Far East because of the *lower cost of production. Ford will be test marketing the Taurus in the Japanese market in the near future.*

Ironically, with the devaluation of the dollar, many importers who depend on foreign components to manufacture their products are having trouble finding domestic alternative resources. Recently, a U.S. color copier company went looking for a supplier to make a low-cost unit but was forced to stay with their overseas component supplier as there was no U.S. competitor.

The world of import/export is ever changing. You must be able to regroup and alter plans to meet current needs. Therefore, you must have different suppliers available to take advantage of new opportunities.

1

The funding for your business can be handled in two ways. You can act as a broker or agent (intermediary) and receive commissions for your effort, or, as is most common for importers, you can purchase goods from overseas sources. In either case, you can start small (even on a part-time basis) and increase your activities as your funds permit. I've had clients who started with only $1,000 and others that needed $150,000 initial seed money.

EXPORTING: YOUR CHANCES OF SUCCESS

Most American firms do not export because they (1) lack information about overseas markets, (2) lack proper financing, or (3) have no long-term commitment to export sales (caused by fear of the unknown and provincialism). Therefore, individuals and companies willing to provide the know-how to firms that haven't exported can develop a profitable business. The opportunities today abound when you look at the statistics:

- Some 90 percent of all U.S. firms sell domestically, only.
- Approximately 2,000 U.S. companies account for 70 percent of U.S. manufactured exports.
- About 250 of the above account for 85 percent of dollar value.
- Exporting accounts for only 5.1 percent of the U.S. GNP; in Japan, 10.5 percent; United Kingdom, 19.3 percent; West Germany, 25.9 percent; and Canada, 25.1 percent.
- Exporters keep more than 5.4 million people employed in the United States—25,000 workers for every $1 billion of exports.

In the last few years the "Made in U.S.A." label has not *automatically* commanded the reputation for high quality, style, and so on. However, American products are still much in demand overseas. In the September 28, 1987 issue of *Business America* (U.S. Department of Commerce) publication, the following appeared: "Sales opportunities in Italy for consumer goods ranging from kitchen utensils, sports clothing to selected foods are good. Italy looks favorably upon U.S. lifestyles . . . leisure and sports fields especially among the youth" is just one example of opportunities awaiting those with the imagination and drive to act.

IMPORTING: YOUR CHANCES OF SUCCESS

Currently U.S. imports have reached levels above $400 billion a year. Motor vehicles and parts, consumer electronics, ADP (data processing) equipment, office machinery and parts, telecommunications equipment, apparel, and footwear are some of the most important product categories.

Japan has become the largest U.S. supplier of manufactured goods, followed by Canada, West Germany, Taiwan and South Korea. This, of course, is no surprise to those following the current debate over the trade deficit.

Interestingly, as foreign exporters reach their quota limits on products, they are switching manufacturers' locations. Recently, several Hong Kong clothing firms have built plants in the Caribbean to ease their quota problems.

As with exports, many companies are just too busy to handle transportation, documentation, and financing when dealing with overseas suppliers. Again, if you select products carefully (in person or through catalogs) and study the domestic market, you can find many opportunities to profit from selling consumer or industrial goods. If you are an established company looking to broaden your supplier base, similar opportunities abound.

Now, before learning about selecting products, studying markets, and using the correct documentation, you should do a bit of self-examination. The next section will help you focus on your strengths and weaknesses for starting such a business.

PREPARING YOURSELF TO BE AN IMPORTER/EXPORTER

Like other trades, the import/export business makes certain demands on its practitioners. Some of them, like initiative, responsibility, and problem solving, are in common with other businesses. Others are special. The greater your needs and desires for success, the more important all these qualities become.

Before you make a firm decision to start your own import/export firm, you should consider whether your personality can deal both with the problems of starting any new business and with the unique demands of international trade.

Below is a questionnaire. Read it carefully, and try to test yourself objectively. The test isn't very scientific. It is only meant to make you think about yourself and your basic nature. After rating yourself, ask a friend to have you rated anonymously by several people who know you—people who can and will evaluate you objectively. The results may startle you, but consider them seriously. *Remember:* You are considering risking your money and your or your company's time; you are considering making contractual promises to others. You are starting something, and you should be able to finish it.

Rating Scale for the Potential Importer/Exporter

Instructions: After each question, place a check mark on the line at the point closest to your answer. The mark doesn't have to be directly over an answer because your rating may lie somewhere between two answers. Be honest with yourself.

1. Are you a self starter?

| I do things my own way. Nobody needs to tell me to get going. | If someone gets me started, I keep going all right. | Easy does it. I don't put myself out unless I have to. |

2. Can you stick with it?

If I make up my mind to do something, I don't let anything stop me.	I usually finish what I start.	If a job doesn't do right, I turn off. Why beat your brains out?

3. How good an organizer are you?

I like to have a plan before I start. I'm usually the one to get things lined up.	I do all right unless things get too goofed up. Then I cop out.	I just take things as they come.

4. Can you take responsibility?

I like to take charge of and see things through.	I'll take over if I have to, but I'd rather let someone else be responsible.	There's always some eager beaver around wanting to show off. I say let him.

5. Can you make decisions?

I can make up my mind in a hurry if necessary, and my decision is usually ok.	I can if I have plenty of time. If I have to make up my mind fast, I usually regret it.	I don't like to be the one who decides things. I'd probably blow it.

6. Can people trust what you say?

They sure can. I don't say things I don't mean.	I try to be on the level, but sometimes I just say what's easiest.	What's the sweat if the other person doesn't know the difference?

7. Are you patient?

I have no difficulty hanging in there, without letting it bother me, until I get things straightened out. I can wait.	I'm ok with a minor delay now and again, but I can't stand foul-ups.	If things don't happen the way I expect them to right *now*, I get very upset.

8. Are you tactful?

I'm concerned about the other person's feelings and I'm particularly careful if another's background is different from mine.	I don't want to hurt anyone's feelings, but sometimes I do when I'm under pressure.	I don't always think, or care, about what I say.

9. Are you reasonably imaginative?

I often think up new, effective ways to get things done.	Once in a while I have a good idea.	I expect others to think of a new or different approach.

10. Are you interested in foreign affairs?

I regularly read about international events in news and business publications.	I listen to the 6 o'clock news and sometimes I'm conscious of international situations.	I think the most important events are right here at home—foreign affairs don't interest me.

You have completed the questionnaire. Are most of your check marks on the left-hand side of the page? That's where they should be. But look them over carefully and be sure none of them is on the left-hand side because of wishful thinking. Compare your answers with those given by the people who know you. If you have weak points, admit to them. You may be able to compensate by training yourself or by obtaining help from a source outside yourself. But if you are weak in too many traits, self-employment and the import/export business are probably not for you.

Now let's consider why some of these qualities are important.

The first six items on the questionnaire deal with *drive*, which has been isolated as an important component of success in any business. Drive is made up of responsibility, vigor, initiative, and perseverance. If you desire to do so, you can develop the drive and the personal capacities that will help you improve your effectiveness and increase your chances of success. Much of the development of such drive depends on setting goals for yourself. That is, you must decide specifically how successful you want to be ("I'll make $100,000 from my import business next year"; "By June 30, I'll convince X manufacturer to let me export his products"). The chapters that follow will help you to define reasonable goals in the import/export business.

The next four items on the questionnaire deal with the additional qualities needed by the importer/exporter. They are patience, tact, imagination, and an interest in foreign affairs.

Patience heads the list of special qualities. In shepherding merchandise to its destination, you will often deal with mail delays, poor routing, strikes, and revolutions, any of which can thoroughly test your reserves of entrepreneurial grit. You may also line up an excellent prospect (e.g., a Japanese customer for yachts) only to discover a requirement your U.S. manufacturer can't meet or can't certify. You must be calm enough not to develop a nervous tic because a shipment is late or not to lose your temper with the Japanese authority who explains to you the standards for imported pleasure boats.

Tact, as well as patience, will serve you well in the import/export business. Initially, you will be dealing with overseas agents and suppliers whom you've never met—you can't just drop by to discuss an order. This lack of a close relationship can sometimes cause misunderstandings. Also, you will be dealing with business people from other cultures that have standards and customs very different from the ones with which you grew up. Relationship building should be a main goal of your business. Dealing with different cultures requires flexibility and adaptability quite different from that found within the United States.

You will also need a dose of *imagination*. Difficulties in exporting to one part of the world may create possibilities for importing from that area. Reevaluation of currencies, changes in governments, and outbreaks of war all contribute a variety of unique circumstances offering profit potential to the imaginative trader. You must be able to analyze a changing marketplace and adapt your product and your selling approach to a variety of situations and potential customers. And sometimes you must have a talent for, as the saying goes, turning a lemon into lemonade.

To bolster your imagination, you need to keep up on the changing situations; that is, you need an *interest in foreign affairs*. For example, early in 1979, the deposal of the Shah of Iran and the ensuing economic collapse virtually halted business activity relating to Iran. In addition, it is quite common for countries in political and economic turmoil to put restrictions on currency. If you read about trouble in a certain area with which you are planning to do business, check with your local Department of Commerce office or with the international department of your bank—they will have the most up-to-date information.

In addition to listening to the news and reading magazines like *Time* or *Newsweek*, the new importer/exporter should become familiar with publications that tell more about the international business climate. These include *Business Week International*, the *Asian Wall Street Journal*, and possibly the *Journal of Commerce*. These should be available in your local library, or you can subscribe to them; they will keep you well informed about world trade situations.

More specific information about import and export opportunities can be had from the *Trade Channel Magazines*, *Made in Europe*, and *Trade Opportunities in Taiwan*. Many other publications of this type could be useful to you, and you can review them at your local Department of Commerce office.

Most transactions between U.S. and foreign business people are carried out in English (as most U.S. citizens speak only one language); however, if you are dealing with nonexecutive people in government and business, you may find the going difficult. Therefore, consider hiring an interpreter. This person should be a native of the country and, if possible, knowledgeable in your product area or specialty. Consulates and embassies are your best source of names. If there is no U.S. representation where you are, contact the Canadian or British officials. *Remember:* "Yes" is not always yes, just as "no" may not be definite. Having someone giving you the *real* meaning behind the words can make the difference between success and failure.

You have now considered the potential the import/export trade has to offer, and you have considered some of the qualities that you will have to possess or develop. You've decided you're made of the right raw material, and you'd like to explore the import/export business a bit further. Read on! Chapter Two describes the first simple, inexpensive steps you must take to set up your new business.

Chapter Two

How to Set Up Your Business

If you have never been in business for yourself, *you should read this chapter carefully.* From the beginning, you want to impress your customers with your professionalism. You also want to set up your office and record keeping in the most efficient ways possible, so they will help rather than hinder you as your business grows. The basic guidelines in this chapter can start you on the road to success before your first customer has signed a contract.

ESTABLISHING THE RIGHT IMAGE

Because your business will be conducted almost exclusively through the mails, always use a conservatively designed letterhead—the simpler, the better. A sample letterhead appears in Figure 2.1. Include your company name (for example, XYZ Trading Company or American Importing Company), address (including U.S.A. after the state), telex number, and bank. Generally, for overseas use, either 11- or 13-pound rag sheet, with *Air Mail* imprinted, is recommended.

The reason for using a light sheet is the high cost of mailing. Simulated parchment might look nice, but postage is expensive, and doubling the weight of your paper could double your postage costs. At this writing, air mail rates are 45¢ for the first one-half ounce outside of the United States, Canada, and Mexico. For mail weighing above two ounces, the rate drops to 42¢ for each one-half ounce or frac-

7

XYZ TRADING COMPANY
4126 Green Street
Los Angeles, CA 90000 U.S.A.

Telephone (213) 000–0000   Bank: Hometown Bank
Fax (213) 100–1000
Telex #000001

Figure 2.1   Acceptable letterhead

tion of each one-half ounce. In Central America, Bermuda, the Bahamas, Columbia, Venezuela, the Caribbean Islands, Miquelon, and St. Pierre, the rate is 45¢ per one-half ounce up to and including two ounces; then 42¢ for each additional half ounce. When calculating air mail charges, always figure any fraction of the next one-half ounce as a full ounce. Also buy a postage scale for convenience and to avoid excessive or insufficient postage. The amount of money saved will more than justify the cost.

In addition to lightweight air mail stationery, purchase a standard 20-pound white bond paper for domestic use. Buy small quantities of each type of stationery (no more than 1,000 sheets and envelopes) because you will be adding the names of organizations and associations to your letterhead and will have to have your stationery regularly reprinted.

Always have your letters professionally typed if you cannot do an adequate job yourself. You will be judged as a company on the appearance and content of your letters since your business will be conducted through the mails. Be sure to discuss specific terminology or phrasing with your typist. Transactions have been terminated because of typing errors as simple as forgetting to put U.S. in front of the dollar ($) sign. In this example, the difference between the Hong Kong and the U.S. dollar is so great that a misunderstanding might cancel a deal.

When buying your stationery, order 1,000 business cards, conservatively designed like your letterhead. If you are planning a trip to the Far East, consider having the cards printed in English and in the language of the country you will visit.

Whether you have an office or use a room in your home, you should rent a post office box. This will safeguard your correspondence even though you will need to pick up your own mail. Your business will be through the mails, and any delayed or lost inquiries *can and will be costly.*

As your business develops, you should rent or buy a telex or fax machine. These are direct line communication machines that enable you to send and receive messages at any hour. They are the workhorses of the import/export business because of the time-zone problems one encounters when using the telephone.

If you are working out of your home, change your personal phone listing to a business listing, or order a second, business only, phone. You will then automatically have a free listing in the yellow pages. If you live in an area where many volumes of the yellow pages exist, place your firm's name in all of them. The price is relatively low and the exposure is beneficial.

Open a business checking and savings account under your new company's name. This will make it simpler to control expenses and receipts for tax purposes and to review the progress of the company. The Small Business Administration publishes several booklets on bookkeeping for new businesses. You should contact the SBA, obtain copies, and review them. Your accountant or banker can also provide sound advice on financial record keeping.

ORGANIZING YOUR FILING SYSTEM

Setting up a filing system is one of the keys to long-term success for the beginner. *It forces you to organize.* Begin with either a standard business desk with a file drawer, or a cardboard drawer from a stationery store. In the drawer, set up your folders by company for correspondence and price lists. The next step is to cross-reference the company names and products. Purchase an index card box from a stationery store and set up the cards as shown in Figure 2.2. Or you can purchase a PC and enter this same information on a disk-storage system. Many PCs can act as telex machines as well as computers. Check with your local computer supply company.

You don't need to rent a warehouse. Your facilities may consist of boxes, shelves, the hall closet, or anything else easy to organize. You should tag your samples with item number and supplier. This careful marking will make it easier to retrieve the specific article requested when an inquiry is received. You *must* have some way to pinpoint the whereabouts of your samples so that you do not needlessly waste time searching for them.

When you file a letter received from overseas, staple the envelope to it first. Foreign countries often have several towns with the same or similar names, and you may have to refer to the postmark to avoid confusion later. Postmarks also show foreign zip codes. Both envelope and foreign letterhead should show the special address sequence used in the originating country; this is helpful because many countries use a different order than most Americans are accustomed to. Several sample addresses follow:

D-200 Hamburg   (City)
Postfach 500749   (Post Office Box)
Holstenstrasse 224   (Street Address)
Federal Republic of Germany   (Country)

Electra House, Temple Place   (Street Address)
Victoria Embankment   (District)
London WC2R 3HP   (City, Zip Code)
England   (Country)

5-5 2-chome Minami-machi   (Street Address)
Mito, Ikasaki 310   (District, City)
Japan   (Country)

Finally, always keep a file copy of outgoing correspondence.

The guidelines set forth in this chapter apply to any business, not just the import/export business. It is essential, however, for you to consider them carefully, particularly if you have never before been in business for yourself, or if you have always depended upon another department to handle clerical duties. The next chapter discusses finding products to market. However if your office procedures are poorly organized or nonexistent, even excellent, highly salable products can fail to bring you profits.

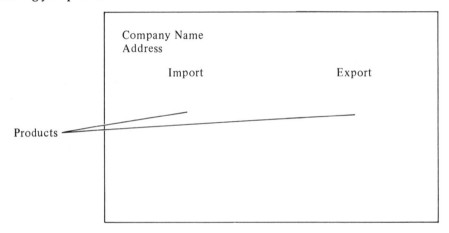

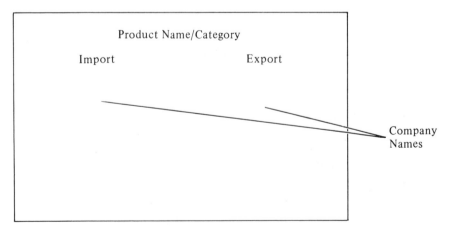

Figure 2.2 Cross-referenced file cards

Chapter Three

Locating Products to Import or Export

In discussing products one must first look at the starting point of the individual. If, for example, your goal is to travel and pay for the journey by selling products you return with, then your viewpoint would be different than that of an established company wishing to expand its operations.

So let's start by reviewing pre-travel plans for individuals wishing to pay for their travels by importing.

1. Work with products you like.
2. Specialize within a category.
3. Buy something you would enjoy selling.
4. Do not be afraid to take the plunge—Buy Now!

What is the best product or service to import/export? Are my company's products/services salable internationally? These are by far the most common questions asked during my seminars. Everyone obviously has different experiences: therefore, choose a product in which you have a genuine interest. This will help sustain your efforts when you have problems.

If you are interested in pottery, be specific. Work with merchandise from one area or region rather than just buying "goods" from every country you go to. Let's say you are a skiing enthusiast and travel to interesting skiing locations. While on a trip you locate a "new" type of warmer for gloves and boots. You have never seen this item in any domestic shop and you believe this would be the perfect item with which to start. At this point, consider these questions:

1. Can I get it out of the country?
2. Will the local price prohibit enough markup?
3. Is it unique, especially for the area I live in?
4. Will it be easy to reorder from a local source?

Finally, take a chance and buy a small quantity. Even if your estimate of the resale value is wrong, you need to get your "feet wet." Unless you fool yourself or are "sold" by a local merchant, your problems should be easily handled.

Now let us move on to discussing a more in-depth approach at sourcing products for international trade.

MATCHING PRODUCT TO MARKET:
THE IMPORTANCE OF MARKET RESEARCH

Before you decide on a product to import or export, you must prepare a market analysis to determine whether the product you are considering offers a promise for profit. Or, if you have no specific product in mind, the analysis can show which products may be most profitable in which markets. Not every product can be successfully exported to every country. For instance, many foreign countries have domestic industries producing goods similar to those of U.S. manufacturers, or new product areas they wish to develop. To protect these industries, the foreign country may use a high protective tariff, thereby making it unprofitable for you to export these goods to them. For example, a market analysis can warn you not to export cuckoo clocks to the Black Forest area of Germany, where they are made, or not to export watches to Switzerland. (The United States also restricts certain exports; see Chapter Twelve for more information.)

Once you have completed your basic studies and have narrowed down your product choices, you must look more closely at related *international trade and economic statistics.*

WHY DO YOU USE TRADE AND ECONOMIC STATISTICS?

To do the type of market analysis you need for success in foreign trade, you must be able to understand and use trade and economic statistics. Statistics can be extremely valuable in isolating attractive foreign markets. They are most useful for comparing several different markets for a particular product and for uncovering local conditions, such as high tariffs, that might prohibit profitable trade in that item.

It is very important that you be able to use statistics to answer these basic marketing questions:

1. Are my import choices currently being sold to the United States or being manufactured in the United States?
2. Which companies in my area are manufacturing my import choices? Does the local production of these goods prohibit their importation because locally made products offer too-strong competition?
3. Which countries offer the best markets for my export choices?

USING TRADE STATISTICS

The easiest method of using international trade statistics is by constructing an import/export grid. This grid identifies major importing countries and major exporting countries along one axis, and product categories along the other. The first step in preparing this grid is to obtain U.S. import/export figures for your product for perhaps the last three of four years. It is essential to consider statistics over a period at least this long to determine if any significant trends are present.

U.S. import/export statistics indicate the total amount, in U.S. dollars, of your product category that has been imported or exported for the years in question. A breakdown by country of origin or destination is given. From this breakdown, you will be able to determine which countries are importing from or exporting to the United States. Table 3.1 addresses U.S. exports of fountain pens, including stylographic pens.

Table 3.2 illustrates a common grid, with exporters listed along the horizontal axis (across the top) and importers along the vertical axis (down the side). Many other configurations are possible, but for simplicity, this is a good model. The figures all refer to exports of photographic apparatus over a three-year period.

U.S. exporters captured varying percentages of the world markets, ranging from 1 to 50 percent. The fact that U.S. producers are supplying 5 percent or more to numerous markets illustrates the strength of the U.S.'s competitive position.

From a high of 55.9 percent in Costa Rica to a low of 16 percent (not all countries shown), U.S.=exported photographic apparatus covers the globe. In contrast, U.S. importers have bought most of their equipment from Belgium, Luxembourg, West Germany, and Switzerland.

U.S. import/export figures are published by the Bureau of the Census in the form of numbered *Foreign Trade Reports*, issued monthly, with an annual supplement. The appropriate number is either FT-135 (U.S. imports) or FT-140 (U.S. exports), and a reference publication entitled *Schedule A* (for FT-135) or *Schedule E* for (FT-410) is the index by which you determine the numbered category that includes your type of product. These reports are on file in the Department of Commerce field offices and in many libraries. They may be purchased on a subscription basis.

Your analysis should not end with a grid of U.S. imports/exports, for this can tell you nothing about those markets being served by exporters in other countries, particularly Western Europe and Japan. By using trade statistics from international organizations such as the Organization for Economic Cooperation and Develop-

TABLE 3.1 EXPORTS OF FOUNTAIN PENS, INCLUDING STYLOGRAPHIC PENS, DECEMBER 1986

	Net Quantity	Value (000 dollars)
CANADA	72,460	243
MEXICO	42,790	260
PANAMA	45,968	228
COLOMB	36,351	125
VENEZ	6,225	98
CHILE	19,424	64
PARAGUA	14,725	83
U KING	97,751	382
IRELAND	86,780	95
NETHLDS	134,318	330
FRANCE	199,892	264
FR GERM	164,295	290
SPAIN	89,428	316
ITALY	72,314	185
TURKEY	29,633	95
IRAQ	222,194	2,048
KUWAIT	27,300	155
S ARAB	695,321	1,229
ARAB EM	99,847	185
MALAYSA	14,546	99
SINGAPR	29,623	92
HG KONG	91,851	312
CHINA T	19,930	64
JAPAN	243,668	672
AUSTRAL	92,381	193
OTH CTY	322,238	653
TOTAL	2,971,253	8,660

Source: U.S. Department of Commerce, Foreign Trade, FT-410, December 1986.

ment (OECD), 2 Rue Andre=Pascal, Paris 16, France, one can conduct two other types of analysis.

The first alternate analysis is to review U.S. imports of a product to see which countries are major exporters to the United States (use FT-135 reports, with *Schedule A*). Having obtained the names of countries exporting to the United States, you can

TABLE 3.2 U.S. SHARES OF EXPORTS FROM 14 SUPPLIER COUNTRIES TO THE WORLD AND TO 102 DESTINATIONS, 1978–80 (THOUSANDS OF DOLLARS)

EXPORTER	TOTAL EXPORTS FROM 14 COUNTRIES	UNITED STATES VALUE	PERCENT OF TOTAL	JAPAN	GERMANY F.R	SWITZER-LAND	FRANCE	UNITED KINGDOM	BELG LUX	ITALY	NETHER-LANDS
DESTINATION											
WORLD											
1978	13084255	1988288	16.2	3620476	1888274	2139459	895362	785440	538037	425836	369808
1979	14715985	2244788	16.3	3913291	2195674	2213837	1104387	929263	648172	526410	434289
1980	17555148	2626479	16.0	4988684	2421581	2409281	1293414	1208412	935839	572088	519175
UNITED STATES											
1978	2010126	NA	0.0	1085123	192809	295231	92352	75910	63748	68834	7385
1979	2013644	NA	0.0	1076051	183313	266953	97049	90560	81358	85664	6583
1980	2350268	NA	0.0	1252132	205222	283887	88236	100842	140189	72057	16383
WORLD EX. EXPORTS TO US											
1978	11074128	1988288	18.0	2535353	1595466	1844228	803010	710530	474289	367001	362423
1979	12702342	2244788	17.7	2837240	2012561	1945884	1007348	838702	567814	460746	427705
1980	15204880	2526479	17.3	3714552	2216359	2125394	1205178	1107571	795640	500011	503812
CANADA											
1978	453558	229309	50.6	114833	22844	16969	13839	34006	8625	7745	873
1979	470158	244952	52.1	114317	21889	17771	13943	34735	9188	8648	730
1980	554941	273880	49.3	159853	22349	17586	13998	33440	14703	11576	3256
ARGENTINA											
1978	60589	16119	26.6	18345	7034	11502	2301	1337	1536	1678	479
1979	106740	28588	27.7	27461	13005	21612	5004	3735	2001	3118	270
1980	174874	48393	27.7	58800	18425	27710	5000	5136	2169	5120	1218
BOLIVIA											
1978	3635	592	19.0	869	909	727	14	33	220	100	45
1979	3037	606	20.0	451	739	806	32	43	194	93	45
1980	3121	507	16.2	396	761	1154	8	45	58	147	16

(Continued)

15

TABLE 3.2 Continued

EXPORTER	TOTAL EXPORTS FROM 14 COUNTRIES	UNITED STATES VALUE	PERCENT OF TOTAL	JAPAN	GERMANY F.R	SWITZER-LAND	FRANCE	UNITED KINGDOM	BELG LUX	ITALY	NETHER-LANDS
BRAZIL											
1978	132341	41993	31.7	29956	11481	26603	11016	4054	1069	3366	1312
1979	154154	53415	34.7	33802	11420	27730	13874	3393	894	5306	2122
1980	151721	38529	25.4	38477	12578	31647	12284	3669	2333	7024	2849
CHILE											
1978	15113	5338	33.1	2824	3189	2471	558	396	752	413	65
1979	21288	6343	29.8	4639	5004	2840	818	317	550	498	81
1980	36198	12292	34.0	11158	5603	2868	1272	559	1085	933	136
COLOMBIA											
1978	17882	7252	40.6	1210	2023	4036	850	609	993	515	233
1979	21884	9447	43.2	1588	2118	4754	799	832	1492	612	75
1980	27124	12511	46.1	1388	2273	5220	998	1748	1457	679	63
COSTA RICA											
1978	4437	2491	56.1	239	422	519	165	35	463	30	22
1979	3970	1901	47.9	307	570	675	137	94	177	38	25
1980	4738	2649	55.9	313	615	475	86	15	413	33	11
CUBA											
1978	5372	13	0.2	1132	1585	207	310	103	1087	482	107
1979	4500	13	0.3	1033	1191	175	101	327	506	486	44
1980	5328	4	0.1	1620	1189	61	129	308	1332	323	53
DOMINICAN REPUBLIC											
1978	4154	2340	56.3	221	529	497	58	66	207	80	NA
1979	3955	2631	86.5	102	195	414	51	31	181	36	1
1980	5561	3713	66.8	178	320	467	74	74	350	38	3

16

then assemble the export statistics of these countries to determine the other markets to which they are presently exporting. That is, a country exporting wicker baskets to the United States is a likely exporter of wicker baskets to other countries.

Another approach is to obtain the import figures of those countries that import the greatest amounts of your product from the United States. These import figures indicate the other countries serving the same markets. That is, if Sweden imports substantial quantities of canned fruit from the United States, it is likely that Sweden also imports canned fruit from other countries.

PROBLEMS WITH TRADE STATISTICS

Although international trade statistics are extremely useful for identifying attractive products and markets and for locating likely competitors, the difficulties and weaknesses of these figures warn against complete dependence on them. Consider the problems:

1. A number of categories of trade statistics both here and in foreign countries are simply too broad to be of value to anyone concerned with a specific product. Some import/export categories contain more than 100 different items, and producers of specialized products are likely to find such basket categories entirely useless.

2. Some countries do not publish trade statistics, and others are several years behind in issuing them.

3. Parts for both repair and assembly purposes are included with finished items in many categories. Such figures are likely to be misleading since a high percentage of the total may be parts destined for foreign assembly plants or to repair end items already in use.

4. Import/export figures are by necessity historical. They say nothing about new products, new marketing techniques, changes in trade restrictions, and other factors of importance. The results achieved by others may be a poor indication of your own trade possibilities.

5. Many exports are sent to free ports and foreign trade zones from which they are reexported to other destinations. For example, Panama appears to be a much more significant market for U.S. products than it actually is because goods are shipped to the free port at Colon for shipment to other Central and South American markets.

However, in spite of the difficulties and weaknesses of using trade statistics, they are a valuable source of information for isolating attractive import/export markets and products.

USING ECONOMIC STATISTICS

A wide variety of economic statistics is available to aid the importer/exporter in preparing statistical profiles of one or more countries. The kinds of information required to construct a useful profile depends on the particular product being exported or imported. For example:

1. An importer/exporter of items purchased by teenagers would be concerned about the size of the population by age group, per capita disposable income, and geographical distribution within a certain country; breakdowns in consumer spending among particular products; disposition of incremental income (additional income above basic expenses); and other economic statistics that may be obtained from a variety of sources.

2. The importer/exporter of coal mining machinery would be concerned about the levels of coal production, wage costs, fuel consumption, and so forth.

3. Other ways in which economic statistics may be used to isolate markets include using the number of wired homes to indicate the potential for electrical appliances and the number of motor vehicles to indicate the extent of the market for automotive accessories. (There is no sense in trying to sell electric hair dryers in an area where homes have no electricity, or mag wheels to people who can afford only bicycles.)

The importer/exporter of consumer products should be extremely concerned with the disposition of incremental income; that is, how do people spend their extra money? The level of family purchasing power is increasing rapidly throughout many parts of the world. Standards of living are rising and traditional spending patterns are being drastically altered. For example, one of the most obvious trends in shifting spending patterns is taking place in Japan.

In other words, a certain level of spending on food, clothing, and housing is necessary to sustain a family. As family income rises above this basic level, expenditures on food, clothing, and housing are not increased proportionately. Instead, expenditures on appliances, automobiles, travel, and education are increased substantially or made for the first time.

Therefore, importers/exporters of basic items such as food and clothing will not benefit from rising consumer incomes to the same extent as will importers/exporters of products suddenly in demand. In some cases, the explosion of demand in Japan will outstrip local production capacity, leaving at least temporary openings for exporters.

PRODUCT CONSIDERATIONS

The number of goods from which you can pick is virtually limitless. You may choose a specific product because you are familiar with it (perhaps you are an amateur chef who is knowledgeable about small kitchen implements) or because you live near a manufacturer (perhaps your home is across town from a manufacturer of phonograph records). Possibly your market analysis boded ill for kitchen implements and you must seek a different product, or possibly you had no product in mind until the market analysis suggested one to you. There are many reasons for choosing your product. Following are some considerations that have proven successful for may importers/exporters.

1. *Specialize.* In the past, individuals have tried to import/export items on a one-shot basis. They would trade in any or all types of goods and commodities. Generally, this proved disastrous because of a lack of expertise both in the goods and in their handling. Therefore, I suggest that you select your products with an eye to specialization. Plan on trading in one general type of merchandise. (Small kitchen implements, cutlery, and pots and pans would be one example of a workable group of products; you might be unwise, however, to try to mix cutlery and automobile accessories.) Try to find a niche or specialty item within a product group. Deal with companies that offer the highest-quality product within your price range. In today's competitive marketplace, quality and specialization, not just price, are necessities for successful international sales. After your initial success with one or two items, begin to develop a line of products. This will enhance your reputation and bring other companies to your business. Avoid representing competing manufacturers, as this will cause your reputation to suffer.

2. *Know your product line.* It is much easier to deal in materials with which you are familiar. Intimate knowledge of the best way to pack, ship, and market a certain product can benefit profits greatly.

3. *Work with local companies.* As an exporter, you wish to provide a great deal of personal service to the manufacturers you represent; therefore, do not contact firms outside of your area. As an importer, you can build up contacts for your products by using local distributors.

4. *Start small.* An individual starting out is usually better off working with small- to medium-sized manufacturers. Stay away from large companies initially (Ford, General Foods, Texaco, etc.) because most have their own export departments or overseas subsidiaries. Companies that already have overseas sales that comprise 15 to 20 percent of their total sales volume usually do not need your services. Also, do not contact agricultural co-ops, weapons manufacturers, or sophisticated electronics equipment companies. Generally, their products require special export licenses, large amounts of capital, and a large network of support personnel.

5. *Consider yourself.* Whether you are importing or exporting, your individual circumstances should guide you. Everyone has special abilities and experiences that lend themselves to certain product categories. For example, if you are an electronics technician, you might consider dealing in

consumer electronic products or possibly electronic testing equipment. On the other hand, never avoid a product category only because you aren't familiar with it. Your main job as an import/export agent is distributing and selling the goods—you can buy any technical expertise you need. Allow your marketing research to be your first guide in dictating your final product choice.

6. *Consumer/technical products.* Whether you choose to deal in consumer products or industrial goods, the basic techniques (documentation, financing, etc.) are the same for both importing and exporting. Any differences are dictated by the product itself. A fashion item may have a limited retail sales life; certain frozen foods have limited shelf lives, thereby necessitating special shipping and handling; highly technical items may require special repair facilities or, as with fashion goods, may have a limited sales life because rapid innovations in technology make them obsolete. Data processing equipment provides an example of this latter situation.

Make certain that the management of the company you are dealing with is flexible about packaging, design, and such. Changing a product to meet overseas needs is common in international trade. Also avoid companies that use exporting as a method of selling *excess* products.

PRODUCT POTENTIAL CHECKLIST

In doing your research, you should carefully review each of the following items as it pertains to the products you are considering.

Domestic market trade regulations. Chapter Eleven discusses controls, licenses, and documentation in more detail.

- Country restrictions
- Currency and tax regulations
- Licensing and other requirements

Foreign market access. This information can be found in country reports such as the *Overseas Business Reports.*

- Tariffs and quotas of importing countries
- Currency restrictions
- Internal taxes
- Political factors

Foreign competitors. Consult *Business International* and *The Economic Intelligence Unit*; foreign consulates, embassies and UN statistical data are also good sources.

- Domestic production, volume, and growth
- Reasons for success
- Strengths (size, special advantages)

Market size, pattern, and growth. Consult *Business International* and *The Economic Intelligence Unit;* foreign consulates, embassies, and UN statistical data are also good sources.

Price structure. For more information, write to U.S. embassies overseas, talk with international freight forwarders, and attend trade fairs. (The U.S. Department of Commerce [ITA] has lists of trade fairs.)

- Prices to end users
- Trade markups
- Transport costs

Reports of interest available from the Department of Commerce include:

- *Commerce Business Daily and Business America*
- Foreign economic trends and their implications for the United States
- *Overseas Business Reports*
- *Commercial News U.S.A.*

OTHER SOURCES OF INFORMATION

There are also several directories, available in your local or University library, that can be most helpful in locating producers of export/import products:

- *Thomas Register of American Manufacturers*
- *Kompass*
- *Bottin International Directory*
- *ABC European Production*
- *Asian Buyers' Guide*
- *Midwest Manufacturers and Industrial Directory*
- *MacRae's Blue Book*

Another excellent source of statistical information are the many international data bases. These organizations will provide a variety of information, on line or in report form, about most major countries of the world and the products that they import or export.

Figures 3.1 through 3.7 are examples of a series of reports available from Trade Inflo (202-785-1945, 800-527-6138).

Observe trade flow with each partner at a glance.

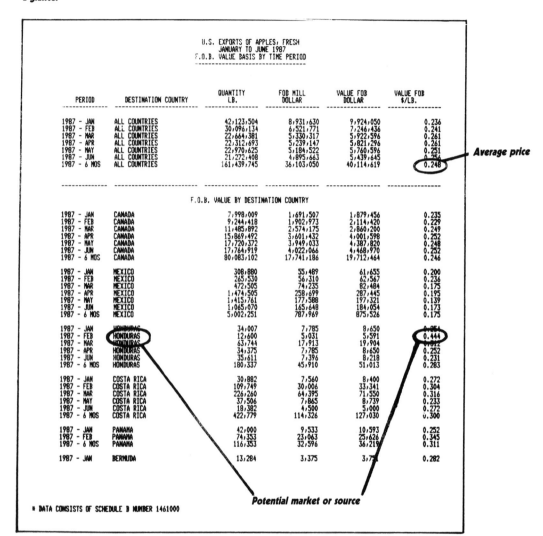

U.S. EXPORTS OF APPLES, FRESH
JANUARY TO JUNE 1987
F.O.B. VALUE BASIS BY TIME PERIOD

PERIOD	DESTINATION COUNTRY	QUANTITY LB.	FOB MILL DOLLAR	VALUE FOB DOLLAR	VALUE FOB $/LB.
1987 - JAN	ALL COUNTRIES	42,123,504	8,931,630	9,924,050	0.236
1987 - FEB	ALL COUNTRIES	30,096,134	6,521,771	7,246,436	0.241
1987 - MAR	ALL COUNTRIES	22,664,381	5,330,317	5,922,596	0.261
1987 - APR	ALL COUNTRIES	22,312,693	5,239,147	5,821,296	0.261
1987 - MAY	ALL COUNTRIES	22,970,625	5,184,522	5,760,596	0.251
1987 - JUN	ALL COUNTRIES	21,272,408	4,895,663	5,439,645	0.254
1987 - 6 MOS	ALL COUNTRIES	161,439,745	36,103,050	40,114,619	0.248

F.O.B. VALUE BY DESTINATION COUNTRY

1987 - JAN	CANADA	7,998,009	1,691,507	1,879,456	0.235
1987 - FEB	CANADA	9,244,418	1,902,973	2,114,420	0.229
1987 - MAR	CANADA	11,485,892	2,574,175	2,860,200	0.249
1987 - APR	CANADA	15,869,492	3,601,432	4,001,598	0.252
1987 - MAY	CANADA	17,720,372	3,949,033	4,387,820	0.248
1987 - JUN	CANADA	17,764,919	4,022,066	4,468,970	0.252
1987 - 6 MOS	CANADA	80,083,102	17,741,186	19,712,464	0.246
1987 - JAN	MEXICO	308,880	55,489	61,655	0.200
1987 - FEB	MEXICO	265,530	56,310	62,567	0.236
1987 - MAR	MEXICO	472,505	74,235	82,484	0.175
1987 - APR	MEXICO	1,474,505	258,699	287,445	0.195
1987 - MAY	MEXICO	1,415,761	177,588	197,321	0.139
1987 - JUN	MEXICO	1,065,070	165,648	184,054	0.173
1987 - 6 MOS	MEXICO	5,002,251	787,969	875,526	0.175
1987 - JAN	HONDURAS	34,007	7,785	8,650	0.254
1987 - FEB	HONDURAS	12,600	5,031	5,591	0.444
1987 - MAR	HONDURAS	63,744	17,913	19,904	0.312
1987 - APR	HONDURAS	34,375	7,785	8,650	0.252
1987 - JUN	HONDURAS	35,611	7,396	8,218	0.231
1987 - 6 MOS	HONDURAS	180,337	45,910	51,013	0.283
1987 - JAN	COSTA RICA	30,882	7,560	8,400	0.272
1987 - FEB	COSTA RICA	109,749	30,006	33,341	0.304
1987 - MAR	COSTA RICA	226,260	64,395	71,550	0.316
1987 - MAY	COSTA RICA	37,506	7,865	8,739	0.233
1987 - JUN	COSTA RICA	18,382	4,500	5,000	0.272
1987 - 6 MOS	COSTA RICA	422,779	114,326	127,030	0.300
1987 - JAN	PANAMA	42,000	9,533	10,593	0.252
1987 - FEB	PANAMA	74,353	23,063	25,626	0.345
1987 - 6 MOS	PANAMA	116,353	32,596	36,219	0.311
1987 - JAN	BERMUDA	13,284	3,375	3,73	0.282

Average price

Potential market or source

ⁿ DATA CONSISTS OF SCHEDULE B NUMBER 1461000

Figure 3.1 Example 1: Country of origin or destination (*Source:* Trade Inflo, Division Steward Trade Data Services Corporation, 1001 Connecticut Avenue, N.W., Suite 901, Washington, D.C. 20036.)

Quickly see who the primary markets are through the ranking. Also see which Countries could be a new developing market.

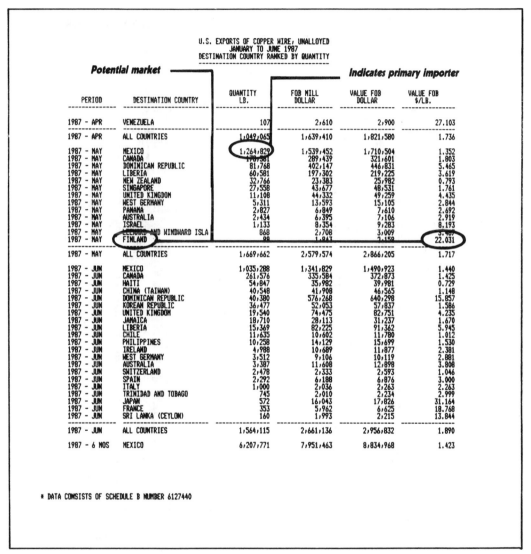

Figure 3.2   Example 2: Ranked by quantity (Source: Trade Inflo, Division Steward Trade Data Services Corporation, 1001 Connecticut Avenue, N.W., Suite 901, Washington, D.C. 20036.)

Notice which countries have the greatest sales or receive the greatest sales volume.

Indicates Japan's primary source

U.S. competitors

Competing prices

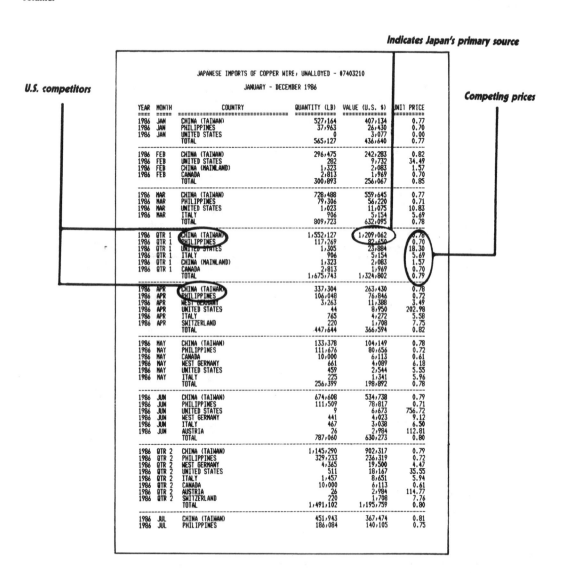

JAPANESE IMPORTS OF COPPER WIRE, UNALLOYED - #7403210

JANUARY - DECEMBER 1986

YEAR	MONTH	COUNTRY	QUANTITY (LB)	VALUE (U.S. $)	UNIT PRICE
1986	JAN	CHINA (TAIWAN)	527,164	407,134	0.77
1986	JAN	PHILIPPINES	37,963	26,430	0.70
1986	JAN	UNITED STATES	0	3,077	0.00
		TOTAL	565,127	436,640	0.77
1986	FEB	CHINA (TAIWAN)	296,475	242,283	0.82
1986	FEB	UNITED STATES	282	9,732	34.49
1986	FEB	CHINA (MAINLAND)	1,323	2,083	1.57
1986	FEB	CANADA	2,813	1,969	0.70
		TOTAL	300,893	256,067	0.85
1986	MAR	CHINA (TAIWAN)	728,488	559,645	0.77
1986	MAR	PHILIPPINES	79,306	56,220	0.71
1986	MAR	UNITED STATES	1,023	11,075	10.83
1986	MAR	ITALY	906	5,154	5.69
		TOTAL	809,723	632,095	0.78
1986	QTR 1	CHINA (TAIWAN)	1,552,127	1,209,062	0.78
1986	QTR 1	PHILIPPINES	117,269	82,650	0.70
1986	QTR 1	UNITED STATES	1,305	23,884	18.30
1986	QTR 1	ITALY	906	5,154	5.69
1986	QTR 1	CHINA (MAINLAND)	1,323	2,083	1.57
1986	QTR 1	CANADA	2,813	1,969	0.70
		TOTAL	1,675,743	1,324,802	0.79
1986	APR	CHINA (TAIWAN)	337,304	263,430	0.78
1986	APR	PHILIPPINES	106,048	76,846	0.72
1986	APR	WEST GERMANY	3,263	11,388	3.49
1986	APR	UNITED STATES	44	8,950	202.98
1986	APR	ITALY	765	4,272	5.58
1986	APR	SWITZERLAND	220	1,708	7.75
		TOTAL	447,644	366,594	0.82
1986	MAY	CHINA (TAIWAN)	133,378	104,149	0.78
1986	MAY	PHILIPPINES	111,676	80,656	0.72
1986	MAY	CANADA	10,000	6,113	0.61
1986	MAY	WEST GERMANY	661	4,089	6.18
1986	MAY	UNITED STATES	459	2,544	5.55
1986	MAY	ITALY	225	1,341	5.96
		TOTAL	256,399	198,892	0.78
1986	JUN	CHINA (TAIWAN)	674,608	534,738	0.79
1986	JUN	PHILIPPINES	111,509	78,817	0.71
1986	JUN	UNITED STATES	9	6,673	756.72
1986	JUN	WEST GERMANY	441	4,023	9.12
1986	JUN	ITALY	467	3,038	6.50
1986	JUN	AUSTRIA	26	2,984	112.81
		TOTAL	787,060	630,273	0.80
1986	QTR 2	CHINA (TAIWAN)	1,145,290	902,317	0.79
1986	QTR 2	PHILIPPINES	329,233	236,319	0.72
1986	QTR 2	WEST GERMANY	4,365	19,500	4.47
1986	QTR 2	UNITED STATES	511	18,167	35.55
1986	QTR 2	ITALY	1,457	8,651	5.94
1986	QTR 2	CANADA	10,000	6,113	0.61
1986	QTR 2	AUSTRIA	26	2,984	114.77
1986	QTR 2	SWITZERLAND	220	1,708	7.76
		TOTAL	1,491,102	1,195,759	0.80
1986	JUL	CHINA (TAIWAN)	451,943	367,474	0.81
1986	JUL	PHILIPPINES	186,084	140,105	0.75

Figure 3.3 Example 3: Ranked by value (*Source*: Trade Inflo, Division Steward Trade Data Services Corporation, 1001 Connecticut Avenue, N.W., Suite 901, Washington, D.C. 20036.)

*Offers greater detail of imports and
exports. It demonstrates the U.S. regions
through which the commodities flow.*

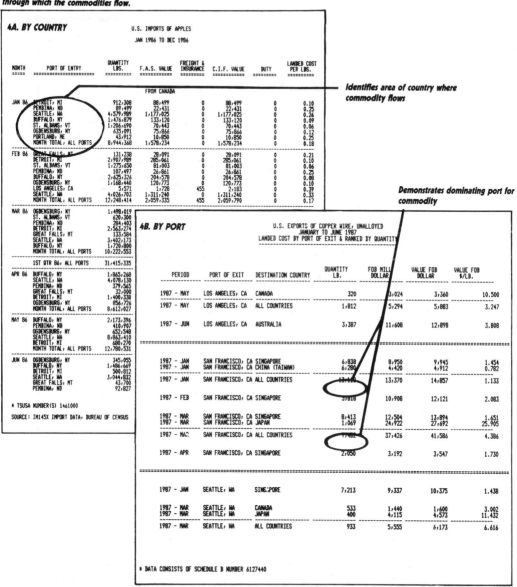

Figure 3.4 Example 4: Port data (U.S. data only) (*Source*: Trade Inflo, Division Steward Trade Data Services Corporation, 1001 Connecticut Avenue, N.W., Suite 901, Washington, D.C. 20036.)

Monitor surges, trends and changes on a monthly basis, 2 complete years and current year

Compare like time periods

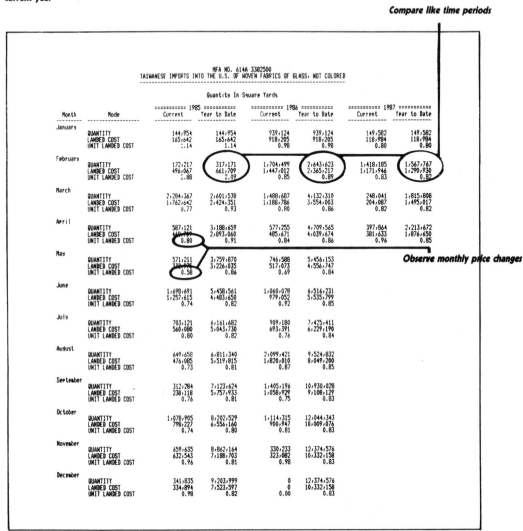

Figure 3.5   Example 5: Surge report   (*Source*: Trade Inflo, Division Steward Trade Data Services Corporation, 1001 Connecticut Avenue, N.W., Suite 901, Washington, D.C. 20036.)

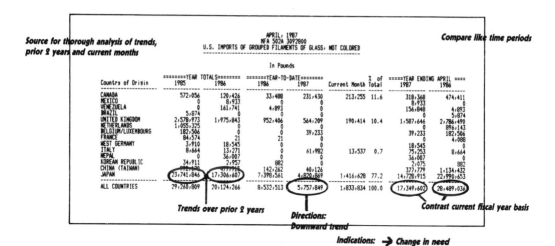

Figure 3.6 Example 6: Year-to-date, year-ending, current month (*Source*: Trade Inflo, Division Steward Trade Data Services Corporation, 1001 Connecticut Avenue, N.W., Suite 901, Washington, D.C. 20036.)

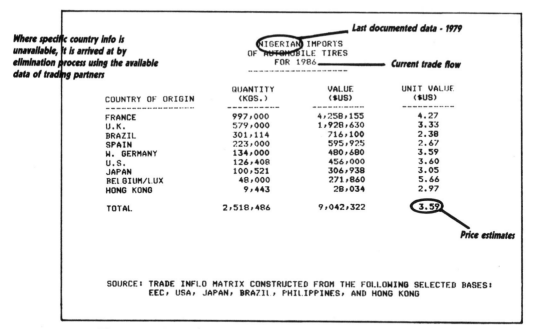

Figure 3.7 Example 7: Country matrix (*Source*: Trade Inflo, Division Steward Trade Data Services Corporation, 1001 Connecticut Avenue, N.W., Suite 901, Washington, D.C. 20036.)

The following list of companies and books will help you locate information on your products for service.

Datapro Research Corporation
1805 Underwood Boulevard
Delran, NJ 08075
800/DATAPRO
(High Tech Information)

The Data Star Information Service
485 Devon Park Drive, Suite 110
Wayne, PA 19087
215-687-6777   800-221-7754

Encyclopedia of Informational Systems and Services
Gale Research Company
Book Tower
Detroit, MI 48226
313-961-2242;   800-223-4253
(Lists 25,000 information systems services worldwide)

Find/SVP
500 Fifth Avenue
New York, NY 10110
212-354-2324

Information Handling Services
1990 M Street, NW, Suite 400
Washington, D.C. 20031
202-331-0961

International Planning Information, Inc. (IPI)
465 Convention Way, Suite 1
Redwood City, CA 94063
415-364-9041

Kompass Online
Windsor Court
East Grinstead House
East Grinstead
West Sussex RH 19 IXA
England
0342/26972

Port Import Export Reporting Service (PIERS)
The Journal of Commerce, Inc.
120 Wall Street
New York, NY 10005
212-425-1616

Trade Inflo
Division Stewart Trade
Data Services Corporation
1001 Connecticut Avenue, N.W.
Suite 901
Washington, D.C. 20036
202-785-1945; 800-527-6138

World Exporter
U.S. Distributor
Trade Data Reports, Inc.
6 West 37th Street
New York, NY 10018
212-563-2772

If you follow the guidelines set forth in this chapter, making liberal use of data from informed individuals, organizations, trade and economic statistics, and the U.S. Department of Commerce, you should be able to assemble a short, workable list of products and a list of countries that seem to offer attractive prospects for those products.

Chapter Four

Help for the New Importer/Exporter

International trade is unique among businesses in that you have access to more free advice and assistance than in any other type of venture. There are several groups anxious to help you because your success furthers theirs:

- International Trade Administration, U.S. Department of Commerce
- Foreign freight forwarders/Customs brokers
- U.S. banks
- Consulates and embassies
- Special foreign trade organizations
- Chambers of commerce
- International trade associations
- Transportation companies (Pan Am, SAS, etc.)
- U.S. Customs Service, U.S. Department of the Treasury

INTERNATIONAL TRADE ADMINISTRATION

The International Trade Administration of the U.S. Department of Commerce is very interested in your success because it helps the federal government increase exports for reasons of balance of payments (the United States suffered nearly a $171 billion trade deficit in 1987). The Administration has offices in 72 cities in the United States and Puerto Rico. (For a listing, see Appendix 1.) Each of them offers the exporter detailed information about the following:

- *Overseas trade missions.* The Administration sponsors teams of business leaders who travel abroad to promote U.S. trade and investment and to exchange business proposals with their foreign counterparts (catalog and video-catalog shows).
- *Trade centers.* Permanent overseas showcases for U.S. goods are placed in major foreign cities, such as London, Frankfurt, Milan, Stockholm, Bangkok, and Tokyo.
- *Sample display service.* Samples are displayed overseas for U.S. firms seeking agents or distributors in such countries as Thailand, Kenya, and the Philippines.
- *Commercial exhibitions.* U.S. product exhibits at international trade fairs abroad help U.S. firms make sales and find new agents.
- *Agency index.* Aimed at prospective foreign buyers, this index lists local distributors of U.S. products.
- *Foreign traders index.* Information on more than 150,000 foreign importing organizations in 135 countries is stored in a computerized file.
- *Export mailing list service.* U.S. firms wishing to make export contacts may obtain lists of foreign organizations interested in specific products or product groups. The lists, selected by computer from the Foreign Traders Index, is available either on pressure-sensitive mailing labels or in standard printout format. (From this source, I obtained a list of importers of office products. Then I sent out a piece of promotional literature describing several items that were quite competitive. The response was enthusiastic and resulted in several large orders for my company.)
- *Data tape service* U.S. firms with computer facilities may purchase magnetic tapes containing information on all firms in selected countries or in all countries covered in the Foreign Traders Index.
- *World trade directory reports.* These reports describe operations of a foreign company—products, size and reputation, capital, and annual turnover.
- *Commercial newsletter.* The newsletter informs over 50,000 business people in fifty nations of new U.S. products, research, and economic trends.
- *Publications.* Hundreds of Department of Commerce publications provide current information on business conditions and opportunities abroad.
- *Foreign trade zones.* The Department of Commerce has established numerous duty-free trade zones for manufacturing and marketing. Locations include New York, New Orleans, San Francisco, Seattle, Mayaguez, Toledo, and Honolulu. (See Chapter Twenty-One for more information.)

- *Business counseling services.* Department of Commerce district offices offer guidance, in-depth counseling, and scheduling of appointments with officials in various agencies. This is a one-stop service designed to give the business person a maximum amount of information in a minimum of time.

Many states also provide aid through their export councils or departments, which work to foster the sale of products from that state. (See Appendix 1 for state trade promotion offices.)

Private industry eager for the international trader's business also offers free assistance. Consider the following sources.

FOREIGN FREIGHT FORWARDERS/CUSTOMS BROKERS

Finding the"right" freight forwarder is like finding the "right" doctor. The freight forwarder must understand you and your particular needs.

Aside from documentation, shipping schedules, insurance, warehousing, and so on, a freight forwarder can assist in choosing the "best" method of transportation for you. Also, many offer consolidation services. That is, several shipments can be placed in a container bound for one port, thereby saving money for each exporter.

Customs brokers can work alone or as employees of freight forwarders. They should be licensed by the federal government (check on it). Also ask what product(s) they specialize in.

The main job for customs brokers is to make entries (see Chapter Nineteen, The Entry Process) for importers. They can advise customers on the best way to bring merchandise through the ports (i.e., assembled versus unassembled-there can be a considerable difference in duty rates). Their charges, as with a freight forwarder, depend on what services are performed. This is a very competitive business, so check prices thoroughly.

To find a reliable freight forwarder/customs broker, check with international clubs and associations in your area. They can usually recommend several sources. In your final selection of a forwarder/broker, consider these points:

- Reputation
- Service (e.g., relationship with the carriers)
- Flexibility
- Knowledge of commodities
- Rates
- "Chemistry"

U.S. BANKS

If your current bank has no international department, have your branch manager recommend two or three alternatives. Ask other companies in foreign trade for recommendations. You may also wish to check with the local international trade association. *Remember:* You are a potentially important customer. Go where you will receive the best *service*. The banking officer you are dealing with is just as important as the institution.

These services offered include:

- Working capital loans
- Short-term advances against shipping and collection documents
- Direct loads to foreign importers by U.S. banks
- Handling of letters of credit and drafts
- Reference checks on overseas firms
- Help in establishing credit reliability
- Assistance in locating markets for your products, using the bank's economic studies of certain areas.

(See Appendix 6 for list of banks doing international business.)

There are many other places, such as those described below where one can find help in solving foreign trade problems. You should, however, use the International Trade Administration, your freight forwarder, and your local bank before you contact any of the others. These three will provide the most help in the least amount of time.

CONSULATES AND EMBASSIES

These agencies specialize in promoting the products and services of their home country. If you live outside Washington, D.C., contact your local consulates. They are located in major cities throughout the United States; check your white pages under Consulates or Trade commissioners. They can provide different services depending on the wealth of the country. That is, some have telex and library facilities you can use to find overseas suppliers. Others can help arrange meetings before you travel. Most can explain particular customs regarding doing business in their country. Many publish monthly or quarterly bulletins on business opportunities in their country. Do not, however, ask them what to *sell* in their country, as they will probably direct you to the U.S. Department of Commerce.

SPECIAL FOREIGN TRADE ORGANIZATIONS

There are several organizations outside the essential trade channels. These groups specialize in a different function than consulates.

JETRO (Japan External Trade Organization) is one of these agencies. Presently they are assisting U.S. companies in penetrating the Japanese market. CEDTC (China External Trade Development Council) is also working with U.S. companies to promote trade with Taiwan.

All of these groups have materials on doing business with their home countries. Many have offices in major cities in the United States. Ask the local consulate if their country has one of these agencies.

CHAMBERS OF COMMERCE

Most cities in the United States have a chamber of commerce. The larger cities have departments to help local business people in exporting. They generally will have a reference library of books and magazines dealing with imports/exports, or they can refer you to one. Many of the organizations have world trade committees to promote the sale of goods from each area. They also have guest speakers from time to time to discuss current overseas business developments. (See Appendix 10 for a list of U.S. and foreign chambers.)

INTERNATIONAL TRADE ASSOCIATIONS

There are more than twenty-five cities that now have World Trade Centers, many within the United States. Normally, wherever you find a World Trade Center, there is a trade association and support facilities nearby. There are many types of trade associations or clubs:

- *Export managers associations* are generally made up of individuals who own or export for themselves or of large companies that export. Many export management people belong to these groups. Manufacturers will frequently contact them looking for someone to handle their overseas business.
- *Foreign trade associations* often have heads of major corporations and city officials as members. They also invite foreign speakers.
- *Freight forwarding organizations* are usually comprised of people in the freight business. They, like the other associations, have speakers who discuss different aspects of international trade relating to transportation.
- *Importing associations* are a variety of different clubs usually representing special product groups, such as metals, shoes, and so on.

Note: See Appendices 1 and 8 for a list of associations fostering foreign trade.

TRANSPORTATION COMPANIES

Some airlines and steamship companies (SAS, EL-AL) provide all types of assistance to clients. They publish reference materials on shipping, where to find products, and the like.

U.S. CUSTOMS SERVICE

As you will find out, the U.S. Customs Service is a very important government agency for the importer, and to some extent the exporter.

Its job is basically divided into two parts:

1. Collect all information regarding products entering or leaving the United States (i.e., location, value, country of origin, etc).

2. Collect duties (taxes) and enforce U.S. laws regarding these same products. For the average business person, however, customs is a place to receive basic information (i.e., duties, quotas, etc.).

The job of actually making a custom entry is best left to the professionals (customs brokers).

I recommend visiting the nearest district office of customs to find out your duty rates, restriction, and quotas (limitation of quantity from a specific country) or calling your customs broker before actually importing merchandise. Along with this, I suggest calling the information office of the U.S. Customs Service for a copy of "Importing into the United States" as a primer on how customs works. *Do not*, however, expect customs officers to actually fill out forms for you. They have neither the personnel nor the time.

Chapter Five

Organizing for Exports

There are several ways to organize an exporting firm, but there are only two that the novice should consider. You will see these two approaches, as well as others, in action as you gain experience as a trader.

Export agents have sales representatives in foreign countries who sell by catalogs and samples. When a sale is completed, the end user pays the export agent, not the exporter's overseas representatives. The agent in turn pays his or her representatives. When you are starting out, this arrangement can pose problems because you appear to have limited resources and experience.

Export management companies handle the foreign business of several noncompeting domestic manufacturers. In effect, the export company acts as the export department for the manufacturer and is paid either on a *commission* or *buy-and-sell* arrangement. This is the approach that is generally most profitable for beginners.

If you are starting out in business and are low in capital reserves, you will probably need to begin on commission. Under this system, you receive a 7.5 to 20.0 percent discount on the wholesale distributor price. The manufacturer is paid by the end user, and you are paid by the manufacturer. For example, if you were selling custom tire rims wholesale for $10, and you receive a 10 percent discount, the price of the rim to you as an exporter would be $9. Since you are working on a commission basis, however, your commission is the amount of the discount, or $1 per rim. When the end user in a foreign country pays the manufacturer $10, the manufacturer pays you $1.

If the buy-and-sell approach is employed, you sell the manufacturer's product under your own name—you might buy the discounted $10 tire rim for $9 and resell

36

it, adding on your export costs in arriving at your selling price. This approach involves sales and credit risks, packaging, shipping, and all correspondence. You, the export management company, purchase at the domestic net wholesale distributor price, less a certain percentage equal to the manufacturer's domestic sales overhead.

As you develop your business, you may decide to change from a commission system to a buy-and-sell system. The buy-and-sell form is a good way to build up business, especially if you are dealing with small manufacturers who cannot afford to tie up their capital in the goods that you export. You buy the products directly from them and *you* assume all the risks.

Sometimes you may lose a client when her or his overseas sales reach 15 to 20 percent of total sales volume. The manufacturer will usually hire his or her own export manager. Losing a client in this way is evidence of your success, and a good reference from your lost client makes your task in seeking out new clients much easier.

After you have developed a clientele with a certain product area, join an export trade association, club, or organization. Aside from being good for your image as a serious member of the profession, your participation in these organizations might bring you more clients.

Appendix 1, State and Local Sources for International Assistance, lists organizations dealing with both importing and exporting.

You have now selected your product(s) and considered the form you want your business to take. The next chapter discusses the distribution of export products—without a prudent approach to these topics, your business cannot survive! (See Chapter Fifteen for a discussion of import pricing.)

Chapter Six

Distributing Your Product Overseas

Once you have chosen you product(s) carefully, you must proceed through the right channels. Your next step is to establish those channels—to contact overseas agents and domestic manufacturers. Your ability to convince manufacturers that you can sell their products profitably will, to a great extent, determine your success in obtaining products to export. Similarly, to be successful with imports, you must display an ability to sell to local distributors.

You have completed your market research and have summed it up by making a list of the goods, with matching countries, that appear to offer the most potential for your import/export business. Now, next to each export product on your list, write the names of manufacturers that produce these products in your area, noting particularly any new firms. Generally, new companies are more apt to let you handle their overseas sales because they lack knowledgeable personnel and they need to maximize sales. (A good source for a list of new local companies is the local city or county clerk's office; most such offices sell lists of newly established businesses.) Then, next to each import product, list the names of distributors. You are now ready to solicit business actively by means of an international and domestic letter-writing campaign.

MAKING OVERSEAS CONTACTS

Figure 6.1 shows a good example of a first-contact letter. *Be sure to indicate product categories you are interested in importing/exporting.* Send this letter to the chambers of

Your letterhead
Date

Director
Chamber of Commerce (or U. N., Trade Association, etc.)
(City)
(Country)

Dear Sir (or Madam):

As an export/import firm involved in many aspects of international trade, we want to establish mutually profitable working arrangements with similar businesses in (name of city). We deal primarily in (product categories).

We would appreciate your supplying us with names and addresses of appropriate firms who could represent us there, as we would represent them in the United States.

Please publish a notice of our interest and offer in your next Chamber of Commerce bulletin. This would be appreciated.

Thank you for your generous assistance.

Sincerely Yours,

Figure 6.1 Sample text for first contact letter

commerce and trade associations of all the countries you are interested in, and also write to local bi-national chambers of commerce, such as the American-Israeli Chamber of Commerce. (Your local chamber of commerce can supply names and addresses.) In addition, send letters to commercial attachés of U. S. embassies (obtain names and addresses from your local U. S. Department of Commerce field office).

Finally, contact trade associations you feel would be important (see *Encyclopedia of Associations*, Gale Research Company, 700 Book Tower, Detroit, Michigan 48226). You might also contact the United Nations to learn of current projects or programs where bids are requested. (Send for the *Business Bulletin*, published monthly by the U. N.'s Development Program. It lists current opportunities for contractors. For detailed information on procedures and background for doing business with the U. N., ask for the "Guide to Firms and Organizations.")

You can reach some firms directly by answering ads in magazines and journals, such as *Business America, Trade Channel Magazines, Made in Europe, Trade Winds, Asian Sources*, and *International Intertrade Index*. (Copies of these magazines can be found in the International Trade Administration offices of the Department of Commerce and in many larger chambers of commerce, public libraries, and university libraries.)

Before sending your first letter, review the following, which should apply to all of your future overseas business correspondence:

1. Write your letters in English. Most overseas companies and organizations have someone on staff who can translate. However, if you receive replies in another language, answer in that language. Most large cities have foreign language translation and typing services.

2. Write your letters in standard English. Stay away from slang, colloquial expressions, and humor. The people who are receiving and reading your letters may have only a rudimentary understanding of English.

3. Make sure your letterhead has U.S.A. included on it. State and zip code are not sufficient for international mail travel.

4. Check your postage carefully. A shortage of only a few cents may delay a transaction weeks or perhaps months.

5. Never send currency through the mail. In certain parts of the world, it is common practice for postal employees to supplement their income by opening letters that contain currency.

6. Send all your letters air mail and request a response the same way. All important documents (purchase orders, sales contracts, etc.) should be sent registered mail or DHL Courier Express.

7. Never send form letters. Since most of your business will be conducted by mail, you will be judged by both the content and the appearance of the letters you send.

8. When sending cables or telexes, follow the same general rules listed above for letters.

MAKING DOMESTIC CONTACTS

Send a "no-cost" letter to each of the local companies manufacturing the product(s) in which you are interested. State that, at no cost to them, you will market their products abroad. Make sure you write to the highest ranking marketing officer (vice president of Sales or Marketing, national sales manager, or the like) and request an appointment. If you receive no answer within two weeks, call for an appointment. *You must be very aggressive.*

Try to make several appointments each week. It is beneficial to speak with the company's top executives, since they are the decision-makers. At the meeting, first explain that you will represent the company free of charge. Emphasize that you can sell its products through your worldwide distributor network. This will not only increase the company's sales, but also lower its production costs. (See the discussion of marginal costing in Chapter Seven for an explanation of how production costs are lowered.) As an alternative course of action, consider the following: Ask the company you work for if you could handle their overseas sales as an independent contractor (e.g. you get paid only on results).

Be sure to bring a *sole agent contract* (Figure 6.2) with you to the meeting. *This is what you want the company executive to sign.* This contract gives you the exclusive right to market their company's products overseas; it is similar to a manufacturer's

This agreement made and entered into by and between:
    Company:
    Address:
hereinafter called the Manufacturer
    AND:
    Your Company:
    Address:
hereinafter called the Export Representative:
    WITNESSETH
The Manufacturer appoints the Export Representative as its exclusive sales representative and export department in and for all countries of the world except the United States.
The Manufacturer agrees to pay the Export Representative a commission of (specify %) on all orders received, excluding the United State and (if another), with or without the Export Representative's intervention. Commission due and payable thirty (30) days after shipment of order.
The Manufacturer shall provide catalogues and samples for the Export Representative's overseas agents and distributors.
Export Representative shall have an obligation to appoint distributors for the sale of the Manufacturer's product.
The Manufacturer will refer copies of any correspondence between Manufacturer and others in the territory assigned to the Export Representative.
The Export Representative, through his agents and distributors, will make every effort to promote the sale of the Manufacturer's products.
This contract shall be in force for a period of five (5) years from this date and shall continue automatically at the end of that time unless cancelled in writing, with a six (6) month notice, by either party.
If there is no business generated in any twelve (12) month period from this date, either party can cancel the contract by notice in writing forthwith.

Signed:_____
                                Manufacturer

Date:_____

Witnessed:_____
                                Notary Public

Signed:_____
                                Export Representative

Date_____

Figure 6.2 Sole agent contract

representative contract. (See Appendices 7 and 9 regarding trademark and patent protection laws.)

One point to consider: Commission rates vary from industry to industry. Make sure you check the industry standards *before* you meet with the company executive.

APPOINTING OVERSEAS DISTRIBUTORS

Within a four- to eight-week period, you should receive responses from your overseas letters. The responses will resemble the illustration in Figure 6.3. They will ask what lines of merchandise you carry, export prices, catalogs, samples, and what you wish to import or export. They may ask for a sole agent contract.

After reviewing the letters you receive from foreign firms seeking to act as your representative, write back to those that appear most promising (basing your judgment on the initial and any subsequent market analysis).

In most countries, people working in international trade can understand English. However, if your products, require a detailed piece of literature to explain operations or benefits, it may be wise to have this information printed in multiple languages (this is especially critical in South America, where both Spanish and Portuguese are spoken). The most common non-English languages in foreign trade are French, Spanish, German, and, more recently, Japanese and Chinese.

If you did not receive the following information initially, request it before appointing your overseas representative. In the same vein, you would supply this information about yourself, if you were asked for it:

Date:_____

Dear Sir (or Madam):

We received your promotional letter describing the products (toys, apparel, etc.) you distribute. We wish to establish relations and are therefore, desirous of making a mutually beneficial alliance with an import-export firm in (name the city).

We handle several (toys, apparel, etc.) lines of products and would like to know what you have to offer and what your country needs in imports.

We wish to enter into agreements for Sole Agency Contracts on specific lines and products.

Anticipating your early reply.

Sincerely Yours,

Figure 6.3   Typical agent letter

1. Products carried
2. Territory covered
3. Commissions expected
4. Number of salespeople
5. Functions performed (agent, importer, exporter, manufacturer, etc.)
6. Companies they do business with in the United States

This last point is most important; you should appoint only representatives having a history of success with similar products. Contact the U. S. firms they are currently dealing with and ask the amount of business (in dollars and in units of merchandise) they are handling, the length of time they have been associated with the U. S. firm, and their credit reliability. This information can protect you from dealing with a disreputable agent. Conversely, you should give this type of information about your company's overseas agents and representatives freely to U. S. companies that ask for it.

Appoint one agent for each country, unless you have information indicating that an agent is able to sell in several countries (e.g., multinational dealers exist in the Middle East. Initially do not appoint more than one agent per country, just as you would not handle competing products of different manufacturers. It is important to treat your overseas agents fairly. Their ability and willingness to sell your products reputably will greatly determine your success in selling your products overseas. Finally, can they perform maintenance, repair, and training, if necessary? Recently, U. S. companies have been losing sales because of lack of service follow-up, especially in rural locations. Before making any final agreement, check Appendix 11 for a more detailed analysis of agency laws, and contact your local foreign trade association for sample contracts or an attorney.

IMPROVING OVERSEAS DISTRIBUTOR PERFORMANCE

Once you have appointed your distributor(s), keeping them motivated is a key factor in their and your success. Some of the most important methods in doing this are:

1. *Communications.* Any changes regarding the product or company should immediately be sent to the distributor—especially those that relate to technology, design, and distribution.
2. *Incentives.* Margins or commissions should be competitive with local conditions. Rewards such as achievement plaques, prizes, and trips are helpful.
3. *Training.* Develop catalogs and samples that suit the local marketplace. If possible, personally show your overseas agent/distributor how the product operates as well as repairs and required maintenance.

Close contact between your company and the foreign distributor will overcome many problems. In Japan, as in many other countries in the Far East, agency terminations are usually blamed on the foreign company and often inhibit one's effort in finding a good replacement.

Finally, the use of lawyers in business is not so ingrained as in the United States; therefore, use them sparingly.

SELLING TO FOREIGN DEPARTMENT STORES IN THE UNITED STATES

One way to get started is to sell to the U. S. buying office of foreign department stores. Contact them in person if you can, with a proposal for unique "Made in the U.S.A." items. Normally they will pay you as the U. S. department store would except where they act as "resident" buyers for a group of stores. In this case, they may use Letters of Credit to transfer the funds to your account.

The following are lists of foreign stores with their own offices and independent resident buying offices:

Buying Offices in the United States Serving Foreign Department Stores

Aaron Schwab International
Los Angeles, CA 90014

Arkwright, Inc.
New York, NY 10036

Associated Merchandising Corp.
New York, NY 10018

Felix Lilienthal & Co., Inc.
New York NY 10016

Independent Retailers Syndicate
New York NY 10001

Kirby Block Marketing Service
New York, NY 10001

McGreevey, Werring & Howell
New York, NY 10001

Maricent International, Inc.
New York NY 10017

Metasco, Inc.
International Division of Allied Stores Corporation
New York, NY 10036

Mutual Buying Service
New York, NY 10036

Products Exchange Company, Inc.
New York, NY 10001

R. W. Cameron and Co.
New York, NY 10017

Retailers Representatives, Inc.
New York, NY 10018

Sears Roebuck International
Skokie, IL 60076

Six Foreign Department Stores with Their Own U. S. Buying Offices

Daimaru, Inc.
New York, NY 10010

Seibu Corporation of America
New York, NY 10020

Takashimaya Company, Ltd.
New York, NY 10017

The Robert Simpson Co., Ltd.
New York, NY 10036

T. Eaton Co., Ltd.
New York, NY 10017

SONAC-Nouvelles Galeries
New York, NY 10036

Chapter Seven

Pricing for Foreign Markets

After you have set up your overseas network by deciding with which overseas agents or distributors you will deal, and have acquired several domestic manufacturers as clients, one day you will receive a request from a foreign representative asking for prices. You must be prepared to establish, or to help your domestic clients establish, a sound approach to pricing. The method generally used to price an export product effectively is called *marginal cost pricing*. Making up the marginal cost price are the following incremental costs:

1. *Costs to produce the export product* over and above costs to produce items sold domestically.
2. *Costs of selling in the foreign market*, such as advertising and credit.
3. *Costs of moving the goods* from factory to final destination.

The total of these costs represents a level below which prices cannot be set without incurring a loss.

It is extremely important for both you and the manufacturer to understand the benefits *you* can provide the manufacturer in selling abroad. By examining the following cost analysis, you can easily see how exporting can significantly improve profits.

COSTS TO PRODUCE THE EXPORT PRODUCT

All manufacturing costs are either fixed or variable. *Fixed costs*, such as executive salaries, rent, and interest payments, change little with the volume of output. *Variable costs*, such as the cost of materials and sales, rise as the volume of output rises. The total cost of each item is generally computed by adding to its variable cost a share of total fixed costs.

Marginal costing includes variable costs, but not fixed costs, in the total cost of each item. That is, *margin* refers to the production capacity beyond the normal limits upon which fixed costs are based. Export products are manufactured within this margin.

For example, assume a small company was operating at 80 percent of its capacity and had *no alternative* for using the idle 20 percent. Further assume that it had to maintain its present minimum work force, which also worked at 80 percent capacity. The factory costs of increasing production by 10 percent might include only raw materials and extra utilities. *No* other costs would increase. Note that labor can be treated as a fixed cost, since the additional output does not cause the payroll to rise. The company could sell the 10 percent production increase without losing money if it recovers the materials cost and the increase in the utilities bill. Any amount greater than this would contribute to the payment of fixed costs, all of which would have been incurred whether production had been increased the 10 percent or not. If, in the absence of other sales alternatives, the company could sell this 10 percent abroad by lowering the export price below the domestic sales price, it might be advantageous to do so.

COSTS OF SELLING IN THE FOREIGN MARKET

It is important to identify and include those out-of-pocket costs that result directly from trying to export a particular product. For example, if significant costs for new packaging or promotional literature are required to market an item overseas, these expenses should be costed directly into the specific export items and not into the entire product line. However, most of the time these costs are figured into the total projected sales volume for that item as a fixed cost. The same is true for travel to foreign markets, advertising and promotion abroad, credit, and other costs that relate directly to the export item. These are really fixed costs that must be covered by the export sales. In determining the f.o.b. (free on board, meaning that you do not pay shipping charges) export price (this does *not* mean that you should *quote* f.o.b.), a projected export sales volume should be estimated and the fixed export costs for this period should be prorated over the number of items to be sold. (See Terms of Sale, later in this chapter, for definitions of some common abbreviations.)

Let the product determine the type of packaging and promotional literature needed. Consumer items such as toiletries and prepared foods need the same creative packaging displayed when these items are sold domestically. Most industrial items, such as food processing or computer equipment, need little in the way of packaging, but detailed explanatory literature is important. In both cases, when you receive a request for prices, send a price list with literature in their language, samples (of small items), or pictures. If samples are requested, send them immediately. The requestor should be billed for the manufacturing costs only.

COSTS OF MOVING THE GOODS

The last group of costs are those traditionally associated with exporting—the costs involved in moving the goods from the factory door to the ultimate foreign consumer. A few of these costs, such as certain types of general marine insurance policies, are fixed, but most of them, including tariffs, shipping, warehousing, commissions, and margins, are variable.

Figure 7.1 is a sample worksheet that will help determine your costs and profits for these transactions. The elements from Figure 7.1 are illustrated in the calculating sheet of Figure 7.2. (Figures 7.1 through 7.5 were taken from *How to Build an Export Business, U. S. Department of Commerce, 1980, Office of Minority Business Enterprises.*)

Great care must be exercised in preparing a price quotation. You must be absolutely certain that you overlook nothing. Therefore, very carefully review all of your figures and double-check the calculations.

If you are acting as an export agent, your commissions will probably be between 5–15 percent. The commission would depend on your negotiation with the manufacturer. As an Export Management Company taking title, you would build in a profit margin somewhat larger because of your financial outlay.

Start your price quotation letter by stating that your company is pleased to submit its firm, fixed price quotation for a specified period of time (the manufacturer will usually give you a period of time the quote is valid). State that the shipping date will remain open until the order is received. If the overseas agent has requested samples or literature, send such by registered air mail (or DHL Courier Express) to insure delivery.

Many times a seller is requested to submit a *pro forma invoice* with his or her quotation (see Figure 7.3). A pro forma invoice is not for payment purposes. It is only a model, which the buyer will use when applying for an import license or arranging for funds.

Before completing your quotation, check the current overseas prices for your product category to make sure you are competitive. It is common for overseas agents to check with several sources of a product before they place an order. (See Figures 7.4 and 7.5 Sample Sales Letter and Purchase Order.)

REFERENCE INFORMATION
  1. Our Reference   _____   2. Customer Reference_____
CUSTOMER INFORMATION
  3. Name_____   5. Cable Address_____
  4. Address_____   6. Telex No._____
      _____
      _____

PRODUCT INFORMATION
  7. Product_____   11. Dimensions_____x_____x_____
  8. No. of units _____   12. Cubic measure ____(square inches)
  9. Net Weight _____   (unit)   ____(square feet)
10. Gross weight_____   13. Total measure_____
                                               14. Schedule B. No._____
PRODUCT CHARGES
15. Price (or cost) per unit_____x units_____   Total_____
16. Profit (or mark-up)   _____
17. Sales Commissions   _____
18.   FOB Factory
FEES—PACKING, MARKING, INLAND FREIGHT
19. Freight Forwarder   _____
20. Financing costs   _____
21. Other charges   _____
22. Export packing   _____
23. Labeling/Marking   _____
24. Inland freight to_____   _____
25. Other charges (identify)_____   _____
26. FOB, Port City Export Packed)
PORT CHARGES/DOCUMENT
27. Unloading (Heavy Lift)   _____
28. Terminal   _____
29. Other (identify)_____   _____
30. Consular document (check, if required) _____   _____
31. Certificate of Origin (check, if required) _____   _____
32. Export License (check, if required)   _____   _____
33. FAS Vessel (or Airplane)
FREIGHT
34. Based on   _____weight _____measure
35. Ocean   _____Air   _____
36. On deck   _____Under deck_____
37. Rate   _____Minimum_____Amount _____
INSURANCE
38. Coverage required   _____
39. Basis_____Rate_____Amount _____
40. CIF, Port of Destination

Figure 7.1 Export costing worksheet
(for preparing export quotations)

YOUR COMPANY, INC.

DATE: July 20, 1988   #76-10
QUOTED TO: ABC Refrigeration, 1500 Pembridge, London MK 46 BN England
REFERENCE: #225–dated July 10, 19XX
FROM PORT: New York
PRICE QUOTATION TERMS: C.I.F. Liverpool
SHIPPING LINE: White Star
PRODUCT DESCRIPTION: Our model 232
SCHEDULE B No: 719.1502

NO. OF UNITS: 5   NET FOB FACTORY PRICE: $920   TOTAL PRICE: $4,600
INLAND FREIGHT:
EXPORT PACKING & STENCILING   85
FREIGHT FORWARDING   200
    CLEARANCE & HANDLING   30
    BOOKING STEAMSHIP SPACE   10
    CONSULAR DOCUMENTATION } not required
    CERTIFICATE OF ORIGIN
    PREPARING EXPORT DECLARATION   5
    PREPARING OCEAN BILL OF LADING   3
    MESSENGER SERVICE   5
    SHIPMENT PAPERS TO U. S. BANK FOR L/C   5
TOTALING FORWARDING AND INLAND FREIGHT CHARGES $343
MARINE INSURANCE INCLUDING WAR RISK $67.50 plus 5% =   71
NET WEIGHT OF SHIPMENT   1,060 pounds
GROSS WEIGHT OF SHIPMENT (units plus crating) 1,140 pounds
DIMENSIONS OF EACH CRATE: 31" x 30" x 40"
EACH CRATE CUBIC FEET: 37,200 cubic inches = 21.5 = 22 cubic feet
TOTAL SHIPMENT CUBIC FEET: 110 or 110 ÷ 35.3145 = 3.11 cubic meters
OCEAN FREIGHT $1.50/cubic ft = $1.50 x 110 = $165 + 5% = $173
TOTAL CIF PRICE LIVERPOOL   165 + 8 $5,187
These items are approximate

Note that this price quotation work sheet differs from the suggested costing sheet, which shows all *possible* charges that could occur. Charges for consular invoices or certificates of origin are not necessary because U. K. customs do not require them.

Figure 7.2 Export Costing Sheet

YOUR COMPANY, INC.
111 MAIN STREET
HOMETOWN, VIRGINIA 22101
555/821-1860
JULY 20, 19XX

ABC Refrigeration Co., Ltd.
P.O. Box 25
1500 Pembridge Crescent
London, England

PRO-FORMA INVOICE

Your Reference: #225
Dated: July 10, 19XX

Five (5) Model 232 water-cooled ice cube makers @ $920 each	$ 4,600
Estimated inland freight, export packing, and forwarding fees	343
F.O B. vessel—New York, NY	$ 4,943
Estimated ocean freight	$ 173
Estimated marine insurance	71
C.I.F. Liverpool	$ 5,187

Export packed in 5 wood crates, 110 total cubic feet
Gross weight: 1140 lbs.
Net weight: 1060 lbs.

Payment terms: Irrevocable letter of credit confirmed by a U. S. bank.
Shipment can be made two (2) weeks after receipt of firm order.

COUNTRY OF ORIGIN: United States of America

We certify that this pro-forma invoice is true and correct.

Your Company, Inc.

Nelson T. Joyner, Jr.
President

Figure 7.3 Pro-forma invoice

YOUR COMPANY, INC.
111 MAIN STREET
HOMETOWN, VIRGINIA 22101
555/821-1860

ABC Refrigeration Company, LTD
150 Pembridge Crescent
London MK 46 4BN, England   Our quote: 76-10
Gentlemen:

Thank for your letter (your reference no. 225) dated July 10, 19XX, which expresses interest in our Model 232 water-cooled ice cube maker. We have attached specification sheets for this model.

Our pro-forma invoice for five of these units C.I.F. Liverpool, England, is enclosed. Our payment terms are irrevocable letter of credit confirmed by a U. S. bank.

We can ship these units within two weeks after receipt of your firm order. The goods will be shipped in wooden crates, steel strapped, containing one Model 232 water-cooled ice cube maker per carton. Marine insurance will be provided warehouse-to-warehouse.

Our Model 232 contains unique features not found on any other product. We have a long list of satisfied customers for this product.

We look forward to receiving your order.

                                        Sincerely,

                                        Nelson T. Joyner, Jr.
                                        President

Figure 7.4   Sample of a cover "sales" letter to be sent with the pro-forma invoice

ABC REFRIGERATION CO., LTD.

Post Office Box 25 / 1500 Pembridge Crescent / London, MK 46 4 BN England

Telephone: 01-355-1414   *PURCHASE ORDER NO. 555*   *Banks:* Union Bank, Ltd.

Telex: 825540   British Bank, Ltd.

Cable: ABCREF   Date: August 1, 19XX

TO SUPPLIER:

Your Company, Inc.
111 Main Street
Hometown, VA 22101

Please fill the following order in accordance with the shipping instructions, packing, delivery and terms that are specified below.

Please notify us by airmail of your acceptance of this order by signing the attached duplicate copy and returning it to us as soon as possible. If you cannot comply with any of the following provisions, please let us know immediately by airmail or TELEX. Then wait for our further comments before proceeding with the order.

ITEM: Model 232 Water-Cooled Ice Maker
QUANTITY: 5
PRICE: US $1,035.20 each C.I.F. Liverpool, England
SHIPPING DATE: On or before September 5, 19XX.
PACKING: For export in wooden crates, steel strapped, containing one Model 232 water-cooled ice cube maker per carton.
SHIPPING MARKS: ABC-London
                      No. 555
                      London via Liverpool
                      No. 1-5/up
EXPORTING ROUTING: From New York to Liverpool via White Star Line
MARINE INSURANCE: Warehouse-to-warehouse, plus all-risk C.I.F. Liverpool, plus 10%.
PAYMENT TERMS: Irrevocable letter of credit, opened by British Bank, Ltd., London, and confirmed by their correspondent bank, Home Town Bank, Hometown Virginia USA.
DOCUMENTS REQUIRED: Upon dispatch of the order, airmail the following to ABC Refrigeration Co., Ltd., 1500 Pembridge crescent, London MK 46 4BN, England, the following documents:

    6 copies commercial invoices. Show country
       of origin on all commercial invoices.
    6 copies of packing lists. Detail net and
       gross weight in pounds.
    Other documents in accordance with the terms
       of the letter of credit.

Sincerely,

R. E. Jones
Managing Director

Figure 7.5   Sample purchase order

TERMS OF SALE

It is very important that a common understanding exists regarding the delivery terms. In the United States, it is customary to ship "f.o.b factory," "freight collect," "prepay and charge," or "c.o.d." but an entirely different set of terms is used in international business. Some terms sound similar, but they have different definitions. Some of the more common terms used in international trade are briefly defined below; more comprehensive lists appear in the glossaries at the end of this book.

- *c.i.f.*: cost, insurance, freight to named overseas port of import. Under this term, the seller quotes a price including the goods, insurance, and all transportation and miscellaneous charges to the point of debarkation from vessel or aircraft.
- *c & f.*: cost and freight to named overseas port of import. Under this term, the seller quotes a price including the cost of transportation to the named point of debarkation.
- *f.a.s.*: free along side at named U. S. port of export. Under this term, the seller quotes a price, including service charges and delivery of the goods along side the vessel.
- *f.o.b.*: free on board. There are a number of classes of f.o.b.:
    - f.o.b. named inland port of origin
    - f.o.b. named port of exportation
    - f.o.b. vessel (named port of export)
  In all classes of f.o.b., the price quoted includes loading the product onto the carrying vessel, but not shipping it.
- *ex* (named point of origin) (e.g., ex factory, ex warehouse, etc.): Under this term, the price quoted applies only at the point of origin, and the seller agrees to place the goods at the disposal of the buyer at the agreed place on the date or within the period fixed. All other charges are for the account of the buyer.

When quoting, make your terms meaningful. A price for industrial machinery quoted "f.o.b. Saginaw, Michigan, not export packed" would be unacceptable to prospective foreign buyers, who would have no way to determine with any accuracy what the export packing costs would be in Saginaw, nor would they know the freight charges from Saginaw to the port of export.

Always quote c.i.f. whenever possible; this is significant when quoting abroad. It shows the foreign buyer what it costs to get your product into a port in his or her country or in a nearby port.

You will need assistance in figuring the c.i.f. price; call your freight forwarder and he or she will be glad to help you. Furnish this person with a description of your product and the weight and cubic measurement when packed. The freight forwarder can then compute the c.i.f. price and usually will not charge you for this service. In fact, most of the information for your price quotation will come from your freight forwarder. This individual will also make most of the necessary shipping arrangements and handle your insurance needs. Other services offered by these people are discussed in later chapters.

When your customer accepts your quote, he or she will send you a purchase order and open a letter of credit in you favor (letters of credit are further discussed in Chapter Eight). Examine the purchase order you receive. Make sure it conforms to your price quote.

Next, inform the manufacturer of the terms and conditions of the purchase order. Make arrangements with the manufacturer for delivery close to the ship's departure date. (A sample export purchase order appears in Figure 7.5.)

Finally, have your foreign freight forwarder prepare all documents for shipping. After the goods are shipped, the freight forwarder will give you the documents necessary for you to receive payment from the bank. In order to receive payment, it is very important that you have complied with all requirements listed in the letter of credit.

Normally, you will be billed by the manufacturer, the freight forwarder, and the shipping (trucking, airline) company within thirty days. You must calculate and then pay commission to your overseas agent(s).

Chapter Eight covers in more detail how to get paid.

Chapter Eight

How to Get Paid

Because exporting requires international financial arrangements and agreements, many would-be exporters hesitate to become involved, or try and become confused. Actually, export terms of sale and payments are quite simple and differ only slightly from domestic financing. The general concepts are about the same and the methods are similar. In either situation, the seller wants to be assured that the buyer will pay, and the buyer wants to be certain that he or she receives what he or she pays for.

There are three types of export financing: short, medium, and long term. Short-term covers 180 days or less; medium-term, 181 days to five years; and long-term, five years or more. This discussion is limited to short-term financing, inasmuch as the beginner is usually not in a position to offer better terms. There are five methods of payment:

1. Cash with order or in advance of order
2. Letters of credit
3. Documentary drafts
4. Open account
5. Consignment

Categories 1 and 2 favor the seller, whereas categories 3, 4, and 5 favor the buyer.

CASH WITH ORDER OR IN ADVANCE OF ORDER

The best terms possible are receiving cash in advance or with orders—you have payment before the foods have left your hands. However, unless there is an extraordinarily favorable sellers' market or a situation where the seller dominates that market, most overseas customers will be reluctant to pay in advance. There are times when insisting upon some cash in advance is prudent. For example, if a foreign customer orders a specially designed piece of equipment that you do not normally carry, you should require the customer to give you at least 25 percent deposit against the total cost of the item before manufacturing begins. By and large, very little business is conducted in this manner.

LETTERS OF CREDIT

It goes without saying that you, the exporter, want to be paid as quickly as possible, whereas your overseas customer may well want to defer payment for as long as possible. The answer, of course, is credit.

Since World War I, U. S. exporters have usually insisted upon letters of credit that were equivalent to cash on shipment. As late as 1963, one-half of all U. S. exports were sold on a letter-of-credit basis; the remainder was sold on open account or draft collection terms. In Third World countries, letters of credit are the rule in conducting export sales.

A letter of credit (illustrated in Figure 8.1) is a financing instrument opened by a foreign buyer with a bank in her or his locality. The letter of credit stipulates the purchase price agreed upon by the buyer and seller, the quantity of merchandise to be shipped, and the type of insurance coverage to protect the merchandise during shipment. The letter of credit names the seller as beneficiary (that is, you are the party who gets paid) and identifies the definite time period the terms remain in force. The letter of credit authorizes the buyers to pay when all the stipulated conditions have been met. Most export letters of credit are made payable in the United States.

A letter of credit gives some assurance to the seller that the buyer is solvent. Most letters of credit are irrevocable and often confirmed when requested by the seller's bank in the United States before they are accepted by the seller. This confirmation obligates the confirming bank to pay you once you have met all the stated conditions in the particular letter of credit.

There are two simple considerations when using letters of credits:

1. Specify as fully as possible to your buyer the amount of credit (payment) needed, the length of time for which this letter of credit should be valid, whether partial shipments are acceptable, and all necessary documents.
2. When the letter of credit is delivered to you through the advising bank, check to see that you can meet all provisions specified. If not, request an amendment by the foreign buyer before proceeding.

Chemical Bank

International Operations
P.O. Box 44, Church Street Station
New York, N.Y. 10008   March   , 19XX

Their Ref. No.   123456   Our Advance no. 000000

To   EXPORT CORPORATION OF AMERICA
                  123 FIRST STREET
                  NEW YORK, NEW YORK 10036

                  EXPORT CONFIRMED

                                                      for Account (same if left blank)
Instructions   BANCO DE BANCO   GOMEZ Y FLORENCIO
                  BOGOTA, COLOMBIA   BOGOTA, COLOMBIA

Gentlemen:
We are instructed by the above mentioned correspondent to advise you that they have ordered in your favor
their irrevocable credit, as indicated above, for a sum or sums not exceeding in all. . . . .
FIFTY THOUSAND DOLLARS UNITED STATES CURRENCY ($50,000.00)

Available by   **At**   SIGHT ON US
your draft(s)
                  For   FULL   Invoice value of merchandise Invoice as:

MACHINE SPARE PARTS,   F.O.B. NEW YORK

YOUR DRAFT(S) MUST BE ACCOUNTED
1.   YOUR COMMERCIAL INVOICE AND 3 COPIES.
2.   FULL SET ON BOARD OCEAN LADING ISSUED TO ORDER BLANK ENDORSED,
     DATED LASTEST APRIL 30, 1900

EVIDENCING SHIPMENT OF THE MERCHANDISE FROM NEW YORK TO BOGOTA.
PARTIAL SHIPMENTS NOT PERMITTED.
INSURANCE COVERED BY BUYERS IN COLOMBIA.

THE ABOVE MENTIONED CORRESPONDENT ENGAGES WITH YOU THAT ALL DRAFTS DRAWN UNDER
AND IN CONFORMITY WITH THE TERMS OF THIS ADVICE WILL BE DULY HONORED UPON
DELIVERY OF DOCUMENTS AS SPECIFIED IF PRESENTED AT THIS OFFICE (COMMERCIAL
LETTER OF CREDIT DEPARTMENT, 55 WATER STREET, SOUTH BUILDING, 17th FLOOR,
NEW YORK CITY, NEW YORK 10041) ON OR BEFORE MAY 10, 19XX.

WE CONFIRM THE CREDIT AND HEREBY UNDERTAKE THAT ALL DRAFTS DRAWN AND PRESENTED AS
ABOVE SPECIFIED WILL BE DULY HONORED.
                                        Very truly yours,

                                        XXXXXXXXXXXXXXXXXXXXXXXXXXXXXXXXXXXXXXXXXXX
                                        Authorized Signature

Provisions applicable to this credit
This credit is subject to the Uniform Customs and Practice for Documentary Credits (1983 Revision) International Chamber of Commerce Publication No. 4

Fig. 8.1 Letter of credit

Letters of credit are most often used when initiating business with a new account, when a check of the importer's credit reveals it would be unwise to make shipment on a less secure basis, or when large purchases are requested by an unknown buyer. When dealing with established accounts, letters of credit can become burdensome, especially considering the competitive financing terms available today. For example, a European company recently made a large sale of aluminum cable to a Mexican company, even though their price was higher than that of a competing U. S. firm. The deciding factor in closing the deal was not the price but the credit extended by the European company, with the assistance of its government, to finance the installation over an extended period of time. This story illustrates a common practice in international trade—you can close more sales if you offer better terms. To be successful, you must often offer your established accounts something better than letter of credit terms.

The specimen shown in Figure 8.1 of an irrevocable and confirmed letter of credit illustrates the various parts of a typical letter of credit. In this sample, the letter of credit was forwarded by the Export Corporation of America (A) by the drawee's bank, Chemical Bank (B), as a result of the letter of credit being issued by the Banco de Banco, Bogota, Colombia (C), for the account of the importer, Gomez y Florencio (D). The date of issue was March X, 19xx (E), and the beneficiary must submit proper documents (e.g., a commercial invoice in triplicate) (F) by April 30, 19XX (G) in order for a sight draft to be honored. Figure 8.2 illustrates a typical letter of credit transaction.

If your relationship with your customer is good, other methods of financing can make business transactions easier. You might want to consider three special types of letters of credit that offer you more flexibility:

1. *Revolving letter of credit.* This is useful when shipping a variety of goods to an established customer. It normally runs for a period less than one year and it provides for prompt reinstatement when drawn against.

2. *Assignable letter of credit.* This type is the same as the normal letter of credit, except that it includes the phrase "and/or assignees" following the name of the beneficiary. This allows the exporter to make his or her domestic purchase by using the overseas buyer's credit. That is, you agree that payment for the letter of credit may be made to your U. S. supplier. This is a way for an exporter to conduct business with limited capital.

3. *Banker's acceptances.* As your business grows you will want to extend credit to your importer. One of the most efficient methods of doing this is through a banker's acceptance. After agreeing to the terms (e.g., 90 days at sight), the importer opens a draft (check) under a letter of credit in favor of the exporter (beneficiary). The exporter presents the draft and the requested shipping documents to the paying bank. The bank reviews the documentation for correctness, then "accepts" the draft to become payable

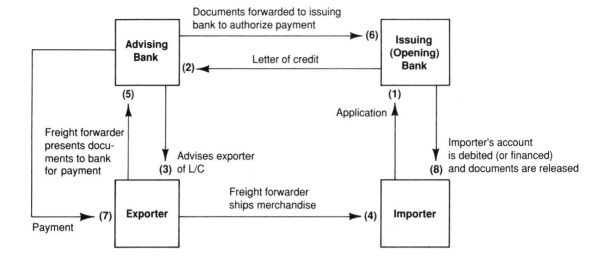

Figure 8.2 Typical letter of credit transaction

(mature) in 90 days, or, if the exporter requires, "accepts" the draft and discounts the amount because of the need for immediate funds.

DOCUMENTARY DRAFTS (BILL OF EXCHANGE)

Drafts are a popular and common method of financing exports. A draft is a written instrument drawn by one party (exporter) on a buyer for certain sum of money at sight (D/P) or at some definite future time. Since World War II, letters of credit have become less popular because of competition.

When using drafts, you and the buyer usually agree beforehand that the transaction will be on a sight draft basis or perhaps on a 60- or 90-day deferred payment basis (60 SD, DA). The overseas importer orders merchandise directly from you, and you arrange to ship the goods. You then take your shipping documents and your own draft, drawn on the importer, to your bank. Your U. S. bank forwards all documents to its correspondent bank overseas. This overseas bank notifies the importer when the documents arrive. If terms are payment at sight, this arrangement would be called a *sight draft document against payment* (S/D, D/A), and the importer would be required to pay immediately to obtain the shipping documents so she or he can pick up the goods.

However, if the importer has agreed to "accept" (pay later) (D/A) the draft, he or she is permitted to obtain the documents by accepting the draft and the merchandise but is not obliged to make payments until the draft matures (e.g., 60 days D/A). The exporter will, of course, have established credit locally and made arran-

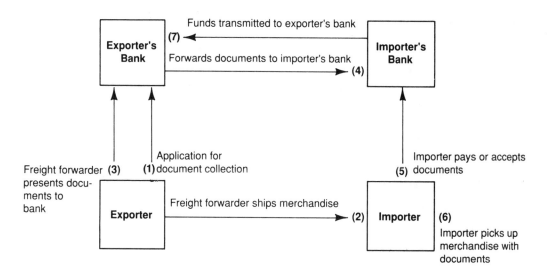

Figure 8.3 Typical documentary draft transaction

gements with his or her bank prior to undertaking the shipment. Figure 8.3 illustrates a typical documentary draft transaction.

Two other types of drafts are used less frequently: *time drafts* and *date drafts*. They are used to give the buyer better financing because they are forms of deferred payment. In the case of Time Draft, the buyer may take possession of the merchandise with payment deferred. With a Date Draft, the seller retains the title of goods until payment. The main problem with this type of financing is the possibility of the buyer being insolvent when the drafts are presented for payment. Therefore, before offering such terms, you should be fairly certain of the buyer's financial stability.

OPEN ACCOUNT

In open account financing, the overseas importer neither provides letters of credit nor honors drafts. The only requirement is that the importer pay the balance of his or her account periodically, or within a certain period of time after the purchase.

Open account financing is usually used between large companies and their subsidiaries (e.g., Ford Motor Company and Ford of Europe). As might be expected, this arrangement requires the exporter to have full confidence in the overseas buyer. Some open account arrangements are on a monthly basis for outstanding bills; however, other types of arrangements (quarterly, semi-annually) are common. Many Third World nations do not allow open accounts in international trade because they could not control their balance of payments if money were to flow freely in and out of the country.

CONSIGNMENT

When goods are exported on consignment, the exporter is not paid until the goods are sold in the overseas marketplace. Consignment is rarely used between independent exporters and importers. There is too much risk for the exporters because they are not paid until all goods are sold. Also, most exporters feel that when an importer has his or her money tied up in inventory, he or she will make a greater sales effort.

DEALING WITH FOREIGN CURRENCY

Generally, a U. S. exporter or importer will have no trouble with currency because the U. S. dollar is one of the most accepted currencies in world trade. However, at times it may be necessary to accept orders and quote prices in other currencies, such as the Spanish *peseta*, the Japanese *yen*, or the Greek *drachma*. If you are faced with this situation, you should contact your bank.

Banks buy and sell convertible currency "at" spot (immediate) or for future delivery. You, as an importer, may contract with a bank to buy the currency for future delivery at a fixed rate of exchange because you know that, at some specific future time, you must make payment in that foreign currency. Conversely, as an exporter you may protect yourself by contracting to sell to a bank, at a fixed rate of exchange, the foreign currency proceeds you expect on a given date. These contracts provide a "hedge" against currency fluctuation. That is, importers and exporters avoid the risk of fluctuating exchange rates and can better determine their true costs and profits when they enter into such a contract. The bank does not charge interest on these contracts because no payments are due in advance of the due date of the contract.

Chapter Nine

Export Financing

The methods of payment described in Chapter Eight can involve varying credit terms. It is important to your success in exporting that you understand the use of credit in overseas transactions.

FACTORS AFFECTING YOUR USE OF CREDIT

First, competition is becoming more intense, and U. S. exporters now must offer attractive terms if they are going to compete with traders of other nations. Second, when you become better acquainted with buyers overseas, and as these buyers prove their credit worthiness, you should be more willing to extend longer credit terms. And third, longer terms have been made less risky for U. S. exporters because of the export credit insurance now available through the U. S. government in association with the insurance industry. Without doubt, this protection against political and commercial risks of doing business abroad has helped many exporters, especially those new to foreign marketing, to be more competitive.

HOW TO GET CREDIT INFORMATION ABOUT YOUR BUYERS

There are several sources of credit information. Your bank is in an excellent position, either directly or through its correspondents, to obtain credit information for

63

you. In addition, it is not uncommon for one exporter to check with another U. S. exporter to find out what his or her experience has been in selling to a particular foreign buyer on credit. These are called *trade checkups*. The U. S. Department of Commerce also maintains information on thousands of buyers around the world. *World Traders Data Reports* (WTDRs) are available through the Department of Commerce's district offices. Private credit institutions, such as Dun and Bradstreet, offer an international service as well.

WHERE TO FIND FINANCING FOR YOUR EXPORT SALES

Many sources of financial assistance are open to you. First, of course, is your own working capital or bank line of credit; that is, *you* might give credit terms to your overseas customer. However, use of your own facilities may restrict your total cash availability even if you were to establish a separate export line of credit with your bank.

Probably the best solution is to contact a bank—about 250 U. S. banks have qualified international banking departments. Perhaps no other country in the world offers such a wide choice of financial institutions that are prepared to provide international financing and marketing assistance to exporters.

Many commercial banks with active international departments have specialists fully familiar with particular foreign countries and experts in different types of commodities and transactions. These banks, located in all major U. S. cities, maintain a wide network of correspondent relationships with smaller banks throughout the United States. This banking network enables any exporter to find assistance (for yourself or your overseas customer) directly or indirectly for export financing needs. These larger banks also maintain correspondent relationships with banks in most foreign countries or operate their own overseas branches, providing a direct channel to your overseas customer.

Exporters should also be aware of factoring houses that deal in accounts receivable of American exporters. Factors may charge higher fees than banks, but they will purchase your receivables, often without recourse (i.e., if your buyer fails to pay, it is the factor's loss, not yours), assuring you of prompt, although discounted, payment for your export sales.

Federal Government Programs

The following finance programs outline where and what type of help one can expect from government and private sources.

- Export-Import Bank of the U. S. (EXIMBANK)
  811 Vermont Avenue, N. W.
  Washington, D.C. 20571
  202-566-8819

This government-owned organization offers insurance, loan guarantees, direct credits, and counseling on a variety of programs to help U. S. exporters.

In the past, large projects and big capital goods orders were the mainstay of their operation. Recently, they have put greater emphasis on supporting small- and medium-size companies selling overseas.

The financing programs cover all types of merchandise and equipment for 181 days to five years. They have opened a Small Business Hotline (800-424-5201) to give advice on which program would be best for your company.

Also offered is FCIA insurance programs against commercial and political risks.

- U. S. Small Business Administration (SBA) (Contact nearest SBA office for assistance.)

The SBA has two basic programs. The first is the Export Revolving Line of Credit program. Under this situation, the SBA can guarantee up to 90 percent of a revolving line of credit to $500,000 for as long as eighteen months. You must be able to meet SBA criteria for small businesses and have been in business for one year. This has not been an outstanding success for the agency.

The second program, which has been more successful, is the SBA EXIMBANK Co-Guarantee Program. The SBA EXIMBANK can jointly guarantee up to 90 percent of export-related loans from $200,000 to $1,000,000.

Finally, the SBA, in cooperation with the Department of Agriculture's Foreign Agricultural Service (FAS), is helping small minority firms build exports of farm products as jobbers, dealers, distributors, and brokers. They accomplish this by sponsoring overseas exhibits and trade fairs, and by supporting regional state organizations that sell overseas.

- Overseas Private Investment Corporation (OPIC)
1129 20th Street, N. W.
Washington, D. C. 20257
202-632-1804

Although they specialize in long-term financing of U. S. business investments in underdeveloped countries, OPIC does make direct loans of $100,000 to $4,000,000 for projects sponsored by small business (defined as a company with $22 million or less in annual revenues or $44 million or less in net worth).

- Private Export Funding Corporation (PEFCO)
  280 Park Avenue
  New York, N.Y. 10017
  212-557-3100

  This is a private company made up of commercial banks that lend money in cooperation with EXIMBANK. These loans are made to foreign purchasers of U. S. exports (goods or services). Transactions are usually $1 million or more. The loan period is 181 days to five years.

- Commodity Credit Corporation (CCC)
  c/o Assistant General Sales Manager
  Export Credits
  Foreign Agricultural Services (FAS)
  14th Street and Independence Avenue, S.W.
  Washington, D. C. 20250
  202-447-3224

  Under this program, the CCC will guarantee payment against default for the port value of the commodity exported. This is done where private institutions may be unwilling to provide financing with the CCC guarantee. Credit terms can extend to three years.

State Government Programs

Because of federal government budget restraints and the retreat of many banks from making export loans, state governments have become active in guaranteeing loans to small and medium businesses. Indiana, Minnesota, Illinois, and California are among the most active states in supporting export financing programs.

Most of these programs have a term of eighteen months or less and are usually for amounts under $500,000. (See Appendix 1: State and Local Sources for International Assistance.)

City Government Programs

- Economic Development Office
  City Hall
  Room 2008
  Los Angeles, CA 90012
  213-488-6154

  The need for trade financing has become so great for small and medium size businesses that cities are moving into this function.

Los Angeles is the first of such programs to offer export financing. The purpose of this program (co-sponsored by EXIMBANK) is to provide one-stop export financing, coordination of federal, state, and local information resources, to identify the needs of small- and medium-sized companies needing financing, and to provide a new distribution channel for EXIMBANK'S financing program.

Private Programs

- AIG Political Risks, Inc.
  70 Pine Street
  New York, NY 70270
  212-770-7000

This is an alternative to FCIA (EXIMBANK) insurance (political and commercial risk). The policies offered are as follows:

1. Performance bond—bid bond
2. Political risk for export transactions
3. Contract repudiation (government contract)
4. Expropriation coverage
5. Transfer risk (money)

This company will insure goods that are under government restrictions (economic and foreign policy consideration). The minimum premium is $50,000 and policy term can be up to five years.

Chapter Ten

Preparing Your Goods for Foreign Shipment

Whether you are exporting for a manufacturer or shipping under your own label, you should make certain that the merchandise is properly prepared both for its destined foreign market and for shipping.

There are four phases of preparation: engineering, production, packing, and marketing. The first of these, engineering, is part of the homework you must do before you offer products for sale overseas.

ENGINEERING

It may be necessary to modify a product in order to sell it successfully overseas. Modifications may make a product conform with country regulations, historical preferences, or local customs. Modifications may also facilitate movement, reduce costs, or compensate for possible differences in electrical current and/or measurement standards.

The most common mistake U.S. exporters make is failing to consider these overseas differences. Some people tend to think that any product that has sold well in the United States will sell well in the same form in other countries. This error is best illustrated by the domestic car manufacturers' approach to selling overseas. Because of great success within the home market, little or no effort was made to

68

build a vehicle that could be used in multiple areas of the world. However, by examining the sales of cars like the Mercedes-Benz, one can see opportunities that U.S. manufacturers failed to address. Only the advent of stricter smog control regulations, foreign competition, and the rising cost of fuel have brought about changes in Detroit's thinking regarding design and performance.

A business associate of mine, in the electronics field, was more flexible than the domestic auto firms just described. Before committing himself to shipping a large quantity of modular components for receivers and transmitters, he obtained a catalog of these products from a friend in Germany. By closely examining the equipment described within that magazine, he stripped down his product to meet the more basic needs of the European market, thus saving both himself and his distributor from a potentially disastrous marketing error.

Thus, to avoid problems of "fit," have your overseas distributor or agent send your local catalogs and pictures of products similar to yours. You must know what has been selling successfully in your market. Then you can help your manufacturers conform with customs, regulations, and standards used overseas. You must be prepared to modify.

Other considerations include the following:

1. Many foreign countries use different electrical standards than those in the United States. It is not unusual to find phase, cycle, or voltages, both in home and commercial usage overseas, that would damage equipment designed for use in the United States, or that would impair its operating efficiency. These will sometimes vary even within a given country. This knowledge will let the exporter know if it is necessary to substitute a special motor and/or arrange for a different drive ratio to achieve a desirable operating RPM or service factor.

2. Many equipment items must be graduated in the metric system to allow them to be integrated with other pieces of equipment or to allow work to be completed in the standard of a country.

3. Since freight charges are usually assessed on a weight or volume basis, whichever provides the greater revenue for the carrier, some consideration must be given to shipping an item disassembled, rather than assembled, in order to lower delivery costs. This may also be necessary to facilitate movement on narrow roads and streets or through doorways and elevators which could otherwise cause transit problems.

4. Local customs or historical preference regarding size, color, speed, source, grade of raw materials, and so on, are other reasons why a redesign might be considered. In addition, many foreign governments have established mandatory standards. These will usually be specified with the request for quotations.

PRODUCTION

The most important thing to remember about production is to process overseas orders as promptly as domestic orders would be processed. It is very difficult to explain, in a different language, to someone halfway around the world the reason for a delayed shipment. If a shipment is delayed, it may be necessary to extend the expiration date of a letter of credit. This added expense to the buyer certainly will not be appreciated, especially if it happens often.

PACKING

Packing is a critical element of your export business. If the product doesn't arrive at its destination in good condition, it is almost as if your product hadn't arrived at all. Both manufacturers and freight forwarders can help with proper packing, since they have had experience with shipping hazards and with the specific product, respectively. Following is a basic packing guide to introduce you to alternative methods of preparing your products for shipment.

Exterior Containers

Fibreboard boxes (Cartons).   The most common economical container continues to be the fibreboard box. This is understandable as shippers seek efficient, but cheap and lightweight containers. (See Figure 10.1.)

Fibreboard comes closest to fitting the description of the ideal shipping container—light in weight, low cost, but able to withstand normal transportation hazards and protect the contents against loss or damage during transportation. The fibreboard box frequently measures up to most of these requirements in domestic transportation, but often fails in overseas movements when proper selection procedures are not followed. It must be recognized that all commodities cannot be suitably packed in fibreboard boxes. Moreover, all fibreboard boxes are not suitable overseas containers. This is particularly true because increases in moisture content of corrugated fibreboard adversely affect its stiffness and compressive strength.

First, the shipper must determine whether or not a fibreboard container is suitable for the particular commodity to be shipped, bearing in mind the item's vulnerability as well as the handling and transportation hazards to be encountered. If the answer is "yes," the shipper must then proceed to use the fibreboard container subject to the following:

1. The underlying factors in the selection of the fibreboard box are resistance to compression, resistance to puncture, strength on the score lines, and—probably the most important—resistance to moisture absorption. Impregnated and multiwall boxes are the most practical. Never use corrugated

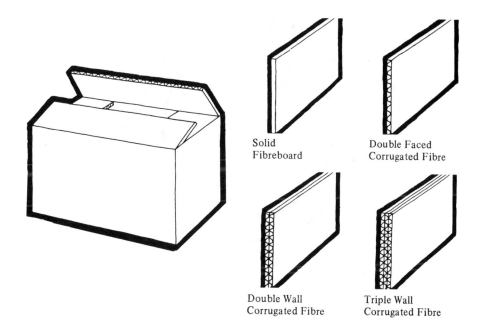

Solid Fibreboard

Double Faced Corrugated Fibre

Double Wall Corrugated Fibre

Triple Wall Corrugated Fibre

Figure 10.1 Fiberboard boxes (cartons) (*Source:* CIGNA P&C Companies, Publisher, Ports of the World, P.O. Box 7728, Philadelphia, PA 19101)

fibreboard boxes with a bursting test strength of less than 275 pounds per square inch (for exporting).

2. Flaps should be stapled or glued with a water-resistant adhesive applied to the entire area of contact between the flaps. For further protection, all seams can be sealed with a water-resistant tape.

3. Keep the weight of the contents within load limits specified in the box maker's certificate that appears on the box. The imprinted certificate should appear on one exterior face of every carton. It indicates bursting strength, size limit, and weight limit (Figure 10.2).

4. Reinforce with two tension straps applied at right angles and crisscrossing at top and bottom, or with two girth straps of filament tape.

5. When the nature of the contents permits, the load should support the walls of the container. Otherwise, the container selected should have sufficient resistance to compression to prevent collapse when it is placed in the bottom tier of a pile of similar boxes. *Never overload.*

6. Full height partitions should be utilized to separate fragile items within the same fibreboard box and/or to increase the stacking strength of the box.

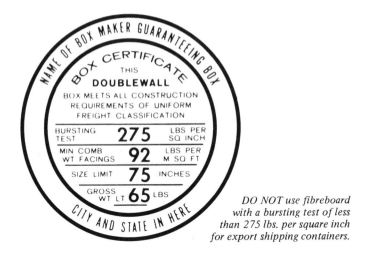

DO NOT use fibreboard with a bursting test of less than 275 lbs. per square inch for export shipping containers.

Figure 10.2 Box certificate (*Source:* CIGNA P&C Companies, Publisher, Ports of the World, P.O. Box 7728, Philadelphia, PA 19101)

7. Do not overlook the savings and the additional security offered by unitizing or palletizing (see page 82) or by overpacking several fibreboard boxes in consolidation containers.

8. Remember, highly pilferable merchandise is never safe in fibreboard boxes.

Nailed wood boxes. The nailed wood box (Figure 10.3) is one of the most satisfactory containers for overseas shipments for commodities of moderate weight.

Among its particular advantages is its ability to support superimposed loads; its ability to contain difficult loads without undue distortion or breaking open; the protection it affords contents from damage due to puncture, breakage, or crushing; and, finally, the fact that it permits interior blocking to hold the contents in place, thus allowing the container to be turned on its side or upside down. The following recommendations should be considered in selecting nailed wood boxes:

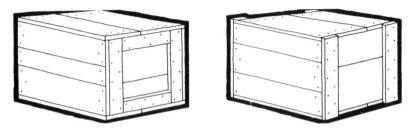

Figure 10.3 Nailed wood boxes (*Source:* CIGNA P&C Companies, Publisher, Ports of the World, P.O. Box 7728, Philadelphia, PA 19101)

1. Boxes should be made up of seasoned lumber with moisture content between 12 and 18 percent. Knots should not be over one-third the width of the board and specifically should not interfere with nailing. Bad cross-graining should also be avoided.

2. Consult appropriate tables for selecting the proper sizes of lumber and nails. Boxes with two or four cleats on each end are particularly recommended for overseas shipment (Table 10.1).

3. Load properly. Many well-designed boxes fail because the load is not properly fitted within the container. Unless the item to be packed is irregular in shape, do not permit any voids or dead space. If the load must be kept upright, equip the box with lift handles, skids, top peaks or gables, or some similar device to assure the box being stowed and handled in an upright position. *Avoid overloading.*

4. Reinforce the boxes with adequate tension metal straps placed one-sixth of the distance from the ends, unless containers are in excess of forty-eight inches in length or over 250 pounds. Then, three or more straps should be used, with one for each additional twenty-four inches. Staples should be used to hold strapping in place when boards are 5/8 inch in thickness or greater.

5. *Do not use second-hand boxes.* They are deficient in strength and do not permit detection of pilferage.

6. Boxes should be equipped with corrugated fasteners or similar devices where contents are substantially valued and susceptible to pilferage.

7. Boxes should be lined with a waterproof barrier material and sealed at the edges with a waterproof tape or adhesive. This will protect both the contents and the interior packing material.

There are two general types of crates: the open or skeleton crate and the fully sheathed crate. Both types are dependent on properly constructed frameworks. Although the drawings in Figure 10.4 illustrate the comparative strength of frame members of open crates under vertical compression, the same principles apply to sheathed crates, as they also require diagonal bracing to make them rigid. Keep in mind that sheathing is provided to protect the contents against exposure to the elements.

The open crate can be used where contents are virtually indestructible and when packing is required only to facilitate handling and stowage. It also serves well as an overpack to consolidate fibreboard boxes or to provide unit pack stiffness to resist crushing. Three-way corner construction should be reinforced with diagonals.

Consider these points in sheathed crate construction:

1. Provide a *substantial* framework (i.e., corner posts or vertical end struts, edge or frame members, intermediate struts and diagonal braces).

TABLE 10.1 LUMBER AND NAIL TABLES FOR NAILED WOOD BOXES

BELOW MEASUREMENTS IN INCHES

Weight of Contents (Pounds) Over	Less	Number of End Cleats	LOAD SUPPORTS CONTAINER WALLS — SOFTWOOD Thickness sides, top & bottom	Thickness ends	Thickness and width of cleats	HARDWOOD Thickness sides, top & bottom	Thickness ends	Thickness and width of cleats	LOAD GIVES LITTLE OR NO CONTAINER SUPPORT — SOFTWOOD Thickness sides, top & bottom	Thickness ends	Thickness and width of cleats	HARDWOOD Thickness sides, top & bottom	Thickness ends	Thickness and width of cleats
0	50	2	$3/8$	$5/8$	$5/8 \times 1\tfrac{3}{4}$	$3/8$	$5/8$	$5/8 \times 1\tfrac{3}{4}$	$1/2$	$3/4$	$3/4 \times 2\tfrac{1}{4}$	$1/2$	$5/8$	$5/8 \times 1\tfrac{3}{4}$
0	50	4	$3/8$	$5/8$	$5/8 \times 1\tfrac{3}{4}$	$3/8$	$5/8$	$5/8 \times 1\tfrac{3}{4}$	$1/2$	$5/8$	$5/8 \times 2\tfrac{1}{4}$	$1/2$	$5/8$	$5/8 \times 1\tfrac{3}{4}$
50	100	2	$1/2$	$3/4$	$3/4 \times 2\tfrac{1}{4}$	$3/8$	$5/8$	$5/8 \times 1\tfrac{3}{4}$	$1/2$	$3/4$	$3/4 \times 2\tfrac{1}{4}$	$1/2$	$5/8$	$5/8 \times 1\tfrac{3}{4}$
50	100	4	$1/2$	$3/4$	$3/4 \times 2\tfrac{1}{4}$	$3/8$	$5/8$	$5/8 \times 1\tfrac{3}{4}$	$5/8$	$5/8$	$5/8 \times 2\tfrac{1}{4}$	$1/2$	$5/8$	$5/8 \times 1\tfrac{3}{4}$
100	250	2	$5/8$	$3/4$	$3/4 \times 2\tfrac{1}{4}$	$1/2$	$3/4$	$3/4 \times 2\tfrac{1}{4}$	$5/8$	$3/4$	$3/4 \times 2\tfrac{5}{8}$	$1/2$	$3/4$	$3/4 \times 2\tfrac{1}{4}$
100	250	4	$5/8$	$5/8$	$5/8 \times 2\tfrac{1}{4}$	$1/2$	$5/8$	$5/8 \times 2\tfrac{1}{4}$	$3/4$	$3/4$	$3/4 \times 2\tfrac{1}{4}$	$1/2$	$5/8$	$5/8 \times 2\tfrac{1}{4}$
250	400	2	$3/4$	$13/16$	$3/4 \times 2\tfrac{5}{8}$	$5/8$	$3/4$	$3/4 \times 2\tfrac{1}{4}$	$3/4$	$1\tfrac{1}{16}$	$1\tfrac{1}{16} \times 3\tfrac{1}{4}$	$5/8$	$13/16$	$13/16 \times 2\tfrac{3}{4}$
250	400	4	$3/4$	$13/16$	$3/4 \times 2\tfrac{5}{8}$	$5/8$	$3/4$	$3/4 \times 2\tfrac{1}{4}$	$3/4$	$3/4$	$1\tfrac{1}{16} \times 3\tfrac{1}{4}$	$5/8$	$3/4$	$3/4 \times 2\tfrac{3}{4}$
400	600	4	$13/16$	$13/16$	$13/16 \times 2\tfrac{5}{8}$	$5/8$	$3/4$	$3/4 \times 2\tfrac{1}{4}$	$13/16$	$13/16$	$1\tfrac{1}{16} \times 3\tfrac{1}{4}$	$3/4$	$13/16$	$13/16 \times 2\tfrac{3}{4}$
600	800	4	$13/16$	$1\tfrac{1}{16}$	$1\tfrac{1}{16} \times 3\tfrac{1}{4}$	$13/16$	$1\tfrac{1}{16}$	$1\tfrac{1}{16} \times 3\tfrac{1}{4}$	$13/16$	$1\tfrac{1}{16}$	$1\tfrac{1}{16} \times 3\tfrac{1}{4}$	$3/4$	$13/16$	$13/16 \times 2\tfrac{3}{4}$
800	1000	4	$1\tfrac{1}{16}$	$1\tfrac{5}{16}$	$1\tfrac{5}{16} \times 4\tfrac{1}{8}$	$1\tfrac{1}{16}$	$1\tfrac{5}{16}$	$1\tfrac{5}{16} \times 4\tfrac{1}{8}$	$1\tfrac{1}{16}$	$1\tfrac{5}{16}$	$1\tfrac{5}{16} \times 4\tfrac{1}{8}$	$7/8$	$1\tfrac{1}{16}$	$1\tfrac{1}{16} \times 3\tfrac{3}{8}$

NAILS—Cement coated nails are preferred for their increased holding power. The size of the nail depends on the thickness of the wood (see above). Use 6d for 5/8'', 7d for 3/4'', 8d for 13/16'', 9d for 1-1/16'' & 12d for 1-5/16''. Do not use nails into wood less than 5/8''. Spacing of nails (fastening sides, tops & bottom to the ends) varies with the size of the nail. Space 6d 2'', 7d 2-1/4'', 8d 2-1/2'', 9d 2-3/4'', and 12d 3-1/2''. (If nailing into end grain, reduce spacing by 1/4''.)

WOOD—Fir, pines, poplar, cottonwood, cedar, hemlock and larch are included in the softwood category. Hardwoods include ash, elm, cherry, oak, hard maple and hickory.

74

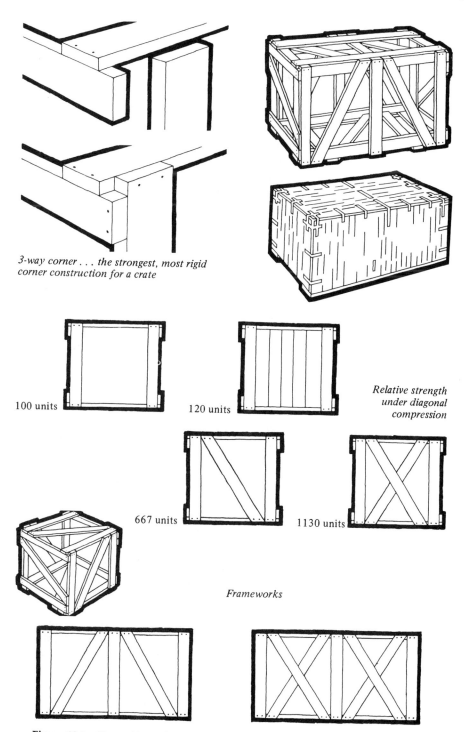

3-way corner . . . the strongest, most rigid corner construction for a crate

100 units

120 units

Relative strength under diagonal compression

667 units

1130 units

Frameworks

Figure 10.4 Crates (*Source:* CIGNA P&C Companies, Publisher, Ports of the World, P.O. Box 7728, Philadelphia, PA 19101)

2. Large crates are usually stowed in lower holds, hence they must bear great superimposed weights. Insure top strength by frequent top joists under sheathing (never more than thirty inches apart). *Do not* depend on end grain nailing *alone* to hold these joists. Provide joist support positioned directly under the joists' ends.

3. Reinforce the flooring at load bearing points when between skids or still members. At the point of greatest weight, you must add more supports.

4. Design for vertical sheathing: sides and ends. The end and side corners should be constructed in a vertical fashion.

5. On skid-type crates, terminate end sheathing at flooring to permit entry of forklifts. Terminate side sheathing 1/2 inch short of skid bottoms to prevent tearing away of sheathing when crate is dragged sideways.

6. On sill-type crates, provide lengthwise rubbing strips at base to facilitate handling and prevent tearing adrift of sheathing when crate is dragged.

7. Where skids are used, be sure they are of sufficient dimensions and of adequate number. Skid ends should always be chamfered (grooved).

8. Reduce cube and interior bracing problems by providing maximum disassembly of the carried item. Spares and disassembled parts should be adequately secured to the crate interior. In so doing, aim at a low center of gravity.

9. Supplement weak end grain nailing of interior bracing by back-up cleats.

10. Line crate interiors (except bottom) with a high-grade waterproof barrier material. Ventilate crates containing machinery or other items susceptible to damage from condensation, with baffled vents or louvre plates covering ventilation hole clusters at ends or sides. Also, space floor boards 3/8 inch apart. Consider use of crate top coating where open freight car or open storage may be encountered.

11. Corners of all crates should be reinforced with lengths of one-inch flat nailed strapping, applied so as to tie together all faces at each corner.

12. Assure yourself that handling facilities are available for your crate at destination and at intermediate points. Provide consignee with opening instructions to reduce accidental damage in unpacking.

Wirebound boxes and crates. Wirebound boxes and crates (Figure 10.5a) have shown themselves useful for a large variety of products not affected by minor distortions of the container, and where the possibility of pilferage is not a primary concern. It is an ideal container for overpacks of solid or corrugated fibreboard boxes (cartons). If the wirebound container is not completely filled or if the contents may be affected by possible distortion of the container, interior blocking or bracing, properly applied, should be used. The ends of wirebound containers should be reinforced to resist adequately the forces that may be applied during handling, thus preventing damage to contents. Shippers should *avoid overloading* and should not use boxes too large for their contents. Other considerations are:

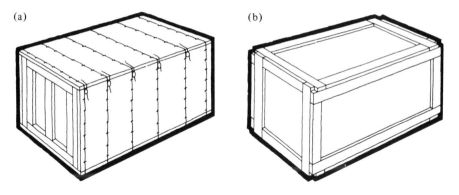

(a) (b)

Figure 10.5 (a) Wirebound boxes and crates, (b) cleated plywood boxes (*Source:* CIGNA P&C Companies, Publisher, Ports of the World, P.O. Box 7728, Philadelphia, PA 19101)

1. Veneer and cleats should be full thickness, straight grained and sound, and free from knots, decay, mildew, or open splits. Sound knots not more than 1-1/2 inches in diameter and less than one-third the width of the piece of veneer are allowable. Wire should be free from rust and scales.
2. Ideal staple spacing is 2-1/2 inches on crates; 2 inches on boxes. A minimum of two staples per slat is recommended.
3. Mitered cleats provide greater resistance to rough handling than tongued and grooved cleats.
4. Observed care in effecting closures to avoid wire fatigue. Use special closure tools.
5. Consult appropriate tables and your box supplier for specifications for export-type containers.
6. Where contents are susceptible to pilferage or exceed 150 pounds, apply one tension strap around tip, bottom, and ends. If weight is over 250 pounds, apply two additional straps 3 inches from each and around top, bottom, and sides; also consider applying straps over intermediate cleats.
7. Line box interior with high-grade waterproof material, properly sealed.

Cleated plywood boxes. Properly assembled and used, cleated plywood panel boxes (Figure 10.5b) have many uses in foreign trade. Their lightness and comparative strength particularly recommend them for air freight shipments. Shippers may abuse these containers, however, by using secondhand units, overloading, applying strapping improperly, allowing long unsupported panels, or failing to nail the box closed properly. Thin panels invite damage to contents through punctures. Follow these points in plywood shipments:

1. Consult appropriate tables to avoid overloading, to determine proper nail

spacing, and to find correct dimensions of plywood and cleats. *Never use secondhand boxes.*

2. Reject rotten, split, or otherwise defective cleats.

3. Apply intermediate cleats to all panels in excess of 24 inches.

4. Apply strapping only over edge and/or intermediate cleats for maximum support. Strapping that spans unframed areas is easily broken and may injure handlers. Employ stapling to hold banding in place on the cleats.

5. If contents are susceptible to water damage, line the box with adequate waterproof or vaporproof barrier material.

Steel drums. New steel drums (Figure 10.6a) are generally excellent for export. Secondhand drums, unless thoroughly reconditioned and tested, may give trouble because of fatigue caused by dents at the chime and previous damages to closures. Also consider the following:

1. Closures must be made as prescribed by the manufacturer. Back up friction-type covers of drums as well as cans or pails with soldering or spot welding at three or more points.

2. Be sure adequate seals are used on locking levers and sealing rings of open-end drums. Failure of seals may result in accidental openings of covers.

3. Consider using tamperproof seals at filling and dispensing holes.

4. Make frequent spot checks of automatic filling machinery by weighing filled drums. Shortages may occur at the source.

5. Do not reuse single or one-trip containers.

6. For hazardous or dangerous substances, be sure the drums are approved for the carriage of the intended cargo.

Fibre drums. Fibre drums (Figure 10.6b) are gaining importance in the export picture. Before using fibre drums, however, it should be determined that open storage en route is not contemplated. Considerations for fibre drums include:

1. High-density materials should not be packed into fibre drums.

2. Fiber drums should be filled to capacity so to add rigidity to the packages.

3. It is advisable to settle or de-aerate materials, particularly light fluffy powders, during the filling operations. Use of a vibrator or mechanical settler is recommended. Bag-lined drums can be de-aerated simply by manually compressing the filled bag.

4. Keep the size of the drum compatible with the weight of the contents to avoid overloading.

5. Closures are important. Be sure sealing rings and locking levers are properly in place and will not be accidentally jarred or pulled loose.

Figure 10.6 (a) Steel drums, (b) fibre drums, (c) barrels, casks or kegs (*Source:* CIGNA P&C Companies, Publisher, Ports of the World, P.O. Box 7728, Philadelphia, PA 19101)

6. Handle the drums with mechanical equipment or roll them on bottom chimes. Fibre drums are not designed to roll on sidewalls. Avoid cutting and chafing the sidewalls.

Barrels, casks, or kegs. The wooden barrel (Figure 10.6c) has been a workhorse of overseas trade, dating back to ancient times. Selection of the wrong barrel for your product can result in leakage, contamination, breakage and many other headaches. The following ar basic recommendations:

1. Tight (liquid) barrels should be stored bung up. Request stowage on bilges. Slack (dry) barrels should be stored on ends. Never store or ship slack barrels on their sides.

2. Provide reinforcing head cleats running from chime to chime at right angles to the headpieces. Cleat thickness should never be greater than chime depth.

3. Use tongue and groove staves with a suitable liner where the contents, such as dry chemicals and powders, may sift. Make sure barrel wood and liner material will not contaminate contents.

4. Keep voids in slack barrels to a minimum. Use headliners (strips of coiled elm fastened inside chime) to give barrel heads added strength.

5. Where tight barrels are employed, hoops should be fastened with not less than three hoop fasteners (dogs) per hoop. Provide for inspection at interim transit points to check for leakage where practicable. If contents are carried in brine, rebrining at interim points may save contents of leaking units.

Multi-wall shipping sacks. Multi-wall shipping sacks or bags (Figure 10.7a) are being used more and more for packaging of powdered, granular, and lump materials, particularly dry chemicals. These sacks are flexible containers generally made from two walls or plies of heavy-duty craft paper to a maximum of six sides. Often, they are made in combination with special coatings, laminations, impregnations, or even plies of textile material, such as burlap, to give them additional strength and added protection to their contents. Because of the flexibility of these containers, special attention must be given to the use of flexible waterproof or moisture-proof barriers in their construction.

There are several types of bags used, the most common being the pasted bottom or sewn bottom open-mouth, and the pasted valve or sewn valve. The pasted bottom and sewn bottom open-mouth-type bags are closed after filling by sewing through all plies with a strip of tape incorporated into the sewn end in such a way that it folds over the end of the sack to control sifting. They can also be closed by

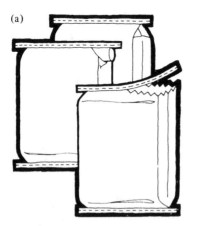
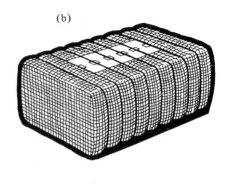

Figure 10.7   (a) Multi-wall shipping sacks, (b) bales (*Source:* CIGNA P&C Companies, Publisher, Ports of the World, P.O. Box 7728, Philadelphia, PA 19101)

gluing. The valve-type bags are closed by manually folding over an external paper sleeve or by the check-valve action of an inner paper sleeve when the bags are full. The internal pressure of the contents causes this, and care must be taken that the bags are sufficiently filled to exert this pressure. It must be recognized that slight leakage will nevertheless occur, particularly when the bags are handled.

The use of these bags for overseas shipments should be limited. This type of container, more than any other, must be adapted to the requirements of the commodity they contain. This requires careful research and intelligent selection. It is recommended that the loaded bag does not exceed fifty pounds. Consideration must be given to the value of the product as well as to its hygroscopic properties and chemical and physical characteristics. Utmost consideration must be given to in-transit hazards, such as atmospheric conditions or exposure to the elements, number of transfers, handling, and warehouse facilities. Of major importance is the question as to whether the contents of the sack will be subjected to contamination if the bags are ruptured or if foreign matter can filter in through the stitching holes.

A good practice for the shipper is to include a supply of open-mouth refill or overslip sacks with each shipment. The number of refill sacks should not be less than 1 percent of the number of sacks in the shipment and preferably 3 percent. The refill sacks should be imprinted with instructions for their use as well as identification of the commodity they will carry. Overslip sacks should be slightly larger than the original sack and constructed of the same number and kind of plies.

Palletizing of a number of sacks, adequately shrink-wrapped and/or banded to the pallet, has been particularly effective in reducing damage and pilferage, and forces use of mechanical handling equipment.

Bales. A well-made bale (Figure 10.7b) may be expected to outturn reasonably well in most export trades. Bear in mind, however, that all bales are subject to pilferage, hook hole, and water damage. Therefore, they are not recommended for highly valued commodities. To minimize losses, follow these recommendations:

1. Where contents may be subject to damage from strapping pressure, use a primary wrap of fibreboard material.
2. Use an inner wrap of creped or pleted waterproof paper. This type of paper is necessary to provide moisture protection and to "give" with the bale distortions without tearing.
3. Provide a heavy outer wrap of burlap or similar cloth able to stand heavy abrasions in transit.
4. Provide "ears" at corners of small bales to facilitate handling without hooks. Bale weights under 300 pounds are less apt to be handled with hooks.
5. A minimum of four flat tension bands should be used. Apply tightly at the maximum bale compression to avoid slipping of end bands.
6. Stencil all shipping and cautionary marks on bale. Do not use tags.

Cushioning. Fragile and brittle items must be suspended or protected against shock and vibration by a cushion that gradually increases resistance against item movement. Selection of the correct cushioning material depends on the item's size, weight, shape, surface finish, and the built-in shock resistance. See Table 10.2 for cushioning characteristics.

Unit Loads

Many products or commodities can be economically palletized or unitized (Figures 10.8 and 10.9) to facilitate handling, stowage, and protection of cargo. *Palletizing* is the assembly of one or more packages on pallet base and securing the load to the pallet. *Unitizing* is the assembly of one or more items into a compact load, secured together and provided with skids and cleats for ease of handling. Often, packing costs can be significantly reduced by palletizing and unitizing. Pallet and unit loads offer the following additional advantages:

1. Handling of palletized or unitized loads requires use of mechanical handling equipment, thereby reducing the manual handling damage hazard.
2. The multiple handling of individual items is eliminated, further reducing possible damage from manual handling.
3. Opportunity for pilferage and theft is reduced. Pallet and unit loads also permit early detection of tampering.
4. Loading and unloading of trailers, boxcars, intermodal containers, barges, ships, and aircraft is faster.
5. Application of waterproofing protection to the load is easily facilitated; the overwrap applied accompanies the load for the entire journey.
6. The incidence of lost or strayed items is reduced.
7. Checking and inventory of shipment are easier.

Palletizing cargo. There are four "standard" pallets that accommodate the different modal/intermodal containers most frequently used in international commerce. The sizes, in inches, of these pallets are 45 X 53 (114 X 137 cm), 45 X 45 (114 X 114 cm), 45 X 33.75 (114 X 83 cm), and 40.91 X 49.09 (104 X 125 cm).

When selecting the pallet, consider the following:

1. Utilize efficiently the space of the intermodal transportation to be used.
2. Keep in mind the uniform unit package dimensions of the item to be shipped.
3. Limit the weight of the palletized load to 2,200 pounds (1,000 kg).

Assemble the individual unit packages on the pallet base without an overhang. The load pattern should minimize voids and be interlocking.

TABLE 10.2 CUSHIONING CHARACTERISTICS (1)

Type Material	Abrasion Resistance	Resilience	Compression	Absorption	Water Resistance	(2) Dusting	Damping Quality(3)
Bound Fibre	Poor	High	Low	Low	High	High	Fair
Cellulosic	Good	Medium	High	(4)	(4)	High	Excellent
Fibrous Glass	(4)	High	Low	Low	High	Low	Fair
Wood Excelsior	Poor	Medium	High	High	(4)	High	Excellent
Hair Felt	(5)	Medium	Low	(5)	(5)	Low	Poor
Solid Fibreboard	Poor	Medium	Low	Low	High	Low	Poor
Wax Shredded Paper	Poor	Low	High	High	Low	High	Excellent
Wrapping Paperboard	Good	Low	High	High	Low	Low	Excellent
Cellular, Plasticized, Polyvinyl Chloride	(4)	High	Low	Nil	High	Low	Good
Rigid or Elastic Polyurethane Foam	(6)	(6)	(6)	(6)	Low	None	(6)
Chemically Blown Cellular Rubber	Good	High	Low	(6)	(6)	Low	Fair
Latex Foam Sponge Rubber	Good	High	Low	High	Low	Low	Fair
Paper Honeycomb	Energy dissipating medium only.						
Corrugated Fibreboard	Used primarily as a die cut, cells pads and trays.						

(1) These ratings are general in nature. Any characteristic can be varied in a customized mode.
(2) Dusting describes the extent of material breakdown in small or dustlike particles in transit.
(3) Damping quality reflects the ability of the material to progressively diminish vibrations or oscillation.
(4) This material is manufactured under different specifications that vary the degree of named characteristics.
(5) Used mainly as padding for large heavy items. Often glued in place.
(6) This is a foam-in-place material that can vary in make-up to meet requirements.

83

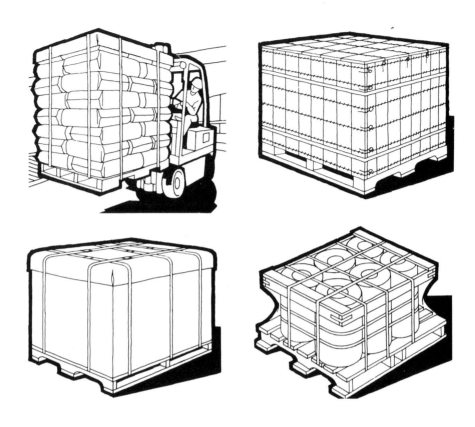

Figure 10.8 Palletizing cargo (*Source:* CIGNA P&C Companies, Publisher, Ports of the World, P.O. Box 7728, Philadelphia, PA 19101)

Insert spacers between the rows or layers of irregularly shaped items. Adhesives can be used between cartons in a uniform load. Secure the load tightly and firmly by using horizontal and vertical strapping. Plastic shrink wrap can be used to stabilize and protect palletized loads.

Provide stacking protection to the top of the pallet by using a lumber, plywood, or fibreboard cap. Loads that are susceptible to compression must also be supported with vertical framing.

Palletized loads susceptible to water damage can be protected by shrink wrap or stretch wrap, overwrapping with barrier material, or consolidated shipping in a weather-tight container.

Unitizing cargo. Assemble individual items into one unit by bolting, nailing, or strapping together. Provide the load with skids to facilitate handling by a forklift, or, if the load is to be handled by a cargo sling, provide vertical cleats on the sides of the load.

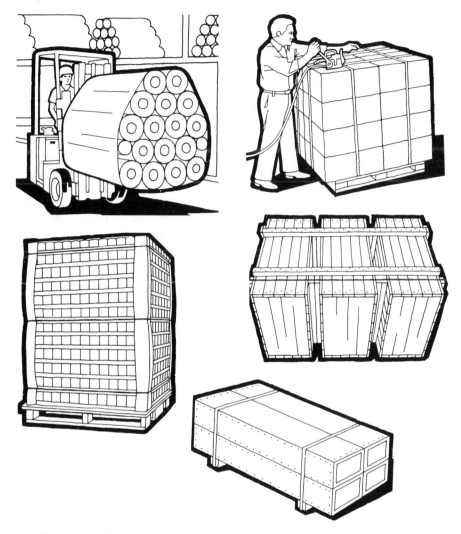

Figure 10.9   Unitizing cargo (*Source:* CIGNA P&C Companies, Publisher, Ports of the World, P.O. Box 7728, Philadelphia, PA 19101)

Insure protection against water damage by using plastic shrink wrap or stretch wrap on individual items before assembly into unit load. Then shrink wrap or stretch wrap to entire load. Use waterproof paper or plastic film overwrap.

Sources of Help

If the manufacturer you are working with is unfamiliar with correct packing methods, contact your freight forwarder for the name(s) of export packing companies to handle your goods. These firms are experts in their field.

MARKING

The primary purpose of marking is to identify the shipment, which enables the carrier to forward it to the ultimate consignee. Old marks, advertising, and other extraneous information only serve to confuse this primary function for freight handlers and carriers. Follow these fundamental marking rules:

1. Unless local regulations prohibit them, use blind marks, particularly where goods are susceptible to pilferage. Change them periodically to avoid familiarity by handlers. Trade names and consignees' or shippers' names should be avoided as they indicate the nature of the contents.
2. Consignee (identification) marks and port marks showing destination and transfer points should be large, clear, and applied by stencil with waterproof ink. They should be applied on three faces of the container, preferably side and/or ends, and top. Legibility is of utmost importance. Letters should be a minimum of two inches high.
3. If commodities require special handling or stowage, the containers should be so marked, and this information should also appear on the bills of lading.
4. Cautionary markings must be permanent and easy to read. (Use the languages of both the origin and destination countries.) The use of stencils is recommended for legibility—do not use crayon, tags, or cards. Figure 10.10 gives an example of markings on an export pack.

If the manufacturer you are working with is unfamiliar with the correct marking procedures, contact your freight forwarder for the name(s) of export packing companies to handle your goods. These firms are experts in marking as well as packing.

Nonhazardous Pictorial Markings

It is recommended that handling instructions always be printed on the exterior pack in the language of the destination country. It is not unusual for a shipment to be handled by another country along the transport path or by freight handlers who cannot read. These potential problems can best be overcome by pictorial markings. The seven symbols depicted under the heading of "International" in Figure 10.11 represent markings that have been accepted by the International Organization for Standardization. The other three symbols under the "U.S." caption are additional markings that have been accepted by the American National Standards Institute, but are not yet included as international standards.

Cautionary markings in various languages appear in Table 10.3.

Hazardous Materials

Unilateral state regulations of international commerce is impractical in today's interdependent world. Procedures that are acceptable in one country and forsaken in

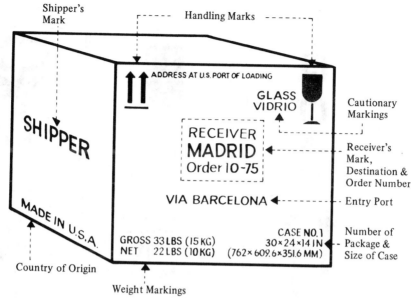

Figure 10.10   Example of markings (*Source:* CIGNA P&C Companies, Publisher, Ports of the World, P.O. Box 7728, Philadelphia, PA 19101)

another inhibit world trade through embargo or unacceptable delay in cargo reaching its ultimate destination. The labels shown in Figure 10.12 are the hazardous material (dangerous goods) identifications adopted by many IMCO (United Nations) member countries to smooth the flow of these type materials in waterborne commerce. The color coding, symbol, and class number are universal.

These labels simply provide a visual signal of dangerous goods in transport. They will cause special handling along the transport path, including embargo, if the commodity is not authorized for carriage. Dangerous goods regulations almost always also require special documentation and packing under strict criteria. Routing through named entry ports is also a frequent requirement. Consequently, when negotiating for entry into foreign trade of these items, always require a complete explanation of the applicable rules.

Important: Do not assume that compliance with domestic regulations will automatically qualify a shipment for passage through en route countries and entry into the destination port. Requirements that are not met can easily be the difference between profit and loss. If the material might be hazardous then in addition to all known required markings and labels furnish pertinent chemical or physical data. This will expedite foreign freight relabelling by forwarders.

EXPORT INSURANCE

Export shipments are usually insured against loss or damage in transit by ocean marine insurance. Inland marine policies cover shipment to the point of departure,

INTERNATIONAL

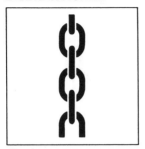

Sling here

Fragile, Handle with care

Use no hooks

This way up

Keep away from heat

Keep dry

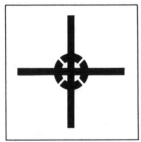

Center of gravity

U.S. STANDARDS

Do not roll

Hand truck here

Keep away from cold

Figure 10.11 Nonhazardous markings (*Source:* CIGNA P&C Companies, Publisher, Ports of the World, P.O. Box 7728, Philadelphia, PA 19101)

TABLE 10.3 CAUTIONARY MARKINGS

English	French	German	Italian	Spanish	Portuguese	Swedish
Handle With Care	Attention	Vorsicht	Attenzione	Manéjese con Cuidado	Tratar Com Cuidado	Varsamt
Glass	Verre	Glas	Vetro	Vidrio	Vidro	Glas
Use No Hooks	Manier Sans Crampons	Ohne Haken handhaben	Manipolare senza graffi	No Se Usan Ganchos	Não Empregue Ganchos	Begagna inga krokar
This Side Up	Cette Face En Haut	Diese Seite oben	Questo lato su	Este Lado Arriba	Este Lado Para Encima	Denna sida upp
Fragile	Fragile	Zerbrechlich	Fragile	Frágil	Fragil	Ömtäligt
Keep in Cool Place	Garder En Lieu Frais	Kuehl aufbewahren	Conservare in luogo fresco	Manténgase En Lugar Fresco	Deve Ser Guardado Em Lugar Fresco	Förvaras kallt
Keep Dry	Protéger Contre Humidité	Vor Naesse schuetzen	Preservare dallé umidità	Manténgase Seco	Não Deve Ser Molhado	Förvaras torrt
Open Here	Ouvrir Ici	Hier oeffnen	Aprire da questa parte	Ábrase Aqui	Abrir Por Este Ponto	Öppnas här

Prepared by Marine and Aviation Services Dept., Insurance Co. of North America.

Class 1
Explosives
(Orange)

Class 1
Explosives
(Orange)

Class 2
Non-Flammable
Gases (Green)

Class 2
Flammable
Gases −OR−
Class 3
Flammable Liquids
(Red)

Class 4
Flammable Solids
(Red & White Stripe)

Class 4
Spontaneously
Combustible
Substances (Red)

Class 4
Water Reactive
Substances
(Blue)

Figure 10.12 Hazardous materials (color of solid or shaded area in parentheses) (*Source:* CIGNA P&C Companies, Publisher, Ports of the World, P.O. Box 7728, Philadelphia, PA 19101)

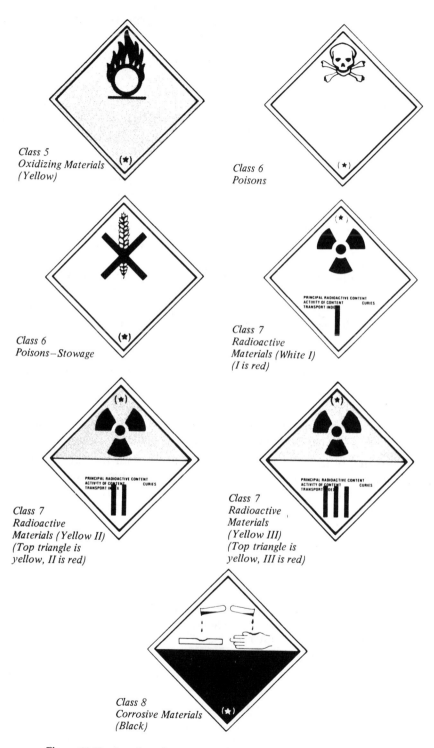

Class 5
Oxidizing Materials
(Yellow)

Class 6
Poisons

Class 6
Poisons—Stowage

Class 7
Radioactive
Materials (White I)
(I is red)

Class 7
Radioactive
Materials (Yellow II)
(Top triangle is
yellow, II is red)

Class 7
Radioactive
Materials
(Yellow III)
(Top triangle is
yellow, III is red)

Class 8
Corrosive Materials
(Black)

Figure 10.12 (continued)

whether seaport, airport, or rail terminal inside the United States. Two types of policies are popular in international trade:

1. Special (one-time) cargo policy, which insures a single shipment.
2. Open and blanket cargo policies, which are in continuous effect and automatically insure all cargo moving at the seller's risk.

The one-time cargo policy is, of course, more expensive since the risk cannot be spread over a number of different shipments. However, if your export business is infrequent, it may be wise to obtain this type of coverage.

Open and blanket cargo policies are similar. The open policy remains in force until it is canceled, covering all shipments of the exporter in transit within specified geographical trade areas. Premiums are paid "as they go" because the amounts can be determined only when the goods are shipped.

Blanket policies are closed contracts. The insured exporter pays a lump sum premium that is fixed in advance. The premium is based on the estimated total amount of shipping expected. It can be adjusted depending on whether the coverage exceeded the originally insured amount or fell below it.

Generally, the open (or floating) policy is more popular with U.S. exporters because

1. If the exporter fails to report that goods have been forwarded from the place of shipment, he or she is automatically covered.
2. The rate schedule attached to this policy gives the premium charge for various commodities and merchandise so that the exact insurance amount can figure into the c.i.f., or landed, sales price.

Your freight forwarder will normally handle your insurance or will recommend someone for you to use. Rates are very competitive, since the forwarder can offer insurance services along with shipping and transportation.

Class	Description
1	Explosives (Class 1.1, 1.2 and 1.3) Explosives (Class 1.4 and 1.5)
2	Non-Flammable and Flammable Gases
3	Flammable Liquids
4	Flammable Solids (Readily combustible) Spontaneously Combustible Substances Water Reactive Substances
5	Oxidizing Materials (Oxidizing maters and/or organic peroxides)
6	Poisonous Materials (Class A, B & C poisons or toxic substances) Poisonous Materials (Harmful stow away from foodstuffs)
7	Radioactive Materials (White I, Yellow II or Yellow III)
8	Corrosive Materials (Acids, corrosive liquids/solids & alkalines)
9	Miscellaneous Hazardous Materials (Those materials which present a danger in transport. No specific label authorized.)

Figure 10.12 (Continued) Hazardous materials (Classes)

Chapter Eleven

Export Licensing and Document Processing

Documentation is very important in processing an order. The papers accompanying a shipment tell what is being shipped, to whom, and how. Figure 11.1 shows the paper flow connected with an export transaction.

Documented papers show the approval of the U.S. government and sometimes of the government of the receiving country, and they provide either or both countries with the raw data that makes up trade statistics. By giving special attention to preparing the documents, you will avoid difficulties at the time of shipment.

In foreign trade, there is no element of the casualness sometimes present in transactions taking place in the U.S. marketplace. If the documentation for a foreign shipment is wrong—even a small detail—the shipment may be refused by customs at the U.S. port of exit or the foreign port of entry; it may be delayed; it may be lost. It is not as easy to correct documentation errors for foreign shipments as it is for shipments within the United States.

A recent *Business Week* article emphasized the problem in U.S. exports to France. Firms in the United States repeatedly send incorrect documentation, so French importers cannot get shipments out of customs; one or two such experiences would be enough to dry up an otherwise promising market.

Shipper

1. Prepares Domestic Bill of Lading for movement of cargo to pier, and sends copy to his forwarder along with packing list.

2. Checks Bill of Lading.:
   - number of packages
   - marks and numbers
   - description of cargo
   - foreign destination
   - gross weights of each package shipped
   - local party to be notified

3. Marks cargo plainly to show:
   - gross and net weights
   - cubic measurement
   - foreign destination
   - identification marks
   - country of origin

Inland Carrier

4. Secures interchange agreement with steamship company on containers.

5. Accepts cargo for transit to the port.

6. Advises freight forwarder or shipper's local representative of cargo's arrival.

7. Obtains the following information from forwarder or representative:
   - name of vessel
   - sailing date
   - pier number and location
   - location of any special permits needed to clear hazardous or over-size cargo for acceptance by ocean terminal.

8. Obtains Dock Receipt from forwarder or other representative to accompany cargo.

9. Contacts terminal operator to make appointment for special handling or equipment, if required, at least 24 hours before delivery.

Forwarder

10. Provides Dock Receipt and special permits, if any, to delivering motor carrier.

11. Checks Dock Receipt for completeness:
    - name of shipper
    - name of vessel
    - ports of loading and discharge
    - number and type of packages
    - description of cargo
    - gross weight, dimensions, and cubic measurement of each package
    - marks and numbers
    - shipper's export declaration number, if required.

Terminal Operator

12. Issues pass to driver at gate house.

13. Assigns driver a checker and an unloading spot.

14. Retains original of Dock Receipt and forwards a copy to the steamship company.

Steamship Company

15. Issues Ocean Bill of Lading to shipper or his agent.

Figure 11.1 Export steps (Source: CIGNA P&C Companies, Publisher, Ports of the World, P.O. Box 7728, Philadelphia, PA 19101)

SHIPPING DOCUMENTS

Shipping documents consist of *export licenses* and *export declarations*. Export licenses are also of two types: *general licenses* and *validated licenses*, along with alterations and special cases.

General Export License

This type of license allows the exporter to ship goods without submitting a license application. The Export Administration Regulations, Section 371, details the various types of licenses (and symbols) under this category. More than 90 percent of licenses granted fall into this category.

Normally, actual licensing is handled by your freight forwarder; however, it is wise to ask the local Department of Commerce which type of license is required before you quote an order. Checking ahead of time will save considerable time and effort, and familiarity on your part can forestall errors by others.

Validated Export Licenses

These licenses apply to products the U.S. government wants to control for foreign policy, short supply, crime, nuclear nonproliferation, and security reasons. A validated export license amounts to special permission to sell such products overseas, or special permission to sell more ordinary products to countries in which the United States has placed trade restrictions. Obtaining this special license is frequently time-consuming and costly.

Figure 11.2 shows a completed application for an export license. Figure 11.3 shows the approved license from the U.S. Departments of Commerce, Office of Export Licensing. Figure 11.4 is an amendment on the reverse side of the export license. Figure 11.5 shows the Statement by Ultimate Consignee and Purchaser. This form and and an Import Certificate (I/Cs) are required documents when applying for a validated license. The first can be gotten from DOC and the second from the overseas buyer (see Section 375.2 of Export Administration Regulations for an explanation). Local U.S. Department of Commerce officers have copies of the regulations and a staff that can explain their meaning. You or your freight forwarder can handle this procedure.

Your local Department of Commerce office can give you a current list of goods and countries requiring validated export licenses; Chapter Twelve provides an introduction to this material. Skimming Chapter Twelve can give you an idea of the scope of U.S. trade relations with other countries. Obtaining some familiarity with these relations should be part of your homework, to be done before you select the product(s) to export and while you are doing market research.

You should also be familiar with the following in order to facilitate planning:

Time needed for acquiring licenses. Most applications, amendments, and reexport requests are acted upon within two weeks after receipt in the Office of Export Licensing (202-377-4811 or 714-660-0144). Those involving strategic commodities, sensitive areas, and/or other security or policy problems may, however, require a longer processing time. Whe processing time extends in excess of ninety days, the Office of Export Licensing will advise the exporter of the circumstances requiring the additional time and give an estimate of when action will be taken.

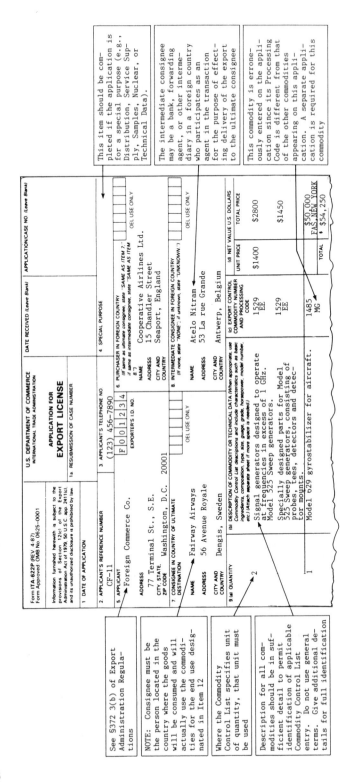

Figure 11.2 Form ITA-622P, Application for Export License

Figure 11.2 (Cont.)

Left margin annotations:

End-use is an important factor. Broad General statements are not satisfactory. Information supplied must show specific use, urgency of need, economic significance, particular facilities served, etc. In other words, furnish precise facts concerning the use that will be made of the items to be shipped, and not statements as to general uses of the items

In complying with the requirement for fullest disclosure of all parties in interest, names and addresses of other parties (agents, middle men, brokers) concerned in the transaction should be disclosed. Also enter here special certifications, etc. required by the Export Administration Regulations. Continue on additional sheets of paper where necessary

Unsigned or facsimile signed applications will be returned without action to the applicant

Right margin annotations:

If the applicant is exporting for other than his own account the name and address of the foreign principal must be shown and an explanation of the transaction given in full

Where applicant did not receive order directly from the foreign purchaser or ultimate consignee, or through his or their agents abroad, the person in the U.S. (Order Party) who conducted direct negotiations with the foreign party and originally received the order, signs (See §372 3(b) of Export Administration Regulations).

Form ITA-622P is issued in sets of six copies. The short second copy is Form ITA-628, titled "Export License," but is not valid until stamped with the Department of Commerce seal, even though it may have been given a license number. The third copy is the acknowledgement copy which will be used to notify you if action on your application cannot be taken in 10 days. You should retain the sextuplicate. All other copies must be submitted to the Office of Export Administration

Form content:

10. FILL IN IF PERSON OTHER THAN APPLICANT IS AUTHORIZED TO RECEIVE LICENSE — OEL USE ONLY

NAME — Deliam Forwarding Company
ADDRESS — 42 Broadway
CITY, STATE, ZIP CODE — New York, New York 10004

11. IF APPLICANT IS NOT THE PRODUCER OF COMMODITY TO BE EXPORTED GIVE NAME AND ADDRESS OF SUPPLIER (If unknown, state "UNKNOWN.") — OEL USE ONLY

Aviation Equipment Co.
700 Market Street
Edam, North Carolina 27406

12. SPECIFIC END-USE OF COMMODITIES OR TECHNICAL DATA BY CONSIGNEE IN ITEM 7 ABOVE. IF KNOWN, GIVE NAME AND ADDRESS OF END-USER IF DIFFERENT FROM ITEM 7.

Urgently needed to effect safety measures at commercial airports at Gavle and Umea, Sweden

13. IF APPLICANT IS NOT EXPORTING FOR HIS OWN ACCOUNT, GIVE NAME AND ADDRESS OF FOREIGN PRINCIPAL AND EXPLAIN FULLY. — OEL USE ONLY

14. FOREIGN AVAILABILITY (Completion Optional) Submission as defined in Part 391 of the Export Administration Regulations is attached. ☐

15. ADDITIONAL INFORMATION (Attach separate sheet if more space is needed)

Order received by Maurice, Inc. from David Black (purchaser's agent), 35 Chandler Street, Seaport, England

16. APPLICANT'S CERTIFICATION. I hereby make application for a license to export, and I certify that (a) to the best of my knowledge, information and belief all statements in this application, including the description of the commodities or technical data and their end users, and any documents submitted in support of this application are correct and complete and that they fully and accurately disclose all the terms of the order and other facts of the export transaction. (b) this application conforms to the instructions accompanying this application and the Export Administration Regulations, (c) I obtained the order from the order party who has completed item 17, or I negotiated with and secured the export order directly from the purchaser or ultimate consignee, or through his or their agent(s) (d) I will retain records pertaining to this transaction and make them available as required by §387 13 of the Export Administration Regulations, (e) I will report promptly to the U.S. Department of Commerce any material changes in the terms of the order or other facts or intentions of the export transaction as reflected in this application and supporting documents, whether the application is still under consideration or a license has been granted; and (f) if the license is granted, I will be strictly accountable for its use in accordance with the Export Administration Regulations and all the terms and conditions of the license.

Type or Print — Foreign Commerce Co. (APPLICANT) (Same as item 5)
SIGN HERE IN INK
Type or Print — U.S. Acirema / Vice President (NAME and TITLE of person whose signature appears on line to the left)
(SIGNATURE of person authorized to execute this application)

17. ORDER PARTY'S CERTIFICATION (See §372 8(b) of the Export Administration Regulations). The undersigned order party certifies to the truth and correctness of items 15(a) and 16(a) above, and that he has no information concerning the export transaction that is undisclosed or inconsistent with representations made to the Department of Commerce and agrees to comply with items 16(d) and 16(e) above.

Type or Print — Maurice, Inc. (Order Party)
SIGN HERE IN INK
Type or Print — Albert Maurice / President (NAME and TITLE of person whose signature appears on line to the left)
(SIGNATURE of person authorized to sign for the Order Party)

This license application and any license issued pursuant thereto are expressly subject to all rules and regulations of the Department of Commerce. Making any false statement or concealing any material fact in connection with this application or altering in any way the validated license issued, is punishable by imprisonment or fine, or both, and by denial of export privileges under the Export Administration Act of 1979 and any other applicable Federal statutes. No export license will be issued unless this form is completed and submitted in accordance with Export Administration Regulation 372.4 (50 U.S.C. app. Sec. 2403; 15 CFR Sec. 372.4).

FOR DEPARTMENT OF COMMERCE USE ONLY

ACTION TAKEN	VALIDITY PERIOD	AUTHORITY	RATING	DV	TECH DATA			
☐ APPROVED / ☐ REJECTED	MONTHS						(Licensing officer)	(No.) (Date)
DOCUMENTATION	POLICY	END-USE CHECK	REEX PORT	SUPPORT DOCUMENT	TYPE OF LICENSE		(Review officer)	(Date)

NOTE: Submit the first five copies of this application, Form ITA-622P (with top stub attached), to the Office of Export Licensing P.O. Box 273, Washington, D.C. 20044, retaining the sextuplicate copy of the form for your files. Remove the long carbon sheet from in front of the sextuplicate copy. Do not remove any other carbon sheets. Reproduction of this form is permissible, providing that content, format, size, and color of paper and ink are the same

NOTE: In separate SEXTUPLICATE copy for applicant's file, hold stub of form with fingers of one hand, grasp SEXTUPLICATE copy and long carbon with other hand, and pull out

COPY-1 OEL FILE COPY

97

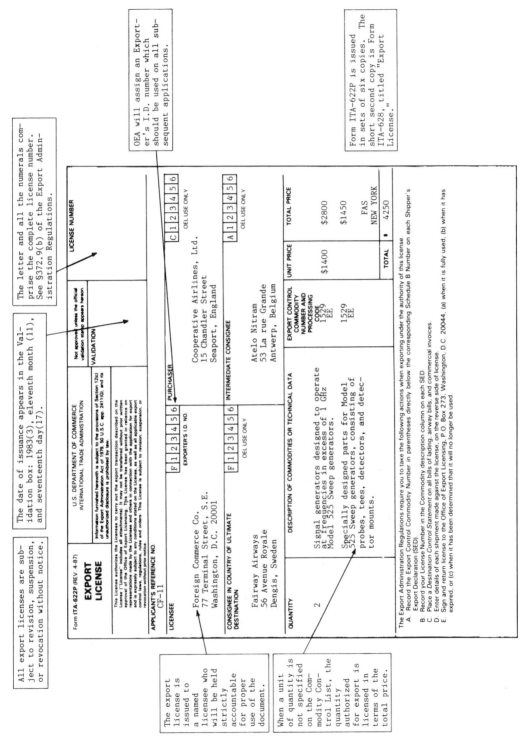

All export licenses are subject to revision, suspension, or revocation without notice.

The date of issuance appears in the Validation box: 1983(3), eleventh month (11), and seventeenth day(17).

The letter and all the numerals comprise the complete license number. See §372.9(b) of the Export Administration Regulations.

OEA will assign an Exporter's I.D. number which should be used on all subsequent applications.

Form ITA-622P is issued in sets of six copies. The short second copy is Form ITA-628, titled "Export License."

The export license is issued to a named licensee who will be held strictly accountable for proper use of the document.

When a unit of quantity is not specified on the Commodity Control List, the quantity authorized for export is licensed in terms of the total price.

Figure 11.3 Form ITA-628, Export License

98

RECORD OF SHIPMENTS

Each Shipment made against this Export License shall be recorded below. If more space is needed, use a continuation sheet. (See Export Administration Regulations §386.2 (d). Shipping tolerances apply only to the unshipped balance remaining on the license at the time of shipment (§386.7)

QUANTITY SHIPPED	DESCRIPTION OF COMMODITIES	DOLLAR VALUE	NAME OF EXPORTING CARRIER	POINT OF EXPORT OR POST OFFICE OF MAILING	DATE OF EXPORT	INITIALS OF PERSON MAKING ENTRY
3*	Signal Generators Model 525	4200*	ss Selfont	N.Y., N.Y.	12/1/84	
	Pts. for Model 525 Sweep Generator	1450	ss Selfont	N.Y., N.Y.	12/1/84	

I certify that shipments have been made under this license as indicated above. There is no material or substantive change in facts on which the license or subsequent amendments were issued. Delium Forwarding Co.

42 Broadway, N.Y., New York   10004

Richard Mann
Signature of Licensee or duly authorized agent

Address

12/1/84

Date

Figure 11.4 Reverse of Form ITA-628P, Export License (Note that the quantity and value originally licensed was amended to permit this export.)

FORM ITA-629P
(REV. 6-84)

U.S. DEPARTMENT OF COMMERCE
INTERNATIONAL TRADE ADMINISTRATION

STATEMENT BY ULTIMATE CONSIGNEE AND PURCHASER

GENERAL INSTRUCTIONS – This form must be submitted by the importer (ultimate consignee shown in Item 1) and by the overseas buyer or purchaser, to the U.S. exporter or seller with whom the order for the commodities described in Item 3 is placed. This completed statement will be submitted in support of one or more export license applications to the U.S. Department of Commerce. **All items on this form must be completed.** Where the information required is unknown or the item does not apply, write in the appropriate words "UNKNOWN" or "NOT APPLICABLE." If more space is needed, attach an additional copy of this form or sheet of paper signed as in Item 8. Submit form within 180 days from latest date in Item 8. Information furnished herewith is subject to the provisions of Section 12(c) of the Export Administration Act of 1979, 50 USC app. 2411(c), and its unauthorized disclosure is prohibited by law.

1. **Ultimate consignee name and address**

   Name
   Fairways Airways

   Street and number
   56 Avenue Royale

   City and Country
   Dengis, Sweden

   Reference *(if desired)*

2. **Request** *(Check one)*

   a. [X] We request that this statement be considered a part of the application for export license filed by

   Foreign Commerce Co., 77 Terminal St., S.E., Washington, D.C. 20001

   U.S. exporter or U.S. person with whom we have placed our order (order party)
   for export to us of the commodities described in item 3.

   b. [ ] We request that this statement be considered a part of every application for export license filed by

   _____
   U.S. exporter or U.S. person with whom we have placed or may place our order (order party)
   for export to us of the type of commodities described in this statement, during the period ending June 30 of the

   second year after the signing of this form, or on _____

3. **Commodities**

   We have placed or may place orders with the person or firm named in Item 2 for the commodities indicated below:

COMMODITY DESCRIPTION	(Fill in only if 2a is checked)	
	QUANTITY	VALUE
Signal generators designed to operate at frequencies in excess of 1 GHz Model 525 Sweep Generators	2	2,800
Specially designed parts for Model 525 Sweep Generators, consisting of probes, tees, detectors and detection mounts		1,450

4. **Disposition or use of commodities by ultimate consignee named in Item 1** *(Check and complete the appropriate box(es))*

   We certify that the commodity(ies) listed in Item 3:

   a. [ ] Will be used by us (as capital equipment) in the form in which received in a manufacturing process in the country named in Item 1 and will not be reexported or incorporated into an end product.

   b. [ ] Will be processed or incorporated by us into the following product(s) _____
   (Specify)

   to be manufactured in the country named in Item 1 for distribution in _____
   (Name

   of country or countries)

   c. [ ] Will be resold by us in the form in which received in the country named in Item 1 for use or consumption therein.

   The specific end-use by my customer will be _____
   (Specify, if known)

   d. [ ] Will be reexported by us in the form in which received to Urgently needed to effect safety _____
   (Name of country(ies))

   e. [X] Other *(Describe fully)* measures at commercial airports at Goyle and Umes, Sweden

   NOTE: If Item (d) is checked, acceptance of this form by the Office of Export Administration as a supporting document for license applications shall not be construed as an authorization to reexport the commodities to which the form applies unless specific approval has been obtained from the Office of Export Administration for such reexport.

(Reproduction of this form is permissible, providing that content, format, size and color of paper are the same)

Please continue form and sign certification on reverse side.

Figure 11.5 Form ITA-629P

5. Nature of business of ultimate consignee named in Item 1 and his relationship with U.S. exporter named in Item 2.

a. The nature of our usual business is ——————————————————————————
(Broker, distributor, fabricator, manufacturer, wholesaler, retailer, etc.)

b. Our business relationship with the U.S. exporter is _____ Contractual _____
(Contractual, franchise, exclusive distributor, distributor,

wholesaler, continuing and regular individual transaction business, etc.)
and we have had this business relationship for ____5____ years.

6. Additional information *(Any other material facts which will be of value considering applications for licenses covered by this statement.)*

7. Assistance in preparing statement *(Names of persons other than employees of consignee or purchaser who assisted in the preparation of this statement.)*

8. **CERTIFICATION OF ULTIMATE CONSIGNEE AND PURCHASER** (This item is to be signed by the ultimate consignee shown in Item 1 and by the purchaser where the latter is not the same as the ultimate consignee. Where the ultimate consignee is unknown, this item should be signed by the purchaser.)

We certify that all of the facts contained in this statement are true and correct to the best of our knowledge and belief and we do not know of any additional facts which are inconsistent with the above statement. We shall promptly send a supplemental statement to the person named in Item 2, disclosing any change of facts or intentions set forth in this statement which occurs after the statement has been prepared and forwarded. Except as specifically authorized by the U.S. Export Administration Regulations, or by prior written approval of the U.S. Department of Commerce, we will not reexport, resell, or otherwise dispose of any commodities listed in Item 3 above: (1) to any country not approved for export as brought to our attention by means of a bill of lading, commercial invoice, or any other means; or (2) to any person if there is reason to believe that it will result directly or indirectly, in disposition of the commodities contrary to the representations made in this statement or contrary to U.S. Export Administration Regulations.

Ultimate Consignee

Signature in ink _John Smith_
(Signature of official of ultimate consignee)

Type or print _John Smith - V.P._
(Name and title of official of ultimate consignee)

Date ____2-8-85____

Purchaser

Signature in ink _Robert Wallace_
(Signature of official of purchaser firm)

Type or print _Robert Wallace_
(Name and title of official of purchaser firm)

Type or print _Cooperative Airlines LTD._
(Name of purchaser firm)

Date ____2-14-85____

9. **CERTIFICATION FOR USE OF U.S. EXPORTER** in certifying that any correction, addition, or alteration on this form was made prior to the signing by the ultimate consignee and purchaser in Item 8.

We certify that no corrections, additions, or alterations were made on this form by us after the form was signed by the (ultimate consignee) (purchaser).

Type or print _Foreign Commerce_
(Name of exporter firm)

____2-4-85____
(Date signed)

Sign here in ink _U.S. Acirema_
(Signature of person authorized to certify for exporter)

Type or print _U.S. Acirema - V.P._
(Name and title of person signing this document)

The making of any false statement, the concealment of any material fact, or failure to file required information may result in denial of participation in U.S. exports. Notarial or governmental certification is not required.

FORM ITA-629P (Rev. 6-84)   USCOMM-DC 84-21766

Figure 11.5

Since a premature request for information may actually interrupt the normal processing of such documents and therefore cause unnecessary delay, the applicant should wait from three to five weeks from the date the document was mailed before requesting information (unless an emergency exists).

Amendments and extensions. A change that constitutes an essentially new transaction, such as a change in ultimate consignee, destination, or commodity, requires a new license. If the change is not significant, however, a license may be amended (e.g., a price increase, extension of validity period, addition of another commodity, etc.). Individual licenses that are issued with the normal one-year validity period may extended for six months if complete shipment cannot be made against the license during the original validity period. Figure 11.6 illustrates the form used when amendments are necessary.

Emergency clearances. There may be times when there is urgent reason for an application to receive immediate attention. In justifiable emergencies, the Office of Export Administration (and certain Department of Commerce district offices), when requested to do so by the applicant or his or her authorized agent and at the applicant's or agent's expense, will send a telegram authorizing clearance of the shipment. Usually, such special clearance can be handled within one working day. The validity of a license issued under this special processing procedure expires on the last day of the month following the month of issuance. Because a license issued on an emergency basis is expected to be used immediately, the validity of such licenses may not be extended.

Exports by mail. When shipping by mail, a Shipper's Export Declaration (Figure 11.7) should be presented to the postmaster at the time of each commercial mailing valued over $1,500. Either the validated license number, or the general license symbol along with the phrase "Export License Not Required," must be marked on the address side of each parcel. Parcel post packages are subject to inspection by customs officers at various international mail points, and packages that do not comply with this marking requirement may be returned to the sender or may be seized by Customs. Exports by mail must also conform to Post Office Department regulations as to size, weight, permissible contents, and the like.

Reexports. The reexport of U.S. commodities, in whole or in part, from the original country of destination to another country may be made without further recourse to the Office of Export Administration *only* if the following conditions exist:

1. The destination control statement on the shipping documents specifically names the countries to which the Office of Export Administration authorizes the reexport.

2. The commodity is exportable directly from the United States to the new country of destination under an appropriate general license authorization.

3. The reexport is to a destination to which direct shipment from the United States is authorized under an unused outstanding validated export license.

4. The reexport is specifically authorized under a special licensing procedure.

In all other instances, the approval of the Office of Export Administration is required before reexport may be made.

In order to obtain authorization to reexport commodities previously exported, Request to Dispose of Commodities or Technical Data Previously Exported, Form ITA-699P (Figure 11.8), should be submitted to the Office of Export Administration.

If the form is not readily available, a letter request may be submitted setting forth all the facts surrounding the proposed reexport, with a certification by the applicant that the facts are true as stated, and that he or she will be strictly accountable to the Office of Export Administration for the use of the authorization to export if the request is granted.

Parts and components. The use of U.S.-origin parts, components, and materials in the manufacture abroad of commodities that will be exported from the country of manufacture to any other country requires prior authorization of the Office of Export Administration. The exception is either the U.S.-origin parts and components or the foreign-produced commodity, were they of U.S. origin, could be shipped from the United States to the new country of destination under General License G-DEST. A request for such authorization should include a description of both the components and the end product, the relative value of each, the country(ies) of ultimate destination, the ultimate consignee, if known, and any other pertinent information.

Once the required license is obtained by the freight forwarder, a general license symbol is stamped on the shipper's export declaration (described below). The freight forwarder generally handles licensing (as well as export declaration and shipping instructions), but it is wise for you to be aware of general requirements and procedures as well as instances requiring special licensing.

Special Licensing Procedures

In addition to individual export licenses, described above, the Office of Export Administration provides certain simplified procedures under which one license application can cover a number of transactions. The most widely used transactions are discussed.

Project license. This license covers the export of all commodities requiring validated licenses that are needed for certain large-scale operations such as construction projects, petroleum development projects, and so on.

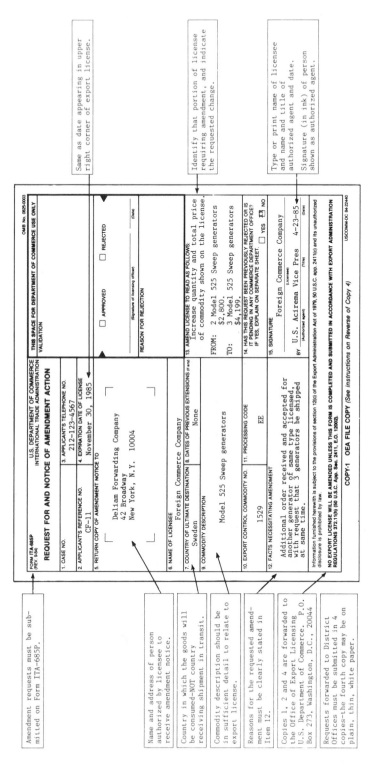

Figure 11.6 Form ITA-685P, Request for and Notice of Amendment Action

104

U.S. DEPARTMENT OF COMMERCE — BUREAU OF THE CENSUS — INTERNATIONAL TRADE ADMINISTRATION

FORM **7525-V** (1-1-88)   **SHIPPER'S EXPORT DECLARATION**   OMB No. 0607-0018

1a. EXPORTER *(Name and address including ZIP code)*

Brown and Company
123 Samantha Road
Toledo, OH

ZIP CODE 43264

2. DATE OF EXPORTATION
1-10-88

3. BILL OF LADING/AIR WAYBILL NO.
00—1234—5678

b. EXPORTER'S EIN (IRS) NO.
12—345678901

c. PARTIES TO TRANSACTION
☐ Related   ☒ Non-related

4a. ULTIMATE CONSIGNEE
Kirk Sales, LTD
162 Belva Street
London, England

b. INTERMEDIATE CONSIGNEE
Tim Service Company
3456 Fred Lane
London, England

5. FORWARDING AGENT
Sharyn Exports
P.O. Box XYZ
New York, NY 10047

6. POINT (STATE) OF ORIGIN OR FTZ NO.
OH

7. COUNTRY OF ULTIMATE DESTINATION
England

8. LOADING PIER *(Vessel only)*

9. MODE OF TRANSPORT *(Specify)*
Air

10. EXPORTING CARRIER
Fairway Air

11. PORT OF EXPORT
Kennedy Airport

12. PORT OF UNLOADING *(Vessel and air only)*
Gatwick, England

13. CONTAINERIZED *(Vessel only)*
☐ Yes   ☐ No

14. SCHEDULE B DESCRIPTION OF COMMODITIES,
15. MARKS, NOS., AND KINDS OF PACKAGES
(Use columns 17—19)

VALUE (U.S. dollars, omit cents)
(Selling price or cost if not sold)

D/F (16)	SCHEDULE B NUMBER (17)	CHECK DIGIT	QUANTITY — SCHEDULE B UNIT(S) (18)	SHIPPING WEIGHT (Kilos) (19)	(20)
	2 Boxes (B/1 and B/2) of Model 525 Signal Generators				
D	8543.20.0000	3	2	6 Kg	2,375
	1 Box (B/3) of Parts for Model 525 Signal Generator (probes, tees, defectors, and defector mounts)				
D	8543.90.9500	4	X	31 Kg	1,854

21. VALIDATED LICENSE NO./GENERAL LICENSE SYMBOL
A 123456

22. ECCN *(When required)*
1529

23. Duly authorized officer or employee
H. Brown
The exporter authorizes the forwarder named above to act as forwarding agent for export control and customs purposes.

24. I certify that all statements made and all information contained herein are true and correct and that I have read and understand the instructions for preparation of this document, set forth in the "**Correct Way to Fill Out the Shipper's Export Declaration.**" I understand that civil and criminal penalties, including forfeiture and sale, may be imposed for making false or fraudulent statements herein, failing to provide the requested information or for violation of U.S. laws on exportation (13 U.S.C. Sec. 305; 22 U.S.C. Sec. 401; 18 U.S.C. Sec. 1001; 50 U.S.C. App. 2410).

Signature *S. Sharyn*
Title President
Date 1-10-88

Confidential - For use solely for official purposes authorized by the Secretary of Commerce (13 U.S.C. 301 (g)).

Export shipments are subject to inspection by U.S. Customs Service and/or Office of Export Enforcement.

25. AUTHENTICATION *(When required)*

This form may be printed by private parties provided it conforms to the official form. For sale by the Superintendent of Documents, Government Printing Office, Washington, D.C. 20402, and local Customs District Directors. The "**Correct Way to Fill Out the Shipper's Export Declaration**" is available from the Bureau of the Census, Washington, D.C. 20233.

Figure 11.7 FORM 7525, Shipper's Export Declaration

FORM ITA-699P (Rev. 7/86)
OMB No. 0625-0009

Information furnished herewith is subject to the provisions of Section 12(c) of the Export Administration Act of 1979, 50 U.S.C. app. 2411(c), and its unauthorized disclosure is prohibited by law.

1. DATE OF REQUEST

U.S. DEPARTMENT OF COMMERCE
INTERNATIONAL TRADE ADMINISTRATION

REQUEST TO DISPOSE OF COMMODITIES OR TECHNICAL DATA PREVIOUSLY EXPORTED

No reexport requiring authorization from the Office of Export Licensing may be authorized unless a completed Form ITA-699P has been received (50 U.S.C. 2401 et. seq. 15 CFR Part 374).

CASE NO. *(Leave Blank)*

2.(a) APPLICANT'S REF. NO.

2.(b) APPLICANT'S TELEPHONE NO.

2.(c) RESUBMISSION OF CASE NO:

3. APPLICANT'S NAME

STREET

CITY, STATE,
ZIP CODE

EXPORTER'S I.D. NO.

4. COMMODITIES OR TECHNICAL DATA PREVIOUSLY EXPORTED UNDER

VALIDATED LICENSE NO. _____

CASE NO. _____

GENERAL LICENSE *(Specify type)* _____

5. NEW ULTIMATE CONSIGNEE

NAME

STREET

CITY AND COUNTRY

OEL USE ONLY

6. ORIGINAL ULTIMATE CONSIGNEE

NAME

STREET

CITY AND COUNTRY

OEL USE ONLY

7. I (WE) HEREBY REQUEST AUTHORIZATION TO ☐ REEXPORT ☐ SELL
☐ OTHER *(Specify)* _____
THE FOLLOWING: *(If this request is being submitted on behalf of another firm or individual, explain in Item 10 below.)*

8.(a) QUANTITY	(b) DESCRIPTION OF COMMODITY OR TECHNICAL DATA	(c) EXPORT CONTROL COMMODITY NO. AND PROCESSING CODE	(d) DOLLAR VALUE

9. END-USE OF COMMODITIES OR TECHNICAL DATA BY NEW ULTIMATE CONSIGNEE *(Describe fully)*

10. ADDITIONAL INFORMATION *(Attach separate sheet if more space is needed)*

11. APPLICANT'S CERTIFICATION - I(We) certify that the above statements are true to the best of my(our) knowledge and belief. If authorization is granted, I(we) will be strictly accountable for its use in accordance with the Export Administration Regulation and all terms and conditions specified on the authorization.

Type or _____ **SIGN HERE** _____ Type or _____
Print (Applicant Same as Item 3) **IN INK** (Signature of person authorized to execute this request) print (Name and title of person whose signature appears on line to left)

FOR DEPARTMENT OF COMMERCE USE ONLY

SPECIAL CONDITIONS

ACTION TAKEN	AUTHORITY	RATING		DV	TECH. DATA			
☐ APPROVED								
☐ REJECTED						(Licensing officer)	(No.)	(Date)
DOCUMENTATION		END-USE CHECK	REEX-PORT	SUPPORT DOCUMENT	TYPE OF LICENSE	(Review officer)		(Date)

NOTE: Submit the first four copies of this request to the Office of Export Licensing. P.O. Box 273, Washington. D.C. 20044, retaining copy five for your files. This form may be reproduced provided the content, format,size and color of paper and ink are the same.

COPY-1
OEA CASE FILE COPY

USCOMM-DC 86-21564

Figure 11.8   FORM ITA-699P, Request to Dispose of Commodities or Technical Data Previously Exported

Distribution license. This single license authorizes exports during one year of certain commodities to consignees in specified countries with which the United States has good relations. The consignees must have been approved in advance as foreign distributors or users.

Service supply license (SL). This license enables persons or firms in the United States or abroad to provide prompt service for equipment (1) exported from the United States, or (2) produced abroad by a manufacturer who uses parts imported from the United States in the manufactured product. It permits the export of spare and replacement parts to consignees in certain approved countries.

Application of Licenses

The export licensing controls described above are administered by the Department of Commerce and apply to (1) exports of commodities and technical data from the United States; (2) reexports of U.S.-origin commodities and technical data from a foreign destination to another foreign destination; (3) U.S.-origin and components used in a foreign country to manufacture a foreign end product for export; and (4) in some instances, the foreign produced direct product of U.S.-origin technical data.

These licensing controls do not extend to exports by U.S. subsidiaries, affiliates, or branches in foreign countries if the commodities exported are (1) of foreign manufacture; (2) contain no U.S. materials; and (3) not based on restricted U.S. technology. However, the Treasury Department does control certain transactions by U.S. nationals (including foreign subsidiaries or branches of U.S. firms) involving foreign-origin commodities destined for Country Groups Q, S, W, Y, or Z. (Country Groups are described in Chapter Twelve.) Such transactions may be subject to the Transaction Control Regulations, the Foreign Assets Control Regulations, the Cuban Assets Control Regulations, or the Rhodesian Sanctions Regulations. Complete information on Treasury controls may be obtained from the Office of Foreign Assets Control, U.S. Department of Treasury, Washington, D.C. 20220.

The controls established by the Office of Export Administration are published in the *Federal Register* and in the U.S. Department of Commerce *Export Administration Regulations*. However, a portion of the material appearing in the *Export Administration Regulations*, the Commodity Control List, is incorporated in the *Federal Register* by reference only.

Subscriptions to the U.S. Department of Commerce *Export Administration Regulations* and supplementary U.S. Department of Commerce *Export Administration Bulletins* may be ordered from the Superintendent of Documents, U.S. Government Printing Office, Washington, D.C. 20402; from any U.S. Department of Commerce district office; or from Room 1905, U.S. Department of Commerce Building, 14th and E Streets, N.W., Washington, D.C. 20230. Subscribers will receive the basic *Export Administration Regulations* and all supplementary *Export Administration Regulations*. A subscription is an inexpensive way to build up an information library on export regulations.

Shipper's Export Declaration

This document has a dual purpose. The government uses it to help move shipments through U.S. Customs because it shows the proper authorization for shipments—that is, general or validated export licenses. In addition, the shipping information and description of the merchandise that it contains becomes part of the statistics upon which the FT-410 reports (Schedule B-Commodity) are based. Explicit shipping instructions are usually included with the above documents. The freight forwarder generally handles licensing, export declaration, and shipping instructions. It is wise, however, for you to be aware of general requirements and procedures, as well as instances requiring special treatment. (See Figure 11.7.)

COLLECTION DOCUMENTS

Collection documents are the documents that are submitted to the importer or the importer's bank in order to receive payment. Collection documents may vary from country to country in method of receiving payment and mode of shipping. Documents may even vary from importer to importer. Several general types of documents will be discussed here.

Commercial invoices. As in a domestic shipment, good business practice dictates that a commercial invoice (Figure 11.9) include the full address of the shipper, seller, and consignee, if different; the respective reference numbers; date of the order; shipping date; mode of shipment; delivery and payment terms; a complete description of the merchandise; and prices, discounts, and quantities.

In addition, it is customary on an export order to indicate the origin of the goods and the export marks. If payment is to be against a letter of credit, reference to the bank and the corresponding credit or advice numbers must be given.

Some countries require special certification, sometimes in the language of that country, incorporated in the invoice. Information about these statements may be obtained from any Department of Commerce district office.

In some instances, it is necessary for the seller to sign his or her invoices and even have them notarized or countersigned by the local chamber of commerce, or both. Many times it is also necessary to have the invoices visaed by the resident consul of the country of destination. Again, this information may be obtained from Department of Commerce district offices.

Consular invoices. A few foreign countries, notably Latin American, require a special form of invoice (Figure 11.10) in addition to the commercial invoice. These documents must be prepared in the language of that country and official forms sold by the respective consulates. They are then visaed by resident consul, thereby certifying the authenticity and correctness of the documents. It is recommended that the shipper's forwarder prepare these documents at time of shipment.

Certificates of origin. Even though the commercial invoice may contain a statement of origin of the merchandise, a few countries require a separate certificate (Figure 11.11) sometimes countersigned by a chamber of commerce and possibly even visaed by the country's resident consul at the port of export. These may be on a special form of the foreign government, or, in other cases, a certificate on the shipper's own letterhead will suffice. Statements of origin are required to establish possible preferential rates of import duties under a most favored nation arrangement.

Inspection certificates. In order to protect themselves, many foreign firms request a certificate of inspection. This may be either an affidavit by the shipper or by an independent inspection form, as dictated by the buyer, certifying to the quality, quantity, and conformity of goods in relation to the order. This is usually done before the goods are shipped.

Bills of lading. These may be overland (truck or rail), air, or ocean bills of lading (Figure 11.12), depending on destination or terms of sales. As in domestic shipment, there are two basic types of bills of lading: "straight" (or nonnegotiable) and "shipper's order" (or negotiable). The latter is used for sight draft or letter of credit shipments. This shipper must endorse the original copy of the "order" bill of lading before it is presented to the bank for collection. The endorsement may either be "in blank" or "to the order of" a third party, such as the negotiating bank. The letter of credit will stipulate which endorsement to use. With the exception of ocean shipments, only one original bill of lading is issued by the carrier. Any number of original ocean bills of lading may be issued depending on the requirements of the buyer. Normally, all original copies are endorsed and submitted to the bank.

According to the rules set forth by the International Chambers of Commerce (*Guide to Incoterms*, 1980 edition), which governs foreign trade terms, documents, and so on, on draft or letter of credit shipments, the only bill of lading that is acceptable is one that is marked "CLEAN ON BOARD." This statement signifies that the carrier has not taken any exception to the condition of the cargo or packing and that the merchandise has actually been loaded aboard the carrying vessel.

Dock receipts, warehouse receipts, and so on. In cases where the shipper is not responsible for moving the merchandise to the foreign destination, but to the U.S. port of export instead, these documents may be requested. They are exactly as their name implies—a receipt to the effect that the stipulated merchandise has been received at the pier or a warehouse for further disposition.

COMMERCIAL INVOICE

SHIPPER/EXPORTER
Brown & Co.
123 Samantha Road
Toledo, OH 43624
U.S.A.

DOCUMENT NO.

EXPORT REFERENCES

CONSIGNEE
Kirk Sales Ltd.
162 Belva Street
London, England

FORWARDING AGENT - REFERENCES
Sharyn Exports
P.O. Box XYZ
New York, NY 10047
POINT AND COUNTRY OF ORIGIN
OH – U.S.A.

NOTIFY PARTY
Bolden Service Company
3456 Fred Lane
London, England

DOMESTIC ROUTING/EXPORT INSTRUCTIONS

PIER OR AIRPORT
Kennedy Airport

EXPORTING CARRIER (Vessel/Airline)
Fairway Air

PORT OF LOADING
New York

ONWARD INLAND ROUTING

AIR/SEA PORT OF DISCHARGE
Gatwick, England

FOR TRANSSHIPMENT TO

PARTICULARS FURNISHED BY SHIPPER

MARKS AND NUMBERS	NO. OF PKGS.	DESCRIPTION OF PACKAGES AND GOODS	GROSS WEIGHT	MEASUREMENT

110

B,1,B,2	2 Boxes	Signal generators operating at frequencies over 1 GHz Model 525 Sweep generators	146
B,3	1 Box	Specially designed parts for Model 525 Sweep generators, consisting of probes, tees, detectors, and detector mounts	68

DELIVERY TERMS

FAS NEW YORK

NET INVOICE VALUE $ 4,250

AMOUNT INSURED $ 4,250

See addendum attached for detailed summary of billing and packing.

CERTIFICATIONS

Form No. 86-525
Printed and Sold by Unz & Co., Division of Scott Printing Corp., 190 Baldwin Ave., Jersey City, N.J. 07306 — N.J. (201) 795-5400 / N.Y. (212) 344-2270 Signed _____
Toll Free (800) 631-3098

Figure 11.9 Commercial invoice

111

DA 59

Supplier (name, address, country)

DECLARATION OF ORIGIN—
for the export of goods to the
REPUBLIC OF SOUTH AFRICA

Consignee (name, address, country)

NOTE TO IMPORTERS

This declaration, properly completed by the supplier, must be furnished in support of the relative bill of entry where goods qualify for and are entered at the rate of duty lower than the general rate

Particulars of transport

Customs date stamp

1 Item No.	2 Marks and numbers	3 No. and desc. of packages	4 Description of goods	5 Country of origin	6 Gross Mass	7 Invoice No./ Ref.

112

I, (name and capacity) ....

duly authorised by the supplier of the goods enumerated above hereby declare that—

1. the goods enumerated opposite item(s) .... in column 1 above have been wholly produced or manufactured in the country stated in column 5 in respect of such goods from raw materials produced in that country;

2. the goods enumerated opposite item(s) .... in column 1 above have been wholly or partly manufactured from imported materials in the country specified in column 5 in respect of such goods; and

2.1 the final process of manufacture has taken place in the said country;

2.2 the cost to the manufacturer of the materials wholly produced or manufactured in the said country plus the cost of labour directly employed in the manufacture of such goods is not less than .... per cent of the total production cost of such goods;

2.3 in calculating the production cost of such goods only the cost to the manufacturer of all materials plus manufacturing wages and salaries, direct manufacturing expenses, overhead factory expenses, cost of inside containers and other expenses incidental to manufacturing, used or expended in the manufacture of such goods have been included and profits and administrative, distribution and selling overhead expenses have been excluded.

Place .... Date .... Signature of Deponent ....

Form No. 10 - 659   Printed and Sold by Unz & Co., Division of Scott Printing Corp., 190 Baldwin Ave., Jersey City, N.J. 07306 — N.J. (201) 795-5400 / N.Y. (212) 344-2270 Toll Free (800) 631-3098

Figure 11.10 Consular invoice

CERTIFICATE OF ORIGIN

SHIPPER/EXPORTER

Brown & Company
123 Samantha Road
Toledo, OH 43624
U.S.A.

DOCUMENT NO.

EXPORT REFERENCES

CONSIGNEE

Kirk Sales Ltd.
162 Belva Street
London, England

FORWARDING AGENT - REFERENCES

Sharyn Exports
P.O. Box XYZ
New York, NY 10047

POINT AND COUNTRY OF ORIGIN

OH – U.S.A.

NOTIFY PARTY

Bolden Service Company
3456 Fred Lane
London, England

DOMESTIC ROUTING/EXPORT INSTRUCTIONS

PIER OR AIRPORT

Kennedy Airport

PORT OF LOADING

New York

EXPORTING CARRIER (Vessel/Airline)

Fairway Air

FOR TRANSSHIPMENT TO

AIR/SEA PORT OF DISCHARGE

Gatwick, England

ONWARD INLAND ROUTING

PARTICULARS FURNISHED BY SHIPPER

MARKS AND NUMBERS	NO. OF PKGS.	DESCRIPTION OF PACKAGES AND GOODS	GROSS WEIGHT	MEASUREMENT

114

B,1,B2	2 Boxes	Signal generators operating at frequencies over 1 GHz Model 525 Sweep generators	146
B,3	1 Box	Specially designed parts for Model 525 Sweep generators, consisting of probes, tees, detectors and detector mounts	68

The undersigned ___Export Coordinator___ (Owner or Agent), does hereby declare for the above named shipper, the goods as described above were shipped on the above date and consigned as indicated and are products of the United States of America.

Dated at _____ on the _____ day of _____ 19 ____

Sworn to before me this _____ day of _____ 19 ____

_____

SIGNATURE OF OWNER OR AGENT

The _____, a recognized Chamber of Commerce under the laws of the State of _____, has examined the manufacturer's invoice or shipper's affidavit concerning the origin of the merchandise, and, according to the best of its knowledge and belief, finds that the products named originated in the United States of North America.

Secretary ___Jim Jones___

Form No. 80-335— Printed and Sold by Unz & Co., Division of Scott Printing Corp., 190 Baldwin Ave., Jersey City, N.J. 07306—N.J. (201) 795-5400 / N.Y. (212) 344-2270 Toll Free (800) 631-3098

Figure 11.11 Certificate of origin

SHORT FORM BILL OF LADING

Non-Negotiable Unless Consigned To Order)

NAME OF CARRIER

SHIPPER/EXPORTER (2) (COMPLETE NAME AND ADDRESS)

Brown & Company
123 Samantha Road
Toledo, OH 43624
U.S.A.

DOCUMENT NO. (5)

EXPORT REFERENCES (6)

CONSIGNEE (3) (COMPLETE NAME AND ADDRESS)

Kirk Sales Ltd.
162 Belva Street
London, England

FORWARDING AGENT-REFERENCES (7) (COMPLETE NAME AND ADDRESS)

Sharyn Exports
P.O. Box XYZ
New York, NY 10047

POINT AND COUNTRY OF ORIGIN (8)

NOTIFY PARTY (4) (COMPLETE NAME AND ADDRESS)

Bolden Service Company
3456 Fred Lane
London, England

DOMESTIC ROUTING/EXPORT INSTRUCTIONS (9)

PIER/TERMINAL (10)
Kennedy Airport

VESSEL (11)   FLAG
Fairway Air

PORT OF LOADING (12)
New York

ONWARD INLAND ROUTING (15)

PORT OF DISCHARGE FROM VESSEL (13)
Gatwick, England

FOR TRANSSHIPMENT TO (14)

	PARTICULARS FURNISHED BY SHIPPER			
MARKS AND NUMBERS	NO. OF PKGS.	DESCRIPTION OF PACKAGES AND GOODS	GROSS WEIGHT	MEASUREMENT
(16)	(17)	(18)	(19)	(20)

116

B, 1, B2	2 Boxes	Signal generators operating at frequencies over 1 GHz. Model 525 Sweep generators.	146
B, 3	1 Box	Specially designed parts for Model 525 Sweep generators, consisting of probes, tees, detectors, and detector mounts.	68

FREIGHT AND CHARGES PAYABLE AT

	PREPAID	COLLECT
TOTAL	$4,250 –	

PREPAID ☐   COLLECT ☐

RECEIVED the goods or the containers, vans, trailers, pallet units or other packages said to contain goods herein mentioned, in apparent good order and condition, except as otherwise indicated, to be transported, delivered or transhipped as provided herein. All of the provisions written, printed or stamped on either side hereof are part of this bill of lading contract.

IN WITNESS WHEREOF, the Master or agent of said vessel has signed ____ bills of lading, all of the same tenor and date, one of which being accomplished, the others to stand void.

_____ FOR THE MASTER

BY

DATED

B/L NO.

Form 80-320 — Printed and Sold by Unz & Co., Division of Scott Printing Corp., 190 Baldwin Ave., Jersey City, N.J. 07306 — N.J. (201) 795-5400 / N.Y. (212) 344-2270
Toll Free (800) 631-3098

Figure 11.12 Bill of lading

117

Certificate of manufacture.   This document is used when a buyer intends to pay for the goods prior to shipment but the lead time for the manufacture of the products is lengthy and the buyer does not desire to allocate the money so far in advance. If the seller feels that the buyer is a good credit risk, the seller will proceed with the manufacture of the products with perhaps only a down payment. After the merchandise is ready, the seller prepares a certificate stating that the ordered goods have been produced in accordance with the contract and have been set aside for the account of the buyer. Commercial invoices and packing list are sent as supporting documents. As soon as payment and shipping instructions have been received, the merchandise is shipped.

Insurance certificates.   Where the seller provides ocean marine insurance, it is necessary to furnish insurance certificates, usually in duplicate, indicating the type and amount of coverage involved. Here again, these are negotiable documents and must be endorsed before submitting them to the bank.

The seller can arrange to obtain an open cargo policy to cover all foreign shipments or the seller can use the open cargo policy which the forwarder maintains.

These are the basic documents involved in foreign shipments. However, a country or individual may require additional ones, which will be specified either in the order or letter of credit. Special care should be taken when reviewing the order or letter of credit to assure that all of the documents required are furnished in the manner prescribed to avoid rejection and other difficulty.

As mentioned previously, freight forwarders and other traffic management firms are capable and willing to prepare these documents for the shipper at moderate cost. Let them!

Another word of caution: Shipping documents must be presented for collection within certain time limits after shipment or they will be considered "stale" and the bank will reject them. It will then be necessary to contact the buyer for permission to honor these late documents before the bank will release payment. It is equally important to make sure the shipment is made within the specified time indicated in the letter of credit, otherwise the credit will expire and it may not be possible to receive payment. In most cases it will be possible to arrange for the buyer to pay for the shipment, but serious delays may be experienced.

Information regarding the documents required and assistance in their preparation may be obtained from any Department of Commerce district office. UNZ & Company, 190 Baldwin Avenue, Jersey City, New Jersey 07306—800-631-5400 or in New Jersey 201-795-5400—provides an excellent catalog of forms. Beginners will find it helpful and should write to the company for a copy.

Chapter Twelve

Country Groups and Commodity Controls

In addition to the licensing procedures described in Chapter Eleven, the U.S. government controls exports by separating all the countries of the world into Country Groups.

For political reasons, the government looks on some of these Country Groups more favorably than on others. Products can be exported freely to some, with more difficulty (special licensing) to others, and not at all to others. Which products are affected? The cross-reference to the Country Group list is the Commodity Control List (CCL) which indicates which products require which licenses to go to which countries.

COUNTRY GROUPS

All destinations for exports (excluding Canada) are divided into the following Country Groups. Canada is not included in any Country Group since exports to that country normally are controlled only in specific short supply or foreign policy situations.

- Group Q—Rumania
- Group S—Libya

119

- Group T—North, Central, and South America; Bermuda and the Caribbean, except Canada and Cuba
- Group V—All countries not included in any other Country Group except Canada, which is not in any group
- Group W—Hungary, Poland
- Group Y—Albania, Bulgaria, Czechoslovakia, Estonia, German Democratic Republic (including East Berlin), Laos, Latvia, Lithuania, Mongolian People's Republic, U.S.S.R.
- Group Z—Cuba, Cambodia, North Korea, Vietnam

Briefly, the policies relating to the licensing of exports to various Country Groups are:

1. *U.S. Possessions*: No export authorization is required for shipments of commodities or technical data intended for use or consumption by persons in Puerto Rico or U.S. territories, dependencies, and possessions. Such shipments are considered domestic shipments.

2. *Canada*: As a general rule, no commodities or technical data require export licenses to Canada for consumption in Canada. Whenever commodities or technical data do require a validated export license for Canada, that requirement is shown in the Export Administration Regulations.

3. *Cuba* (in Country Group Z): U.S. restrictions on trade with Cuba have been in effect since 1960. Under the embargo, exports to Cuba are kept to an absolute minimum consistent with humanitarian considerations. Commodities meeting the provisions of certain general licenses, such as gift and baggage licenses, may be sent to Cuba, as may publications, periodicals, and technical data exportable under General License GTDA. All other exports require validated export licenses, and applications are therefore generally rejected.

4. *North Korea, North Vietnam, South Vietnam, and Cambodia* (in Country Group Z): There is an embargo on commercial shipments to these countries. However, personal baggage, publications, periodicals, and technical data exportable under General License GTDA may be shipped to these areas.

5. *U.S.S.R., East European countries, the Mongolian People's Republic, and Laos* (in Country Group Y); *Rumania* (in Country Group Q); and *Poland* and *Hungary* (in Country Group W): For the past several years the U.S. government has permitted nonstrategic trade with the U.S.S.R., other Warsaw Pact countries, Albania, the Mongolian People's Republic, and Laos. You may export commodities that are essentially peaceful end uses under General License G-DEST. Where a validated license is required, OEA

reviews the proposed transaction to determine whether it would contribute significantly to the military potential of the countries mentioned above in a way that would be detrimental to U.S. national security. This review includes, but is not limited to, the following considerations:

- What kinds and quantities of commodities or technologies are to be shipped?
- What is their potential military or civilian use?
- Are the same or comparable commodities or technologies available abroad without restriction?
- What is the country of destination?
- Who are the ultimate end users?
- What is the intended end use of the commodities or technologies?

6. *Afghanistan* (in Country Group V): The Soviet military presence in Afghanistan requires special attention to exports because commodities or technical data entering Afghanistan may be diverted to the U.S.S.R. Accordingly, the validated licensing requirements for the U.S.S.R. extend to shipments to Afghanistan, and license applications are examined to verify use by the Afghan civil economy.

7. *People's Republic of China* (in Country Group V): Although China is in the same export category as certain other friendly countries, national security controls are maintained on truly sensitive technology, and licensing decisions may be coordinated with COCOM. OEA's decision on whether or not to license a particular shipment is based on whether the commodity or technology falls into the "green," the "intermediate" or the "red" technology zone.

- *Green:* Equipment and technology in this zone generally are approved for export by Commerce without interagency review because the items pose only a minimal strategic risk. (Special China notes on selected CCL entries identify green zone items.)
- *Intermediate:* Equipment and technology in this zone are reviewed on a case-by-case basis and generally are approved for export unless such items pose a clear threat to U.S. national security.
- *Red:* Equipment and technology in this zone have direct strategic military applications, and such items generally are not approved for export.

8. *South Africa and Namibia* (in Country Group V): There is an embargo on exports and reexports to South Africa and Namibia of items controlled under the United Nations arms embargo of South Africa. In addition, there is an embargo on exports and reexports to military or police entities of U.S.-origin commodities controlled for national security, nuclear nonproliferation, or crime control reasons; this embargo also covers related technical data, automotive vehicles, watercraft, parts and accessories thereof, and

tires. Special licensing policies apply to all exports of aircraft and helicopters and to exports of computers for some government consignees. Otherwise, export controls for the Republic of South Africa and Namibia are generally the same as for other destinations in Country Groups T and V.

9. *Libya* (in Country Group S): There is an embargo on national-security controlled exports to Libya. Validated license requirements exist for all other commodities except for medicine and medical supplies, food and agricultural commodities, and exports to Libya from other countries of foreign nonstrategic products of U.S.-origin technical data.

10. *Other Countries* (in Country Group T or V): OEA generally approves applications for export to T and V countries. Applications for T and V destinations are required primarily to ensure that the commodity to be exported will not be reexported to an unauthorized or restricted destination.

COMMODITY CONTROL

The Commodity Control List is the key to determining whether a specific shipment is exportable under an established general license authorization, or whether a validated export license (for which an application must be filed) is needed. For all of the commodities licensed by the Bureau of East-West Trade, the CCL shows the destinations for which each commodity requires a license document. It also shows whether any special requirement must be met in connection with the submission of a license application.

The CCL is keyed to the Schedule B Commodity Classification System, which is known to most exporters because it must be used to prepare the Shipper's Export Declaration.

USING THE COMMODITY CONTROL LIST

Each commodity on the CCL is identified in the first column by its Export Control Commodity (ECC) Number. This number is composed of the first one to five digits of the seven-digit Schedule B (*Schedule B, Statistical Classification of Domestic and Foreign Commodities Exported from the United States*, available from the U.S. Government Printing Office) commodity classification number applicable to the commodity, and by italicized digits in parentheses indicating the sequence of that entry among all those entries that have the same preceding digit(s). This number is followed by a code letter indicating the Country Groups for which a validated license is required. (In the example below for Capacitance Strain Gages designed for operation at temperatures of plus 600°F and over, this code letter is "J," indicating that a validated license is required to export this commodity to Country Groups Q, S, W, Y, and Z.)

To determine whether a specific commodity requires a validated license, first find the Schedule B number under which it is classified. (If assistance is necessary, it is obtainable from the Foreign Trade Division, Bureau of the Census, Washington, D.C. 20233.) Then, using that number as the key, locate the commodity on the CCL. As an example, the Schedule B number for Capacitance Strain Gages is 729.5266; therefore, the ECC Number is 7295 (48). The CCL shows that for No. 7295 (48), a validated license is required for shipments to Country Groups Q, S, W, Y, and Z, while exports to Country Groups T and V can be made under General License G-DEST. However, the column titled "GLV $ Value Limits" shows that individual dollar-value shipments of these gages may be made in amounts up to $100 to Country Group Q under the provisions of General License GLV. There is no GLV value shown for Country Groups T and V since shipments of these gages to T and V destinations are exportable under General License G-DEST. No GLV value is shown for Country Groups S, W, Y, or Z since General License GLV is *not* applicable to those destinations.

Chapter Thirteen

Import Organizations

The import business is one of the oldest trades, dating back to a period before the invention of money when people bartered for goods. The trade was and still is open to anyone with the perseverance and willingness to learn the mechanics. Importing is not limited to the exotic paraphernalia found in the local import store. Overseas manufacturers provide the U.S. market with a vast array of both consumer and technical products. By using your ingenuity and doing a thorough job of market research, you can tap what constitutes a $400 billion gold mine. Consider the following examples:

- More than two dozen name-brand foreign cars are sold in the United States. As with domestic cars, whole lines of accessories are made to enhance the vehicles' appearance. Such auto accessories are fine products for the novice importer, as are accessories for recreational vehicles, mopeds, and bicycles.
- Foreign-make wearing apparel, food, and home furnishings continue to be popular in the United States. *Made in Europe, Asian Sources* magazine can give you an idea of current styles and prices.
- Health and beauty products from Europe have great appeal for the U.S. consumer; they form a product category of excellent potential for the novice.
- Electronics is a growing industry abroad, as it is in the United States. The novice should investigate electronic products both for consumer and technical markets.

Magazines that discuss new business opportunities, such as *Trade Channels*, can provide the novice with ideas for products that are salable in the current marketplace. There are many other business-opportunity publications that you should check out.

IMPORTING AND EXPORTING: WORKING TOGETHER

The beginner who is just getting involved in exporting can easily combine importing with it. Importing and exporting are just opposite sides of the same coin. Either can be operated independently, or they can work together. Neither is more profitable; importing, however, puts a greater burden on the novice because imported products must be distributed and sold. In contrast, the exporter functions as an intermediary between the manufacturer and the overseas representative who does the distributing and selling.

These next ten chapters review pricing, selling, financing, transportation, customs clearance, and more, as they pertain to importing. All are important, but the key to your import success is found in *marketing*. Finding products, identifying customers, promoting products, and selling them are the basis for a lucrative importing business. Expertise in financing can be found at your bank; transportation help comes from freight forwarders and transportation companies; documentation assistance is obtainable from a customs broker. Do not let the technicalities of importing interfere with your marketing efforts. Pay the experts for what they know; save your time to sell your products.

Before perusing the following chapters, you should quickly review the introductory chapters, particularly those on market research and on making overseas and domestic contacts (Chapters Three and Six, respectively). Just as with exporting, it is critical for the new importing practitioner to do his or her homework thoroughly before making commitments. There is always some risk involved in every business dealing, and it is every business person's responsibility to lessen the risk as much as possible by intelligent forethought. Consider also that, whereas you previously were thinking about trade from the standpoint of the exporter who had to deal with the foreign importer, you have now switched places. To an exporter somewhere in the world, *you* are the foreign importer. Reviewing Chapters Five through Twelve with this in mind can greatly enhance your understanding of the import business.

BASIC ORGANIZATIONS FOR AN IMPORT FIRM

There are several types of import organizations with which the beginner should be familiar. Although you may start out as an import agent, expansion into an organization requiring capital and experience may be in the future.

Import agents generally buy on orders received, and as *commission agents* they either receive a fixed commission from the seller or act as brokers, collecting fees just for bringing two parties together.

When operating on fixed commissions, the agent usually checks the credit-worthiness and intent of the U.S. buyer, delivers the documents, collects the proceeds, and remits them to the foreign exporter less a commission. At no time during the operation does the agent assume title for the goods.

When the agent acts as broker, you normally represent the seller. However, during extraordinary periods (war, bad weather), both buyer and seller may pay for the agent's services (providing munitions during wartime is a good example).

Most import agents have small organizations with fewer than ten employees. They keep catalogs and samples of noncompetitive lines to show to their local clients. This is the best form for the beginner, since it protects you from risk.

Most large buyers, however, prefer to deal with a merchant who has a local stock of merchandise. This way, the buyer can see exactly what she or he is getting, and there is no delay in delivery. Commodity merchants especially prefer access to a local stock because most merchants trade on the exchanges and they want to provide excellent pricing and quick delivery. If you, as a beginner, wishes, you can use the money and connections gained from commissions for setting up a warehouse with showrooms and sales staff, and thereby become an import merchant.

Import merchants have warehouse facilities and a fairly large sales staff. They may specialize in one commodity (coffee, tea, spices, textiles, and other traditional imports), buying and selling the goods on their own behalf, or they may act as a broker, never taking title to the goods. That is, import merchants may buy only on orders received. They are the oldest type of U.S. importing organization, and are plentiful in the established eastern and western seaports.

Import distributors are very popular when the product requires backup support (farm machinery, computers, or anything else where sales must be closely supported with good service). These firms are usually fairly large organizations that are sometimes directly or indirectly owned by a foreign manufacturer. Many of the Japanese consumer electronic firms have set up this type of company to handle all U.S. distribution. Most such firms have large warehousing facilities, service departments, showrooms, and sales staff.

Advertising and promotion usually play an important role in these operations. In some cases, the foreign source controls sales promotion, and in other instances the import division does it all.

As with the import merchant, many distributors specialize in certain goods. For example, representing a half dozen noncompeting food lines is a common practice.

International trading companies are usually found in Europe, Japan, and the United States. Generally, they are large organizations with good marketing coverage and financial stability. In Japan, they control the domestic distribution networks for many types of products, and exporters must sell through them. In the

United States, bank export trading companies have not been particularly successful. It will probably be some time before the trading company concept catches on.

Manufacturers sometimes import to augment their product lines. The manufacturer who imports is usually a large company, like U.S. Steel, that relies on a continuous flow of raw materials from overseas. Oftentimes a permanent division of that corporation is stationed overseas. The larger steel, petroleum, and copper companies provide examples of this type of importer.

The type of organization usually appears on the firm's letterhead. When dealing with foreign import organizations, do not be surprised if the same company or family name appears repeatedly from letterhead to letterhead. In many parts of the world, certain families or ethic groups dominate a particular industry, so that all functions regarding that product are under one company or family name.

STEPS ALONG THE WAY

Whatever import organization you select, you must be prepared to follow your imports through a series of steps in order to bring them into the United States. A comprehensive list appears in Figure 13.1, showing what is expected of each of the services with which you will deal.

Steamship Company
1. Notifies consignee two days prior to ship's arrival
2. Provides freight release to terminal operator

Broker
3. Obtains customs release, freight release, Department of Agriculture clearances, etc.; coordinates contacting motor carrier
4. Forwards to motor carrier an original of the Domestic Bill of Lading and an Original Delivery Order, which authorizes pick-up of import cargo
5. Checks Bill of Lading for completeness:
   - Number of packages
   - description of cargo
   - marks and numbers
   - inland destination
   - gross weights of each commodity shipped
   - consignee
6. Checks Delivery Order for completeness:
   - forwarder's name
   - shipper's name
   - ultimate consignee's name
   - motor carrier making pick-up

Figure 13.1 Import steps (*Source*: CIGNA P&C Companies, Publisher, ports of the World, P.O. Box 7728, Philadelphia PA 19101.)

- vessel
- arrival date
- voyage number
- ocean bill of lading number
- pier number and location
- marks and numbers
- number of packages
- description of goods
- gross weights
- legible signatures

Motor Carrier

7. Secures interchange agreement with steamship company on containers
8. Ascertains expiration of free time and availability of cargo for pick-up before dispatching driver to pier
9. Provides driver with original and copy of Delivery Order before departure for pier
10. Checks Bill of Lading and Delivery Order for completeness, as above
11. Dispatches driver to pier

Terminal Operator

12. Issues pass to driver at gate house
13. Checks Delivery Order for completeness and legibility, as above
14. Verifies motor carrier's credit rating for loading charges
15. Makes arrangements for payment of demurrage, if any has accrued

Customs

16. Verifies contents to invoices, examination is required

Terminal Operator

17. Calls driver for loading
18. Assigns checker and loading spot

Customs

19. Performs all necessary functions prior to the release of cargo

Terminal Operator

20. Loads cargo onto vehicle with pier personnel (Checker notes exceptions and shortages)
21. Retains original Delivery Order

Driver

22. Assists in and/or supervises loading of vehicle
23. Signs tally and loading ticket (exceptions and shortages noted)
24. Reports back to delivery office, if required
25. Retains copy of Delivery Order
26. Surrenders gate pass at gate house

Motor Carrier

27. Advises broker of completion of cargo pick-up

Figure 13.1   (Cont.)

Chapter Fourteen

Pricing and Distribution Channels

Once you, the importer, have selected the product or product category in which you plan to deal, and have considered the domestic contacts (wholesalers, retailers, manufacturer's representatives) you must make in order to sell the merchandise, you can approach the pricing of imports in more detail. Before you offer anything for sale, you should analyze your costs carefully, just as you would before quoting a price on an export order. As it does for the exporter, a cost analysis helps to select products that offer the greatest potential for profit.

Let's say that, after completing your international product research, you decide that women's handbags should sell well in your area. At this point, you write to the overseas distributors or manufacturers to obtain a price list, pictures, sample (if available), delivery schedules, and terms.

When writing for prices, ask for the c.i.f. (cost, insurance, freight) price to your nearest port (or airport, as the case may be). This will make your landed cost (cost of getting merchandise to your nearest port) computations simpler because insurance and freight are included in the price. However, if f.o.b. terms are the only terms available, ask your foreign freight forwarder for the cost of transporting goods to your locale. Very often, the exporter will give you only an f.o.b. price, and you must handle shipping and customs through your freight forwarder to customs broker. Finally, make certain your pricing is current—check the date on the price list. When the handbag samples arrive, take them to department stores, specialty shops, and boutiques, and compare them to the domestic products. Speak with local manufacturer's representatives and buyers about the market for these handbags.

Then prepare a landed cost survey, which is very similar to the cost survey you prepared when you quoted your export order. This alerts you to the product's profitability or lack of same, so you can adjust your price or decide whether to im-

129

LANDED COST SURVEY
for XYZ Importing Co.
New York, N.Y.

Supplier: John Hauser, Southampton, England
Quantity: 200 leather handbags

GROSS SALES PRICE	$5555.00
Less Cash Discount (10%)	<u>555.50</u>
Net Sales Price	$4999.50
LANDED COST	
Purchase Price (200 @ $25 each)	5000.00
Packing (1 per case)	—
Inland Freight to Foreign Port	—
Inland Freight	—
Duty (Customs)($4,620 @ 9.0%)	
($5,555 less 10% discount, $29.15	
insurance $350.00 freight)	415.80
Brokerage Clearance Fees	100.00
Banking Charges - Letter of Credit	100.00
Custom Bond Fee	40.00
Merchandise Processing Fee (.17%)	7.85
Harbor Maintenance Fee (.04%)	<u>1.89</u>
	SUB TOTAL 656.54
TOTAL LANDED COSTS (c.i.f. LA)	$5,656.54
EXPENSES	
Repacking	—
Freight Out (Truck)	50.00
Advertising	—
Interest	—
ABI Fees (Automated Broker Interface)	<u>10.00</u>
TOTAL EXPENSES	60.00
TOTAL LANDED COSTS AND EXPENSES	
($5000.00 + $656.54 + $60.00)	5716.64

Unit Cost: Approximately $28.58 each   Suggested Selling Price: $55.00
Net Profit: $5284.00

Figure 14.1 Landed Cost Survey

port. A survey prepared for women's handbags is provided in Figures 14.1 and 14.2.

Keep in mind when pricing that reselling a $.25 item for $2.50 is difficult, if not impossible, in today's marketplace. Balance of trade, reevaluation of the dollar, and so on, have made exaggerated profits unrealistic. If possible, stay with items that offer a reasonably steady profit.

For mail order items, a minimum of 300 percent markup after calculating shipping costs is needed. When dealing with wholesale quantities on high-cost con-

DEPARTMENT OF THE TREASURY
UNITED STATES CUSTOMS SERVICE

ENTRY SUMMARY

1. Entry No. M51 0001234-4	2. Entry Type Code 01	3. Entry Summary Date 24
4. Entry Date	5. Port Code	
6. Bond No. 422	7. Bond Type Code 9	8. Broker / Importer File No. 1234

9. Ultimate Consignee Name and Address

10. Consignee No.

11. Importer of Record Name and Address
XYZ Co., Inc.
7 Dream St.
Los Angeles, CA 90011

12. Importer No. 95-0123651

CA STATE

13. Exporting Country GB	14. Export Date 122787
15. Country of Origin GB	16. Missing Documents
17. I.T. No.	18. I.T. Date

19. B L or AWB No. LPL 1010	20. Mode of Transportation 11	21. Manufacturer I.D. GBJOHHOU6543LON	22. Reference No. 33-0000333
23. Importing Carrier JSS Los Angeles, V015	24. Foreign Port of Lading 41374	25. Location of Goods/G.O. No. CAL PAC Terminal	
26. U.S. Port of Unlading 2709	27. Import Date 011288		

28. Line No.	29. Description of Merchandise / 30. A. T.S.U.S.A. No. B. ADA CVD Case No.	31. A. Gross Weight B. Manifest Qty.	32. Net Quantity in T.S.U.S.A. Units	33. A. Entered Value B. CHGS C. Relationship	34. A. T.S.U.S.A. Rate B. ADA/CVD Rate C. I.R.C Rate D. Visa No.	35. Duty and I.R. Tax Dollars	Cents
	20 ctns						
001	Luggage & handbags, whether or not fitted with bottle, dining, drinking, manicure, sewing, traveling or similar sets; and flat goods; of leather; Luggage & handbags; Valued over $20 EACH						
	706.0900	400	200 NO	4620 C379 N	9%	415	80
	MPF				.17%	7	85
	Inv. Val. USD	5555.					
	Less N/D/C	934.65					
		4620.35					
	N.E.V. USD	4620.					
	Block 39 Summary						
	Merchandise Processing Fee		499	7.85			
	Harbor Maintenance Fee		501	1.85			

36. Declaration of Importer of Record (Owner or Purchaser) or Authorized Agent

I declare that I am the
[ ] importer of record and that the actual owner, purchaser, or consignee for customs purposes is as shown above. OR [X] owner or purchaser or agent thereof.
I further declare that the merchandise
[ ] was obtained pursuant to a purchase or agreement to purchase and that the prices set forth in the invoice are true. OR [X] was not obtained pursuant to a purchase or agreement to purchase and the statements in the invoice as to value or price are true to the best of my knowledge and belief.

I also declare that the statements in the documents herein filed fully disclose to the best of my knowledge and belief the true prices, values, quantities, rebates, drawbacks, fees, commissions, and royalties and are true and correct, and that all goods or services provided to the seller of the merchandise either free or at reduced cost are fully disclosed. I will immediately furnish to the appropriate customs officer any information showing a different state of facts.

Notice required by Paperwork Reduction Act of 1980. This information is needed to ensure that importers/exporters are complying with U.S. Customs laws, to allow us to compute and collect the right amount of money, to enforce other agency requirements, and to collect accurate statistical information on imports. Your response is mandatory.

U.S. CUSTOMS USE		TOTALS	
A. Liq. Code	B. Ascertained Duty	37. Duty 415	80
	C. Ascertained Tax	38. Tax	
	D. Ascertained Other	39. Other 9	70
	E. Ascertained Total	40. Total 425	50

41. Signature of Declarant, Title, and Date
A. W. Attorney in fact 011988

Customs Form 7501 (030984)

RECORD

Figure 14.2 Entry Summary 7501 (shows the form properly prepared for leather handbags described in Figure 14.1)

sumer items, a 50 to 75 percent markup is reasonable. A 15 to 25 percent markup is sufficient on industrial items, but be leery when the markup is too low. Each item should be judged on its individual merit. Markups differ depending on the item, and one should not (and indeed cannot afford to) generalize.

In large corporations, a traffic manager or clerk would be responsible for handling these calculations. You, the individual, can receive all the specialized help you need from your banker and your customs broker. U.S. Customs is also helpful, and import regulations are spelled out in detail in a book entitled *Custom House Guide*, published by North American Publishing Company, Philadelphia, PA.

Before you complete a transaction for fashion goods, sophisticated equipment, or anything requiring exacting specifications (close tolerance, special materials, etc.), stipulate in your letter of credit, purchase order, and/or draft instructions that a certificate of inspection is required for the overseas exporter to be paid. This will provide a safeguard to insure that you receive what you are paying for.

It is extremely important for the beginner *not* to buy anything without a domestic purchase order in hand. That is, never order an item from overseas that you have not already sold to a domestic source. Adhering to this rule will save you both money and headaches. Once you have built up sufficient sales, warehousing becomes practical—but not until that point. How do you build up sufficient sales? By means of a good distributor network.

DISTRIBUTION

As an exporter, you had only to ship the goods; the foreign importer handled the end distribution. Importing presents an aspect that never troubles the exporter— you, as an importer, must sell or somehow distribute products to the end users. There are several ways of distributing or selling products; not all of them work for the beginner.

Retail stores.   Selling to retail stores is one of the most financially rewarding methods of distribution. However, to be successful, one must understand the merchants' viewpoint in buying.

Small stores.   For most small stores, the same individual is both owner and buyer. When you make a presentation, you must be ready to give maximum service (delivery, labeling, etc.). Have an attractive product and, *most importantly,* an excellent sales presentation. This final point requires several important steps. First, dress in a neat, professional-looking manner. Next, arrange the appointment to suit the buyer's needs (day and time). Have a display case to show off your products. (These can be bought through sales magazines and merchandise marts located around the United States.) Finally, prepare a price list and catalog. Make them as professional as you an afford. Include the following information on your price sheet: minimum order, discounts if any (2-10 net 30), and delivery charges, if applicable. If you are not going to make up a separate catalog sheet, then include a picture, dimensions, and weight on your price list. With the use of computer-assisted layout systems available at copy shops, you can do a good job at reasonable prices.

Starting with small, independent stores allows you to make errors on a minor scale that would be disastrous in a department store (delivery problems, etc.).

Mass merchandising. Selling to large stores requires the same preparation as a small store does. First, you must locate the buyer, either by calling the central purchasing department or through books like *Stores of the World*, which list buyers' names and telephone numbers. Buyers are very busy people. Always make an appointment; never drop in. Some stores do have an open-house day when they will see anyone, but it is on a first-come basis and is usually very crowded.

Make sure you know your product, quality, materials, and so forth. Nothing makes you seem unprofessional faster than not knowing the merchandise.

Some department stores may require cooperative advertising money. That is, they will buy your goods only if you are willing to share the advertising costs; Others may charge you for shelf space. Avoid these type of situations initially.

If you have sold other stores successfully, mention this to the buyer. The buyers may need others to co-sign their orders and like to refer their bosses to other people with whom you have done business.

Direct Mail

This is the industry term for the type of advertising most consumers refer to as *junk mail*. Despite its unpopularity, it is an effective sales technique when properly done, particularly for single products or product categories.

Mail Order

This sales approach is different from direct mail because the sellers, large organizations, generally stock many different types of items, not just items from a single product category, and illustrate them in catalogs. Familiar examples are Sears, Fingerhut, and Speigel. These operations have many of their own overseas buying offices and contacts for importing. If you have a unique consumer idea, it is definitely worth trying to contact one of these large mail-order concerns or possibly starting your own catalog.

Distributor Network

One avenue available to the beginning importer is a broad network of wholesalers, manufacturer's representatives, jobbers (also sometimes known as dealers or distributors). By contacting members of these trades, you can become part of the distribution network which looks like this:

1. Consumer products → manufacturer → wholesaler → retailer → public
2. Industrial products → manufacturer → manufacturer's representative → distributor → end user

When you're selling through wholesalers, manufacturer's representatives, dealers, and so on, check your price spread carefully. For example:

Your Landed Cost is	$18..50
Wholesaler pays	25.00
Retailer pays	50.00
Customer pays	$100–$300

It is conceivable to have an 800 percent markup from your cost to the final price. Make sure that you not only understand the price spread of your product, but the normal markups taken along the distribution network. This will guide you in deciding where to enter the network. If a similar product retails for $50 (not $100 to $300), as in the above example, you might consider selling directly to the store and eliminating the wholesaler or manufacturer's representative's markup and/or commission.

You can find the names of manufacturer's representatives, wholesalers, and mass merchandisers dealing in your product category in the following directories:

Manufacturers Agents Annual Directory. The Agent and Representative, 626 North Garfield Avenue, Alhambra, CA 91802.

Directory of Manufacturers Agents. (Useful for contacting industrial distributors.) McGraw-Hill Book Co., 1221 Avenue of the Americas, New York, NY 10022.

Verified Directory of Manufacturers Representatives, 8th ed. Manufacturers Agent Publishing Co., 663 Fifth Avenue, New York, NY 10022.

Major Mass Market Merchandisers. The Salesman's Guide, Inc., 1182 Broadway, New York, NY 10001.

Sheldons Jobbing Trade Annual. 92nd ed. Pheton-Sheldon Publications, Inc., 32 Union Square, New York, NY 10003.

Directory of Industrial Distributors (1971–1972). Industrial Distribution, McGraw-Hill Book Co., 122a Avenue of the Americas, New York, NY 10020.

Your local library should be able to provide copies of some or all of these publications. Write to those prospective distributors that deal in your product category. In your letters, state what you are offering (include a picture if possible), price, delivery, discounts, how the product is packaged and shipped, and how long the offer is in effect. This is the basic technique in marketing your imported goods.

Chapter Fifteen

Financing Imports

The beginning importer is in a better position than the beginner in many other business fields. You can start with small amounts of capital, simply by acting as a commission merchant and not ordering anything that does not already have an eager buyer at home. After operating in this fashion for a time, during which you develop a better sense of what you can sell and how you can sell it, you may begin using commissions to finance your own import ventures. If you are successful on this limited scale and have also built a functional distribution network that you know works for your product line, you may eventually wish to finance larger overseas purchases than what your bank account permits. When you reach this point, you must consider how best to approach your banker to finance your imports.

When you first visit your banker, be prepared to give an accurate personal financial statement. (Figure 15.1 is a sample.) Have a definite projection neatly typed—something like the Landed Cost survey in Chapter Fourteen—and include a cost and profit analysis. The more information you can give on your prospective customers, the better. You must prove to the banker that you have done your homework and that you know what you are doing.

TRANSFERRABLE LETTER OF CREDIT

This method is sometimes used when the importer has limited financial resources. After selling your product, ask the company to open a transfer L/C. In this way, the

135

PERSONAL FINANCIAL STATEMENT

As of _____ 19____

Received at _____ Branch

Name _____

Employed by _____ Years _____

Address _____

Position _____ Age _____ Name of Spouse _____

If Employed Less Than
1 Year, Previous Employer

The undersigned, for the purpose of procuring and establishing credit from time to time with you and to induce you to permit the undersigned to become indebted to you on notes, endorsements, guarantees, overdrafts or otherwise, furnishes the following (or in lieu thereof the attached) which is the most recent statement prepared by or for the undersigned as being a full, true and correct statement of the financial condition of the undersigned on the date indicated, and agrees to notify you immediately of the extent and character of any material change in said financial condition, and also agrees that if the undersigned, or any endorser or guarantor of any of the obligations of the undersigned, at any time fails in business or becomes insolvent, or commits an act of bankruptcy, or dies, or if a writ of attachment, garnishment, execution or other legal process be issued against property of the undersigned or if any assessment for taxes against the undersigned, other than taxes on real property, is made by the federal or state government or any department thereof, or if any of the representations made below prove to be untrue, or if the undersigned fails to notify you of any material change as above agreed, or if such change occurs, or if the business, or any interest therein, of the undersigned is sold, then and in such case, all of the obligations of the undersigned to you or held by you shall immediately be due and payable, without demand or notice. This statement shall be construed by you to be a continuing statement of the condition of the undersigned, and a new and original statement of all assets and liabilities upon each and every transaction in and by which the undersigned hereafter becomes indebted to you, until the undersigned advises in writing to the contrary.

ASSETS	DOLLARS	cents
Cash in B of _____ (Branch)		
Cash in _____ (Other—give name)		
Accounts Receivable-Good		
Stocks and Bonds (Schedule B)		
Notes Receivable-Good		
Cash Surrender Value Life Insurance		

LIABILITIES	DOLLARS	cents
Notes payable B of _____ (Branch)		
Notes payable _____ (Other)		
Accounts payable		
Taxes payable		
Contracts payable _____ (To whom)		
Contracts payable _____ (To whom)		

136

Autos _____ (Year-Make) _____ (Year-Make) _____

Real Estate (Schedule A) _____

Other Assets (describe)

1. _____
2. _____
3. _____
4. _____
5. _____

TOTAL ASSETS

Real Estate indebtedness (Schedule A) _____

Other Liabilities (describe)

1. _____
2. _____
3. _____
4. _____

TOTAL LIABILITIES

NET WORTH

TOTAL

ANNUAL INCOME   and ANNUAL EXPENDITURES (Excluding Ordinary Living Expenses)

Salary _____

Salary (wife or husband) _____

Securities Income _____

Rentals _____

Other (describe)

1. _____
2. _____
3. _____
4. _____
5. _____

TOTAL INCOME

Real Estate payment (s) _____

Rent _____

Income Taxes _____

Insurance Premiums _____

Property Taxes _____

Other (describe-include instalment payments

other than real estate)

1. _____
2. _____
3. _____

TOTAL EXPENDITURES

LESS-TOTAL EXPENDITURES

NET CASH INCOME
(exclusive of ordinary living expenses) _____

Figure 15.1 Personal financial statement

137

importer (middleman) use these credits to pay his or her supplier as long as the terms of the original L/C are met. Usually used with a finished product, this transferability of credits can be done only once to one or more third parties.

BACK-TO-BACK LETTER OF CREDIT

Another letter of credit useful to the novice is the back-to-back type. In this situation, the end user opens a L/C in favor of the importer; the importer than asks his or her bank for a companion (almost identical) L/C to be issued to the supplier. Therefore, the original L/C acts as the financial basis for the second L/C. Many banks do not look favorably upon this type of financing if other options are available.

There are many publications available to help you prepare your financial statement, and a visit to your accountant may be the best solution. If you are considering borrowing money to expand your business, your accountant can offer suggestions that will far exceed his or her fee in savings to you.

Remember that bankers are not mysterious. They are business people just like you are, except that they are in the business of lending money for the purpose of financing attractive proposals. The suggestions they make can save considerable expense and time. If they refuse your request, you should consider objectively the reasons for the refusal and ask yourself if the venture you are proposing is indeed as attractive as you believe it to be.

If possible, go to a bank where you have established previous good credit and where the bankers know you. If you have been working with exports through the bank and have therefore previously checked it out in terms of the service the banking officers give you, you are more likely to receive better attention and more help than if you choose a bank with which you have never dealt.

FOREIGN BANKS IN THE UNITED STATES

Many foreign banks offer extended financing for overseas buyers. These purchasing programs are usually underwritten by the exporting country.

One such program is the BANCOMEXT (BNCE). This program allows Mexican banks to offer financing from 90 days to 5 years at preferred interest rates. The financing amount depends on the Mexican content of the goods imported. (Over 50 percent: 100 percent of invoices up to one year and 85 percent after a year; between 30 to 50 percent: a case-by-case determination. Terms and conditions: nonmanufactured, 90 days; raw materials, parts, and accessories, 180 days; durable goods, up to 2 years, etc.)

To take advantage of this type of program, you would contact the U.S. branch of a Mexican bank (e.g., Banco National De Mexico, Bancomer, SNC, Banca Serfin, SNC) and make out an application.

Many other countries offer similar programs to help their exporters sell overseas. Check and compare finance programs, as well as products, before making your initial purchases.

Chapter Sixteen

Transporting Imports

When you export products, you are usually responsible for packing and shipping them properly and for meeting any particular requirements set by your overseas buyer. For assistance, you often rely on your freight forwarder or transportation company for packing and shipping.

When you import goods, you usually rely on the overseas exporter to provide you with the same service—he or she quotes you a c.i.f. price and is responsible for moving the merchandise to a U.S. port of entry. It is from that point that you, or someone acting for you, takes possession of the goods and moves them to their final destination. Since the overseas exporter has apprised you of the carrier, the date of shipment, and the expected date of arrival, you can arrange for the transportation services you need.

In some instances, however, you may have to make shipping arrangements yourself for goods from overseas, in which case you must rely more heavily on the services of a freight forwarder. Very often, your overseas supplier sends you only f.o.b. prices (though you, as an exporter, would always strive to quote c.i.f. prices and arrange for shipping to your overseas buyer). If this occurs, you must notify the exporter which freight forwarder you will be using; the freight forwarder will provide you with costs, handle the overseas shipment, and deliver the shipment wherever you wish.

METHODS OF TRANSPORTATION

One often sees pictures of ships marked Exxon or Texaco and trucks marked with the name of some particular store. As a beginner, of course, you cannot afford to own the transportation. You will rent space on ships, planes, trucks, and trains, and you will use the parcel post system. The type of transportation you require will be determined by the quantity, cost, and size of each shipment, the distance it must travel, and the nature of the goods. For example, importers of perishables must make certain they obtain overseas transportation and rapid dispatch at the pier on arrival in order to prevent spoilage. Obviously, close attention must be paid to routing and scheduling dates. Importers of seasonal merchandise must likewise make sure that schedules are met. As anyone who has worked in a department or specialty store knows, sales promotions generally run on time. Late goods are usually returned to the vendors because most sales contracts have a clause specifying arrival dates.

Your location also has a direct bearing on transportation. The closer you are to the docking site or airport, the easier it is to supervise the movement of the goods. The further you are from a metropolitan port, the more dependent you are on the freight forwarder or customs broker. Generally, an importer enters into a contract with a broker so that, regardless of where the goods land, the broker can handle the entry documentation and delivery of goods to the ultimate buyer.

Ocean freight. The majority of goods from foreign countries, excluding Canada and Mexico, come by ocean freight. It is the most economical way to ship large quantities. Steamship companies charge by weight or measurement, depending on which produces the greatest revenue. Therefore, articles such as fishing weights would probably be charged by weight, whereas modular housing would be charged by size (cubic feet).

Air freight. Air freight is becoming more popular as rates are reduced. Speed of delivery is a major attraction, but it is also often easier to ship fragile, expensive items by air, since less packaging is required for security during air shipment and since most such items are lightweight (e.g., watches and art work).

Air freight rates are based on the commodity shipped and the distance traveled. Within these constraints, weight and volume, as with ocean freight, will determine the final cost. Rates are normally set on a sliding scale. As the weight goes up from the minimum, the price per pound goes down.

As with passenger transportation, air carriers are trying to increase the use of their cargo services. To this end, freight forwarders are allowed to pool the shipments of smaller shippers, thus taking advantage of the lower rates applied to large quantities. The freight forwarders, acting in this instance as consolidators, book several shipments to one destination, then book the cargo on an air carrier to obtain the best rates. They then pass on the savings to the shippers.

Quotations from air carriers are from airport to airport. You should compare air quotations with ocean freight plus truck or rail quotations, considering also delivery schedules and the nature of the goods, before you make a final decision.

Parcel post. Samples and other small, inexpensive packages are best dispatched by parcel post. Air parcel post is best, since it speeds delivery by two or three weeks.

Truck and rail. From Canada or Mexico, for all but small shipments, truck and rail are better than air. Occasionally, due to customs formalities, air might be faster from Mexico.

A call to a truck carrier will give you the latest rates. Trains require carload lots, so it might be advisable to check with a local inland freight forwarder for better rail rates.

INSURANCE

All shipments should be insured either by yourself or by the shipper. If you have obtained c.i.f. pricing from your supplier, you will not have to worry about insurance, since it is included in the price you pay for the merchandise. However, be aware that there are some insurance coverages taken out by foreign sellers that United States importers do not find satisfactory. Therefore, before you accept a deal with a c.i.f. price, check to see that the coverage meets your needs.

If you make infrequent purchases from a particular source, the price you pay may not include insurance. In such cases, or if the offered coverage is unacceptable, you should obtain an open marine policy from a local company or through your customs broker. (Since 90 percent of import shipments come by sea, such policies are generally termed "marine," although they usually cover other means of transportation as well.)

Generally, it is easier to process a claim through a U.S. insurance company rather than a foreign company. Also, it is preferable to have one company underwrite all risks for collection purposes. Most marine insurance companies, however, will not grant an open policy until your volume and experience are established. Therefore, you will have to arrange coverage through your broker or rely on the foreign shipper.

Regardless of how you acquire marine insurance, you must have protection against "General Average Agreement," which, simply stated, means that if the ship on which your freight is being carried sustains damage, or if any other cargo is damaged due to collision, fire, and so on, the ship owner has the option of collecting a share of the damage from each firm that has cargo on board. This claim becomes a lien on your cargo, and any such lien must be satisfied before you can obtain your cargo.

Finally, you should also acquire an open inland marine policy, which covers shipments of goods after discharge at seaport, international airport, or rail terminal to their ultimate destination inside the United States.

Chapter Seventeen

Shipping Documentation

Just as the U.S. government controls to which foreign countries exports are freely sent, it also controls from which countries imports are freely received. It also levies an import tax, called a *duty*, and it collects data for trade statistics. These ends are accomplished by means of a *commercial invoice*, and several other documents that tell U.S. Customs what a shipment contains, where the products were manufactured, and how much they are worth.

DOCUMENT PREPARATION AND HANDLING

Before a shipment can move through Customs, the importer *must* have the correct documentation. Many of these documents should be familiar to the reader who has reviewed Chapter Eleven, which deals with export documentation. Other documents are three copies of the original *bill of lading* or air bill and, if requested, an *insurance certificate* and a *certificate of origin*. If importing from GSP countries (see Chapter Twenty), then a certificate of country of origin, UN Form A, is required. (Note: Where products from certain countries are admitted duty free, check with U.S. Customs for details; Appendix 3 has region and district offices.) For textiles you need the country A declaration and quota declaration from the shipper.

Normally, arrangements for all documentation are handled through the banks. The letter of credit and purchase order will state what documents are necessary, as well as the amount of money required for the transaction. These documents can be sent to the importer or the importer's broker; they are never sent directly to Customs.

Each shipment should have only one consignee (that is, it should be addressed just to you). U.S. Customs requires invoices in English or an English translation attached to the document. (See Chapter Eleven, Figure 11.9 for a sample invoice.) There is no particular required form for the commercial invoice, as long as it meets standard commercial practices and the government requirements listed below:

1. Description of merchandise.
    a. The name by which each item of merchandise is known to the trade in the country of production or exportation
    b. The grade or quality of each item of merchandise
    c. The marks, numbers, or symbols under which each item of merchandise is sold by the seller or manufacturer to the trade in the country of exportation
    d. The marks and numbers of the package in which merchandise is packed
2. The quantities in weights and measures of the country of origin or that of the United States.
3. The purchase price of the merchandise in the currency of purchase or, in the case of nonpurchased material, the price that the seller would have received or was willing to receive in the currency in which the transactions are usually made.
4. The currency used, in the case of purchased merchandise.
5. All charges upon the merchandise, itemized by name and amount when known to the seller or shipper, or all charges by name included in invoice prices when amounts for such charges are unknown to the seller or shipper.
6. All rebates, drawbacks, and bounties, separately itemized, allowed upon the exportation of the merchandise. Any rebate or grant given the manufacturer must also be itemized on the invoice by name and amount.
7. Any costs for items such as dies, molds, patterns, engineering work, financial assistance, and so on, that assist in production but are not included in invoice price. If "assists" were involved, also state by whom they were supplied, if they were supplied without cost, if they were rented, or if they were invoiced separately; attach a copy of the invoice.
8. If merchandise is imported from a country that has a currency for which two or more rates of exchange have been certified by the Federal Reserve Bank of New York, the exact exchange rate or rates used in converting the U.S. dollars received for such merchandise into foreign currency should be shown on the invoice.
9. In the case of certain special classes of items, additional information must be shown on the commercial invoice. The classes are diverse, including such items as beads (invoice must tell length of string, size of beads in mil-

limeters, and material of which beads are composed), fish livers (invoice must tell if livers contain extra oil, and if so, what kind), and boiled wool (invoice must certify that a certain boiling process was followed in the country of origin). The importer should check with the U.S. Customs Office for details and exact requirements.

PRO FORMA INVOICES

When a commercial invoice is required but is not available at the time a foreign shipment arrives at U.S. Customs, the *importer* (*not* the foreign exporter) may prepare a *pro forma* invoice. This "invoice" contains generally the same information required on the proper commercial invoice, which is prepared by the exporter.

In addition to the pro forma invoice, the importer must also give a bond which guarantees that he or she will file the required invoice with the district or port director of Customs within six months from the date of entry of this shipment. If the invoice does not arrive in that time, the importer will incur a liability under the bond.

The pro forma invoice is a device that speeds the movement of goods through Customs. It may be made out in substantially the form shown in Figure 7.3 in Chapter Seven.

INSTALLMENT SHIPMENTS

Installments of a shipment covered by a single order or contract and shipped from one consignor to one consignee may be included in one invoice if the installments arrive at the port of entry by any means of transportation within a period of not to exceed ten consecutive days. Otherwise, shipments must be invoiced separately.

An invoice to cover an installment shipment should be prepared in the same manner as an invoice for a single shipment, and obviously it must fit the invoicing requirements for the class of goods involved. If it is practical to do so the invoice should show the quantities, values, and other invoice data with respect to each installment, and it should identify the carrier on which each installment was shipped.

INVOICING ERRORS

It is necessary for you, the U.S. importer, to be familiar with invoicing requirements so that you can assist the foreign exporters with whom you deal to fill out invoices properly. If your exporters make an error, *you* will pay the penalty that Customs imposes, and *you* will pay storage charges for the goods while Customs awaits the proper documents.

Prevention of invoicing errors can best be accomplished by a clear understanding of the terms of sale (i.e., description of goods, quantity, price, currency, rebates, etc.) between buyer and seller. Most countries have commercial invoice requirements similar to those described earlier in this chapter and experienced foreign exporters should have no difficulty in providing the necessary material. Still, errors are made. The common errors made by foreign shippers are the following:

1. The shipper assumes that a commission, royalty, or other charge against the goods is a so-called "nondutiable" item and omits it from the invoice.
2. A foreign shipper who purchases goods and sells them to a U.S. importer at a delivered price shows on the invoice the cost of goods to him or her instead of the delivered price (which includes freight and insurance).
3. A foreign shipper manufactures goods partly with the use of material supplied by the U.S. importer, but invoices the goods at the actual cost to the manufacturer without including the value of the materials supplied by the importer.
4. The foreign manufacturer ships replacement goods to the customer in the United States and invoices the goods at the net price without showing the full price less the allowance for defective goods previously shipped and returned.
5. A foreign shipper who sells goods at list price, less a discount, invoices them at the net price, and fails to show the discount.
6. A foreign shipper sells goods at a delivered price but invoices them at a price f.o.b. the place of shipment and omits the subsequent charges.
7. Currently customs uses transaction value, the price paid or payable as the preferred basis of appraisement.
8. A foreign shipper indicates in the invoice that the importer is the purchaser, whereas he or she is in fact either an agent who is receiving a commission for selling the goods or a party who will receive part of the proceeds of the sale of the goods sold for the joint account of the shipper and consignee.

FURTHER INFORMATION

This chapter does not pretend to answer all questions about invoices and other documentation. Chapter Eighteen continues the discussion, but the importer in need of assistance should contact a U.S. consular office, a Treasury representative, or a district director of Customs.

Chapter Eighteen

The Entry Process

The U.S. government regulates imports through the use of documents, physical inspection of shipments, and appraisal of goods. When a shipment arrives at a seaport or airport, the carrier sends a notice to the importer or customs broker. Usually five days are allowed for an entry to be made—that is, for you or your broker to present the required documents and to pay the duty and other customs fees. If entry is not made within five days, the goods are moved to a warehouse under Customs custody, and you are charged storage. If you have not removed your goods within one year, the government can auction the materials to pay for storage. Usually, this sale does not occur because the exporter notifies you of when and on what ship or flight the goods are being sent so the shipment can be met without delay. The exporter (through the banks) sends you all the documents necessary for you to secure the goods at the pier.

From a commercial standpoint, all goods arriving at U.S. ports require a formal entry, with the exception of those valued at a less than U.S. $1,250.

There are four steps in the processing of import shipments:

1. Entry, or filing of documents
2. Inspection and control
3. Classification and valuation, or setting the duty rate
4. Liquidation, or final determination of the duty

Functions 2, 3, and 4 are performed by U.S. Customs. By law this process must be completed within one year (can be extended to four years).

ENTRY

Before an entry can be made, the importer or broker must be in possession of certain documents. The most common required documents are:

1. Commercial invoice, which the exporter fills out
2. Bill of Lading, which the exporter or forwarder fills out
3. Entry forms, which the importer or broker fills out

On the entry form, you estimate the duty you will have to pay. You can then pay Customs immediately, and you may post a bond that guarantees against your possible failure to pay duties, taxes, or penalties at a later date. Two types of bonds are employed: (1) Single Transaction Bond (STB), which applies to entry through only one port; and (2) Continuous Bond, which covers all U.S. ports. Surety may also be posted in the form of cash. For most situations, your customs broker can arrange for a surety bond.

Because most transactions are financed through letters of credit, you must pay your bank to receive the documents you will need to clear Customs.

Caution: Bear in mind that the importer who files the preceding documents with Customs vouches for the truth of the documents, as well as the accuracy of the entry and other documents that are filed with the entries. The presentation of any false documents, information, or statement (by whomever prepared) can subject the importer to severe penalties, whether or not the United States has been deprived of any revenue. These penalties are, by statute, equivalent to the domestic value of the imported merchandise, including all expenses of transportation and insurance and the duties applicable to the merchandise (only in cases of fraud).

The importer is also subject to similar penalties for failure to disclose all the details of the transaction pursuant to which the merchandise was exported to the United States. This includes any financial aid or other assistance provided to the manufacturer or exporter, and full information as to the status of any agent involved in the transaction, including the amount of commission or other reimbursement paid to such agent.

It is apparent that importing merchandise into the United States, especially from the Far East, can be complicated by language problems and by special characteristics of business in foreign countries. Importers are encouraged to consult with their Customs broker and, if necessary, Import Specialist Team member on classification matters.

INSPECTION AND CONTROL

After the proper documents are filed, Customs inspectors may take a sample of the goods to the Customs plant or send a sample to the Import Specialist Teams. Its classification is then ascertained.

LIABILITY FOR DUTIES

Duties, taxes, and other customs fees on imports cannot be prepaid in a foreign country before exportation to the United States. In the usual case, liability for the payment of duty becomes fixed at the time an entry is filed with the district director of Customs. The person or firm in whose name the entry is filed is the one who must pay. If the entry is made by a Customs broker in his or her own name, the broker is exempt from paying any increased or additional duties found due on the goods, as long as he or she (1) names the actual owner of the goods in the entry, (2) obtains an owner's declaration in which the owner agrees to pay any increased or additional duties, and (3) files the owner's declaration with the district director of Customs within ninety days of the date of entry, together with the owner's bond.

When Customs enters unclaimed goods for warehousing, the liability for the payment of duties may be transferred to any person who purchases the goods and desires to withdraw them in his or her own name.

LIQUIDATION

Liquidation is the final determination of the exact amount of duty owed on the shipment. You will be notified if Customs officials disagree with your estimate of value and duty that you stated on your entry form. Remember that you estimated value and duty on your entry form; Customs officials also make an initial judgment when they first obtain samples of the shipment. If the importer and Customs disagree, a protest can be filed within ninety days after the liquidation date with the Import Specialist who has up to two years to make a decision. Protests can be made with the National Import Specialist, 6 World Trade Ctr., NY 10048 or you can hire an attorney for the Court of International Trade. Most of the time, importers and Customs agree, and goods enter the United States within a week.

TYPES OF ENTRY

There are twenty-two different kinds of Customs entries. The following are the most prevalent:

1. *Consumption Entry* is the most common type. It is used when goods are intended for resale within the country or are brought directly into the importer's stock.

2. *Immediate Transportation Entry* is used when the importer desires to have his or her merchandise forwarded from the port of entry to an interior destination of Customs clearance. Usually the customs broker will arrange shipment under bond without appraisement.

3. *Warehouse Entry* allows you to store certain commodities in a Customs-bonded warehouse for five years (no perishables or explosives).

4. *Warehouse Withdrawal for Consumption Entry* makes it possible to pay duty only on portions of a shipment at a time. The importer leaves the shipment in a Customs-bonded warehouse; the Customs broker withdraws a portion of the goods as it is needed and pays duty only on that portion.

5. *Immediate Exportation Entry* allows goods to be routed via a U.S. port to a foreign country. The steamer pier may serve as a bonded warehouse when the transship period is short.

6. *Baggage Declaration and Entry* is filed when a U.S. citizen returns from a trip abroad.

Following acceptance of the entry and payment of duties, the shipment is examined (only 10 percent of all goods are inspected) to make certain it contains what you state it to contain, and then it is released, providing no legal or regulatory violations have occurred.

If you are planning to receive a large shipment, you will find the services of a Customs broker extremely valuable. Small shipments coming through the mails usually do not require such services. The following two sections discuss the handling of both small and large shipments.

MAIL AND PARCEL POST: DO IT YOURSELF

Small shipments are best consigned to you by parcel post. Customs will simply clear the shipment and have the mail carrier collect any duty owed. The mails are most useful for small, inexpensive objects because you save on shipping charges and there is no need to clear parcels valued at under $1,250 personally. The only requirement, made jointly by Customs and the Postal Service, is that all parcel post packages have a Customs declaration securely attached, giving both an accurate description and the value of the contents. Commercial shipments must also be accompanied by a commercial invoice enclosed in (or securely attached to) the parcel bearing the declaration, and the package must be marked on the address side, "Invoice Enclosed." If the shipment contains more than one package, each package should be numbered and marked "Invoice in Package #____." Shipments that do not comply with these requirements will be delayed through Customs. All shipments of commercial textiles require a formal bonded consumption entry.

Packages other than parcel post (such as letter-class mail), printed matter, commercial papers, and samples must be marked, on the address side, "May be opened for customs purposes before delivery."

If the value of the mail importation exceeds $1,250, the addressee is notified to prepare and file documentation for a formal Customs entry at the nearest Customs port.

A nominal charge, currently $5, is collected from the addressee on all dutiable or taxable mail. A merchandise processing fee of 0.17 percent will be collected on all formal entries (over $1,250).

OCEAN, AIR, AND TRUCK:
HIRE A CUSTOMS BROKER

Shipments on all three types of carrier require similar handling. All shipments should be consigned to you directly and marked to the attention of your Customs broker. Air and truck shipments should show on the airway bill or the freight bill that the shipment is to be sent to you "In Bond," consigned to your address.

As a beginning importer, you should depend heavily on your broker for handling paperwork. Familiarity with the documentation is necessary, but the primary purpose of the importer is to sell merchandise, not to process paperwork.

Goods may be entered by the consignee named in the bill of lading under which they are shipped (you), or the bill of lading may be endorsed over to a broker or carrier who can then enter the goods. In most instances, entry is made by a person or firm certified by the carrier bringing the goods to the port of entry to be the owner of the goods for Customs purposes. (The broker will have all the paperwork you collected when you paid the bank fo the goods: bill of lading, insurance certificate, and so on. He or she will present these to the carrier to collect the goods.)

If you live close to the point of Customs clearance and regularly import shipments valued at less than $1,250, you can probably clear the parcels yourself, without posting bond with Customs. If you live some distance away, however, or if you import more expensive merchandise, you will find it less expensive, less trouble, and less time-consuming to employ a Customs broker. These individuals know the Customs regulations and are familiar with the requirements of the local Customs office. They will post bond in your behalf, pay duty, clear the shipment, and forward the shipment to you. They will also invoice you for all charges plus a nominal fee, which rarely exceeds $100 per $1,000 or merchandise value (except for textiles).

As with any business dealing, always precheck your broker's charges, freight costs, insurance, and Customs duty. Confirming costs in advance will avoid the disaster of extra charges being billed to you after you have sold the goods. Appendix 5 contains a list of freight forwarders and Customs brokers. Always check with several of these firms and compare prices and services.

DUTIABLE STATUS

One of the basic determinations an importer must make when deciding whether to import an item is its duty status. All items are classified as either dutiable or free from duty.

There are three types of duty levied: specific, ad valorem, and compound. *Specific duties* are assessed as an amount per unit of item, such as 10 per pound or 5 per yard. *Ad valorem duties* are a fixed percentage, such as 10 percent of total value or 25 percent of total value. The *compound duty* is a combination of specific and ad valorem duties. For example, wool valued at under $4 per pound is dutiable at 23.5 percent, plus 25 per pound; wool worth over $4 per pound is dutiable at 23.5 percent, just like the cheaper wool, but the specific rate jumps to 37.5 per pound.

No comprehensive discussion of the rates of duty provided for in the Tariff Schedules of the United States could be attempted in a book of this limited scope. If you need information about the classification and rate of duty (or free status) of specified goods, you may write to the district director at the port of entry at which your goods will be entered.

When requesting information, you must supply the following information:

1. A complete description of the goods. Send samples, sketches, diagrams, or other illustrations if the goods cannot be described in writing.
2. The method of manufacture or fabrication.
3. Specifications and analyses.
4. Quantities and costs of the component materials—with percentages, if possible.
5. Whatever information you have as to the:
   a. Commercial designation of your goods in the United States.
   b. Principal use of your goods in the United States.

If you are positive that any of the foregoing will not be of use in determining the status of your goods, you may disregard it, but omitting necessary information will delay a decision. Send samples along with the description whenever you can.

The decision you receive can be relied upon for placing or accepting orders for goods to be imported to the United States. The decision will not be changed without prior public notice.

Statutory rates of duty, which are not listed here because they are constantly changing, apply to products of the following countries or areas, whether imported directly or indirectly:

Afghanistan	Kurile Islands
Bulgaria	Latvia
Cuba	Lithuania
Czechoslovakia	Outer Mongolia
Estonia	Southern Sakhalin
German Democratic Republic and East Berlin	Tanna Tuva
Communist Indochina	U.S.S.R.
Communist Korea	

Products of other countries are subject to reduced duty rates as set forth in the Tariff Schedules of the United States.

CURRENCY CONVERSION

The conversion of foreign currency for Customs purposes must be based on the New York market buying rate for the foreign currency involved, as determined and certified by the Federal Reserve Bank of New York. The rates for widely used currencies are certified each day. Other rates are certified only by request of Customs officers, for the dates needed.

The date of exportation of the goods determines the rate of exchange to be used in converting foreign currency for Customs purposes. The currencies of certain foreign countries listed in the Customs Regulations are converted at a value measured by the buying rate first certified by the Bank for a day in the quarter in which the day of exportation falls. These include most (but not all) the more widely used foreign currencies. Ordinarily, conversions involving the currency of other countries will be made at the buying rate certified by the Bank for the particular day on which exportation occurred, even though a different rate may have been used in payment of the goods.

TEMPORARY FREE IMPORTATION

You, the importer, should be aware that some goods, primarily samples and displays, may be admitted into the United States without the payment of duty, under bond for their exportation within one year from the date of importation. The categories are as follows:

1. Merchandise imported to be repaired, altered, or processed in the United States, as long as (a) the end product does not contain alcohol, perfume, or wheat; (2) a complete accounting of articles is made and any waste is given to Customs; and (c) the results of the processing are exported or destroyed within the bonded period.

2. Models of women's wearing apparel imported by manufacturers for use solely as models in their own establishment.

3. Samples solely for use in taking orders for merchandise; articles solely for examination with a view to reproduction (except printing plates); and motion picture advertising films.

4. Articles intended solely for testing, experimental, or review purposes (plans, specifications, drawings, photos, etc.). Such articles may be destroyed during the bonded period rather than exported.

5. Containers for covering or holding merchandise during transportation and suitable for reuse for that purpose.
6. Articles imported by illustrators and photographers for use solely as models in their own establishments, in the illustration of catalogs, pamphlets, or advertising matter.
7. Professional equipment, tools of trade, repair components for such equipment and tools, and articles of special design for temporary use in the manufacture or production of items for export.
8. Theatrical scenery, properties, and apparel for temporary use in theatrical exhibitions.

This law also allows for foreign residents to import articles such as cars, boats, works of art, films, and animals for their use while visiting the United States, participating in an exhibition, lecturing, promoting business, and the like.

If after a year the goods are not exported, the bond will be forfeited or the articles will be seized, unless they are destroyed under Customs supervision or unless satisfactory proof of destruction is furnished to the district director of Customs with whom the Customs entry was filed.

Specific information regarding articles that can be imported free should be obtained from a district director.

REFUNDS (DRAWBACK)

The exportation of imported goods after they have been released from Customs custody does not result in a refund of the duties paid on the goods. There are four exceptions:

1. When articles manufactured or produced in the United States with the use of imported merchandise are exported, a refund of 99 percent of the duties paid on the imported merchandise is refundable.
2. When the imported goods do not conform to the sample or specifications on the basis of which they were ordered, or were shipped without the consent of the consignee, the importer may secure a refund of 99 percent of the duties paid by returning the goods to Customs custody within 90 days (or longer if authorized) after they were released and exporting them under Customs supervision.
3. When goods are exported in the same condition as they were imported or destroyed within three years from the date of importation, you can get 99 percent of duty.
4. When imported goods found not to be entitled to admission into the commerce of the United States are exported under Customs supervision, a

refund of the entire amount of duties paid on the rejected goods is allowable.

A refund of the entire amount of duties is allowable in the following circumstances:

1. Imported goods are exported from a bonded Customs warehouse or from continuous Customs custody elsewhere than in a bonded warehouse within the warehousing period.
2. Imported goods are withdrawn for supplies, maintenance, or repair for vessels and aircraft under certain conditions.
3. Imported goods, found not to be entitled to admission into the commerce of the United States are destroyed under Customs supervision.

A refund of the entire amount of duties may also be made when articles entered under bond under any provision of the Customs law are destroyed under Customs supervision during the period of the bond and when articles in a Customs bonded warehouse are voluntarily abandoned to the government by the consignee.

EXCESS GOODS AND SHORTAGES

Showing the contents of each package on the invoice, the orderly packing of the goods, the proper marking and numbering of the packages in which the goods are packed, and the placing of the corresponding marks and numbers on the invoice facilitate the allowance in duties for goods that do not arrive and the ascertainment of whether any excess goods are contained in the shipment.

If any package that has been designated for examination is found by the Customs officer to contain any article not specified in the invoice, and there is reason to believe that such article was omitted from the invoice with fraudulent intent on the part of the seller, shipper, owner, or agent, the contents of the entire package in which the excess goods are found are subject to seizure and possible forfeiture.

On the other hand, when no such fraudulent intent is apparent, penalties do not accrue, but the duties due, if any, on the excess goods will be collected.

When a deficiency in quantity, weight, or measure is found by the Customs officer in the examination of any package that has been designated for examination, an allowance in duty will be made for the deficiency.

Allowance in duty is made for deficiencies in packages not designated for examination, provided that before liquidation of the entry becomes final, the importer notices the district director of Customs of the shortage and establishes to the satisfaction of the director that the missing goods were not delivered.

DAMAGE OR DETERIORATION

Goods that are found by the Customs officer to have been entirely without commercial value because of damage or deterioration at the time of arrival in the United States are treated as a "nonimportation." No duties are assessed on such goods. When damage or deterioration is present with respect to part of the shipment only, allowance in duties is not made unless the importer segregates the damaged or deteriorated part from the remainder of the shipment under customs supervision.

When the shipment consists of fruits, vegetables, or other perishable merchandise, allowance in duties cannot be made unless the importer files an application for allowance with the district director of Customs. This must be done within ninety-six hours after the unloading of the merchandise, and before it has been removed from Customs custody.

On shipments consisting of any article partly or wholly manufactured of iron or steel, or any manufacture of iron or steel, allowance or reduction of duty for partial damage or loss in consequence of discoloration or rust is precluded by law.

TARE

In ascertaining the quantity of goods dutiable on net weight, a deduction is made from the gross weight for tare packaging). The following schedule tares are provided for in the Customs Regulations:

- Apple boxes—8 pounds per box (includes paper wrappers, if any, on the apples)
- China clay in so-called half-ton casks—72 pounds per cask
- Figs in skeleton case—Actual tare for outer containers plus 13 percent of the gross weight of the inside wooden boxes and figs
- Fresh tomatoes—4 ounces per 100 paper wrappings
- Lemons and oranges—10 ounces per box and 5 ounces per half box for paper wrappings, and actual tare for outer containers
- Ocher, dry, in casks—8 percent of the gross weight; in oil in casks—12 percent of the gross weight
- Pimientos in tins imported from Spain—
    30 pounds for case of 6 tins, 3 kilos each
    36.72 pounds, case of 24 tins, 28 ounces each
    17.72 pounds, case of 24 tins, 15 ounces each
    8.62 pounds, case of 24 tins, 7 ounces each
    5.33 pounds, case of 24 tins, 4 ounces each
- Sugar—2.5 pounds per bag for standard bags

- Tobacco, leaf not stemmed—13 pounds per bale

For other goods dutiable on the net weight, an actual tare will be determined. An accurate tare stated on the invoice is acceptable for Customs purposes in certain circumstances.

If the consignee files a timely application with the district director of Customs, an allowance may be made in any case for excessive moisture and impurities not usually found in or upon the particular kind of goods.

Chapter Nineteen

Marking

U.S. Customs laws require that each imported article produced abroad be legibly marked in a conspicuous place, with the name of the country of origin (the country in which the article was grown, manufactured, or produced) in English so the ultimate U.S. purchaser can see it. For example, a toy might be marked "Made in Venezuela."

Most established foreign export companies are familiar with U.S. marking requirements. However, if you are dealing with a unique item (e.g., a new invention), you may save yourself much difficulty if you communicate marking information to your overseas source.

WHEN MARKING IS NOT REQUIRED

The following articles and classes or kinds of articles do not require marking. However, the outermost containers in which such articles ordinarily reach the ultimate purchaser in the United States must be marked.

Art, works of

Articles classification items 850.40, 850.70, 851.30 and 853.30, TSUS

Bagging, waste

Bags, jute

158

Bands, steel

Beads, unstrung

Bearings, ball

Blanks, metal, to be plated

Bolts, nuts, and washers

Briarwood in blocks

Briquettes, coal or coke

Buckles

Burlap

Buttons

Cards, playing

Cellophane and celluloid

Chemicals, drugs, etc., in capsules, pills, etc.

Cigars and cigarettes

Covers, straw bottle

Dies, diamond wire, unmounted

Dowels, wooden

Effects, theatrical

Eggs

Feathers

Firewood

Flowing

Flowers, artificial, except bunches

Glass, cut for clocks, hand mirrors, etc.

Glides, furniture

Hairnets

Hides, raw

Hooks, fish

Hoops (wood), barrel

Laths

Leather, except finished

Lumber, sawed

Metal bars

Mica

Monuments

Nails, spikes, and staples

Natural products, such as vegetables and animals

Nets, bottle wire

Paper, newsprint, stencil, stock

Parchment and vellum

Parts for machines imported from same country as parts

Pickets, wooden

Pins, tuning

Pipes, iron or steel, and fittings

Plants, shrubs, and other nursery stock

Plugs, tie

Poles, bamboo

Poles, electric-light, telephone, etc.

Posts (wood), fence

Pulpwood

Rags

Railway materials

Ribbon

Rivets

Rope

Scrap and waste

Screws

Shims, trace

Shingles (wood), except red cedar

Skins, fur, dressed or dyed

Skins, raw fur

Sponges

Springs, watch

Stamps, postage

Staves (wood), barrel

Steel, hoop

Sugar, maple

Ties (wood), railroad

Tiles, not over 1 inch in greatest dimension

Timbers, sawed

Tips, penholder

Trees, Christmas

Weights, in sets

Wicking, candle

Wire, except barbed

Unless an article you are importing is specifically named in the above list, it would be advisable for you to obtain information from a district director of Customs, regional commissioner of Customs, or port director of Customs before concluding that it is exempt from marking.

The following items are also exempt from marking:

- Items for use by the importer and not intended for sale (such as samples)
- Items to be processed in the United States
- Items obviously from a specific country

The following classes of articles are also exempted from marking to indicate the country of origin, although their containers must be marked:

- Articles that are incapable of being marked
- Articles that cannot be marked prior to shipment to the United States without injury
- Articles that cannot be marked prior to shipment to the United States except at an expense economically prohibitive of their importation
- Crude substances
- Articles produced more than twenty years prior to their importation

When the marking of the container of an article reasonably indicates the country of origin of the article, the article itself is exempt from such marking. This exemption applies only when the articles will reach the ultimate purchaser in an unopened container. For example, dried flower sachets that reach the retail purchaser in sealed containers marked clearly to indicate the country of origin come within this exemption. Materials to be used in building or manufacture by the builder or manufacturer who will receive the materials in unopened cases likewise come within this exemption.

The following articles and their containers are not subject to the requirements of marking to indicate the country of their origin or to the special marking requirements set out in this chapter:

- Articles entered or withdrawn for immediate exportation or for transportation and exportation
- Products of U.S. fisheries that are free of duty

- Products of possessions of the United States
- Products of the United States exported and returned
- Articles valued at not more than $1 which are passed without entry

WHEN MARKING IS REQUIRED

Except as specifically set out in the preceding section of this chapter, every other imported article must be marked legibly and in a conspicuous place in such manner that it will indicate to an ultimate purchaser in the United States the English name of the country of origin of the article.

It is not feasible to state who will be the ultimate purchaser in every circumstance. Broadly stated, an *ultimate purchaser* may be defined as the last person in the United States who will receive the article in its imported form. Generally, if an imported article will be used in manufacture, the manufacturer is the ultimate purchaser. If an article is to be sold at retail, the U.S. consumer is the ultimate purchaser. A person who subjects an imported article to a process that results in a substantial transformation of the article, even though the process may not result in a new or different article, may be an ultimate purchaser in certain circumstances. But if the process is a minor one, which leaves the identity of the imported article intact, the consumer remains the ultimate purchaser.

If either an article or a container requires marking, the marking is considered adequate if it remains legible until the article reaches the ultimate purchaser.

If the imported article is combined with articles of different origin before delivery to the ultimate purchaser the marking must clearly show that the origin is only that of the imported article and not that of any other article. For example, if bottles imported from England are to be filled in the United States, they must be marked "Bottle made in England." Imported labels that are affixed to U.S. products should so indicate, such as "Label printed in Japan."

If the imported article is substantially changed in the United States, as when bristles are inserted into imported hairbrush blocks or toothbrush handles, only the country of origin mark must appear.

Although it is permissible to mark articles (or their containers) with the name of the country of origin after importation, under Customs supervision, and at the expense of the importer, marking after importation almost invariably results in delay, inconvenience, and expense, which could have been avoided had the articles (or their containers) been marked at the time of manufacture.

SPECIAL MARKING REQUIREMENTS

The following articles must be marked legibly and conspicuously by die stamping, cast-in-the-mold lettering, etching, engraving, or by means of metal plates attached by welding, screws, or rivets to the article. Details on these groups of items can be obtained by consulting the Tariff Schedules of the United States, and the importer is advised to do so.

Knives of all kinds and their parts, including handles

Clippers, shears, and scissors of all kinds

Razors and blades

Pliers of all kinds

Surgical and dental instruments

Scientific and laboratory instruments

Drawing instruments

Thermostatic bottles, jars, etc.

Watch and clock movements, cases, and dials

Lamps

Electron microscopes

Weighing machines

Some articles (consult Tariff Schedules) must be marked to show the name of the manufacturer or purchaser.

Gold and silver articles have certain marking requirements that are administered by the Department of Justice, Washington, DC 10530, who should be contacted with questions.

If you intend to import to the United States any of the above articles or articles possibly related to them, you should request specific advice from a district or port director of Customs or a regional commissioner of Customs as to the exact marking requirements.

If you are in doubt about whether your goods (or their containers) must be marked, how to mark them, what is to be regarded as the country of their origin, or if you need information on any other aspect of marking, contact the above Customs authorities.

IMPROPER MARKING

The U.S. government is obviously concerned about informing its citizens of the origin of the goods they purchase. It follows, therefore, that there are federal regulations against markings that give the purchaser a false impression of origin. Regulations state that any imported article of foreign origin that bears a name or mark calculated to induce the public to believe that it was manufactured anywhere other than the country or locality in which it was in fact manufactured shall not be admitted to entry at any customhouse in the United States.

In general, the words *United States*, the letters U.S.A., or the name of an city or locality in the United States appearing on an imported article or its container are deemed to be calculated to induce the public to believe that the article was manufactured in the United States—unless the name to indicate the country or origin (in letters of comparable size) appears in close proximity to the name that indicates a domestic origin. For example, Colombian crockery called "Los Angeles" brand dinnerware would be considered misleading unless a "Made in Colombia" mark appeared everywhere the brand name "Los Angeles" appeared.

An imported article bearing a prohibited name or mark is subject to seizure and forfeiture. However, if you, the importer, files a petition prior to final disposition of the article, the district or port director of Customs may release it upon the condition that the prohibited marking be removed and that the article or containers be properly marked. Or the article may be exported or destroyed.

If books are being imported, the words *Printed in*, followed by the name of the country of origin, and the words *Printed in*, followed by the name and address of the foreign printer and the name of the country of origin, or words of similar significance, should appear on the front or back of the title page or cover (not covered by a dust cover or jacket), or on a page near the front or back of the book.

Chapter Twenty

Government Import Restrictions

Chapter Twelve discussed U.S. government export restrictions, which take the form of Country Groups and commodity controls. To the same end, as you read in Chapter Eighteen the government levies higher duties against goods from certain countries. This chapter discusses government protection of its citizens through a list of items whose importation is prohibited or restricted, controls over import quantities by means of import quotas, protection for U.S. industries in the form of the so-called antidumping regulations and import "preferences" (GSP) shown to developing nations.

Generally, import licenses are not required for merchandise entering the United States. There are thousands of products that can be imported freely and with no restrictions, and the beginner is well-advised to concentrate on these. They are almost all types of consumer products found in retail stores, such as clothing, televisions, most automotive products, radios, all types of appliances, and gifts. Industrial products that can be imported freely include machinery, heating units, most food products, and construction equipment.

The following section discusses prohibited and restricted articles. It is unlikely that many of these articles would be of interest to the beginner, but a summary is included so you will know what products to avoid and what agencies to contact if you have questions.

PROHIBITED AND RESTRICTED ARTICLES

The importation of certain articles is either prohibited or restricted. Their shipment to the United States may result in seizure or forfeiture. In addition to Customs regulations, many of these prohibitions and restrictions on importations are subject to the laws and regulations administered by one or more other government agencies, with which Customs cooperates in enforcement. For example, such laws and regulations may prohibit entry; limit entry to certain ports; restrict routing, storage, or use; or require treatment, labeling, or processing as a condition of release. Customs clearance is given only if these various additional requirements are met. The restrictions apply to all types of importations, including those made by mail and those placed in foreign-trade zones (discussed in Chapter Twenty-One).

A list of categories of restricted goods follows, along with the agency that administers the restriction. A local Customs office an give you more information, as can the agencies themselves.

- *Alcoholic beverages and confectionery*
  Bureau of Alcohol, Tobacco, and Firearms
  Department of the Treasury
  Washington, D.C. 20226

- *Arms, ammunition, explosives, and implements of war*
  Bureau of Alcohol, Tobacco, and Firearms
  Department of the Treasury
  Washington, D.C. 20226

- *Automobiles and equipment*
  Environmental Protection Agency
  Washington, D.C. 20460

- *Coins, currencies, stamps, and other monetary instruments*
  U.S. Secret Service
  Department of the Treasury
  Washington, D.C. 20223

- *Eggs and egg products*
  Veterinary Services
  Animal and Plant Health Inspection Service
  U.S. Department of Agriculture
  Washington, D.C. 20250

- *Electronic products, radiation standards*
  Federal Communications Commission
  Washington, D.C. 20559

- *Food, drugs, cosmetics*
  U.S. Consumer Product Safety Commission
  Washington, D.C. 20207
  and
  Department of Health, Education and Welfare
  Food and Drug Administration
  Rockville, Maryland 20857

- *Products from certain Communist countries*
  Foreign Assets Control
  Department of the Treasury
  Washington, D.C. 20220

- *Animals*
  Bureau of Epidemology
  Veterinary Public Health Service
  Atlanta, Georgia 30333

- *Fruits, vegetables, plants, insects*
  Fruit and Vegetable Division
  Consumer and Marketing Service
  Department of Agriculture
  Washington, D.C. 20250
  and
  Plant Protection and Quarantine Programs
  U.S. Department of Agriculture
  Hyattsville, Maryland 20782

- *Livestock and meat*
  Department of Agriculture
  Hyattsville, Maryland 20782

- *Narcotics*
  Drug Enforcement Administration
  Department of Justice
  Washington, D.C. 20537

- *Pesticides and toxic substances*
  Environmental Protection Agency
  Washington, D.C. 20460

- *Wild animals, endangered species*
  U.S. Fish and Wildlife Service
  Department of the Interior
  Washington, D.C. 20240

- *Wool, fur, textile, and fabric products*
  Federal Trade Commission
  Washington, D.C. 20580

- *Mild and cream, viruses and serums, rags, brushes*
  Public Health Service
  Department of Health, Education, and Welfare
  Rockville, Maryland 20857

IMPORT QUOTAS

Various import quotas, established by directives from the Committee for the Implementation of Textile Agreements, by legislation, and by presidential proclamations, are administered by the district director. These quotas are of two types: tariff-rate and absolute. Figure 20.1 lists commodities that are affected.

Tariff-rate quotas.   Tariff-rate quotas provide for the entry of a specified quantity of the quota product at a reduced rate of duty during a given period. For example, Australian beef was imported under this type of quota in order to reduce the domestic price to the consumer. There is no limitation of the amount of the product that may be entered during the quota period, but quantities entered in excess of the quota for the period are subject to higher duty rates. In most cases, products of Communist-controlled areas are not entitled to the benefits of tariff-rate quotas.

Absolute quotas.   Absolute quotas are quantitative; that is, no more than the amount specified may be permitted entry during a quota period. This type of quota has been used to protect steel and other industries for political purposes. Some absolute quotas are global, whereas others are allocated to specified foreign countries. Imports in excess of a specified quota may be exported or detained for entry in a subsequent quota period.

General.   The usual Customs procedures generally applicable to other imports apply with respect to commodities subject to quota limitations.

The quota status of a commodity subject to a tariff-rate quota cannot be determined in advance of its entry. The quota rates of duty are ordinarily assessed on such commodities entered from the beginning of the quota period until such time in the period as it is determined that imports are nearing the quota level. District

Commodities Subject to Import Quotas
Administered by the District Director of Customs
as provided for in the Tariff Schedules of the United States

Tariff Rate Quotas

- Whole milk, fluid, fresh or sour
- Fish, fresh, chilled, or frozen, filleted, etc., cod, haddock, hake, pollock, cusk, and rosefish
- Tuna fish, described in item 112.30 Tariff Schedules
- Potatoes, white or Irish; certified seed and other than certified seed
- Whiskbrooms wholly or in part of broom corn
- Other brooms wholly or in part of broom corn
- Motorcycles, over 700 cc engine displacement

Absolute Quotas

- Animal feeds containing milk or milk derivatives
- Butter substitutes, containing over 45 percent of butterfat, provided for in item 116.30, Tariff Schedules, and butter oil
- Buttermix containing over 5.5 percent but not over 45 percent by weight of butterfat
- Cheese, natural Cheddar made from unpasteurized milk and aged not less than 9 months
- Chocolate, containing 5.5 percent or less by weight of butterfat
- Chocolate crumb and other related articles containing over 5.5 percent by weight of butterfat
- Cream, fluid or frozen, fresh or sour
- Milk and cream, condensed or evaporated
- Ice cream
- Cotton having a staple length under 1 1/8" (except harsh or rough cotton having a staple length of under 3/4", and other than linters)
- Cotton (other than linters) having a staple length of 1 1/8" or more
- Cotton card strips made from cotton having a staple length under 1 3/15" and comber waste, lap waste, sliver waste, and roving waste, whether or not advanced
- Fibers of cotton processed but not spun
- Peanuts, shelled or not shelled, blanched, or otherwise prepared or preserved (except peanut butter)
- Sugar, syrups, and molasses described in items 115.20, 115.30, 156.45, 183.01, and 183.05 Tariff Schedules
- Steel, bars, rods, stainless, alloy tool steel
- Coffee

Figure 20.1 Examples of import quotas

directors of Customs are then instructed to require the deposit of estimated duties at the over-quota duty rate and to report the time of official acceptance of each entry. A final determination of the date and time when the quota is filled is made, and all district directors are advised accordingly.

Other quotas. Quotas on certain other products are administered by specific agencies. Fuel oil and oil product quotas are administered by the Director, Oil Imports, Federal Energy Administration, P.O. Box 7414, Ben Franklin Station, Washington, D.C. 20461. Quotas on watches and watch movements are administered by the Office of Import Programs, Special Import Programs Division, U.S. Department of Commerce, Washington,D.C. 20230. Dairy product quotas are administered by the Department of Agriculture. Detailed information can be obtained from the Import Branch, Foreign Agricultural Service, U.S. Department of Agriculture, Washington, D.C. 20250.

ANTIDUMPING REGULATIONS

Dumping is the practice of selling foreign merchandise in the United States at less than fair value, thereby causing injury to domestic industries. The determination as to whether dumping is occurring is ordinarily based on a comparison between the net, f.o.b. factory price to the U.S. importer and the net, f.o.b. factory price to purchasers in the home market. If the sales to the United States are on a c.i.f. delivered basis or on an f.o.b. seaport basis, the necessary deductions are made in order to arrive at an f.o.b. factory price. If the merchandise is not sold in the home market, or if the amount sold in the home market is so small as to be an inadequate basis for comparison,then comparison is made between the prices to the United States and the prices for exportation to third countries. If the merchandise is sold only to the United States or if the merchandise sold in the homemarket or to third countries is not sufficiently similar to the merchandise sold to the United States to furnish a satisfactory basis for comparison, then comparison is made between the price to the United States and the constructed value. Constructed value is the sum of:

1. Cost of materials, labor, and fabrication
2. Usual general expenses, such as factory and administrative overhead, and the usual profit realized in the manufacture of merchandise of the same general character
3. Cost of packing and other expenses incident to preparing the merchandise for shipment to the United States.

In most cases, an importer should be able to satisfy himself or herself that merchandise is not being purchased at less than fair value by comparing net, f.o.b. factory prices to the United States with the net, f.o.b. factory prices in the home market or to third countries.

GENERALIZED SYSTEM OF PREFERENCES (GSP)

A wide range of products, classifiable under approximately 2,750 different item numbers prefixed with A or A* in the Tariff Schedules of the United States, may qualify for duty-free entry if imported into the United States directly from any of the designated developing countries and territories. These countries are listed below; entries in the list may change from time to time.

Requests for information concerning the addition to, or deletion from, the list of eligible merchandise or countries should be directed to the Chairman, Trade Policy Staff Committee, Office of the Special Representative for Trade Negotiations, 1800 G Street, N.W. Washington, D.C. 20506.

Independent Countries

Angola	Costa Rica	Kenya
Antigua and Barbuda***	Cyprus	Kiribati
Argentina	Djibouti	Korea, Republic of
Bahamas***	Dominica***	Lebanon
Bahrain	Dominican Republic	Lesotho
Bangladesh	Ecuador	Liberia
Barbados***	Egypt	Madagascar
Belize***	El Salvador	Malawi
Bhutan	Equatorial Guinea	Malaysia**
Bolivia*	Fiji	Maldives
Botswana	Gambia	Mali
Brazil	Ghana	Malta
Brunei Darussalam**	Grenada***	Mauritania
Burkina Faso	Guatemala	Mauritius
Burma	Guinea	Mexico
Burundi	Guinea Bissau	Morocco
Cameroon	Guyana***	Mozambique
Cape Verde	Haiti	Nauru
Central African	Honduras	Nepal
Republic	India	Nicaragua
Chad	Indonesia**	Niger
Chile	Israel	Oman
Colombia*	Ivory Coast	Pakistan
Comoros	Jamaica***	Panama
Congo	Jordan	Papua and New Guinea

Paraguay
Peru*
Philippines**
Portugal
Romania
Rwanda
Saint Lucia***
Saint Vincent
  and the Grenadines***
Sao Tome and Principe
Senegal
Seychelles
Sierra Leone
Singapore**

Solomon Islands
Somalia
Sri Lanka
Sudan
Surinam
Swaziland
Syria
Taiwan
Tanzania
Thailand**
Togo
Tonga
Trinidad and Tobago***
Tunisia

Turkey
Tuvalu
Uganda
Upper Volta
Uruguay
Vanuatu
Venezuela*
Western Samoa
Yemen Arab Republic
  (Sanaa)
Yugoslavia
Zaire
Zambia
Zimbabwe

Non-Independent Countries and Territories

Anguilla
Bermuda
British Indian
  Ocean Territory
Cayman Islands
Christmas Island
  (Australia)
Cocos (Keeling)
  Islands
Cook Islands
Falkland Islands
  (Islas Malvinas)

French Polynesia
Gibraltar
Heard Island and
  McDonald Islands
Hong Kong
Macau
Montserrat***
Netherlands Antilles
New Caledonia
Niue
Norfolk Island
Pitcairn Islands

Saint Christopher-
  Nevis***
Saint Helena
Tokelau
Trust Territory of
the
  Pacific Island
Turks and
  Caicos Islands
Virgin Islands,
  British
Wallis and Futuna
Western Sahara

* Member countries of the Cartagena Agreement—Andean Group (treated as one country).
**Association of South East Asian Nations—ASEAN (treated as one country).
***Member countries of the Caribbean Common Market—CARICON (treated as one country).

CIVIL AND CRIMINAL FRAUD LAWS

Importers who submit false or fraudulent documents to Customs may have to forfeit their merchandise and pay a penalty equal to the domestic value of the merchandise. These structures are provided by the Tariff Act of 1930. In addition, a criminal fraud statute provides a maximum of two years' imprisonment, or a $5,000 fine, or both, for each violation involving an importation or attempted importation.

Both of these fraud statutes were enacted by Congress to discourage persons from evading the payment of lawful duties owed to the United States. They are enforced by special agents assigned to the Office of Investigations who operate throughout the United States and in the major trading centers of the world.

Chapter Twenty-One

Foreign Trade Zones

Manufacturers and exporters familiar with the advantages of continental free ports, free-trade zones, and entrepot (trade and shipment) facilities will be interested to learn that a number of foreign-trade zones have been established in the United States to encourage the consignment and reexport trade.

Foreign exporters planning to expand or open up new United States outlets may forward their goods to a foreign-trade zone in the United States to be held for an unlimited period while awaiting a favorable market in the United States or nearby countries without being subject to customs entry, payment of duty or tax, or bond.

The zones provide similar advantages for U.S. importers. For example, apparel may be brought into and held in trade zones. The importer thus obtains flexibility—the stock can be labeled as it is sold. Should a customer cancel part of an order, the importer is not in the position of having to relabel stock in order to sell it to another store.

You might also wish to buy equipment in one country and sell it in another. Used machinery purchased in Europe might be stored in a U.S. foreign trade zone, refurbished there, and then sold in South America. The importer would only have to pay storage fees—no duty would apply.

Merchandise brought into foreign trade zones may be stored, sold, exhibited, broken up, repacked, assembled, distributed, sorted, graded, cleaned, mixed with foreign or domestic merchandise, otherwise manipulated, or manufactured. The resulting merchandise may thereafter be either exported or transferred into customs

174

territory. When foreign goods, in their condition at time of entry into the zone or after processing there, are transferred into Customs territory of the United States, the goods must be entered at the custom house. If entered for consumption, duties and taxes will be assessed on the entered articles according to the condition of the foreign merchandise at the time of entry into the zone, it if has been placed in the status of privileged foreign merchandise proper to manipulation or manufacture, or on the basis of the condition at the time of entry for consumption, if the foreign merchandise was in nonprivileged status at the time of processing.

An important feature of foreign trade zones is that the goods may be brought to the threshold of the market, making immediate delivery certain and avoiding possible cancellation of orders due to shipping delays after a favorable market has closed.

Production of articles in zones by the combined use of domestic and foreign materials makes it unnecessary either to send the domestic materials abroad for manufacture or the duty-paid bonded importation of the foreign materials into this country. Duties on the foreign goods involved in such processing or manufacture are payable only on the actual quantity of such foreign goods incorporated in merchandise transferred from a zone for entry into the commerce of the United States. If there is any unrecoverable waste resulting from manufacture or manipulation, allowances are made for it, thereby eliminating payment of duty except on the articles that are actually entered. If there is any recoverable waste, it is dutiable only in its condition as such and in the quantity entered.

A second notable feature under the zone act is the authority to exhibit merchandise within a zone. Zone facilities may be utilized for the full exhibition of foreign merchandise without bond, for an unlimited length of time, and with no requirement of exportation or duty payment. Thus, the owner of goods in a zone may now display his or her goods where they are stored, establish showrooms on his or her own, or join with other importers in displaying merchandise in a permanent exhibition established in the zone. And, since the owner may also store and process merchandise in a zone, she or he is not limited to mere display of samples, but may sell from stock in wholesale quantities.

The owner of foreign merchandise that has not been manipulated or manufactured in any way that would effect a change in its U.S. tariff classification, had it been taken into Customs territory, may, upon request to the district director of Customs, have its dutiable status fixed and liquidated. This dutiable status will apply irrespective of when the merchandise is entered into Customs territory and even though its condition or form may have been changed by processing in the zone, as indicated above.

Domestic merchandise may be taken into a zone and, providing its identity is maintained in accordance with regulations, may be returned to Customs territory free of quotas, duty, or tax, even though while in the zone it may have been combined with or made part of other articles. However, domestic distilled spirits, wine, and beer, and a limited number of other kinds of merchandise, may not be processed while in the zone.

Savings may result from manipulations and manufacture in a zone. For example, many products, shipped to the zone in bulk, can be dried, sorted, graded, or cleaned and bagged or packed, permitting savings of duties and taxes on moisture taken from content or on dirt removed and culls thrown out. From incoming shipment of packaged or bottled goods, damaged packages or broken bottles can be removed. Where exportation results during shipment or while goods are stored in the zone, contents of barrels or other containers can be regauged and savings obtained, as no duties are payable on the portions lost or removed. In other words, barrels or other containers can be gauged at the time of transfer to Customs territory, to insure that duties will not be charged on any portion of their contents that has been lost due to evaporation, leakage, breakage, or otherwise.

Savings in shipping charges, duties, and taxes may result from such operations as shipping unassembled or disassembled furniture, machinery, and so on, to the zone and then assembling or reassembling them there.

Merchandise may be remarked or relabeled in the zone to conform to requirements for entry into the commerce of the United States if otherwise up to standard. Remarking or relabeling that would be misleading is not permitted in the zone.

Standard foods and drugs may, in certain cases, be reconditioned to meet the requirements of the Food, Drug, and Cosmetics Act.

There is no time limit as to how long foreign merchandise may be sorted in a zone, or when it must be entered into customs territory, reexported, or destroyed.

Foreign merchandise in Customs-bonded warehouses may be transferred to the zone at any time before the limitation on its retention in the bonded warehouse expires, but such a transfer to the zone may be made only for the purpose of eventual exportation or destruction.

When foreign merchandise is transferred to the zone from Customs-bonded warehouses, the bond is canceled and all obligations in regard to duty payment, or as to the time when the merchandise is to be reexported, are terminated. Similarly, the owner of domestic merchandise stored in internal revenue-bonded warehouses may transfer her or his goods to a zone and obtain cancellation of bonds. In addition, domestic goods moved into a zone for export are considered exported upon entering the zone for purpose of excise and other internal revenue tax rebates. A manufacturer, operating in Customs territory and using dutiable imported materials in his or her product, may also obtain drawbacks of duties paid or cancellation of bond, upon transferring the product to the zone for export and complying with the appropriate regulations.

Thus, the owner does not need to wait until he or she finds a foreign customer, or until the customer is ready for delivery, to obtain these benefits.

Foreign-trade zones are listed below. Information as to rates and charges, and details as to how individual foreign trade zones can be utilized, may be obtained by writing to the U.S. Foreign Trade Zone Manager.

U.S. FOREIGN TRADE ZONES

Zone No. 1, New York City
Operator: S & F Warehouse, Inc.
Brooklyn Navy Yard, Bldg. 77
Brooklyn, N.W. 11205
Sol Braun (718) 834-0400
Grantee: City of New York

Zone No. 2, New Orleans
Grantee/Operator: Board of Commissioners of the Port of New Orleans
P.O. Box 60046,
New Orleans, LA 70160
Robert Dee (504) 897-0189

Zone No. 3, San Francisco
Operator: Foreign Trade Services, Inc.
Pier 23
San Francisco, CA 94111
Ed Osgood (415) 391-0176
Grantee: San Francisco Port Commission

Zone No. 5, Seattle
Grantee/Operator: Port of Seattle Commission
P.O. Box 1209
Seattle, WA 98111
Jack Fox (206) 382-3257

Zone No. 7, Mayaguez, Puerto Rico
Grantee/Operator: Puerto Rico
G.P.O. Box 2350
San Juan, P.R. 00936
Jose Cobian (809) 765-2784

Zone No. 8, Toledo
Grantee: Toledo-Lucas County Port Authority
One Maritime Plaza
Toledo, HO 43604-1866
John Loftus (419) 243-8251

*This list gives the address and phone number of the contact person for each zone project, with the city or county location appearing after the zone number. When the contact person is not an employee of the grantee, the name of the grantee organization is given. Further information on any particular zone can be obtained from the contact persons. If assistance is needed from FTZ Staff, U.S. Department of Commerce, please call (202) 377-2862.

Zone No. 9, Honolulu
Grantee/Operator: State of Hawaii
Pier 2
Honolulu, HI 96813
Homer Maxey (808) 548-5435

Zone No. 12, McAllen, Texas
Grantee/Operator: McAllen Trade Zone, Inc.
6401 S. 33rd Street
McAllen, TX
Frank Birkhead (512) 682-4306

Zone No. 14, Little Rock
Operator: Little Rock Port Authority
7500 Lindsey Rd.
Little Rock, AR 72206
Robert Brave (501) 490-1468
Grantee: Arkansas Dept. of Industrial Development

Zone No. 15, Kansas City, Missouri
Grantee/Operator: Greater Kansas City FTZ, Inc.
120 W. 12th St., Suite 650
Kansas City, MO 64105
Robert Drost (816) 421-7666

Zone No. 16, Sault Ste. Marie, Michigan
Grantee/Operator: Economic Development Corp. of Sault Ste. Marie
1301 W. Easterday
Sault Ste. Marie, MI 49783
James F. Hendricks (906) 635-9131

Zone No. 17, Kansas City, Kansas
Grantee/Operator: Greater Kansas City FTZ, Inc.
120 W. 12th St., Suite 650
Kansas, MO 64105
Robert Drost (816) 421-7666

Zone No. 18, San Jose, California
Grantee: City of San Jose
801 North First St.
Rm. 408, City Hall
San Jose, CA 95110
Ted Daigle (408) 277-4744

Zone No. 19, Omaha
Grantee/Opertor: Dock Board of the City of Omaha
Omaha-Douglas Civic Center
1819 Farnam St., Rm. 701
Omaha, NE 68183
Ken Johnson (402) 444-5165

Zone No. 20, Suffolk, Virginia
Grantee: Virginia Port Authority
600 World Trade Center
Norfolk, VA 23510
John Hunter (804) 623-8080

Zone No. 21, Dorchester County, S.C.
Operator: Carolina Trade Zone
2725 W. 5th North St.
Summerville, S.C. 19483
A.M. Quattlebaum (803) 871-4870
Grantee: South Carolina State Ports Authority

Zone No. 22, Chicago
Grantee: Illinois International Port District
12700 Butler Drive
Lake Calumet Harbor
Chicago, IL 60633
Franklynn Albert (312) 646-4400

Zone No. 23, Buffalo
Grantee: County of Erie
Erie County Industrial Development Agency
Suite 300, Liberty Bldg.
424 Main St.
Buffalo, NY 14202
Phillip R. Jacobs (716) 856-6525

Zone No. 24, Pittston, Pennsylvania
Grantee/Operator: Eastern Distribution Center, Inc.
1151 Oak Street
Pittston, PA 18640-3795
James G. Pettinger (717) 655-5581

Zone No. 25, Port Everglades, Florida
Grantee/Operator: Port Everglades Port Authority
P.O. Box 13136
Port Everglades, FL 33316
Thomas E. Ezzo (305)523-3404

Zone No. 26, Shenandoah, Georgia
Grantee: Georgia Foreign Trade Zone, Inc.
230 Peachtree St., N.W.
P. O. Box 1776
Atlanta, GA 30301
Michael H. Lott (404) 581-4008

Zone No. 27, Boston
Grantee: Massachusetts Port Authority
10 Park Plaza
Boston, MA 02116
Elliot K. Friedman (617) 973-5500

Zone No. 28, New Bedford, Massachusetts
Grantee/Operator: City of New Bedford
Mayor's Office of Community Development
133 William St., Rm. 215
New Bedford, MA 02740
Richard M. Bennett (617) 999-2931 Ext. 367

Zone 29, Louisville
Grantee/Operator: Louisville & Jefferson County
Riverport Authority
6219 Cane Run Road
Louisville, KY 40258
Robert M. Timmerman (502)935-6024

Zone No. 30, Salt Lake City
Grantee: Redevelopment Agency of Salt Lake City
285 West North Pemple
Suite 200
Salt Lake City, UT 84103
Michael Chitwood (801) 328-3211

Zone No. 31. Granite City, Illinois
Grantee/Operator: Tri-City Regional Port District
2801 Rock Road
Granite City, IL 62040
Robert Wydra (618) 877-8444

Zone No. 32, Miami
> Grantee: Greater Miami Foreign Trade Zone, Inc.
> 1601 Biscayne Blvd.
> Miami, FL 33132
> Sandra Gonzalez (305) 350-7700

Zone No. 33, Pittsburgh
> Grantee: Regional Industrial Dev. Corp. of Southwestern Pennsylvania
> Suite 1220, Frick Building
> Pittsburgh, PA 15219
> Frank Brooks Robinson (412) 471-3939

Zone No. 34, Niagra County, New York
> Grantee/Operator: County of Niagra
> County Office Bldg.
> 59 Park Ave.
> Lockport, NY 14094
> Theodore J. Belling (716) 439-6033

Zone No. 35, Philadelphia
> Grantee: The Philadelphia Port Corporation
> 1020 Public Ledger Bldg.
> 6th & Chestnut Streets
> Tom Tamasco (215) 928-9100

Zone No. 36, Galveston
> Operator: Port of Galveston
> Galveston Wharves
> P.O. Box 328
> Galveston, TX 77550
> John Massey, Jr. (409) 766-6112
> Grantee: City of Galveston

Zone No. 37, Orange County, New York
> Operator: Foreign Trade Dev. Co. of Orange Cty., Inc.
> P.O. Box 6147, Stewart Airport
> Newburgh, NY 12550
> Nick Cignarale (914) 564-7700
> Grantee: County of Orange

Zone No. 38, Spartanburg County, S.C.
> Operator: Carolina Trade Zone
> 2725 W. 5th North St.
> Summerville, S.C. 29483
> A. M. Quattlebaum (803) 871-4870
> Grantee: South Carolina State Ports Authority

Zone No. 39, Dallas/Fort Worth
  Grantee: Dallas/Fort Worth Regional Airport Board
  P. O. Drawer DFW
  Dallas/Fort Worth Airport, TX 75261
  Dennis Konopatzke (214) 574-3121

Zone No. 40, Cleveland
  Grantee: Cleveland Port Authority
  101 Erieside Avenue
  Cleveland, OH 44114
  John L. Townley (216) 241-8004

Zone No. 41, Milwaukee
  Grantee: Foreign Trade Zone of Wisconsin, Ltd.
  2150 E. College Avenue
  Cudahy, WI 53110
  Vincent J. Boever (414) 764-2111

Zone No. 42, Orlando
  Grantee/Operator: Greater Orlando Aviation Authority
  4101 East 9th Street
  Orlando, FL 32812
  William Blood (305) 859-9485

Zone No. 43, Battle Creek, Michigan
  Grantee/Operator: BC/CAL/KAL Inland Port Authority of S. Central
  Michigan Development Corp.
  P.O. Box 1438
  Marilyn E. Parks (616) 968-8197

Zone No. 44, Morris County, N.J.
  Grantee: N.J. Dept. of Commerce & Economic Dev.
  Office of Int'l Trade
  744 Broad St.
  Newark, NJ 07102
  Joseph Brade (210) 648-3518

Zone No. 45, Portland, Oregon
  Grantee/Operator: Port of Portland
  P.O. Box 3529
  Portland, OR 97208
  Peggy J. Krause (503) 231-5000 x220

Zone No. 46, Cincinnati
  Grantee/Operator: Greater Cincinnati FTZ, Inc.
  120 W. 5th Street
  Cincinnati, OH 45202
  Joe Kramer (513) 579-3143

Zone No. 47, Campbell County, Kentucky
  Grantee/Operator: Greater Cincinnati FTZ, Inc.
  120 W. 5th Street
  Cincinnati, OH 45202
  Joe Kramer (513) 579-3143

Zone No. 48, Tucson, Arizona
  Grantee/Operator: Papago-Tucson FTZ Corp.
  San Xavier Development Authority
  P.O. Box 11246
  Mission Station, AR 85734
  William Tatom (602) 881-0439

Zone No. 49, Newark/Elizabeth, New Jersey
  Grantee/Operator: Port Authority of NY and NJ
  One World Trade Center
  Rm. 64 West
  New York, NY 10048
  Catherine Durda (212) 466-7985

Zone No. 50, Long Beach, California
  Grantee: Board of Harbor Commissioners of the Port of Long Beach
  P.O. Box 570
  Long Beach, CA 90801-0570
  Rick Aschieris (213) 590-4104

Zone No. 51, Duluth, Minnesota
  Grantee/Operator: Seaway Port Authority of Duluth
  1200 Port Terminal Drive
  P.O. Box 8677
  Duluth, MN 55808
  Henry K. Hanka (218) 727-8525

Zone No. 52, Suffolk County, New York
  Grantee/Operator: County of Suffolk
  1 Trade Zone Drive
  Ronkonkoma, N.Y. 11779
  Jim Mackey (516) 588-5757

Zone No. 53, Rogers County, Oklahoma
Grantee/Operator: City of Tulsa-Rogers Cty. Port Auth. Tulsa Port of Catoosa
5350 Cimarron Road
Catoosa, OK 74105
Robert W. Portiss (918) 266-2291

Zone No. 54, Clinton County, New York
Grantee/Operator: Clinton County Area Dev. Corp.
P.O. Box 19
Plattsburgh, NY 12901
Francis Lapham (518) 563-3100

Zone No. 55, Burlington, Vermont
Grantee/Operator: Greater Burlington Industrial Corp.
P.O. Box 786
Burlington, VT 05402
C. Harry Behney (802) 862-5726

Zone No. 56, Oakland, California
Operator: Oakland International Trade Center, Inc.
633 Hengenberger Rd.
Oakland, CA 94621
Dayton Ballenger (415) 639-7405
Grantee: City of Oakland

Zone No. 57, Mecklenburg County, N.C.
Operator: Piedmont Distribution Center
P.O. Box 7123
Charlotte, N.C. 28217
Richard Primm (704) 588-2868
Grantee: North Carolina Department of Commerce

Zone No. 58, Bangor, Maine
Grantee/Operator: City of Bangor
Economic Dept., City Hall
Bangor, ME 04401
Edward McKeon (207) 947-0341

Zone No. 59, Lincoln, Nebraska
Grantee/Operator: Lincoln Chamber of Commerce
1221 North Street
Suite 606
Lincoln, NE 68508
Duane Vicary (402) 476-7511

Zone No. 60, Nogales, Arizona
 Operator: Rivas Realty
 3450 Tucson-Nogales Highway
 Nogales, AR 85621
 Herman Rivas (602) 287-3411
 Grantee: Border Industrial Development, Inc.

Zone No. 61, San Juan, Puerto Rico
 Grantee/Operator: Puerto Rico Commercial Dev. Co.
 Commonwealth of Puerto Rico
 G.P.O. Box 4943
 San Juan, PR 00936
 Miguel Sigueroa (809) 721-1273

Zone No. 62 Brownsville, Texas
 Grantee/Operator: Brownsville Navigation District Port of Brownsville
 P.O. Box 3070
 Brownsville, TX 78520
 Al Cisneros (512) 831-4592

Zone No. 63, Prince George's County, Maryland
 Grantee: Prince George's County Government
 The Collington Center
 16201 Trade Zone Ave
 Suite 104
 Upper Marlboro, MD 20772
 Don L. Spicer (301) 390-8123

Zone No. 62, Jacksonville, Florida
 Grantee: Jacksonville Port Authority
 P.O. Box 3005
 Jacksonville, FL 32206
 Bruce Cashon (904) 630-3070

Zone No. 65, Panama City, Florida
 Grantee/Operator: Panama City Port Authority
 P.O. Box 15095
 Panama City, FL 32406
 Tommy L. Berry (904) 763-8471

Zone No. 66, Wilmington, North Carolina
 Operator: N.C. State Port Authority
 2202 Burnett Blvd.
 Wilmington, NC 28403
 Patsy Everhart (191) 763-1621
 Grantee: North Carolina Dept. of Commerce

Zone No. 67, Morehead City, North Carolina
Operator: N.C. State Port Authority
2202 Burnett Blvd.
Wilmington, NC 28402
Patsy Everhart (191) 763-1621
Grantee: North Carolina Dept. of Commerce

Zone No. 68, El Paso, Texas
Operator: El Paso International Airport
El Paso, TX 79925
Robert C. Jacob, Jr. (915) 772-4271
Grantee: City of El Paso

Zone No. 70, Detroit
Grantee/Operator: Greater Detroit Foreign-Trade Zone, Inc.
100 Renaissance Ctr.
Suite 2020
Detroit, MI 48243
James Kellow (313) 259-8077

Zone No. 71, Windsor Locks, Connecticut
Grantee: Industrial Development Commission of Windsor Locks
Town Office Building
50 Church Street
P.O. Box L
Windsor Locks, CT 06096
R. Clifford Randall (203) 627-1444

Zone No. 72, Indianapolis
Operator: Indianapolis Economic Development Corporation
48 Monument Circle
Indianapolis, IN 46203
David P. Bennett (317) 236-6246
Grantee: Indianapolis Airport Authority

Zone No. 73, Baltimore/Washington Int'l Airport
Operator: All Cargo Expediting Services, Inc.
P.O. Box 28673
BWI Airport, MD 21240
Robert J. Schott (301) 859-4449
Grantee: Maryland Dept. of Transportation

Zone No. 74, Baltimore
Grantee: City of Baltimore
c/o Baltimore Economic Development Corp.
36 South Charles St.
Baltimore, MD 21201
Paul Gilbert (301) 837-9305

Zone No. 75, Phoenix
Grantee: City of Phoenix
Community & Economic Dev. Adm.
Suite D
920 E. Madison St.
Phoenix, AZ 85034
Edward R. Standage (602) 261-8707

Zone No. 76, Bridgeport, Connecticut
Grantee/Operator: City of Bridgeport
City Hall
45 Lyon Terrace
Bridgeport, CT 06604
Michael Freimuth (203) 576-7135

Zone No. 77, Memphis
Operator: Mid-South Terminals Company, Ltd.
P.O. Box 13286
Memphis, TN 38113
Thomas D. Murphree, (901) 774-4889
Grantee: The City of Memphis

Zone No. 78, Nashville
Grantee: Metropolitan Nashville-Davidson
County Port Authority
172 Second Ave. North
Suite 212
Nashville, TN 37201
Horace Bass (615) 259-7468

Zone No. 79, Tampa
Grantee: City of Tampa
Office of Urban Dev.
City Hall
315 E. Kennedy Blvd.
Tampa, FL 33602
George Unanue (813) 223-8381

Zone No. 80, San Antonio
Grantee: City of San Antonio
P.O. Box 9066
San Antonio, TX 78285
Kenneth W. Daly (512) 299-8080

Zone No. 81, Portsmouth, New Hampshire
Grantee/Operator: New Hampshire State Port Authority
555 Market Street
P.O. Box 506
Portsmouth, NH 03801
George Smith (603) 436-8500

Zone No. 82, Mobile
Operator: Mobile Airport Authority
Bldg. 11, Brookley Complex
Mobile, AL 36615
Don Dupont (205) 438-7334

Zone No. 83, Huntsville, Alabama
Grantee/Operator: Huntsville-Madison County Airport Authority
P.O. Box 6006
Huntsville, AL 35806
J.E. Mitchell, Jr. (205) 772-9395

Zone No. 84, Harris County, Texas
Grantee: Port of Houston Authority
P.O. Box 2562
Houston, TX 77252
Jack Beasley (713) 670-2400

Zone No. 85, Everett, Washington
Grantee: Puget Sound Foreign-Trade Zone Association
c/o Economic Development Partnership for Washington
18000 Pacific Highway South
Suite 400
Seattle, WA 98188
Bill Grinstein (206) 433-1629 Attn: Nance Hughes

Zone No. 86, Tacoma, Washington
Grantee: Puget Sound Foreign-Trade Zone Association
c/o Economic Development Partnership for Washington
18000 Pacific Highway South
Suite 400
Seattle, WA 98188
Bill Grinstein (206) 433-1629 Attn: Nance Highes

Zone No. 87, Lake Charles, Louisiana
Grantee/Operator: Lake Charles Harbor & Terminal District
P.O. Box AAA
Lake Charles, LA 70602
James E. Sudduth (318) 439-3661

Zone No., 88, Great Falls, Montana
Grantee/Operator: Economic Growth Council of Great Falls
P.O. Box 1273
Great Falls, MT 59403
Joseph C. Mudd (406) 761-5036

Zone No. 89, Clark County, Nevada
Grantee/Operator: Nevada Development Authority
3900 Paradise Road, Suite 155
Las Vegas, NV 89109
Al Dague (702) 739-8222

Zone No. 90, Onondaga, New York
Grantee: County of Onondaga
c/o Greater Syracuse Chamber of Commerce
100 E. Onondaga Street
Syracuse, NY 13202
Joseph D. Russo (315) 470-1334

Zone No. 91, Newport, Vermont
Grantee/Operator: Northeastern Vermont Dev. Assoc.
44 Main Street
St. Johnsbury, VT 05819
Henry W. Merrill, Jr. (802) 748-5181

Zone No. 92, Harrison County, Mississippi
Grantee: Greater Gulfport/Bilozi Foreign-Trade Zone, Inc.
3825 Ridgewood Rd.
Jackson, MS 39211-6453
Noel Guthrie (601) 982-6606

Zone No. 93, Raleigh/Durham, North Carolina
Grantee: Triangle J Council of Governments
100 Park Drive
P.O. Box 12276
Research Triangle Park, NC 27709
Pamela Davison (919) 549-0551

Zone No. 94, Laredo, Texas
Operator: Laredo International Airport
Operator of Foreign-Trade Zone No. 94
518 Flightline, Building #132
Laredo, TX 78041
Jose L. Flores (512) 722-4933
Grantee: City of Laredo

Zone No. 95, Starr County, Texas
Grantee/Operator: Starr County Industrial Foundation
P.O. Drawer H
Rio Grande City, TX 78582
Sam Vale (512) 487-5606

Zone No. 96, Eagle Pass, Texas
Grantee/Operator: City of Eagle Pass
P.O. Box C
City Manager's Office
Eagle Pass, TX 78852
Alfonso Gonzales (512) 773-1111

Zone No. 97, Del Rio, Texas
Grantee/Operator: City of Del Rio
City Manager's Office
P.O. Drawer DD
Del Rio, TX 78840
Jeff Pomeranz (512) 774-2781

Zone No. 98, Birmingham, Alabama
Grantee/Operator: City of Birmingham
Mayor's Office, City of Birmingham
Birmingham City Hall
Birmingham, AL 35203
Virginia Riley (205) 254-2277

Zone No. 99, Wilmington, Delaware
Grantee/Operator: State of Delaware
Delaware Development Office
Dover, DE 19901
Dorothy Sbriglia (302) 736-4271

Zone No. 100, Dayton, Ohio
Grantee/Operator: Greater Dayton Foreign-Trade Zone, Inc.
1880 Kettering Tower
Dayton, OH 45423-1880
Gary D. Geisel (513) 226-1444

Zone No. 101, Clinton County, Ohio
    Grantee/Operator: Airborne FTZ, Inc.
    145 Hunter Drive
    Wilmington, OH 45177
    Mike Kuli (513) 382-5591

Zone No. 102, St. Louis
    Grantee/Operator: St. Louis County Port Authority
    130 South Bemiston
    Clayton, MO 63105
    Wayne Weidemann (314) 721-0900

Zone No. 103, Grand Forks, North Dakota
    Grantee/Operator: Grand Forks Dev. Foundation
    P. O. Box 1177
    204 North 3rd
    Grand Forks, ND 58201
    Robert W. Nelson (701) 772-7271

Zone No. 104, Savannah, Georgia
    Grantee/Operator: Savannah Airport Commission
    P. O. Box 2723
    Savannah, GA 31402-2723
    Don Fishero (912) 964-0904 or 964-0514

Zone No. 105, Providence and North Kingstown, Rhode Island
    Grantee: Rhode Island Port Authority and Economic Dev. Corp.
    7 Jackson Walkway
    Providence, RI 02903
    Ted Spinard (401) 277-2601

Zone No. 106, Oklahoma City, Oklahoma
    Grantee: The City of Oklahoma City
    c/o Community Dev. Dept.
    200 N. Walker
    4th Floor
    Oklahoma City, OK 73102
    Carolyn Lyon (405) 231-2583

Zone No. 107, Des Moines, Iowa
    Operator: Centennial Warehouse Corporation
    10400 Hickman Rd.
    Des Moines, IA 50322
    Fred Caruthers (515) 278-9517
    Grantee: The Iowa Foreign Trade Zone Corporation

Zone No. 108, Valdez, Alaska
> Grantee: The City of Valdez, Alaska
> Port of Valdez
> 200 S.W. Market St.
> Suite 985
> Portland, OR 97201-5713
> Vern Chase (503) 227-4567

Zone No. 109, Watertown, New York
> Grantee: The County of Jefferson
> c/o Jefferson Industrial Dev. Agency
> 175 Arsenal St.
> Watertown, NY 13601
> John Nichols (315) 785-3226

Zone No. 110, Albuquerque, New Mexico
> Operator: Foreign-Trade Zone of New Mexico
> FTZ Operators, Inc.
> 1617 Broadway N.E.
> P.O. Box 26928
> Albuquerque, NM 87125
> Bob Wittington (505) 842-0088
> Grantee: The City of Albuquerque

Zone No. 111, JFK Int'l Airport, New York
> Operator: Port Authority of New York and New Jersey
> Kennedy Int'l Airport
> Business Adm. Div.
> Bldg. 141
> Gerald Drasheff (212) 656-4402
> Grantee: The City of New York

Zone No. 112, Colorado Springs, Colorado
> Operator: Front Range Foreign-Trade Zone, Inc.
> 4675 Aerospace Boulevard
> Colorado Springs, CO 80925
> Charlie Luse (303) 390-5666
> Grantee: Colorado Springs Foreign-Trade Zone, Inc.

Zone No. 113, Ellis County, Texas
> Operator: Trade Zone Operations, Inc.
> 100 Center Drive
> Midlothian, TX 76065
> Larry White (214) 299-6301
> Grantee: Midlothian Chamber of Commerce

Zone No. 114, Peoria, Illinois
    Grantee: Economic Development Council, Inc.
    230 S.W. Adams
    Peoria, IL 61602
    Don Rigley (309) 676-0755

Zone No. 115, Beaumont, Texas
    Operator: Foreign-Trade Zone of Southeast Texas, Inc.
    M-Bank Port Arthur
    8200 Hwy. 69
    Suite 403
    Port Arthur, TX 77640
    Dolly Johnson (409) 722-7831

Zone No. 116, Port Arthur, Texas
    Grantee: Foreign-Trade Zone of Southeast Texas, Inc.
    M-Bank Port Arthur
    8200 Hwy. 69
    Suite 403
    Port Arthur, TX 77640
    Dolly Johnson (409) 722-7831

Zone No. 117, Orange, Texas
    Grantee: Foreign-Trade Zone of Southeast Texas, Inc.
    M-Bank Port Arthur
    8200 Hwy, 69
    Suite 403
    Port Arthur, TX 77640
    Dolly Johnson (409) 722-7831

Zone No. 118, Ogdensburg, New York
    Grantee: Ogdensburg Bridge and Port Authority
    Ogdensburg, NY 13669
    Salvatore Pisani (315) 393-4080

Zone No. 119, Minneapolis-St. Paul, Minnesota
    Grantee: Greater Metropolitan FTZ Commission, c/o MCDA
    331 Second Ave. S.
    Suite 600
    Midland Square Bldg.
    Minneapolis, MN 55401
    Dennis Rock (612) 342-1211

Zone No. 120, Cowlitz County, Washington
    Grantee: Cowlitz Economic Development Council
    1338 Commerce, Suite 211
    Longview, WA 98632
    John C. Thompson (206) 423-9921

Zone No. 121, Albany, New York
  Grantee: Capital District Regional Planning Commission
  214 Canal Square
  2nd Floor
  Schenectady, NY 12305
  Chungchin Chen (518) 393-1715

Zone No. 122, Corpus Christi, Texas
  Grantee/Operator: Port of Corpus Christi Authority
  P.O. Box 1541
  Corpus Christi, TX 78403
  Thomas S. Moore (512) 882-5633

Zone No. 123, Denver, Colorado
  Operator: Aspen Distribution
  5401 Oswego St.
  P.O. Box 39108
  Denver CO 80239
  Don Cooper (303) 371-2511
  Grantee: City and County of Denver

Zone No. 124, Gramercy, Louisiana
  Grantee: South Louisiana Port Commission
  P.O. Drawer K
  La Place, LA 70068-1109
  Richard J. Clements (540) 652-9278

Zone No. 125, South Bend, Indiana
  Operator: Material Trans Action
  2741 N. Foundation Dr.
  South Bend, IN 46634-1877
  Kenneth Kanczuzewski (219) 233-2666
  Grantee: St. Joseph County Airport Authority

Zone No. 126, Sparks, Nevada
  Grantee: Nevada Development Authority
  Nevada Foreign-Trade Zone
  P.O. Box 11710
  Reno, NV 89510
  Kevin Day (702) 784-3844

Zone No. 127, West Columbia, South Carolina
  Operator: Columbia Metropolitan Airport
  3000 Aviation Way,
  W. Columbia, SC 29169-2190
  Donnie B. Turbeville (803) 794-3427
  Grantee: South Carolina State Ports Authority

Zone No. 128, Whatcom County, Washington
Grantee: Lummi Indian Business Council
2616 Kwina
Bellingham, WA 98266
Leroy Deardorff (206) 734-8180

Zone 129, Bellingham, Washington
Grantee: Port of Bellingham
P.O. Box 1737
Bellingham, WA 98227
Hugh Wilson (206) 676-2500

Zone No. 130, Blaine, Washington
Grantee: Port of Bellingham
P.O. Box 1737
Bellingham, WA 98227
Hugh Wilson (206) 676-2500

Zone No. 131, Sumas, Washington
Grantee: Port of Bellingham
P.O. Box 1737
Bellingham, WA 98227
Hugh Wilson (206) 676-2500

Zone No. 132, Coos County, Oregon
Grantee: International Port of Coos Bay Commission
Oregon Int'l. Port of Coos Bay
Port Bldg
Front & Market St.
Coos Bay, OR 97420
Frank G. Martin (503) 267-7678

Zone No. 133, Quad-City, Iowa/Illinois
Grantee: Quad-City Foreign-Trade Zone, Inc.
First National Bank of the Quad-Cities
Suite 406
Quad-City, IL 61201
Richard R. Weeks (309) 788-7436 or (319) 326-1005

Zone No. 134, Chattanooga, Tennessee
Grantee: Partners for Economic Progress, Inc.
1001 Market Street
Chattanooga, TN 37402
Robert McAuley (615) 756-2121

Zone No. 135, Palm Beach County, Florida
Grantee: Port of Palm Beach District
P.O. Box 761 Palm Beach, FL 33480
Colonel Frank Donahue (305) 832-4556

Zone No. 136, Brevard County, Florida
Grantee: Canaveral Port Authority
P/.O. Box 267, Port Canaveral Station
Cape Canaveral, FL 32920
Ken Karpinski (305) 783-7831

Zone No. 137. Washington Dullas Int'l Airport, Virginia
Grantee: Washington Dullas Foreign-Trade Zone
P.O. Box 17349
Washington Dullas Int'l Airport
Washington, DC 20041
Thomas Morr (703) 661-8040

Zone No. 138, Franklin County, Ohio
Grantee: Rickenbacker Port Authority
375 South High Street
17th Floor
Columbus, OH 43215
Eric N. Waldron (614) 461-9046

Zone No. 139, Sierra Vista, Arizona
Grantee: Sierra Vista Economic Development Foundation, Inc.
P.O. Box 2380
Sierra Vista, AZ 85636
Joseph Luce (602) 459-6070

Zone No. 140, Flint, Michigan
Grantee: City Of Flint
Bishop International Airport
G-3425 West Bristol Road
Flint, MI 48507
Robert Hidley (313) 766-8620

Zone No. 141, Monroe County, New York
Grantee: County of Monroe, New York
Monroe County Foreign-Trade Zone
55 St. Paul Street
Rochester, NY 14604
Charles Goodwin (716) 454-2220

Chapter Twenty-Two

Special Trade Programs

U. S.–ISRAEL FREE TRADE AREA AGREEMENT

The purpose of this pact between the United States and Israel is to create a free trade area that will eliminate all Customs duties and most nontariff barriers between each country by 1995. Initially, metal working, machine tools, and many electronics components became duty-free in 1985 when the agreement went into effect.

Israel offers many unique products for those new to importing, as well as a market for sophisticated, high-tech items produced in the United States.

Check with the American–Israel Chamber of Commerce, U. S. Department of Commerce, Director, Israel Information Center, Office of the Near East, Washington, D. C. 20230, telephone 202-377-4652 and the Israeli Government Investment and Export Authority. (They have a booklet, "Guide to the Israel–U. S. Free Trade Area Agreement," which is full of information on the agreement and on products currently coming into the United States from Israel.) See Figure 22.1.

UNITED STATES–CANADA FREE TRADE AGREEMENT

Recently signed, but not yet ratified by Congress, this agreement is an important step in easing trade tensions between the United States and Canada (lumber, fishing rights, etc.). The purpose of this agreement, like the one reached with Israel, is to create a free trade area between the countries. Currently we do $124 billion in bilateral trade, making our exchange of goods the most between any two nations.

U.S. CERTIFICATE OF ORIGIN
FOR EXPORTS TO ISRAEL

1. Goods consigned from exporter's business (name, address):	Reference No.
	U.S.—ISRAEL FREE TRADE AREA
	CERTIFICATE OF ORIGIN
	(Combined declaration and certificate)
2. Goods consigned to (consignee's name, address)	
	(See notes over leaf)
3. Means of transport and route (as far as known)	4. For official use

5. Item number	6. Marks and numbers of packages	7. Number and kind of packages, description of goods	8. Origin criterion (see notes over leaf)	9. Gross Weight or other quantity	10. Number and date of invoices

11. CERTIFICATION

The _____ a recognized chamber of commerce, board of trade, or _____ under the laws of the State of _____ has examined the manufacturer's invoice or shipper's affidavit concerning the origin of the merchandise and, according to the best of its knowledge and belief, finds that the products named originated in the United States of America.

_____
Certifying Official

12. DECLARATION BY THE EXPORTER

The undersigned hereby declares that the above details and statements are correct; that all the goods were produced in the United States of America and that they comply with the origin requirements specified for those goods in the U.S.—Israel Free Trade Area Agreement for goods exported to Israel.

_____
Signature of Exporter

Sworn to before me this _____ day of _____ 19_____

_____
Signature of Notary Public

Form 10-380P Printed and Sold by UNACO, 190 Baldwin Ave., Jersey City, NJ 07306 • (800) 631-3098 • (201) 795-5400

198

ATTACHMENT

Specimens of Certificates of Origin

An original of Attachment I shall be used for exports of the United States and an original of Attachment II shall be used for exports of Israel.

NOTES

1. Conditions. The main conditions[1] for admission under the Free Trade Area (FTA) Agreement between the United States of America and Israel (the Agreement) are:

   (a) The goods must be consigned direct from the United States of America to Israel but in most cases shipment through one or more intermediate countries is accepted provided that the goods did not enter into the commerce of that country and otherwise complied with the direct shipment requirements of the Agreement.

   (b) The goods comply with the origin criteria specified in the Agreement. Indication of the origin requirements is given in paragraph 2.

   (c) Each article in a consignment must qualify separately in its own right concerning the rules of origin and direct shipment.

2. Origin requirements for goods originating in the United States of America. The Agreement shall apply to any article if:

   (a) That article is wholly the growth, product, or manufacture of the United States of America or is a new or different article of commerce that has been grown, produced, or manufactured in the United States of America.

   (b) The sum of (a) the cost or value of the materials produced in the United States of America plus (b) the direct cost of processing operations performed in the United States of America is not less than 35 percent of the appraised value of the article at the time it is entered into Israel.

   No article shall be considered a new or different article of commerce under the Agreement and no material shall be eligible for inclusion as domestic content under the Agreement by virtue of having merely undergone (a) the simple combining or packaging operations or (b) mere dilution with water or with another substance that does not materially alter the characteristics of the article or material.

   The expression "wholly the growth, product, or manufacture of the United States of America" refers both to any article which has been entirely grown, produced, or manufactured in the United States of America and to all materials incorporated in an article which have been entirely grown, produced, or manufactured in the United States, as distinguished from articles or materials imported into the United States of America from a third country, whether or not such articles or materials were substantially transformed into new or different articles of commerce after their importation into the United States of America.

   "Country of origin" requires that an article or material, not wholly the growth, product, or manufacture of the United States of America, be substantially transformed into a new and different article of commerce, having a new name, character, or use, distinct from the article or material from which it was so transformed.

   For purpose of determining the 35 percent U.S.A. content requirement under the Agreement, the cost or value of materials which are used in the production of an article in the United States of America, and which are the products of Israel, may be counted in an amount up to 15 percent of the appraised value of the article. Such materials must in fact be products of Israel under the country or origin criteria set forth in the Agreement.

3. Entries to be made in Box 8.

   Products must be either wholly obtained in accordance with the rules of the Free Trade Agreement or sufficiently worked or processed to fulfill the requirements of the Free Trade Area Agreement.

   (1) Products wholly grown, produced, or manufactured in the United States: enter the letter P in Box 8.

   (2) Products sufficiently worked or processed in the United States of America: enter in Box 8 a Y value for the sum of the cost or value of the domestic materials and the direct cost of processing expressed as a percentage of the ex-factory price of the exported products. (Example: Y=35%.)

4. The declaration of the exporter on this certificate shall be notarized by a notary public and certified by an appropriately constituted local business organization, such as chamber of commerce or board of trade.

---

[1] The conditions specified on this Form are for reference purposes only and do not change in any way or manner the binding rules of origin as specified in Annex III to the FTA Agreement between the United States of America and Israel.

Figure 22.1 U.S. Certificate of Origin for Israel

Target dates for Tariff Removal are in three categories:

1. Immediate removal beginning on January 1, 1989
2. Five equal cuts of 20 percent a year beginning on January 1, 1989.
3. Ten equal cuts of 10 percent a year beginning on January 1, 1989.

The above stages of elimination of tariffs will depend on the type of products involved (i.e., EDP and related equipment, furs, and motorcycles would be in the first group; after-market automobile parts, chemicals, etc., in the second group; and beef, consumer appliances, costume jewelry, etc., in the third group).

For further information regarding products and services traded between these two countries, contact U. S. Department of Commerce, Office of Canada, Room 3033, Washington, D. C., 20230, telephone 202-377-3101, the Canadian Consulate nearest you, or the Canadian Embassy in Washington.

CARIBBEAN BASIN INITIATIVE

This program, started in 1984, offers U. S. importers and investors some unique opportunities. The centerpiece of the program revolves around a twelve-year duty-free access for products from the Caribbean. Under this program, almost all merchandise can be imported without regard to quotas. Also, U. S. citizens will be allowed tax deductions for expenses of business conventions held in eligible countries.

With more than twenty countries involved (Caribbean and Central American), the opportunity to buy and sell products from this part of the world is outstanding.

It is recommended that you send away for the CBI Information Kit ($1.75), Caribbean Basin Business Information Center, U. S. Department of Commerce, Room 3027, Washington, D. C. 20231, telephone 202-377-2527. This booklet will give you a complete background on products available from these countries and what they buy from the United States.

MEXICAN IN-BOND PROGRAM

Started in 1965, this program has offered low-labor cost to U. S. manufacturers while affording the Mexican government and people a source of revenue beneficial to both countries. There are almost 1,000 plants stretching the U. S.–Mexican border area. This program allows firms to send U. S. raw materials into Mexico, have them manufactured into finished products, and returned to the United States; the U.S. firms pay duty on the added-value, labor.

Manufacturers from the United States are allowed 100 percent ownership; duty-free entry of machinery and equipment for operation, with the exception of textile and apparel; no restriction on what items a *maquiladora* (in bond plant) can produce for export; and authorization to lease land and plant facilities within Mexico's coastal and border zones under a thirty-year, beneficial trust arrangement. For further information, contact U. S. Department of Commerce, Mexican Desk Officer, Room 3028, Washington, D. C. 20230, telephone 202-377-4464 or the nearest Mexican Consulate officer and ask for the booklet, "Mexico—Its In-Bond Industry—Your Investment Opportunity."

The Appendices that follow provide you with the names, addresses, and definitions you will need to get started in the import/export trade. Now that you've read this book, the next step is up to you.

Appendix 1

State and Local Sources for International Assistance

Alabama

Alabama Development Office
State Capitol
Montgomery, Ala. 36130
(205) 263-0048

Alabama Intl. Trade Center
University of Alabama
P.O. Box 870396
University, Ala. 35487-0396
(205) 348-7621

Alabama State Docks
P.O. Box 1588
Mobile, Ala. 36633
(205) 690-6112

Alabama World Trade Assn.
Ste. 131, 250 N. Water St.
Mobile, Ala. 36602
(205) 433-3174

Birmingham Area Chamber of Commerce
P.O. Box 10127
Birmingham, Ala. 35202
(201) 323-5461

Center for Intl. Trade & Commerce
Ste. 131, 250 N. Water St.
Mobile, Ala. 36602
(205) 433-1151

North Alabama Intl. Trade Assn.
Madison County Commission
7th Floor
Madison County Courthouse
Huntsville, Ala. 35801
(205) 532-3570

U.S. Dept. of Commerce (ITA)
Room 302, 2015 2nd Ave. N.
Birmingham, Ala. 35203
(205) 731-1331

Source: "Business America," U.S. Dept. of Commerce, International Trade Administration, July 16, 1990.

Alaska

State of Alaska
Dept. of Commerce & Econ. Dev.
P.O. Box D
Juneau, Alaska 99811
(907) 465-2500

State of Alaska, Governor's Office of Intl. Trade
3601 C St., Ste. 798
Anchorage, Alaska 99503
(907) 561-5585

Alaska State Chamber of Commerce
310 Second St.
Juneau, Alaska 99801
(907) 586-2323

Anchorage Chamber of Commerce
437 E St., Ste. 300
Anchorage, Alaska 99501
(907) 272-2401

Fairbanks Chamber of Commerce
709 Second Ave.
Fairbanks, Alaska 99701
(907) 452-1105

U.S. Department of Commerce (ITA)
222 West 7th Ave., Box 32
Anchorage, Alaska 99513-5041
(907) 271-5041

University of Alaska
Alaska Center for Intl. Business
4201 Tudor Centre Dr., Ste. 120
Anchorage, Alaska 99508
(907) 561-2322

World Trade Center Alaska
4201 Tudor Centre Dr., Ste. 300
Anchorage, Alaska 99508
(907) 561-1615

Arizona

Amer. Graduate School of Intl. Management
Thunderbird Campus
Glendale, Ariz. 85306
(602) 978-7115

Arizona Dept. of Commerce
3800 N. Central
Phoenix, Ariz. 85012
(602) 280-1300

Ariz. District Export Council
4617 E. Ocotillo Rd.
Paradise Valley, Ariz. 85253
(602) 840-7439

Ariz. Mexico Commission
1700 W. Washington, State Office Tower
Phoenix, Ariz. 85007
(602) 542-1345

Ariz. World Trade Assn.
c/o Phoenix Chamber of Commerce
34 W. Monroe
Phoenix, Ariz. 85003
(602) 254-5521

Consular Corps of Arizona
8331 E. Rose Lane
Scottsdale, Ariz. 85253
(602) 947-6011

Sunbelt World Trade Assn.
P.O. Box 42995
Tucson, Ariz. 85733
(602) 885-7866

U.S. Dept. of Commerce (ITA)
3412 Federal Bldg.
230 N. 1st Ave.
Phoenix, Ariz. 85025
(602) 379-3285

Arkansas

Ark. Assn. of Planning & Dev. District
P.O. Box 187
Lonoke, Ark. 72086
(501) 676-2721

Ark. District Export Council
Savers Building, Ste. 811
Capitol at Spring St.
Little Rock, Ark. 72201
(501) 378-5794

Ark. Industrial Dev. Commission
#1 State Capitol Mall
Little Rock, Ark. 72201
(501) 371-7678

Ark. Intl. Center, University of Arkansas at
Little Rock
33rd and University
Little Rock, Ark. 72204
(501) 569-3782

Ark. State Chamber of Commerce
P.O. Box 3645
Little Rock, Ark. 72203-3645
(501) 374-9225

Little Rock Chamber of Commerce
#1 Spring St.
Little Rock, Ark. 72201
(501) 374-4871

World Trade Club
1100 TCBY Tower, 425 W. Capitol
Little Rock, Ark. 72201
(501) 688-8229

World Trade Club of Northeast Ark.
Office of Business Research, P.O. Box 970
State University, Ark. 72467
(501) 972-3823

U.S. Dept of Commerce (ITA)
Savers Bldg., Ste. 811
Capitol at Spring St.
Little Rock, Ark. 72201
(501) 378-5794

California

British-American Chamber of Commerce
Stewart Home, Exec. Dir.
41 Sutter St., Ste. 303
San Francisco, Calif. 94104
(415) 296-8645

Calif. Assn. of Port Authorities
1510-14th St.
Sacramento, Calif. 95814
(916) 446-6339

Calif. Chamber of Commerce, Trade Dept.
1201 K St., 12th Floor, P.O. Box 1736
Sacramento, Calif. 95812-1736
(916) 444-6670

Claif. Council for Intl. Trade
700 Montgomery St., Ste. 305
San Francisco, Calif. 94111
(415) 788-4127

Calif. Export Finance Office
World Trade Center, Box 250-S
San Francisco, Calif. 94111
(415) 556-5868

Calif. Export Finance Office
107 S. Broadway, Ste. 8039
Los Angeles, Calif. 90012
(213) 620-2433

Calif. State Dept. of Commerce
1121 L St., Ste. 600
Sacramento, Calif. 95814
(916) 322-1394

Calif. State World Trade Commission
1121 L St. Ste. 310
Sacramento, Calif. 95814
(916) 324-5511

Coordination Council for North American
Affairs on Taiwan
555 Montgomerty St., Ste. 501
San Francisco, Calif. 94111
(415) 362-7680

Coordination Council for North American
Affairs, Cultural Division (Taiwan)
530 Bush St., Ste. 401
San Francisco, Calif. 94108
(415) 398-4979

Econ. Dev. Corp. County of Los Angeles
221 S. Figueroa St., Ste. 100
Los Angeles, Calif. 90112
(213) 625-7752

Export Managers Assn. of Calif.
14549 Victory Blvd., Ste. 5
Van Nuys, Calif. 91411
(818) 782-3350

Foreign Trade Assn. of S. Calif.
900 Wilshire Blvd., Ste. 1434
Los Angeles, Calif. 90017
(213) 672-0634

French-American Chamber of Commerce
Jean Ward Jacote, Exec. Dir., 425 Bush St., Ste. 401
San Francisco, Calif. 94108
(415) 398-2449

German-American Chamber of Commerce
of the Pacific Coast, Inc.
465 California St., Ste. 910
San Francisco, Calif. 94104
(415) 392-2262

Inland Pacific World Trade Committee
1035 W. Bonnie Brae
Ontario, Calif. 91762
(714) 984-3680

Intl. Business Assn. of S. Calif. Long Beach
Chamber of Commerce
One World Trade Center, Ste. 350
Long Beach, Calif. 90831-0350
(213) 436-1251

L.A. Chamber of Commerce
404 Bixel St.
Los Angeles, Calif. 90017
(213) 629-0602

Greater L.A. World Trade Center Assn.
One World Trade Center, Ste. 295
Long Beach, Calif. 90831-0295
(213) 495-7070

Hong Kong Econ. and Trade Office
180 Sutter St., 4th Fl.
San Francisco, Calif. 94104
(415) 397-2215

JETRO San Francisco
360 Post St., Ste. 501
San Francisco, Calif. 94108
(415) 392-1333

Marine Exchange of the San Francisco Bay Region
303 World Trade Center
San Francisco, Calif. 94111
(415) 982-7788

New Zealand-American Assn.
POB 2888
San Francisco, Calif. 94126

Northern Calif. District Export Council
450 Golden Gate Ave., Box 36013
San Francisco, Calif. 94102
(415) 556-5870

Oakland Chamber of Commerce
475-14th St.
Oakland, Calif. 94612
(415) 874-4800

Oakland World Trade Assn.
475-14th St.
Oakland, Calif. 94612-1900
(415) 388-8829

Orange County Intl. Marketing Assn.
Cal State Fullerton
Dept. of Marketing
Fullerton, Calif. 92634
(714) 773-2223

Pacific Indonesian
Chamber of Commerce
1946 Embarcadero, Ste. 200
Oakland, Calif. 94606
(415) 536-1967

Pan American Society of San Francisco
312 Sutter St., Ste. 604
San Francisco, Calif. 94108
(415) 788-4764

San Diego Chamber of Commerce
110 West "C" St., Ste. 1600
San Diego, Calif. 92101
(619) 232-0124

County of San Diego
Intl. Trade Commission
1600 Pacific Highway, Room 375
(Mail Station A-227)
San Diego, Calif. 92101

San Diego District Export Council
6363 Greenwich Drive, Ste. 145
San Diego, Calif. 92122
(619) 557-5395

San Diego Unified Port District
3165 Pacific Highway
San Diego, Calif. 92112
(619) 291-3900

San Diego World Trade Assn.
6363 Greenwich Dr., Ste. 140
San Diego, Calif. 92122
(619) 453-4605

San Francisco Custom Brokers
& Freight Forwarders Assn.
303 World Trade Center
San Francisco, Calif. 94111
(415) 982-7788

San Francisco Intl. Managers Assn.
P.O. Box 2425
Custom House
San Francisco, Calif. 94126
(415) 461-3286

San Francisco Intl. Trade Council
465 California St., 9th Flr.
San Francisco, Calif. 94104
(415) 392-4511

San Francisco World Trade Assn.,
San Francisco Chamber of Commerce
465 California St., 9th Flr.
San Francisco, Calif. 94104
(415) 392-4511, ext. 801

San Mateo County Econ. Dev. Assn.—World
Trade Council
840 Malcolm Rd., Ste. 100
Burlingame, Calif. 94010
(415) 692-7632

Santa Clara Valley World Trade Assn.
P.O. Box 4180
Santa Clara, Calif. 95054
(408) 986-1406

S. Calif. District Export Council
11000 Wilshire Blvd., Rm. 9200
Los Angeles, Calif. 90024
(213) 575-7115

Southwestern College
Small Business & Intl. Trade Center
7101 Siempre Viva Rd., Ste. 200
Otay Mesa, Calif. 92073
(619) 661-1135

U.S.-Arab Chamber of Commerce (Pacific)
One Hallidie Plaza, Ste. 504
San Francisco, Calif. 94102
(415) 398-9200

U.S. Dept. of Commerce (ITA)
11000 Wilshire Blvd., Rm. 9200
Los Angeles, Calif. 90024
(213) 575-7203

U.S. Dept. of Commerce (ITA)
6363 Greenwich Dr., Ste. 145
San Diego, Calif. 92122
(619) 557-5395

U.S. Dept. of Commerce (ITA)
450 Golden Gate Ave., Box 36013
San Francisco, Calif. 94102
(415) 556-5868

U.S. Dept. of Commerce (ITA)
116-A W. 4th St., Ste. 1
Santa Ana, Calif. 92701
(714) 836-2461

U.S. Small Buisness Administration
880 Front St., Rm. 4529
San Diego, Calif. 92188
(619) 557-7272

U.S. Small Business Administration
450 Golden Gate Ave., Box 36044
San Francisco, Calif. 94102
(415) 556-4724

World Trade Center Assn. of Orange County
One Park Plaza, Ste. 150
Irvine, Calif. 92714
(714) 724-9822

Colorado

Colo. Assn. of Commerce and Industry
1776 Lincoln St., Ste. 1200
Denver, Colo. 80203
(303) 831-7411

Colo. Intl. Trade Office
1625 Broadway, Ste. 680
Denver, Colo. 80202
(303) 892-3850

Denver Chamber of Commerce
1600 Sherman St.
Denver, Colo. 80203
(303) 894-8500

Intl. Business Assn. of the Rockies
10200 W. 44th Ave., Ste. 304
Wheat Ridge, Colo. 80033
(303) 422-7905

Rocky Mt. World Trade Center Assn.
World Trade Center, 1625 Broadway, Ste. 680
Denver, Colo. 80202
(303) 592-5760

U.S. Dept. of Commerce (ITA)
World Trade Center, 1625 Broadway, Ste. 680
Denver, Colo. 80202
(303) 844-3246

U.S. Small Business Admin.
999 18th Street, Ste. 701
Denver, Colo. 80202
(303) 294-7872

Connecticut

Conn. Business & Industry Assn.
370 Asylum St.
Hartford, Conn. 06103-2022
(203) 547-1661

Conn. Dept. Econ. Devel. Intl. Division
865 Brook St.
Rocky Hill, Conn. 06067-3405
(203) 258-4256

Conn. District Export Council
450 Main St., Room 610B
Hartford, Conn. 06103

Conn. Foreign Trade Assn.
611 Access Rd.
Stratford, Conn. 06497
(203) 336-7323

Conn. Intl. Trade Assn.
P.O. Box 317
Windsor Locks, Conn. 06096
(203) 272-9175

Conn. Small Business Devel. Center
Room 422, U-41SB
368 Fairfield Rd.
Storrs, Conn. 06268
(203) 486-4135

Greater Hartford Chamber of Commerce
250 Constitution Plaza
Hartford, Conn. 06103
(203) 525-4451

Greater New Haven Chamber of Commerce
195 Church St.
New Haven, Conn. 06510
(203) 787-6735

Middlesex County Chamber of Commerce
393 Main St.
Middletwon, Conn. 06457
(203) 347-6924

Southwestern Area Chamber of Commerce
and Industry Assn. of Conn., Inc.
One Landmark Square
Stamford, Conn. 06901
(203) 359-3220

U.S. Dept. of Commerce (ITA)
450 Main St., Room 610B
Hartford, Conn. 06103
(203) 240-3530

U.S. Small Business Admin.
330 Main St.
Hartford, Conn. 06106
(203) 240-4670

Westconn Intl. Trade Assn. Inc.
P.O. Box 3063
Stamford, Conn. 06905
(203) 468-2863

Delaware

Delaware Dept. of Agriculture
2320 S. DuPont Highway
Dover, Del. 19901
(302) 736-4811

Delaware Dev. Office
Business Dev. Office
P.O. Box 1401
Dover, Del. 19903
(302) 736-4271

Delaware-Eastern Pa. District Export Council
475 Allendale Rd., Ste. 202
King of Prussia, Pa. 19406
(215) 962-4980

U.S. Department of Commerce (ITA)
475 Allendale Rd., Ste. 202
King of Prussia, Pa. 19406
(215) 962-4980

World Trade Center Institute (Del.)
DuPont Bldg., Ste. 1022
Wilmington, Del. 19899
(302) 656-7905

District of Columbia

D.C. Office of Intl. Business
1250 I St., Ste. 1003
Washington, D.C. 20005
(202) 727-1576

U.S. Dept. of Commerce (ITA) Branch Office
Room 1066, Hoover Bldg.
Washington, D.C. 20230
(202) 377-3181

Greater Washington Board of Trade
1129 20th St. N.W.
Washington, D.C. 20036
(202) 857-5900

World Trade Center, Washington
1101 King St.
Alexandria, Va. 22314
(703) 684-6622

Florida

Beacon Council
Intl. Business Development
One World Trade Plaza
Ste. 2400
80 S.W. 8th St.
Miami, Fla. 33130
(305) 536-8000

Coral Gables Chamber of Commerce
Intl. Trade Committee
50 Aragon St.
Coral Gables, Fla. 33134
(305) 446-1657

District Export Council
U.S. Department of Commerce
51 S.W. First Ave., Room 224
Miami, Fla. 33130
(305) 536-5267

Florida Bar International Section
650 Apalachee Parkway
Tallahassee, Fla. 32399-2300
(904) 561-5600

Florida Council of Intl. Dev.
2701 LeJeune Rd., Ste. 330
Coral Gables, Fla. 33134
(305) 448-4035

Florida Customs Brokers
& Forwarders Assn.
P.O. Box 522022
Miami, Fla. 33152
(305) 871-7177

Florida Delegation, Southeast U.S./Japan Assn.
2701 LeJeune Rd., Ste. 330
Coral Gables, Fla. 33134
(305) 448-4035

Florida Dept. of Commerce
Bureau of Intl. Trade and Dev.
331 Collins Building
Tallahassee, Fla. 32399-2000
(904) 488-6124

Florida Department of Commerce
Office for Latin American Trade
2701 LeJeune Rd., Ste. 330
Coral Gables, Fla. 33134
(305) 446-8106

Florida Exporters & Importers Assn.
One World Trade Plaza, Ste. 1800, 80 S.W. 8th St.
Miami, Fla. 33130
(305) 579-0094

Florida Intl. Agricultural Trade Council
Mayo Building, Room 412
Tallahassee, Fla. 32399-0800
(904) 488-4366

Florida Intl. Bankers Assn.
One World Trade Plaza, Ste. 1800, 80 S.W. 8th St.
Miami, Fla. 33130
(305) 579-0064

Florida/Korea Economic Cooperation Committee
2701 LeJeune Rd., Ste. 330
Coral Gables, Fla. 33134
(305) 448-4035

Florida Ports Council
2701 Ponce de Leon Blvd., Ste. 203
Coral Gables, Fla. 33134
(305) 446-7297

Jacksonville Chamber of Commerce Intl. Dev. Dept.
P.O. Box 329
Jacksonville, Fla. 32201
(904) 353-0300

Jacksonville Customs Brokers & Forwarders Assn.
P.O. Box 3342
Jacksonville, Fla. 32206
(904) 356-9646

Greater Miami Chamber of Commerce
Intl. Econ. Development
Omni Complex, 1601 Biscayne Blvd.
Miami, Fla. 33132
(305) 350-7700

Miami Foreign Trade Assn.
2501 N.W. 72nd Ave.
Miami, Fla. 33122
(305) 592-4893

Greater Orlando Chamber of Commerce
Intl. Business, P.O. Box 1234
Orlando, Fla. 32802
(407) 425-1234

Orlando World Trade Assn.
c/o Greater Orlando Chamber of Commerce
P.O. Box 1234
Orlando, Fla. 32802
(407) 425-1234

Polk Intl. Trade Assoc.
600 N. Broadway St., Ste. 300
P.O. Box 1839
Bartow, Fla. 33830
(813) 534-6066

Tampa Bay Intl. Trade Council
Cliff Topping, Exec. Dir., P.O. Box 420
Tampa, Fla. 33601
(813) 228-7777

U.S. Department of Commerce (ITA)
51 S.W. First Ave., Room 224
Miami, Fla. 33130
(305) 536-5267

World Trade Center Miami
One World Trade Plaza, Ste. 1800
80 S.W. 8th St.
Miami, Fla. 33130
(305) 579-0064

World Trade Council of N.W. Florida
P.O. Box 1972
Pensacola, Fla. 32589-1972
(904) 444-1222

Georgia

Business Council of Georgia
233 Peachtree St., Ste. 200
Atlanta, Ga. 30303
(404) 223-2264

Georgia Dept of Agriculture
Capitol Square, 328 Agriculture Building
Atlanta, Ga. 30334
(404) 656-3740

Georgia Dept. of Industry, Trade, and Tourism
285 Peachtree Center Ave., Stes. 1000 & 1100
P.O. Box 1776
Atlanta, Ga. 30303
(404) 656-3556

Georgia Ports Authority
P.O. Box 2406
Savannah, Ga. 31412
(912) 964-1721

U.S. Dept. of Commerce (ITA)
1365 Peachtree St., N.E., Ste. 504
Atlanta, Ga. 30309
(404) 347-7000
Note: as of Aug. 15, the location will be:
Plaza Square N.
4360 Chamblee-Dunwoody Rd., Ste. 310
Atlanta, Ga. 30341

U.S. Dept. of Commerce (ITA)
120 Barnard St.
Savannah, Ga. 31401
(912) 944-4204

Hawaii

Chamber of Commerce of Hawaii
735 Bishop St.
Honolulu, Hawaii 96813
(808) 522-8800

Economic Development Corp. of Honolulu
1001 Bishop St., Ste. 735
Honolulu, Hawaii 96813
(808) 545-4533

Foreign Trade Zone No. 9
521 Ala Moana Blvd., Pier 2
Honolulu, Hawaii 96813
(808) 548-5435

State of Hawaii, Dept. of Bus. and Econ. Dev.
Trade and Ind. Dev. Branch
P.O. Box 2359
Honolulu, Hawaii 96804
(808) 548-7719

Pacific Basin Dev. Council
567 S. King St., Ste. 325
Honolulu, Hawaii 96813
(808) 523-9325

U.S. Dept. of Commerce (ITA)
300 Ala Moana Blvd., Box 50026
Honolulu, Hawaii 96817
(808) 541-1782

Idaho

District Export Council
Idaho Wheat Commission
1109 Main St., Ste. 310
Boise, Idaho 83702
(208) 334-2353

Division of Intl. Business
Idaho Dept. of Commerce
700 W. State St.
Boise, Idaho 83720
(208) 334-2470

Intl. Trade Committee
Boise Area Chamber of Commerce
P.O. Box 2368
Boise, Idaho 83701
(208) 334-5515

U.S. Dept. of Commerce (ITA)
700 W. State St., 2nd Floor
Boise, Idaho 83720
(208) 334-3857

Illinois

Automotive Exporters Club of Chicago
3205 S. Shields Ave.
Chicago, Ill. 60616
(312) 567-6500
Toll Free (1-800) 666-1552

Carnets U.S. Council for Intl. Business
1930 Thoreau Dr., Ste. 101
Schaumburg, Ill. 60173
(708) 490-9696

Central Illinois Coord., Committee for Intl. Trade
205 Arcade Bldg.
725 Wright St.
Champaign, Ill. 61820
(217) 333-1465

Chicago Assn. of Commerce & Industry
World Trade Div.
200 N. LaSalle
Chicago, Ill. 60603
(312) 580-6900

Chicago Convention and Tourism Bureau, Inc.
McCormick Place-on-the-Lake
Chicago, Ill. 60616
(312) 567-8500

Chicago Council on Foreign Relations
116 S. Michigan Ave., 10th Fl.
Chicago, Ill. 60603
(312) 726-3860

Chicago Midwest Credit Management Assn.
315 South N.W., Hwy.
Park Ridge, Ill. 60068
(708) 696-3000

Customs Brokers and Foreign Freight
Forwarders Assn. of Chicago, Inc.
P.O. Box 66584/AMP O'Hare
Chicago, Ill. 60666
(708) 678-5400

Econ. Dev. Commission
1503 Merchandise Mart
Chicago, Ill. 60654
(312) 744-9550

Foreign Credit Insurance Assn.
20 N. Clark St., Ste. 910
Chicago, Ill. 60602
(312) 641-1915

Ill. Ambassadors
233 S. Wacker Drive., 633 Sears Tower
Chicago, Ill. 60606
(312) 715-0734

Ill. Dept. of Commerce and Community Affairs
Intl. Business Div.
310 S. Michigan Ave., Ste. 1000
Chicago, Ill. 60604
(312) 793-7164

Ill. District Export Council
55 E. Monroe, Rm. 1406
Chicago, Ill. 60603
(312) 353-4450

Ill. Export Council
321 N. Clark St., Ste. 550
Chicago, Ill. 60610
(312) 793-1WTC

Ill. Export Dev. Authority
321 N. Clark St., Ste. 550
Chicago, Ill. 60610
(312) 793-4982

Ill. Intl. Port District
3600 E. 95th St.
95th St. at Lake Front
Chicago, Ill. 60617
(312) 646-4400

Ill. Manufacturers' Assn.
175 W. Jackson Blvd., Ste. 1321
Chicago, Ill. 60604
(312) 372-7373

Ill. State Bar Assn.
75 E. Wacker Dr., Ste. 2100
Chicago, Ill. 60601
(312) 726-8775

Ill. Quad City Chamber of Commerce
622 19th St.
Moline, Ill. 61265
(309) 762-3661

Institute for Intl. Education
401 N. Wabash Ave., Ste. 722
Chicago, Ill. 60611
(312) 644-1400

Intl. Air Cargo Assn. of Chicago
P.O. Box 66235/AMF O'Hare
Chicago, Ill. 60666
(312) 782-8122

Intl. Trade Assn. of Greater Chicago
P.O. Box 454
Elk Grove Village, Ill. 60009-0454
(708) 980-4109

Intl. Trade Club of Chicago
203 N. Wabash, Ste. 1102
Chicago, Ill. 60601
(312) 368-9197

Intl. Visitors Center
520 N. Michigan Ave., Ste. 522
Chicago, Ill. 60611
(312) 645-1836

Library of Intl. Relations
77 S. Wacker Dr.
Chicago, Ill. 60605
(312) 567-5234

Mid-America Intl. Agri-Trade Council
(MIATCO)
Drayton Mayers, Exec. Dir.
820 Davis St.
Evanston, Ill. 60201
(708) 866-7300

U.S. Dept. of Commerce (ITA)
55 E. Monroe, Ste. 1406
Chicago, Ill. 60603
(312) 353-4450

U.S. Dept. of Commerce (ITA)
Branch Office
c/o Rockford Area Chamber of Commerce
P.O. Box 1747
Rockford, Ill. 81110-0247
(815) 987-8123 or 8128

U.S. Dept. of Commerce (ITA)
Branch Office
c/o W.R. Harper College
Roselle and Algonquin Rd.
Palatine, Ill. 60067
(312) 397-2000, ext. 2532

U.S. Great Lakes Shipping Assn.
3434 E. 95th St.
Chicago, Ill. 60617
(312) 978-0342

U.S. Small Business Admin. District Export
Develop/SCORE
219 S. Dearborn St., Ste. 437
Chicago, Ill. 60604
(312) 353-4528

World Trade Council of Northern Ill.
515 N. Court
Rockford, Ill. 61103
(815) 987-8100

Indiana

Forum for Intl. Professional Services
Attn: President
One N. Capitol, Ste. 200
Indianapolis, Ind. 46204
(317) 264-3100

Greater Ft. Wayne Chamber of Commerce
826 Ewing St.
Ft. Wayne, Ind. 46802
(219) 424-1435

Indiana-Asean Council, Inc.
One American Square, Box 82017
Indianapolis, Ind. 46282
(317) 685-1341

Indiana Chamber of Commerce
Econ. and Business Dev.
One N. Capitol, Ste. 200
Indianapolis, Ind. 46204-2248
(317) 264-6892

Indiana Dept. of Commerce
Dir. of Intl. Trade
Business Dev. Div.
One N. Capitol, Ste. 700
Indianapolis, Ind. 46204-2288
(317) 232-3527

Michiana World Trade Club
P.O. Box 1715-A
South Bend, Ind. 46634
(219) 289-7323

Tri State World Trade Council
Old Post Office Place
100 N.W. 2nd St., Ste. 202
Evansville, Ind. 47708
(812) 425-8147

U.S. Dept. of Commerce (ITA)
One N. Capitol, Ste. 520
Indianapolis, Ind. 46204-2227
(317) 226-6214

World Trade Club of Indiana, Inc.
One N. Capitol
Ste. 200
Indianapolis, Ind. 46204-2248
(317) 264-6892

Iowa

Cedar Falls Chamber of Commerce
Northeast Iowa Intl. Trade Council
10 Main St., P.O. Box 367
Cedar Falls, Iowa 50613
(319) 266-3593

Cedar Rapids Area Chamber of Commerce
Intl. Trade Office
424 1st Ave., N.E. 52401
P.O. Box 4860
Cedar Rapids, Iowa 52407

Greater Des Moines Chamber of Commerce
300 Saddlery Bldg.
309 Court Ave.
Des Moines, Iowa 50309
(515) 286-4950

Iowa Dept. of Agriculture
Intl. Mkting. Div.
Wallace Bldg.
Des Moines, Iowa 50319
(515) 281-6190

Iowa Dept of Econ. Dev.
Intl. Mkting. Div.
200 E. Grand Ave.
Des Moines, Iowa 50309
(515) 281-3251

Iowa Intl. Trade Center
312-8th St.
Des Moines, Iowa 50309
(515) 246-6013

Midwest Agribusiness Trade and Information
Center (MATRIC)
312-8th St., Ste. 240
Des Moines, Iowa 50309
(515) 246-6027

Sioux City Chamber of Commerce
Siouxland Intl. Trade Council
101 Pierce St.
Sioux City, Iowa 51101
(712) 255-7903

U.S. Dept. of Commerce (ITA) Branch Office
424 1st Ave. N.E.
Cedar Rapids, Iowa 52401
(319) 362-8418

U.S. Dept of Commerce (ITA)
210 Walnut St., Room 817
Des Moines, Iowa 50309
(515) 284-4222

U.S. Small Business Admin.
210 Walnut St., Room 749
Des Moines, Iowa 50309
(515) 284-4522

U.S. Small Business Admin.
373 Collins Rd. N.E.
Cedar Rapids, Iowa 52402
(319) 393-8630

Kansas

Mid-America World Trade Center
301 N. Main St., Epic Center-Ste. 1810
Wichita, Kans. 67202
(316) 291-8475

Kansas Dept. of Commerce
Trade Development Div.
400 SW 8th St., Ste. 500
Topeka, Kans. 66603
(913) 296-4027

Sedgwick County Foreign Trade, Zone #161
525 N. Main St.
Wichita, Kans. 67203
(316) 383-7575

U.S. Dept. of Commerce (ITA)
Wichita Branch Office, River Park Place, Ste. 580
727 N. Waco
Wichita, Kans. 67203
(316) 269-6160

U.S. Small Business Administration
110 E. Waterman
Wichita, Kans. 67202
(316) 269-6273

Whichita Area Chamber of Commerce
350 W. Douglas
Wichita, Kans. 67202
(316) 265-7771

World Trade Council of Wichita
Barton School of Business, Campus Box 88
Wichita State Univ.
Wichita, Kans. 67208
(316) 689-3176

Kentucky

Bluegrass Area Dev. District
3220 Nicholasville Rd.
Lexington, Ky. 40503
(606) 272-6656

Kentuckiana World Commerce Council
P.O. Box 58456
Louisville, Ky. 40258
(502) 583-5551

Ky. Cabinet for Econ. Dev.
Office of Intl. Mkting., Capital Plaza Tower
Frankfort, Ky. 40601
(502) 564-2170

Ky. District Export Council
James Hansen, Vice Chairman
First Nat. Bank of Louisville
P.O. Box 3600
Louisville, Ky. 40233
(502) 581-4228

Louisville/Jefferson County Office of Econ. Dev.
200 Brown & Williamson Tower
401 S. Fourth St.
Louisville, Ky. 40202
(502) 625-3051

Northern Kentucky Intl. Trade Assn.
7505 Sussex Drive
Florence, Ky. 41042
(606) 283-1885

U.S. Dept. of Commerce (ITA)
Courthouse Building
601 W. Broadway, Room 636B
Louisville, Ky. 40202
(502) 582-5066

Louisiana

Chamber of Commerce/New Orleans
and River Region
301 Camp St.
New Orleans, La. 70130
(504) 527-6900

La. Dept. of Econ. Devel.
Office of Intl. Trade, Finance and Devel.
P.O. Box 94185
Baton Rouge, La. 70804-9185
(504) 342-5362

Port of New Orleans
P.O. Box 60046
New Orleans, La. 70160
(504) 528-3259

U.S. Dept. of Commerce (ITA)
432 World Trade Center, 2 Canal St.
New Orleans, La. 70130
(504) 589-6546

World Trade Center of New Orleans
Executive Offices, Ste. 2900, 2 Canal St.
New Orleans, La. 70130
(504) 529-1601

World Trade Club of Greater New Orleans
1132 World Trade Center
2 Canal St.
New Orleans, La. 70130
(504) 525-7201

Maine

Greater Bangor Chamber of Commerce
519 Main St.
P.O. Box 1443
Bangor, Maine 04401
(207) 947-0307

Biddeford-Saco Chamber of Commerce and
Industry
170 Main St.
Biddeford, Maine 04005
(207) 282-1567

Caribou Chamber of Commerce
111 High St.
P.O. Box 357
Caribou, Maine 04736
(207) 498-6156

Lewiston-Auburn Area Chamber of Commerce
179 Lisbon St.
Lewiston, Maine 04240
(207) 783-2249

Maine Chamber of Commerce & Industry
126 Sewall St.
Augusta, Maine 04330
(207) 623-4568

Maine State Dev. Office
State House, Station 59
Augusta, Maine 04333
(207) 289-2656

Oxford Hills Area Dev. Corp.
174 Main St.
Norway, Maine 04268
(207) 743-2425

Greater Portland Chamber of Commerce
142 Free St.
Portland, Maine 04101
(207) 772-2811

U.S. Dept. of Commerce (ITA)
Branch Office
77 Sewall St.
Augusta, Maine 04330
(207) 622-8249

Maryland

Greater Baltimore Committee, Inc.
Ste. 900, 2 Hopkins Plaza
Baltimore, Md. 21201
(301) 727-2820

Baltimore Econ. Dev. Corp.
36 S. Charles St., Ste. 2400
Baltimore, Md. 21201
(301) 837-9305

Baltimore/Washington Common Market
Washington/Baltimore Regional Assn.
Suite 202, 1129 20th St. N.W.
Washington, D.C. 20036
(202) 861-0400

Md. Chamber of Commerce
275 West St., Ste. 400
Annapolis, Md. 21401-3480
(301) 269-0642

Md. Dept. of Econ. and Community Dev.
45 Calvert St.
Annapolis, Md. 21401
(301) 269-3176

Md. Econ. Growth Associates, Inc. (MEGA)
Legg Mason Tower, Ste. 2220
111 S. Clavert St.
Baltimore, Md. 21202
(301) 724-0447

Md. Industrial Dev. Financing Auth. (MIDFA)
Dept. of Econ. Employment Dev.
World Trade Center, 401 E. Pratt St.
Baltimore, Md. 21202
(301) 689-4264

Md. Manufacturing Assn.
Catonsville Community College
800 South Rolling Rd.
Catonsville, Md. 21228
(301) 455-4392

Md. Office of Intl. Trade (MOIT)
7th Floor, World Trade Center
401 E. Pratt St.
Baltimore, Md. 21202
(301) 333-4295

Md. Small Business Dev. Center
123 W. 24th St.
Baltimore, Md. 21210
(301) 889-5772

Md. Port Administration
World Trade Center, 401 E. Pratt St.
Baltimore, Md. 21202-3041
(301) 333-4500

U.S. Chamber of Commerce
1615 H St. N.W.
Washington, D.C. 20062
(202) 463-5486

U.S. Dept of Commerce (ITA)
Room 415, U.S. Customhouse, 40 S. Gay St.
Baltimore, Md. 21202
(301) 962-3560

U.S. Small Business Administration
Suite 453, 10 N. Calvert St.
Baltimore, Md. 21202
(301) 962-2054

Massachusetts

Associated Industries of Mass.
441 Stuart St., 5th Fl.
Boston, Mass. 02116
(617) 262-1180

Greater Boston Chamber of Commerce
Federal Reserve Plaza, 600 Atlantic Ave., 13th Fl.
Boston, Mass. 02210-2200
(617) 227-4500

Central Berkshire Chamber of Commerce
Berkshire Common
Pittsfield, Mass. 01201
(413) 499-4000

Greater Chicopee Chamber of Commerce
93 Church St.
Chicopee, Mass. 01020
(413) 594-2101

Econ. Dev. and Industrial Corp. of Boston
38 Chauncy St.
Boston, Mass. 02111
(617) 725-3342

Fall River Area Chamber of Commerce
200 Pocasset St., P.O. Box 1871
Fall River, Mass. 02722
(508) 676-8266

Intl. Business Center of New England, Inc.
World Trade Center Boston, Ste. 323
Boston, Mass. 02210
(617) 439-5280

Lawrence Chamber of Commerce
264 Essex Street
Lawrence, Mass. 01840
(508) 686-9404

Mass Office of Intl. Trade
100 Cambridge St., Ste. 902
Boston, Mass. 02202
(617) 367-1830

Mass. Office of Business Dev.
100 Cambridge St.—13th Fl.
Boston, Mass. 02202
(617) 727-8380

Metro South Chamber of Commerce
60 School St.
Brockton, Mass. 02401
(508) 586-0500

Metrowest Chamber of Commerce
1617 Worcester Road
Ste. 201
Framingham, Mass. 01701
(508) 879-5600

Lynn Area Chamber of Commerce
170 Union St.
Lynn, Mass. 01901
(617) 592-2900

New England Council, Inc.
581 Boylston St., 7th Fl.
Boston, Mass. 02116
(617) 437-0304

North Central Mass.
Chamber of Commerce
80 Erdman Way
Leominster, Mass. 01453
(508) 343-6487

Northern Berkshire
Chamber of Commerce
69 Main St.
North Adams, Mass. 02147
(413) 663-3735

Smaller Business Assn. of New England, Inc.
69 Hickory Drive
Waltham, Mass. 02254
(617) 890-9070

Greater Springfield Chamber of Commerce
600 Bay State W. Plaza
1500 Main St., Ste. 600
Springfield, Mass. 01115
(413) 734-5671

Tri-Community Chamber of Commerce
11 Main St.
Southbridge, Mass. 01550
(508) 764-3283

U.S. Dept. of Commerce (ITA)
World Trade Center, Ste. 307
Boston, Mass. 02210
(617) 565-8563

Watertown Chamber of Commerce
75 Main St.
Watertown, Mass. 02172
(617) 926-1017

Worcester Area Chamber of Commerce
33 Waldo St.
Worcester, Mass. 01608
(508) 753-2924

Michigan

Ann Arbor Council for Intl. Business
207 E. Washington St.
Ann Arbor, Mich. 48104
(313) 662-0550

BC/CAL/KAL Inland Port Auth. of South
Central Mich. Dev. Corp.
4950 W. Dickman Road
Battle Creek, Mich. 49015
(616) 962-7530

Greater Detroit Chamber of Commerce
600 W. Lafayette Blvd.
Detroit, Mich. 48226
(313) 964-4000

Detroit Customhouse Brokers & Foreign
Freight Forwarders Assn.
c/o Intl. Customs Consultants, Inc.
3874 Penobscot Building
Detroit, Mich. 48226
(313) 964-2190

Detroit/Wayne County Port Auth.
174 S. Clark St.
Detroit, Mich. 48209
(313) 841-6700

Greater Grand Rapids Chamber of Commerce
17 Fountain St. NW
Grand Rapids, Mich. 49503
(616) 771-0300

Great Lakes Trade Adjustment
Assistance Center
School of Bus. Admin., Univ. of Michigan
2901 Baxter Rd.
Ann Arbor, Mich. 48226
(313) 763-4085

KITCO
P.O. Box 1169
Kalamazoo, Mich. 49007
(616) 381-4000

Mich. Dept. of Agriculture
Manufacturing Dev.
P.O. Box 30017
Lansing, Mich. 48909
(517) 373-1054

Mich. Dept. of Commerce
World Trade Services Div.
P.O. Box 30225
Lansing, Mich. 48909
(517) 373-0601

Mich. District Export Council
1140 McNamara Bldg.
Detroit, Mich. 48226
(313) 226-3650

Mich. Manufacturers Assn.
124 E. Kalamazoo
Lansing, Mich. 48933
(517) 372-5900

Mich. Small Business Dev. Center
2727 Second Ave.
Detroit, Mich. 48021
(313) 577-4848

Mich. State Chamber of Commerce
Small Business Programs
600 S. Walnut
Lansing, Mich. 48933
(517) 371-2100

Mich. State University
205 Intl. Center
East Lansing, Mich. 48824-1035
(517) 353-4336

Muskegon Econ. Growth Alliance (MEGA)
349 W. Webster
Muskegon, Mich. 49440
(616) 722-3751

Operation Action U.P.
100 Portage St.
Houghton, Mich. 49931
(906) 482-3210

Twin Cities Area Chamber of Commerce
185 E. Main St.
P.O. Box 1208
Benton Harbor, Mich. 49023
(616) 925-0044

U.S. Customs
2nd Floor, McNamara Bldg.
Detroit, Mich. 48226
(313) 226-3177

U.S. Dept. of Commerce (ITA)
1140 McNamara Bldg.
477 Michigan Ave.
Detroit, Mich. 48226
(313) 226-3650

U.S. Dept. of Commerce (ITA)
300 Monroe NW, Room 406A
Grand Rapids, Mich. 49503
(616) 456-2411

U.S. Small Bus. Admin.
515 McNamara Bldg.
Detroit, Mich. 48226
(313) 226-7240

W. Mich. World Trade Assn.
17 Fountain St. NW
Grand Rapids, Mich. 49503
(616) 771-0319

World Trade Center
Townsend Lathrup
Ste. 1510
150 W. Jefferson Ave.
Detroit, Mich. 48226
(313) 965-6500

World Trade Club
of the Gr. Detroit
Chamber of Commerce
600 W. Lafayette Blvd.
Detroit, Mich. 48226
(313) 964-4000

Minnesota

Minn. Export Finance Authority
1000 World Trade Center, 30 E. 7th St.
St. Paul, Minn. 55101
(612) 297-4658

Minn. Trade Office
1000 World Trade Center, 30 E. 7th St.
St. Paul, Minn. 55101
(612) 297-4227

Minn. World Trade Assn.
P.O. Box 24069
Apple Valley, Minn. 55124
(612) 431-1289

Minn. World Trade Center Corporation
400 Minn. World Trade Center
30 E. 7th St.
St. Paul, Minn. 55101
(612) 297-1580

Seway Port Authority of Duluth
P.O. Box 16877
Duluth, Minn. 55816-0877
(218) 727-8525

U.S. Dept of Commerce (ITA)
108 Federal Building
110 S. 4th St.
Minneapolis, Minn. 55401
(612) 348-1638

Mississippi

Greenville Port Commission
P.O. Box 446
Greenville, Miss. 38702
(601) 335-2683

International Trade Club of Miss., Inc.
P.O. Box 16353
Jackson, Miss. 39236
(601) 949-0245

Jackson County Port Authority
P.O. Box 70
Pascagoula, Miss. 39568
(601) 762-4041

Miss. Dept. of Econ. & Community Dev.
P.O. Box 849
Jackson, Miss. 39205
(601) 359-3552

Miss. State Port Authority
P.O. Box 40
Gulfport, Miss. 39502
(601) 865-4300

U.S. Dept. of Commerce (ITA)
300 Woodrow Wilson Blvd., #328
Jackson, Miss. 39213
(601) 965-4388

Missouri

Intl. Trade Club of Greater Kansas City
920 Main St., Ste. 600
Kansas City, Mo. 64105
(816) 221-1460

Missouri Dept of Agriculture
Intl. Marketing Div., P.O. Box 630
Jefferson City, Mo. 65102
(314) 751-5611

Missouri Dept of Commerce
Intl. Business Office, P.O. Box 118
Jefferson City, Mo. 65102
(314) 751-4855

Missouri District Export Council
7911 Forsyth Blvd., Ste. 610
St. Louis, Mo. 63105
(314) 425-3305

U.S. Dept. of Commerce (ITA)
601 E. 12th St.
Kansas City, Mo. 64106
(816) 426-3142

U.S. Dept. of Commerce (ITA)
7911 Forsyth Blvd., Ste. 610
St. Louis, Mo. 63105
(314) 425-3302

World Trade Club of St. Louis, Inc.
412 S. Clay Ave.
St. Louis, Mo. 63122
(314) 965-9940

Montana

Mont. Dept. of Agriculture
Capital Station
Helena, Mont. 59621
(406) 444-2402

Mont. Dept. of Commerce, Business Dev. Div.
1424-9th Ave.
Helena, Mont. 59620
(406) 444-3923

U.S. Dept. of Commerce (ITA)
Boise Branch Office, 700 W. ST., 2nd Floor
Boise, Idaho 83720
(208) 334-3857

Nebraska

Midwest Intl. Trade Assn.
P.O. Box 37402
Omaha, Neb. 68137
(402) 333-6572

Nebraska Dept. of Econ. Devel.
301 Centennial Mall S.
Lincoln, Neb. 68509
(402) 471-3111

Omaha Chamber of Commerce
1301 Harney St.
Omaha, Neb. 68102
(402) 346-5000

U.S. Dept. of Commerce (ITA)
11133 "O" St.
Omaha, Neb. 68137
(402) 221-3664

U.S. Small Business Admin
11145 Mill Valley Rd.
Omaha, Neb. 68154
(402) 221-3607

Nevada

Commission on Econ. Dev.
Capitol Complex
Carson City, Nev. 89710
(702) 687-4325

Econ. Dev. Auth. of W. Nev.
5190 Neil Rd., #11
Reno, Nev. 89502
(702) 829-3700

Las Vegas Chamber of Commerce
2301 E. Sahara St.
Las Vegas, Nev. 89104
(702) 457-8450

Latin Chamber of Commerce
P.O. Box 7534
Las Vegas, Nev. 89125-2534
(702) 385-7367

Nevada Devel. Auth.
3900 Paradise Rd., #155
Las Vegas, Nev. 89109
(702) 791-0000

Nev. District Export Council
P.O. Box 11007
Reno, Nev. 89520
(702) 784-3844

Nev. World Trade Council
P.O. Box 2882
Carson City, Nev. 89702
(702) 687-4250

Greater Reno/Sparks Chamber of Commerce
405 Marsh Ave.
Reno, Nev. 89509
(702) 786-3030

U.S. Dept. of Commerce (ITA)
1755 E. Plumb Lane, #152
Reno, Nev. 89502
(702) 784-5203

New Hampshire

Greater Manchester Chamber of Commerce
889 Elm St.
Manchester, N.H. 03101
(603) 625-5753

(State of) New Hampshire Dept. of Resources
and Econ. Dev.
P.O. Box 856
Concord, N.H. 03301
(603) 271-2341

N.H. Assn. of Commerce and Industry
1 Tara Blvd., Ste. 211
Nashua, N.H. 03062
(603) 891-2471

Greater Portsmouth Chamber of Commerce
500 Market St., Box 239
Portsmouth, N.H. 03801
(603) 436-1118

U.S. Dept. of Commerce (ITA)
World Trade Center, Ste. 306
Boston, Mass. 02210
(617) 565-8563

New Jersey

Center for Intl. Business Education (CIBE)
James H. Levin Bldg.
Kilmer Campus, Rutgers Univ., P.O. Box 5062
New Brunswick, N.J. 08903-5062
(201) 932-5639

Delaware River Port Auth., World Trade Div.
Bridge Plaza
Camden, N.J. 08101
(609) 963-6420

Intl. Round Table
Bergen County Community College
400 Paramus Rd.
Paramus, N.J. 07652
(201) 477-7167

(Metro) Newark Chamber of Commerce
40 Clinton St.
Newark, N.J. 07102-3795

N.J. Business and Industry Assn.
102 W. State St.
Trenton, N.J. 08608
(609) 393-7707

(State of) N.J. Div of Intl. Trade
744 Broad St., Rm. 1709
Newark, N.J. 07102
(201) 466-8499

N.J./N.Y. Port Auth.
One World Trade Center, 63-S
New York, N.Y. 10048
(212) 466-8499

N.J. Small Business Dev. Center
Rutgers, State Univ. Grad. School
of Management
180 University Ave.
Newark, N.J. 07102
(201) 648-5950

Princeton Chamber of Commerce
Intl. Business Dev. Council
100-300 Village Blvd.
Princeton Forrestal Village
Princeton, N.J. 08540
(609) 520-1776

U.S. Dept. of Commerce (ITA)
3131 Princeton Pike
Bldg. 6, Ste. 100
Trenton, N.J. 08648
(609) 989-2100

New Mexico

(State of) New Mexico Economic Dev.
and Tourism Dept.
Trade Division
1100 St. Francis Dr.
Joseph M. Montoya Bldg.
Santa Fe, N.M. 87503
(505) 827-0307

New Mexico Dept. of Agriculture
Intl. Marketing Program
Box 30005, Dept. 5600
New Mexico State Univ. Campus
Las Cruces, N.M. 88003
(505) 646-4929

New Mexico Intl. Trade Council
c/o SW Intl. Technology
and Trading Co., Ltd.
4300 Silver, S.E.
Albuquerque, N.M. 87108
(505) 821-2318

New Mexico Small Business Dev. Center
P.O. Box 4187
Santa Fe, N.M. 87502-4187
(505) 438-1362

New Mexico Trade Fdn.
c/o Econ. Dev. and Tourism Dept.
1100 St. Francis Dr.
Joseph M. Montoya Bldg.
Santa Fe, N.M. 87503
(505) 827-0264

U.S. Dept. of Commerce (ITA)
Branch Office
c/o Small Business Administration
625 Silver, S.W.
3rd Floor
Albuquerque, N.M. 87102
(505) 766-2070

U.S. Dept. of Commerce (ITA)
Branch Office
c/o Econ. Dev. and Tourism Dept.
1100 St. Francis Dr.
Joseph Montoya Bldg.
Santa Fe, N.M. 87503
(505) 988-6261

U.S. Small Business Administration
625 Silver, S.W., 3rd Fl.
Albuquerque, N.M. 87102
(505) 766-1879

New York

Greater Buffalo Chamber of Commerce
Develop./Govt. Relations
107 Delaware Ave.
Buffalo, N.Y. 14202
(716) 852-7100

Buffalo World Trade Assn.
P.O. Box 591
Williamsville, N.Y. 14221
(716) 631-5602

Canada-U.S. Trade Center
Dept. of Geography
Fronczak Hall
Buffalo, N.Y. 14260
(716) 636-2299

Foreign Credit Insurance Assn.
Sharyn H. Hess, Asst. V.P.
40 Rector St., 11th Floor
New York, N.Y. 10006
(212) 306-5000

Intl. Executives Assn., Inc.
13 E. 37th St., 8th Fl.
New York, N.Y. 10016
(212) 683-9755

Long Island Assn. Inc.
80 Hauppaugo Rd.
Commack, N.Y. 11725
(516) 499-4400

Mohawk Valley World Trade Council
P.O. Box 4126
Utica, N.Y. 13504
(800) 848-8483

Nat. Assn. of Credit Mgrs. (NACM)
Finance Credit Intl. Business (FCIB)
520 8th Ave.
New York, N.Y. 10018
(212) 947-5368

Nat. Assn. of Credit Management
(NACM)—Upstate New York
250 Delaware Ave., Ste. 4
Buffalo, N.Y. 14202
(716) 854-7018

Nat. Customs Brokers & Forwarders Assn.
of America, Inc.
One World Trade Center, Rm. 1153
New York, N.Y. 10048
(212) 432-0050

N.Y. Chamber of Commerce & Industry
200 Madison Ave.
New York, N.Y. 10016
(212) 561-2028

N.Y. State Dept. of Commerce
Dept. of Econ. Dev.
1515 Broadway
New York, N.Y. 10036
(212) 827-6100

Overseas Automotive Club, Inc.
Secretary
P.O. Box 1638
300 Sylvan Ave.
Englewood Cliffs, N.J. 07632
(201) 894-6810

Port Auth. of N.Y. and N.J.
Trade Devel. Office
Rm. 64E, One World Trade Center
New York, N.Y. 10048
(212) 466-8333

Greater Rochester Metro
Chamber of Commerce
World Trade Dept.
Intl. Trade & Transportation
55 St. Paul St.
Rochester, N.Y. 14604
(716) 454-2220

Southern Tier World Commerce Assn.
c/o School of Management
SUNY Binghamton
P.O. Box 60000
Binghamton, N.Y. 13902-6000
(607) 777-2342

Greater Syracuse Chamber of Commerce
Intl. Trade Council
100 E. Onondaga St.
Syracuse, N.Y. 13202
(315) 470-1343

Tappan Zee Intl. Trade Assn.
One Blue Hill Plaza
Pearl River, N.Y. 10965
(914) 735-7040

U.S. Council for Intl. Business
1212 Ave. of the Americas
New York, N.Y. 10036
(212) 354-4480

U.S. Dept. of Commerce (ITA)
1312 Fed. Bldg.
Buffalo, N.Y. 14202
(716) 846-4101

U.S. Dept. of Commerce (ITA)
26 Federal Plaza
Rm. 3718
New York, N.Y. 10278
(212) 264-0634

U.S. Dept. of Commerce (ITA)
111 E. Ave.
Ste. 220
Rochester, N.Y. 14604
(716) 263-6480

U.S. Small Bus. Admin.
26 Fed. Plaza, Rm. 3130
New York, N.Y. 10278
(212) 264-4507

U.S. Small Bus. Admin., Officer
100 S. Clinton St.
Syracuse, N.Y. 13260
(315) 423-5383

Westchester County Assn. Inc.
World Trade Club of Westchester
235 Mamaroneck Ave.
White Plains, N.Y. 10605
(914) 948-6444

Western N.Y. Intl. Trade Council
P.O. Box 1271
Buffalo, N.Y. 14240
(716) 852-7160

World Commerce Assn. of Central N.Y.
100 E. Onandaga St.
Syracuse, N.Y. 13202
(315) 470-1343

World Trade Institute
One World Trade Center
New York, N.Y. 10048
(212) 466-4044

North Carolina

N.C. Dept of Agriculture
P.O. Box 27647
Raleigh, N.C. 27611
(919) 733-7912

N.C. Dept. of Econ. and Community Dev.
Intl. Division
430 N. Salisbury St.
Raleigh, N.C. 27611
(919) 733-7193

N.C. District Export Council
P.O. Box 2690
High Point, N.C. 27261
(919) 889-6621

N.C. State University Intl. Trade Center
P.O. Box 7401
Raleigh, N.C. 27695-7401
(919) 737-3793

N.C. World Trade Assn.
Reg. Dev. Institute, E. Carolina University
Willis Bldg., Corner First & Reade St.
Greenville, N.C. 27858
(919) 757-6650

Research Triangle World Trade Center
1007 Slater Road, Ste. 200
Morrisville, N.C. 27560
(919) 941-5120

U.S. Dept. of Commerce (ITA)
P.O. Box 1950
Greensboro, N.C. 27402
(919) 333-5345

North Dakota

Fargo Chamber of Commerce
321 N. 4th St.
Fargo, N.D. 58108
(701) 237-5678

N.D. Econ. Devel. Commission
Liberty Memorial Bldg.
State Capital Grounds
Bismarck, N.D. 58505
(701) 224-2810

U.S. Dept. of Commerce (ITA)
11133 "O" St.
Omaha, Neb. 68137
(402) 221-3664

U.S. Small Business Admin.
P.O. Fed. Bldg., Box 3086
Fargo, N.D. 58108
(701) 239-5131

Ohio

Akron Reg. Dev. Board
Intl. Business and Trade Assn.
One Cascade Plaza, Ste. 800
Akron, Ohio 44308
(216) 379-3157

Greater Cincinnati Chamber of Commerce
300 Carew Tower
441 Vine St.
Cincinnati, Ohio 45202
(513) 579-3170

Cincinnati Council on World Affairs
Tri-State Building, Ste. #300
432 Walnut St.
Cincinnati, Ohio 45202
(513) 621-2320

Port of Cleveland
Cleveland-Cuyahoga County Port Auth.
101 Erieside Ave.
Cleveland, Ohio 44114-1095
(216) 241-8004

Cleveland Council on World Affairs
539 Hanna Bldg.
1422 Euclid Ave.
Cleveland, Ohio 44115
(216) 781-3730

Cleveland World Trade Assn.
Trade & Business Dev.
690 Huntington Bldg.
Cleveland, Ohio 44115
(216) 621-3300

Columbus Area Chamber of Commerce
Intl. Trade Dev. Office
37 N. High St.
Columbus, Ohio 43215
(614) 221-1321

Columbus Council on World Affairs
Two Nationwide Plaza, 280 N. High St.
Columbus, Ohio 43215
(614) 249-8450

Dayton Council on World Affairs
Wright Brothers Branch
P.O. Box 9190
Dayton, Ohio 45409
(513) 229-2319

Miami Valley Intl. Trade Assn.
P.O. Box 291945
Dayton, Ohio 45429
(513) 439-9465

N. Central Ohio Intl. Trade Club
c/o Warren Rupp, Inc.
P.O. Box 1568
Mansfield, Ohio 44901
(419) 524-8388

N. Ohio District Export Council
Ste. 600, 668 Euclid Ave.
Cleveland, Ohio 44114
(216) 522-4750

Ohio Dept. of Agriculture
Ohio Dept. Bldg., Room 607
65 S. Front St.
Columbus, Ohio 43215
(614) 466-2732

Ohio Dept. of Dev., Intl. Trade Division
77 S. High St., 29th Floor
Columbus, Ohio 43215
(614) 466-5017

Ohio Foreign Commerce Assn., Inc.
21010 Center Ridge Rd., Ste. 702
Rocky River, Ohio 44116
(216) 333-6069

S. Ohio District Export Council
9504 Fed. Office Bldg.
550 Main St.
Cincinnati, Ohio 45202
(513) 684-2944

Toledo Area Intl. Trade Assn.
218 Huron St.
Toledo, Ohio 43604
(419) 243-8191

Port of Toledo, Dir. of Trade Dev.
Toledo-Lucas County Port Auth.
One Maritime Plaza
Toledo, Ohio 43604-1866
(419) 243-8251

U.S. Customs Service
Room 116, Dayton Intl. Airport
Vandalia, Ohio 45377
(513) 225-2877

U.S. Customs Service
55 Erieview Plaza
Cleveland, Ohio 44114
(216) 522-4284

U.S. Customs Service
8511 Fed. Office Bldg.
550 Main St.
Cincinnati, Ohio 45202
(513) 684-3682

U.S. Customs Service
4600 17th Ave.
Room 221
Columbus, Ohio 43219
(614) 469-6670

U.S. Department of Commerce (ITA)
Great Lakes Region IV
9504 Fed. Office Bldg.
550 Main St.
Cincinnati, Ohio 45202
(513) 684-2944

U.S. Dept. of Commerce (ITA)
Ste. 600, 668 Euclid Ave.
Cleveland, Ohio 44114
(216) 522-4750

U.S. Small Business Administration
317 AJC Fed. Bldg.
1240 E. 9th St.
Cleveland, Ohio 44199
(216) 522-4194

Youngstown Area Chamber of Commerce
World Trade Committee
200 Wick Bldg.
Youngstown, Ohio 44503-1474
(216) 744-2131

Oklahoma

Center for Intl. Trade Dev.
Oklahoma State University
109 Cordell N.
Stillwater, Okla. 74078
(405) 744-7693

Foreign Zone #53
Tulsa Port of Catoosa
5555 Bird Creek Ave.
Catoosa, Okla. 74015
(918) 266-5830

Foreign Trade Zone #106
Foreign Trade Zone Administrator
City of Oklahoma City Planning and Econ. Dev.
300 S.W. 7th St.
Oklahoma City, Okla. 73109
(405) 297-2583

Metro. Tulsa Chamber of Commerce
Econ. Dev. Division
616 S. Boston Ave.
Tulsa, Okla. 74119
(918) 585-1201

Muskogee City-County Port Authority
Foreign Trade Zone #164
Route 6, Port 50
Muskogee, Okla. 74401
(918) 682-7886

Oklahoma City Intl. Trade Assn.
P.O. Box 1936
Oklahoma City, Okla. 73101
(405) 478-3530

Oklahoma Dept. of Agriculture
Market Dev. Division
2800 Lincoln Blvd.
Oklahoma City, Okla. 73105
(405) 521-3864

Oklahoma Dept of Commerce
6601 Broadway Extension
Oklahoma City, Okla. 73116
(405) 841-5217

Oklahoma District Export Council
6601 Broadway Extension
Oklahoma City, Okla. 73116
(405) 231-5302

Oklahoma State Chamber of Commerce
4020 Lincoln Blvd.
Oklahoma City, Okla. 73105
(405) 424-4003

Small Business Development Center
6420 S.E. 15th
Midwest City, Okla. 73110
(405) 841-5224

Tulsa International Council
616 S. Boston Ave.
Tulsa, Okla. 74119
(918) 584-4685

Tulsa Port of Catoosa
5350 Cimarron Rd.
Catoosa, Okla. 74015
(918) 266-2291

Tulsa World Trade Assn.
616 S. Boston Ave.
Tulsa, Okla. 74119
(918) 585-1201, Ext. 234

U.S. Dept. of Commerce (ITA)
6601 Broadway Extension
Oklahoma City, Okla. 73116
(405) 231-5302

Oregon

Central Oregon Intl. Trade Council
2600 NW College Way
Bend, Ore. 97701

Intl. Trade Insititute
One World Trade Center
121 SW Salmon, Ste. 230
Portland, Ore. 97204
(503) 725-3246

Mid Willamette Valley Council of Governments
105 High St., S.E.
Salem, Ore. 96301

Oregon Dept. of Agriculture
One World Trade Center
121 SW Salmon, Ste. 240
Portland, Ore. 97204
(503) 229-6734

Oregon District Export Council
One World Trade Center
121 SW Salamon, Ste. 242
Portland, Ore. 97204
(503) 228-6501

Oregon Econ. Devel. Dept., Intl. Trade Division
One World Trade Center
121 SW Salamon, Ste. 300
Portland, Ore. 97204
(503) 229-5625

Oregon Trade & Marketing Center, Inc.
One World Trade Center
121 SW Salamon, Ste. 200
Portland, Ore. 97204
(503) 274-7475

Pacific Northwest Intl. Trade Assn.
200 SW Market, Ste. 190
Portland, Ore. 97201
(503) 228-4361

Portland Chamber of Commerce
221 NW 2nd Ave.
Portland, Ore. 97209
(503) 228-9411

Small Business Intl. Trade Program
One World Trade Center
121 SW Salamon, Ste. 210
Portland, Ore. 97204
(503) 274-7482

Southern Oregon Intl. Trade Council
290 NE "C" St.
Grants Pass, Ore. 97526

U.S. Dept. of Commerce (ITA)
One World Trade Center
121 SW Salmon
Ste. 242
Portland, Ore. 97204
(503) 326-3001

Western Wood Products Assn.
522 SW 5th Ave.
Portland, Ore. 97204
(503) 224-3930

Willamette Intl. Trade Center
Room 209, 1059 Willamette
Eugene, Ore. 97401
(503) 686-0195

World Trade Center Portland
One World Trade Center
121 SW Salmon, Ste. 250
Portland, Ore. 97204
(503) 464-8888

Pennsylvania

Airport Area Chamber of Commerce
986 Brodhead Rd.
Moon Township
Coraopolis, Pa. 15106
(412) 264-6270

American Soc. of Intl. Executives, Inc.
18 Sentry Parkway, Ste. One
Blue Bell, Pa. 19422
(215) 540-2295

Berks County Chamber of Commerce
P.O. Box 1698, 645 Penn St.
Reading, Pa. 19603
(215) 376-6766

Del. County Chamber of Commerce
602 E. Baltimore Pike
Media, Pa. 19063
(215) 565-3677

Del.-Eastern Pa. District Export Council
475 Allendale Rd., Ste. 202
King of Prussia, Pa. 19406
(215) 962-4980

Del. River Port Auth.
World Trade Division
Bridge Plaza
Camden, N.J. 08101
(215) 925-8780, ext. 2264

Econ. Dev. Council of NE Pa.
1151 Oak St.
Pittston, Pa. 18640
(717) 655-5581

Erie-Western Pa. Port Auth.
17 W. Dobbins Landing
Erie, Pa. 16507-1424
(814) 455-7557

Foreign Trade Zone #33
Regional Industrial Dev. Corp.
1220 Frick Bldg.
Pittsburgh, Pa. 15219
(412) 471-3939

Greater Willow Grove Chamber of Commerce
603 N. Easton Rd.
P.O. Box 100
Willow Grove, Pa. 19090
(215) 657-2227

Intl. Business Forum
1520 Locust St.
Philadelphia, Pa. 19102
(215) 732-3250

Intl. Trade Committee
Erie Excellence Council
928 West 19th St.
Erie, Pa. 16502
(814) 455-6533

Intl. Trade Executives Club of Pittsburgh
2002 Federal Bldg.
1000 Liberty Ave.
Pittsburgh, Pa. 15222
(412) 644-2850

Lancaster Chamber of Commerce and Industry
Southern Market Center
100 S. Queen St.
P.O. Box 1558
Lancasater, Pa. 17603-1558
(717) 397-3531

Lehigh Univ. Small Business Dev. Center
Intl. Trade Dev. Program
310 Broadway
Bethlehem, Pa. 18015
(215) 758-4630

Montgomery County Dept. of Commerce
#3 Stony Creek Office Center
151 W. Marshall Road
Norristown, Pa. 19401
(215) 278-5950

North Central Pa. Regional Planning
& Dev. Commission
P.O. Box 488
651 Montmorenci Ave.
Ridgeway, Pa. 15853
(814) 772-6901 or (814) 773-3162

Northern Tier Reg. Planning
and Dev. Commission
507 Main St.
Towanda, Pa. 18848
(717) 265-9103

NW Pa. Reg. Planning & Dev. Commission
614 11th St.
Franklin, Pa. 16323
[Erie] (814) 871-7322; [Franklin] (814) 437-3024

Pa. Dept. of Agriculture
Bureau of Markets
2301 N. Cameron St.
Harrisburg, Pa. 17110
(717) 783-3181

Pa. Dept. of Commerce, Office of Intl. Dev.
Bureau of Intl. Trade, 433 Forum Bldg.
Harrisburg, Pa. 17120
(717) 787-7190

Pa. Dept. of Commerce, Bureau of Intl. Dev.
433 Forum Bldg.
Harrisburg, Pa. 17120
(717) 783-5107

Pa. State Univ. Small Business Dev. Center
Export Development Program
of South Central Pa.
Middletown, Pa. 17057
(717) 948-6069

Greater Philadelphia Chamber of Commerce
1346 Chestnut St., Ste. 800
Philadelphia, Pa. 19107
(215) 545-1234

Philadelphia Industrial Dev. Corp.
123 So. Broad St., 22nd Floor
Philadelphia,. Pa. 19109
(215) 875-3508

Pittsburgh Council for Intl. Visitors
Rm. 263, Thackeray Hall, 139 University Place
Pittsburgh, Pa. 15260
(412) 624-7800

Greater Pittsburgh World Trade Assn.
Greater Pittsburgh Chamber of Commerce
3 Gateway Center, 14th Floor
Pittsburgh, Pa. 15222
(412) 392-4500

SEDA-Council of Governments
Timberhaven Rd #1
Lewisburg, Pa. 17838
(717) 524-4491

Small Business Dev. Center
Clarion Univ. of Pa.
Dana Still Bldg.
Clarion, Pa. 16214
(814) 226-2060

Small Business Dev. Center
Duquense Univ.
Rockwell Hall, Room 10
Concourse
600 Forbes Ave.
Pittsburgh, Pa. 15282
(412) 434-6233

Small Business Dev. Center
Indiana Univ. of Pa.
202 McElhaney Hall
Indiana, Pa. 15705
(412) 357-2929

Small Business Dev. Center
St. Francis College
Loretto, Pa. 15940
(814) 472-3200

Small Business Dev. Center
St. Vincent College
Latrobe, Pa. 15650
(412) 537-4572

Small Business Dev. Center
Univ. of Pittsburgh
343 Mervis Hall
Pittsburgh, Pa. 15260
(412) 648-1544

Southern Alleghenies Commission
541 58th St.
Altoona, Pa. 16602
(814) 949-6500

SW Pa. Econ. Dev. District
12300 Perry Highway
Wexford, Pa. 15090
(412) 935-6122

U.S. Customs Service
822 Federal Bldg.
1000 Liberty Ave.
Pittsburgh, Pa. 15222
(412) 644-3589

U.S. Dept. of Commerce (ITA)
Erie Associate Office
3537 W. 12th St.
Erie, Pa. 16505
(814) 459-3335

U.S. Dept. of Commerce (ITA)
475 Allendale Rd.
Ste. 202
King of Prussia, Pa. 19406
(215) 962-4980

U.S. Dept. of Commerce (ITA)
2002 Federal Bldg.
1000 Liberty Ave.
Pittsburgh, Pa. 15222
(412) 644-2850

U.S. Small Business Admin.
475 Allendale Rd.
Ste. 201
King of Prussia, Pa. 19406
(215) 962-3815

U.S. Small Business Admin.
Fifth Floor, 960 Penn Ave.
Pittsburgh, Pa. 15222
(412) 644-5438

Univ. of Scranton Small Business Dev. Center
415 N. Washington Ave.
Scranton, Pa. 18510
(717) 961-7588

Western Pa. District Export Council
1000 Liberty Ave.
Pittsburgh, Pa. 15222
(412) 644-2850

Wharton Export Network
Wharton School
Univ. of Pennsylvania
3733 Spruce St.
413 Vance Hall
Philadelphia, Pa. 19104
(215) 898-4187

Wilkes College Small Business Dev. Center
Hollenbeck Hall
192 S. Franklin St.
Wilkes Barre, Pa. 18766

Women's Intl. Trade Assn.
P.O. Box 40004
Philadelphia, Pa. 19106
(215) 922-6610

World Trade Assn. of Philadelphia
P.O. Box 58640
Philadelphia, Pa. 19102
(215) 988-0711

Puerto Rico

District Export Council
Diversified Farming Complex, Firm Delivery
Ponce, P.R. 00731
(809) 836-1818

P.R. Chamber of Commerce
P.O. Box 3789
San Juan, P.R. 00904
(809) 721-6060

P.R. Department of Commerce
P.O. Box 4275
San Juan, P.R. 00905
(809) 721-3290

P.R. Econ. Devel. Admin.
GPO Box 2350
San Jaun, P.R. 00936
(809) 758-4747

P.R. Manufacturers Assn.
P.O. Box 2410
Hato Rey, P.R. 00919
(809) 759-9445

P.R. Products Assn.
GPO Box 3631
San Juan, P.R. 00936
(809) 753-8484

U.S. Dept. of Commerce (ITA)
Rm. G-55, Federal Building
Hato Rey, P.R. 00918
(809) 766-5555

Rhode Island

Greater Providence Chamber of Commerce
30 Exchange Terrace
Providence, R.I. 02903
(501) 521-5000

R.I. Dept. of Econ. Dev.
7 Jackson Walkway
Providence, R.I. 02903
(401) 277-2601

U.S. Dept. of Commerce (ITA)
Branch Office, 7 Jackson Walkway
Providence, R.I. 02903
(401) 528-5104

South Carolina

Charleston-Trident Chamber of Commerce
Intl. Dept.
P.O. Box 975
Charleston, S.C. 29402
(803) 577-2510

Greater Columbia Chamber of Commerce
P.O. Box 1360
Columbia, S.C. 29202
(803) 733-1110

Greater Greenville Chamber of Commerce
P.O. Box 10048
Greenville, S.C. 29603
(803) 242-1050

Jobs-Economic Dev. Authority, Program Mgr.
1201 Main St., Ste. 1750
Columbia, S.C. 29201
(803) 737-0079

Low Country Intl. Trade Assn.
P.O. Box 159
Charleston, S.C. 29402
(803) 724-3566

Midlands Intl. Trade Assn.
101 Trade Zone Drive, Ste. 1A
West Columbia, S.C. 29169-3911
(803) 822-5039

Pee Dee Intl. Trade Assn. (Florence)
P.O. Box 25
Darlington, S.C. 29532
(803) 393-4341

Small Business Dev. Center
College of Business
Univ. of South Carolina
Columbia, S.C. 29208
(803) 777-5118

S.C. Dist. Export Council
1835 Assembly St.
Ste. 172
Columbia, S.C. 29201
(803) 765-5345

S.C. State Dev. Board
Intl. Business Div.
P.O. Box 927
Columbia, S.C. 29202
(803) 737-0400

S.C. State Ports Authority
P.O. Box 817
Charleston, S.C. 29402
(803) 577-8100

Western S.C. Intl. Trade Assn.
P.O. Box 2081
Greenville, S.C. 29602-2081
(803) 574-4400

U.S. Dept. of Commerce (ITA)
1835 Assembly St., Ste. 172
Columbia, S.C. 29201
(803) 765-5345

South Dakota

Rapid City Area Chamber of Commerce
P.O. Box 747
Rapid City, S.D. 57709
(605) 343-1744

Sioux Falls Chamber of Commerce
315 S. Phillips St.
Sioux Falls, S.D. 57101
(605) 336-1620

S.D. Governor's Office of Econ. Dev.,
Export & Mktg. Div.
Capitol Lake Plaza
Pierre, S.D. 57501
(605) 773-5032

U.S. Dept. of Commerce (ITA)
11133 "O" St.
Omaha, Neb. 68137
(402) 221-3664

U.S. Small Business Admin.
101 S. Main Ave.
Sioux Falls, S.D. 57102
(605) 336-2980, ext. 231

Tennessee

E. Tenn Intl. Commerce Council
P.O. Box 2688
Knoxville, Tenn. 37901

Memphis Area Chamber of Commerce
P.O. Box 224
Memphis, Tenn. 38101
(901) 575-3500

Memphis World Trade Club
P.O. Box 3577
Memphis, Tenn. 38173
(901) 678-2500

Middle Tenn. World Trade Club
P.O. Box 100574
Nashville, Tenn. 37210-0574

Mid-South Exporters' Roundtable
P.O. Box 3521
Memphis, Tenn. 38173
(901) 320-2210

Tenn. Dept. of Agriculture
Ellington Agricultural Center
P.O. Box 40627
Melrose Sta.
Nashville, Tenn. 37204
(615) 360-0160

Tenn. District Export Office
Pen Trading Co., P.O. Box 2128
Brentwood, Tenn. 37027
(615) 371-7350

Tenn. Export Office
320 6th Ave. N., 7th Floor
Nashville, Tenn. 37219-5308
(615) 741-5870

World Trade Club of Chattanooga
1001 Market St.
Chattanooga, Tenn. 37402

U.S. Dept. of Commerce (ITA)
22 N. Front St., Ste. 200
Memphis, Tenn. 38103
(901) 544-4137

U.S. Dept. of Commerce (ITA)
Ste. 1114, 404 James Robertson Pkwy.
Nashville, Tenn. 37129-1505
(615) 736-5161

Texas

Austin Foreign Trade Council
P.O. Box 4533
Austin, Tex. 78765
(512) 928-3706

Austin World Affairs Council
P.O. Box 1967
Austin, Tex. 78767
(512) 469-0158

Port of Beaumont
P.O. Drawer 2297
Beaumont, Tex. 77704
(409) 835-5367

Brownsville Econ. Dev. Council
1600 E. Elizabeth
Brownsville, Tex. 78520
(512) 541-1183

Brownsville Minority Business Development Center
2100 Boca Chica Tower, Suite 301
Brownsville, Tex. 78521-2265
(512) 546-3400

Brownsville Navigation District
P.O. Box 3070
Brownsville, Tex. 78523-3070
(512) 542-4341

Cameron County Private Industry Council
285 Kings Hwy.
Brownsville, Tex. 78521
(512) 542-4351

Center for Govt. Contracts
1400 Woodlock Forest Dr.
Ste. 500
The Woodlands, Tex. 77380
(713) 367-5777

Port of Corpus Christi Auth.
P.O. Box 1541
Corpus Christi, Tex. 78403
(512) 882-5633

Corpus Christi Area Econ. Dev. Corp.
1201 N. Shoreline
P.O. Box 640
Corpus Christi, Tex. 78403-0640
(512) 883-5571

Port of Corpus Christi Foreign Trade Zone
P.O. Box 1541
Corpus Christi, Tex. 78403
(512) 882-5633

Corpus Christi Small Business Development Center
P.O. Box 640
Corpus Christi, Tex. 78403
(512) 883-5571

Council for S. Texas Econ. Progress (COSTEP)
1701 W. Business Hwy. 83
Texas Commerce Bank
Ste. 600
McAllen, Tex. 78501
(512) 682-1201

City of Dallas
Office of Intl. Affairs
City Hall, 5EN
1500 Marilla
Dallas, Tex. 75201
(214) 670-3319

Dallas Council on World Affairs
P.O. Box 58232
Dallas, Tex. 75258
(214) 748-5663

Dallas/Fort Worth Airport Board
Development/FTZ
P.O. Box DFW
DFW Airport, Tex. 75261
(214) 574-3079

Dallas Partnership
Greater Dallas Chamber of Commerce
Intl. Bus. Dev., 1201 Elm St.
Ste. 2000
Dallas, Tex. 75270
(214) 746-6739

Foreign Credit Insurance Assn.
600 Travis, Ste. 2860
Houston, Tex. 77002
(713) 227-0987

Port of Houston Authority
1519 Capitol Ave.
Houston, Tex. 77001
(713) 226-2100

Greater Houston Partnership
World Trade Division, 100 Milam, 25th Floor
Houston, Tex. 77002
(713) 658-2408

Intl. Small Business Dev. Center
P.O. Box 58299
Dallas, Tex. 75258
(214) 653-1777

Intl. Trade Assn. of Dallas/Fort Worth
President
P.O. Box 58009
Dallas, Tex. 75258
(214) 748-3777

Intl. Trade Resource Center
Ste. 150, 2050 Stemmons Freeway
Dallas, Tex. 75258
(214) 653-1113

McAllen Foreign Trade Zone
Joyce Dean, V.P. of Operations
6401 S. 33rd St.
McAllen, Tex. 78503
(512) 682-4306

McAllen Minority Business Development
Center
1701 W. Business Hwy. 83, Ste. 1023
McAllen, Tex. 78501
(512) 687-5224

N. Harris County College
Small Business Dev. Center
20000 Kingwood Dr.
Kingwood, Tex. 77339
(713) 359-1624

N. Texas District Export Council
c/o Bell Helicopter Textron
P.O. Box 482
Forth Worth, Tex. 76101
(817) 280-3622

Port of Port Arthur
Box 1428
Port Arthur, Tex. 77640
(409) 983-2011

(Greater) San Antonio
Chamber of Commerce
Intl. Trade Center
P.O. Box 1628
San Antonio, Tex. 78296
(512) 229-2113

San Antonio World Trade Center
118 Broadway, Ste. 600
San Antonio, Tex. 78205
(512) 225-5877

S. Plains Assn. of Governments (SPAG)
P.O. Box 3730
Lubbock, Tex. 79452
(806) 762-8721

S. Texas District Export Council
515 Rusk
Rm. 2625
Houston, Tex. 77002
(713) 228-0500

Tex. Dept. of Agriculture
Export Services Div.
P.O. Box 12847
Capitol Sta.
Austin, Tex. 78711
(512) 463-7624

Texas Dept of Commerce
Office of Intl. Trade
P.O. Box 12728, Capitol Sta.
816 Congress
Austin, Tex. 78711
(512) 472-5059
*The Department maintains
export assistance centers
in a number of Texas cities.*

Texas Dept. of Commerce
Export Finance
P.O. Box 12728, Capital Sta.
816 Congress
Austin, Tex. 78711
(512) 320-9662
*The export finance division has
marketing representatives
in 10 Texas cities.*

U.S. Chamber of Commerce
4835 LBJ Freeway, Ste. 750
Dallas, Tex. 75244
(214) 387-0404

U.S. Customs Service
P.O. Box 61050
DFW Airport, Tex. 75261
(214) 574-2170

U.S. Dept. of Commerce (ITA)
Austin Branch
P.O. Box 12728, 816 Congress
Austin, Tex. 78701
(512) 482-5939

U.S. Dept. of Commerce (ITA)
1100 Commerce St., Rm. 7A5
Dallas, Tex. 75242
(214) 767-0542

U.S. Dept of Commerce (ITA)
515 Rusk St., Rm. 2625
Houston, Tex. 77002
(713) 229-2578

U.S. Small Business Administration
400 Mann, Room 403
Government Plaza Bldg.
Corpus Christi, Tex. 78401
(512) 888-3301

U.S. Small Business Administration
Harlingen District Office
222 E. Van Buren St., Ste. 500
Harlingen, Tex. 78550
(512) 427-8533

Utah

Cache County Chamber of Commerce
Executive Director
160 N. Main St.
Logan, Utah 84321-4541
(801) 752-2162

Cedar City Chamber of Commerce
Executive Director
P.O. Box 220
Cedar City, Utah 84720
(801) 586-4022

St. George Chamber of Commerce
Executive Director
97 E. 100 N.
St. George, Utah 84770
(801) 628-1658

Salt Lake Intermountain Port Authority
2110 State St., S2100
Salt Lake City, Utah 84190-3710
(801) 468-3246

U.S. Dept. of Commerce (ITA)
Room 105, 324 S. State St.
Salt Lake City, Utah 84111
(801) 524-5116

Utah Dept. of Community & Econ. Devel.
Ste. 200, 324 S. State St.
Salt Lake City, Utah 84111
(801) 538-8737

U.S. Small Business Administration
2237 Federal Building, 125 S. State St.
Salt Lake City, Utah 84138
(801) 524-6831

Utah Valley Economic Devel. Assn.
100 East Center St., Ste. 2500
Provo, Utah 84606
(801) 370-8100

World Trade Assn. of Utah
P.O. Box 53522
Salt Lake City, Utah 84116

Vermont

Lake Champlain Regional
Chamber of Commerce
209 Battery St.
P.O. Box 453
Burlington, Vt. 05402
(802) 863-3489

(State of) Vermont Agency of Dev.
and Community Affairs
Pavillion Office Bldg.
109 State St.
Montpelier, Vt. 05602
(802) 828-3221

U.S. Dept. of Commerce (ITA)
World Trade Center, Ste. 307
Boston, Mass. 02210
(617) 565-8563

Virginia

Fairfax County Chamber of Commerce
8391 Old Courthouse Rd.
Ste. #300
Vienna, Va. 22182
(703) 749-0400

Hampton Roads Maritime Assn.
P.O. Box 3487
Norfolk, Va. 23514
(804) 622-3487

Institute for Econ. Competitiveness
Radford University
Radford, Va. 23142
(703) 831-5000

Intl. Trade Assn. of N. Virginia
P.O. Box 2982
Reston, Va. 22090
(703) 860-8795

Intl. Trade Assn. of W. Virginia
P.O. Box 936
Lexington, Va. 24450
(703) 463-1095

Jefferson Intl. Business Club
269 Monroe Hall
University of Virginia
Charlottesville, Va. 22903
(804) 924-4568

Norfolk Airport Authority
Cargo Dev.
Norfolk International Airport
Norfolk, Va. 23518
(804) 857-3351

Piedmont World Trade Council
P.O. Box 1374
Lynchburg, Va. 24505
(804) 528-7511

Richmond Export-Import Club
P.O. Box 12135
Richmond, Va. 23241
(804) 853-0900

U.S. Dept. of Commerce (ITA)
8010 Federal Bldg.
400 N. 8th St.
Richmond, Va. 23240
(804) 771-2246

Va. Chamber of Commerce
9 S. Fifth St.
Richmond, Va. 23219
(804) 644-1607

Va. Dept. of Agriculture
& Consumer Affairs
1100 Bank St.
Rm. 710
Richmond, Va. 23219
(804) 786-3501

Va. Dept. of World Trade
6000 World Trade Center
Norfolk, Va. 23510
(804) 683-2849

Va District Export Council
P.O. Box 10190
Richmond, Va. 23240
(804) 771-2246

Va. Port Authority
6000 World Trade Center
Norfolk, Va. 23510
(804) 683-8000

Washington

Commencement Bay
Intl. Trade Council
Tacoma-Pierce County
Chamber of Commerce
P.O. Box 1933
Tacoma, Wash. 98401
(206) 627-2175

Cowlitz Economic Dev. Council
1338 Commerce Ave.
Ste. 211
Longview, Wash. 98632

Export Assistance Center of Wash.
2001 Sixth Ave.
Ste. 1700
Seattle, Wash. 98121
(206) 464-7123

IMPACT (Agricultural Marketing)
Washington State Univ.
Hulbert Hall, Room 104
Wash. St. University
Pullman, Wash. 99164-6214
(509) 335-6653

Inland N.W. World Trade Council
P.O. Box 1124
Spokane, Wash. 99210
(509) 456-3243

International Business Center
ASR Building
13555 Bel-Red Road, Ste. 208B
Bellevue, Wash. 98005
(206) 562-6154

International Trade Institute
North Seattle Community College
9600 College Way N.
Seattle, Wash. 98103
(206) 527-3732

National Marine Fisheries Service
Fisheries Development Div.
7600 Sand Point Way N.E.
Bin C15700
Seattle, Wash. 98115
(206) 526-6117

N.W. Trade Adjustment Assistance Center
900 Fourth Ave., Ste. 2430
Seattle, Wash. 98164
(206) 622-2730

Pacific Northwest/Caribbean Basin Trade Assn.
5120 W. Third Ave.
Kennewick, Wash. 99336
(509) 783-3337

Seattle Chamber of Commerce
Trade and Transportation Div.
600 Univeristy St., Ste. 1200
Seattle, Wash. 98101
(206) 389-7269

Spokane Chamber of Commerce
P.O. Box 2147
Spokane, Wash. 99210
(509) 624-1393

Tri-Ports Export Services
One Clover Island
Kennewick, Wash. 99336
(509) 586-1188

U.S. Dept. of Commerce (ITA)
3131 Elliott Ave., Ste. 290
Seattle, Wash. 98121
(206) 442-5615

U.S. Dept. of Commerce (ITA)—Spokane Branch
P.O. Box 2170
Spokane, Wash. 99210
(509) 353-2922

Greater Vancouver Chamber of Commerce
404 E. 15th St.
Vancouver, Wash. 98663
(206) 694-2588

Wash. Council on Intl. Trade
2615 Fourth Ave., Ste. 350
Seattle, Wash. 98121
(206) 443-3826

Washington Public Ports Assn.
P.O. Box 1518
Olympia, Wash. 98507
(206) 943-0760

Wash. State Dept. of Trade and Econ. Dev.
2001 Sixth Ave., 26th Floor
Seattle, Wash. 98121
(206) 464-7076

World Affairs Council
515 Madison St., Ste. 501
Seattle, Wash. 98104
(206) 682-6986

Wash. State Intl. Trade Fair
999 Third Ave., Ste. 1020
Seattle, Wash. 98104
(206) 682-6900

World Trade Ctr. of Tacoma
3600 Port of Tacoma Road
Tacoma, Wash. 98424
(206) 383-9474

World Trade Club of Seattle
P.O. Box 21488
Seattle, Wash. 98111
(206) 624-9586

West Virginia

Appalachian Export Center for Hardwoods
West Virginia University
P.O. Box 6061
Morgantown, W. Va. 26506-6061
(304) 293-7577

Governor's Office of Community and Ind. Dev.
Intl. Division, Room 531, Building #6
1900 Washington St. E.
Charleston, W. Va. 25305
(304) 348-2001

Institute for Intl. Trade Dev.
Exporter's Assistance Program
1050 Fourth Ave.
Huntington, W. Va. 25755-2131
(304) 696-2451

U.S. Dept. of Commerce (ITA)
P.O. Box 26
Charleston, W. Va. 25321
(304) 347-5123

W. Va. Chamber of Commerce
P.O. Box 2789
Charleston, W. Va. 25330
(304) 342-1115

W. Va. Export Council
P.O. Box 26
Charleston, W. Va. 25321
(304) 343-3726

W. Va. Manufacturers Assn.
405 Capitol St.
Charleston, W. Va. 25301
(304) 342-2123

Wisconsin

Foreign Trade Zone of Wis. Ltd.
1925 E. Kelly Lane
Cudahy, Wis. 53110
(414) 764-2111

Milwaukee Assn. of Commerce
756 N. Milwaukee St.
Milwaukee, Wis. 53202
(414) 273-3000

Milwaukee World Trade Assn
756 N. Milwaukee St.
Milwaukee, Wis. 53202
(414) 273-3000

Port of Milwaukee
500 N. Harbor Dr.
Milwaukee, Wis. 53202
(414) 278-3511

Small Business Dev. Center
432 N. Lake St.
Madison, Wis. 53706
(608) 263-7766

U.S. Dept. of Commerce (ITA)
517 E. Wisconsin Ave., Ste. 606
Milwaukee, Wis. 53202
(414) 297-3473

Wis. Dept. of Development
P.O. Box 7970
123 W. Washington Ave.
Madison, Wis. 53707
(608) 266-1767

Wis. World Trade Center
Pfister Hotel
424 E. Wisconsin Ave.
Milwaukee, Wis. 53202
(414) 274-3840

Wyoming

U.S. Dept. of Commerce (ITA)
World Trade Center
1625 Broadway, Ste. 680
Denver, Colo. 80202
(303) 844-3246

State of Wyoming
Office of the Governor
Capitol Building
Cheyenne, Wyo. 82002
(307) 777-6412

Sources of Assistance by State

STATE TRADE DEVELOPMENT SERVICES

State	Seminars/ conferences	One-on-one counseling	Market studies prepared	Language bank	Referrals to local export services	Newsletter	How-to handbook	Sales leads disseminated	Trade shows	Trade missions	Foreign offices reps.	Operational financing program
WYOMING											•	
WISCONSIN	•	•				•	•	•	•	•	•	•
WEST VIRGINIA	•										•	
WASHINGTON	•	•	•	•	•	•			•	•	•	•
VIRGINIA	•	•	•				•			•	•	
VERMONT	•										•	
UTAH	•	•					•	•	•		•	•
TEXAS	•	•					•	•	•		•	
TENNESSEE	•	•	•			•	•	•	•	•		
SOUTH DAKOTA	•	•	•	•				•				
SOUTH CAROLINA	•					•	•	•	•	•	•	
RHODE ISLAND	•	•				•	•	•	•	•	•	
PENNSYLVANIA	•	•	•			•	•	•	•		•	
OREGON	•	•					•	•	•			
OKLAHOMA	•	•	•	•	•	•	•	•	•			
OHIO	•	•	•	•	•	•		•	•	•	•	•
NORTH DAKOTA	•	•						•	•			
NORTH CAROLINA	•	•	•	•	•			•	•	•	•	
NEW YORK	•	•			•	•		•	•	•	•	
NEW MEXICO	•	•			•		•	•	•			
NEW JERSEY	•	•			•	•		•		•	•	
NEW HAMPSHIRE	•	•			•		•	•				
NEVADA	•			•		•				•		
NEBRASKA	•	•		•		•		•			•	
MONTANA	•	•	•		•			•	•	•		
MISSOURI	•	•			•	•	•	•	•	•	•	
MISSISSIPPI	•	•	•		•	•	•	•	•	•		•
MINNESOTA	•	•			•			•	•	•		•
MICHIGAN	•	•	•		•		•	•	•	•	•	
MASSACHUSETTS	•	•	•		•			•				
MARYLAND	•	•			•		•		•	•		
MAINE	•						•		•			
LOUISIANA (d)												
KENTUCKY	•	•			•		•	•	•	•	•	
KANSAS	•	•			•	•	•	•	•	•		
IOWA	•	•	•	•			•	•	•	•		
INDIANA	•	•		•			•	•	•	•	•	
ILLINOIS	•	•	•		•		•	•	•	•		•
IDAHO	•						•	•	•	•		•
HAWAII	•	•			•		•	•	•			
GEORGIA	•	•	•		•		•	•	•	• (c)		
FLORIDA	•	•	•				•	•	•	• (c)		
DELAWARE	•				•		•	•				
CONNECTICUT	•	•	•		•	•	•	•		•		
COLORADO	•	•	•		•		•	•	•		•	
CALIFORNIA	•	•		•			• (a)	• (b)	•	•		•
ARKANSAS	•	•	•	•	•	•	•	•	•	•		
ARIZONA	•	•	•		•			•	•	•		
ALASKA								•	•	•		
ALABAMA	•	•			•		•	•	•	•	•	

Notes: See next page for notes and explanation of programs.

231

STATE TRADE DEVELOPMENT SERVICES: EXPLANATION AND FOOTNOTES

- Seminars/conferences—State sponsors seminars for exporters, either basic, specific function, or specific market.
- One-on-one counseling—State staff provides actual export counseling to individual businesses in addition to making appropriate referrals.
- Market studies prepared—State staff prepares specific market studies for individual companies.
- Language bank—State program to match foreign-speaking visitors with bilingual local residents who provide volunteer translation services.
- Referrals to local export services— Matching exporters with exporter services, e.g. matchmaker fair, export service directory, individual referrals, etc.
- Newsletter—State publishes an international trade newsletter.
- How-to-handbook—State publishes a basic how-to-export handbook.
- Sales leads disseminated—State collects and distributes sales leads to in-State businesses.
- Trade shows—State assists with and accompanies or represents businesses on trade shows.

- Trade missions—State assists with and accompanies business on trade missions.
- Foreign offices/reps—State office or contractual representative located abroad.
- Operational financing program—State export financing assistance program that is currently operational.

Footnotes:

(a) California issues a bimonthly column to local chambers and trade groups for publication in their newsletters.

(b) California produces a "road map" to low cost and free trade services.

(c) Georgia's foreign offices are only active in attracting reverse investment.

(d) Louisiana has recently established a new Office of International Trade, Finance and Development within the Department of Commerce and Industry. The Office is expected to offer a full range of trade promotion services.

Source: National Association of State Development Agencies, State Export Program Database, January, 1985.

Appendix 2

U. S. Ports of Entry

Following is an alphabetical list of the Customs ports of entry arranged by states, including Puerto Rico and the Virgin Islands. District shown in boldface; regional headquarters are preceded by a bullet.

ALABAMA

Birmingham
Huntsville
Mobile

ALASKA

Alcan
Anchorage
Alton Cache
Fairbanks
Juneau
Ketchikan
Sitka

Skagway
Valdez
Wrangell

ARIZONA

Douglas
Lukeville
Naco
Nogales
Phoenix
San Luis
Sasabe

ARKANSAS

Little Rock-
 N. Little Rock

CALIFORNIA

Andrade
Calexico
Eureka
Fresno
• **Los Angeles—Long
 Beach**
Port San Luis
San Diego

Source: "Importing into the U. S." Department of Treasury, U. S. Customs Service, Washington, D. C., June 1986.

San Francisco-Oakland
Tecate
San Ysidro

COLORADO

Denver

CONNECTICUT

Bridgeport
New Haven
New London

DELAWARE

Wilmington
  (See Philadelphia)

DISTRICT OF COLUMBIA

Washington

FLORIDA

Apalachicola
Boca Grande
Carrabelle
Fernandina Beach
 Jacksonville
Key West
• **Miami**
Orlando
Panama City
Pensacola
Port Canaveral
Port Everglades
Port St. Joe
St. Petersburg

Tampa
West Palm Beach

GEORGIA

Atlanta
Brunswick
Savannah

HAWAII

Honolulu
Hilo
Kahului
Nawiliwili-Port Allen

IDAHO

Eastport
Porthill
Boise

ILLINOIS

• **Chicago**
Peoria
Rock Island-Moline*
  (see Davenport)

INDIANA

Evansville/Owensboro,
  Ky.
Indianapolis
Lawrenceburg/
  Cincinnati, Ohio

IOWA

Davenport-Rock
Island-Moline*

Des Moines

KANSAS

Wichita

KENTUCKY

Louisville
Owensboro/
  Evansville, Ind.

LOUISIANA

Baton Rouge
Gramercy
Lake Charles
Morgan City
• **New Orleans**
Shreveport/
  Bossier City*

MAINE

Bangor
Bar Harbor
Bath
Belfast
Bridgewater
Calais
Eastport
Fort Fairfield
Fort Kent
Houlton
Jackman
Jonesport
Limestone
Madawaska
Portland

Rockland
Van Buren
Vanceboro

MARYLAND

Annapolis
Baltimore
Cambridge

MASSACHUSETTS

- **Boston**
Fall River
Gloucester
Lawrence
New Bedford
Plymouth
Salem
Springfield
Worcester

MICHIGAN

Battle Creek
Detroit
Grand Rapids
Muskegon
Port Huron
Saginaw-Bay City/Flint
Sault Ste. Marie

MINNESOTA

Baudette
Duluth
  and Superior, Wis.
Grand Portage

International
  Falls-Ranier
Minneapolis-St. Paul
Noyes
Pinecreek
Roseau
Warroad

MISSISSIPPI

Greenville
Gulfport
Pascagoula
Vicksburg

MISSOURI

Kansas City
St. Joseph
St. Louis
Springfield
  (Temporary)

MONTANA

Butte
Del Bonita
Great Falls
Morgan
Opheim
Piean Raymond
Roosville
Scobey
Sweetgrass
Turner
Whitetail
Whitlash

NEBRASKA

Omaha

NEVADA

Las Vegas
Reno

NEW HAMPSHIRE

Plymouth

NEW JERSEY

Perth Amboy(See
  New York/Newark)

NEW MEXICO

Albuquerque
Columbus

NEW YORK

Albany
Alexandria Bay
Buffalo-Niagara Falls
Cape Vincent
Champlain-
  Rouses Point
Chateaugay
Clayton
Fort Covington
Massena
- **New York Kennedy**
    Airport Area
    Newark Area
    New York Seaport Area
Ogdensburg

Oswego
Rochester
Sodus Point
Syracuse
Trout River
Utica

NORTH CAROLINA

Beaufort-Morehead City
Charlotte
Durham
Reidsville
Wilmington
Winston-Salem

NORTH DAKOTA

Ambrose
Antler
Carbury
Dunseith
Fortuna
Hannah
Hansboro
Maida
Neche
Noonan
Northgate
Pembina
Portal
Sarles
Sherwood
St. John
Walhalla
Westhope

OHIO

Akron
Ashtabula/Conneaut
Cincinnati/
  Lawrenceburg, Ind.
Cleveland
Columbus
Dayton
Toledo/Sandusky

OKLAHOMA

Oklahoma City
Tulsa

OREGON

Coos Bay
Newport
Portland*

PENNSYLVANIA

Chester (see Phila.)
Erie
Harrisburg
**Philadelphia/Chester/
  Wilmington**
Pittsburgh
Wilkes-Barre/Scranton

PUERTO RICO

Aguadilla
Fajardo
Guanica
Humacao
Jobos

Mayaguez
Ponce
San Juan

RHODE ISLAND

Newport
Providence

SOUTH CAROLINA

Charleston
Georgetown
Greenville-Spartanburg

TENNESSEE

Chattanooga
Knoxville
Memphis
Nashville

TEXAS

Amarillo
Austin
Beaumont*
Brownsville
Corpus Christi
Dallas/Ft. Worth
Del Rio
Eagle Pass
El Paso
Fabens
Freeport
Hidalgo
• **Houston/Galveston**

Laredo

Lubbock

Orange*

Port Authur*

Port Lavaca-Point
  Comfort

Presidio

Progreso

Rio Grande City

Roma

Sabine*

San Antonio

UTAH

Salt Lake City

VERMONT

Beecher Falls

Burlington

Derby Line

Highgate
  Springs/Alburg

Norton

Richford

St. Albans

VIRGIN ISLANDS

**Charlotte Amalie,
  St. Thomas**

Christiansted

Coral Bay

Cruz Bay

Frederiksted

VIRGINIA

Alexandria

Cape Charles City

**Norfolk-Newport
  News**

Reedville

Richmond-Petersburg

WASHINGTON

Aberdeen

Anacortes*

Bellingham*

Blaine

Boundary

Danville

Everett*

Ferry

Friday Harbor*

Frontier

Laurier

Lonview*

Lynden

Metaline Falls

Neah Bay*

Nighthawk

Olympia*

Oroville

Point Roberts

Port Angeles*

Port Townsend*

Seattle*

Spokane

Sumas

Tacoma*

WEST VIRGINIA

Charleston

WISCONSIN

Ashland

Green Bay

Manitowoc

Marinette

Milwaukee

Racine

Sheboygan

*Consolidated Ports:
  Columbia River port of entry includes Longview, Washington, and Portland Oregon.
  Beaumont, Orange, Port Arthur, Sabine port of entry includes ports of the same name.
  Port of Puget Sound includes Tacoma, Seattle, Port Angeles, Port Townsend, Neah Bay, Friday, Harbor, Everett,
    Bellingham, Anacortes, and Olympia in the State of Washington.
  Port of Philadelphia includes Wilmington and Chester.
  Port of Rock Island includes Moline and Davenport, Iowa.
  Port of Shreveport includes Bossier city, La.
Designated User-free Airports: Allentown-Bethlehem-Easton, PA, Fargo, ND, Lebanon, NH, Santa Teresa, NM, Wilmington,
OH, and Southwest Florida Regional Airport, Fort Myers, FL.

Appendix 3

Customs Regions and Districts

Headquarters

U. S. Customs Service
1301 Constitution
  Ave., N. W.
Washington, D. C. 20229

**Northeast
Region—Boston Mass.
02110**

Districts:

Portland, Maine 04112
St. Albans, Vt. 05478
Boston, Mass. 02109
Providence, R. I. 02903
Buffalo, N. Y. 14202
Ogdensburg,
  N. Y. 13669
Bridgeport, Conn. 06601
Philadelphia, Pa. 19106

Baltimore, Md. 21202
Norfolk, Va. 23510
Washington, D.C. 20041

**New York Region—New
York, N. Y. 10048**

New York Seaport
  Area New York, N. Y.
  10048

Source: "Importing into the U. S." Department of Treasury, U. S. Customs Service, Washington, D. C., June 1986.

Kennedy Airport Area
Jamaica, N. Y. 11430

Newark Area Newark
N. J. 07114

Southeast
Region—Miami, Fla.
33131

Districts

Wilmington, N. C. 28401

San Juan, P. R. 00903

Charleston, S. C. 29402

Savannah, Ga. 31401

Tampa, Fla. 33602

Miami, Fla. 33131

St. Thomas, V. I. 00801

South Central
Region—New Orleans,
La. 70130

Districts:

Mobile Ala. 36601

New Orleans, La. 70130

Southwest
Region—Houston, Tex.
77057

Districts:

Port Authur, Tex. 77642

Houston/Galeveston,
Tex. 77052

Laredo, Tex. 78041-3130

El Paso, Tex. 79985

Dallas/Fort Worth,
Tex. 75261

Pacific Region
—Los Angeles, Calif.
90012

Districts:

Nogales, Ariz. 85621

San Diego, Calif. 92189

Los Angeles/Long
Beach, Calif. 90731

San Francisco,
Calif. 94126

Honolulu, Hawaii 96806

Portland, Oreg. 97209

Seattle, Wash. 98174

Anchorage,
Alaska 90501

Great Falls, Mont. 59401

North Central
Region—Chicago, Ill.
60605-5790

Districts:

Chicago, Ill. 60607

Pembina, N. Dak. 58271

Minneapolis-
St. Paul, Minn. 55401

Duluth, Minn. 55802

Milwaukee, Wis. 53202

Cleveland, Ohio 44114

St. Louis, Mo. 63105

Detroit, Mich.
48226-2568

Appendix 4

U. S. Customs Offices in Foreign Countries

Austria

Customs Attaché
American Embassy
Boltzmanngasse 16
A-1091
Vienna
Tel: 513-5511

Belgium

Customs Attaché
U. S. Mission to the
European Communities
(USEC)
No. 40 Blvd. du Regent
1000 Brussels
Tel: 513-4450 Ext. 2779

Brazil

Customs Attaché
American Embassy
Avenida Das Nocoes
Lote 3
Brasilia
Tele: 223-0120

Source: "Importing into the U. S." Department of Treasury, U. S. Customs Service, Washington, D. C., June 1986.

240

Canada

Customs Attaché
American Embassy
95 Sparks, St.
Suite 1130
Ottawa, Ont. K1P5T1
Tel: (613) 238-5335 X 322

England

Customs Attaché
American Embassy
24/31 Grosvenor Square
London, W. 1
Tel: 1/493-4599

France

Customs Attaché
American Embassy
58 bis Rue la Boetie
Room 210
75008 Paris
Tel: 296-1202
Ext. 2392/2393

Hong Kong, B.B.C.

Senior Customs Representative
American Consulate
    General
St. John's Building-11th
    Floor
33 Garden Road
Tel: 5-239011 Ext. 244

Italy

Customs Attaché
American Embassy
Via V. Veneto 119
Rome
Tel: 6/4674 Ext. 475 or
413

Japan

Customs Attaché
American Embassy
Minato-Ku Akasaka
1-chome
13 go, No. 14
Tokyo
Tel: 583-7141 Ext. 7205

Korea

Customs Attaché
82 SeJong Ro
Chongro-Ku
Seoul
Tel: 732-2601 Ext. 4563

Mexico

Customs Attaché
American Embassy
Paseo de la Reforma 305
Colonia Cuahtemoc
Mexico, D. F., Mexico
Tel: (905) 211-0042 Ext.
3687

Pakistan

Senior Customs Rep.
American Consulate
General
8 Abdullah Haroon Road
Karachi
Tel: 51-50-81

Panama

Customs Attaché
Calle 38 & Avenida
Balboa
Panama, R. P.
Tel: 271777

Thailand

Customs Attaché
American Embassy
95 Wireless Road
Bangkok
Tel: 252-5040

West Germany

Customs Attaché
American Embassy
Mahlemer Avenue 5300
Bonn-Bad Godesberg
Tel: 228/3392207
 228/3312853

Appendix 5

Customs Brokers and Freight Forwarders

ALABAMA

MOBILE, ALABAMA

Alcoa Steamship Co., Inc.
P. O. Box 256
Mobile, AL 36601
Phone: 205 433-9581

Brining, John, M., Co., Inc.
P. O. Box 403
Mobile, AL 33601
Phone: 205 433-7467

M. G. Mahler & Co., Inc.
P. O. Box 2242
Mobile AL 36652

W. R. Zanes & Co.
International Trade Center
Suite 325
Mobile AL 36601

ARIZONA

PHOENIX, ARIZONA

Byrnes, W. J. & Co.
P. O. Box 20623
Phoenix, AZ 85036
Phone: 602 244-1752

TUCSON, ARIZONA

Byrnes, W. J. & Co.
P. O. Box 22044
Tucson, AZ 85734

CALIFORNIA

BURLINGAME, CALIFORNIA

McGregor Sea & Air Services Ltd.
1588 Gilbreth Road
Burlingame, CA 94010
Phone: 415 692-7500

Source: American Export Register, 1989 edition. Thomas International Publishing Company, One Penn Plaza, New York, NY 10119.

242

Rausch, Ted L. Co.
1304 Rollins Road
Burlingame, CA 94010

Trans/World Shippers, Inc.
P. O. Box 5449
Carson, CA 90749
Phone: 213 799-9999

Zerwekh, Edward S. Co.
1161 Watson Center Road
Carson, CA 90745
Phone: 213 830-5404

COMPTON, CALIFORNIA

Dow, Frank P. Co.

615 W. Walnut Street
Compton, CA 90220
Phone: 213 638-0335

EL SEGUNDO, CALIFORNIA

Alpha Cargo Service Corp.
1222 E. Imperial Avenue
El Segundo, CA 90245
Phone: 213 678-3037

Packair Airfreight, Inc.
1550 E. Franklin Avenue
El Segundo, CA 90245
Phone: 213 772-8000

Schenkers International Forwarders
221 Rosecrans Avenue
El Segundo, CA 90245
Phone: 213 973-8700

Shiloh International, Inc.
1222 E. Imperial Avenue
El Segundo, CA 90245
Phone: 213 678-3037

Schroff, Karl & Associates, Inc.
1700 E. Holly Avenue
El Segundo, CA 90245
Phone: 213 773-7523

INGLEWOOD, CALIFORNIA

Behring International, Inc.
10834 S. La Cienega Boulevard
Ingelwood, CA 90304
Phone: 213 776-7800

Fritz, Arthur J. Co. of Los Angeles
1039 W. Hilcrest
Inglewood, CA 90307
Phone: 213 776-7620

Interamerican World Transport Corp.
426 W. Florence Avenue
Ingelwood, CA 90301
Phone: 213 671-2387

Lep Transport, Inc.
746 S. Glaslow Avenue
Inglewood, CA 90301
Phone: 213 670-6740

LTH International (USA), Ltd.
915 W. Hyde Park Blvd.
Inglewood, CA 90302
Phone: 213 673-9100

Panalpina, Inc.
343 N. Oak, Street
Inglewood, CA 90308
Phone: 213 678-2601

Perryman, Mojonier Co.
9720 S. La Cienega Boulevard
Ingelwood, CA 90301
Phone: 213 649-0070

Radix Group Intl.
8728 Aviation Boulevard
Ingelwood, CA 90301
Phone: 213 776-2365

LONG BEACH, CALIFORNIA

A & W International Customs Brokers
215 Long Beach Boulevard
Suite 907
Long Beach, CA 90802
Phone: 213-491-1177

Aero-Brokers, Inc.
P. O. Box 92934
Long Beach, CA 90809-2934

International Customs Service, Inc.
3447 Atlantic Avenue, Suite 300
Long Beach, CA 90503
Phone: 213 427-0101

Martin Lewis Transcargo, Inc.
2240 N. Figueroa Street
Long Beach, CA 90065-1098
Phone: 213 225-2347

Rausch, Ted L. Co.
110 W. Ocean Boulevard
Long Beach, CA 90802
Phone: 213 435-8231

LOS ANGELES, CALIFORNIA

Byrnes, W. J. & Co.
5758 W. Century Boulevard
Los Angeles, CA 90045
Phone: 213 568-0877

Byrnes, W. J. & Co.
P. O. Box 90595
Los Angeles, CA 90009
Phone: 213 776-1638

Coopersmith, L. E.
3460 Wilshire Boulevard, Suite 700
Los Angeles, CA 90010
Phone: 213 380-3770

Oceanland Service, Inc.
416 W. 8th Street, Suite 806
Los Angeles, CA 90014
Phone: 213 622-4076

Pacheco International Corp.
11207 S. La Cienega Blvd.
Los Angeles, CA 90045
Phone: 213 776-5500

Rausch, Ted L. Co.
8621 Bellianca Avenue
Los Angeles, CA 90045
Phone: 213 471-8498

Shenk, David W. & Co.
8610 Airport Boulevard
Los Angeles, CA 90045
Phone: 213 776-1040

Wiley, James G. Co.
408 S. Spring Street
Los Angeles, CA 90013
Phone: 213 628-8344

MILLBRAE, CALIFORNIA

ASG International, Inc.
340 Adrian Road
Millbrae, CA 94680
Phone: 415 692-9020

NORWALK, CALIFORNIA

Custom Crating, Inc.
P. O. Box 1190
Norwalk, CA 90650
Phone: 213 774-5631

SACRAMENTO, CALIFORNIA

Rausch, Ted. L. Co.
World Trade Center
Stone Boulevard West
Sacramento, CA L95691
Phone: 916 371-6502

SAN DIEGO, CALIFORNIA

Four Winds Pickfords
P. O. Box 85771
San Diego, CA 92138
Phone: 619 450-0650

SAN FRANCISCO, CALIFORNIA

Barinco International Corporation
P. O. Box 2250
San Francisco, CA 94126
Phone: 415 362-4944

Berry & McCarthy Shipping Co.
1350 Marin Street
San Francisco, CA 94124
Phone: 415 821-6800

Byrnes, W. J. & Co.
P. O. Box 280205
San Francisco, CA 94128-0205
Phone: 415 692-1142

Chun, R. T.
21 Columbus Avenue
San Francisco, CA 94111
Phone: 415 362-3119

Circle Air Freight
260 Townsend Street
San Francisco, CA 94107
Phone: 415 978-0640

Fritz Company
735 Market Street, Suite 500
San Francisco, CA 94103
Phone 415 541-8200

Myers, F. W. & Co., Inc.
165 Mitchell Avenue
So. San Francisco, CA 94080
Phone 415 952-1611

Rausch, Ted. L. Co.
655 4th Street
San Francisco, CA 94107
Phone: 415 957-5810

SAN PEDRO, CALIFORNIA

Withrow, Wayne M. & Co.
29000 S. Western Avenue
San Pedro, CA 90732
Phone: 213 775-6663

COLORADO

DENVER, COLORADO

Byrnes, W. J. & Co.
P. O. Box 38707
Denver, CO 80238
Phone: 303 320-5921

Sluys, Ralph V. Customs Broker
12000 E. 47th Avenue, Suite 100
Denver, CO 80239
Phone: 303 337-1160

CONNECTICUT

STAMFORD, CONNECTICUT

Cleveland Air Sea, Inc.
15 Rockland Road
Stamford, CT 06854
Phone: 203 853-6298

DISTRICT OF COLUMBIA

Cosimano, G., Inc.
P. O. Box 17092
Washington, D. C. 20041
Phone: 703 471-9824

FLORIDA

FT. LAUDERDALE, FLORIDA

Manaco International Forwarders, Inc.
Port Everglades
Amman Building, Suite 8
Eisenhower Boulevard
Ft. Lauderdale, FL 33316
Phone: 305 463-6910

Reynolds, J. P. Co.
P. O. Box 13071
Ft. Lauderdale, FL 33316
Phone: 305 522-3763

JACKSONVILLE, FLORIDA

James, John S.
P. O. Box 3342
Jacksonville, FL 32206
Phone: 904 356-9646

Sunshine Forwarders, Inc.
P. O. Box 8
Jacksonville, FL 32201
Phone: 904 353-1741

Wilk Forwarding Co.
P. O. Box 6418
Jacksonville, FL 32236
Phone: 904 389-5588

MELBOURNE, FLORIDA

Air Compac International
P. O. Box 1330
Melbourne, FL 32901
Phone: 305 725-1311

MIAMI, FLORIDA

Benson's Forwarding Service
P. O. Box 522370
Miami, FL 33152
Phone: 305 593-0642

Fritz, Arthur J. & Co.
P. O. Box 52-2502
Miami, FL 33152
Phone: 305 592-6330

Glukstad, Sig M. Inc.
P. O. Box 523730
Miami, FL 33153
Phone: 305 594-0038

Intercobal, Inc.
7220 N. W. 36th Street
Miami, FL 33166

Miami International Forwarders, Inc.
1573 N. W. 82nd Avenue
Miami, FL 33126
Phone: 305 594-0038

PAFCO Forwarders, Inc.
157 N. E. 8th Street
Phone: 305 381-6795

Penson Florida Co.
2315 N. W. 107th Avenue, B-15
Miami, FL 33172
Phone: 305 591-8700

Radix Group International
7232 N. W. 56th Street
Miami, FL 33166
Phone: 305 887-2349

GEORGIA

ATLANTA, GEORGIA

Carroll, W. G. & Co., Inc.
P. O. Box 20729
Atlanta, GA 30320
Phone: 404 761-2929

Sunshine Forwarders, Inc.
100 Hammond Drive, Suite 106
Atlanta, GA 30328
Phone: 404 252-0844

SAVANNAH GEORGIA

The Hipage Co.
P. O. Box 31402
Savannah, GA 31402
Phone: 912 233-9991

James, John S. Co.
P. O. Box 2166
Savannah, GA 31498
Phone: 912 232-0211

Mobley, E. L. Inc.
P. O. Box 1686
Savannah, GA 31402
Phone: 912 234-0686

Robinson, Harper Co.
31 West Congress Street, Suite 303
Savannah, GA 31401
Phone: 912 234-4451

HAWAII

HONOLULU, HAWAII

Aero-Brokers, Inc.
P. O. Box 29131
Honolulu, HI 96820

Fritz, Arthur J. & Co.
333 Queen Street, Suite 206
Honolulu, HI 96813
Phone: 808 533-6080

IDAHO

EASTPORT, IDAHO

Jensen, Norman G. Inc.
Eastport, ID 83286
Phone: 208 267-3794

ILLINOIS

ARLINGTON HEIGHTS, ILLINOIS

Radix Group International
2355 S. Arlington Heights Road
Arlington Heights, IL 60005
Phone: 321 364-8200

CHICAGO ILLINOIS

Alltransport
300 S. Wacker Drive
Chicago, IL 60606
Phone: 312 322-7900

Borinquen Express Co.
1501 N. Milwaukee Avenue
Chicago, Il 60622
Phone: 312 227-1710

Davies, Turner & Co.
111 W. Monroe Street
Chicago, IL 60603
Phone: 312 346-8292

Dow, Frank P. Co.
P. O. Box 66293
Chicago, IL 60666
Phone: 312 671-7800

Fritz, Arthur J. & Co., Inc.
P. O. Box 66215, AMF O'Hare
Chicago, IL 60660
Phone: 312 350-5900

LEF International, Inc.
P. O. Box 66017
Chicago, IL 66066
Phone: 312 299-4000

Nettles & Co., Inc.
P. O. Box 66508
Chicago, IL 60666
Phone: 312 692-5090

Quast & Co., Inc.
327 S. La Salle Street
Chicago, IL 60604
Phone: 312 435-3870

Thomas, Phil & Son International
332 S. Michigan Avenue
Chicago, IL 60604
Phone: 321 427-7317

DES PLAINES, ILLINOIS

Air Express International Agency, Inc.
1500 Birchwood Street
Des Plaines, IL 60018
Phone: 312 297-1070

ELK GROVE, ILLINOIS

Eagle International, Ltd.
2101 Lunt Avenue
Elk Grove, Il 60007
Phone: 312 228-7766

ROSEMONT, ILLINOIS

Schroff, Karl, & Associates, Inc.
9757 W. Farrague Street
Rosemont, IL 60018
Phone: 312 992-4100

Myers, F. W. & Co., Inc.
9982 Bryn Mawr
Rosemont, IL 60018
Phone: 312 427-0004

SHILLER PARK ILLINOIS

Besler, E. & Co.
9864 W. Leland Avenue
Schiller Park, IL 60176
Phone: 312 671-3620

Carr, John v. & Son, Inc.
4825 N. Scott Street, Suite 319
Schiller Park, IL 60176
Phone: 312 671-5248

WILMETTE, ILLINOIS

American Industries
P. O. Box 434
Wilmette, IL 60091
Phone: 312 372-8241

INDIANA

EVANSVILLE, INDIANA

Atlas Van Lines International Corp.
P. O. Box 509
Evansville, IN 47703-0509
Phone: 812 424-2222

FORT WAYNE, INDIANA

NAVTRANS International Freight
Forwarding, Inc.
P. O. Box 988
Fort Wayne, IN 46801
Phone: 219 429-3720

INDIANAPOLIS, INDIANA

Circle Air Freight
5701 Progress Road
Indianapolis, IN 46241
Phone: 317 247-5506

Quast & Co.
P. O. Box 41954
Indianapolis, IN 46421
Phone: 317 243-8361

Williams, Kenneth M. & Associates, Inc.
P. O. Box 51607
Indianapolis, IN 46251
Phone: 317 243-7575

KENTUCKY

ERLANGER, KENTUCKY

MSAS Cargo International
1455 Jamike Drive
Erlanger, KY 41018
Phone: 606 371-3850

LOUISVILLE, KENTUCKY

Meuter, W. F.
P. O. Box 1
Louisville, KY 40201
Phone: 502 636-0381

LOUISIANA

NEW ORLEANS, LOUISIANA

Air Express International Corp.
P. O. Box 20005
New Orleans, LA 70141
Phone: 504-464-9671

Allen, J. W. & Co., Inc.
414 Whitney Building
New Orleans, LA 70130
Phone: 504 581-0181

Alltransport, Inc.
503 International Trade Mart
2 Canal Street
New Orleans, LA 70130
Phone: 504 523-4014

Baster Company Custom House Brokers,
Inc.
832 Whitney Building
New Orleans, LA 70130
Phone: 504 523-7769

Cosmos Shipping Co., Inc.
336 Camp Street
New Orleans, LA 70130
Phone: 504 468-2800

Dorf International, Inc.
212 Charles Street
New Orleans, LA 70130
Phone: 504 568-0379

Fritz, Arthur J. & Co.
204 Decatur Street
New Orleans, LA 70130
Phone: 504 529-7557

Gogarty, H. A.
International Trade Mart
New Orleans, LA 70130
Phone: 504 586-9888

Hoxter, P. F.
1437 World Trade Center
2 Canal Street
New Orleans, LA 70130
Phone: 504 525-1231

Intlcobal, Inc.
P. O. Box 2711
New Orleans, LA 70176-2711
Phone: 504 362-6972

Maher, M. G. & Co., Inc.
442 Canal Street
New Orleans, LA 70130
Phone: 504 581-3320

Pan American Shipping Co.
International Building
611 Gravier Street
Suite 606
New Orleans, LA 70130
Phone: 504 581-5836

Richeson, W. L. & Sons, Inc.
422 Canal Street
New Orleans, LA 70130
Phone: 504 529-5641

Surface Freight Corporation
P. O. Box 20005
New Orleans International Airport
New Orleans, LA 70141
Phone: 504 729-5581

Universal Transport Corporation
2 Canal Street
New Orleans, LA 70130
Phone: 504 524-6766

Westfeldt Bros. Forwarders, Inc.
P. O. Box 51750
New Orleans, LA 70151
Phone: 504 586-0087

Zanes, W. R. & Co. of Louisiana, Inc.
223 Tchoupitoulas Street
New Orleans, LA 70130
Phone: 504 524-1309

ST. ROSE, LOUISIANA

Robinson, Harper & Co.
125 Mallard Street, Suite D.
St. Rose, Louisiana 70087
Phone: 504 464-1588

MAINE

BANGOR, MAINE

Henderson, F. H., Inc.
P. O. Box 1779
Bangor, ME 04401
Phone: 207 942-6332

CALAIS, MAINE

Fenderson, F. H. Inc.
12 Main Street
Calais, ME 04619
Phone: 207 454-7503

FORT KENT, MAINE

Fenderson, F. H. Inc.
P. O. Box 86
Fort Kent, ME 04743
Phone: 207 834-6155

HOULTON, MAINE

Fenderson, F. H. Inc.
18 Market Square
Houlton, ME 04730
Phone: 207 532-7315

JACKMAN, MAINE

Fenderson, F. H. Inc.
P. O. Drawer 488
Jackman, ME 04945
Phone: 207 668-2611

MADAWASKA, MAINE

Fenderson, F. H. Inc.
P. O. Box 226
Madawaska, ME 04756
Phone: 207 728-6382

PORTLAND, MAINE

Chase, Leavitt & Co.
P. O. Box 589
Portland, ME 04112
Phone: 207 772-3751

Fenderson, F. H. Inc.
P. O. Box 271 DTI
Portland, ME 04112
Phone: 207 772-1848

Moran J. F. Co., Inc.
42 Commercial Street
Portland, ME 04101
Phone: 207 772-6515

MARYLAND

BALTIMORE MARYLAND

Aarid Enterprise Corp.
1340 Chesapeake Avenue
Baltimore, MD 21226
Phone: 301 355-8200

Alltransport, Inc.
World Trade Center, Suite 753
Baltimore, MD 21202
Phone: 301 385-1077

Anchor International
P. O. Box 28387
Baltimore, MD 21234
Phone: 301 882-6400

Fritz, Arthur J. & Co.
5 Light Street, Suite 700
Baltimore MD 21201
Phone: 201 539-1660

Blaser & Mericle, Inc.
16 S. Calvert Street, Suite 902
Baltimore, MD 21202
Phone: 301 837-1535

Bruzzone Shipping, Inc.
31 Calvert Street
Baltimore, MD 21202
Phone: 301 837-2280

Connor, John S. Inc.
33 S. Gay Street
Baltimore, MD 20202
Phone: 301 332-4800

Footner & Co., Inc.
210 E. Redwood Street
Baltimore, MD 21202
Phone: 301 727-0732

Hobelmann International, Inc.
211 E. Pleasant Street
Baltimore, MD 21202
Phone: 301 685-1000

Intercobal, Inc.
1227 Hesse Avenue
Baltimore, MD 21237
Phone: 301 687-1034

Kelly, Robert E.
BWI Commerce Park
2605 Cabover Drive
Baltimore, MD 21076
Phone: 301 761-1122

Kraus, D. Lee & Co.
713 W. Pratt Street
Baltimore, MD 21201
Phone: 301 837-5490

Masson, William H. Inc.
11 E. Mt. Royal Avenue
Baltimore, MD 21202
Phone: 301 539-0911

Robinson, Harper & Co.
222 E. Redwood Street, Suite 600
Baltimore, MD 21202
Phone: 301 539-1586

Ruckert Terminal Corp.
P. O. Box 5163
Baltimore, MD 21224
Phone: 301 276-1013

Shapiro, Samuel & Co., Inc.
401 E. Pratt Street
Baltimore, MD 21202
Phone: 301 539-0540

Traffic Dispatch International, Inc.
31 S. Calvert Street
Baltimore, MD 21202
Phone: 301 837-1087

Trans-World Shipping Service
300 Water Street
Baltimore, MD 21202
Phone: 301 727-7930

HANOVER, MARYLAND

Kelly, Robert E.
BWI Commerce Park
7509 Connelley Drive, Suite 0
Hanover, MD 21076
Phone: 301 766-5888

HARMANS, MARYLAND

Ntersm F, W, & Co., Inc.
7484 Candlewood Road
Harmans, MD 21077
Phone: 301 859-4250

HYATTSVILLE, MARYLAND

Bailey Customs House Brokers & Freight
Forwarders
P. O. Box 996
Hyattsville, MD 20783
Phone: 301 439-6400

MASSACHUSETTS
BOSTON, MASSACHUSETTS

Air Express International
Logan Airport
Air Cargo Terminal
Boston, MA 02128
Phone: 617 567-7928

Conkey, John A. & Co., Inc.
67 Broad Street
Boston, MA 02109
Phone: 617 439-4466

Downing, T. D. Co.
115 Broad Street
Boston, MA 02110
Phone: 617 426-4800

Proctor, W. N. Co., Inc.
P. O. Box 192
Boston, MA 02101
Phone: 617 596-5082

Stone & Downer Co.
Logan International Airport
Edison Building, Room 102
Boston, MA 02128
Phone: 617 569-5829

Advance Brokers, Ltd.
P. O. Box 447
East Boston, MA 02128
Phone: 617 561-0300

Fenderson, F. H. Inc.
Logan International Airport
239 Prescott Street, Suite 314
East Boston, MA 02128
Phone: 617 569-7880

Moran, J. F. Co., Inc.
Central Airfreight Terminal
Logan International Airport
East Boston, MA 02128
Phone: 617 569-7115

Saratoga Forwarding Co., Inc.
P. O. Box 239
East Boston, MA 02128
Phone: 617 567-2022

EVERETT, MASSACHUSETTS

Demetrios Air Freight Co., Inc.
413 2nd Street
Everett, MA 02149
Phone: 617 387-4700

PEABODY, MASSACHUSETTS

Intercontinental Forwarders, Inc.
1 International Way
Peabody, MA 01960
Phone: 617 535-5020

MICHIGAN

ALLEN PARK, MICHIGAN

Altransnco Customs Brokers
10501 Allen Road, Suite 206
Allen Park, MI 48101
Phone: 313 388-0300

DETROIT, MICHIGAN

Carr, John, V. & Son, Inc.
P. O. Box 479A
Detroit, MI 48232
Phone: 313 965-1540

Filbin, W. R. & Co.
2436 Bagley Avenue
Detroit, MI 48216
Phone: 313 964-1144

Leonard Brothers International, Ltd.
7060 W. Fort Street
Detroit, MI 48209
Phone: 313 588-6504

Trans-Overseas Corporation
P. O. Box 42494
Detroit, MI 48242
Phone: 313 946-8750

Whelan, W. F. Co.
P. O. Box 42422
Detroit, MI 48242
Phone: 313 946-5112

ROMULUS, MICHIGAN

Export-Import Service Co., Inc.
28265 Beverly Road
Romulus, MI 48174
Phone: 313 292-3440

McGregor Sea & Air Services, Ltd.
Air Cargo Center
28479 Highland Road
Romulus, MI 48174
Phone: 313 946-8120

TAYLOR, MICHIGAN

Coughlin, F. X. Co.
27050 Wick Road
Taylor, MI 48180
Phone: 313 946-9510

Fritz & Co., Inc.
27150 Trolley Industrial Drive
Taylor, MI 48180
Phone: 313-295 2030

MINNESOTA

MINNEAPOLIS, MINNESOTA

Jensen, Norman G., Inc.
3006 Hennepin Avenue
Minneapolis, MN 55408
Phone: 612 827-3761

MISSOURI

KANSAS CITY, MISSOURI

Circle Air Freight
19701 N. Conant Avenue
Kansas City, MO 64195
Phone: 816 891-8600

MONTANA

EUREKA, MONTANA

Sluys, Ralph V. Custom Brokers
P. O. Box 744
Eureka, MT 59917
Phone: 406: 889-3550

GREAT FALLS, MONTANA

Sluys, Ralph V., Customs Broker
P. O. Box, 1963
Great Falls, MT 59403
Phone: 406 452-0152

SWEETGRASS, MONTANA

American Brokers
P. O. Box 147
Sweetgrass, MT 59484
Phone: 406 335-2030

Moberly, W. Y. Inc.
P. O. Box 164
Sweetgrass, MT 59484
Phone: 406 335-2211

NEBRASKA

OMAHA, NEBRASKA

Union Pacific Railroad
1416 Dodge Street
Omaha, NE 68179
Phone: 402 271-5373

NEW JERSEY

CARLSTADT, NEW JERSEY

Abarim Freight Service
120 Kero Road
Carlstadt, NJ 07072
Phone: 201 939-3000

CRESSKILL, NEW JERSEY

Transport Masters International, Inc.
P. O. Box 418
Cresskill, NJ 07626
Phone: 201 569-4300

HILLSIDE, NEW JERSEY

Air Express International
465 Mudet Street
Hillside, NJ 07205
Phone: 201 688-6700

JERSEY CITY, NEW JERSEY

Holt, C. J. & Co., Inc.
3000 Kennedy Boulevard
Jersey City, NJ 07306
Phone: 201 792-9555

The Wilson Group USA, Inc.
1 Exchange Place
Jersey City, NJ 07302
Phone: 201 432-8800

NEWARK, NEW JERSEY

Circlee Air Freight
22 Rutherford Street
Newark, NJ 07105
Phone: 201 589-8200

Emery Air Freight
Newark International Airport
100 Port Street
Newark, NJ 07114
Phone: 201 961-3576

Import-Export Service of NJ, Inc.
972 Broad Street
Newark, NJ 07102
Phone: 201 622-0326

Redden, Charles A. Inc.
International Plaza Building
International Way
Newark, NJ 07114
Phone: 201 242-7200

Right-O-Way, Inc.
57 Charles Street
Newark, NJ 07105
Phone: 201 621-7383

RAMSEY, NEW JERSEY

Intercobra, Inc.
10 S. Franklin Tpke.
Ramsey, NJ 07446
Phone: 201 825-3330

RUTHERFORD, NEW JERSEY

Transmodel Associates, Inc.
85 Orient Way
Rutherford, NJ 07070
Phone: 201 896-1222

SOUTH KEARNY, NEW JERSEY

Brody Associates, Inc.
P. O. Box 85
South Kearny, N. J.
Phone: 201 589-5045

NEW YORK

ALEXANDRIA BAY, NEW YORK

Fenderson, Inc.
P. O. Box 596
Alexandria Bay, NY 13607
Phone: 315 482-2203

Myers, F. W. & Co. Inc.
RFD Wellesley Island
Alexandria Bay, NY
Phone: 315 482-2471

BAYSIDE, NEW YORK

Coleman, T. A. & Co., Inc.
212-22 48th Avenue
Bayside, NY 11384
Phone: 718-631-0660

BUFFALO, NEW YORK

Carrl, John V., & Son, Inc.
P. O. Box 268
Buffalo, NY 14201
Phone: 716 881-6550

Filbin, W. R. & Co.
1010 Niagara Street
Buffalo, NY 14213
Phone: 716 886-8101

Tower, C. J. & Son
128 Dearborn Street
Buffalo, NY 14207
Phone: 716 874-1300

CHAMPLAIN, NEW YORK

Fenderson, F. H. Inc.
P. O. Box 8
Champlain, NY 12919
Phone: 518 298-8265

INWOOD, NEW YORK

Behring Shipping Co., Inc.
600 Bayview Avenue
Inwood, NY 11696
Phone: 516 371-1505

JAMAICA, NEW YORK

Air-Sea Forwarders, Inc.
147-65 Farmers Boulevard
Jamaica, NY 11434
Phone: 718 723-7400

Aviation Transport, Inc.
JFK International Airport
Cargo Building 66
Jamaica, NY 11430
Phone: 718 1995-4747

British Airways Cargo
Building 66
JFK International Airport
Jamaica, NY 11430

Grace International Customs Brokers, Inc.
145-119 Buy B. Brewer Boulevard
Jamaica, NY 11434
Phone: 718 723-6400

Intercobal, Inc.
147-15 183rd Street
Jamaica, NY 11434
Phone: 718 432-9320

Cargo Building 80
Kennedy International Airport
Jamaica, NY 11430
Phone: 718 656-7430

McGregor Sea and Air Services Ltd.
167-17 146th Road
Jamaica, NY 11434
Phone: 718 632-7000

Mercer, W. & Co., Inc.
P. O. Box 885
JFK International Airport
Jamaica, NY 11430
Phone: 718-767-5840

Ryder International Freight &
Customs Service
175-11 148th Avenue
Jamaica, NY 11434
Phone: 718 653-0200

LAWRENCE, NEW YORK

Circle Airfreight Corporation
1 Johnson Road
Lawrence, NY 11559
Phone: 718 995-5050

LYNBROOK, NEW YORK

Robinson, Harper & Co.
No. 8 Freer Street, Room 155
Lynbrook, NY 11563
Phone: 718 656-5770

MASPETH, NEW YORK

Seven Brothers International, Inc.
57-48 49th Street
Maspeth, NY 11378
Phone: 718 366-8700

NEW YORK CITY, NEW YORK

Accelerated Shipping Corporation
54 Stone Street
New York, NY 10004
Phone: 212 475-0402

Ad. M. Schmid & Co.
7 Dey Street, Suite 900-B
New York, NY 10007
Phone 212 349-7307

Alpha International
30 Vexey Street
New York, NY 10007
Phone: 212 267-3700

Atlas Forwarding Co., Inc.
45 John Street
New York, NY 10038
Phone: 212 349-4911

B.L.G. Inc.
90 West Street
New York, NY 10006
Phone: 212 946-5281

The Bartel Shipping Co., Inc.
7 Dey Street
New York, NY 10007
Phone: 212 946-4371

Bemo Shipping Co., Inc.
25 Hudson Street, 10th Floor
New York, NY 10013
Phone: 212 941-2100

Brauner International Corp.
One World Trade Center
New York, NY 10048
Phone: 212 432-0080

Bruzzone Shipping, Inc.
132 Nassau Street
New York, NY 10038
Phone: 212 608-3830

Corbett International, Inc.
30 Vesey Street
New York, NY 10007
Phone: 212 349-4638

Cosmos Shipping Co., Inc.
39 Broadway
New York, NY 10006
Phone: 212 809-9330

Dansas Alltransport
17 Battery Place North
New York, NY 10004
Phone: 212 943-0230

Davies, Turner & Co.
1 World Trade Center, Suite 1729
New York, NY 10048
Phone: 212 432-0660

Direct Container Line, Inc.
Five World Trade Center, Suite 926
New York, NY 10048
Phone: 212 432-0580

Dow, Frank P. Co., Inc.
One World Trade Center Suite 2649
New York, NY 10048
Phone: 212 432-1747

Excel Shipping Corp.
One World Trade Center, Suite 1913
New York, NY 10048
Phone 212 432-0850

Gehrig, Hoban, & Co., Inc.
One World Trade Center, Suite 1617
New York, NY 10048
Phone: 212 432-1530

Haniel- Phoeni Transport, Inc.
105 Washington Street
New York, NY 10006
Phone: 212-269-0540

Happel, Charles, Inc.
90 West Street
New York, NY 10006
Phone: 212 422-8443

Hartrodt-Schmidt, Inc.
150 Broadway, Suite 1310
New York, NY 10038
Phone: 212 233-7105

Hauser, D., Inc.
1 World Trace Center, Suite 1535
New York, NY 10048
Phone: 212-432-0022

Helstrom International, Inc.
7 Dey Street
New York, NY 10007
Phone: 212 227-6740

The Hippage Co., Inc.
170 Broadway, Suite 812
New York, NY 10006
Phone: 212 372-1025

Hudsons Shipping Co., Inc.
90 West Street
New York, NY 10006
Phone: 212 349-8240

International Sea & Air Shipping Corp.
25 Ann Street
New York, NY 10038
Phone: 212 766-1616

Intercobal, Inc.
1 World Trade Center, Suite 1247
New York, NY 10048
Phone: 212 432-9320

Keating, W. R. & Co.
25 Hudson Street
New York, NY 10013
Phone: 212 226-3560

Laufer Shipping, Co., Inc.
305 Broadway, Suite 403
New York, NY 10007
Phone: 212 513-1444

Lykes Bros. Steamship Co., Inc.
17 Battery Place
New York, NY 10004
Phone: 212-943-6363

Maron Shipping Agency, Inc.
20 Vesey Street
New York NY 10007
Phone: 212 619-5400

Meyers, F. W. (Atlantic) & Co.
1 World Trade Center, Suite 3211
New York, NY 10048
Phone: 212 432-0670

Natural Nydegger Transport Corp.
1 World Trade Center, Suite 1565
New York, NY 10048
Phone: 212 432-1640

Neth, W. P. Co. Inc.
53 Park Place
New York, NY 10007
Phone: 212 964-6855

New Era Shipping Co., Inc.
114 Liberty Street, Suite 1007
New York, NY 10006
Phone: 212 233-8280

Nordstrom Freighting Corp.
21 West Street
New York, NY 10006
Phone 212 425-6740

Otterbourg, Steindler, Housten & Rosen
230 Park Avenue
New York, NY 10069
Phone: 212 661-9100

Penson & Co.
25 Hudson Street
New York, NY 10013
Phone 212 219-2988

Phelps, W.A. & Co., Inc.
1 World Trade Center, Suite 1963
New York, NY 10048
Phone: 212 775-1000

Phoenix Shipping Co., Inc.
105 Washington Street
New York, NY 10048
Phone: 212 269-0540

Radix Group International
158 William Street
New York, NY 10038
Phone: 212 185-2340

Robbins Fleisig Forwarding, Inc.
9 Murray Street
New York, NY 10007
Phone: 212 732-0900

Robinson, Harper & Co.
1 World Trade Center, Suite 2321
New York, NY 10048
Phone 212 775-7200

Robinson, H.W. & Co., Inc.
1 World Trade Center
New York, NY 10048
Phone 212-432-1350

Rohner, Gehrig & Co., Inc.
One Whitehall Street
New York, NY 10004
Phone: 212 269-8900

S.A.I.M.A. America, Inc.
39 Broadway
New York, NY 10006
Phone 212 344-1930

Saint John, H.W. & Co.
33 Rector Street
New York, NY 10006
Phone: 212 269-7680

Schenkers International Forwarders, Inc.
1 World Trade Center, Suite 1867
New York, NY 10048
Phone: 212 432-3000

Schroff, Karl & Associates, Inc.
90 West Street
New York, NY 10006
Phone: 212 732-1434

Silvey Shipping Co., Inc.
130 William Street, Suite 807
New York, NY 10038
Phone 212 732-7790

Snedeker, Milton, Corp.
105 Chamber Street
New York, NY 10007
Phone: 212-2276-7555

Spadaro International Services
401 Broadway, Suite 609
New York, NY 10013
Phone 212 226-3316

Surface Air International
20 Vesey Street
New York, NY 10007
Phone: 212 943-1100

Trans World Shipping Corp.
53 Park Place
New York, NY 10007
Phone: 212 267-4800

Terramar Shipping Co., Inc.
1 World Trade Center, Suite 1551
New York, NY 10048
Phone: 212 432-0770

United Forwarders Service, Inc.
15 Maiden Lane
New York, NY 10038
Phone: 212 349-6400

United States Forwarding Corp.
1 World Trade Center, Suite 2109
New York, NY 10048
Phone: 212 432-0090

West India Shipping Co., Inc.
280 Park Avenue
New York, NY 10017
Phone: 212 697-4919

STATEN ISLAND, NEW YORK

Trocciola, Burno J.
1002 Drumgoole Road, West
Staten Island, NY 10312
Phone: 718 356-3316

NORTH CAROLINA

CHARLOTTE, NORTH CAROLINA

Southern Overseas Corp.
P. O. Box 19086
Charlotte, NC 28219
Phone: 704 527-2414

WILMINGTON, NORTH CAROLINA

Waters Shipping Co.
P. O. Box 118
Wilmington, NC 28401
Phone: 919 763-8491

OHIO

CLEVELAND, OHIO

Blaser & Mericle, Inc.
P. O. Box 81309
Cleveland, OH 44135
Phone: 216 267-1800

Teimouri, R.S. & Co., Inc.
1 Leaker Building
Cleveland, OH 44114
Phone: 216 678-0560

COLUMBUS, OHIO

Fenton, A. W., Co., Inc.
P. O. Box 19937
Columbus, OH 43219
Phone: 614 258-2500

DAYTON, OHIO

Fenton, A. W. Co.
420 Dellrose Avenue
Dayton, OH 45403
Phone: 513 253-2030

MIDDLEBURG HEIGHTS, OHIO

Harper, Robinson, & Co.
17901 Sheldon Road
Middleburg Heights, OH 44130
Phone: 216 433-7575

McGregor Sea & Air Services, Ltd.
18751 Sheldon Road
Middleburg Heights, OH 44130
Phone: 216 433-1340

TOLEDO, OHIO

Blaser & Mericle Inc.
1946 N. 13th Street, Suite 360
Toledo, OH 43624
Phone: 419 244-4081

Danzas Seaway, Seaway
Forwarding Corp.
714 Washington Street
Toledo, OH 43624
Phone: 419 242-7318

Lipinski, J.S. Co.
35 West Capistrano
Toledo, OH 43612
Phone: 419 476-7977

OREGON

PORTLAND, OREGON

Fritz, Arthur J. & Co.
3601 N. W. Yeon Avenue, 204
Portland, OR 97208
Phone: 503 222-1451

Rausch, Ted L. Co. of Oregon
5362 N.E. 112Th
Portland, OR 97230
Phone: 503 257-0510

PENNSYLVANIA

ERIE, PENNSYLVANIA

Hosford Co., The
P. O. Box 8285
Erie, PA 16505
Phone: 814 455-6533

FOLCROFT, PENNSYLVANIA

Air Express International
111 Darby Commons Court
Folcroft, PA 19032
Phone: 215 534-7800

PHILADELPHIA, PENNSYLVANIA

Aghoian-Tague, Inc.
44 South Second Street
Philadelphia, PA 19153
Phone: 215 925-8000

Amco Customs Brokerage Co.
Cargo Building 2
Philadelphia International Airport
Philadelphia, PA 19153
Phone: 215 365-3307

Davies, Turner & Co.
113 Chestnut Street
Philadelphia, PA 19106
Phone: 215 925-3300

Friedman, Morris, Co.
320 Walnut Street
Philadelphia, PA 19106
Phone: 215 925-4200

Keer, Mauer, Inc.
209 Chestnut Street
Philadelphia, PA 19106
Phone: 215 629-1616

Merion, Milton C. Inc.
918 Lafayette Building
Philadelphia, PA 19106
Phone: 215 923-7766

Quaker Export Packaging Co., Inc.
901 Poplar Street
Philadelphia, PA 19123-1998
Phone: 215 236-5800

PUERTO RICO

SAN JUAN, PUERTO RICO

Caribe Shipping Co., Inc.
P. O. Box 3267
Old San Juan, PR 00904
Phone: 809 724-5800

Matos, Felix L.
P. O. Box 4263
Old San Juan, PR 00905
Phone: 809 725-5375

RHODE ISLAND

PROVIDENCE, RHODE ISLAND

Goff & Page Co.
P. O. Box 9248
Providence, RI 02940
Phone: 401 785-9100

SOUTH CAROLINA

CHARLESTON, S. CAROLINA

Costal Forwarders, Inc.
1085 Morrison Drive
Charleston, SC 29402
Phone: 803-722-1703

Carroll, W. G. & Co., Inc.
P. O. Box 685
Charleston, SC 29402
Phone: 803 722-8574

Fritz, Arthur J. & Co., Inc.
1071 Morrison Drive
Charleston, SC 29402
Phone: 803 722-8334

Hasman & Baxt, Inc.
P. O. Box 1409
Charleston, SC 29402
Phone: 803 577-0337

The Hippage Co., Inc.
P. O. Box 841
Charleston, SC 29401
Phone: 803 723-4846

International Forwarders, Inc.
P. O. Box 550
Charleston, SC 29402
Phone: 803 722-2731

James, John S.
P. O. Box 1017
Charleston, SC 19402
Phone: 803 722-2751

Transport International, Inc.
P. O. Box 746
Charleston, SC 29402
Phone: 803 723-0688

TENNESSEE

MEMPHIS, TENNESSEE

Alexander, V. & Co.
P. O. Box 30250
Memphis, TN 38130
Phone: 901 795-7761

TEXAS

BEAUMONT, TEXAS

Schurig, H. E. & Co., Inc
P. O. Box 2341
Beaumont, TX 77704
Phone: 409 833-8669

BROWNSVILLE, TEXAS

Soto Forwarding Agency
P. O. Box 4199
Brownsville, TX 78520
Phone: 512 542-7203

CORPUS CHRISTI, TEXAS

Valls, Ralph & Son, Inc.
P. O. Box 2505
Corpus Christi, TX 78403
Phone 512 884-4096

DALLAS, TEXAS

Harper, Robingson & Co.
P. O. Box 61024
Dallas, Texas 75261
Phone 214 574-2841

Sekin, Darrell J. & Co., Inc.
P. O. Box 655464
Dallas, TX 75267
Phone: 214 456-0730

EL PASO, TEXAS

ABACO Custom House Broker, Inc.
P. O. Box 9705
El Paso, TX 79905
Phone: 915 542-0701

Brown, Alcantar & Brown, Inc.
P. O. Box 1161
El Paso, TX 79947
Phone: 915 532-3461

GALVESTON, TEXAS

Sachurig, H.E. & Co., Inc.
P. O. Box 332
Galveston, TX 77553
Phone: 409 762-7685
United States National Bank Building
Room 1018
Galveston, TX 77550
Phone: 409 963-2305

GRAPEVINE, TEXAS

Radix Group International
169 Schribner Street
Grapevine, TX 76051
Phone: 817 481-7568

HIDALGO, TEXAS

B & D Custom House Brokers, Inc.
P. O. Drawer M.
Hidalgo, TX 78557
Phone: 843-2253

HOUSTON, TEXAS

Air Express International Agency, Inc.
Interncontinental Airport
Houston, TX 77205
Phone: 713 443-0710
Circle Air Freight
P. O. Box 60428
Houston, TX 77205
Phone: 713 443-0921
Coopersmith, L. E. Inc.
15700 Export Plaza Drive
Houston, TX 77032
Phone: 713 987-9870

Dorf International, Inc.
9370 Wallisville Road
Suite 1000
Houston, TX 77013
Phone: 713 673-8399

Dow, Frank P. Co.
P. O. Box 53180
Houston, TX 77052
Phone: 713 233-9419

Fritz, Arthur J. & Co.
P. O. Box 52860
Houston, TX 77052
Phone: 713-868-6200

HLZ Import Services, Inc.
P. O. Box 60295 AMF
Houston, TX 77205
Phone: 713-443-1537

Harper Robinson & Co.
P. O. Box 77205 AMF
Houston, TX 77060
Phone: 713 820-5526

Intlcobal, Inc.
P. O. Box 130350
Houston, TX 77219
Phone: 713 955-0833

Lambay/Summers, Air Freight
P. O. Box 60627
Houston, TX 77205
Phone: 713 433-0601

Labay/Summers International, Inc.
P. O. Box 52170
Houston, TX 77052
Phone: 713 237-9431

McGregor Sea & Air Services, Ltd
2700 Greens Road, Building F
Houston, TX 77032
Phone: 713 590-6000

Schurig, H. E. & Co., Inc.
P. O. Box 54
Houston, TX 77074
Phone: 713 224-8541

Seacon Express, Inc.
P. O. Box 15705
Houston, TX 77220
Phone: 713 227-0421

Soto, A. X.
P. O. Box 52067
Houston, TX 77052
Phone: 713 237-8203

Surface Air International, Inc.
2700 Green Road, Building K
Houston, TX 77032
Phone: 713 675-2255

Zane, W. R. & Co.
Houston International Airport
Houston, TX 77205

Ziegler, H. L., Inc.
P. O. Box 53180
Houston, TX 77052
Phone: 713 688-5800

LAKE JACKSON, TEXAS

Ziegler, H. L., Inc.
P. O. Box 480
Lake Jackson, TX 77566
Phone: 409 297-8178

LAREDO, TEXAS

American Brokerage Co.
Mann Road & Station Maria
Laredo, TX 78041
Phone: 512 723-7821

Freidin, Sidney, Inc.
P. O. Box 1029
Laredo, TX 78040
Phone: 512 723-8271

Munoz, Estaban
P. O. Box 1491
Laredo, TX 78040
Phone: 512 724-8311

MEDERLAND, TEXAS

Keer, mauer, Inc.
1220 Dixie Boulevard
Mederland, TX 77627
Phone: 713 727-3974

PRESIDIO, TEXAS

Hendrix, Miles & Hendrix, Inc.
P. O. Box 840
Presidio, TX 79845
Phone: 915 229-3208

VERMONT

DERBY LINE, VERMONT

Fenderson, F. H. Inc.
RR #1, 3 Herrick Road
Derby Line, VT 05830-9701
Phone: 802 873-3131

HIGHGATE SPRINGS, VERMONT

Fenderson, F. H. Inc.
P. O. Box 225
Highgate Springs, VT 05460
Phone: 802 868-7369

NORTON, VERMONT

Fenderson, F. H. Inc.
P. O. Box 51
Norton, VT 05907
Phone: 802 822-5227

SAINT ALBANS, VERMONT

Myers, F. W. & Co., Inc.
P. O. Box 229
Saint Albans, VT 05478
Phone: 802 868-7352

VIRGINIA

NORFOLK, VIRGINIA

Alltransport, Inc.
101 St. Paul Boulevard, Suite 1414
Norfolk, VA 23510
Phone: 804 625-2375

Bemo Shipping Co., Inc.
P. O. Box 13084
Norfolk, VA 23506-0084
Phone: 804 466-0136

Connor, John S. Inc.
340 Montecello Arcade
Suite 322
208 E. Plume Street
Norfolk, Va 23514
Phone: 804 627-3910

The Hippage Co., Inc.
227 E. Plume Street
Norfolk, VA 23510
Phone: 804 625-5307

Intercobal, Inc.
304 E. Plume Street
Norfolk, VA 23510
Phone: 804 625-5307

Myers, F. W. & Co., Inc.
109 East Main Street, Suite 600
Norfolk, VA 23510
Phone: 804 627-7425

Penson & Co.
P. O. Box 3221
Norfolk, VA 23514
Phone: 804 625-0526

Schenkers International Forwarders, Inc.
P. O. Box 3174
Norfolk, VA 23514
Phone: 804 853-0900

Stone, W. M. Co., Inc.
P. O. Box 3447
Norfolk, VA 23514
Phone: 804 622-3293

WASHINGTON

BLAINE, WASHINGTON

Border Brokerage Co.
P. O. Box B
Blaine, WA 98230
Phone: 206 332-5222

Fritz, Arthur J. & Co., Inc.
P. O. Drawer G
Blaine, WA 98230
Phone: 206 332-5001

LONGVIEW, WASHINGTON

Bush, George S. & Co., Inc.
P. O. Box 1400
Longview, WA 98632
Phone: 206 425-5061

Jensen, Norman G. Inc.
P. O. Box 908
Longview, WA 98632
Phone: 206 425-1543

SEATTLE, WASHINGTON

Airborne Freight Corporation
190 Queen Anne Avenue North
Seattle, WA 98111
Phone: 206 285-4600

Bush, George S. & Co., Inc.
1400 Exchange Building
821 2nd Avenue
Seattle, WA 98104
Phone: 206 623-2563

Dow, Frank P. & Co.
P. O. Box 3074
Seattle, WA 98114
Phone: 206 622-1360

Gladish & Associates
1511 Third Avenue, Suite 808
Seattle, WA 98101
Phone: 206 623-1023

Jensen, Norman G. Inc.
810 Third Avenue
Seattle, WA 98104
Phone: 206 442-9456

Rausch, Ted L. Co.
1415 Western Avenue
Seattle, WA 98101
Phone: 206 682-1492

Schroff Karl, & Associates, Inc.
P. O. Box 69168
Seattle, WA 98188
Phone: 206 292-0600

WENATCHEE, WASHINGTON

Aero-Brokers (Trading Co.) Inc.
P. O. Box 3627
Wenatchee, WA 98801-0058

WISCONSIN

MILWAUKEE, WISCONSIN

Byrnes & Co.
P. O. Box 21948
Milwaukee, WI 53221
Phone: 414 769-7222

Circle Air Freight
241 W. Edgerton Avenue
Milwaukee, WI 53207
Phone: 414 482-2400

Foreign Forwarding, Inc.
10300 W. Hampton Avenue
Milwaukee, WI 53225
Phone: 414 461-6230

The Hippage Co., Inc.
P. O. Box 14124
Milwaukee, WI 53214
Phone: 414 475-4100

Appendix 6

Banks in World Trade

ALABAMA

BIRMINGHAM, ALABAMA

AmSouth Bank, N.A.
1900 5th Avenue N.
Birmingham, AL 35203
Phone: 205 326-5486

South Trust Bank of Alabama
P.O. Box 2554
Birmingham, AL 35290
Phone: 205 254-5218

MOBILE, ALABAMA

AmSouth Bank, N.A.
31 N. Royal Street
Mobile, AL 36621

First Alabama Bank
P.O. Drawer 2527
Mobile, AL 36622
Phone: 205 690-1244

ARIZONA

PHOENIX

Arizona Bank
P.O. Box 2511
Phoenix, AZ 85002
Phone: 602 262-2391

Source: American Export Register, 1989 Edition, Thomas International Publishing Company, One Penn Plaza, New York, NY 10119.

The First Interstate Bank of Arizona
P.O. Box 20551
Phoenix, AZ 85036
Phone: 602 271-6143

Valley National Bank
P.O. Box 71
Phoenix, AZ 85001
Phone: 602 261-2900

ARKANSAS

LITTLE ROCK, ARKANSAS

First Commercial Bank, N.A.
P.O. Box 1471
Little Rock, AR 72203
Phone: 501 371-7338

Northern Bank & Trust Co.
P.O. Box 1681
Little Rock, AR
Phone: 501 378-1080

CALIFORNIA

LOS ANGELES, CALIFORNIA

Banco Di Napoli
33 Grand Avenue
Los Angeles, CA 90071
Phone: 213 617-8111

Lloyds Bank of California
612 S. Flower Street
Los Angeles, CA 90017
Phone: 213 613-2000

Mitsui Manufacturers Bank
515 S. Figueroa Street, 4th FLoor
Los Angeles, CA 90071
Phone: 213 489-8647

Security Pacific National Bank
P.O. Box 2238, Terminal Annex
Los Angeles, CA 90051
Phone: 213 613-5817

Union Bank
Fifth & Figueroa
Los Angeles, CA 90071
Phone: 213 687-6877

United California Bank
707 Wilshire Boulevard
Los Angeles, CA 90017
Phone: 213 615-4111

SAN DIEGO, CALIFORNIA

San Diego Trust & Savings Bank
P.O. Box 1871
San Diego, CA 92112
Phone: 619 238-4715

SAN FRANCISCO, CALIFORNIA

Bank of America
555 California Street
San Francisco 94104
Phone: 415 622-3456

Bank of California, N.A.
400 California Street
San Francisco 94104
Phone: 415 765-3218

Barclays Bank of California
111 Pine Street
San Francisco 94111
Phone: 415 981-8090

California First Bank
350 California Street
San Francisco 94104
Phone: 415 445-0200

Crocker National Bank
1 Montgomery Street
San Francisco 94104
Phone: 415 983-3280

Wells Fargo Bank, N.A.
464 California Street
San Francisco 94104
Phone: 415 396-0123

Wildwood International Banking
P.O. Box 3949
San Francisco 94119
Phone: 415 445-8000

COLORADO

DENVER, COLORADO

First Interstate Bank of Denver
633 17th Street
Denver, CO 80270
Phone: 303 293-2211

Colorado National Bank of Denver
P.O. Box 5168
Denver, CO 80217
Phone: 303 892-1862

United Bank of Denver, N.A.
1700 Broadway
Denver, CO 80274-0085
Phone: 303 861-8811

CONNECTICUT

BRIDGEPORT, CONNECTICUT

Citytrust
961 Main Street
Bridgeport, CT 06601
Phone: 203 384-5212

Connecticut National Bank
888 Main Street
Bridgeport, CT 06603
Phone: 203 579-3131

HARTFORD, CONNECTICUT

The Connecticut Bank & Trust CO.
1 Constitution Plaza
Hartford, CT 06115
Phone: 203 244-5000

Connecticut National Bank
777 Main Street
Hartford, CT 06115
Phone: 203 718-2000

NEW HAVEN, CONNECTICUT

First Bank
1 Church Street
New Haven, CT 06502
Phone: 203 773-7439

STAMFORD, CONNECTICUT

Union Trust Co.
300 Main Street
Stamford, CT 06904
Phone: 203 348-6211

WATERBURY, CONNECTICUT

Colonial Bank & Trust Co.
P.O. Box 2149
Waterbury, CT 06730
Phone: 203 574-7000

DELAWARE

WILMINGTON, DELAWARE

Bank of Delaware
901 Market Street
Wilmington, DE 19801
Phone: 302 4429-1566

Wilmington Trust Co.
10th & Market Streets
Wilmington, DE 18999
Phone: 302 428-7000

DISTRICT OF COLUMBIA

American Security Bank, N.A.
15th Street & Pennsylvania Avenue, N.W.
Washington, D.C. 20013
Phone: 202 624-4000

National Bank of Washington
619 14th Street, N.W.
Washington, D.C. 20005
Phone: 202 537-2000

National Savings & Trust CO.
15th Street & New York Avenue,
N.W.
Washington, D.C.
Phone: 202 659-5900

Riggs National Bank
800 17th Street, N.W.
Washington, D. C. 20006
Phone: 202 462-0028

FLORIDA

JACKSONVILLE, FLORIDA

First Union National Bank of Florida
200 W. Forsyth Street
Jacksonville, FL 32231-0010
Phone: 904 361-7749

Florida First National Bank
General Mail Center
Jacksonville, FL 32232
Phone: 904 359-5111

MIAMI, FLORIDA

Barnett Bank of Miami, N.A.
800 Brickell Avenue
Miami, FL 33131
Phone: 305 350-7122

Flagship Bank
11 Lincoln Road Mall
Miami, Beach FL 33139
Phone: 305 674-5111

Florida National Bank
69 E. Flager Street, Suite 722
Miami, FL 33131
Phone: 305 545-3154

Pan American Bancshares, Inc.
P.O. Box 010831
Miami, FL 33101
Phone: 305 577-5600

Southeast Bank, N.A.
Southeast Financial Center
Miami, FL 33131
Phone: 305 375-7500

ORLANDO, FLORIDA

Sun Bank, N.A.
P.O. Box 3833
Orlando, FL 32897
Phone: 305 2337-4141

TAMPA, FLORIDA

First National Bank of Florida
P.O. Box 1810
Tampa, FL 33601
Phone: 813 224-1514

NCNB National Bank of Florida
P.O. Box 25900
Tampa, FL 33630
Phone: 813 224-5151

GEORGIA

ATLANTA, GEORGIA

Bank South, N.A.
P.O. Box 4387
Atlanta, GA 30302
Phone: 404 529-3789

The First National Bank of Atlanta
2 Peachtree Street
Atlanta, GA 30383
Phone: 404 588-5000

Trust Co. Bank
25 Park Place, N.E.
Atlanta, GA 30303
Phone: 404 588-7711

HAWAII

HONOLULU, HAWAII

Bank of Hawaii
111 S. King Street
Honolulu, HI 96846
Phone: 808 537-8111

First Hawaiian Bank
P.O. Box 3200
Honolulu, HI 96847
Phone: 808 525-8721

ILLINOIS

CHICAGO, ILLINOIS

American National Bank of Chicago
33 N. LaSalle Street, Room 1400
Chicago, IL 60602
Phone: 312 661-5000

Chicago-Tokyo Bank
40 N. Dearborn Street
Chicago, IL 60602
Phone: 312 236-1200

Continental Illinois National Bank & Trust Co.
231 La Salle Street
Chicago, IL 60693
Phone: 312 828-2345

Exchange National Bank of Chicago
La Salle & Adams Streets
Chicago, IL 60690
Phone: 321 781-8000

First National Bank of Chicago
1 First National Plaza
Chicago, IL 60670
Phone: 312 732-4000

Harris Trust & Savings Bank
111 W. Monroe Street
Chicago, IL 60690
Phone: 312 461-2121

Lake View Trust & Savings Bank
3201 N. Ashland Avenue
Chicago, IL 60657
Phone: 312 525-2180

La Salle National Bank
135 S. La Salle Street, Room 2060
Chicago, IL 60603
Phone: 312 443-2000

Exchange National Bank of Chicago
La Salle & Adams Streets
Chicago, IL 60690
Phone: 321 781-8000

First National Bank of Chicago
1 First National Plaza
Chicago, IL 60670
Phone: 312-732-4000

Harris Trust & Savings Bank
111 W. Monroe Street
Chicago, IL 60690
Phone 312 461-2121

Lake View Trust & Savings Bank
3201 N. Ashland Avenue
Chicago, IL 60657
Phone: 312 525-2180

La Salle National Bank
135 S. La Salle Street, Room 2060
Chicago, IL 60603
Phone: 312 443-2000

The Northern Trust Co.
50 S. La Salle Street
Chicago, IL 60675
Phone: 312 630-6000

INDIANA

FT. WAYNE, INDIANA

Fort Wayne National Bank
110 W. Berry Street
Ft. Wayne, IN 46802
Phone: 219 426-0555

INDIANAPOLIS, INDIANA

American Fletcher National Bank
111 Monument Circle
Indianapolis, IN 46277
Phone: 317 639-7943

Indiana National Bank
One Indiana Square
Indianapolis, IN 46266
Phone: 317 266-6068

Merchants National Bank & Trust Co.
One Merchants Plaza, Suite 77S
Indianapolis, IN 46255
Phone: 317 267-7000

IOWA

DES MOINES, IOWA

Northwest Bank International
666 Walnut Street
Des Moines, IA 50304
Phone: 5 245-3131

KANSAS

WICHITA, KANSAS

Fourth National Bank & Trust Co.
P.O. Box 4, Wichita, KS 67201
Phone: 316 261-4444

KENTUCKY

LOUISVILLE, KENTUCKY

Citizens Fidelity Bank & Trust Co.
Citizens Plaza
Louisville, KY 40296
Phone: 502 581-2100

First National Bank of Louisville
P.O. Box 36000
Louisville, KY 40232
Phone: 502 566-2000

Liberty National Bank & Trust Co.
P.O. Box 32580
Louisville, KY 40232
Phone: 502 566-2297

LOUISIANA

NEW ORLEANS, LOUISIANA

First National Bank of Commerce
P.O. Box 60279
New Orleans, LA 70160
Phone: 502 561-1322

MARYLAND

BALTIMORE, MARYLAND

Equitable Bank, N.A.
P.O. Box 1556
Baltimore, MD 20213
Phone: 301 547-4709

First National Bank of Maryland
14 Light Street
Baltimore, MD 21203
Phone: 301 244-4520

Maryland National Bank
10 Light Street
Baltimore, MD 21202
Phone: 301 244-5000

Signet Bank/Maryland
P.O. Box 1077
Baltimore, MD 21203
Phone: 301 625-4022

MASSACHUSETTS

BOSTON, MASSACHUSETTS

Bank of Boston
100 Federal Street
Boston, MA 02110
Phone: 617 434-2200

N. E. Merchants National Bank
28 State Street
Boston, MA 02109
Phone: 617 742-4000

State Street Bank & Trust Co.
225 Franklin Street
Boston, MA 01201
Phone: 617 786-3000

DEDHAM, MASSACHUSETTS

Baybank Norfolk County Trust Co.
858 Washington Street
Dedham, MA 02026
Phone: 617 329-3700

QUINCY, MASSACHUSETTS

Multibank International
1400 Hancock Street
Quincy, MA 02169
Phone: 617 847-3275

WORCESTER, MASSACHUSETTS

Worcester County National Bank
P.O. Box 529
Worcester, MA 01608
Phone: 508 793-4000

MICHIGAN

DETROIT, MICHIGAN

City National Bank of Michigan
P.O. Box 2659, Detroit, MI 48231
Phone: 313 965-1900

Coamerica Bank
211 W. Fort Avenue
Detroit, MI 48264
Phone: 313 222-3300

First of American Bank - Detroit, N.A.
645 Griswold Street
Detroit, MI 48226
Phone: 313 965-1900

Manufacturers National Bank of
Detroit
100 Renaissance Center, 12th Floor
Detroit, MI 48243
Phone: 313 222-3160

Michigan National Bank
300 River Place, Suite 6000
Detroit, MI 48207
313 568-4565

National Bank of Detroit
P.O. Box 116
Detroit, MI 48232
Phone: 313 225-1000

GRAND RAPIDS, MICHIGAN

Old Kent Bank & Trust Co.
1 Vandenberg Center
Grand Rapids, MI 49503
Phone: 616 774-1026

Union Bank & Trust Co., N.A.
200 Ottawa, N.W.
Grand Rapids, MI 49503
Phone: 616 451-7000

LANSING, MICHIGAN

Michigan National Bank
124 W. Allegan
Lansing, MI 48901
Phone: 517 377-3111

MINNESOTA

MINNEAPOLIS, MINNESOTA

First Bank of Minneapolis
120 S. 6th Street
Minneapolis, MN 55480
Phone: 612 370-4141

MISSISSIPPI

JACKSON, MISSISSIPPI

Deposit Guaranty National Bank
P.O. Box 1200
Jackson, MS 39205
Phone: 601 354-8211

Trustmark National Bank
P.O. Box 291
Jackson, MS 39205
Phone 601 354-5861

MISSOURI
KANSAS CITY, MISSOURI

Boatmen's First National Bank of
Kansas City
P.O. Box 38
Kansas City, MO 64183
Phone: 816 221-2800

Commercial Bank of Kansas City,
N.A.
P.O. Box 248
Kansas City,MO 64141
Phone: 816 234-2581

Centerre Bank of Kansas City, N.A.
900 Walnut Street
Kansas City, MO 64106
Phone: 816 474-6211

United Missouri Bank of Kansas City
P.O. Box 226
Kansas City, MO 64141
Phone: 816 556-7000

ST. LOUIS, MISSOURI

Boatmen's National Bank
100 N. Broadway
St. Louis, MO 63102
Phone: 314 425-3651

Centerre Bank, N.A.
1 Centerre Plaza
St. Louis, Mo 63101
Phone: 314 554-6000

Mercantile Trust Co., N.A.
721 Locust Street
St. Louis, MO 63166
Phone: 314 425-3770

NEBRASKA
LINCOLN, NEBRASKA

First National Bank & Trust Co of Lincoln
P.O. Box 81008, Lincoln, NE 68501
Phone: 402 471-1231

National Bank of Commerce Trust &
Savings Assoc.
P.O. Box 82408
Lincoln, NE 68501
Phone: 402 472-4321

OMAHA, NEBRASKA

Northwest Bank Omaha, N.A.
1919 Douglas Street
Omaha, NE 68102
Phone: 402 536-2113

Omaha National Bank
P.O. Box 3443
Omaha, NE 68102
Phone: 402 348-6000

NEW JERSEY
EDISON, NEW JERSEY

Midatlantic National Bank
499 Thornall Street
Edison, NJ 08818
Phone: 201 321-8230

ELIABETH, NEW JERSEY

National State Bank
68 Broad Street
Elizabeth, NJ 08207
Phone: 201 354-3400

HACKENSACK, NEW JERSEY

United Jersey Bank
210 Main Street
Hackensack, NJ 07601
Phone: 2021 646-0500

JERSEY CITY, NEW JERSEY

First National Bank
1 Exchange Place
Jersey City, NJ 07303
Phone: 201 547-7000

MORRISTOWN, NEW JERSEY

American National Bank & Trust Co.
225 South Street
Morristown, NJ 07960
Phone: 201 285-2035

Horizon Bank
334 Madison Avenue
Morristown, NJ 07960
Phone; 201 285-2785

NEWARK, NEW JERSEY

Fidelity Union Trust Co.
765 Broad Street
Newark, NJ 07101
Phone: 201 430-4000

First National State Bank of New
Jersey
550 Broad Street, 19th Floor
Newark, NJ 07102
Phone: 201 565-3095

PARAMUS, NEW JERSEY

Garden State National Bank
10 Forest Avenue
Paramus, NJ 07652
Phone: 201 368-7000

RUTHERFORD, NEW JERSEY

National Community Bank
P.O. Box 250, Rutherford, NJ 08080
Phone: 201 845-1000

TRENTON, NEW JERSEY

New Jersey National Bank
P.O. Box 671, Trenton, NJ 08628
Phone: 609 771-5644

WEST PATERSON, NEW JERSEY

Midatlantic National Bank/North
P.O. Box 2177
West Paterson, NJ 07509
Phone: 201 881-5300

NEW YORK

NEW YORK, NEW YORK
Allied Bank International
116 E. 55th Street
New York, NY 10022
Phone 212 546-0600

American Express International Banking
Corp.
American Plaza
125 Broad Street
New York, NY 10004
Phone: 212 323-2000

Julius Baer Banking Co.
330 Madison Avenue
New York, NY 10017
Phone: 212 949-9044

Banca Serfin, S.N.C.
88 Pine Street
Wall Street Plaza, 24th Fl.
New York, NY 10005
Phone: 212 635-2320

Banco Di Napoli
277 Park Avenue
New York, NY 10172
Phone: 212 644-8400

Banco Popular de Puerto Rico
7 W. 51 Street
New York, NY 10019
Phone: 212 315-2800

Banco Santander
375 Park Avenue, 29th Fl.
New York, NY 10152
Phone: 212 826-9281

Bancomer, S.N.C.
15 E. 54 St.
New York, NY 10022
Phone: 212 759-7600

Bankers Trust Co.
280 Park Avenue
New York, NY 10017
Phone: 212 775-2500

Bank Bumi Daya
350 Park Avenue, 7th Fl.
New York, NY 10022
Phone: 212 735-5289

Bank of East Asia, Ltd.
450 Park Avenue
New York, NY 10022
Phone: 212 980-0510

Bank Leumi Trust Co. of New York
579 Fifth Avenue
New York, NY 10017
Phone: 212 382-4010

Bank of New York
48 Wall Street
New York, NY 10015
Phone: 212 530-1784

Banque Nationale de Paris
499 Park Avenue
New York, NY 10022
Phone: 212 750-1400

Brown Brother Harriman & Co.
59 Wall Street
New York, NY 10005
Phone: 212 483-1818

Chase Manhattan Bank, N.A.
1 Chase Manhattan Plaza
New York, NY 10015
Phone: 212 552-2222

Chemical Bank
277 Park Avenue
New York, NY 10172
Phone: 212 310-7120

Citibank, N.A.
399 Park Avenue
New York, NY 10043
Phone: 212 559-1000

DNC American Banking Corp.
600 Fifth Avenue
New York, NY 10020
Phone: 212 315-6500

European American Bank & Trust Co.
10 Hanover Square
New York, NY 10005
Phone: 212 437-4300

French American Banking Corp.
120 Broadway
New York, NY 10271
Phone: 212 964-4127

The Fuji Bank & Trust Co.
1 World Trade Center, Suite 8023
New York, NY 10048
Phone: 212 938-6666

Irving Trust Co.
1 Wall Street
New York, NY 10015
Phone: 212 487-2121

Israel Discount Bank of New York
511 Fifth Avenue
New York, NY 10017
Phone: 212 551-8500

Israel Discount Bank of New York
1350 Broadway
New York, NY 10018
Phone: 212 551-8500

ITC/FIBA, Inc.
P.O. Box 605, FDR Sta.
New York, NY 10150
Phone: 212 355-1818

Kansallis-Osake-Pankki
575 Fifth Avenue
New York, NY 10017
Phone: 212 972-4545

Krung Thai Bank
452 Fifth Avenue
New York, NY 10018
Phone 212 704-0001

Manufacturers Hanover Trust Co.
4 New York Plaza
New York, NY 10015
Phone: 212 623-7939

Marine Midland Bank
140 Broadway
New York, NY 10015
Phone: 212 440-1000

Moran Guaranty Trust Co. of New York
23 Wall Street
New York, NY 10015
Phone: 212 483-2323

National Commercial Bank
245 Park Avenue
New York, NY 10167
Phone: 212 916-9000

National Westminster Bank, USA
75 Water Street
New York, NY 10038
Phone: 212 602-2100

Republic National Bank of New York
452 Fifth Avenue
New York, NY 10018
Phone: 212 930-6000

Harry Schroder Banking Trust Co.
1 State Street
New York, NY 10015
Phone: 212 269-6500

Sterling National Bank & Trust Co.
540 Madison Avenue
New York, NY 10022
Phone: 212 826-2200

United Bank, Ltd.
30 Wall Street
New York,NY 10028
Phone: 212 943-1275

United States Trust Co. of New York
45 Wall Street
New York, NY 10005
Phone: 212 806-4500

ROCHESTER, NEW YORK

Central Trust Co.
44 Exchange Street
Rochester, NY 14614
Phone: 716 546-4500

Lincoln First Bank of Rochester
1 Lincoln First Square
Rochester, NY 14642
Phone: 716 262-2000

Norstar Bank, N.A.
1 East Avenue
Rochester, NY 14638
Phone: 716 546-9250

SYRACUSE, NEW YORK

Merchants National Bank & Trust Co. of Syracuse
P.O. Box 4950
Syracuse, NY 13221
Phone: 315 472-5561

NORTH CAROLINA

CHARLOTTE, NORTH CAROLINA

NCNB North Carolina National Bank
P.O. Box 120
Charlotte, NC 28255
Phone: 704 374-5000

NORTH WILKESBORO, NORTH CAROLINA

The Northwestern Bank
P.O. Box 310
North Wilkesboro,NC 28674
Phone: 919 651-5000

WINSTON SALEM, NORTH CAROLINA

Wachovia Bank & Trust Co.
P.O. Box 3099
Winston Salem, NC 27150
Phone: 919 748-5000

AKRON, OHIO

National City Bank
1 Cascade Plaza
Akron, OH 44308
Phone 216 375-8300

CINCINNATI, OHIO

Central Trust Co., N.A.
5th & Main Streets
Cincinnati, OH 45202
Phone 513 651-8911

First National Bank
5th & Walnut Streets
Cincinnati, OH 45202
Phone: 513 632-4137

CLEVELAND, OHIO

Central National Bank of Cleveland
800 Superior Avenue
Cleveland, OH 44114
Phone: 216 344-3000

Huntington National Bank
917 Euclid Avenue
Cleveland, OH 44115

National City Bank
623 Euclid Avenue
Cleveland, OH 44114
Phone: 216 861-4900

COLUMBUS, OHIO

Huntington Nat'l Bank of Columbus
17 S. High Street
Columbus, OH 43216
Phone: 614 469-7000

DAYTON, OHIO

First National Bank
1 First National Plaza
Dayton, OH 45202
Phone: 513 226-2000

Society Bank, N.A.
34 N. Main Street
Dayton, OH 45402
Phone: 513 226-6139

Winter National Bank & Trust Co.
Winter Bank Tower
Dayton, OH 45401
Phone: 513 449-8600

TOLEDO, OHIO

First National Bank of Toledo
606 Madison Avenue
Toledo, OH 43604
Phone: 419 259-6894

Ohio Citizens Bank
P.O. Box 1688
Toledo, OH 43603
Phone: 419 259-7700

Trustcorp, Inc.
3 Sea Gate
Toledo, OH 43603
Phone: 419 259-8153

OKLAHOMA

OKLAHOMA CITY, OKLAHOMA

First National Bank & Trust Co.
Oklahoma City, OK 73102
Phone: 405 272-4000

Liberty National Bank & Trust Co.
100 Broadway
Oklahoma City, OK 73102
Phone: 405 231-6000

TULSA, OKLAHOMA

Bank of Oklahoma, N.A.
P.O. Box 2300
Tulsa, OK 74192
Phone: 918 588-6886

First National Bank & Trust Co.
P.O. Box 1, Tulsa, OK 74193
Phone: 918 586-1000

OREGON

PORTLAND, OREGON

The Oregon Bank
1001 S.W. 5th Avenue
Portland, OR 97204
Phone: 503 222-7762

Seattle First International Bank
101 S.W. Main Street, Suite 1600
Portland, OR 97204
Phone: 503 225-9086

United States National Bank of
Oregon
321 S.W. 6th Avenue
Portland OR 97208
Phone: 503 225-5016

PENNSYLVANIA

ERIE, PENNSYLVANIA

The First National Bank of
Pennsylvania
717 State Street
Erie, PA 16566
Phone: 814 871-3400

HARRISBURG, PENNSYLVANIA

The Commonwealth National Bank
10 S. Market Street
Harrisburg, PA 17108
Phone 717 780-3115

Dauphine Deposit Bank & Trust Co.
213 Market Street
Harrisburg, PA 17101
Phone: 717 255-2121

LANCASTER, PENNSYLVANIA

Hamilton Bank
100 N. Queen Street
Lancaster, PA 17604
Phone: 717 291-3304

PHILADELPHIA, PA 19102

Continental Bank
Centre Square
1500 Market Street
Philadelphia, PA 19102
Phone: 215 564-7000

Fidelity Bank
Broad & Walnut Streets
Philadelphia, PA 19109
Phone: 215 985-8783

First Pennsylvania Bank, N.A.
Centre Square
15th & Market Streets
Philadelphia, PA 19101
Phone: 215 786-5000

Industrial Valley Bank
Industrial Valley Bank Building
1700 Market Street
Philadelphia, PA 19103
Phone: 215 561-3000

Meridian Bank
1700 Arch Street
Philadelphia, PA 19101
Phone: 215 854-3842

Philadelphia National Bank
Broad & Chestnut Streets
Philadelphia, PA 19101
Phone: 215 629-3100

Provident National Bank
P.O. Box 7648
Philadelphia, PA 19101
Phone: 215 585-5000

PITTSBURGH, PENNSYLVANIA

Equibank, N.A.
2 Oliver Plaza
Pittsburgh, PA 15222
Phone: 412 288-5423

Pittsburgh National Bank
Fifth Avenue & Wood Street
Pittsburgh, PA 15222

PUERTO RICO

SAN JUAN, PUERTO RICO

Banco de Ponce
GPO Box G-3108
San Juan, PR 00936
Phone: 809 759-7000

Banco Popular de Puerto Rico
GPO 2708
San Juan, PR 00936
Phone: 809 759-8900

RHODE ISLAND

PROVIDENCE, RHODE ISLAND

Fleet National Bank
111 Westminster St.
Providence, RI 02903
Phone: 401 278-5715

Old Stone Bank
1 Old Stone Square
Providence, RI 02903
Phone 401 278-2252

Rhode Island Hospital Trust
National Bank
1 Hospital Trust Plaza
Providence, RI 02903
Phone: 401 278-8133

SOUTH CAROLINA

COLUMBIA, SOUTH CAROLINA

Bankers Trust of South Carolina
P.O. Box 448
Columbia, SC 29202
Phone: 803 771-2110

Citizens & Southern National Bank
1801 Main St.
Columbia, SC 29201
Phone: 803 765-8146

South Carolina National Bank
1426 Main Street
Columbia, SC 29226
Phone: 803 771-3511

TENNESSEE

CHATTANOOGA, TENNESSEE

American National Bank & Trust Co.
P.O. Box 1638
Chattanooga, TN 37401
Phone: 615 757-3654

First Tennessee Bank, N.A.
701 Market Street
Chattanooga, TN 37401
Phone: 615 757-4011

KNOXVILLE, TENNESSEE

First Tennessee Bank
800 S. Gay Street
Knoxville, TN 37901
Phone: 615 971-2100

MEMPHIS, TENNESSEE

First Tennessee Bank, N.A.
P.O. Box 84
Memphis, TN 38101
Phone: 901 523-4436

National Bank of Commerce
1 Commerce Square
Memphis, TN 38150
Phone: 901 523-3116

Union Planters National Bank
67 Madison Avenue
Memphis, TN 38103
Phone: 901 523-6828

NASHVILLE, TENNESSEE

Commerce Union Bank
1 Commerce Place
Nashville, TN 37219
Phone: 615 749-3333

First American National Bank
First American Center
Nashville, TN 37237
Phone: 615 748-2821

Third National Bank in Nashville
201 4th Avenue North
Nashville, TN 37244
Phone: 615 748-4832

TEXAS

DALLAS, TEXAS

Banc Texas, P.O. Box 2249
Dallas, TX 75221
Phone: 214 969-6111

First Republic Bank Trade, Inc.
P.O. Box 83000, Dallas, TX 75283-1260
Phone: 214 977-3064

Interfirst Bank Dallas
P.O. Box 83480, Dallas, TX 75283
Phone: 214 744-8161

M Bank Dallas, 1704 Main Street
Dallas, TX 75201
Phone: 214 698-6000

EL PASO, TEXAS

El Paso National Bank
P.O. Box 140
El Paso, TX 79980
Phone: 915 546-6500

M Bank El Paso
P.O. Box 1072
El Paso, TX 79958
Phone: 915 532-9922

FORT WORTH, TEXAS

Interfirst Bank Fort Worth
P.O. Box 2260
Fort Worth, TX 76113
Phone: 817 390-6161

Texas American Bank
P.O. Box 2050
Fort Worth TX 76102
Phone: 817 228-8011

HOUSTON, TEXAS

First City National Bank of Houston
P.O. Box 2557
Houston, TX 77252
Phone: 713 658-6670

First Republic Bank Houston, N.A.
700 Louisiana Street
Houston, TX 77002
Phone: 713 247-6213

M Bank Houston
910 Travis
Houston, TX 77002
Phone: 713 751-6100

Texas Commerce Bank
P.O. Box 2558
Houston, TX 77252
Phone: 713 757-6000

Texas Commerce Bank, N.A.
712 Main Street
Houston, TX 77002
Phone: 713 236-4865

SAN ANTONIO, TEXAS

Interfirst Bank, N.W.
P.O. Box 1230
San Antonio, TX 78295
Phone: 512 733-1300

NBC Bank San Antonio, N.A.
430 Soledad
San Antonio, TX 78205
Phone: 512 225-2511

UTAH

SALT LAKE CITY, UTAH

Zion First National Bank
310 S. Main Street
Salt Lake City UT 84101
Phone: 801 524-4690

FALLS CHURCH, VIRGINIA

First Virginia Bank
6400 Arlington Boulevard
Falls Church, VA 22046
Phone: 703 241-4831

NORFOLK, VIRGINIA

Virginia National Bank
P.O. Box 600
Norfolk, VA 23501
Phone: 804 441-4821

RICHMOND, VIRGINIA

Bank of Virginia Co.
P.O. Box 23260
Richmond, VA 25970
Phone: 804 771-7000

Central Fidelity Bank
1021 E. Cary Street
Richmond, VA 23219
Phone: 804 697-6860

Sovran Bank
12th & Main Streets
Richmond, VA 23261
Phone: 804 788-2120

United Virginia Bank
900 E. Main Street
Richmond, VA 23219
Phone: 804 782-7416

WASHINGTON

SEATTLE, WASHINGTON

First Interstate Bank of Washington
P.O. Box 160
Seattle, WA 981111
Phone: 206 292-3318

Pacific National Bank of Washington
1215 4th Avenue
Seattle, WA 98161
Phone: 206 292-3111

Peoples National Bank of Washington
1414 4th Avenue
Seattle, WA 98111
Phone: 206 344-2300

Ranier National Bank
P.O. Box 3966
Seattle, WA 98124
Phone: 206 621-4111

WISCONSIN

MILWAUKEE, WISCONSIN

First Wisconsin National Bank of
Milwaukee
777 E. Wisconsin Avenue
Milwaukee, WI 53202
Phone: 414 765-4321

M & I Marshall & Ilsley Bank
P.O. Box 2035
Milwaukee, WI 53201
Phone: 414 765-7700

Marine Bank, N.A.
P.O. Box 750
Milwaukee, WI 53201
Phone: 414 765-3000

Appendix 7

Foreign Patent Protection: Treaties and National Laws

U.S. businessmen seeking patent protection abroad can benefit in many countries from the Patent Cooperation Treaty (PCT) and the European Patent Convention (EPC). Acceptance of applications under both treaties began in July 1978. These conventions benefit U.S. businessmen primarily by simplifying the procedures for obtaining foreign patent protection, but do not confer automatic protection in any country for U.S. patents. In countries not adhering to these conventions, U.S. businessmen must, as in the past, file a separate application in each country where patent protection is desired.

The Commerce Department's Domestic Policy Review Advisory Committee on Industrial Innovation, in the Report of its Subcommittee on Patent and Information Policy, refers to well-documented evidence of a positive relationship between increased exports and patent filings abroad, i.e., the more patents, the more subsequent exports. Since 1971, U.S. nationals have filed an average of about 100,000 applications and received about 75,000 patents annually abroad. About 55 percent of this activity has occurred in Western Europe, 10 percent in Japan, 10 percent in Eastern Europe. While patents do not eliminate risks in international transaction, continued ability of U.S. firms to penetrate foreign markets will be enhanced by a patent program to protect their inventions and innovations abroad. In terms of expanded trade, it may be noted that, of the $143.6 billion of total U.S. exports in 1978,

Source: "Foreign Business Practices," U.S. Department of Commerce, International Trade Administration, Washington, D.C., April 1985.

more than $94.5 billion (about 66 percent) consisted of manufactured goods embodying patented subject matter.

The importance of foreign patenting by U.S. exporters also will increase as countries improve their technical capabilities and become more competitive in world markets, especially in high-technology product industries. In 1978 the Massachusetts Institute of Technology's Center for Policy Alternatives undertook a study for the Commerce Department on the relationship of patenting to export performance in high-technology industries. Strong correlations were found between a high level of U.S. patents awarded to nationals of 21 countries in 23 industries (including fabricated metal products, scientific instruments, nonelectrical machinery sectors, chemical product groups, electrical and electronic groups, and transport sectors) and the large volume of exports from those countries and industries. U. S. exporters, therefore, are well advised to look into the cost-efficiency and red-tape-cutting benefits which are available under these new patent treaties.

Patents are also a well-recognized vehicle for transfer of technology. By offering protection against piracy or infringement of new products and processes, they encourage capital investments in research and development and provide a firm basis for the licensing and sale of technology and related know-how. Since 1971, U.S. receipts of royalties and related management and service fees from licensing of patents and technology have increased by about 130 percent. In that year, the total was $2.4 billion ($618 million from unaffiliated licensing transactions and $1.8 billion from direct investment licensing). In 1978, the total income reached $5.5 billion ($1.1 billion, unaffiliated, and $4.4 billion, direct investment). Our payments for foreign technology licensed in this country were $241 million in 1971, and $565 million in 1978, about equally divided between unaffiliated and direct investment sources. Patenting abroad thus has not only been a stimulus to exports but also to a favorable technological balance of payments, with royalty and fee income exceeding our payments by 10 to 1.

The Patent Cooperation Treaty (PCT) is currently adhered to by the United States and 34 other countries (see Annex A).

The PCT is administered by the World Intellectual Property Organization (WIPO), which has published a *PCT Applicants Guide* containing detailed information on the Treaty for those interested in filing international applications, a PCT Gazette, and brochures containing a text of the PCT, its regulations, and Administrative Instructions. These publications may be purchased from WIPO at 34 Chemin des Colombettes. 1211 Geneva 20, Switzerland.

Basically, the treaty provides centralized filing procedures and a standardized international application format. Under the PCT, a U.S. national or resident may file an international patent application at the U.S. Patent and Trademark Office (PTO) and designate in that application the member countries in which he desires patent protection. This filing has the same effect as if that person had filed several or many individual applications for the same invention in those member countries. After filing, the application is subjected to a search of the prior art by an international searching authority, which for the U.S. applicant, is also the U.S Patent and Trademark Office. The applicant, when he receives the International Search Report, can then decide whether he wishes to continue with the national patent granting procedures of his application in the countries he has designated. The PCT benefits the U.S applicant by enabling him to make a single filing in the United States of an international application in English and according to a uniform format. This should minimize the expenditure of time and money particularly with respect to such formal requirements as certifications, consul stamps, and other foreign legal procedures.

The U.S. applicant also is provided additional time (up to 20 months, instead of the ordinary 12 months) within which to submit translations and national fees to foreign countries. During this time, he will have available the International Search Report containing prior art citations (patents and other published technology which might disclose the invention) which may further aid him in deciding whether to proceed in one or more foreign countries.

As a long-range benefit, the Treaty should provide a focal point for continued cooperation among the world's patent offices toward the improvement of patent practices, to the advantage of U.S. exporters. The Treaty also is designed to benefit developing nations by providing for the establishment of information services to facilitate acquisition of technology and technical information. Additionally, it calls for a committee to organize and supervise technical assistance programs to aid developing countries in improving their patent systems. To the extent that developing countries improve their patent system, so also should their market potential become increasingly attractive for U.S. investment of foreign technology, know-how and capital.

The PCT makes no substantive changes as to patent-ability of an invention in an individual member country. The patent grant ultimately rests with the member country. The main purpose of the PCT, then, is facilitation in the filing of patent applications in other than one's own country. It deals with procedural matters and does not result in the issuance of international patents.

Under the European Patent Convention, any party, including a U. S. nation, may file an application with the European Patent Office (EPO) in Munich, Germany, or its Branch Office at The Hague, Netherlands, designating those member countries where patent protection is desired. First, the application is examined for formalities by the EPO. If it is found acceptable, a search is then conducted. The application is published 18 months after the official date. The search report, when it is completed, will accompany the application. Within six months of publication of the search report, the applicant must file a "request for examination"; otherwise, the application will be considered withdrawn. If such a request is made, the application is then examined by the EPO for novelty and inventive merit, resulting in either refusal or grant of a patent. The grant of a patent is published in the *European Patent Bulletin*, and for 9 months thereafter anyone may file an opposition. If an opposition is filed, the application will be re-examined and the patent either sustained, modified, or revoked. Appeal procedures are available regarding opposition decisions. Duration of the European patent in the countries designated by the applicant is 20 years from the effective filing date.

An EPC patent has the same effect in the designated countries as if the patent had been granted by the individual member country in terms of uniform examination and on questions of validity. Questions of infringement, however, are left to member states under their national laws. Thus, the EPC introduces a step toward progressive unity in the filing of applications and grants of patents, but does not go so far as to remove all rights from member countries relating to patents. Belgium, France, Federal Republic of Germany, Italy, Luxembourg, Netherlands, Sweden, Switzerland, and the United Kingdom are now members of the EPC. *A Guide for Applicants—How to Get A European Patent* may be secured by writing to the European Patent Office (EPO), Motoroma-Haus, Rosenheimer Strasse 30, Munich, Germany.

The members of the European Common Market also are working toward establishment of a single community patent which would be granted for the nine member countries. A treaty was signed on December 15, 1975, but has not yet come into force.

The centerpiece of international treaties on patent rights is still the oldest and most important of those in existence—the Paris Convention for the Protection of Industrial Property (commonly known as the "Paris Convention") founded in 1883. The United States has been a party since 1887. Presently, 88 countries are members. The Convention applies not only to patents, but also to trademarks, industrial designs, utility models, trade names, and, under the 1967 Stockholm Revision, to inventors' certificates. The main provisions concern national treatment and the right of priority (see Annex B).

Under the national treatment provision, the Convention provides that, with regard to the protection of the aforementioned types of industrial property, each member country must grant the same protection to nationals of other member countries as it grants to its own nations. This provision guarantees that foreign applicants will be treated at least as well as domestic applicants in pursuing protection of their industrial property rights. Under the right of priority provision, on the basis of a regular application first filed in one of the member countries, the applicant may, within a certain period (12 months for patents), apply for protection in any of the member countries and have such later filed applications regarded as if they were filed on the same date as the first application.

The Convention also contained provisions designed to protect patent owners against arbitrary forfeiture of their patents if not used or worked. It also establishes the principle of independence of patents, meaning that once a patent has been granted, it subsequent revocations or expiration in the country of original filing does not affect its validity in other countries. The Convention also provides safeguards against invalidation of a patent merely because the patented product was imported into the country of destination.

This Convention may well continue as the best guarantee to patentees that their rights will be protected in foreign markets, at least insofar as any given foreign market offers sound protections to its own nations. There have been six major revisions since its establishment in 1883 and through the years there have been numerous suggestions for further liberalizing its provisions, the vast majority being aimed at making foreign patenting more attractive on a worldwide scale.

The United States also belongs to an Inter-American Convention on Inventions, Patents, Designs and Industrial Models, signed at Buenos Aires in 1910. The Convention, adhered to by 12 Latin American countries, adopts the principles of national treatment, right of priority, and independence of patents along the lines of the Paris Union Convention.

The United States also has concluded a number of bilateral arrangements with countries, some of which are not members of the above Conventions, under which U.S. citizens receive national treatment and other protection against discriminatory practices in acquiring and maintaining patent rights.

Most countries, including those that have become independent since the end of World War II, have patent laws. There are only a few without a system of patent protection. Many former colonies, now independent countries, provide patent protection only on the basis of a patent first acquired in the former parent country. Examples are Ghana, where a "confirmation patent" is issued, based on a patent first acquired in the United Kingdom, and Burma, where Indian patents are recognized as being in force.

There are certain countries that provide, in addition to regular patents of invention, so-called "introduction," "revalidation," or "importation" patents. These can be applied for on an invention already patented elsewhere by the same patent owner or, after a period of time, by a local national. Such patents expire at the duration of their basic foreign patents. Their purpose is to permit an invention to be introduced and protected, notwithstanding its prior patenting in other countries.

The USSR, Bulgaria, Poland, Rumania, Albania, and Algeria provide for issuance of so-called "inventor's certificates," as well as patents. The inventor's certificate system is used extensively in the USSR. Under its procedures, an inventor offers his invention outright to the state, which assumes its ownership and exclusive use. If used by the state, it entitles the inventor to a cash reward or other specific benefit. In such dual system countries, the inventor generally has the right to choose between applying for an inventor's certificate or a patent. Local inventors in Eastern Europe generally apply for inventors' certificates; foreigners apply for patent rights because of certain impracticalities in acquiring inventors' certificates.

(A country-by-country summary of world patent laws follows.)

Afghanistan—No patent law. Some common law protection available for inventions and designs against imitation.

African Intellectual Property Organization—Member countries, Benin, Cameroon, Central African Empire, Chad, Congo, Gabon, Ivory Coast, Mauritania, Niger, Senegal, Togo, and Upper Volta. Inquiries and applications should be directed to the Office Africain de la Propriete Intellectuelle (OAPI) located in Yaounde, Cameroon.

Invention patents valid in all member countries 10 years after application. Prior publicity anywhere prejudicial. No novelty examination. No opposition provision. Compulsory licensing possible 3 years after patent grant or if working interrupted for any 3-year period. French patents in force prior to dates of independence of the various countries may receive protection for 20 years from application filing date if revalidated with OAPI before March 31, 1967.

Albania—Invention patents valid 15 years from application date; inventor's certificates also granted. Chemical manufacturing processes patentable, but not chemicals; medical and some biological inventions eligible only for certificates. Prior publication or use anywhere prejudicial. Novelty examination. Opposition period 3 months. No provision for working. Compulsory licensing possible.

Algeria—Invention patents valid 20 years from application filing date. Confirmation patents valid 10 years from filing date of foreign patents upon which based. Inventors' certificates also granted. Prior publicity anywhere prejudicial. No novelty examination opposition. Confirmation patent must be worked 1 year from grant and not discontinued for more than a year; otherwise can be cancelled. Compulsory license or invention patents possible 3 years from grant or 4 years from application date if not adequately worked. French patents valid in Algeria on July 3, 1962 remain in force if continuously worked by Algerian enterprise.

Antigua—Patents valid 14 years from application filing date. Confirmation patents, coterminous with U. K. patents also granted; must be filed for within 3 years of latter. No novelty examination. For independent patents, public use in Antigua prejudicial. No working. Compulsory licensing possible.

Argentina—Invention patents granted for 5, 10, or 15 years; 15 years after grant only for important inventions. Patents of importation good for up to 10 years. Pharmaceutical manufacturing processes patentable. Prior publication anywhere, or grant of foreign patent (except for Argentine import patents), or public use in Argentina prejudicial. Novelty examination. No opposition provision. Working required 2 years after grant, not be interrupted for any 2-year period. No compulsory licensing provision. Importation or advertised offer of sale may constitute working.

Australia—Invention patents valid 16 years after application, renewable up to 10 years where inadequately remunerated. Prior publication, public use, or disclosure in Australia prejudicial. Novelty examination. If no examination requested within 5 years of application filing date, application will lapse. Opposition period 3 months. Compulsory licensing possible 3 years after grant if inadequately worked; revocation possible 2 years after first compulsory license. Patent registration should be marked on product.

Austria—Invention patents valid 18 years after application. Prior published description anywhere, or use or exhibition in Austria prejudicial. Novelty examination. Opposition period 4 months. Compulsory licensing possible 3 years after grant or years after application, if inadequately worked.

Bahamas—Patents granted before June 1, 1967 (new Act effective date), valid 7 years, renewable twice for 7 years each time. Under new Act, invention patents valid 16 years from application filing date. Publication, public use, or knowledge prejudicial. No novelty examination, opposition, compulsory licensing, or working requirement.

Bahrain—Patents valid 15 years from application filing; renewable 5 years. Usually granted as revalidations of foreign patents for term-duration of latter. No examination, working, or compulsory licensing provisions.

Bangladesh—Patents granted in Pakistan before independence date (March 25, 1971) and still in force then can be maintained for their original duration in Bangladesh upon payment of necessary fees. New applications may be filed in Dacca. Patents valid 16 years from application date. Novelty examination. Four months opposition period. Compulsory licensing possible.

Barbados—Invention patents valid 14 years from application date, renewable for 7 years. Provisional protection available 9 months. Public use in Barbados prejudicial. No novelty examination. Opposition period 2 months. Compulsory licensing possible.

Belgium—Invention patents valid 20 years after application; patents of importation valid up to 20 years. Patentable inventions must be industrially or commercially workable. Prior commercial use in Belgium or patenting or publication anywhere prejudicial except for import patents. No novelty examination; form only. No opposition provision. Working required 4 years after application filing (1 year for countries not party to Paris Union) not to be interrupted for any 12-month period. Compulsory licensing provisions.

Belize—Patents valid 14 years from application filing date, renewable 7 or 14 years. Coterminous with prior corresponding foreign patent, if latter exists. Confirmation patents based on and coterminous with U.K. patents granted, if applied for within 3 years. No novelty examination, working or compulsory licensing provisions.

Bermuda—Invention patent valid 16 years from patent grant, renewable 7 year periods. Patents also available as confirmation of U.K patents, if applied for within 3 years of latter's grant date. Coterminous duration with latter. No novelty examination. For independent patents, use and sale in Bermuda prejudicial. No opposition for independent patents; 2 month for confirmation patents. No working provisions but compulsory licensing possible.

Bolivia—Invention patents valid up to 15 years after grant, including renewals; confirmation patents valid up to 15 years. Prior knowledge, description, working or nonpatent publication anywhere prejudicial. Foreign patent not prejudicial, if application filed within 1 year of foreign application. No novelty examination. Published twice in 1 month at 15-day intervals for opposition. Compulsory licensing possible 2 years after grant, if inadequately worked or, if working interrupted for any 1-year period. Importation or advertised offer to license may constitute working.

Botswana—Confirmation patents based on prior registration in South Africa. U.K. patents automatically in force, recordation unnecessary.

Brazil—Present law effective December 31, 1971, patents granted before then valid for terms stated in patent grant. Invention patents are valid 15 years from application filing date. Use or publication anywhere prejudicial. Application published 18 months from earliest priority or filing date. Applicant can request examination with 24 months; otherwise application deemed abandoned. Opposition period 90 days. Working required within 3 years after grant and not interrupted for longer than 1 year, otherwise subject to compulsory license. Failure to work within 4 years, or if license issued after 5 years, working is discontinued for 2 consecutive years, patent considered lapsed.

Brunei—Patents granted as confirmation of and coterminous with U.K., Malaysia, or Singapore patents, to be applied for within 3 years of grant in latter countries. No novelty examination, working, or compulsory licensing provisions.

Bulgaria—Invention patents valid 15 years after application; law also provides for inventor's certificates. Some medical and biological inventions eligible only for certificates. Prior publication or public knowledge anywhere prejudicial. Novelty examination. No opposition. Working and licensing provision; 3 years after grant or 4 years after application. Importation may qualify.

Burma—No patent law. Indian patents valid.

Burundi—Invention patents valid 20 years from application filing date; importation patents valid to 20 years. Public use anywhere prejudicial. No novelty examination or opposition. Patent must be worked within 2 years otherwise can be cancelled. No compulsory licensing provision.

Canada—Patents valid 17 years after grant. Chemical manufacturing processes patentable. Prior knowledge, use, patent, or description anywhere, or public use or sale in Canada more than 2 years prior to Canadian application prejudicial. Canadian application must be filed either before grant of first foreign patent or within 12 months of first foreign application. Novelty examination. Opposition period not provided, but protest may be filed. Compulsory licensing may be ordered by Patent Commissioner 3 years after grant, and if licenses are insufficient, patent may be revoked. Patent registration should be marked on product.

Chile—Invention patents valid up to 15 years after grant, including renewals. If invention is patented abroad, patent is coterminous with original foreign patent. Prior public knowledge, use, sale or publication anywhere, or importation into Chile prejudicial. Foreign patent not prejudicial, if inventions not commercially known in Chile. Novelty examination. 1 month opposition period. No working or compulsory licensing provisions. Patent registration must be marked on product.

China, People's Republic of—Patent Law promulgated March 12, 1984 will become effective April 1, 1985. Meanwhile, no patent law. Parties may apply for inventor's certificate on invention which, if granted, entails cash awards and other benefits to applicant based on the invention's value to the state. Foreigners presumably may apply for inventor's certificates. State retains ownership under inventor's certificate registrations. New US-PRC Trade Agreement contains provisions for PRC recognition of U.S. patent rights and protection of such rights in contracts (art. VI). The new law shall grant patent protection for 15 years from date of filing application. Foreigners may file applications based on reciprocity or relevant treaty or convention. 12 month priority period recognized from date of foreign filing. Pharmaceutical products and substances obtained by means of chemical process are excluded from patentability. However, the processes themselves may be patented. Working of patent required from 3 years of issuance. Compulsory licenses available in case of non-working. Preliminary and novelty examination conducted. Novelty requires idea to be new, not only not known in China, but to the world.

Colombia—Invention patents granted for 5 years from grant, renewable for additional 5 years if subject matter sufficiently worked in Colombia. Use or publication anywhere prejudicial to novelty. Foreign patents must be filed prior to 1 year following application in country of origin. Formalities and novelty examination conducted. Pharmaceutical products, foodstuffs and beverages not patentable, however processes may be patented. Opposition period 90 days following publication of application. Working required within 3 years following issuance of patent. Working not to be interrupted more than 1 year. Compulsory licenses may be granted if patent not adequately worked in Colombia.

Costa Rica—Invention patents valid 20 years after grant; confirmation patents coterminous with basic patent up to 20 years. Prior public knowledge or use in Costa Rica prejudicial for confirmation patents, anywhere for other patents. Novelty examination. Opposition period 30 days. Working required 2 years after grant, not to be interrupted for any 3-year period, no compulsory licensing provision.

Cyprus—Patents only obtainable as confirmation of U.K. patents. Request must be made within 3 years of U.K. patent grant date.

Czechoslovakia—Invention and dependent patents valid 15 years after application. Chemical and medicinal manufacturing processes, patentable; certain medical treatments and biological inventions eligible only for inventors' certificates. Prior public knowledge anywhere via publication, patent description, or display prejudicial. Novelty examination. Opposition period 3 months. No working requirement, but use of patent in public interest may be ordered 4 years after filing or 3 years after grant, whichever is later. Compulsory licenses may be granted.

Denmark—Invention and dependent patents valid 17 years after application, addition patents coterminous with basic patent. Prior published description or public use anywhere prejudicial. Novelty examinations. Opposition period 3 month. Compulsory licensing possible 3 years after grant or 4 years from application filing date, if inadequately worked.

Dominican Republic—Invention and revalidation patents valid up to 15 years after grant, including renewals. Medicines and chemicals patentable if approved by Medical Board. Public knowledge or use anywhere prejudicial. No novelty examination. Foreign patenting or importation no bar. No opposition provision. Working required 5 years after application, not to be interrupted for any 3-year period. No compulsory licensing provision.

Ecuador—Invention patents valid up to 12 years after grant. Importation patents, valid up to 12 years, apply regionally or over whole country. Revalidation patent based on, and coterminous with, patent owned in United States of certain Latin American countries. Prior existence or public knowledge in Ecuador prejudicial. Opposition period 90 days; if working, 2 years after grant; if inadequately worked, or if working interrupted for any 2-year period patent may lapse. Compulsory licensing possible if patent not worked.

Egypt—Invention patents valid 15 years after application, renewable 5 years; food and drug process patents valid 10 years. Public use or publication in Egypt prejudicial. No novelty examination. Opposition period 2 months. Compulsory licensing possible 3 years after grant if inadequately worked, if working interrupted for any 2-year period, of if needed to work another invention. Revocation possible 2 years after first compulsory license.

El Salvador—Invention patents valid up to 15 years after grant, renewable 5 years in exceptional cases. Prior publication (except in foreign patent documents) or public use anywhere prejudicial. No novelty examination. Patent an be applied for based on foreign patent, if no other publication occurred. Opposition period 90 days. Patent must be worked within 3 years of grant and working not interrupted for more than 3 years; otherwise subject to compulsory licensing. Patent markings on products are compulsory.

Ethiopia—No patent law. Publication of cautionary notices in local press and informing government of existence of foreign patent may afford some protection.

Fiji—Patents valid for 14 years from the grant, or until corresponding first foreign patent expires. Confirmation patents coterminous with U.K. patents also granted. No novelty examination. Use or publicity in Fiji prejudicial. No working or compulsory licensing provisions.

Finland—Invention patents valid 17 years after application. Prior publication in any form anywhere, or public disclosure prejudicial. Novelty examination. Opposition period 3 months. Compulsory licensing or revocation possible 3 years after grant, if inadequately worked, or if needed to work another patent.

France—Invention patents valid 20 years from filing date. Law also provides for "Certificates of Utility," issued for 6 years. Public knowledge anywhere, including publication of a corresponding patent in an official journal, prejudicial. Novelty examination for invention patent, not utility certificate applications. Compulsory licensing possible 3 years after grant or 4 years after patent filing date, if inadequately worked, or if working discontinued for any 3-year period. Special legislation applies to patenting of pharmaceutical cases. If no request made during that period, application converted to one for "certificate of utility." No opposition provision but application laid open for 18 months to permit public comment. Patents applied for before new law effective date (1-1-69) remain subject to former law.

Gambia—Patents only obtainable as confirmation of U.K. patents, Request must be made within 3 years of U.K. patent grant date.

German Democratic Republic—Exclusive non-exclusive (economic) and addition patents granted. Patents valid for 18 years from application date, except for patents of addition which are valid for the remaining term of the main patent. Publication, use in East Germany, described in a printed publication anywhere prejudicial to novelty. Exclusive patents vest ownership rights on registrant, non-exclusive patent vests rights on registrant and also on any third parties authorized by the Patent Office. Patents must be worked in East Germany. No provision for compulsory licensing. However, government may, based on public need after indemnification, order restriction or revocation of the patent. Patent Court of Leipzig has jurisdiction in infringement cases.

Germany, Federal Republic—Invention patents valid 18 years after application if filed before Jan. 1, 1978; 20 years if filed after Dec. 31, 1977. Prior public use in Germany or printed descriptions anywhere (including patent applications and registered utility models) prejudicial, if filed before Jan. 1, 1978; absolute novelty; not made available anywhere, if filed after Dec. 31, 1977. All applications given preliminary screening. Applications opened for public inspection for 18 months after filing. Applicant can postpone full novelty examination request for 7 years; if no request made by that time, application lapses. Opposition period 3 months. Compulsory licensing possible at any time; revocation adequately worked. Patenting in United States constitutes working in Germany.

Ghana—Patents only obtainable as confirmation of U.K. patents, except those for pharmaceuticals. Request must be made within 3 years of U.K. patent grant date.

Greece—Patents valid 15 years after application. No novelty examination. No opposition provisions. Revocation possible 3 years after grant, if inadequately worked; compulsory licensing possible if needed to work another patent. Advertised offers of licensing may be considered working. Owners of corresponding U.S. patents exempted from working requirement.

Guatemala—Invention patents valid 15 years after grant; importation patents coterminous with basic patent up to 15 years. Inventions to be patentable must meet positive criteria listed in the patent law; prior public knowledge in Guatemala prejudicial for importation patents, anywhere for other patents. Novelty examination. Opposition may be filed within 40 days after first publications. Compulsory licensing possible 1 year after grant if inadequately worked or if working interrupted for any 3-month period.

Guyana—Invention patents valid 16 years after application. Publication, working, sale, or use in Guyana prejudicial. Novelty examination. Opposition period 2 months. Compulsory licensing or revocation possible after 3 years if inadequately worked. Patent registration should be marked on product. Confirmation patents based on U.K. registration also issued.

Haiti—Invention and revalidation patents valid up to 20 years with grant, including renewals, addition patents coterminous with basic patent. Public use or publication anywhere more than 1 year prior to application prejudicial. No novelty examination, opposition, compulsory licensing or working provisions.

Honduras—Invention patents valid up to 20 years after grant. For foreigners, granted only for life of basic foreign patent. Prior publication or use in Honduras prejudicial for import patents, anywhere for other patents. Novelty examination. Opposition period 90 days. If patent is not worked within 1 year after grant, patent lapses. Patent notice marking necessary to maintain infringement actions.

Hong Kong—Patents only obtainable as confirmation of patents granted in the United Kingdom. Application for protection must be filed within 5 years of U.K. patent issue date. Hong Kong patent expires with corresponding U.K. patent.

Hungary—Patents valid 20 years from application filing date. Application first examined for formalities and published, if accepted. Applicant or others then have 4 years to request complete novelty examination, otherwise application considered abandoned. Prior use or publication anywhere prejudicial. Opposition period 3 months after full examination. Compulsory licensing if patent not worked within 4 years of filing or 3 years from grant whichever is later.

Iceland—Invention patents valid 15 years after grant. Prior publication anywhere, including use or display in Iceland, prejudicial. Novelty examination. Opposition period 12 weeks. Compulsory licensing possible 5 years after grant if inadequately worked or 3 years after grant if needed to work another patent.

India—Invention patents valid 14 years after application, other than for foods and drugs. Food and drug process patents valid 7 years from filing date. Prior public knowledge or use in India prejudicial. Novelty examination. Opposition period 4 months. Compulsory licensing possible 3 years after grant for inadequate working. All patented articles must be marked with number and year of patent. Reciprocal priority rights granted on basis of applications filed in certain Commonwealth countries. Not member of Paris Union. Patents granted before April 20, 1972 exist 16 years from filing.

Indonesia—Pending passage of patent legislation, applications may be filed with the Indonesian Justice Ministry. Although applications will not be acted on until a patent law is passed, they will reportedly be considered regular applications.

Iran—Invention patents valid up to 20 years after application; addition or improvement patents coterminous with foreign patents. Except for import patents, prior publication in official publications or journals anywhere, prejudicial. No novelty examination. Opposition period not specified. Revocation possible 5 years after grant if inadequately worked. No compulsory licensing provision.

Iraq—Invention patents valid 15 years from date of application, patents of importation for unexpired term of their foreign basic patents up to 15 years. Prior public knowledge or use anywhere prejudicial. No opposition provision. Patent must be worked within 3 years and not discontinued for 2 years, otherwise subject to compulsory license or revocation.

Ireland—Invention patents valid 16 years, renewable under exceptional conditions up to 10 years when inadequately remunerated. Prior public use or knowledge anywhere prejudicial. Novelty examination. Opposition period 3 months. Compulsory licensing possible 3 years after grant or 4 years after application date, if inadequately worked. Revocation possible 2 years after first compulsory license. Importation does not constitute working. Patent registration should be marked on product.

Israel—Invention patents valid 20 years after application. Prior publication use, or sale anywhere prejudicial. Novelty possible 3 years after grant or 4 years after application date, if inadequately worked; revocation possible 2 years after first compulsory license.

Italy—Invention patents valid 20 years after application. Prior public knowledge anywhere prejudicial. No novelty examination or opposition provisions. Compulsory licensing possible if inadequately worked 3 years after grant, or 4 years after application or if working interrupted for any 3-year period. Exhibition but not importation may constitute working.

Jamaica—Invention patent valid 14 years after application, renewable 7 years, confirmation patents based on foreign patents coterminous with original. Prior publication or public use in Jamaica prejudicial, except for confirmation patents. No novelty examination. No opposition provision. No working or compulsory licensing provisions.

Japan—Invention patents valid 15 years from date application published, cannot exceed 20 years application filing date. Application open to public inspection 18 months from filing date. Examination can be postponed 7 years at applicant's request; if no request for examination made at that time application lapses. Publication anywhere or public knowledge or use in Japan prejudicial. Novelty examination. Opposition period 2 months. Compulsory licensing possible 3 years after registration or 4 years after filing, if inadequately worked or if needed to work another patent.

Jordan—Invention patents valid 16 years after application. Prior publication, use or sale in Jordan prejudicial. Novelty examination. Opposition period 2 months.

Compulsory licensing examination. Opposition period 2 months. Compulsory licensing or revocation possible 3 years after grant, if inadequately worked.

Kenya—Patents only obtainable as confirmation of U.K. patents. Request must be made within 3 years of U.K. patent grant date.

Korea, Republic of—Invention patents valid 12 years after grant or 15 years after application, whichever is less. Public knowledge or use in Korea, or appearance in publications distributed in Korea prejudicial. Novelty examination. Opposition period 2 months. Compulsory licensing or cancellation possible 3 years after grant if inadequately worked or if working interrupted for any 3-year period. Patent registration must be marked on product.

Kuwait—Inventions patents granted for 15 years from application date, extendable for 5 additional years. Patents of addition granted for remaining term of main patent. Patents for special processes or means for foodstuffs, medicines or pharmaceutical preparations granted for 10 years. Novelty: invention not published or publicly known in Kuwait for 20 years preceding application. No novelty examination, only for compliance with formal requirements. Working within 3 years following grant not to be interrupted for more than 2 years, otherwise compulsory licenses may be issued.

Lebanon—Invention patents valid 15 years after application. Prior publication anywhere prejudicial. No novelty examination. No opposition provision. Working required 2 years after grant. For nationals of Paris Union countries, however, allowance period is 3 years. No compulsory licensing provisions. Direct offer to license party capable of working the invention may constitute working, but importation does not.

Lesotho—Confirmation patents based on Republic of South Africa patents; issued for remaining term of corresponding patent in latter country. U.K. patent automatically protected for its duration; no local registration or confirmation required. Marking of article to indicate patent desirable.

Liberia—Invention patents valid 15 years after grant. Prior public knowledge, publication, or use in Liberia prejudicial. No specific exclusion from patentability. No novelty examination. No opposition provision. Working required 3 years after grant.

Libya—Invention patents valid 15 years after application, renewable 5 years. Processes for making foodstuffs, medicines, or pharmaceutical preparations patentable for 10 years. Public use of publication in Libya prejudicial. No novelty examination. Opposition period 2 months. Working required in Libya or country of origin within 3 years; 2-year extension possible. Compulsory licensing may be ordered at any time.

Liechtenstein—Swiss patents automatically valid without any required formalities.

Luxembourg—Invention patents valid 10 years after application. Prior public knowledge or use anywhere prejudicial. No novelty examination or opposition provision. Compulsory licensing possible after 3 years, nonworking for 3 years can also result in revocation.

Malawi—Invention patents valid 16 years from application filing date. Prior pubic use or knowledge in Malawi, or imprinted publications anywhere prejudicial. No novelty examination. Opposition period 3 months. Compulsory license can be ordered if patent sufficiently worked within 3 years.

Malaysia—Federation consisting of former areas of Malaya, Sabah, and Sarawak, each still has separate patent law. In Malaya and Sabah, U.K. patent is applicable; it must be registered separately within 3 years of U.K. grant, in each territory to be in force; remains in force for the duration of U.K. registration. In Sarawak, application may be filed any time based on patent in the United Kingdom, Singapore, or Malaya.

Malta—Invention patents valid 14 years from application, renewable 7 years. Publicity anywhere prejudicial. No novelty examination. Opposition period 2 months. Compulsory licensing possible, if not worked in 3 years.

Mauritius—Invention patents valid 14 years from application, renewable for like period. Publicity or use in Mauritius prejudicial. No novelty examination. Opposition period 1 month. No working or compulsory licensing.

Mexico—Inventions protected by patents or certificates of invention at applicant's option. Patents grant exclusive rights to owner to use or authorize others to use invention. Inventors' certificates are available for non-patentable products (chemicals, nuclear inventions, and anti-pollutant devices). Owner of inventor's certificate is under obligation to grant nonexclusive license to any third party wanting to use it, but retains right to continue working the invention. Decisions on payments left to parties but government may intervene if no decision reached. Patents, patents of improvement, and certificates granted for 10 years from this issue date. Recent prior publication or use anywhere prejudicial. No opposition provisions.

Working of invention is required within 3 years from issue of patent. Patent will lapse, if working not commenced within 4 years from issue and no compulsory license granted. Importation of patent product does not constitute working. Patent subject to compulsory license if (1) not worked within 3 years of issue, (2) working suspended more than 6 months, (3) working fails to meet national demand, and (4) export markets exist which are not being supplied by working of the patent. Government determines duration, scope, and royalties payable under such patent license.

Monaco—Invention patents valid 20 years after application. Publicity or use anywhere prejudicial. No novelty examination or opposition. Working required within 3 years after grant otherwise subject to compulsory licensing.

Morocco—Although country consists of former French Morocco, Tangier Zone and Spanish Zone, no unified patent law yet exists. Separate application for the former French Morocco must be filed with Industrial Property Office at Casablanca, and for Tangier, with Industrial Property Bureau in that area. Situation in ex-Spanish Zone unclear.

For Morocco, invention patents valid 20 years after application. Prior public knowledge anywhere prejudicial. No opposition provision. Working required 3 years after grant for nationals of Paris Union countries, 3 years after application for others; working not to be interrupted for any 3-year period. Reasonable offer to license or sell may constitute working; importation may be prejudicial. No compulsory licensing provision.

For Tangier Zone, invention patents valid 20 years and importation patent 10 years from application. Public use or publication anywhere prejudicial for basic invention patents. No novelty examination or opposition provision. Working required within 3 years, otherwise subject to compulsory licensing.

Namibia (South-West Africa)—Patent matters administered by South African Patent Office. Invention patents valid 14 years from application filing date, renewable 7 to 14-year periods. No novelty examination. Prior use in Namibia, or abroad more than 2 years before filing, prejudicial. No opposition. Compulsory license possible if not worked within 2 years.

Nauru—Patents granted as confirmation of and coterminous with Australian patents. Must be applied for within 3 years of latter's grant date. No working or compulsory licensing provisions.

Nepal—Invention patents valid 15 years after grant, extendable for two additional 15-year periods. Applications screened for novelty regarding known use in Nepal; rejected if criteria not met.

Netherlands—Invention patents granted after Jan. 1, 1978, valid 20 years from effective filing date. Patents granted before Jan. 1, 1964, or based on applications pending that date, valid 18 years from day of grant. Patents applied for after Jan. 1, 1964 and granted before Jan. 1, 1978, valid 20 years from filing day or 10 years from grant, whichever is longer. Prior publication, public knowledge, or use anywhere prejudicial. Novelty examination. Applicant has 7 years after filing to request complete examination; if no request made by then, application lapses. Opposition period 4 months. Compulsory licensing possible 3 years after grant if inadequately worked; at any time if needed to work another patent. Patent registration should be marked on product.

Netherlands law applied in Netherlands Antilles and Suriname.

New Zealand—Invention patents valid 16 years after application; renewable up to 10 years. Recent prior publication in patent specification anywhere, or publication or use in New Zealand prejudicial. Novelty examination. Opposition period 3 months. Working required within 3 years after grant. Subject to compulsory licensing at any time for foods and medicines; revocation after 2 years, if licensing unsatisfactory.

Nicaragua—Invention patents valid 10 years after grant. Public knowledge in Nicaragua prejudicial. Processes patentable, but not products. Examination. Opposition period 30 days. Working required 1 year after grant, not to be interrupted for any 1-year period. Sworn affidavit and advertised offer of sale or license constitutes working. No compulsory licensing provision. Patent registration should be marked on product.

Nigeria—Patents granted under former law as confirmation of U.K. patents continue until term expires. New law effective December 1, 1971. Invention patents valid 20 years after application. Use or publication anywhere prejudicial. No novelty examination or opposition provisions. Compulsory licensing possible 3 years from grant or 4 years from application date, if inadequately worked.

Norway—Since 1980 invention patents are valid for 20 years from application date. Patents granted between January 1, 1968 and January 1, 1980 have a 20-year validity term. Patents granted before 1968 have a 17-year validity. Prior publication and use anywhere prejudicial. Novelty and formal examination. Opposition period 3 months. Compulsory licensing possible 3 years after grant or 4 years after application if inadequately worked, if working interrupted or if needed to work another patent.

Oman, Qatar, United Arab Emirate (Abu Dhabi, Dubai)—No patent laws. Cautionary notice in certain Lebanese newspapers circulating in these states may afford some protection.

Pakistan—Invention patents valid 16 years after application. Prior public knowledge or use in Pakistan prejudicial. Novelty examination. Opposition period 4 months. Working required within 4 years of grant, otherwise compulsory licensing possible. Patent registration should be marked on product. Not member of Paris Union, but reciprocal priority right granted to applications filed in certain commonwealth countries.

Panama—Invention patents valid up to 20 years. Revalidation patents coterminous with foreign patents up to 15 years. Prior public knowledge in Panama prejudicial. No novelty examination. Opposition period 90 days. Patents may lapse if not worked when one-third of term has passed, working not required for revalidation patents. No compulsory licensing provision.

Paraguay—Invention patents valid 15 years after application; confirmation patents coterminous with basic patents up to 15 years. Publication of foreign patent 1 year prior to Paraguayan application, or prior working or public disclosure in Paraguay prejudicial. No novelty examination. No opposition provision. Compulsory licensing possible if not worked for any 3-year period.

Peru—Invention patents valid 10 years from grant. Provisional patents based on foreign patents, valid 1 year only for person domiciled in Peru. Renewed foreign patents valid for unexpired term of foreign patent but not in excess of 10 years' duration. Formal and novelty examination. Prior use in Peru or publication anywhere and not later than 1 year from filing date of first foreign application, prejudicial. Opposition period 30 days after application last published. Working required within 2 years of grant; period extendable 2 years. Compulsory licensing possible if patentee importing product, local working insufficient, or needed to work another patent.

Poland—Regular patents valid 15 years from application filing date. Applications published 18 months after examination for formalities. Full examination must be requested within 6 months' publication. Applicant can request provisional examination and grant of provisional examination and grant of provisional patent for 5-year duration. Has 4 years after application date to request full examination and conversion to regular patent, if provisional patent sought first. Law also embodies inventor's certificate system, similar to Soviet Union, with state assuming ownership of inventions thereunder and granting awards, based on invention's use.

Portugal—Invention patents valid 15 years after grant. Prior publication anywhere or pubic use in Portugal prejudicial. Novelty examination in case of opposition. Opposition period 3 months. Compulsory licensing possible 3 years after grant, if inadequately worked, if working interrupted for any 3-year period, or if needed to work another patent.

Romania—Invention patents valid 15 years after application; patents of addition for period of basic patent but no less than 10 years. Inventors' certificates provided for in law. Filing acceptable if invention not previously filed or patented in Romania or publicly revealed anywhere. No opposition provision. Working required 4 years after application or 3 years after grant; otherwise subject to compulsory licensing.

Rwanda—Invention patents valid 20 years after application. Importation patents coterminous with corresponding foreign patents, not to exceed 20 years. Public use in Rwanda or publication anywhere prejudicial. No novelty examination or opposition. Patent must be worked within 2 years from date worked abroad, otherwise can be cancelled. No compulsory licensing.

Ryukyu Island (Okinawa)—Reverted to Japan, May 15, 1972. Japanese patent law extends to this area.

San Marinoa—Industrial property rights obtained in Italy applicable.

Saudi Arabia—No patent law. Can publish cautionary ownership notice of foreign patent in local "Official Gazette" or newspaper for such rights this may offer in seeking court action against infringers.

Sierra Leone—Patents only obtainable as confirmation of U.K. patents. Request must be made within 3 years of U.K. patent grant date.

Singapore—Patents only obtainable as confirmation of U.K. patents. Requests must be made within 3 years of U.K. patent grant.

Somalia—Patents granted for 15 years from filing date. Prior knowledge of inventions anywhere prejudicial. Patent must be worked within three years of grant and working not interrupted for three consecutive years.

South Africa—Patents valid 20 years after application. Prior public knowledge, use, or working in South Africa, or publication anywhere prejudicial. No novelty examination. Opposition period 3 months. Compulsory licensing possible 3 years after grant or 4 years after application, whichever is later, if inadequately worked, if needed to work another patent, or for foods, plants, or medicines. Importation does not constitute working. Patent registration should be marked on product.

Spain—Invention patents valid 20 years after grant. Patents of importation valid 10 years and may be applied for by anyone. Recent public knowledge or working in Spain prejudicial for import patents, anywhere for other patents. No novelty examination. No opposition provision. Compulsory licensing required 3 years after grant if not worked. Importation patents must be worked annually to remain in force.

Sri Lanka—Invention patents valid for 15 years after grant. Prior public knowledge anywhere via publication, description or use, prejudicial. Examination for compliance for formalities and novelty. Opposition not provided for. Working and compulsory licensing not provided for in new Code (August 8, 1979). However the Code's transitory provisions may require compulsory licenses or revocation of the patent if not worked properly within 3 years following application of priority date.

Sudan—No patents issued. Can publish cautionary ownership notice of foreign patent in local "Official Gazette" for such rights this may offer in seeking court action against infringers.

Swaziland—Confirmation patents based on prior registration in South Africa. U.K. Patents automatically in force.

Sweden—Invention patents valid 20 years after application. Prior publication or public use anywhere prejudicial. Novelty examination. Opposition period 3 months. Compulsory licensing possible 3 years after grant or 4 years after application, if inadequately worked, or if needed to supplement an earlier patent.

Switzerland—Invention patents valid 20 years after application. Prior public knowledge in Switzerland or published disclosure anywhere prejudicial. Textile and timepiece inventions subject to novelty examination. Compulsory licensing possible 3 years after grant, if inadequately worked, or if needed to work another patent. Working in United States satisfies working requirement.

Syria—Invention patents valid 15 years after application. Prior public knowledge anywhere prejudicial. No novelty examination. No opposition provisions. Working required 2 years after grant. No compulsory licensing provision.

Taiwan—Invention patents valid 15 years after publication; addition patents coterminous with basic patent. Prior publication or public use prejudicial. Novelty examination. Opposition period 3 months. Compulsory licensing or revocation possible, if inadequately worked within 3 years from grant. Patent registration should be marked on product.

Tanzania—Consists of former Tanganyika and Zanzibar areas, now joined as independent state; former separate laws for each area still in effect. In fomer Tanganyika, confirmation of U.K. patents only for term of U.K. patent; application for confirmation patent must be made within 3 years of U.K. patent grant. In former Zanzibar, same situation prevails, except that registration in that area may be invalidated by manufacture, use, and sale of invention subject-matter before priority date of U.K. patent.

Thailand—New patent law, published March 16, 1979, entered into force September 12, 1979. Invention patents valid for 15 years from application filing date. Public use in Thailand or disclosure of invention anywhere prejudicial to novelty. Foreign applicants may apply only if their countries permit Thai nationals to file applications. Foreign applications may be ordered to be accompanied by an examination conducted by a foreign government or other appropriate organizations dealing with patents. If the application meets certain basic formalities and substantive criteria, it is published. The applicant must then submit a request for novelty examination within 5 years after publication, otherwise the application is considered abandoned. Third parties may file oppositions within 180 days of the application's publication. Compulsory licensing possible 3 years after patent issues, if not properly worked. After 6 years of non-working, patent may be revoked by government. Product design patents issued for 7 years from application date. Imports of patented products are prohibited, except as specifically permitted, on request, by the government.

Trinidad and Tobago—Invention patents valid 14 years after grant, renewable for 7 years. Prior public use in Trinidad or Tobago, prejudicial. No novelty examination or opposition. Compulsory licensing possible.

Tunisia—Invention patents valid up to 20 years after application. Prior publication, public knowledge, or public use anywhere prejudicial. No novelty examination. Opposition period 2 months. Working required 3 years after grant (2 years for non-Paris Union nationals), not to be interrupted for any 2-year period. Importation not considered working; could invalidate patent. No compulsory licensing provision.

Turkey—Patents valid up to 15 years after application. Prior publication anywhere prejudicial. Novelty examination. No opposition provision. compulsory licensing possible 3 years after grant, if inadequately worked or if working interrupted for any 2-year period.

Uganda—Patents only obtainable as confirmation of U.K. patents. Request must be made within 3 years of U.K. patent grant date.

United Arab Emirates—See Oman, Qatar.

United Kingdom—For patents dated before June 1, 1967, duration is 16 years from filing date. Can be extended for 10 years on applications filed before June 1, 1978 and up to four years on applications filed after June 1, 1978. For patents dated after June 1, 1967, duration 20 years from filing date on original patent. For applications filed after June 1, 1978, patent duration is 20 years from filing date. Prior public disclosure in the United Kingdom or abroad prejudicial. Novelty examination.

Compulsory licensing possible three years after grant, if inadequately worked for patents on applications filed before June 1, 1978.

Certain newly independent countries in the British Commonwealth have already established or are in the process of developing their own national patent codes. In the meantime, some such countries continued to use pre-independence procedures and facilities in providing patent protection within their respective territories. These countries, as well as those of the British Commonwealth that now have separate patent laws, are covered separately and alphabetically in this article. Generally, in such countries the patent protection available is by registered confirmation of a U.K. patent which must take place within 3 years of the original U.K. grant.

Uruguay—Invention and related improvement patents valid 15 years after grant; revalidation patents granted for unexpired term of foreign patents but not to exceed 15 years, must be applied for within 3 years of basic patent. Prior public knowledge anywhere prejudicial. Novelty examination. Opposition period 20 days. Compulsory licensing possible 3 years after grant, if not worked. Importation or nominal working does not constitute working.

USSR—Soviet law provides for granting of either patents or inventor's certificates for new inventions. Patents are granted for 15 years' duration after application, inventor's certificates have unlimited duration. Full examination is made for novelty and usefulness, based on prior Soviet and foreign patents and publications and prior Soviet inventors' certificates. No opposition provision. No working provision. Compulsory licensing possible.

Venezuela—Invention and improvement patents issued for 5 or 10 years after grant at owner's request. Revalidation patents (based on prior foreign filing) coterminous with basic patents issued up to 10 years. Patents of introduction available to non-owner of foreign patent; are granted for a 5-year-term, but do not protect against imports. Publication in Venezuela or public knowledge anywhere prejudicial for invention and improvement patents. Prior public knowledge in Venezuela prejudicial for introduction and revalidation patents. Novelty examination for invention and improvement patents. Opposition period 60 days. Working for all patents must be effected 2 years after grant. Thereafter, working must continue for 2 consecutive years for 10-year patent and 1 year for 5-year patent.

Exploitation in Venezuela in lieu of manufacture constitutes working for invention, improvement, and revalidation patents. Introduction patents must be worked by local manufacturer. No compulsory licensing provision. Failure to meet working requirements may result in revocation. Patent registration must be marked on product. Not member of Paris Union but owner of foreign patent has priority right to obtain Venezualan patent if he applies within 12 months of foreign patent grant.

Yemen Arab Republic—Patent applications accepted under Law No. 45 of 1976, although no patent yet issued to foreigners.

Yemen, People's Democratic Republic(formerly Aden)—Grants patents only as confirmation of U.K. patents, to be applied for within 3 years of U.K. grant.

Yugoslavia—Patents valid 15 years after application publication. Publication or description anywhere, or sale, use, or display in Yugoslavia prejudicial. Novelty examination. Opposition period 3 months. Compulsory licensing possible 3 years after grant if inadequately worked, if working interrupted for any 3-year period, or if needed to work another patent. Revocation possible 2 years after first compulsory license.

Zaire (Kinshasa)—Inventions patents valid 20 years after application and importation patents coterminous with basic foreign patents. Prior patents or publication anywhere (except for import patents) or public use in Zaire prejudicial. No novelty examination, opposition, compulsory licensing or working provisions.

Zambia—Patents previously registered in old Federation of Rhodesia and Nyasaland in force in Zambia for remainder of unexpired term. Patents valid 16 years after application. Printed publication anywhere or public knowledge or use of intention in Zambia prejudicial. No novelty examination. Opposition period 3 months from advertisement of acceptance of patent specifications. Compulsory licensing possible 3 years after grant, (no grace period on patents relating to food or medicines), if inadequately worked.

Zimbabwe-Rhodesia—Invention patents valid 20 years after applications. Use or working in Zimbabwe-Rhodesia or publication anywhere prejudicial. Novelty examination. Opposition period 3 months. Compulsory licensing possible 3 years from grant date or 4 years from application date, if not adequately worked.

KEY PATENT TERMS

Coterminous—Refers to duration of special types of patents (e.g. confirmation, revalidation, or importation patents) issued in a country on the basis of a regular patent first obtained in another country. Such special patents are conterminous (i.e., they expire) with the basic patents.

Novelty Examination—Refers to requirements in a country's patent law under which a patent application must be examined by authorities to determine whether the invention is new (novel), as defined in the statute.

Opposition Period—Specific period of time allowed to any aggrieved third part to file documents opposing a patent application or grant for purpose of seeking its rejection or cancellation.

Prejudicial—Refers to those conditions (prior knowledge, use, publication, etc.) which can destroy the novelty of an invention and thus render it unpatentable under the country's patent law.

Appendix 8

Associations Fostering Foreign Trade

ASIAN-U.S. Business Council
  (U.S. Section)
Chamber of Commerce
  of the United States
International Division
1615 H Street, NW.
Washington, DC 20062
Telephone: (202) 463-5486

Advisory Council on Japan-
  U.S. Economic Relations
(U.S. Section)
Chamber of Commerce of USA
International Division
1615 H Street, NW.
Washington, DC 20062
Telephone: (202) 463-5489

Academy of International Business
World Trade Education Center
Cleveland State University
Cleveland, OH 44115
Telephone: (216) 687-3733

Affiliated Advertising Agencies
  International
World Headquarters
1393 East Iliff Avenue
Aurora, CO 80014
Telephone: (303) 750-1231

Source: "A Basic Guide to Exporting," U.S. Department of Commerce, International Trade Administration, U.S. and Foreign Commercial Services, Washington, D.C., September 1986.

American Arbitration Association
140 West 51st Street
New York, NY 10020
Telephone: (212) 484-4000

American Association of Exporters
and Importers
30th Floor, 11 West 42nd Street
New York, NY 10036
Telephone: (212) 944-2230

American Enterprise Institute
for Public PolicyResearch
1150 17th Street, NW., Suite 1200
Washington, DC 20036
Telephone: (202) 862-58001

American Importers Association
11 West 42nd Street
New York, NY 10036
Telephone: (212) 944-2230

American Institute
of Marine Underwriters
14 Wall Street, 21st Floor
New York, NY 10005
Telephone: (212) 233-0550

American Management Association
440 1st Street, NW.
Washington, DC 20001
Telephone: (202) 347-3092

American National Metric Council
1010 Vermont Avenue, NW.
Washington, DC 20005
Telephone: (202) 628-5757

American Society of International
Executives
1777 Walton, Suite 419
Blue Bell, PA 19422
Telephone: (215) 643-3040

American Society of International
Law
2223 Massachusetts Avenue, NW.
Washington, DC 20008
Telephone: (202) 265-4313

Bankers Association for Foreign Trade
1101 16th Street, NW., Suite 501
Washington, DC 20036
Telephone: (202) 833-3060

Brazil-U.S. Business Council (U.S.
Section)
Chamber of Commerce
of the United States
International Division
1615 H Street, NW.
Washington, DC 20062
Telephone: (202) 463-5485

Brookings Institution (The)
1775 Massachusetts Avenue, NW.
Washington, DC 20036
Telephone: (202) 797-6000

Bulgarian-U.S. Economic Council
(U.S Section)
Chamber of Commerce
of the United States
International Division
1615 H Street, NW.
Washington, DC 20062
Telephone: (202) 463-5482

Caribbean Central American Action
1333 New Hampshire Avenue, NW.
Washington, DC 20036
Telephone: (202) 466-7464

Caribbean Council
2016 O Street, NW.
Washington, DC 20036
Telephone: (202) 775-1136
Chamber of Commerce of the United
States
1615 H Street, NW.
Washington, DC 20062
Telephone: (202) 659-6000

Coalition for Employment
Through Exports, Inc.
1801 K Street, NW.
9th Floor
Washington, DC 20006
Telephone: (202)296-6107

Committee
  for Economic Development
1700 K Street, NW
Washington, DC 20006
Telephone: (202) 296-5860

Committee on Canada-United States
  Relations
(U.S. Section)
Chamber of Commerce of the United
States
International Division
1615 H Street, NW.
Washington, DC 20062
Telephone: (202) 463-5488

Conference Board (The)
845 Third Avenue
New York, NY 10022
Telephone: (212) 759-09001

Council of the Americas
680 Park Avenue
New York, NY 10021
Telephone: (212) 628-3200

Council on Foreign Relations, Inc.
58 East 68th Street
New York, NY 10021
Telephone: (212) 734-0400

Customs and International
  Trade Bar Association
c/o 40 Siegel Mandell and Davidson
1 Whitehall Street
New York, NY 10004
Telephone: (212) 425-0060

Czechoslovak-U.S. Economic Council
  (U.S. Section)
  Chamber of Commerce
  of the United States
  International Division
1615 H Street, NW.
Washington,DC 20062
Telephone: (202) 463-5482

Egypt-U.S. Business Council (U.S.
Section)
  Chamber of Commerce
  of the United States
  International Division
1615 H Street, NW.
Washington, DC 20062
Telephone: (202) 463-5487

Emergency Committee
  for American Trade
1211 Connecticut Avenue, Suite 801
Washington, DC 20036
Telephone: (202) 659-5147

Foreign Credit Interchange Bureau—
  National Assoc Of Credit Managers
475 Park Avenue South
New York, NY 10016
Telephone: (212) 578-4410

Foreign Policy Association
205 Lexington Avenue
New York, NY 10016
Telephone: (212) 481-8450

Fund for Multi-National Management
  Education
  (FMME)
680 Park Avenue
New York, NY 10021
Telephone: (212) 535-9386

Hungarian-U.S. Economic Council
  (U.S. Section)
  Chamber of Commerce
  of the United States
International Division
615 H Street, NW.
Washington, DC 20062
Telephone (202) 463-5482

Ibero American Chamber of Commerce
2100 M Street, NW., Suite 607
Washington, DC 20037
Telephone: (202) 296-0335

India-U.S. Business Council
  (U.S. Section)
  Chamber of Commerce
  of the United States
International Division
1615 H Street, NW.
Washington, DC 20062
Telephone: (202) 463-5492

Institute for International
  Development
354 Maple Avenue West
Vienna, VA 22108
Telephone: (703) 281-5040

International Advertising Association
475 Fifth Avenue
New York, NY 10077
Telephone: (212) 684-1583

International Airforwarders
  and Agents Association
Box 627
Rockville Center, NY 11571
Telephone: (516) 536-6229

International Bank
  for Reconstruction
  and Development
1818 H Street, NW.
Washington, DC 20006
Telephone: (202) 477-1234

International Cargo Gear Bureau
17 Battery Place
New York, NY 10004
Telephone: (212) 425-27501

International Economic
  Policy Association
1625 Eye Street, NW.
Washington, DC 20006
Telephone: (202) 331-1974

International Executives Association, Inc.
114 East 32nd Street
New York, NY 10016
Telephone: (212) 683-9755

International Finance Corporation
1818 H Street, NW.
Washington, DC 20433
Telephone: (202) 477-1234

International Insurance Advisory Council
  (U.S. Section)
  Chamber of Commerce
  of the United States
International Division
1615 H Street, NW
Washington, DC 20062
Telephone: (202) 463-5480

International Trade Council
750 13th Street, SE.
Washington, DC 20003
Telephone: (202) 547-1727

Israel-U.S. Business Council (U.S. Section)
  Chamber of Commerce
  of the United States
International Division
615 H Street, NW.
Washington,DC 20062
Telephone: (202) 463-5478

National Association
  of Export Management
  Companies, Inc.
200 Madison Ave
New York, NY 10016
Telephone: (212) 561-2025

National Association of Manufacturers
1776 F Street, NW.
Washington, DC 20006
Telephone: (202) 626-3700

National Association
  of State Development Agencies
Hall of State, Suite 345
444 North Capitol, NW.
Washington, DC 20001
Telephone: (202) 624-5411

National Committee
  on International Trade
  Documentation (The)
350 Broadway
New York,NY 10013
Telephone: (212) 925-1400

National Council
  for U.S. China Trade (The)
Suite 350
1050 17th Street, NW.
Washington, DC 20036
Telephone: (202) 429-0340

National Customs Brokers
  and Forwarders Association
  of America
One World Trade Center, Suite 1109
New York, NY 10048
Telephone: (212) 432-0050

National Export Traffic League
234 Fifth Avenue
New York, NY 10001
Telephone: (212) 697-5895

National Foreign Trade Council
11 West 42nd Street, 30th Floor
New York, NY 10036
Telephone: (22) 944-2230

National Industrial Council
1776 F Street, NW.
Washington, DC 20006
Telephone: (202) 626-3853

Nigeria-U.S. Economic Council
  (U.S. Section)
  Chamber of Commerce
  of the United States
International Division
1615 H Street, NW.
Washington, DC 20062
Telephone: (202) 463-5734

Organization of American States
19th & Constitution Avenue, NW.
Washington, DC 20006
Telephone: (202) 789-3000

Overseas Development Council
1717 Massachusetts Avenue, NW.
Suite 501
Washington, DC 20036
Telephone: (202) 234-8701

Pan American Development Fund
1889 F Street, NW.
Washington, DC 20006
Telephone (202) 789-3969

Partners of the Americas
1424 K Street, NW.
Washington, DC 20005
Telephone (202) 628-3300

Partnership for Productivity
  International
2441 18th Street, NW.
Washington, DC 20009
Telephone: (202) 234-0340

Polish-U.S Economic Council
  (U.S. Section)
  Chamber of Commerce
  of the United States
International Division
1615 H Street, NW.
Washington, DC 20062
Telephone (202) 463-5482

Private Export Funding Corporation
280 Park Avenue
New York, NY 10017
Telephone: (202) 557-3100

Romanian-U.S. Economic Council
 (U.S. Section)
 Chamber of Commerce
 of the United States
International Division
1615 H Street, NW.
Washington, DC 20062
Telephone: (202) 463-5482

Suday-U.S. Business Council
 (U.S. Section)
 Chamber of Commerce
 of the United States
International Division
1615 H Street, NW.
Washington, DC 20062
Telephone: (202)463-5487

Trade Relations Council
 of the United States, Inc.
1001 Connecticut Avenue, NW.
Room 901
Washington, DC 20036
Telephone: (202) 785-4194

The U.S.-U.S.S.R. Trade
 and Economic Council
805 3rd Avenue, 14th Floor
New York, NY 10022
Telephone: (202) 644-4550

The U.S.-Yugoslav Economic Council,
 Inc.
1511 K Street, NW., Suite 431
Washington, DC 20005
Telephone: (202) 737-9652

The U.S.A.-Republic
 of China Economic Council
200 Main Street
Crystal Lake, IL 60014
Telephone: (815) 459-5875

United States of America
 Business and Industry
 Advisory Committee
1212 Avenue of the Americas
Ne York, NY 10036
Telephone: (212) 354-4480

Washington Agribusiness
 Promotion Council
14th & Independence Avenue, Room 3120
Auditors Building
Washington, DC 20250
Telephone: (202) 382-8006

World Trade Institute
1 World Trade Center 55 West
New York, NY 10048
Telephone: (212) 466-4044

Appendix 9

Foreign Trademark Protection: Treaties and National Laws

American exporters should not underestimate the importance of trademark protection for their goods and services in foreign markets of present and potential interest. A trademark provides specific, unique identity for the products and services of a firm in foreign markets, as it does in the United States, and also serves as the focal point around which that firm can develop its sales program. The mark also symbolizes to the buying public the goodwill and reputation inherent in the firm and the quality of the products and services which it provides.

In 1978 $143.6 billion worth the U.S. goods were exported. About $94.5 billion (66 percent) consisted of manufactured goods, i.e., those which trademarks serve to identify. The remaining percentage was represented by fungible goods (i.e., grains, ores, raw materials shipped in bulk), some of which also shared in goodwill of the same type represented by a trademark, either because the buyer relied on the reputation of the seller's trade name or because, as in the case of grain and coal shipments and the like, the tankers themselves carried the trademark of the exporters.

Presently, about 40,000 trademark applications are filed annually by U.S. firms in about 80 countries which report such figures. Also, about 475,000 registrations of marks are in force in the U.S. Patent and Trademark Office, 37,000 being registered annually in the USPTO.

Source: "Foreign Business Practices," U.S. Department of Commerce, International Trade Administration, Washington, D.C., April 1985.

The United States is a party to several treaties under the terms of which U.S. firms are entitled to receive, in about 95 countries, treatment under trademark laws which is no less beneficial than that which those countries extend to their own nationals (national treatment). The United States is not a party to any agreement whereby a U.S. trademark registration is automatically recognized and protected in a foreign country or vice verse. Thus, while U.S. nationals have the right to secure trademark registrations in countries with which the United States has treaty arrangements, they must nevertheless proceed country-by-country under the laws of each to obtain these rights.

The most significant multilateral agreement on trademark rights, to which the United States and 89 other countries are party, is the "International Convention for the Protection of Industrial Property" (Paris Convention). The United States also is bound by the "General Inter-American Convention for Trademark and Commercial Protection of 1929," to which eleven other Western Hemisphere countries are party.

Both of these Conventions embody the national treatment principle, as well as certain other advantages for the U.S. business official seeking trademark protection abroad. Such rights include a "right of priority," which is created by filing a first trademark application in the United States or another member country, followed by the filing of one or more corresponding applications in other Convention countries within the next six months. The effect is to give the later filed cases the same effect for purposes of priority as if filed on the same date as the first. Thus, an intervening use of filing of the same mark by another—a "pirate," for example is defeated.

Also, under a revision of the Paris Convention, a U.S. national may apply for the registration of a trademark in any adherent country, if it is otherwise a proper application, without the need of a prior "home county" registration of the same mark in the United States. The revision also strengthens protection for marks for services, as well as those for goods.

There are several international agreements in effect under which trademark applications can be filed in a central office for protection in a number of countries. Although the United States is not yet party to any of these agreements, it is desirable for a firm seeking trademark protection abroad to consider the extent to which a U.S. firm may use these central filing procedures.

The "Madrid Agreement Concerning the International Registration of Trademarks" is adhered to by 22 countries. Under its provisions, the filing and protection of a trademark registered nationally in the country of origin (home country) of a firm can be automatically extended by the owner to one or more of the other countries by a single international application filed with the World Intellectual Property Organization (WIPO) Central Bureau in Geneva, Switzerland, through the intermediary of the applicant's home country office. Upon receipt of the application, the Bureau registers and publishes the application in an international journal and transmits copies to other countries selected by the owner for processing and, if qualified, registration by each in accordance with its own laws. Countries have a right to refuse protection if a notice of refusal or possible refusal is communicated to WIPO within one year from date of publication of the international registration. The international registration is dependent on the prior "home country" registration for an initial period of 5 years. Thus, if the home registration is canceled, the effects in the other countries are also invalidated. After that time, such marks may no longer be terminated by a single action directed against the prior home mark.

In June 1973, the United States participated in a negotiating conference which adopted a new "Trademark Registration Treaty" (TRT), providing for simplified central filing procedures, but with some procedural differences from the Madrid Agreement. The TRT provides that, for a single fee, a trademark application can be filed directly with the WIPO Central Bureau in Geneva. Unlike filings under the Madrid Agreement the applicant will not need a prior home registration and need not proceed through the "home country" office. The filing of a TRT application will have the effect of a filing in each country designated by the applicant. The mark, after filing, will then be published and circulated by WIPO member countries whereupon each country designated by the applicant has 15 months within which to notify the refusal or possible refusal of registration under its national law. The grounds of refusal are the same as those under the national law except that no member country will be able to refuse a mark on grounds of nonuse, nor cancel it on such grounds for at least 3 years after its registration.

The TRT is effective as from August 7, 1980 with respect to five states which have deposited instruments of accession: Congo, Gabon, Togo Republic, Upper Volta, and the USSR. The United States signed the TRT, but will have to amend its trademark law to provide for registration based on intention to use a mark, in order to ratify the treaty.

Prompt registration of trademarks is advantageous for U.S. exporters in those countries where they intend to do business, or where their products may be marketed by others. In almost all foreign countries, trademark applicants are not required to present evidence of use of a mark prior to registration. In fact, in many countries, the first person to apply for and acquire registration of a mark is recognized as its rightful owner. In the British Commonwealth countries and certain others, the applicant must either show use, or specify intended use. In the latter case, the mark must be used within a certain period after registration in order to maintain rights.

In other countries, such as France, the first applicant is entitled to registration and protection of a mark regardless of whether it may have been previously used by another party. In those countries which have no prior use requirement, registration of marks owned in the United States are sometimes acquired by persons without authority of the U.S. owner. Such persons then use these registrations to prevent the owners of the trademark rights in the United States from importing their goods, or to compel them to license the marks to the registrants, or to employ the latter as local distributors in order to do business in their countries.

Unlike patents, trademark registrations can be renewed indefinitely. Their initial duration and renewal periods vary from country to country. In countries with laws patterned on the British system, the initial term is usually 7 years, renewable for 14 years thereafter. In most countries the initial and renewal terms are the same—generally ranging between 10 and 20 years.

Most countries require a trademark to be used within a specified period after its registration; otherwise it is subject to cancellation. Various countries, primarily those in the British Commonwealth, have a requirement in their trademark laws under which certain aspects of a trademark license must be recorded in the Trademark Office. This requirement to record a license as a "registered user" registers the fact that the licensor may control the quality of the licensee's trademarked products. In some countries, the entire license agreement itself must be registered with the government to be enforceable.

The most widely used trademark classification system is that currently established under the "Arrangement of Nice Concerning the International Classification of Goods and Services to Which Trade Marks Apply," adopted June 15, 1957. It consists of 34 product and 7 service classes. The system is used by the United States and about 60 other countries.

For more detailed data on step-by-step procedures to be followed in protecting their trademark rights abroad, exporters should seek advice and assistance from competent counsel relative to the laws of the countries in which they desire to do business.

Summaries of trademark laws throughout the world follow.

Afghanistan—Registrations valid 10 years from application filing date, renewable for similar periods. First applicant entitled to registration. Prior user may contest registration within three years. After three years, no claims against valid registration heard by Commercial Court. No use requirement unless ordered by government.

African Intellectual Property Organization (OAPI)—Members of OAPI are Benin, Cameroon, Central African Republic, Chad, Congo, Gabon, Ivory Coast, Mauritania Niger, Senegal, Togo and Upper Volta. Accord applies to trademarks as well as patents and industrial designs, establishes common system for offering protection in member countries through filing with Central Office, Yaounde, Cameroon.

Trademark application filed with, and registration granted by, Central Office has protection of national law in each member country, valid for 20 years from date of deposit (filing date). Renewable for indefinite period. No examination or opposition. Registration incontestable on prior user grounds after 3 years. Mark must be registered to be recognized as owner's property right in member countries. Marks registered by Central Office may be annulled by Civil Tribunals of member countries in their territories, if such marks found to be contrary to public order, lacking distinctiveness, or liable to public deception. Transfers and assignments must be entered with the special Central Office Register to be enforceable.

Albania—Registrations valid 10 years from registration date, renewable like periods. First applicant, as user, entitled registration. Applications examined, no opposition provisions. Prior home registration required for foreign marks to be accepted for registration. Duration of foreign mark registration cannot exceed prior home registration.

Algeria—Registrations valid 10 years from application filing date, renewable for like periods. Registrations in force July 3, 1962 valid to 15 years, provided registrant made "continuous use" request before December 14, 1966. First applicant entitled to registration. No examination or opposition proceedings. Immediate publication after registration. Requests for cancellation on grounds of confusion of conflict with another's mark permissible within 5 years of contested registration's date.

Argentina—Registration valid 10 years from registration date; renewable for similar periods. First applicant is entitled to registration. Applications are subject to examination and are published for opposition which must be filed within 30 days. Trademark cancellation may be brought within 10 years from registration on the grounds the trademark was obtained contrary to the law; contrary to proprietary rights of third parties; or based on failure to use the trademark within 5 years prior to renewal action. Declaration of use within 5 years prior to renewal is required.

Australia—Registration valid 7 years from application filing date; renewable 14-year periods. First applicant, as user or intended user, entitled registration. Trademark registrable Part A must distinguish applicant's goods from others. After 7 years, mark becomes incontestable on most grounds. Trademark registrable Part B need not be distinctive but capable, in use, of becoming distinctive. Part B registration has no incontestability rights after 7 years' validity, as does Part A. Certification marks registrable Part C. Defensive marks, if already registered Part A, registrable Part D. Applications examined; published opposition, 3 months. Mark may be cancelled upon proof registered without intent to use or, if no bona fide use within 3 years after registration. "Registered Use" provisions. Australian Trade Marks Act extends to Norfolk Island and Nauru.

Austria—Registration valid for 10 years from registration date; renewable for like periods. First applicant entitled to registration. Applications subject to examination, no opposition provisions. Prior user may seek cancellation within 5 years from registration date. Trademark may be cancelled on grounds of non-use after 5 years following registration.

Bahamas—Registrations valid 14 years from application date, renewable similar periods. First applicant entitled to registration. First user rights recognized but mark registered 7 years becomes valid, unless proven to be obtained by fraud. Infringement action possible only if mark registered. Applications examined, published for 1 month opposition. Mark cancellable if not used within 5 years of registration.

Bahrain—Registrations valid 5 years, renewable similar period. First user, or intended user, entitled to registration. Foreign applicant must include certified copy of foreign registration. Bahraini registration may remain in force for duration of foreign registration. Applications published for 30-day opposition period. Mark cancellable if not used on goods for which registered for 2 years preceding the application for revocation by a third party. Registration is prerequisite to infringement proceedings.

Bangladesh (formerly East Pakistan)—Trademarks registered in Pakistan before March 26, 1971 invalidated in Bangladesh. Revalidation of such marks obtainable only if applied for before Sept. 13, 1974. Revalidations retroactive to registration date in Pakistan for period originally granted under Pakistan law. Applications pending in Pakistan March 26, 1971, not valid in Bangladesh. New applications must be filed in Chittagong. Text of Pakistan law has been adopted.

Barbados—Registrations valid 7 years, renewable for 14 years. Persons claiming ownership of mark as first user, may apply for registration. One-month opposition period. No use requirement.

Belgium (see Benelux)

Benelux—Benelux Trademarks Treaty and Uniform Trademark Law, effective Jan. 1, 1971. Establishes Benelux Trademarks Office at The Hague covering Belgium. Netherlands and Luxembourg. Registration effective in all three countries only on the basis of a single application. Not possible to file for, or secure, registration in any separate country. Registration valid 10 years from application date; renewable like periods. First application entitled registration. No opposition provisions. Registration effected if application meets formal requirements. Registrations must be used within 3 years of issue or during uninterrupted five-year period.

Bolivia—Registration valid 10 years from registration date; renewable for similar periods. First applicant entitled to registration. Applications published for opposition within 50 days. Right of ownership becomes conclusive after registration is valid for 18 months. No use requirement, except for pharmaceutical and chemical products.

Bophuthatswana—Formerly a territory in South Africa. Adopted South African trademark law. Marks registered in South Africa and in effect before December 5, 1977 are valid for original duration term. First user entitled to registration for applications filed after that date. Two-month opposition period. Registrations valid 10 years from application date, renewable similar periods. Marks subject to cancellation if not used within 5 years after registration. Registered user, and Part A (distinctive marks) and Part B (capable of distinctiveness) appear in the law. Part A registration incontestable after 7 years.

Botswana—Registration possible on basis of prior registration in South Africa or United Kingdom; valid for unexpired term of prior registration. Renewable with home registration. No examination or opposition.

Brazil—Registrations valid 10 yeas from issue date; renewable like periods. First applicant entitled to registration. Applicants examined published 60 days opposition. Mark must be used within 2 years and not discontinued for more than 2 consecutive years. Mark registered more than 5 years immune from annulment action. Mark covering pharmaceutical product must be licensed by Brazilian Health Department before registration.

Bulgaria—Registrations valid 10 years from application date; renewable for similar periods. First applicant entitled to registration and exclusive use of mark. No opposition or examination. Prior user may contest application, if he files own trademark application within 3 months of objection date. Mark not used for 5 years may be canceled.

Burma—No trademark law. Possible to acquire legally recognized ownership as first user under common law. May record Declaration of Ownership in Office of Registrar of Deeds, Rangoon, and publish "caution notice" in newspapers.

Burundi—Registrations granted for unlimited duration. Person applying as first public user receives registration. No examination or opposition. Registration presumes valid property right unless proof to contrary is submitted to authorities.

Canada—Registration valid for 15 years from date of registration or last renewal; renewable for like periods indefinitely. Person first to use the trademark, or who made mark known in Canada, or who previously registered and used the mark in a Paris Union country, or who intends to use the trademark in Canada, is entitled to registration. In the latter instance, applicant must show use of the trademark before it will be registered. Applications examined for proper form and content; published for opposition within 1 month. If no successful opposition, application is allowed. A mark not used for 3 consecutive years may be cancelled. Registered User provisions.

Central American Agreement—The Agreement was concluded June 1, 1968 by Costa Rica, Guatemala and Nicaragua, in regard to trademarks, tradenames, advertising slogans, and repression of unfair competition in these areas. In the countries which have ratified, it, and where it is now in force (Costa Rica, Guatemala,and Nicaragua), national laws on subject matter officially are not now in effect. However, a trademark applicant must still file for registration and have the application processed separately in each country where he desires protection. The Agreement makes no provision for multiple protection based on a single application. Nor is there a central office to receive applications and effect registrations for all member countries. Under the Agreement's provisions, registrations are valid for 10 years, and renewable for like periods. Marks registered in the member countries before June 1, 1968 and still in force shall continue for their original duration and may be renewed under the provision of the Agreement. Applications are examined and, if accepted, published for opposition for a 2 month period. No compulsory licensing of registered marks except for chemical, pharmaceutical, medical, and food products. Government does have right to order compulsory licensing in other special circumstances in public interest. Ownership of a trade name is required by registration under same procedural requirements governing trademarks. Procedures are also established for registration of advertising slogans and signs and for prevention of acts of unfair competition relating to trademarks, trade names, and advertising slogans and signs.

Chile—Registrations valid 10 years from registration date; renewable for similar periods. First applicant entitled to registration, if first to use mark continuously. Opposition period is 25 days after publication. Two years after registration, mark generally becomes incontestable, if mark has been in use. No compulsory use requirement.

China, People's Republic—Registration of trademark granted to first applicant. Marks registered by local enterprises have no fixed duration; valid until withdrawn by the registrant. Marks registered by foreign parties valid for period of 10 years and renewable further 10-year periods. The owner of a registered trademark acquires exclusive right to its use in PRC.

U.S. nationals may apply for and receive registrations, as of January 1, 1978. The requirement of reciprocity between PRC and country of nationality of applicant is considered by PRC to be met by the United States since PRC foreign trading corporation is already permitted to apply for and register trademarks in this country.

U.S. firms desiring to file applications or correspond with PRC on trademark matters should write to: Trademark registration Agency, China Council for the Promotion of International Trade (CCPIT), Beijing, People's Republic of China. In trademark Matters, CCPIT acts as foreign firm's agent with Central Administrative Bureau for Industry and Commerce (CABIC), which, according to 1963 Regulations, is responsible for administering PRC Trademark Regulations.

U.S. trademarks applied for and registered in PRC may include English words. Foreign trademarks registered there are not limited to Chinese and may use any language. Applications are subject to formal examination, published in Official Bulletin for opposition purposes; opposition to be filed within 3 months following publication. Registrations subject to cancellation if not used for 3 consecutive years.

A trademark registration may be cancelled where quality of product does not meet governmental requirements, where it is altered without governmental authority, where registration has not been used for one full year and no permission for such nonuse has been granted and where third party applies for cancellation and, after examination of reasons for this request by the government, it approves the cancellation. For trademark registration purposes, there are 78 classes of goods.

Colombia—Registrations valid 5 years from registration date, renewable for 5-year periods. First application entitled to registration. Prior use can serve rightful ownership grounds for contesting another's application or registration of similar mark. Applications examined, published for opposition within 30 days. registration subject to cancellation, if not used within 5 years.

Costa Rica (see Central American Agreement)

Cyprus—Registrations valid 7 years from application date; renewable for 14-year periods. Person claiming proprietorship of mark may apply for its registration. First user rights recognized. Applications examined; published opposition 2 months. A mark registered under Part A of Register and not contested for 7 years may not be challenged except upon proof it was obtained by fraud of deception. Mark not used 5 years may be cancelled, unless nonuse was due to special circumstances.

Czechoslovakia—Registrations valid 10 years from application filing date; renewable for similar periods. First application entitled to registration. Another party proving prior use in Czechoslovakia for same class of goods may apply for cancellation within 3 years of registration date. Applications examined. No opposition or use requirement.

Denmark—Registrations valid 10 years from registration date, renewable for similar periods. First applicant entitled to registration. Party claiming prior use mark after registration may, within 5 years of registration date, secure cancellation from courts upon proof of such use. Examination provisions; opposition period 2 months. No use requirement.

Dominican Republic—Registration granted for 5, 10, 15, or 20 years from registration date, at applicant's option, renewable for similar periods. First applicant entitled to registration. Examination, but no opposition provisions. When trademark applicant finds previously registered similar mark, first registration may be cancelled if used less than one-quarter time during which newly-applied for mark has been used by applicant. Cancellation of registration on grounds of similarity to mark previously registered must be sought within 3 years after registration of contested mark. Registered mark must be used within 1 year of registration date.

Ecuador—Registration valid for 5 years from application date; renewable for 5-year periods. First applicant entitled to registration. Applications examined for formal compliance and registrability; opposition may be filed within 30 days following publication in the Official Gazette. Use of mark compulsory; evidence of use required to apply for trademark renewal.

Egypt—Registrations valid 10 years from application filing date, renewable for similar periods. First applicant is entitled to registration. Contestable on prior use grounds for up to 5 years. Applications examined; published opposition 3 months. Registration not contestable after 5 years, if used continuously during that period.

El Salvador—Registrations valid for 20 years; renewable for similar periods. First applicant is entitled to registration. Applications examined, published for opposition, which must occur within 90 days. If mark not used, or use discontinued within 1 year after registration, it can be cancelled. Foreign-owned mark used outside country meets the requirement. Customs authorities may prohibit import goods bearing infringing marks.

Finland—Registration valid 10 years from registration date; renewable for similar periods. First applicant entitled to registration. Examination provisions; opposition period 2 months after publication. Contestability on prior use grounds permissible within 5 years of registration date. Mark not used for 5 years may be cancelled.

France—Present trademark law effective August 1, 1965, as amended to January 10, 1978. Registrations valid for 10 years from application filing date. As transitory measure, all registrations effected before August 1, 1965 enjoy 15-year protection from application filing date. First applicant obtains registration, exclusive ownership of mark even though previously used by others. Only exception: owner of mark already very well known in France as belonging to him rather than registrant may sue registrant for cancellation within 5 years after registrant's application date. Examination for registrability, but not prior marks; no opposition proceedings. Mark not used for 5 consecutive years subject to cancellation.

Former French Colony, now independent country, of Mali continues to apply earlier French Trademark Law (1857) to jurisdiction. Applications should be filed directly in country. In Guinea, mark must first be registered in France to be registered and protected there. French 1965 law applies to Martinique, Guadeloupe, French Guiana, St. Pierre, Miquelon, and French Polynesian Islands.

Gambia—First user entitled to registration. Trademarks registered in United Kingdom are registrable on coterminous basis. Applications subject to formal and registrability examinations. Marks registered for 14 years from application date and renewable for like periods. Opposition may be filed within 3-9 months after publication of application. Trademarks are subject to cancellation on grounds of non-use during 5 years following registration. Trademarks become uncontestable after 7 years.

German Democratic Republic—Registrations valid 10 years from application date, renewable for like periods. First applicant entitled to registration. Prior user, upon proof, may have registration cancelled. Applications examined; no provision for opposition. No use requirement, but mark may be cancelled if business in which used expires. No time limitation for cancellation action.

German, Federal Republic—Registrations valid for 10 years from application filing date, renewable for similar periods. First applicant is entitled to registration. Registration, not prior use, confers proprietary rights. Examination procedures for registrability, not prior marks. Applications published for 3 months' opposition. Mark must be used within 5 years of registration date, otherwise subject to cancellation.

Ghana—Registrations valid 7 years from application filing date, renewable for 14-year periods. Register consists of Part A (distinctive marks) and Part B (marks capable of becoming distinctive). First person applying as user or intended user of mark is entitled to registration. Application examined, published for opposition, which must occur within 2 months. Registration cancelled if not used 5 years. "Registered user" provision.

Greece—Registrations valid for 10 years from application filing date, renewable for similar periods. First applicant is entitled to registration. Examination procedures, opposition period 6 months. Prior user has rights if he proves mark is sufficiently known in his business in Greece, has 3 years from registration date to seek cancellation, but term begins only after first sale by registrant. Registration may be cancelled if registrant fails to place on market goods bearing the mark within 3 years of registration date (1 year for periodicals and 4 years for pharmaceutical marks), or if registrant has discontinued business or not offered products bearing mark for sale for 2 years (1 year periodical marks).

Guatemala (see Central American Agreement)

Guinea Bissau (see Portugal)

Guinea—Trademarks protected by laws similar to French law. Should be filed with Registry of the Tribunal of First Instance of Conakry.

Guyana (formerly British Guiana)—Registrations valid 7 years from application filing date; renewable for similar periods. Person applying as first user is entitled to registration. Owner of United Kingdom registration may also apply registration on this basis. One-month opposition period. Registered mark not used 5 years may be cancelled. Register consists of Part A (for distinctive marks), B (for marks capable of becoming distinctive), and C (registration based on those in the United Kingdom). "Registered user" provisions.

Haiti—Registrations valid 10 years from registration date are renewable for similar periods. First applicant is entitled to registration. Prior user may seek cancellation within 5 years of registration date. Applications published for opposition, which must be made within 2 months. For opposition to be accepted, opposer must also file application for contested mark, if not already registered. Mark may be cancelled if not used within 5 years.

Honduras—Registrations valid 10 years from registration date; renewable for similar periods. First applicant is entitled to registration. Applications published three times, at 10-day intervals, for opposition, which must be filed within 15 days of 1st publication. Mark must be used for more than a year after registration, otherwise considered abandoned unless revalidated upon fee payment.

Hong Kong (see United Kingdom)

Hungary—Registration valid 10 years from application filing date, renewable for similar periods. First applicant is entitled to registration. Registered mark must be used within 5 years otherwise may be cancelled. Applications examined. No opposition provisions.

Iceland—Registrations valid 10 years from registration date; renewable for similar periods. First applicant is entitled to registration. Prior user may contest registration within 5 years of registration date. Examination procedures. Publication for 2 months opposition. No compulsory use.

India—Registrations valid 7 years from application filing date; renewable for similar periods. First applicant who claims ownership through use is entitled to registration. Under certain conditions, proven prior user may also have right to register mark at same time. Register divided into Part A (distinctive marks) and Part B (marks capable of becoming distinctive). Certification and defensive marks registrable under Part A. Applications examined, published three months opposition. Any mark, except defensive mark, may be cancelled if not used continuously for 5 years, unless nonuse was due to circumstances over which registrant had no control. "Registered User" provisions.

Indonesia—Registrations valid 10 years from registration date, renewable for similar periods. Registrations and renewals made before Nov. 11, 1961 are valid 10 years. Exclusive rights to mark are based on its first use in Indonesia. First applicant considered first user. To preserve first user status, registrant must use mark within 6 months of registration date. Examination, but no opposition provisions. Adverse decisions on application appealable to District Court, Jakarta. Cancellation petitions also may be filed with that Court, but within 9 months of registration's publication date. Mark must be used within 6 months of registration. Exclusive right valid for mark for only 3 consecutive years from last use.

Iran—Registrations valid 10 years from application filing date; renewable for similar periods. First applicant is entitled to registration. Prior user claimant must contest it within three years. Applications made public for inspection; opposition; also examined. Allowed applications published for opposition within 30 days. Registration, if not used by registrant in Iran or abroad within three years of effective date, may be cancelled.

Iraq—Registrations valid 15 years from application filing date; renewable for similar periods. Registered mark becomes incontestable after 5 years. Applicant, as user or intended user, is entitled to registration. Applications given preliminary search; published opposition three consecutive times; opposition must be filed within 90 days of last publication date. Registration not used for 2 consecutive years may be cancelled unless owner proves nonuse was due to circumstances over which he had no control.

Ireland—Registrations valid 7 years from application filing date; renewable for 14-year periods. First applicant as user, or intended user, is entitled to registration. Marks are registered Part A (distinctive) or Part B (capable of becoming distinctive). Certification marks registrable under Part A. Part A registration is incontestable after 7 years except on grounds that the mark was acquired through fraud, consists of immoral or deceptive subject matter. Examination procedures; 1-month opposition period. Mark subject to cancellation if not used for 5 years.

Israel—Registration valid 7 years from application filing date, renewable for 14-year periods. First applicant or prior user is entitled to registration, whichever is earlier. Registration is contestable on prior user grounds within 5 years. Examination procedures; opposition period, 3 months. Mark subject to cancellation, if not used within 2 years. "Registered user" provision.

Italy—Registration valid 20 years from application filing date; renewable for similar periods. First applicant is entitled to registration. Prior users have contestability rights for 5 years. To secure cancellation of registrations, he must show that prior use of mark was sufficient for it to be publicly known before contested mark's registration date. No examination or opposition provisions. Mark must be used within 3 years of registration date, must also be used continuously for 3 years.

Jamaica—Registrations valid 7 years from application filing date; renewable for 14-year periods. Register divided into Part A (distinctive) and Part B (capable of becoming distinctive). Part A registrations are conclusive as to validity after 7 years. First applicant as user, or intended user, is entitled to registration. Examination procedures; 1 month opposition period. Registration cancellable if unused for 5 years. "Registered User" provisions.

Japan—Registrations are valid 10 years from registration date, renewable for similar periods. First applicant is entitled to registration. Another person widely using mark before first application filed may be permitted to continue such use even after registered by someone else. Examination procedure, 1-month opposition period. Registration cancellable if not used for 3 consecutive years (unless there was good reason for such nonuse); or if it is deemed similar to someone else's "well known" mark; or if used in a deceptive manner; or if otherwise registered contrary to law. Incontestable after 5 years except on grounds of misleading use or deception.

Jordan—Registration valid 7 years from application filing date, renewable for 14-year periods. First applicant as user, or intended user, is entitled to registration. Examination procedures. Opposition period 3 months. Registration may be cancelled on grounds of nonuse or no bona fide intention to use during 2 years preceding cancellation petition, unless nonuse was due to conditions over which registrant had no control. Mark is incontestable 5 years after registration date. Unless mark has been registered, no infringement damages may be recovered.

Kenya—Registration valid 7 years from application date; renewable for 14-year periods. Register divided into Part A (distinctive) and Part B (capable of becoming distinctive). First applicant as user or intended user is entitled to registration. Examination procedures. Opposition period 60 days. Registration cancellable if mark not used in 5 years. "Registered User" provisions.

Korea (South)—Registration valid for 10 years from registration date; renewable for similar periods. First applicant entitled to registration. Examination limited to compliance with formal requirements. Opposition may be filed by anybody within 30 days following publication. Trademark owners of similar registrations may file opposition within 1 year. Trademark cancellable if not used within 1 year following registration. Cancellation action limited to 5 years from date of registration.

Kuwait—Registrations valid 10 years from application filing date renewable for the same period. First applicant is entitled to registration. Registration incontestable after 5 years. Accepted applications published for opposition in three consecutive issues of the *Official Gazette*. Oppositions must be filed within 30 days of last publication. Mark may be cancelled if not used for 5 consecutive years.

Lebanon—Registrations valid for 15, 30, 45, or 60 years at applicant's option; renewable for identical periods. First applicant entitled to registration, but rights of prior user recognized if exercise within 5 years following registration. Trademark subject to formal examination; no provisions for opposition. No compulsory use provisions in force.

Lesotho—Registration possible on basis of prior registration in South Africa or the United Kingdom; valid for unexpired term of prior registration. Renewable with home registration. No examination or opposition.

Liberia—Registrations valid for 15 years; renewable for similar periods. Infringement action not possible if based on unregistered mark. First applicant is entitled to registration, but must prove mark not in use by anyone else. Examination procedures, but no opposition provisions. Mark must be used within 1 years of registration date; otherwise cancellable. Also cancellable if owner neglects legal action against infringer or adopts new similar mark.

Libya—Registration valid 10 years after application filing date, renewable for similar periods. First applicant is entitled to registration. Examination procedures, opposition period 3 months. Registration incontestable after 5 years. Cancellable if not used for five consecutive years without justification.

Liechtenstein—Registrations valid 20 years from application filing date; renewable for similar periods. First applicant is entitled to registration. No examination or opposition procedures. Prior user rights recognized. Mark cancellable if not used for 3 consecutive years.

Luxembourg (See Benelux)

Malawi (Nyasaland)—Marks registered with the former Federation of Rhodesia and Nyasaland before January 1, 1964 are effective in Malawi for their original term. Certificate of Registration for such marks should be secured and entered in the Malawi Register. Federation separated in 1963 into Malawi, Zambia, and Southern Rhodesia. Marks registrable in Malawi 7 years from application filing date, renewable for 14 years. First applicant, as use or intended user, is entitled to registration. Register divided into Part A (distinctive), Part B (capable of becoming distinctive), C (certification), and D (defensive). Examination procedures. Opposition period is 2 months. Registration cancellable if not used 5 years. Part A registration remaining valid for 7 years is incontestable on prior user grounds. "Registered User" provisions.

Malaysia—Malaysian nation established Sept. 16, 1963, consists of former Malaya, Sarawak, and Sabah (North Borneo). No central trademark law yet adopted; each separate state continues to enforce the law in effect in its area before that date. Office of Registrar of Trademarks and Patents for Malaysia is at Kuala Lumpur. Registrar of Trademarks and Patents in Singapore reportedly serving as Registrar for Sabah. Sarawak Registrar is at Kuching. Registrations for each area are valid 7 years from application filing date; renewable for 14-year periods. Registers in all areas divided into Part A (distinctive) and Part B (capable of becoming distinctive). Associated, defensive,and certification marks are registrable. First applicant as user is entitled to registration. Examination procedure, opposition period 1 month after publication. Mark not used for 5 years cancellable. "Registered User" provisions.

Mali—Applications for registration may be filed at Registry of Tribunal of First Instance of Bamako. Marks registered in France before independence (April 4, 1960) should be re-registered. Registrations valid 15 years.

Malta—Registration valid 14 years from registration date; renewable for similar periods. Applicant as first user is entitled to registration. Examination procedures, opposition period 2 months from publication. No use requirement.

Mauritius—Marks registrable on the basis of prior United Kingdom registration or independently. Independent registrations valid 7 years from registration date; renewable for 14-year periods, U.K.-based registration valid and renewable for term of basic registration. First user entitled to registration. No use requirement.

Mexico—Trademarks registered for 5 years from application filing date and renewable for indefinitely similar periods. Registered mark must be used within 3 years of registration; otherwise subject to cancellation. Registration notice must appear on mark to be enforceable. Applications examined; if questions arise for examiners, applicant given 15 to 45 days to modify application; otherwise registration denied. Government may require registration and use of trademarks on any product or products. marketing of specific products under generic names may be ordered. After December 30, 1984 every trademark of foreign origin or owned by a foreigner, used on articles made in Mexico, must be used jointly with a mark originally registered in Mexico; both marks to be displayed equally. Compliance with this requirement may be postponed for another year. All contracts for licensing and use of foreign-owned marks on locally produced goods must contain this co-use requirement. Owner of mark registered in Mexico may authorize other parties to use his mark and record the "authorized user" contracts with the government for legal recognition and enforcement. Cancellation of registered marks may be sought on grounds that such marks are similar to a prior registration; are false indications of origin; or were applied for by local agent without prior permission of foreign owner. Mark may also be cancelled when government determines that owner has improperly priced or represented quality of product or service covered by mark, to public detriment.

Monaco—Registrations valid 15 years from application filing date; renewable for similar periods. Exclusive right in trademark secured by use. No substantive examination or opposition procedures or compulsory use. Prior user may contest registration within 5 years if mark being effectively used by such user.

Morocco (formerly French Zone)—Former French and Spanish Zones of Morocco, and Tangier Zone, formed Kingdom of Morocco in 1956. No unified trademark legislation yet adopted. Protection in ex-French Zone should be sought through the Moroccan Industrial Property Office, Casablanca. For information on former Spanish and Tangier Zones, see separate summaries. Registrations issued by Office Marocain are valid 20 years from registration date and renewable for similar periods. First applicant is entitled to registration. Prior user may contest registration up to 5 years. No substantive examination or opposition proceedings. Registered mark must be used in Morocco or abroad; otherwise may be cancelled.

Morocco (formerly Spanish Zone)—Registrations in Spain filed before 1956 remain valid for original durations. No facilities for securing new registrations are apparent.

Mozambique—Portuguese law applied.

Nepal—Mark must be registered to be protected. No limitation on duration. First applicant is entitled to registration ; no opposition proceedings.

Netherlands (see Benelux)

New Zealand—Registration valid 7 years from application filing date; renewable for 14-year periods. First registrant, as user or intended user, is entitled to registration. Examination procedures. Opposition period 3 months. Marks registrable as Part A (distinctive) and Part B (capable of becoming distinctive). Part A registrations are incontestable on prior user grounds after 7 years. Certification, association, and defensive marks are registrable. Mark may be cancelled if proven it was registered without intent to use and it was not used up to 1 month before application filed or, if not used within 5 years before cancellation sought. "Registered User" provisions.

Trademarks registered in New Zealand reportedly have validity in the Cook and Tokelau Island; those registered in New Zealand before January 1, 1962 also have effect in Western Samoa.

Nicaragua (see Central American Agreement)

Nigeria—Registrations valid 7 years from application date; renewable for 14-year periods. Register divided into Parts A (distinctive) and B (capable of distinctiveness). First applicant, as user or intended user, is entitled to registration. Opposition period is 1 months from publication. Registration cancellable if not used for 5 years. "Registered user" provisions.

Norway—Registrations valid 10 years from registration date; renewable for similar period. First applicant is entitled to registration. Registration contestable on first user grounds within 5 years of registration date. Rights to mark, if "well known" as belonging to proprietor, may be acquired without registration. Examination procedures. Opposition period is 2 months after publication. No compulsory use.

Oman—There are no trademark laws in effect in the Sultanate of Oman. Protection is afforded by advertising cautionary notice in a high circulation Lebanese newspaper.

Pakistan—Adopted provisions of India Trade Marks Act of 1940. Registrations valid 7 years after application filing date; renewable fo 15-year periods. First applicant, as user or intended user, is entitled to registration. Proven prior user may continue to use mark registered to another and may be entitled to concurrent registration. Applications examined; opposition period is 4 months after publication. Registered mark not used on a continuous 5-year basis is cancellable. Registration remaining valid for 7 years is incontestable. "Registered User" provisions.

Panama—Registration valid for 10 years renewable for like periods. Marks owned and used abroad by foreigners may be registered only on the basis of prior home registration. Examination conducted on registrability and compliance with formal requirements. Opposition must be filed within 3 months following publication of application in the Industrial Property Bulletin. Use of trademark must begin no later than 1 year from registration date.

Paraguay—Registration valid 10 years from registration date, renewable for similar periods. First applicant is entitled to registration. Registration only basis upon which proprietary trademark rights established. Applications examined only as to form; opposition period is 30 days after publication. No compulsory use except as ordered by the government in individual cases. Infringement action cannot be brought by registrant after 2 years of the first occurrence of infringement or after 1 year from day registrant first knew about infringement.

Peru—Registrations valid 5 years from application filing date; renewable for similar periods only if mark used in any Andean Pact county. First applicant is entitled to registration. Applications examined, published for 20 days' opposition. Mark must be used to be renewed.

Philippines—Registration valid 20 years from registration date; renewable similar periods. To maintain registration, owner must file, at 5-year anniversaries, affidavit that mark still used. First user entitled to registration which becomes prima facie evidence of ownership. Examination procedures; opposition period 30 days after publication. Marks registrable in Principal or Supplemental Register. Registered marks recordable at customs for seizure infringing imports.

Poland—Registrations valid 10 years from application date; renewable similar periods. First applicant entitled to registration and recognized ownership. First user may, upon proof, have application rejected or registration cancelled. Applications examined; published for opposition. No compulsory use. Infringement actions must be taken within 3 years after occurrence of infringing act. Prior home registration requirement for U.S. applicants.

Portugal—Registrations valid 10 years from registration date; renewable for similar periods. First applicant is entitled to registration. Prior user claimant may file for cancellation within 6 months of original contested registration's date, providing he has not used mark for more than 6 months without applying for own registration. Examination procedures. Applications published 3 months' opposition. Registration may lapse if not used 3 consecutive years. Portuguese registration can be recorded for protection in former colonies of Angola, Mozambique, Cape Verde Islands, Timor, St. Thomas, Princess Islands, and Guinea Bissau.

Qatar—Registration valid 10 years from application date; renewable for like periods. First applicant is entitled to registration. Formal and registrability examination of application is conducted. Oppositions may be filed within 4 months following publication of application in the Trademark Gazette. Trademark may be cancelled for non-use during 5 consecutive years. Cancellation procedure available during 5 years from registration date.

Romania—Registrations valid 20 years from application filing date; renewable for similar periods. First applicant is entitled to registration. Applications examined, opposition period 3 months. Registrations incontestable after 5 years, except if obtained on fraudulent basis, are deceptive, or consist of official emblems or insignia. No use provisions.

Rwanda—Mark must be registered to be protected. First user is entitled to registration and enforcement of rights. Duration unlimited. No examination, opposition or compulsory use.

Ryukyu Islands (Okinawa)—Reverted to Japan, May 15, 1972. Japanese Trademark Law applies.

San Marino—No separate trademark law. Trademark rights obtained in Italy applicable.

Saudi Arabia—Registrations valid 10 years from application date; renewable for similar periods. First applicant is entitled to registration. Registration is incontestable after 5 years. Applications, after acceptance, published for opposition for 6 months. Person who can prove that he used mark for year before it was first registered may continue to use it. Customs authorities may seize imported goods bearing marks infringing those registered in Saudi Arabia. No compulsory use.

Sierra Leone—Registration valid 14 years from application filing date; renewable for similar periods. U.K. registration may be registered in Sierra Leone concurrently with original registrations. Register divided into Part A (distinctive marks), Part B (marks capable of becoming distinctive). First applicant, as user, is entitled to registration. Applications examined, published opposition for 3 months. "Registered User" provisions.

Singapore—Registrations valid 7 years from application filing date; renewable for 14-year periods. Register divided into Part A (distinctive marks) and Part B (marks capable of becoming distinctive). First applicant, as user or intended user, is entitled to registration. Applications examined, published opposition for 2 months. Registration is cancellable if mark not used for 5 years. Mark may be registered independently without prior U.K. registration, except for textile products, "Registered User" provisions.

Somali Republic—Consists of former British Somaliland and Italian Territory of Somalia. Registrations valid 20 years from application date. Renewable similar periods. Cancellable if not used 3 consecutive years. No opposition provisions.

South Africa—Registrations valid 10 years from application filing date; renewable for similar periods. Registrations on applications filed before January 1, 1964 are valid 14 years; renewable for 10-year periods. First applicant, as user or intended user, is entitled to registration. Under certain conditions, mark being used by more than one person may be registered to several parties for concurrent use. Marks registrable as Part A (distinctive) and B (capable of becoming distinctive). Part A registration, if valid 7 years, becomes incontestable on prior use grounds. Applications examined, published for 2 months' opposition. Also, under informal procedures Registrar may decide conflicting opposition cases with the consent of both parties. Mark cancellable if not used within 5 years. "Registered User" provisions.

Spain—Registrations valid 20 years from registration date; renewable for similar periods. First applicant is entitled to registration. Registrations incontestable on prior use grounds after 3 years, if continuously used by registrant and valid during that period. Applications examined; published for 2 months opposition. Cancellable, if not used 5 consecutive years, unless such nonuse was due to *force majeure*.

Sri Lanka—Registration valid 10 years from application date; renewable for 10 year periods. User or intended user of mark may apply for its registration. Another person proving first user at later date may have registration cancelled. Register has Part A (distinctive marks) and Part B (marks capable of becoming distinctive). Mark incontestable after 7 years. Applications examined, published opposition 3 months. Mark not used 5 consecutive years may be cancelled upon request of an interested party unless nonuse is due to conditions over which registrant had no control.

Sudan—Registrations valid 10 years from application date; renewable like periods. First applicant entitled to registration. Applications examined, published for opposition (6 months for local residents, 8 months for foreigners). Mark must be used during 5 consecutive years preceding allegation of non-use by petition to cancel; otherwise may be cancelled.

Surinam—Registrations valid 20 years from registration date; renewal similar periods. Examination, 6 months' opposition after registration. First user rights recognized. Mark cancellable if not used 3 consecutive years.

Swaziland—Registrations coterminous with those in United Kingdom or South Africa. No examination or opposition procedures. "Registered User" provisions.

Sweden—Registrations valid 10 years from registration date; renewable for similar periods. First applicant entitled to registration. Registration incontestable on prior user grounds after 5 years. Rights may be acquired without registration where mark achieves wide reputation through established use of owner. Applications examined, published opposition 2 months. Registration cancellable if not used 5 consecutive years.

Switzerland—Registrations valid 20 years from application filing date; renewable for similar periods. Ownership based on first use, but mark must be registered to be enforced. Applications examined as to form and, if satisfactory, allowed. No opposition procedures. Marks must be used within 3 years of registration, and consecutively for 3 years thereafter, otherwise may be cancelled.

Syrian Arab Republic—Registrations valid 10 years from registration date. Applications examined; no opposition provisions. First applicant is entitled to registration. First user may contest registration within 5 years, otherwise mark becomes incontestable on prior user grounds unless shown that registrant knew about prior use when application was filed. No compulsory use.

Taiwan—Registration valid 10 years from registration date; renewable like periods. First applicant entitled to registration. Applications examined, published for 3-month opposition period. Registrations must be used within 1 year of registration and use not discontinued for 2 years.

Tangier Zone—Continues to maintain Industrial Property Bureau in Tangier to receive applications, issue registrations. Registrations valid 20 years from application filing date; renewable for similar periods. First applicant entitled registration. First user, desiring to contest registration, must first file application for his mark. Applications published opposition 2 months. Registration cancellable, if not used 5 years.

Tanzania—Comprises the former areas of Tanganyika and Zanzibar. Until a permanent Constitution is finalized, trademark laws of each area remain in force. Each has register divided into Part A (distinctive marks); Part B (marks capable of becoming distinctive). First applicant is entitled to registration. Applications examined. Marks for cotton goods or metal wares must be registered first in United Kingdom. Applications published for Registration may be cancelled in either country, if not used within 5 years. Registrations are valid for 7 years in Tanganyika, in Zanzibar for 14 years, from application filing date. Renewal period is for 14 years in both areas.

Thailand—Registrations valid 10 years from application filing date; renewable for similar periods. First person applying as owner of mark is entitled to registration. Ownership based on proven first use. Infringement proceedings may be instituted on behalf of unregistered mark. Applications examined, published 3 months opposition. Registration not used 5 years cancellable.

Transkei—Formerly a territory in South Africa. Adopted South African Trademark Law. Marks registered in South Africa, and in effect before October 26, 1976, are valid for duration of term. First user entitled to registration, for applications filed after that date. Two-month opposition period. Registrations valid 10 years from application date; renewable similar periods. Marks subject to cancellation if not used within 5 years after registration. Registered user, Part A (distinctive marks), and Part B (capable of distinctiveness) appear in the law. Part A registration incontestable after 7 years.

Trinidad and Tobago—Registrations valid 14 years from application filing date. Renewable for similar periods. Marks registrable as Part A (distinctive marks) or Part B (marks capable of becoming distinctive). First applicant, as user or intended user, is entitled to registration. Applications examined, published opposition 3 months. Marks registered in United Kingdom qualify for registration. Registration cancellable if not used 5 years. "Registered User" provisions.

Tunisia—Registration valid 15 years from application filing date; renewable for similar periods. Person applying as first user of mark is entitled to registration. No examination, opposition, or compulsory use.

Turkey—Registrations valid 10 years from application date; renewable for similar periods. First applicant is entitled to registration. Registration contestable on prior user grounds within 3 years. Applications examined as to form, registrability. No opposition provisions. Ordinarily mark not used 3 years is subject to cancellation; nationals of Paris Union countries are exempt from such use requirements. Prior home registration requirement.

Uganda—Registrations valid 7 years from application date; renewable 14-year periods. First applicant, as user or intended user, entitled to registration. Register divided Parts A and B as in United Kingdom law. Applications examined, published for 60 days' opposition period. Mark cancellable if not used within 5 years. "Registered User" provisions.

United Arab Emirates (Abu Dhabi, Dubai, Sharjah, Ajman, Umm al Qaiwain, Ras Al-Khaimah and Fujairah)—Ras Al-Khaimah is the only Emirate to enact a trademark law. In other Emirates, cautionary notice published in certain Lebanese daily papers may afford some protection.

In Ras Al-Khaimah, registration valid 10 years from application filing date; renewable for similar periods. Applications, if acceptable, published for 60-day opposition period. Registered mark must be used for 5 consecutive years, otherwise subject to cancellation. Registration incontestable after 5 years of use.

In Dubai, Court Ruled, in a 1978 case, that even though there is no trademark law, sufficient protection must still be afforded to the owner of a trademark against those who imitate his mark and engage in unfair competition in use of such imitation, if that rightful owner has proof of his mark's prior use and reputation in Dubai, and registrations elsewhere.

United Kingdom—Registrations valid seven years from application filing date; renewable for 14-year periods. First applicant, as user or intended user is entitled to registration. Marks registrable as Part A (distinctive) or Part B (capable of becoming distinctive) of Register. If valid seven years, Part A registration becomes incontestable on prior user grounds. Applications examined, published for opposition within 1 month. Application refused for Part A may be amended for possible registration as Part B. Registration cancellable anytime on proof that it was obtained by fraud, consists of scandalous matter, is misleading or deceptive, has lost distinctiveness, or is otherwise contrary to law. Applicant may obtain preliminary advice from registrar whether mark qualified for Part A or B. If advised that mark is registrable and applies within 3 months, but application rejected, filing fee is refunded. Mark removable from register if not used continuously for five years. "Registered user" provisions.

Many newly-independent states which were formerly British Colonies now have new and independent trademark laws. Some still recognize or require prior U.K. registration. These countries are summarized separately. Present British colonies and possessions generally fall into following broad categories regarding trademark protection afforded: 1) Areas which provide protection only on the basis of existing registration in the United Kingdom, such as British Honduras, Falkland Islands, Gilbert Islands, Grenada, Gibraltar, St. Helena, Solomon Islands, Seychelles. Trademark Registrations in these areas usually run for the duration of basic U.K. registrations; 2) areas where one can apply for independent registration or secure protection based on existing registration in the United Kingdom, such as Antigua, Bermuda, British Virgin Islands, Brunei, Dominica, Fiji Islands, Monserrat, Nevis, Anguilla, St. Vincent and St. Lucia. Registrations in these areas are usually granted for 7 or 14-year periods. In Hong Kong, trademark registrations must be applied for on an independent basis under 1954 ordinance. Register is divided into Part A (distinctive marks) and Part B (capable of becoming distinctive). Registrations valid 7 years (14 years if registered before January 1, 1955) renewable for 14-year periods. Mark becomes incontestable prior user grounds after 7 years registration. Application examined, published for opposition 2 months. Must be used within 5 years. "Registered User" provisions.

Uruguay—Registrations valid 10 years from registration date; renewable for similar periods. First applicant is entitled to registration. Contestable on prior user grounds up to 2 years after registration date. Applications examined, published in *Official Gazette*. Oppositions must be filed within 20 days of the 1st publication. No compulsory use.

USSR—Marks registered for term specified by applicant up to 10 years from application filing date; renewable on same basis. First applicant entitled registration. Unregistered mark not enforceable. Application examined; if satisfactory, allowed. No opposition proceedings. Patent Bureau of the USSR chamber of Commerce acts as agent for foreign applicants. Approved application reserved 3 months; if not completed by applicant, it is considered abandoned. Registered mark must be used within 5 years of registration; otherwise cancellable. Advertising of mark in USSR publication or Western publication appearing in USSR qualifies as use, as does use on goods at approved exhibition in USSR.

Venda—Formerly a territory in South Africa, now independent, as of September 13, 1979. Expected to adopt South African trademark law, with transition and other provisions similar to those in Transkei and Bophuthatswana.

Venezuela—Registrations valid for 15 years from registration date; renewable for similar periods. First applicant is entitled to registration. Registered mark is contestable on prior use grounds up to 2 years after registration date. Applications examined; if satisfactory, published for opposition within 30 days. Registration not used continuously 2 years is subject to cancellation.

Western Samoa—Two registration systems, one based on overseas and other on nonoverseas registrations. Owner of foreign mark acquired after December 18, 1972 may apply for registration within 2 years of earlier registration date. Mark registered before that date may be registered by December 19, 1974, if complies with law's criteria. "Bona fide local users" of a mark have priority over other applicants, and owners of New Zealand registrations registered before January 1, 1962 have priority over other applicants, if marks applied for before December 19, 1973. Registrations based on overseas marks have duration coterminous with latter. Registrations not so based on 14 year duration; renewable like periods. Applications examined, published 3 months opposition period. Mark must be used within 5 years of registration.

Yemen (People's Democratic Republic)—No trademark law, except in Aden territory, where U.K. registrations may be registered for duration original registration. In other parts of the country, publication of cautionary notice of mark in newspaper is only means of securing any protection that may be available.

Yemen Arab Republic—No trademark law. Publication cautionary notice in local newspaper may afford some protection.

Yugoslavia—Registrations issued on an unlimited basis so long as registrant continued to pay required advance fees for years of protection desired. Registrations usually renewed on 10-year basis. First applicant is entitled to registration. Registration may be contested on prior user grounds within 3 years of registration date. Applications examined as to form registrability, existence of conflicting registrations; if satisfactory, allowed. No opposition provisions. No compulsory use.

Zaire—Registration is valid for 10 years from application date; renewals, for similar 10 year periods. National guaranty marks are granted for unlimited time. First applicant is entitled to registration; foreigners may apply on the basis of reciprocity. No provisions for opposition; trademark may be canceled if not used within 3 months following registration.

Zambia—Marks previously registered for the former Federation of Rhodesia and Nyasaland remain in effect in Zambia for their original term. Marks are registrable in Zambia for 7 years from application filing date; renewable for 14 years. First applicant, as user or intended user, is entitled to registration. Register is divided into Part A (distinctive marks), B (marks capable of becoming distinctive), C (certification marks), and D (defensive marks). Applications examined, if satisfactory published for opposition within 2 months. Registration valid for 7 years is incontestable on prior user grounds. "Registered User" provisions.

Zimbabwe—Registrations valid 10 years from application date; renewable for similar periods. First applicant, as user, or intended user, entitled to registration. Register divided into Parts A and B similar to U.K. law. Applications examined, published 2 months for opposition. Mark must be used within 5 years registration date. Cancellation of Part A registration may be sought after 5 years of registration date. "Registered User" provisions.

Appendix 10

Chambers of Commerce

American Chambers of Commerce Abroad

ARGENTINA

President:
Floyd W. Boyd, Jr.
President
Amoco Argentina Oil Co.
Maipu 942, 15th Floor
1340 Buenos Aires, Argentina
PHONE: (541) 34-4011
TELEX: (390) 22127 or 21369 AMOBA
CABLE: AMOCOAR

Executive Director:
Harry Marples
General Manager
The American Chamber of Commerce
  in Argentina
Av. Pte. Roque Saenz Pena 567, P6
1352 Buenos Aires, Argentina
PHONE: 331-3436
CABLE: USCHAMBCOM
TELEX: 22347 MINAG ARS (c/o A.
Perry)

56 - Number of AmChams (does not include unofficial AmChams)

51 - Number of Countries with AmChams (does not include unofficial Amchams)

72 - Number of AmCham Offices (includes branch offices and unofficial AmChams)

3 - Number of Regional AmCham Organizations

Source: U.S. Chamber of Commerce, International Division, Washington, D.C.

AUSTRALIA

President:
John M. McPhail, President
The American Chamber of Commerce
  in Australia
3rd Floor
50 Pitt Street
Sydney, N.S.W., 2000, Australia
PHONE: 241-1907
TELEX: 72729 ATTIAU
CABLE: AMCHAM SYDNEY
FAX: 2350109 c/o AT&T

Executive Director:
Kevin Bannon, Executive Director
The American Chamber of Commerce
  in Australia
3rd Floor, 50 Pitt Street
Sydney, N.S.W. 2000, Australia
PHONE: 241-1907
CABLE: AMCHAM SYDNEY
TELEX: 72729 ATTIAU

Branch Office - Adelaide

Beverly Kirkby, Manager
The American Chamber of Commerce
  in Australia
1st Floor, 68 Grenfell Street
Adelaide, S.A. 5000, Australia
PHONE: 224-0761

Branch Office - Brisbane

Dianne Hopkins
Brisbane Manager
The American Chamber of Commerce
  in Australia
23rd Floor, 66 Queen Street
Brisbane, Queensland 4000, Australia
PHONE: 221-8542

Branch Office - Brisbane

Randall G. Upton
Melbourne Manager
The American Chamber of Commerce
  in Australia
Level 41, 80 Collins Street
Melbourne, Victoria 3000, Australia
PHONE: 654-5100

Branch Office - Perth

Clair Nielsen
Manager
The American Chamber of Commerce
  in Australia
6th Floor, 231 Adelaide Terrace
Perth, W.A. 6000, Australia
PHONE: 325-9540

AUSTRIA

President:
Guido K. Klestil
President
The American Chamber of Commerce
  in Austria
Tuerkenstrasse 9
A-1090 Vienna, Austria
PHONE: (222) 31 57 51/2
TELEX: 134206 (ATTN: Mrs. Bacher)
FAX: (222) 31 01 632

Executive Director:
Dr. Patricia A. Helletzgruber
Secretary General
The American Chamber of Commerce
  in Austria
Tuerkenstrasse 9
A-1090 Vienna, Austria
PHONE: (222) 31 57 51/2
TELEX: 134206 (Attn: Mrs. Bacher)
FAX: (222) 31 01 632

BELGIUM

President
Eric G. Friberg
Managing Director
McKINSEY & COMPANY, INC.
BELGIUM
Avenue Palmerston 14
1040 Bruxelles, Belgium

Executive Director:
Jo Ann Broger
General Manager
The American Chamber of Commerce
   in Belgium
Avenue des Arts 50, Boite 5
B-1040, Brussels, Belgium
PHONE: (2) 513 7 70/9
TELEX: 64913 AMCHAM B
FAX: (2) 513 79 28

BOLIVIA

President:
Carlos Calvo, General Manager
Expobol S.A., Casilla 335
Edificio Hermann - Piso 18
Plaza Venezuela
La Paz, Bolivia
PHONE: (5912) 372121
TELEX: (336) 2634 EXPBOL

Executive Director:
Carlos Barrero, General Manager
American Chamber of Commerce
   of Bolivia
Casilla 828
La Paz, Bolivia
PHONE: 34-2523
TELEX: 2674 PLAZA BV

BRAZIL - RIO JANEIRO

President:
Wilbur C. Andrews, Jr.
Vice President
Mercantile Trust Co. N.A.
P.O. Box 1642
Rua da Assambleia 10, Conj. 2622
20.011 Rio de Janeiro, RJ - Brazil
PHONE: 252-1064; 242-3550
TELEX: 2130238 METC BR

Executive Director:
Augusto de Moura Diniz, Jr.
Executive Vice President
American Chamber of Commerce for
   Brazil - Rio de Janeiro
Caixa Postal 916
Praca Pio X-15, 5th Floor
20.040 Rio de Janeiro, RJ - Brazil
PHONE: 203-2477
CABLE: AMERCHACOM
TELEX: 2134084 AMCH BR

Branch Office - Salvador

President:
Hans Leusen, President
TABARAMA-Tabacos do Brasil Ltda.
Caixa Postal 508
40.000 Salvador, Bahia, Brazil
PHONE: 241-1844
TELEX: 711009

Executive Director:
Ricardo Rubeiz
Executive Secretary
American Chamber of Commerce for
   Brazil - Salvador
Rua da Espanha, 2, Salas 604-606
40.000 Salvador, Bahia, Brazil
PHONE: 242-0077; 242-5606

BRAZIL - SAO PAULO

President:
R. Christopher Lund
President
Grupo de Lund
Editoras Associadas
Av. Brigadeiro Tobias, 356 - 5 andar
01032 - Sao Paulo, SP - BRAZIL
PHONE: 228-8248
TELEX: 1130562 TLPBBR

Executive Director:
Ercole A. Carpentieri, Jr.
Executive Vice President
American Chamber of Commerce for
   Brazil--Sao Paulo, SP - Brazil
PHONE: 246-9199
CABLE: AMERCHACOM
TELEX: 1136190 AMCH BR

CHILE

President:
Lawrence D. Hayes, President
Cia. Minera Disputada de las Condes
Av. Pedro de Valdivia 291
Santigo, Chile
PHONE: 223-3037
TELEX: 341621 TMDNC CZ

Executive Director:
Maria Isabel Jaramillo, Manager
Chamber of Commerce of the U.S.A.
   in the Republic of Chile
Huerfanos 669, Oficina 614
P.O. Box 4131
Santiago, Chile
PHONE: 393163
CABLE: AMCHAMBER
TELEX: 440001 ITT Booth (include
address)

CHINA (PRC)

President:
Michael E. Bickford
General Manager
Weyerhaeuser China, Ltd.
c/o Jianguo Hotel, Room 174
Jianguo Menwai Dajie
Beijing, People's Republic of China
PHONE: 5002233, ext. 174
TELEX: 22439 JGHBJ CN

COLOMBIA (Unofficial)

Chairman:
John W. Cunningham
President
Crown Litometal S.A.
Apartado Aereo 4084
Bogota, Colombia
PHONE: 238-4506; 238-4512
TELEX: 45224 CROWN CO
CABLE: CROWN

Executive Director:
Oscar A. Bradford, President
Colombian-American Chamber of
Commerce
Apartado Aereo 8008, Calle 35 No. 616
Bogota, Colombia
PHONE: 285-7800
CABLE: CAMBOLAM BOGOTA
TELEX: 43326; 45411 CAMC CO

Branch Office - Cali

President:
Jorge Ernesto Holguin
Caicedo Holguines Abogados
Apartado Aereo 101
Cali, Valle, Colombia
PHONE: 689-506; 689-409
TELEX: 55442
CABLE: VERITATEM

Executive Director:
Leyda Lucia Perez B.
Executive Director
Colombian-American chamber of
Commerce
Apartado Aereo 5943
Cali, Valle, Colombia
PHONE: 813-685; 822-942
TELEX: 55442 CCCAC

COSTA RICA

President:
Samuel Giberga, President
Olympic Fibers, S.A.
P.O. Box 7604
San Jose, Costa Rica
PHONE: 506-390344
TELEX: 7007 OFSA CR

Executive Director:
Gail Smith, Manager
Costa Rican-American Chamber
 of Commerce
Calle 3, Avenidas 1 y 3
Apartado 4946
San Jose, 1000 Costa Rica
PHONE: 332133
TELEX: 7007 OFSA CR
CABLE: AMCHAM

COTE D'IVOIRE

President:
Douglas Leavens, President
American Chamber of Commerce -
 Cote d'Ivoire
01 B.P. 3394 Abidjan 01
Cote d'Ivoire, Africa
PHONE: 326766; 326785
TELEX: 22435 DAM CI

Executive Director:
E.T. Hunt Talmage, III
Secretary
American Chamber of Commerce -
 Cote d'Ivoire,
01 B.P. 708, Abidjan 01
Cote d'Ivoire, Africa
PHONE: 326766; 326785
TELEX: 22435 DAM CI

DOMINICAN REPUBLIC

President:
Frank Rainieri, Vice President
Compania de Desarrollo Turistico,
Residencial y Industrial, S.A.
Ave Tiradentes Esq. San Martin
Edificio Texaco
Santo Domingo, Dominican Republic
PHONE: 565-0011
TELEX: 0415

Executive Director:
Wilson A. Rood
Executive Director
American Chamber of Commerce
 of the Dominican Republic
Hotel Santo Domingo
Avenida Independencia
P.O. Box 95-2
Santo Domingo, Dominican Republic
PHONE: 533-7292
CABLE: AMCHAM
TELEX: 0415 TREISA

ECUADOR

President:
Antonio Teran S., Director
Confiandina Cia. Ltda.
P.O. Box 9103 Suc. Almagro
Quito, Ecuador
PHONE: 523-152; 523-693

Executive Director:
Karl Newlands
Executive Director
Ecuadorian-American Chamber
  of Commerce
P.O. Box 2432
Quito, Ecuador
PHONE: 543-512
CABLE: ECUAME
TELEX: 22298 ECUME EDd

ECUADOR - GUAYAQUIL

President:
Ignacio Kozhaya, President
Fundaciones Industriales S.A.
(FISA)
Escobedo 1402 y Chile
P.O. Box 4767
Guayaquil, Ecuador
PHONE: 529855; 516708

Executive Director:
Cosme Ottati, Executive Director
Ecuadorian-American Chamber of
Commerce
Imbabura 214 y Panama, Piso 2
P.O. Box 11305
Guayaquil, Ecuador
PHONE: 312760; 312865
CABLE: EACH
TELEX: 43851 CAECAM ED

EGYPT

President:
Harvey D. Attra
President and General Manager
Esso Suez Inc.
3 Abu El Feda Street
Zamalek, Cairo, Egypt
PHONE: 3403150
TELEX: 21148
FAX: 3403110

Executive Director:
American Chamber of Commerce
  in Egypt
Cairo Marriott Hotel, Suite 1537
P.O. Box 33 Zamalek
Cairo, Egypt
PHONE: 3408888
TELEX: 20870

EL SALVADOR

President:
Rafael Brito, General Manager
Citibank, N.A.
Edificio Torre Robel, 2 piso
Boulevard de los Heroes
San Salvador, El Salvador
PHONE: 24-3011
TELEX: 20134

Executive Director:
Donald D. Drysdale
Executive Director
American Chamber of Commerce
  of El Salvador
65 Avenida Sur, No. 159
P.O. Box (05) 9
San Salvador, El Salvador
PHONE: 239604; 232419
TELEX: 20768 VERITATEM

FRANCE

President
John F. Crawford, Partner
Surrey & Morse
53, Avenue Montaigne
75008 Paris, France
PHONE: (1) 359-2349

Executive Director:
W. Barrett Dower
Executive Director
The American Chamber of
Commerce in France
21 Avenue George V
F-75008 Paris, France
PHONE: (1) 47 23 70 28
 (1) 47 23 80 26
TELEX: 650286 Royale F
FAX: (1) 42 25 03 29

GERMANY

President:
Albert O. Hicks
Manager
ACS-Aviation Consulting Services
GmbH
Raabestrasse 15
6000 Frankfurt 50
West Germany

Executive Director:
John D. Brennan
General Manager
The American Chamber of Commerce
 in Germany
Rossmarkt 12, Postfach 100 162
D-6000 Frankfurt/Main 1, Germany
PHONE: (69) 28 34 01
 (ltd.: 28 17 00)
TELEX: 4189679 acc d
FAX: (69) 28 56 32

Branch Office - Berlin

Robert H. Lochner, Representative
American Chamber of Commerce
 in Germany
Budapesterstrasse 31
D-1000 Berlin 30, Germany
PHONE: (30) 21 55 86
FAX: (30) 262 26 00

Branch Office - Munich

William H. King
Managing Director
Deutsch Marathon Petroleum Gmbh
Neutrum Strasse #5
8000 Munich 2, West Germany
PHONE: (49) 89 230 7300
TELEX: 529382
FAX: 230 7316

Branch Office - Koln

Franz J. Bohr
American Chamber of Commerce
 Representative in Germany
Brauweiler Weg 88
5000 Koln 41, Germany
PHONE: 0221/481681

Branch Office - Stuttgart

Wilford J. Kramer
American Chamber of Commerce
 Representative in Germany
Leiblweg 28
7000 Stuttgart 1, Germany
PHONE: 0711/813741

GREECE

Co-President:
Charles J. Politis
President
APCO Industries S.A.
Group Corporate Offices
18 Academias Street
Athens 134, Greece
PHONE: 3618-008
TELEX: 212404 APCO GR

Co-President:
Demetre N. Petsiavas
General Manager
Petsiavas N., A.E.
11 Nicodemon & Voulis Streets
Athens 119, Greece
PHONE: 323.0451
TElEX: 215983 NPSA GR

Executive Director:
Symeon G. Tsomokos
General Manager
American-Hellenic Chamber
   of Commerce
17 Valaoritou Street
2nd Floor
 134, Greece
PHONE: (1) 36 18 385
   (1) 36 36 407
TELEX: 223063 AmCh GR

GUAM

President:
Eloise R. Baza, President
Guam Chamber of Commerce
107 Ada Plaza Center
P.O. Box 283
Agana, Guam 96910
PHONE: 472-6311; 472-8001
TELEX: 7216160 BOOTH GM
CABLE: CHAMAGANA

GUATEMALA

President:
Joe Schlosser
General Manager
DHL de Guatemala
Edificio El Patio
Suite 401
7 Av. 2-42, Zona 9
Guatemala, Guatemala

PHONE: 323023
TELEX: 5711 DHLDGU GU/5021
DHLOPS GU

Executive Director:
Thelma Padilla
Executive Manager
American Chamber of Commerce
   in Guatemala
Apartado Postal 832
7 Ave, 14-44, Zona 9
Edificio la Galeria
Nivel 2, Oficina 19
Guatamala City, Guatamala
PHONE: 312235
CABLE: AMCHAM GUATEMALA CITY
TELEX: 5415 DORADO GU

HAITI

President:
Gladys Coupet
General Manager
Citibank, Haiti
P.O. Box 1688
Port-au-Prince, Haiti
PHONE: 6-2600
TELEX: 2030124

Executive Director:
Joanne M. Elie
Executive Director
Haitian-American Chamber of
   Commerce & Industry
Complexe 384, Delmas (59)
P.O. Box 13486 - Delmas
Port-au-Prince, Haiti
PHONE: 6-3164
CABLE: HAMCHAM
TELEX: 2030001 (Public Booth, include
address)

HONDURAS

President:
Eduardo Aragon
Vice President
United Fruit Company
Rod. Tela Railroad Co.
Apartado Postal No. 155
Tegucigalpa, Honduras
PHONE: 33259; 332354
TELEX: 8305 TELA RAIL CO

Executive Director:
Sonia Reyes Noyola
General Manager
Honduran-American Chamber
  of Commerce
Hotel Honduras Maya
Apartado Postal 1838
Tegucigalpa, Honduras
PHONE: 323191, ext. 1056
TELEX: 1145 MAYA HO

Branch Office - San Pedro Sula

Jacqueline M. Sanders de Solis
Manager
Honduran-American Chamber
  of Commerce
Edificio Samara
2 Piso, Of. #5
Boulevard Morazan 16 Ave. S.O.
P.O. Box 1209
San Pedro Sula, Honduras
PHONE: 522401; 522790
TELEX: 5693 INRECORP HO

HONG KONG

President:
Paul F. M. Cheng
Managing Director-Asia
Spencer Stuart & Associates
  (H.K.) Ltd.
St. George's Boulevard
2 Ice House Street
(GPO Box 7157)
Hong Kong
PHONE: 2183730
CABLE: AMCHAM

Executive Director:
Ralph Spencer
Executive Director
The American Chamber of Commerce
  in Hong Kong
1030 Swire House
Hong Kong
PHONE: 5-260165
CABLE: AMCHAM
TELEX: 83664 Amcc Hx

INDONESIA

President:
Nick P. Petroff, President
American Chamber of Commerce
  in Indonesia
The Landmark Centre
22nd floor
J1. Jendral Sudirman Kav. 70A
Jakarta, Indonesia
PHONE: 5780656 (direct)
  5780800, ext. 2222
TELEX: 48116 CIBSEM IAD
  Attn: Amcham Indonesia

Acting Executive Director:
Nick P. Petroff
Acting Executive Director
American Chamber of Commerce
  in Indonesia
Citibank Building
8th Floor
J1. M.H. Thamrin 55
Jakarta, Indonesia
PHONE: 332602
TELEX: 48116 CIBSEM IA

IRELAND

President:
Francis J. Barrett, Retired
Partner, Arthur Andersen & Co.
c/o U.S. Chamber of Commerce
  in Ireland
20 College Green, Dublin 2
PHONE: 793733
TELEX: 31187 UCIL EI

Executive Director:
Robert P. Chalker, Executive Director
The American Chamber of Commerce
  in Ireland
20 College Green
Dublin 2, Ireland
PHONE: (1) 79 37 33
TELEX: 31187 UCIL EI

ISRAEL

President:
Joshua Maor, President
Israel-American Chamber of
  Commerce and Industry
35 Shaul Hamelech Blvd.
P.O. Box 33174
64927 Tel Aviv, Israel
PHONE: (3) 25 23 41/2
TELEX: 32139 BETAM IL

Executive Director:
Nina Admoni, Executive Director
Israel-American Chamber of
  Commerce & Industry
35 Shaul Hamelech Blvd.
P.O. Box 33174, Tel Aviv, Israel
PHONE: (3) 25 23 41/2
TELEX: 32139 BETAM IL
FAX: (3) 25 59 28

ITALY

President:
Michael N. Bitsas, Partner
Continental European Headquarters
Peat, Marwick, Mitchell & Co.
Via San Paolo 15
20121 Milano, Italy
PHONE: 39-2 8690661
TELEX: 23675

Executive Director:
Herman H. Burdick, General Secretary
The American Chamber of Commerce
  in Italy
Via Cantu 1
20123 Milano, Italy
PHONE: (2) 86 90 661
TELEX: 352128 AMCHAM I
FAX: (2) 80 57 737

JAMAICA

President:
Kenneth N. Sherwood
Chairman and Chief Executive Officer
Restaurant Associates Limited
20 Hope Road
Kingston 10, Jamaica
PHONE: 929-1372
TELEX: 3521 AERO JAMAICA

Executive Director:
William Whiting, Executive Director
American Chamber of Commerce
  of Jamaica
The Wyndham Hotel
77 Knutsford Blvd.
Kingston 5, Jamaica
PHONE: 926-5430
TELEX: 2409 WYNDOTEL JA

JAPAN

President:
Joseph A. Grimes, Jr.
Vice President, Asia-Pacific
Honeywell, Inc., Nagai Internat'l
Bldg.
2-12-19 Shibuya - Shibuya-ku
Tokyo 150, Japan
PHONE: 3-409-1611
TELEX: 22902
FAX: 407-6567

Executive Director:
Richard E. Cropp, Executive Director
The American Chamber of Commerce
  of Japan
Fukide Building, No. 2
4-1-21 Toranomon, Minato-Ku
Tokyo 105, Japan
PHONE: (03) 433-5381
CABLE: AMCHAM TOKYO
TELEX: 2425104 KYLE J

JAPAN-OKINAWA

President:
George C. Flanagan
President
The American Chamber of Commerce
  in Okinawa
Sheraton Okinawa Hotel
Room 125, 1529 Kishaba
Kitanakagusuku-Son P.O. Box 235,
Okinawa City 904, Japan
PHONE: 098935-2684
TELEX: J79828 SHEROKA,
Attn. Amcham
CABLE: AMCHAM OKINAWA
FAX: 098935-3546 Attn. Amcham

KOREA

President:
Thomas M. Brown
President
Westinghouse Electric (Asia) S.A.
14th Floor, Kyobo Bldg.
1, 1-ka Chongro, Chongro-ku
Seoul 100, Korea
PHONE: 733-2371/5
TELEX: K22043 WELSASE
FAX: 736-2177

Executive Director:
James W. Booth
Executive Vice President
The American Chamber of Commerce
  in Korea
Room 307, Chosun Hotel
Seoul, Korea
PHONE: 753-6471; 753-6516
CABLE: AMCHAMBER
TELEX: 23745; 28432; 24256 Chosun

MALAYSIA

President:
Donald Jerome
President
Motorola Malaysia
P.O. Box 1001, Jalan Semangat
46960 Petaling Jaya
Selangor, Malaysia
PHONE: 761166
TELEX: MA 37695

Executive Director:
Erin Ariff
Executive Secretary
American Business Council of
Malaysia
905, 9th Floor, Wisma AIA
Jalan Ampang
Kuala Lumpur, Malaysia
PHONE: 01-281223; 01-281224
TELEX: MA 32388 AIA

MEXICO

President:
Stephen B. Friedman
President and General Director
American Express Co.
(Mexico) S.A. de C.V.
Patriotisma 635
03170 Mexico, D.F. Mexico
PHONE: 598-7966
TELEX: 1771170

Executive Director:
John M. Bruton
Executive Vice President
American Chamber of Commerce
of Mexico, A.C.
Lucerna 78-4
Mexico 6, D.F., Mexico
PHONE: 705-0995
CABLE: AMCHAMMEX
TELEX: 1777609, 1771300 AMCHAME

Branch Office - Guadalajara

President:
Adolf B. Horn, Jr.
Managing Director
Helados Bing, S.A.
Apdo. 31-72
45070 Guadalajara, Jalisco, Mexico
PHONE: 158822

Executive Director:
Graciela Pulido Hernandez
Manager
American Chamber of Commerce
of Mexico - Guadalajara
Avenida 16 de Septiembre 730-1209
Guadalajara, Jalisco, Mexico
PHONE: 14300; 148068
TELEX: 068-4241 ACHAME

Branch Office - Monterrey

President:
James Despain
Managing Director
Conek, S.A. de C.V.
Apartado Postal 2781
Monterrey, Nuevo Leon, Mexico

Executive Director::
Kathleen Marks Gibler
Manager
Amnerican Chamber of Commerce
  of Mexico, A.C. (Monterrey)
Picachos 760, Despachos 4 y 6
Colonia Obispado
Monterrey, Nuevo Leon, Mexico
PHONE: 484749; 485574
TELEX: 383087 AMCHAME

MOROCCO

President:
Jean-Pierre Bernex
General Manager
Colgate Palmolive Maroc
11 Avenue des Forces Armees
Royales
Casablanca, Morocco

Executive Director:
Susan Ouaknine
Executive Secretary
The American Chamber of Commerce
  in Morocco
Immeuble "Xerox"
30, Avenue des Forces Armees
  Royales
Casablanca, Morocco
PHONE: 224149
TELEX: 24852 XEROX M

NETHERLANDS

President:
Peter J. Legro
Managing Director
Transavia Holland
z/o The American Chamber of
Commerce in the Netherlands
2517 KJ The Hague, The Netherlands
PHONE: 023-339020
TELEX: 41219

Executive Director:
J.J. van Steenbergen
General Manager
The American Chamber of Commerce
  in the Netherlands
Carnegieplein 5
2517 KJ The Hauge, The Netherlands
PHONE: (70) 65 98 08/9
TELEX: 31058 Amcoc NL
FAX: 70-646992

NEW ZEALAND

President:
Darrell L. Huffman
Managing Director
Griffin & Sons Ltd.
P.O. Box 30-747, Lower Hutt
Wellington, New Zealand
PHONE: (04) 694459
TELEX: NZ 3809

Executive Director:
John L. Gordon
Executive Director
The American Chamber of Commerce
  in New Zealand
P.O. Box 3408
Wellington, New Zealand
PHONE: (04) 767081-J. L. Gordon
  (04) 727-549 Amcham
CABLE: AMCHAM
TELEX: 3514 INBUSMAC NZ

NICARAGUA

President:
Julio Vigil, President
Vigil y Caligaris
Apartado 202
Managua, Nicaragua
PHONE: 62-486
TELEX: 1255 VIGIL

Executive Director:
The American Chamber of Commerce
of Nicaragua
Apartado 202
Managua, Nicaragua
PHONE: 2-486
TELEX: 1255 Vigil

PAKISTAN

President:
Mr. Rudolf J. Gebert
President
American Business Council of
Pakistan
Shaheen Commercial Complex
3rd Floor
M.R. Kayani Road
GPO Box 1322
Karachi, Pakistan
PHONE: 526436
TELEX: 25620 Chase PK

Executive Director:
S. R. A. Hashmi
Secretary
American Business Council
of Pakistan
Shaheen Commercial Complex
3rd Floor
M.R. Kayani Road
GPO Box 1322
Karachi, Pakistan
PHONE: 526436
TELEX: 25620 CHASE PK

PANAMA

President:
Alexander Psychoyos
President

Tagaropulos, S.A.
Apartado 6-4000 El Dorado
Panama, Republica de Panama
PHONE: 6306292
TELEX: 328-2068; 328-3683542

Executive Director:
Fred Denton
Executive Director
American Chamber of Commerce
and Industry of Panama
Apdo. 168
Estafeta Balboa
Panama, Republica de Panama
PHONE: 69-3881
TELEX: 3232 (ITT) or
2984 (INTEL) BOSBANK PA

PARAGUAY

President:
Dr. Guillermo Peroni
Senior Partner
Peroni, Sosa and Sosa and Altamirano,
Abogados
Generlisimo Franco 2012
Asuncion, Paraguay
PHONE: 210-405
TELEX: 638 PY LAWYERS

Executive Director:
Lilian Velazquez, Manager
Paraguayan-American Chamber of
Commerce
Ntra. Senora de la Asuncion 719, piso 8
Asuncion, Paraguay
PHONE: 95-125
TELEX: 638

PERU

President:
Charles G. Preble, President
Southern Peru Copper Corp.
P.O. Box 2640
Lima 100, Peru
PHONE: 36-1565; 36-4708
TELEX: 20168 PE

Executive Director:
John B. Ottiker, General Manager
American Chamber of Commerce of
Peru
Av. Ricardo Palma 836
Lima 18, Peru
PHONE: 47-9349
TELEX: 21165 BANKAMER PE

PHILIPPINES

President:
George W. Drysdale, President
Marsman & Company, Inc.
Sen. Gil Puyat Ave.
Cor. Washington St.
P.O. Box 297
Makati, Metro Manila
Philippines
PHONE: 872031; 889731
TELEX: (RCA) 22060 MSN PN
   (ITT) 45207 MARSMAN PM
CABLE: MARSMANINC

Executive Director:
J. Marsh Thomson
Executive Vice President
The American Chamber of Commerce
   of the Philippines
P.O. Box 1578, MCC
Manila, The Philippines
PHONE: 818-7911
CABLE: AMCHAMCOM
TELEX: (ITT)45181 Amcham Ph
FAX: 011-632-471-267

PORTUGAL

President:
Robert R. Langelier
Director Gerente General
General Motors de Portugal
Av Marcechal Gomes de Costa 33
1800 Lisboa, Portugal
PHONE: (19) 85 39 96
TELEX: 12599 Autorex P

Executive Director:
Dr. Henrique M. Brito do Rio
General Secretary
American Chamber of 0Commerce
   in Portugal
Rua De D. Estefania, 155, 5 ESQ.
Lisbon 1000, Portugal
PHONE: (1) 57 25 61
   (1) 57 82 08
TELEX: 42356 Amcham P

SAUDI ARABIA - DHAHRAN

President:
David D. Bosch
President
American Businessmen's Association,
   Eastern Province
c/o ARAMCO
P.O. Box 1329
Dhahran, Saudi Arabia 31311
TELEX: 801220

Executive Director:
William Hostetler
c/o ARAMCO
P.O. Box 1255
Dhahran, Saudi Arabia 31311
PHONE: 875-3138
TELEX: 801220

SAUDI ARABIA - JEDDAH

President:
John Mulholland
Chariman, Issues Committee
The American Businessmen of Jeddah
P.O. Box 12264
Jeddah, Saudi Arabia
PHONE: 651-9068
TELEX: 604697 SJ

Executive Director:
Ernest G. Gabbard
Chairman, Issues Committee
The American Businessmen of Jeddah
P.O. Box 5019
Jeddah, Saudi Arabia
PHONE: 682-2102
TELEX: 401906 SJ

SAUDI ARABIA - RIYADH

President & Executive Director:
Frank Hardy
Chairman
American Businessmen's Group
   of Riyadh
P.O. Box 8273
Riyadh 11482, Saudi Arabia 07045

SINGAPORE

Chairman:
Thomas J. Bolam, Chairman
American Business Council of
Singapore
c/o Esso Singapore Private, Ltd.
P.O. Box 2824
Maxwell Road Post Office
Singapore 9048
PHONE: 235-0077
TELEX: 50296

Executive Director:
Joyce Rasmussen
Executive Director
American Business Council of Singapore
354 Orchard Road; #10-12 Shaw House
Singapore 0923
PHONE: 235-0077
TELEX: 50296 ABC SIN

SOUTH AFRICA

President:
I.W. Leach General Manager
Caterpillar (Africe) (Pty) Limited
P.O. Box 197
Isando, 1600 - South Africa

Executive Director:
Adrian Botha, Executive Director
The American Chamber of Commerce
   in South Africa
P.O. Box 62280
Johannesburg, South Afica
PHONE: 838-3134
TELEX: 4-29883 SA

President:
Steven K. Winegar
President and Managing
   Director
Bristol-Myers Inc.
Apartado 50989
28080 Madrid, Spain
PHONE: 729 48 88

Executive Director:
Jose A. Manrique, Executive Director
The American Chamber of Commerce
   in Spain
Avda. Diagonal 477
08036 Barcelona, Spain
PHONE: (3) 321 81 95/6
FAX: (3) 209 16 55

Branch Office - Madrid

Maria Nieves Hermida
Assistant Executive Director
The American Chamber of Commerce
  in Spain
Hotel EuroBuilding
Padre Damian 23, Madrid 16, Spain
PHONE: 4586520

SWITZERLAND

President:
Robert Studer
Executive Vice President
Union Bank of Switzerland
P.O. Box 654
8021 Zurich, Switzerland
PHONE: 2341111
TELEX: 813811
FAX: 2364643

Executive Director:
Walter H. Diggelmann
Executive Director
Swiss-American Chamber of
Commerce
Talacker 41
8001 Zurich, Switzerland
PHONE: (1) 211 24 54
TELEX: 813448 IPCO CH
FAX: (1) 211 95 72

TAIWAN

President:
James K. M. Wang, President
Sung-I Industries, Ltd.
10/F 550, Chung Hsiao E. Rd
Sec. 4

Taipei, Taiwan, R.O.C.
PHONE: 709-1690
TELEX: 11715 QUALITY
CABLE: AMCHAM TAIPE

Executive Director:
Herbert Gale Peabody
Executive Director
The American Chamber of Commerce
  in Taiwan
P.O. Box 17-277
Taipei, Taiwan
PHONE: 5512515
CABLE: AMCHAM TAIPEI
TELEX: 27841 AMCHAM

THAILAND

President:
Roy W. Weiland
Managing Director
Esso Standard Thailand Ltd.
1016 Rama IV Road
P.O. Box 189
Bangkok 10500, Thailand
PHONE: 236-0300
TELEX: 82661 ESSO TH
CABLE: ESSOEAST Bangkok

Executive Director:
Thomas A. Seale, Executive Director
The American Chamber of Commerce
  in Thailand
P.O. Box 11-1095
140 Wireless Road
7th Floor, Kian Gwan Building
Bangkok, Thailand
PHONE: 2519266
CABLE: AMERCHAM
TELEX: 82827 KGCOM TH

UNITED ARAB EMIRATES

President:
Mr. E. H. Old, President
American Businessmen's Group
  of Dubai
P.O. Box 2155
Dubai, United Arab Emirates
PHONE: 971-4-442790
TELEX: 45544 CALTX

Executive Director:
Mrs. Nike Lugman
Executive Director
The American Business Council of
Dubai
International Trade Center, Suite 1609
P.O. Box 9281, Dubai - UAE
PHONE: 377735
TELEX: 48244 SERVE EM

URUGUAY

President:
Pedro Nicolas Baridon, President
Indelsa
Calle Paraguay 1547, Oficina 1605
Montevideo, Uruguay
PHONE: (5982) 916602
TELEX: 22448 INGENET UY

Executive Director:
Carlos Boubet
Manager
Chamber of Commerce Uruguay-U.S.A.
Calle Bartolome Mitre 1337
Casilla de Correo 809
Montevideo, Uruguay
PHONE: 986934; 906052
CABLE: AMCHAM
TELEX: 6674 BAPEN UY]

UNITED KINGDOM

President:
Charles K. Alexander
Vice President
Manufacturers Hanover Trust
The Adelphi, 1-11 John Adams Street
London WC2N 6HT

Executive Director:
Harry G. Cressman
Director General
The American Chamber of
Commerce   (United Kingdom)
75 Brook Street
London WIY 2EB, England
PHONE: (1) 1 493 03 81
CABLE: AMCHAM LONDON WI
TELEX: 23675 AM CHAM

VENEZUELA

President:
Orlando G. Hernandez
President and General Manager
Cyanamid de Venezuela
Apartado 5991
Caracas 1010-A, Venezuela
PHONE: 241-0882; 241-4705
TELEX: 25214

Executive Director:
Michael E. Heggie
Executive Director
Venezuelan-American Chamber of
  Commerce & Industry
Torre Credival, Piso 10
2da Avenida de Campo Alegre
Apartado 5181
Caracas, 1010-A Venezuela
PHONE: 313007; 312076
TELEX: 28399 CAVEA VC

REGIONAL AMCHAM ORGANIZATIONS

AACCLA

Robert W. Chandler, Jr.
Vice President
Chase Manhattan Overseas
Corporation
100 Chopin Plaza, 12th Floor
Miami, FL 33131
PHONE: (305) 579-9479
TELEX: 153198 CMOC UT

Executive Director:
Keith L. Miceli, Executive Vice
President
Association of American Chambers of
   Commerce in Latin America
1615 H Street, N.W.
Washington, D.C. 20062
PHONE: (202) 43-5485
CABLE: COCUSA
TELEX: 248302 CCUS UR

APCAC

Chairman:
Harvey Goldstein, Chairman
Asia-Pacific Council of American
   Chambers of Commerce
c/o Resource Management Int'l Inc.
J1. Sultan Hasanuddin 28
Kebayoran Baru
Jakarta Selatan, Indonesia
PHONE: 734-588
TELEX: 47129 RMI IA
FAX: 001-62-21-734-566

Executive Director:
Ann Wise, Executive Director
Asia-Pacific Council of American
   Chambers of Commerce
c/o Honeywell Inc.
Nagai International Building
2-12-19 Shibuya, Shibuyu-Ku
Tokyo 150, Japan
PHONE: (03) 409-1800
TELEX: J22902 YAMATAKE

EUROPEAN COUNCIL

Chairman:
Albert O. Hicks, Chairman
European Council of American
   Chambers of Commerce
Manager
ACS - Aviation Consulting
   Services GmbH
Raabestrasse 15
6000 Frankfurt 50, West Germany
PHONE: (69) 6872100

Executive Director:
John D. Brennan, Secretary General
The American Chamber of Commerce
   in Germany
Rossmarkt 12, Postfach 100 12
D-6000 Frankfurt/Main 1, West Germany
PHONE: 28-34-01
CABLE: AMECOC

Foreign Chambers of Commerce and Associations in the United States

ARGENTINA

Argentine-American Chamber of Commerce
50 West 34th Street
6th Floor, Room C2
New York, NY 10001
(212) 564-3855

AUSTRIA

U.S.-Austrian Chamber of Commerce, Inc.
165 West 46th Street
New York, NY 10036
(212) 819-0117

BELGIUM

Belgian-American Chamber of Commerce in the U.S., Inc.
350 5th Avenue
Suite 703
New York, NY 10118
(212) 967-9898

BRAZIL

Brazilian-American Chamber of Commerce, Inc.
22 West 48th Street
Room 404
New York, NY 10036
(212) 575-9030

Brazilian-American Chamber of Commerce
1111 South Bay Shore Drive
Miami, FL 33131
(305) 377-6700

Brazil-California Trade Association
350 South Figueroa Street
Suite 226
Los Angeles, CA 90071
(213) 627-0634

CHILE

North-American Chamber of Commerce, Inc.
220 East 81st Street
New York, NY 10028
(212) 288-5691

CHINA

Chinese Chamber of Commerce New York
Confucius Plaza
33 Bowery
Room C203
New York, NY 10002
(212) 226-2795

Chinese Chamber of Commerce of San Francisco
730 Sacramento Street
San Francisco, CA 94108
(415) 982-3000

COLOMBIA

Colombian-American Association, Inc.
111 Broadway
Room 1408
New York, NY 10006
(212) 233-7776

DENMARK

Danish-American Chamber of Commerce
825 3rd Avenue
New York, NY 10019

DOMINICAN REPUBLIC

Dominican Republic Export
Promotion Center
One World Trade Center
Room 86065
New York, NY 10048

ECUADOR

Ecuadorean-American Association,
Inc.
115 Broadway
Room 1408
New York, NY 10006
(212) 233-7776

EGYPT

Egyptian-American Chamber of
Commerce
One World Trade Center
Suite 8741
New York, NY 10048
(212) 466-1866

FINLAND

Finnish-American Chamber of
Commerce
540 Madison Avenue
18th Floor
New York, NY 10022
(212) 832-2588

Finnish-American Chamber of
Commerce of the Midwest
35 East Wacker Drive
Suite 1900
Chicago, IL 60601
(312) 34-1150

FRANCE

French-American Chamber of Commerce
in the U.S.
509 Madison Avenue
Suite 1900
New York, NY 10022

GERMANY

German-American Chamber of
Commerce
666 Fifth Avenue
New York, NY 10103
(212) 974-8830

German-American Chamber of
Commerce of Chicago
104 South Michigan Avenue
Chicago, IL 60603-5978
(312) 782-8557

German-American Chamber of
Commerce of Los Angeles, Inc.
One Park Plaza Building
3250 Wilshire Boulevard
Suite 1112
Los Angeles, CA 90010

German-American Chamber of
Commerce of the Pacific Coast, Inc.
465 California Street
Suite 910
San Francisco, CA 94104

German-American Chamber of
Commerce
One Farragut Square South
Washington, D.C. 20006
(202) 347-0247

GREECE

Hellenic-American Chamber of
Commerce
29 Broadway
Room 1508
New York, NY 10006
(212) 934-8594

INDIA

India Chamber of Commerce of
America
445 Park Avenue
New York, NY 10022
(212) 755-7181

Indo-American Chamber of
Commerce
c/o The Bank of India
19 South La Salle Street
Chicago, IL 0603
(312) 621-1200

INDONESIA

American-Indonesian Chamber of
Commerce, Inc.
12 East 41st Street
Suite 701
New York, NY 10017
(212) 637-4505

IRELAND

Ireland-United States Council for
Commerce and Industry, Inc.
460 Park Avenue
New York, NY 10022
(212) 751-2660

ISRAEL

American-Israel Chamber of Commerce
and Industry, Inc.
500 Fifth Avenue
Room 5416
New York, NY 10036
(212) 354-6510

American-Israel Chamber of Commerce
and Industry, Inc.
Cleveland Center
10800 Brookpark Road
Cleveland, Ohio 44130
(216) 267-1200

America-Israel Chamber of Commerce
and Industry, Inc.
Metropolitan Chicago
180 North Michigan Avenue
Suite 911
Chicago, IL 60601
(312) 641-2937

Western States Chamber of Commerce
with Israel
6505 Wilshire Boulevard
Suite 201
Los Angeles, CA 90048
(213) 658-7910

Italian Chamber of Commerce of Chicago
126 West Grand Avenue
Chicago, IL 60610
(312) 661-1336

Italy-American Chamber of Commerce,
Inc.
350 Fifth Avenue
Suite 3015
New York, NY 10118
(212) 279-5520

JAPAN

Honolulu-Japanese Chamber of
Commerce
2454 South Beretania Street
Honolulu, Hawaii 96826

Japan Business Association of
Southern California
345 South Figueroa Street
Suite 206
Los Angeles, CA 90071
(213) 485-0160

Japanese Chamber of Commerce and
Industry of Chicago
401 North Michigan Avenue
Room 602
Chicago, IL 60611
(312) 332-6199

Japanese Chamber of Commerce of
New York, Inc.
145 West 57th Street
New York, NY 10019
(212) 246-9774

Japanese Chamber of Commerce of
Northern California
World Affairs Center
312 Sutter Street
Room 408
San Francisco, CA 94108
(415) 986-6140

Japanese Chamber of Commerce of
Southern California
244 South San Pedro Street
Room 504
Los Angeles, CA 90012
(213) 626-3067

KOREA

Korean Chamber of Commerce
981 South Western Avenue
Room 201
Los Angeles, CA 90006
(213) 733-4410

U.S.-Korea Society
725 Park Avenue
New York, NY 10021
(212) 517-7730

LEBANON

United States-Lebanese Chamber of
Commerce
One World Trade Center
Suite 1345
New York, NY 10048
(212) 432-1133

MEXICO

Mexican Chamber of Commerce of
Arizona
P.O. Box 626
Phoenix, AZ 85001
(602) 252-6448

Mexican Chamber of Commerce of the
County of Los Angeles
125 Paseo de La Plaza
Room 404
Los Angeles, CA 90012
(213) 688-7330

Mexican Chamber of Commerce of the
U.S., Inc.
655 Madison Avenue
The Woolworth Building
16th Floor
New York, NY 10021
(212) 759-9505

Mexican Institute for Foreign Trade
9 East 53rd Street
25th Floor
New York, NY 10022
(212) 759-9505

United States-Mexico Chamber of
Commerce
1900 "L" Street, NW
Suite 612
Washington, D.C. 20036
(202) 296-5198

U.S.-Mexico Quadripartite
Commission
Center for Inter-American Relations
680 Park Avenue
New York, NY 10021
(212) 249-8950

NETHERLANDS

Netherlands Chamber of Commerce
in the U.S., Inc.
One Rockefeller Plaza 11th Floor
New York, NY 10020
(212) 265-6460

NIGERIA

Nigerian-American Chamber of
Commerce, Inc.
575 Lexington Avenue
New York, NY 10022
(212) 715-7200

NORWAY

Norwegian-American Chamber of
Commerce, Inc.
Midwest Chicago Chapter
360 North Michigan Avenue
Suite 1908
Chicago, IL 60601
(312) 782-7750

Norwegian-American Chamber of
Commerce, Inc.
World Trade Center
350 South Figueroa Street
Suite 360
Los Angeles, CA 90017
(213) 626-0388

Norwegian-American Chamber of
Commerce, Inc.
Upper Midwest Chapter
229 Foshay Tower
Minneapolis, MN 55402
(612) 332-3338

Norwegian-American Chamber of
Comerce, Inc.
825 3rd Avenue
New York, NY 10022
(212) 421-9210

Norwegian-American Chamber of
Commerce, Inc.
1301 5th Avenue
Suite 2727
Seattle, WA 98101
(206) 682-5250

Norwegian-American Chamber of
Commerce
Two Embarcadero Center
Suite 2930
San Francisco, CA 94111
(415) 986-0766

PAKISTAN

U.S.-Pakistan Economic Council
c/o Morton Zuckerman
17 Battery Place
New York, NY 10004
(212) 943-5828

PERU

Peruvian-American Association
50 West 34th Street
6th Floor, Suite C2
New York, NY 10001
(212) 564-3855

PHILIPPINES

Philippine-American Chamber of
Commerce, Inc.
711 3rd Avenue
17th Floor
New York, NY 10017

Philippine-American Chamber of
Commerce
c/o Philippine Consulate
447 Sutter Street
San Francisco, CA 94108
(415) 433-6666

PORTUGAL

Portugal-U.S. Chamber of Commerce
5 West 45th Street
4th Floor
New York, NY 10036
(212) 354-4627

PUERTO RICO

Puerto Rico Chamber of Commerce
in the U.S.
200 Madison Avenue
New York, NY 10016
(212) 561-2028

SAUDI ARABIA

Saudi Arabian Council of Chambers of
Commerce and Industry
c/o Hamed Jared, Washington
Representative
Embassy of Saudi Arabia
601 New Hampshire Avenue, NW
Washington, D.C. 20037
(202) 342-3800

SPAIN

Spain-U.S. Chamber of Commerce
350 5th Avenue
Room 3514
New York, NY 10118
(212) 967-2170

SWEDEN

Swedish-American Chamber of
Commerce, Inc.
825 3rd Avenue
New York, NY 10022
(212) 838-5530

Swedish-American Chamber of
Commerce of the Western U.S., Inc.
Ferry Building
World Trade Center
Suite 268
San Francisco, CA 94111
(415) 781-4188

TRINIDAD

Trinidad and Tobago Chamber of
Commerce of the U.S.A., Inc.
c/o Trintoc Services Limited
400 Madison Avenue
Room 803
New York, NY 10017
(212) 759-3388

UNITED KINGDOM

British-American Chamber of
Commerce
275 Madison Avenue
Room 1714
New York, NY 10016
(212) 889-0680

British-American Chamber of
Commerce
3150 California Street
San Francisco, CA 94115
(415) 567-6128

British-American Chamber of
Commerce and Trade Center
of the Pacific Southwest
1640 5th Street
Suite 224
Santa Monica, CA 90401
(213) 394-4977

VENEZUELA

Venezuelan-American Association of the
U.S., Inc.
115 Broadway
Room 1110
New York, NY 10006
(212) 233-7776

YUGOSLAVIA

U.S.-Yugoslav Economic Council
818 18th Street, NW
Suite 818
Washington, D.C. 20006
(202) 857-0170

REGIONAL ORGANIZATIONS

AFRICA

African-American Chamber of
Commerce, Inc.
P.O. Box 5298
FDR Station
New York, NY 10150
(212) 829-3492

ASIA

ASIAN-U.S. TRADE COUNCIL
40 East 49th Street
New York, NY 10017
(212) 688-2755

Asia Society
725 Park Avenue
New York, NY 10021
(21) 288-6400

Asia Society
1785 Massachusetts Avenue, NW
Washington, D.C. 20036
(202) 387-6500

LATIN AMERICA

Chamber of Commerce of Latin
America in the U.S., Inc.
One World Trade Center
Suite 2343
New York, NY 10048
(212) 432-9313

Council of the Americas
680 Park Avenue
New York, NY 10021
(212) 628-3200

Houston-Inter-American Chamber of
Commerce
1520 Texas Avenue
Suite 1D
Houston, TX 77002

Latin American Chamber of
Commerce
P.O. Box 30240
New Orleans, LA 70190
(504) 527-6936

Latin Chamber of Commerce
1417 West Flagler Street
Miami, FL 33135

Latin American Manufacturing
Association
4919 New Jersey Avenue, SE
Washington, D.C. 20003
(202) 546-3808

Pan American Chamber of
Commerce and Trade Council
Business Information Center
16 Graceland Drive
San Rafael, CA 94901
(415) 454-2555

Pan American Society of San
Francisco
World Affairs Center
312 Sutter Street
San Francisco, CA 94108

Pan American Society of the U.S., Inc.
680 Park Avenue
New York, NY 10021
(212) 744-6868

MIDDLE EAST

American-Arab Association of
Commerce & Industry
420 Lexington Avenue
Suite 2431
New York, NY 10017
(212) 986-7229

Mid-America-Arab Chamber of
Commerce, Inc.
135 South La Salle Street
Suite 2050
Chicago, IL 60603
(312) 782-4654

National Council on U.S.-Arab Relations
1625 Eye Street, NW
Suite 904
Washington, D.C. 20006
(202) 293-0800

U.S.-Arab Chamber of Commerce
One World Trade Center
Suite 4657
New York, NY 10048
(212) 432-0655

U.S.-Arab Chamber of Commerce
1625 Eye Street, NW
Suite 812
Washington, D.C. 20006
(202) 293-3162

U.S.-Arab Chamber of Commerce, Pacific
1231 Market Street
San Francisco, CA 94101
(415) 552-8202

U.S.-Arab Chamber of Commerce
505 North Belt Drive
Suite 405
Houston, TX 77060
(713) 447-2563

Local Chambers of Commerce Which Maintain International Trade Services

Alabama

Birmingham Area C/C
P.O. Box 10127
Birmingham, Alabama 35020
205/323-5461

South Baldwin C/C
P.O. Box 1117
Foley, Alabama 36536
205/943-3291

Colbert County C/C
P.O. Box 1006
Tuscumbia, Alabama 35674
205/383-4531

Decatur C/C
P.O. Box 2003
Decatur, Alabama 35602
205/353-5312

Dothan-Houston County C/C
P.O. Box 638
Dothan, Alabama 36302
205/792-5138

Jasper Area C/C
P.O. Box 972
Jasper Area, Alabama 35501
205/384-4571

Greater Valley Area C/C
P.O. Box 205
Lanett, Alabama 36863
205/642-1411

Mobile C/C
P.O. Box 2187
Mobile, Alabama 36652
205/433-6951

Montgomery Area C/C
P.O. Box 76
Montgomery, Alabama 36101
205/834-5200

Scottsboro-Jackson County C/C
P.O. Box 973
Scottsboro, Alabama 35768
205/259-5500

Selma & Dallas County C/C
P.O. Drawer D
Selma, Alabama 36701
205/875-7241

Alaska

Alaska State C/C
310 Second Street
Juneau, Alaska 99801
907/586-2323

Anchorage C/C
415 F Street
Anchorage, Alaska 99501
907/272-2401

Greater Fairbanks C/C
P.O. Box 74446
Fairbanks, Alaska 99707
907/452-1105

Kodiak Area C/C
P.O. Box 1485
Kodiak, Alaska 99615
907/486-5557

Arizona

Nogales-Santa Cruz County C/C
Kino Park
Nogeles, Arizona 85621
602/287-385

Tempe C/C
504 E. Southern Ave.
Tempe, Arizona 85282
602/967-7891

Tucson C/C
P.O. Box 991
Tucson, Arizona 85701
602/792-1212

Wickenburg C/C
P.O. Drawer cc
Wickenburg, Arizona 85358

Phoenix Metropolitan C/C
34 W. Monroe Street, 9th Floor
Phoenix, Arizona 85003
602/254-5521

Arkansas

Fort Smith C/C
613 Grison Ave.
Fort Smith, Arkansas 72901
501/783-6118

Metropolitan C/C
One Spring Street
Little Rock, Arkansas 72901
501/374-4871

Russellville C/C
P.O. Box 822
Russellville, Arkansas 72801
501/968-2530

California

Alhambra C/C
104 S. First Street
Alhambra, California 91801
818/282-8481

Coronado C/C
720 Orange Ave.
Coronado, California 92118
615/435-9260

Downey C/C
8497 2nd Street
Downey, California 90240
213/923-2191

El Segundo C/C
P.O. Box 544
El Segundo, California 90245
213/322-1220

Escondido C/C
P.O. Box C
Escondido, California 92025
619/745-2125

Gardena Valley C/C
1919 W. Redondo Beach Blvd.
Suite 701
Gardena, California 90247
213/532-9905

Glendale C/C
200 S. Louise Street
Glendale, California 91205
818/240-7870

Inglewood Area C/C
330 E. Queen Street
Inglewood, California 90301
213/677-1121

Long Beach Area C/C
50 Oceangate Plaza
Long Beach, California 90802
213/436-1251

Los Angeles Area C/C
P.O. Box 3696
Los Angeles, California 90051
213/629-0722

Oakland C/C
1939 Harrison Street, #400
Oakland, California 94612
415/827-9514

Monrovia C/C
111 W. Colorado Boulevard
Monrovia, California 91016
818-358/1159

Pico Rivera C/C
9122 E. Washington Boulevard
P.O. Box 985
Pico Rivera, California 90660
213/949-2473

Sacramento Metropolitan C/C
P.O. Box 1017
Sacramento, California 95805
916/443-3771

California C/C
P.O. Box 1736
Sacramento, California 95808
916/447-7111

San Fernando Valley Region C/C
8238 Louise Ave.
Northridge, California 91325
818/708-2391

Gtr. San Diego C/C
110 West C. Street, Suite 1600
San Diego, California 92101
619/232-0124

Orange County C/C
401 Bank of America Tower
One City Boulevard, W.
Orange, California 92668
714/634-2900

San Fernando C/C
747 San Fernando Road
San Fernando, California 91340
818/361-1184

San Francisco C/C
465 California Street
San Francisco, California 94104
415/392-4511

San Jose C/C
P.O. Box 6178
San Jose, California 95105
408/998-7000

Torrance Area C/C
3400 Torrance Boulevard, Suite 100
Torrance, California 90503
213/540-5858

Greater Van Nuys Area C/C
7240 Hayvenhurst Ave.
Van Nuys, California 91406
213/876-2366

Vista C/C
201 Washington Street
Vista, California 92083
619/726-1122

Colorado

Boulder C/C
P.O. Box 73
Boulder, Colorado 80306
303/442-1044

Canon City C/C
P.O. Box 366
Canon City, Colorado 81212
303/275-2331

Colorado Springs C/C
P.O. Box B
110 Chase Stone Center
Colorado Springs, Colorado 80901
303/635-1551

Denver C/C
1301 Welton Street
Denver, Colorado 80204
303/776-5295

Longmont C/C
455 Kimbark Street
Longmont, Colorado 80501
303/776-5295

Montrose C/C
550 N. Townsend
Montrose, Colorado 81401
303/249-5515

Connecticut

Glastonbury C/C
2400 Main Street
Glastonbury, Connecticut 06830
203/923-7154

Greater Danbury C/C
72 West Street
Danbury, Connecticut 06810
203/743-5565

C/C of the Town of Greenwich
175 Greenwich Ave.
Greenwich, Connecticut 06830
203/869-3500

Greater Hartford C/C
250 Constitution Plaza
Hartford, Connecticut 06103
203/525-4451

Greater Meridan C/C, Inc.
17 Church Street
Meridan, Connecticut 06450
203/235-7901

Middlesex County C/C
P.O. Box 997
Middletown, Connecticut 06457
203/347-6924

New Britain C/C
One Central Park Plaza
New Britain, Connecticut 06051
203/229-1665

The Greater New Haven C/C
P.O. Box 1445
New Haven, Connecticut 06051
203/787-6735

Southwestern Area Commerce &
Industry Association of
  Connecticut, Inc.
One Landmark Square, Suite 230
Stamford, Connecticut 06901
203/359-3220

Greater Waterbury C/C
P.O. Box 1469
Waterbury, Connecticut 06721
203/757-0701

Greater Willimantic C/C
P.O. Box 43
Willimantic, Connecticut 06226
203/423-6389

Delaware

Central Delaware C/C
P.O. Box 576
Dover, Delaware 19903
320/734-7513

Delaware State C/C
1102 West Street
Wilmington, Delaware 19801
302/655-7221

Florida

Coral Gables C/C
50 Aragon Avenue
Coral Gables, Florida 32301
305/446-1657

Daytona Beach Area C/C
P.O. Box 2775

Daytona Beach, Florida 32015
904/255-0981

Deerfield Beach C/C
1601 E. Hillsboro Boulevard
Deerfield Beach, Florida 33441
305/427-1050

Fort Lauderdale Area C/C
P.O. Box 14516
Fort Lauderdale, Florida 33302
305/462-6000

Daytona Beach Shores C/C
3616 S. Atlantis Avenue
Daytona Beach Shores, Florida 32019
904/71-7163

St. Lucie County C/C
2200 Virginia Avenue
Fort Pierce, Florida 33450
305/461-2700

Greater Hollywood C/C
P.O. Box 2345
Hollywood, Florida 33022
305/920-3330

Jacksonville Area C/C
P.O. Box 329
Jacksonville, Florida 32201
904/353-0300

Lake Placid C/C
P.O. Box 187
Lake Placid, Florida 33852
813/465-4331

Lake Wales C/C
P.O. Box 191
Lake Wales, Florida 33853-0191
813/676-3445

North Dade C/C
P.O. Box 69-3116
Miami, Florida 33269-0116
305/652-3374

Greater Miami C/C
1601 Biscayne Boulevard
Miami, Florida 33132
305/350-7700

Northern Palm Beach Co. C/C
1983 Pga Boulevard
Palm Beach Garden, Florida 33480
305/694-2300

Orlando Area C/C
P.O. Box 1234
Orlando, Florida 32802
305/425-1234

Pensacola Area C/C
P.O. Box 550
Pensacola, Florida 32593
904/438-4081

Greater Plant City C/C
303 North Warnell Street
Plant City, Florida 33565
813/754-3707

Florida C/C
P.O. Box 11309
Tallahassee, Florida 32301
904/222-2831

Greater Tampa C/C
P.O. Box 420
Tampa, Florida 33601
813/228-7777

Georgia

Atlanta C/C
1300 North Omni International
Atlanta, Georgia 30303
404/521-0845

Georgia C/C
1200 Commerce Building
Atlanta, Georgia 30335
404/524-8481

C/C of Greater Augusta
P.O. Box 657
Augusta, Georgia 30903
404/722-0421

Bainbridge/Decatur C/C
P.O. Box 736
Bainbridge, Georgia 31717
912/246-4774

La Grange Area C/C
P.O. Box 636
La Grange, Georgia 30241
404/884-8671

Gwinnett C/C
P.O. Box 1245
Lawrenceville, Georgia 30246
404/963-5128

Greater Macon C/C
P.O. Box 169
Macon, Georgia 31298
912/741-8023

Savannah Area C/C
301 W. Broad Street
Savannah, Georgia 31499
912/233-307

Valdosta-Lowndes C/C
P.O. Box 790
Valdosta, Georgia 31601
912/247-8100

Guam

Guam C/C
P.O. Box 283
107 ADA Plaza Center
Agana, Guam 96910
671/472-6202

Hawaii

The C/C of Hawaii
735 Bishop Street
Honolulu, Hawaii 96813
808/531-4111

Kauai C/C
P.O. Box 1969
Lihue, Hawaii 96766
808/245-7363

Idaho

Greater Boise C/C
P.O. Box 2360
Boise, Idaho 83701
208/344-5515

Illinois

Charleston Area C/C
P.O. Box 99
Charleston, Illinois 61920
217/345-7041

Illinois State C/C
20 North Wacker Drive, Suite 1960
Chicago, Illinois 60606
312/372-7373

Chicago Assn. of Commerce & Industry
130 South Michigan Avenue
Chicago, Illinois 60603
312/786-0111

Freeport Area C/C
10 N. Galena Avenue
Freeport, Illinois 61032
815/235-9831

Mattoon Assn. of Commerce
1701 Wabash Avenue
Mattoon, Illinois 61938
217/235-5661

Mendota C/C
P.O. Box 370
Mendota, Illinois 61342
815/539-6507

Peoria C/C
230 S. W. Adams Street
Peoria, Illinois 61602
309/676-0755

Rockford Area C/C
815 East State Street
Rockford, Illinois 61101
815/987-8100

Skokie C/C
P.O. Box 53
Skokie, Illinois 60077
312/673-0204

Greater Springfield C/C
3 W. Old State Capitol Plaza
Springfield, Illinois 62701
217/525-1173

St. Charles C/C
4 E. Main Street
St. Charles, Illinois 60174
312/584-8384

Greater Wheaton C/C
211 W. Wesley Street
Wheaton, Illinois 60187
312/668-2739

Indiana

Connersville C/C
100 S. Vine
Connersville, Indiana 47331
317/825-2561

The Greater Elkhart C/C, Inc.
P.O. Box 428
514 S. Main Street
Elkhart, Indiana 46515
219/293-1531

Metropolitan Evansville C/C
329 Main Street
Evansville, Indiana 47708
812/425-8147

Greater Fort Wayne C/C
326 Weing Street
Fort Wayne, Indiana 46802
219/424-1435

Indiana State C/C
1 N. Capitol Avenue, Suite 200
Indianapolis, Indiana 46204
317/634-6407

Indianapolis C/C
320 N. Meridian Street, Suite 928
Indianapolis, Indiana 46204
317/267-2901

Greater Lafayette C/C
P.O. Box 348
Lafayette, Indiana 47902
317/742-4041

Logansport-Cass County C/C
312 E. Broadway, Suite 108, Logan Sq.
Logansport, Indiana 46947
219/753-6388

Munci-Dela County C/C
500 N. Walnut Street
Muncie, Indiana 47305
317/288-6681

Greater Seymour C/C
P.O. Box 312
Seymour, Indiana 47274
812/522-3681

South Bend-Mishawaka C/C
P.O. Box 1677
South Bend, Indiana 46634
219/234-0051

Daviess County C/C
P.O. Box 430
Washington, Indiana 47501
812/254-5262

Iowa

Cedar Rapids-Marion Area C/C
P.O. Box 4860
Cedar Rapids, Iowa 52407
319/398-5320

Council Bluffs C/C
P.O. Box 1565
Council Bluffs, Iowa 51502
712/325-1000

Davenport C/C
404 Main Street
Davenport, Iowa 52801
319/322-1706

Dubuque Area C/C
880 Locust
Dubuque, Iowa 52001
319/557-9200

Greater Des Moines C/C
Eight and High Streets
Des Moines, Iowa 50307
515/286-4950

Grinnell Area C/C
P.O. Box 338
Grinnell, Iowa 50112
515/236-6555

Fort Madison C/C
P.O. Box 277
Fort Madison, Iowa 52627
319/372-5471

Siouxland Assn.-Bus. & Industry
101 Pierce Street
Sioux City, Iowa 51101
712/255-7903

Waterloo C/C
229 W. 5th Street
Waterloo, Iowa 50704

Kansas

Kansas City, Kansas Area C/C
P.O. Box 1310
Kansas City, Kansas 66117
913/371-3070

Leavenworth Area C/C
P.O. Box 44
Leavenworth, Kansas 66048
913/682-4112

McPherson C/C
P.O. Box 616
McPherson, Kansas 67460
316/241-1333

Salina Area C/C
P.O. Box 596
Salina, Kansas 67401
913/827-9301

Greater Topeka C/C
722 Kansas
Topeka, Kansas 66603
913/234-2644

Wichita Area C/C
350 W. Douglas Avenue
Wichita, Kansas 67202
316/265-7771

Kentucky

Louisville Area C/C
One Riverfront Plaza
Louisville, Kentucky 40202
502/566-50000

Marshall County C/C
Route 7, Box 145
Benton, Kentucky 42025
502/527-7665

Bowling Green-Warren Co.C/C
P.O. Box 51
Bowling Green, Kentucky 42101
502/781-3200

Glasgow-Barren County C/C
301 W. Main Street
Glasgow, Kentucky 42141
502/651-3161

Northern Kentucky C/C
1717 Dixie Hwy
Covington, Kentucky 41011
606/341-9500

Greater Lexington C/C
421 N. Broadway
Lexington, Kentucky 40508
606/254-4447

Somerset-Pulasky County C/C
P.O. Box 126
Somerset, Kentucky 42501
606/679-7323

Louisiana

Jennings Assn. of Commerce
P.O. Box 1209
Jennings, Louisiana 70546
318/824-0933

Greater Lafayette C/C
P.O. Drawer 51307
Lafayette, Louisiana 70505
318/433-3632

Greater Lake Charles C/C
P.O. Box 3109
Lake Charles, Louisiana 70602
318/433-3632

New Orleans Area C/C
P.O. Box 30240
New Orleans, Louisiana 70190
504/527-6936

Shreveport C/C
P.O. Box 20074
Shreveport, Louisiana 71120
318/226-8521

Slidell C/C
520 Old Spanish Trail
Slidell, Louisiana 70458
504/643-5678

Maine

Kennebec Valley C/C
P.O. Box E
Augusta, Maine 04330
207/623-4559

Lewiston-Auburn Area C/C
40 Pine Street
Lewiston, Maine 04240
207/783-2249

Maryland

Maryland State C/C
60 West Street
Annapolis, Maryland 21401
301/727-2820

Greater Baltimore Committee
2 Hopkins Plaza, Suite 900
Baltimore, Maryland 21201
301/727-2820

C/C of Frederick County, Inc.
26 S. Market Street
Frederick, Maryland 21701
301/662-4164

Hagerstown-Washington County C/C
14 Public Square
Hagerstown, Maryland 21740
301/739-2015

Baltimore County C/C
100 W. Pennsylvania Avenue
Towson, Maryland 21204
301/825-6200

Massachusetts

Greater Boston C/C
125 High Street
Boston, Massachusetts 02110
617/426-1250

New England Council C/C
120 Boylston Street
Boston, Massachusetts 02601
617/542-2580

Regional C/C
One Center Street
Brockton, Massachusetts 02401
508/58-0500

Greater Gardner C/C
301 Central Street
Gardner, Massachusetts 01440
508/632-1780

Cape Cod C/C
Hyannis, Massachusetts 02601
508/362-3225

Greater Holyoke C/C
69 Suffolk Street
Holyoke, Massachusetts 01040
413/534-3376

Greater Lawrence C/C
264 Essex Street
Lawrence, Massachusetts 01840
508/686-0900

New Bedford Area C/C
P.O. Box G-827
New Bedford, Massachusetts 02742
508/999-5231

South Shore C/C
36 Miller Stile Road
Quincy, Massachusetts 02169
617/479-1111

Greater Springfield C/C
1500 Main Street, Suite 600
Springfield, Massachusetts 01115
413/734-5671

Watertown C/C
P.O. Box 45
Watertown, Massachusetts 02172
617/926-1017

Worchester Area C/C
350 Mechanics Tower
Worcester, Massachusetts 0108
508/753-2924

Michigan

Alpena Area C/C
P.O. Box 65
Alpena, Michigan 49707

Greater Detroit C/C
150 Michigan Avenue
Detroit, Michigan 48226
313/471-4176

Flint Area C/C
708 Root Street
Flint, Michigan 48503
313/232-7101

Grand Rapids Area C/C
17 Fountain Street, NW
Grand Rapids, Michigan 49503
1/459-7221

Greenville Area C/C
327 Lafayette Street
Greenville, Michigan 48838
616/754-5697

Michigan State C/C
New Business and Trade Center
200 N. Washington Square, Suite 400
Lansing, Michigan 48933
517/371-2100

Macomb County C/C
10 North Avenue, P.O. Box 855
Mount Clemens, Michigan 48043
313/463-1528

Mount Pleasant C/C
300 E. Broadway
Mount Pleasant, Michigan 48858
517/772-2396

Royal Oak-Madison Hts./Berkeley
C/C
103 W. Fifth Street
Royal Oak, Michigan 48067
313/547-4000

Minnesota

Bloomington C/C
8200 Humboldt Avenue S.
Bloomington, Minnesota 55431
612/888-8818

Brooklyn Center C.C
3300 County Road 10
Brooklyn Center, Minnesota 55429
612/566-8650

Fridley C/C
7362 University Avenue N.E.
Fridley, Minnesota 55432
612/571-9781

Hastings Area C/C
220 Sibley Street
Hastings, Minnesota 55033
612/437-6775

Hutchinson C/C
218 N. Main Street
Hutchinson, Minnesota 55350
612/587-5252

Marshall Area C/C
501 W. Main
Marshall, Minnesota 56256
507/532-4484

Greater Minneapolis C/C
15 S. Fifth Street
Minneapolis, Minnesota 55402
612/370-9132

St. Paul Area C/C
Suite 300, The Osborne Building
St. Paul, Minnesota 55102
612/222-5561

Waseca C/C
123 N. State Street
Waseca, Minnesota 56258
507/835-3260

White Bear Lake Area C/C
2184 4th Street
White Brear Lake, Minnesota 55110
612/429-7666

Windom Area C/C
P.O. Box 8
Windom, Minnesota 56101
507/831-2752

Mississippi

Biloxi C/C
1036 Fred Haisa Boulevard
Biloxi, Mississippi 39533
601/374-2717

Cleveland-Bolivar County C/C
P.O. Box 490
Cleveland, Mississippi 38732
601/843-2712

Jackson C/C
P.O. Box 22548
Jackson, Mississippi 39205
601/948-7575

Mississippi Marketing Council
P.O. Box 849
Jackson, Mississippi 39205
601/359-3444

Natchez-Adams County C/C
300 N. Commerce
Natchez, Mississippi 39120
601/445-4611

Missouri

Camdenton Area C/C
P.O. Box 785
Camdenton, Missouri 65020
314/346/2227

Greater Kansas City C/C
Main Center, 920 Main Street
Kansas City, Missouri 64105
816/221-2424

Springfield Area C/C
P.O. Box 1687
Springfield, Missouri 65805
417/82-4467

St. Louis Regional Commerce &
Growth Association
10 Broadway
St. Louis, Missouri 6310
314/231-5555

Montana

Billings C/C
P.O. Box 2519
Billings, Montana 59103
406/245-4111

Glendive C/C
P.O. Box 930
Glendive, Montana 59330
406/365-5601

Great Falls C/C
P.O. Box 2127
Great Falls, Montana 59403
406/761-4434

Miles City Area C/C
P.O. Box 730
Miles City, Montana 59301
406/232-2890

Nebraska

Beatrice C/C
P.O. Box 703
Beatrice, Nebraska 68310
402/223-2336

Lincoln C/C
1221 N. Street, Room 606
Lincoln, Nebraska 68508
402/476-7511

Greater Omaha C/C
1606 Douglas Street
Omaha, Nebraska 68102
402/346-5000

Nevada

Greater Las Vegas C/C
2301 E. Sahara Avenue
Las Vegas, Nevada 89104
702/457-4664

Las Vegas C/C
1023 E. Lake Mead
N. Las Vegas, Nevada 89030
702/642-9595

Latin C/C
P.O. Box 7534
Las Vegas, Nevada 89125
702/385-7367

Greater Reno C/C
P.O. Box 3499
Reno, Nevada 89595
702/786-3030

New Hampshire

Exeter Area C/C
120 Water Street
Exeter, New Hampshire 03833
603/722-2411

Merrimack C/C
P.O. Box 254
Merrimack, New Hampshire 03054
603/424-3669

Greater Portsmouth C/C
P.O. Box 239
Portsmouth, New Hampshire 03801
603/436-1116

New Jersey

Eastern Union County C/C
P.O. Box 300
Elizabeth, New Jersey 07207
201/352-0900

Greater Newark C/C
50 Park Place
Newark, New Jersey 07102
201/624-6888

New Jersey State C/C
5 Commerce Street
Newark, New Jersey 07102
201/623-7070

Hudson County C/C
911 Bergen Avenue
Jersey City, New Jersey 07306
201/653-7400

Mercer County C/C
240 West State Freeway 1404
Trenton, New Jersey 08608
609/393-4143

Morris County C/C
230 Madison Avenue
P.O. Box 1700
Convent Station, New Jersey 07961
201/539-3882

Vineland C/C
P.O. Box 489
Vineland, New Jersey 08360
609/691-7400

Burlington County C/C
P.O. Box 2006
Willingboro, New Jersey 08040
609/877-6879

Woodbridge Metropolitan C/C
655 Amboy Avenue
Woodbridge, New Jersey 07095
201/636-4040

New Mexico

Greater Albuquerque C/C
401 Second Street, NW
Albuquerque, New Mexico 87102
505/842-0220

Las Cruces C/C
760 W. Picacho
Las Cruces, New Mexico 88004
505/524-1968

New York

Albany-Colonie Regional C/C
14 Corporate Woods Boulevard
Albany, New York 12211
518/434-1214

Broome County C/C
P.O. Box 995
Binghampton, New York 13902
607/772-8860

Brooklyn C/C
26 Court Street
Brooklyn, New York 11242
714/875-10000

Cortland County C/C
50 Main Street
Cortland, New York 13045
607/756-5005

Chemumg County C/C
P.O. Box 1115
Elmira, New York 14902
607/734-5137

Huntington Twp. C/C
151 W. Carver Street
Huntington, New York 11743
516/423-6100

Long Island Assn., Inc.
80 Hauppauge Road
Commack, New York 11725
516/499-4400

East Orange C/C
72 Broadway
Newburgh, New York 12550
914/562-5100

Mount Vernon C/C
26 E. First Street, Suite 308
Mount Vernon, New York 10550
914/667-7500

New York C/C and Industry
200 Madison Avenue
New York, New York 10016
212/561-2020

Niagara Falls C/C
401 Buffalo Avenue
Niagara Falls, New York 14303
716/285-9141

Poughkeepsie Area C/C
80 Washington Street
Poughkeepsie, New York 12601
914/454-1700

Rochester Area C/C
55 St. Paul Street
Rochester, New York 14604
716/454-2220

Rome Area C/C
218 Liberty Plaza
Rome, New York 13440
315/337-1700

Greater Saratoga C/C
494 Broadway
Saratoga Springs, New York 12866
518/587-0945

Greater Syracuse C/C
1500 One Mony Plaza
Syracuse, New York 13202
315/422-1343

The County C/C
222 Mamaroneck Avenue
White Plains, New York 10605
914/948-2110

North Carolina

Alamance County C/C
P.O. Box 450
Burlington, North Carolina 27215
919/228-1338

Catawala County C/C
P.O. Box 1828
Hickory, North Carolina 28232
704/328-6111

Greensboro Area C/C
P.O. Box 3246
Greensboro, North Carolina 27402
919/275-8675

Greater Charlotte C/C
P.O. Box 32785
Charlotte, North Carolina 28232
704/377-6911

Reidsville C/C
P.O. Box 1020
Reidsville, North Carolina 27320
919/349-8481

Rocky Mount Area C/C
P.O. Box 392
Rocky Mount, North Carolina
27802-0392
919/442-5111

Greater Wilmington C/C
P.O. Box 330
Wilmington, North Carolina 28401
919/72-2611

Greater Winston-Salem C/C
P.O. Box 1408
Winston-Salem, North Carolina 27102
919/725-2361

North Dakota

Fargo C/C
321 N. Fourth Street
P.O. Box 2443
Fargo, North Dakota 58106
701/725-2361

Ohio

Akron Regional Development Board
Eight Floor, One Cascade Plaza
Akron, Ohio 44306
216/379-3157

Bellevue Area C/C
202 W. Main Street
Bellevue, Ohio 44911
419/483-2182

Bucyrus Area C/C
334 S. Sandusky Avenue
Buycrus, Ohio 44820
419/562-4811

Greater Canton C/C
229 Wells Avenue, N.W.
Canton, Ohio 44703
216/456-7253

Greater Cincinnati C/C
120 W. Fifth Street
Cincinnati, Ohio 45202
513/579-3143

Greater Cleveland Growth Association
690 Union Commerce Building
Cleveland, Ohio 44115
216/621-3300

The Columbus Area C/C
P.O. Box 1527
Columbus, Ohio 43216
614/221-1321

Dayton Area C/C
1980 Winters Bank Tower
Dayton, Ohio 45423
513/226-1444

Defiance Area C/C
P.O. Box 130
Defiance, Ohio 43512
419/782-7946

Greater Hamilton C/C
Six Court Street
Hamilton, Ohio 45011
513/895-5638

Lancaster Area C/C
P.O. Box 193
Lancaster, Ohio 43130
614/653-8251

Lima Area C/C
53 Town Square
Lima, Ohio 45801
419/222-6045

Greater Lorain C/C
204 Fifth Street
Lorain, Ohio 4052
216/244-2292

Middletown Area C/C
36 City Centre Plaza
Middletown, Ohio 45042
513/422-4551

Newark Area C/C
P.O. Box 702
Newark, Ohio 43055
614/345-9757

Piqua Area C/C
P.O. Box 1142
Piqua, Ohio 45356
513/773-2765

Salem Area C/C
417 E. State Street
Salem, Ohio 44460
216/337-3473

Springfield Area C/C
333 N. Limestone Street
Suite 201
Springfield, Ohio 45501
513/325-7621

Toledo Area International Trade
    Association
218 Huron Street
Toledo, Ohio 43604
419/243-8191

Troy C/C
P.O. Box 56
Troy, Ohio 45373
513/339-1716

Youngstown Area C/C
200 Wick Building
Youngstown, Ohio 44503
216/744-2131

Oklahoma

Duncan C/C
P.O. Box 600
Duncan, Oklahoma 73533
405/255-3644

Lawton C/C
P.O. Box 1376
Lawton, Oklahoma 73502
405/355-3541

Metropolitan Tulsa C/C
616 South Boston Avenue
Tulsa, Oklahoma 74119
918/585-1201

Oklahoma City C/C
One Santa Fe Plaza
Oklahoma City, Oklahoma 73102
405/278-8900

Pauls Valley C/C
P.O. Box 638
Pauls Valley, Oklahoma 73075

Stillwater C/C
P.O. Box 1687
Stillwater, Oklahoma 74076
405/372-5573

Oregon

Eugene Area C/C
P.O. Box 1107
Eugene, Oregon 97440
503/484-1314

Gresham Area C/C
P.O. Box 696
Gresham, Oregon 97030
503/65-1131

Salem Area C/C
220 Cottage Street, N.E.
Salem, Oregon 97301
503/581-1466

Portland C/C
824 S.W. Fifth Avenue
Portland, Oregon 97204
503/228-9411

Pennsylvania

Allentown-Lehigh Co. C/C
P.O. Box 1229
Allentown, Pennsylvania 18105
215/437-9661

Beaver Valley C/C
1008 Seventh Avenue
Beaver Falls, Pennsylvania 15010
412/846-6750

Bloomsburg Area C/C
233 Market Street
Bloomsburg, Pennsylvania 17815
717/764-2522

Greater Philadelphia C/C
1617 J.F.K. Boulevard
Philadelphia, Pennsylvania 19103
215/545-1234

Greater Pittsburgh C/C
Three Gateway Center
Suite 1400
Pittsburgh, Pennsylvania 15222
412/392-4506

Greater Wilkes Barre C/C
92 W. Franklin Street
Wilkes Barre, Pennsylvania 18701
717/823-2101

Lower Bucks County C/C
409 Hood Boulevard
Fairless Hills, Pennsylvania 19030
215/943-7400

Pennsylvania C/C
222 North Third Street
Harrisburg, Pennsylvania 17101
717/255-3281

C/C of Reading and Berks County
541 Court Street, P.O. Box 1698
Reading, Pennsylvania 19603
215/376-6766

Greater Scranton C/C
426 Mulberry Street
Scranton, Pennsylvania 18503
717/342-7711

State College Area C/C
444 East College Avenue
State College, Pennsylvania 16801
814/237-7644

Warren County C/C
P.O. Box 942
Warren, Pennsylvania 16365
814/723-3050

Greater Washington Area C/C
Millcraft Center, 90 W, Chestnut St.
Washington, Pennsylvania 15301
412/225-3010

York Area C/C
P.O. Box 1229
York, Pennsylvania 17405
717/848-4000

Puerto Rico

Puerto Rico C/C
P.O. Box 6789
San Juan, Puerto Rico 00904
809/721-6060

Rhode Island

Greater Providence C/C
10 Durrance Street
Providence, Rhode Island 02903
401/521-5000

South Carolina

Beaufort C/C
P.O. Box 910
Beaufort, South Carolina 29902
803/524-3163

Kingstree C/C, Inc.
130 E. Main Street
Kingstree, South Carolina 29556
803/354-6431

Rock Hill Area C/C
P.O. Box 590
Rock Hill, South Carolina 29731
803/324-7500

Spartanburg C/C
P.O. Box 1636
Spartanburg, South Carolina 29304
803/585-8722

Tennessee

Greater Chattanooga C/C
1001 Market Street
Chattanooga, Tennessee 37402
615/756-2121

Dyersburg-Dyer County C/C
P.O. Box 443
Dyersburg, Tennessee 38024
901/285-3435

Greater Knoxville C/C
P.O. Box 2229
Knoxville, Tennessee 37901
615/637-4550

Johnson City-Washington County
   C/C
P.O. Box 180
Johnson City, Tennessee 37601
615/926-2141

Memphis Area C/C
P.O. Box 224
Memphis, Tennessee 38101
901/523-2322

Morristown Area C/C
P.O. Box 9
Morristown, Tennessee 37814
615/586-6283

Nashville Area C/C
161 Fourth Avenue, N.
Nashville, Tennessee 37219
615/259-3900

Putnam County C/C
302 South Jefferson
Cookerville, Tennessee 38501
15/526-2211

Shelbyville-Bedford Co. C/C
100 N. Cannon Boulevard
Shelbyville, Tennessee 37160
615/684-3482

Texas

Amarillo C/C
301 Polk Street
Amarillo, Texas 79101
806/374-5238

Mexican-American C/C
P.O. Box 1173
Austin, Texas 78767
512/476-7502

Austin C/C
P.O. Box 1967
Austin, Texas 78767
512/478-6289

Beaumont C/C
P.O. Box 3150
Beaumont, Texas 77704
713/836-856l

Big Spring Area C/C
P.O. Box 1391
Big Spring, Texas 79721
915/263-7641

Corpus Christi C/C
P.O. Box 640
Corpus Christi, Texas 78403
512/882-6161

De Soto C/C
P.O. Box 100
Desoto, Texas 75115
214/224-3565

Fort Worth C/C
700 Throckmorton Street
Fort Worth, Texas 76102
817/336-2491

Gainesville C/C
P.O. Box 518
Gainesville, Texas 76240
817/665-2831

Harlingen Area C/C
311 E. Tyler, P.O. Box 189
Harlingen, Texas
512/423-5440

Houston C/C
1110 Milam Building, 25th Floor
Houston, Texas 77002
713/651-1313

North Channel Area C/C
P.O. Box 9652
Houston, Texas 77213
713/455-3860

Humble Area C/C
P.O. Box 3337
Humble, Texas 77338
713/446-2128

Huntsville-Walker Co. C/C
P.O. Box 538
Huntsville, Texas 77340
409/295-8113

Lubbock C/C
P.O. Box 561
Lubbock, Texas 79408
806/763-4666

Odessa C/C
P.O. Box 3626
Odessa, Texas 79760
512/552-2959

Port Lavaca C/C
P.O. Box 528
Port Lavaca, Texas 77979
512/552-2959

Greater San Antonio C/C
P.O. Box 1628
San Antonio, Texas 78206
512/229-2100

Sinton C/C
P.O. Box 217
Sinton, Texas 78387
512/364-2307

Victoria C/C
P.O. Box 2465
Victoria, Texas 77902
512/573-5277

Utah

Bountiful Area C/C
P.O. Box 99
Bountiful, Utah 84010
801/295-6944

Salt Lake Area C/C
19 East Second, South
Salt Lake City, Utah 84111
801/364-3631

Vermont

Burlington C/C
P.O. Box 453
Burlington, Vermont 05402
802/863-3489

Montpelier C/C
P.O. Box 37
Montpelier, Vermont 05602
802/223-3443

Virgin Islands

St. Thomas and St. John C/C
P.O. Box 324
St. Thomas, U.S. Virgin Islands 00801
809/776-0100

Virginia

Arlington c/C
4600 N. Fairfax Drive
Arlington, Virginia 22203
703/525-2400

Charlottesville-Albemarle C/C
P.O. Box 1564
Charlottesville, Virginia 22902
804/295-3141

City of Fairfax C/C
10856 Main Street
Fairfax, Virginia 22030
703/591-5550

Greater Manassas C/C
P.O. Box 495
Manassas, Virginia 22110
703/379-4813

Norfolk C.C
420 Bank Street
Norfolk, Virginia 23501
804/622-2312

Peninsula C/C
1800 W. Mercury Boulevard
Hampton, Virginia 23666
804-838-4182

Metropolitan Richmond C/C
201 E. Franklin Street
Richmond, Virginia 23219
804/648-1234

Virginia State C/C
611 E. Franklin Street
Richmond, Virginia 23219
804/643-7491

Winchester-Fredrick County Chamber
    of Commerce
2 North Cameron Street
Winchester, Virginia 22601
703/662-4118

Washington

Bellevue C/C
100 116th Avenue, SE
Bellevue, Washington 98005
206/454-2464

Chehalis C/C
P.O. Box 666
Chehalis, Washington 98532
206/748-8885

Pullman C/C
North 415 Grand
Pullman, Washington 99163
509/334-3565

Greater Renton C/C
300 Ranier Avenue, North
Renton, Washington 98055
206/226-4560

Seattle C/C
215 Columbia Street
Seattle, Washington 98104
206/447-7263

Tacoma Area C/C
P.O. Box 1933
Tacoma, Washington 98401
206/627-2175

Walla Walla Area C/C
P.O. Box 644
Walla Walla, Washington 99362
509/525-0850

Westport-Grayland C/C
P.O. Box 306
Westport, Washington 98595
206/268-9422

Greater Yakima C/C
P.O. Box 1490
Yakima, Washington 98907
509/248-2021

West Virginia

Beckley-Raleigh County C/C
P.O. Box 1798
Beckley, West Virginia 25801
304/252-7328

West Virginia C/C
P.O. Box 2789
Charleston, West Virginia 25330
304/342-1115

Huntington Area C/C
P.O. Box 1509
Huntington, West Virginia 25716
304/525-5131

Princeton-Mercer County C/C
P.O.Box 750
Princeton, West Virginia 24740
304/487-1502

Weirton C/C
3370 Main Street
Weirton, West Virginia 26062
304/748-7212

Wisconsin

Fox Cities C/C
P.O. Box 1855
Appleton, Wisconsin 54913
414/734-7101

Greater La Crosse C/C
P.O. Box 219
La Crosse, Wisconsin 54601
608/748-4880

Maintowoc-Two Rivers C/C
P.O. Box 603
Manitowoc, Wisconsin 54220
414/684-5575

Metropolitan Milwaukee Association
    of Commerce
756 N. Milwaukee Street
Milwaukee, Wisconsin 53202
414/273-3000

Racine C/C
731 Main Street
Racine, Wisconsin 53403
414/633-2451

Sparta Area C/C
P.O. Box 26
Sparta, Wisconsin 54656
608/269-4123

Superior Area C/C
1419 Towor Avenue
Superior, Wisconsin 54880
715/394-7716

Wausau Area C/C
P.O. Box 569
Wausau, Wisconsin 54401
715/845-6231

West Bend C/C
P.O. Box 522
West Bend, Wisconsin 53095
414/338-2666

Wyoming

Casper Area C/C
P.O. Box 399
Casper, Wyoming 82602
307/234-5311

Jackson Hole Area C/C
P.O. Box E.
Jackson, Wyoming 83001
307/733-3316

Laramie C/C
P.O. Box 1166
Laramie, Wyoming 82070
307/745-7339

Powell C/C
P.O.Box 814
Powell, Wyoming 82435
307/754-3494

Edited by Alessandra Onorati

Appendix 11

Laws Restraining Termination of Agency Agreements

In the course of its contact with business officials who have, or have had, a foreign representative or agent, the Commerce Department has found that one issue stands out as the most troublesome; namely, laws in a growing number of countries allow onerous economic remedies or sanctions to be lodged against principals who terminate, or fail to renew, agency or distributor agreements without legal justification. These laws, which typically override the provisions of the contract if there is a conflict, can make the severing of an undesirable relationship with a foreign agent or distributor very painful for the principal in terms of the indemnification he is obliged to make. Occasionally, a termination, even if carried out according to the requirements of the local law, may result in protracted litigation or an unwarranted settlement, when the foreign agent utilizes the nuisance possibilities in the often ambiguous legislation.

The proliferation of these agency termination laws can, in part, be traced back to the sudden increase in international trade that occurred following World War II. This surge of international business created an urgent demand for sales representation all over the world. Good agents and distributors were in short supply and

Source: Foreign Business Practices, U.S. Department of Commerce, International Trade Administration, Washington, D.C., April 1985.

there simply were not enough capable ones available to help provide the indispensable local outlets for the export product of the developed countries. As a result, in many instances little or no discretion was used to select foreign agents and distributors, the agreements, were often hastily drawn and the terms were inadequately understood by the local agents. A great number of those relationships ended in dissatisfaction and failure. These failures resulted in large numbers of terminations or modifications of contracts and replacements of agents by their principals.

In addition to this historical problem, other circumstances gave rise to continuing conflicts between the principal and the agent. The agency agreement is a contract and all contracts carry an unwritten question mark as to their future execution. This question eventually impinges upon the duration and execution of the agreement as well as the parties; expectation of the mutual profit involved. It is issues such as these which determine whether the relationship is a success or a failure, and whether it will endure or terminate.

Actions taken by the principal in changing the management, policy, or corporate structure may have effects which determine whether the parties to an agency contract are satisfied with the relationship and whether it may require modification or termination. With the passage of time, agency relationships may deteriorate and whether termination or a substantial overhaul of the agency or distributorship may be in order to improve its productivity, efficiency, or some other feature. Furthermore, imponderable and unforeseen circumstances, such as are sometimes described as *force majeure*, may play havoc with the best laid plans. Domestic market changes may limit the agent or the principal in the ability to perform their respective rights and obligations under the agreement. Legislative enactment of an economic or financial nature may damage beyond recovery a business deal, thereby forcing the termination of the business operation. And finally, political occurrences and social upheavals may require the cancellation or termination of the contract.

Since the local agents in foreign countries were often dissatisfied with the consequences described above, the governments in many countries, and particularly the Latin American countries, were put under political pressure to enact legislation to protect their nationals against what they considered arbitrary behavior by the foreign principals to an agency agreement. As a result, a growing number of nations have enacted contract termination laws, which unilaterally penalize the foreign principals by making it difficult to terminate the agency relationships without severe economic hardship. These laws restrict the freedom of the contracting parties to fashion the terms of their agreements to suit themselves, and are weighted in favor of the agent in the event of a contract termination. In fact, they make it practically impossible to terminate a foreign agency agreement without incurring substantial expenditures.

However, many countries have not followed this trend and have no special legislation penalizing or precluding the termination of agency agreements. The laws of these countries generally uphold the principle that parties to any agency contract are free to establish their mutually agreed legal terms and conditions. This freedom includes the right to express the intentions of the contracting parties as to termination, and violation of the contract terms usually subjects the offending party to damages. Most of the countries in this category operate under Anglo-Saxon common law principles, although some civil law countries in Latin America, Europe, Africa, and Asia also support the right to contractual freedom on the issue of agency terminations.

In countries that have agency termination legislation, the thrust of the laws is to go beyond the written or implied agreement to the underlying basis of the principal-agent relationship. They assume that the agent or distributor has a proprietary interest in the local market he has developed, as well as in the creation of goodwill for the principal's products or services. An economic value is then assigned to this abstract interest of the agent in an amount proportional to that of the duration of the agency. Accordingly, unless the deprivation is for a justified cause specified by the law, the agent is entitled to receive monetary compensation when his legally protected interest is terminated by the principal.

Even though these laws exact financial penalties for "unjust" terminations they do nothing to eradicate the causes for dissatisfaction that lead to an eventual termination. Therefore, in most cases they do little more than penalize foreign principals who wish to terminate their relationship with local agents.

These laws often discriminate against foreign principals, by exempting domestic principals from the obligations they place on foreign principals. At times, this discriminatory effect appears to be contrary to the provision of these countries' own constitutions and their mercantile and civil codes, which guarantee equal treatment for nationals and foreigners in the exercise of business in the country. These agency laws, when addressed solely to foreign principals, may indeed violate the spirit, if not the letter of commercial treaties or conventions, which guarantee national or non-discriminatory treatment for nationals of the signatory parties in their business relations in the host country.

CHARACTERISTICS OF THESE LAWS

A survey of these agency termination laws indicates that they have many common characteristics. For example:

- All these laws tend to strengthen the agent's position under the contract, obliging the principal to compensate the agent according to scheduled rates for damages or losses caused by termination of the agency agreement without just cause. These protective laws define the words "just cause" or the equivalent, in situations where there has been termination of the contract according to law or the terms of the agency contract. Such laws then list and describe the reasons and situations under which an agency agreement may be validly terminated, i.e., incompetence of the agent or a serious decrease in sales or distribution due to circumstances attributable to the agent. The contract terms are valid if they do not violate any specific provisions of the protective laws.

- Laws declaring unwaivable the compensation and perhaps other rights granted to the agent by the protective legislation.
- Laws that establish the law of the enacting state as the sole applicable law; these preclude the parties from validly electing some other country's law to govern the contract.
- Laws placing agents on the same footing as employees, thus entitling them to the benefits of the local labor laws governing dismissal and compensation for discharging employees without just cause.
- Laws requiring that the agent be given notice of the termination some time prior to its effective date. Some of these laws require compensating the agent for the accrual of commissions during the notice period. Other laws require the principal to compensate the agent for the goodwill generated by the agent during the life of the agency agreement. In certain cases the compensation may take the form of a pension.
- Laws that allow an agent to contest a notice of termination by submitting the controversy to arbitration to determine whether the principal has a just cause for ending the relationship.
- Laws condoning the refusal to extend an expired agency agreement only upon a showing of just cause.

Given the fact that many countries now have these agency termination laws in effect, the principal can best minimize the risks involved by addressing the problems these laws create at the time the agency is established. This can be done by being aware of the particulars of these laws and then by taking great care in two aspects of creating a foreign agency-(1) selection of the agent or distributor, and (2) negotiation and drafting of the terms of the representational agreement.

HOW COMMERCE CAN HELP

The Department of Commerce can help when a potential principal wants to take advantage of either or both of these precautionary measures. The International Trade Administration offers a number of services intended to help U.S. business in the selection and appointment of foreign representatives.The Office of Trade Finance can provide information, assistance, and advice regarding the scope of foreign laws on agencies including those affecting terminations, and can supply guides and illustrative material on the preparation of a representational contract. The ITA services for finding and selecting an agent are as follows:

Trade List Service: Names and addresses of foreign distributors, agents, purchasers, and other firms, classified by the product they handle and the services they offer, are made available to U.S. firms through printed Trade lists. Some of the lists are produced from information in the Foreign Traders Index. Others are prepared from data compiled in connection with export promotion programs and from other sources.

The availability of new or revised trade lists is announced regularly in the Department's biweekly Commerce Publications Update. A catalog of Trade Lists is available from Commerce District Offices or from: U.S. Department of Commerce. Office of Trade Information Services, Room ITA 1837, Washington, D.C. 20203

Agent Distributor Service: The Agent Distributor Service (ADS) helps U.S. firms find agents or distributors for their products in almost every country in the world. U.S. Commercial Officers overseas will identify up to six foreign firms that expressed interest in a specific U.S. proposal, for a nominal fee. Application forms may be obtained from any Commerce Department District Office. Trade specialists at District Offices will help a U.S. firm prepare an application. They will offer guidance and determine whether there are factors to discourage a business relationship.

World Traders Data Report Service: A World Traders Data Report (WTDR) is a trade profile that contains detailed commercial information, including financial references, on an individual foreign firm. WTDRS are prepared by the U.S. Foreign Service. A typical report includes background information on the firm, type of organization, year established, number of employees, size of firm, sales area, method of operation, lines handled, name of officers, general reputation in trade and financial circles, and names of the firm's trading connections, WTDRS are available from: U.S. Department of Commerce. Office of Trade Information Services, Room 1315, Washington, D.C. 20230

The complete name and address of the foreign firm must be submitted when ordering WTDRS. U.S. firms may contact the Commerce Department's Office of Trade Information Services in Washington, D.C., or the nearest Commerce District Office, where a trade specialist will assist in completing a request.

PROTECTING THE PRINCIPAL

As to the principal's ability to safeguard his position though the contents of the representational agreement itself, the following should be noted:

The agency agreement should be in writing. The rights and obligations resulting from a written agreement require no extraneous proof and are necessary to record, or prove the terms of a contract in many countries. Failure to reduce such contracts to writing may subject the contract and, consequently, the relationship, to the arbitrary whim of local law.

The agreement should set forth the benefits to both parties. Well-balanced agreements should not place an excessive or profitless burden on one of the parties. Otherwise, performance of the agreement may be impossible to enforce against the party who has no apparent benefit from it. This is particularly true if the enforcement is against a local agent.

A clear definition and meaning must be given to all contract terms. The accepted meaning of contractual terms is a frequent source of confusion and misunderstanding in foreign trade contracts. Many English words, having similar external spelling formation as foreign words, may have entirely different meaning. There should always be an English version of the agreement, which is expressly allowed to prevail in cases of doubt or controversy as to the meaning of contractual terms. To avoid any conflict on this matter the parties may adopt as controlling "The Revised American Foreign Trade Definitions." These definitions have been prepared by the Chamber of Commerce of the United States, 1615 H Street, N.W., Washington, D.C. 20006, with the assistance of The National Council of American Importers, Inc., and the National Foreign Trade Council. Another aid to the certainty of terms is to conform the meaning of contractual terms to the definitions supplied by the International Chamber of Commerce in its publication entitled "INCOTERMS" (1212 Avenue of Americas, New York, N.Y. 10036).

The rights and obligations of the parties should always be expressly stated. Some of the restrictions placed on the agency contract by foreign laws may be waived, provided that these waivers are expressly agreed to in the agency contract. The agency contract should also contain a description of the rights and duties of each party, the nature, character, and duration of the relationship and, where possible, the causes of conditions under which the agreement may be terminated.

Jurisdictional clause. Many foreign laws require that any adjudication of conflicts which arise pursuant to the representational agreement be referred to local courts. On the other hand, if local laws allow, it is advisable to specify in the contract the jurisdiction to handle any legal disputes which might arise, since the principal can thereby avoid exposure of such conflicts to unfamiliar laws and legal systems.

Arbitration. This could prove to be a useful avenue for avoiding litigation in foreign countries. Basic arbitration rules and principles are generally the same everywhere. A clause in the contract may be a general arbitration statement or a decision to arbitrate only specific issues. Such clauses should also contain an identification of the arbitration body or forum, and a statement as to the chosen arbitration rules and procedures. Model arbitration clauses may be obtained upon request from the American Arbitration Assn., 140 West 51st St., New York, N.Y. 10020, or the International Chamber of Commerce, 1212 Avenue of the Americas, New York, N.Y. 10036.

The impact of foreign laws on the contract should be carefully considered. What is a legally valid clause in one country may be nugatory or invalid in another. The drafter must therefore be familiar with the legal rules applicable to his contract, because the omission or invalidation of a particular clause may cause important issues under the contract to be decided according to the vicissitudes, or occasional chaos, of local laws.

CENTRAL AND SOUTH AMERICA

Argentina—Principal-agent relations are basically governed by the Civil and Commercial Codes. No special legislation has been enacted to regulate the termination of agency agreements.

Law No. 20575 of January 2, 1974 requires that representatives of foreign principals be registered in the appropriate section of the Foreign Investment Register. A copy of the contract must accompany the petition for registration.

When the representative is a natural person the agency may be regulated by Law No. 11,544 of 1929, as amended. In particular, Law 14,546 of 1958 extends Labor Law benefits to business agents. The parties may not elect foreign laws to govern the agreement. If a contract is executed abroad to avoid Argentine law, it will not be enforced by Argentine courts.

The Civil and Commercial Codes permit a principal to terminate an agency agreement at his discretion. However, the terminating party may be liable for damages resulting from a wrongful termination. All agreements, whether for a definite or an indefinite term, should include a notice of termination clause.

Labor laws similarly require the service of a termination notice sometime prior to the actual termination date; otherwise, the principal may be liable to the employee for earnings that would have accrued during the notification period. In all termination cases, except for those based on a just cause, the agent is entitled to one month's compensation for each year of service, payable in a lump sum.

Bolivia —The principal-agent relationship is governed by articles 1248—1259 of the Commercial Code, as enacted by the law of March 29, 1977. The parties are free to agree to the terms of their contract within the limits of the code provisions.

Except when otherwise provided by the agency agreement, an agent may not carry on the same line of business for two or more competing principals, and a principal may not appoint more than one agent in the same territory for the same line of goods. The contract must be recorded with the commercial Registrar and include (1) scope of the representative's authority, (2) agent's field of activity, (3) duration of the representation, (4) territory of the agency, and (5) agent's remuneration. Choice of law clauses are not valid; only Bolivian law applies. The agent is entitled to a commission when the principal transacts business within the territory assigned to the agent, unless otherwise provided in the agency contract.

A principal may terminate the agency agreement without incurring liability in any of the following situations: (1) breach by the agent of any obligation in the agency contract; (2) an act, or failure to act, by the agent that adversely affects the interest of the other party to the agreement; (3) an apparent decrease in business operations, which is contrary to contractual provisions and attributable to the fault of the agent; and (4) bankruptcy, incapacity or disability of either the agent or principal.

The agent may retain amounts due his principal and exercise a privileged security interest in the principal's goods or property to the extent of his unpaid commissions. Legal actions based on the agency contract are subject to a 5-year statute of limitations.

Brazil—The principal-agent relationship is governed by Law No. 4886, in force as of December 10, 1965. Although the parties may freely stipulate the terms of their agency contracts, provisions on the following must be included: the conditions and general requirements of the representation; an identification of the products subject to the representation; the period of representation, whether definite or indefinite; the terms and time of payment for carrying out the representation; the zone in which the representation will be exercised (including (1) whether the principal is excluded from doing business within the zone. (2) whether such exclusivity is partially or wholly guaranteed, and for what period. and (3) the restrictions, if any, to zone exclusivity). A provision for the indemnity due the agent upon the principal's terminating the agreement without notice is also required, and this indemnity must not be less than one-twentieth of the compensation earned during the representation.

Agency agreements may be terminated for just cause. Under Law No. 4886 the definition of just cause is limited to the following: the agent's negligence; the agent's breach of the contract; acts by the agent damaging to the principal; and conviction of the agent for a serious criminal offense.

Fixed term agreements terminate on the date provided. Indefinite terms agreements are terminable without just cause after the first 6 months. In all cases, except when other provisions for termination have been agreed upon, service of notice prior to termination is obligatory. If the principal fails to serve such notice, compensation is due the agent amounting to one-third of the earnings accrued during the last 3 months just prior to termination.

Chile—No special protective legislation has been enacted to regulate the termination of agency agreements. The principal-agent relationship is governed by the terms of the agency contract within the limits of Civil and Commercial Code provisions.

Under the Codes, the principal may revoke the agency at any time, either by means of serving termination notice on the agent or merely by appointing another agent. The Commercial Register requires recordation of agency agreements, and notification of termination of agencies. The Registrar may also require that local third party rights be preserved and unaffected by the termination.

Agency and distributorship agreements may also terminate automatically by (1) expiration of the contract term; (2) resignation of the agent; (3) death of the principal or agent; (4) bankruptcy or insolvency or either party; (5) legal incompetence of either party; (6) marriage of a woman agent; and (7) termination of the functions of the principal, if the agency was based on the exercise of such functions.

Colombia—The Commercial Code of Colombia as set forth in Decree No. 410 of March 27, 1971, governs commercial agencies and distributorships. This includes provisions covering the termination of agency agreements and establishing liability for unjust termination by the principal.

Although the parties are free to stipulate the terms of their mutual arrangement, the agency contract must provide for the scope of the agent's authority, the duration of the relationship and the territory encompassed by the agency. Unless otherwise provided in the contract the agency is presumed to be exclusive. Colombian law is the only law that may apply to the agency agreement and, therefore, choice of law clauses are not recognized.

If the principal should terminate the agency contract, the agent has the right to claim, as compensation from the principal for each year of contract duration, an amount equal to 1/12 (one twelfth) of the average commission or remuneration received during the previous 3 years, or the yearly average of everything received if the contract duration is shorter than 3 years.

If the principal terminates the agency relationship without just cause, the agent may also claim compensation for his success in establishing or building up goodwill for the principal's business. The amount of such compensation will be terminated by the Courts, taking into account the amount of time the agent has represented the principal under the agreement and the volume and importance of the principal's business conducted by the agent.

The causes justifying termination of the agency agreement by the principal are: (1) a breach by the agent of his contractual or legal obligation to the principal, (2) an act or default by the agent which results in damage to the principal's business interests, (3) the agent's insolvency or bankruptcy, or (4) liquidation by the principal of the business activity on which the agency contract is based.

If the agency is terminated for any of these listed reasons, the principal is not obliged to compensate the agent.

Costa Rica—Civil and Commercial Codes govern the agency contract. Termination of agency, distributorship and manufacturing agreements and remedies attached thereto are regulated by Law No. 6209 of February 24, 1978, in effect as of April 3, 1978, as amended by Executive Decree No. 8599 of May 5, 1978.

Under the codes the parties may freely stipulate the terms of their contract. However, choice of law clauses and contractual waivers by the representative of any rights granted to him by Law 6209 are not valid.

The law established a 2-year statue of limitations for claims arising under contracts regulated by Law 6209. This law extends to local manufacturers the same rights and protection as previously available to agents, distributors, and manufacturers. This rule applies when the Costa Rican manufacturer uses foreign materials and technologies to make or package goods or merchandise bearing a foreign trademark.

A principal may be held liable to compensate the representative distributor or manufacturer for the unilateral termination, without just cause, or when the principal refuses, without just cause, to renew a definite term contract at expiration. Law 6209 defines the following situations as "just cause" under which a principal may, without incurring damage liability, unilaterally terminate the contract or refuse to renew an expired definite term agreement: (1) commission of a crime by the representative, distributor, or manufacturer against the principal's property or good reputation; (2) negligence or ineptitude of the representative judicially declared by a local court, or continuous stagnation or substantial decrease in sales due to the fault of the representative (import and sale quotas establish a prima facie case against the charge of negligence or ineptitude); (3) breach by the representative of his duty of secrecy and loyalty to the principal; (4) any other serious act by the representative, distributor, or manufacturer in breach of his contractual duty resulting in harm to the principal.

When the representational, distributorship, or manufacturing contract is unilaterally terminated, or when the principal refuses, without just cause, to renew an expired definite term agreement, the principal must indemnify the agent, distributor, or manufacturer with an amount equal to four times the monthly gross profit average resulting from multiplying such gross profit averages by the number of years or fractions thereof of contract duration.

For representational contracts the monthly gross profit average shall be computed by adding up the last four years, commissions divided by the number of months of contract duration.

For distributors or co-distributors, monthly gross profit averages shall be computed by adding up the last 2 years' profits, divided by the number of months of contract duration.

For manufacturers, monthly gross profit averages shall be computed by adding up the last 4 years' profits divided by the number of months of contract duration.

The maximum indemnity shall not exceed the total of 36 months indemnification.

Compensation may also include expenses incurred by the representative in setting up the agency and the cost of items purchased to operate the agency. The Ministry of Economy, Commerce and Industry determines the amount to be paid as compensation.

Until the indemnity is paid, the principal must post a warranty bond to cover the amount of the claim. Failure to post bond or pay the adjudicated indemnification may result in prohibition of the importation of the principal's goods into the country.

Dominican Republic—Agency contracts are governed by the Civil and Commercial Codes. The dissolution of agency contracts is regulated by Law No. 173 of April 16, 1966, as amended by Law No. 263 of December 31, 1971, and Law 622 of December 28, 1973 (effective as of December 29, 1973). These laws afford the agent or representative specific remedies for unjust termination of the agency agreement, if the agreement has been registered with the Exchange Department of the Central Bank of the Dominican Republic within 15 days of its execution.

Although the parties to an agency agreement are free to stipulate as to its terms, the law invalidates any waiver by the local agent of his rights. These rights obligate the principal or any substitute, intermediary, or replacement acting on the principal's behalf and any person or firm acquiring the right to act under the agreement to compensate the agent for his damages in the event (1) the agent is unjustifiably dismissed or substituted; (2) the principal, his assignee, or representative terminates or refuses to renew the agreement without just cause; or (3) the principal, his assignee, or representative takes over the agent's business without just cause.

The agent's damages for unjust termination or refusal to renew an agency agreement may cover all losses the agent has suffered because of his previous efforts on behalf of the principal's business, including: (1) labor law employee compensation obligations of the agent, (2) the actual value of all investments and expenses the agent incurred in setting up and running the business, (3) the value of the agent's inventories and stock, and (4) the value of the agent's lost profits. The principal may also be obliged to pay an additional amount equal to the total of the agent's gross profit for the previous 5 years. If the agency has been in effect for less than 5 years, the compensation is set at five times the average annual profit during the previous years of actual representation.

Just cause for a principal's refusal to renew, or for terminating, an agency agreement is set forth in the law as follows: (1) breach by the agent of any of the essential obligations of the contract, or (2) any action or commission by the agent which substantially harms the principal's interest in the promotion or development of his business.

Ecuador—The principal-agent relationship is governed by Supreme Decree 1038—A. Official Register 245, of December 28, 1976, effective December 31, 1976. This law is entitled: "Law on Protection for Representatives, Agents, and Dealers of Foreign Corporations in Ecuador." Foreign noncorporate or private individual principals are also subject to the provisions of Decree 1038—A

Notwithstanding any contract clause providing otherwise, a principal may not unilaterally modify, terminate, or refuse to renew an agency or distributorship agreement, except for "just cause" judicially determined.

"Just cause" under which a principal may validly terminate a representational agreement is limited to: (1) the agent's failure to discharge his legal or contractual obligations; (2) any act or omission by the agent that substantially and adversely affects the principal's interest in the promotion, marketing, or distribution of his merchandise or services; (3) the agent's insolvency or bankruptcy; and (4) termination of the business. A principal may be held liable to compensate the agent in the event of an unjust termination of the contract. A court will take account of the following factors in assessing damages: (1) value of items purchased and expenses incurred by the agent in setting up and operating the business; (2) value of the agent's unsalable inventories and stock; (3) value of the business goodwill promoted by the agent to be determined in consideration to the following: (a) duration of the relationship, (b) actual volume of sales by the agent vis-a-vis the principal's business, (c) amount of Ecuador's market share acquired by the agent's efforts; and (d) any other equitable factor available to determine the damages suffered by the agent because of the unjust termination of the agreement.

All controversies between a principal and agent must be decided by the local courts having jurisdiction over the agent. The Civil and Commercial Codes apply concerning matters not covered by Supreme Decree 1038—A.

El Salvador—The law regulating principals and agents is found in the Commercial Code (arts 392-399b.), as amended by Decree No. 247 of January 9, 1973.

Agency and distributorship contracts may be terminated by either the principal or the agent by giving written notice 3 months prior to termination. However, a principal may not terminate, modify, or refuse to renew an agency contract without just cause. If a contract is unilaterally and unjustly terminated, the injured party has a right to claim damages.

An agent or distributor whose representation is unjustifiably terminated may claim (1) the unrecoverable expenses which he has incurred for the benefit of the agency; (2) the value of the physical assets of the agency which have no alternative use, including equipment, fixtures, furniture, and implements; (3) the value of this unsalable merchandise, stock, and accessories; (4) an amount equal to his gross profit experience, not to exceed the latest 3 years of representation; and (5) the value of credit has extended to purchasers of the principal's products.

As amended, the Code defines just cause for termination as a (1) breach by the agent of the contract; (2) the agents fraud or abuse of the principal's trust; (3) the agent's incompetence or negligence; (4) a continued decrease in sales for reasons attributable to the agent; (5) the disclosure by the agent of confidential information; or (6) any act of the agent reflecting adversely on the agency, the principal's products, or their sale and distribution.

If the principal is found to have dismissed an agent without just cause, the principal may not import his products, trademarks, or services into El Salvador until the compensation lawfully due to the agent is paid in full.

All controversies between a principal and his agent must be decided by the local court having jurisdiction over the agent.

Guatemala—The principal-agent relationship is governed by Decree No. 78-71, of September 25, 1971, supplemented by nonabrogated provisions of Decree No.

270 of May 1970 and applicable provisions of the Civil and Commercial Codes. The agency contract may only be terminated by written consent of the parties, by expiration of the contract according to its terms, for just cause according to the terms of Decree 78-71, by the agent by giving 3-months' notice to the principal, and by the principal upon agreement to pay compensation to the agent.

The word "agent" while including independent distributors and representatives, does not apply to commercial agents, resale wholesalers, or dependent distributors, when they are subject to either a broader contractual obligation to the principal or a typical labor law agreement.

Just cause for the principal's terminating the agreement is defined as any of the following: (1) a breach by the agent of any of his contractual obligations to the principal, (2) the commission by the agent of a criminal offense against the person or property of the principal, (3) the unjustified refusal by the agent to render accounts due or proceeds of liquidation in accord with the terms of the contract, (4) the agent's disclosure to third parties of confidential information entrusted to him by the principal or (5) a decrease in sales of the principal's products or services due to the agent's negligence or incompetence as determined by a Court of Law.

In the event of an unjust termination by the principal, the agent may claim as compensation an amount including (1) direct promotional expense incurred by the agent in carrying out the agency, (2) the cost of all unrecoverable investments made by the agent in pursuit of the contract, (3) the value of any unsold merchandise in the agent's possession, provided it is in good condition, (4) 50 percent of the presumed gross profits on the sale of such unsold merchandise, and (5) an amount equal to the gross profits to the agent during the period the contract has run, or during the previous 3 years, whichever is less. The principal is also liable to the agent for all Labor Law compensation claims dismissed employees of the agent may have as a result of the termination.

The parties may mutually consent to the amount of compensation due the agent for unjust termination by the principal, and in case of an unresolved dispute as to such amount the issue will be determined by the courts. If the principal has been sued by the agent for unjust termination, he may be prohibited from conducting business in Guatemala, either directly or indirectly, until the suit is settled or the agent's claim is paid. The principal may avoid this prohibition on doing business in Guatemala by posting a bond to guarantee payment of the amount of any possible damage claim against him. A continuation of business under prohibition and without securing such bond will subject the principal to a fine ranging from $50 to $5,000 (50 to 5,000 quetzales).

Haiti—No special legislation has been enacted to regulate the termination of agency and distributorship agreements. The principal-agent relationship is regulated by Presidential Decree of September 26, 1960, supplemented by applicable provisions of the Civil and Commercial Codes. Labor Law provisions apply when the agent is a natural person subject to an employment contract.

The parties are free to stipulate the conditions and obligations of their agreement, including agency termination clauses, subject to the limitations of the 1960 Decree as well as to Codes and Labor Laws.

Under the provisions of the Decree, only Haitian national or Haitian corporations may act as agents for foreign principals. Foreign visiting businessmen, as well as foreign traveling agents, must obtain authorization to operate in Haiti and be accompanied by a licensed Haitian agent while visiting clients or soliciting business. Additionally, all merchandise imports may be made only through Haitian representatives established in Haiti.

Under the Codes, the agency contract should include an identification of the agency territory, a list of the respective duties and obligations of the agent and principal, the remuneration to be paid to the agent, the duration of the agreement, the requirements for service of a termination notice, and the jurisdiction governing the agreement. Under the labor laws a waiver of legal rights is not recognized. Notice of contract termination is required except when the contract is terminated for just cause. The amount of notice that must be given in advance of the termination date varies from 8 days for contracts having been in effect for 3 months to 1 year, to 2 months' notice when a contract has been in effect for more than 10 years. Failure to give the appropriate notice subjects the principal to liability for the remuneration to which the agent would have otherwise been entitled had such notice been given.

Honduras—The principal-agent relationship is governed by Law-Decree No. 549 of November 24, 1977 (effective December 27, 1977), supplemented by applicable provisions of the Commercial and Civil Codes.

Only Honduran nationals, or Honduran legal entities who are members of the corresponding local Chamber of Commerce, may engage in the profession of representing national or foreign firms. Except in cases where the parties agree to submit to arbitration or conciliation procedures, the parties must submit to the jurisdiction of the laws and courts of Honduras concerning all actions arising under the agency relationship. Any contract clause to the contrary is invalid.

A principal may not terminate, modify, or refuse to renew the agency or distributorship contract except for just cause. Termination without just cause subjects the principal to liability for the damages suffered by the agent. Compensation for such damages may include: 5 years' gross profits, or five times average gross profits in contracts of less than 5 years' duration; the value of the agent's investment in premises, equipment, installation, furniture, and utensils, which have no alternative use; the agent's outlay for unsaleable merchandise, stock and accessories; the value of that portion of goodwill generated by the agent's own effort, determined by considering the duration of the agent, the proportional share of the principal's sales or service volume in relation to the agent's total business, the share of the Honduran market which the product or service represents, and any other factor quantifying goodwill.

The following are, under Article 12 of the Law, valid justifications for termination of the agency agreement: (1) the agent's breach of an essential contract clause or obligation assumed under the contract; (2) fraud or abuse of the principal's trust;

(3) continued decrease in sales or services due to the agent's fault, ineptitude, or negligence; (4) the agent's refusal to render accounts to the principal; (5) disclosure by the agent of confidential information; (6) bankruptcy, insolvency, or interdiction of the agent; and (7) any other act attributable to the agent which adversely reflects on the principal's business operation. If the principal is found to have dismissed the representative without "just cause," he may be precluded from importing into Honduras his products, trademarks or services until the agent's adjudicated claim is satisfied.

Mexico—No special legislation protects the agent in case of termination of agency agreements. The principal-agent relationship is governed by the Civil and Commercial Codes. These Codes permit a principal, unless otherwise provided in the contract, to revoke the agency at his discretion. However, a wrongful or premature termination of the agency may make the principal liable for compensatory damages. Appointment of a new agent for the business amounts to a revocation of the old agency contract.

On the other hand, by virtue of Article 285 of the Federal Labor Law of April 1, 1970, natural persons acting as agents may claim the same protection from dismissal as is afforded to employees, including the right to compensation for an unjust termination of the employer-employee relationship. In the case of fixed term agreements which do not exceed 1 year, the compensation specified for premature and unjust termination is set at one-half the value of the remuneration plus 20 days' remuneration for every year of service after the first year. In the case of indefinite term contracts, the compensation amounts to 20 days' remuneration for each year of services rendered. The agent is also entitled to receive an additional 3 months' earnings plus accrued remuneration from the date of dismissal to the actual date the principal pays him all the compensatory damages due.

Nicaragua—Civil and Commercial Codes govern agency agreements. Decree No. 13, enacted January 5, 1980 by the Nicaraguan Government of National Reconstruction, regulates the relationship between foreign principals and their local concessionaires, establishes rules for the termination of agency agreements and provides items of damage compensation due to the representative upon the justified termination by the principal of the principal-agent relationship. Decree No. 13 is entitled: "Law on Agents, Representatives and Distributors of Foreign Firms." This decree is a revised version of former Law No. 287 of February 2, 1972 which was repealed by Decree No. 70 of April 1979. The law defines as concessionaire any person or firm which, by either express or implied contract, is appointed by a foreign principal as its agent, representative, or distributor for the sales or distribution of products or services in Nicaragua.

The parties are free to stipulate the terms of the agency contract; however, a principal may not unilaterally amend, revoke, or waive any of the agent's rights recognized by this law. Decree No. 13 obligates the foreign principal or any substitute, intermediary or replacement, as well as any person or firm acting on the principal's behalf, to compensate the agent for damages caused in the event the principal, his assignee, or representative without just cause (1) dismisses or substitutes the agent, (2) unilaterally modifies or terminates the agreement, (3) refuses to renew an expired agreement, (4) takes over the agency, or (5) increases the number of representatives in Nicaragua.

The agent's compensation is determined based on the value of the agent's unrecoverable investments and expenses he has incurred in furtherance of the agency. Such compensation also includes the agent's constructive loss which is to be determined by the number of years and volume of business of his agency, and the gross earnings of the concessionaire during the last 3 years of his agency. Furthermore, the agent retains his right to all claims against the principal that are given him by equity and may require the principal to buy back his stock at a cost including the purchase price, freight, taxes, and other expenses the agent may have had to incur to obtain and maintain such stock. In cases where the principal has increased the number of representatives without just cause or mutual agreement, the agent may claim compensation equal to eighty percent of the constructive loss compensation that would have been due him had the agency been unjustly terminated. The parties, however, may mutually consent to the amount of compensation due to the agent for unjustified termination by the principal, and in the case of an unresolved dispute as to such amount, the issue will be determined by the courts. Any claim maintained by the agent must be filed with the courts within 2 years of the act giving rise to such claim. To guarantee full payment to the agent on a favorable determination of his claim by the courts, the agent may retain as a preferential creditor all the principal's merchandise he has on hand. Furthermore, the Ministry of Industry and Commerce may suspend the principal's right to import goods into Nicaragua until he has compensated the agent in full or guaranteed such payment upon settlement by the courts.

Just cause for a principal's terminating or refusing to renew an agency agreement includes: (1) any crime committed by the agent against the property or interests of the principal. (2) noncompliance by the agent with any of the terms of the agency contract, (3) continued reduction in the sale or distribution of the principal's products due to the negligence of the agent, (4) any acts attributable to the agent which adversely affect the import, sale, or distribution of the principal's products, and (5) the bankruptcy of the agent.

Decree 13 also carries a temporary provision under which for the next 2 years foreign principals may subscribe temporary agency contracts for periods not exceeding 2 years, provided these contracts do not violate the rights already acquired by agents under the general provisions of this law. Principals who assumed the direct and exclusive distribution of their own products and services in Nicaragua from agents with whom they had agency agreements for more than 1 year on April 21, 1979, must compensate their agents according to the compensation table prescribed by the earlier law enacted on February 19, 1972. (N.B. Compensation under the earlier law varied from 25 percent of the agent's expected gross earnings for a 3-year period if the contract was in effect from 3 to 12 months, to 100 percent of the agent's gross earnings during the previous 3 years if the contract was in effect for more than 3 years). Agents whose contracts were unilaterally rescinded, dissolved, or not renewed during the period April 21, 1979 to January 5, 1980, will be considered codistributors if the principals designated other agents during the above period. The principal, however, can put an end to this relationship by paying the compensation that the agent, representative, or distributor was entitled to as of April 21, 1979.

Panama—The agency contract is regulated by the Civil and Commercial Codes. Termination of the agency contract and remedies for unauthorized termination are governed by Executive Decree No. 344 of 1969, as amended on November 18, 1969, and the rules of practice found in Decree No. 9 of February 7, 1970, as amended by Decree No. 48 of April 6, 1971.

The parties may freely stipulate their contract terms. However, provisions for the waivers of rights or mutual consent terminations are valid only when approved by the Ministry of Commerce.

If a principal can establish just cause, he may without liability terminate, modify, or refuse to renew his agency agreements. If the termination is unjustified, the principal may be liable to compensate the agent the average yearly gross profits for contracts of fewer than 5 years' duration, twice the average annual gross profits for contracts of more than 5 but fewer than 10 years' duration, three times the average annual gross profits for contracts of more than 10 years' but fewer than 15 years' duration, four times the average annual gross profits for contracts of more than 15 years' but fewer than 20 years' duration, five times the average annual gross profits for contracts with more than 20 years' duration. Such relief may include the principal's purchase at cost of the agent's unsalable merchandise.

Once it is determined that an agent was unjustly dismissed by his principal, the principal may not export goods to Panama until the compensation lawfully due the agent is paid. Just cause for termination of the agreement by the principal is defined as the agent's breach of contract, his fraud or abuse of the principal's trust, his negligence or ineptitude, the continued decline in sales or distribution attributable to the agent, his disclosure of secret information, or any act by the agent harmful to the represented firm or products.

Paraguay—No special laws have been enacted to regulate the termination of agency or distributorship agreements. The Civil and Commercial Codes contain provisions regulating the principal-agent relationship. By Law of October 5, 1903. Paraguay adopted the Argentine Code of Commerce, which became effective on January 1, 1904.

The terms of the representational contract govern the operation of the agency agreement, but the parties are free, within the limits of the Civil and Commercial Codes, to agree to their own terms, including clauses providing for termination of the agency or distributorship. However, a principal may be held liable to the agent for damages if he terminates a definite term agreement before its date of expiration, without just cause. This claimable compensation may amount to no fewer than one-half of the otherwise accruable commissions. In all cases, it is customary to give the other party a termination notice. An agency may not validly waive any rights that the Codes establish in their favor.

Peru—There are no laws providing for special compensation to be paid the agent in the event of a terminated agency contract. Representational agreements are regulated by the Commercial Code under the Chapter entitled "De La Commission Mercantil" and by the Civil Code in the Chapter entitled "Del Mandato." Article 273 of the Commercial Code grants the principal the right to terminate or revoke an agency agreement at any time, without need of termination notice to the agent. Similarly, Article 1650 of the Civil Code allows the principal to revoke the agency agreement at any time. Accordingly, except when otherwise provided in the agency contract, a principal may terminate the agency relationship at any time. However, definite term agreements expire at the date of expiration of the contract.

The principal-agent relationship may also terminate due to death, bankruptcy, or insolvency of the principal or the agent, as well as upon termination of the business.

Puerto Rico—The Puerto Rican Civil and Commercial Codes govern the law of agency. Law No. 75 of June 24, 1964, as amended by Law No. 104 of June 28, 1965 and Law No. 105 of June 1966, supplement the Codes on the regulation of the principal-agent relationship. Parties are free to agree on conditions and terms of their representation. However, except for just cause, a party may not unilaterally terminate the representation, refuse to renew an expired agency agreement, or perform any act detrimental to the permanence of the established relationship. Termination of the agency agreement without just cause is considered a tortuous act and makes the offending party liable to pay compensation to the injured party. Clauses waiving any of the agent's rights provided by law are invalid.

In the event of unjust termination of the agency by the principal, the agent has 3 years from the date of actual termination, or the occurrence of an act detrimental to the permanence of the representation, to file a claim for compensation. This compensation may include (1) the actual value of expenses incurred by the agent in setting up and running the business, (2) the value of the agent's inventories and stock, (3) the loss of the agent's profits, and (4) the value of his goodwill. The agent may also claim an amount equal to his profit experience for the previous 5 years, or, if the agency existed for fewer than 5 years, five times the average annual profit.

Just cause for the principal's termination of the agreement is defined as (1) the agent's nonperformance of essential obligations under the contract or (2) any act or omission by the agent which substantially and adversely affects the principal's interest in the promotion, marketing, or distribution of the merchandise or service in question.

Venezuela—The Civil and Commercial Codes govern the rights and duties of an agent operating in his own name for the account of his principal. When an agency agreement for a fixed term expires according to its terms, no notice is required. However, a notice is required for the termination of an agency agreement of indefinite term. When the principal unjustly terminates an agency, in which the agent has made a substantial investment, the principal is liable to the agent for his losses.

The Labor Law of November 3, 1947, as amended by Decree No. 123 of June 1974, regulates the treatment of employees. This law may entitle unjustly discharged gents to the same benefits as discharged employees. Furthermore, Venezuelan courts will not recognize the agent's waiver of these employee rights. Under the Labor Law, an employee may obtain compensation for wrongful or unjust dismissal from his job. This amounts to half a month's current salary for each year of employment, plus severance pay of 15 days' wages for each year of employment (severance may not exceed 8 months' wages).

MIDDLE EAST AND MEDITERRANEAN

Algeria—All foreign commerce operations are governed by Law 78-02 of February 11, 1978 and regulations of Circular No. 09-CAB of March 27, 1982. The law establishes a clear state monopoly of foreign commerce, providing that all import-export operations with foreign enterprises may only be concluded by the State or local governments or a state company. However, the government may, under special circumstances, grant import authorization to certain foreign enterprises and to private Algerian company representatives. All agency representational contracts are considered null and void as of the date of Law 78-02. This includes all contracts for commissions whether exclusive or not. Intermediaries (agents) are formally outlawed and criminal penalties are provided for violations of this law. However, under circular no. 09-CAB of March 27, 1982 the following activities may be considered "nonintermediary": (a) assemblers, general contractors, combined export management; (b) providers of products or supplies as consolidators, dealers, or exclusive agents; (c) trading or commercial companies, (foreign import-export firms). On the other hand foreign enterprises working in Algeria for the exclusive benefit of the state, local governments, or state companies may under regulated circumstances set up offices or appoint representatives to represent them in dealings and operations with the corresponding administrations and organizations, as well as to exercise, in a private capacity, advisory or assistance services in external trade operations.

Bahrain—The agent-distributor profession is regulated by an Amiri decree of October 1975. Under this decree all commercial representatives or agents must be registered with the Ministry of Commerce, Agriculture and Economy; the Amiri Cabinet may regulate the nature and number of foreign agencies a representative may hold. All agents must be Bahraini nationals of good financial and moral standing. Legal persons operating as agents or distributors must be registered as Bahraini corporations, have at least 50 percent Bahraini equity participation and have their head office in Bahrain. A principal for any specific activity may have only one agent operating in the territory of Bahrain. This representative is entitled to commission on all sales occurring within his territory. Either party may only terminate the representation agreement based on just cause verified by the Directorate of Commerce and Economy. Otherwise the other party may claim damage compensation for unjust termination of the agreement. Additionally, the principal may be further sanctioned by having his product banned from Bahrain. Chamber decisions may be appealed to the civil courts.

Cyprus—No specific legislation has been enacted to regulate the termination of agency agreements. The principal-agent relationship is governed by the agency agreement within provisions of the Cyprus Law of Contracts which is basically inspired on English Common Law principals.

According to custom, indefinite term agreements are terminated by giving the agent reasonable termination notice or, in lieu thereof, a reasonable amount in compensation for the termination. A number of intervening factors such as the nature of the business, duration of the representation and the volume of agency operations, may have a variable effect on the extent of the termination notice or in the amount of reasonable compensation to be paid the agent.

Egypt—Foreign agency and commercial broker representation in the private and public sectors is governed by Law No. 120 August 5, 1982 in force since May 5, 1983. No special legislation has been enacted to protect the agent in case of contract termination. The principal-agent relationship is governed by the will of the parties as expressed in the agreement, so long as it does not conflict with the Law. The agreement must indicate the nature of the agents work, responsibilities of the parties, commission stipulated, manner of payment commissions and currency of payment. Only Egyptian legal entities or individuals born of Egyptian fathers, and long-standing naturalized Egyptians may represent foreign principals. Representatives must be registered with and approved by the Ministry of Economy and Foreign Trade. Corporate representatives must by chartered in Egypt and have a totality of Egyptian stockholders and management. Total Egyptian executive and managerial participation is required for partnerships. Furthermore, all commercial representatives must have been permanent residents of Egypt for at least 10 years and have a permanent place of business there. Foreign principals must contract directly with their Egyptian representatives. An agent may represent several principals provided such representations are recorded with the Ministry of Economy and Foreign Trade. Foreign principals represented by agents in the public sector may not appoint private agents until after the expiration of the public sector's agent's agreement.

Foreign principals may provide scientific, technical, and consulting services, when duly registered and authorized by the Ministry of Economy and Foreign Trade, only if engaged in trading activities and operating a commercial agency in Egypt. The Agent's authorization to practice the profession may be cancelled for violation of the country's laws, practices or willful submission of false information.

Israel—The principal-agent relationship is governed by the Agencies Act of 1965, supplemented by then unabrogated provisions of the Ottoman Civil Code. The parties are free to stipulate the terms of the agreement which will govern the agency relationship. General common law principles of agency law apply to the termination or cancellation of agency agreements. Agencies may be terminated by the will of either party; the terms of the agency contract; by death or incapacity of any of the parties; by termination of the business; and bankruptcy or insolvency of either party. Although formal publication to advise third parties of the termination of the agency relationship is not required, it is advisable to place a timely notification in a local paper to prevent possible third party liability.

Arbitration of commercial disputes is allowed. The International Chamber of Commerce, or any other body chosen by the parties, may be agreed upon to arbitrate a commercial dispute. However, as a rule Government agencies may not agree to submit to arbitration.

Iraq—Commission agents are governed by Law No. 11 of February 1983 entitled: "Law for Regulating Commercial Agencies and Mediation," Law 11 of 1983 abrogated Law No. 8. of 1976 and Law 208 of 1969.

Only government-approved Commission agents may be appointed for private sector operations, once approved and registered with the Ministry of Trade and duly recorded in the Commercial Agents and Intermediaries Register. All representation contracts must also be registered with the Ministry. Principals should notify Iraqui authorities regarding the appointment of agents or intermediaries. Documentary proof of the appointment should be supplied. Agents may represent more than one principal. Any person acting as a commercial agent or intermediary prior to securing government authorization and registration may be subject to life imprisonment. Commission agents may not intervene in public sector transactions involving government offices and public sector enterprises. Transactions of this nature are handled directly by the pertinent public sector with the foreign manufacturer or supplier or through Iraqui commercial or consular representatives abroad.

Jordan—The "Commercial Agents and Intermediaries Law, No. 20-74 of May 1, 1974" regulates commercial agents and intermediaries; while previous Law No. 29, 1968, remains in effect only insofar as it is not in conflict with the 1974 law. Although the principal-agent relationship is governed by the mutual will of the parties expressed by their agreement, only Jordanian law applies to the agency contract (choice of law clauses are void) and the Jordanian courts have exclusive jurisdiction to interpret it. Only natural or legal persons of Jordanian nationality may represent foreign principals and corporate representatives must be chartered in Jordan and have a majority of Jordanian stockholders. Furthermore, all commercial representatives must be permanent residents of Jordan and have a permanent place of business in the Kingdom of Jordan. The foreign principal must contract directly with the Jordanian agent or intermediary.

Except when the authorities revoke the agency, the principal is liable to his agent for damages, if he terminates the commercial agency agreement (1) without just cause of (2) at a time other than its natural expiration date. Such damages may include the projected profits the agent would have earned if the contract had expired according to its own terms. When the national law or the contract terms are silent or ambiguous on the issue of termination or damages, the parties may apply local law or custom.

Kuwait—Commercial agencies, distributorships and commission agents are governed by provisions of Chapter V, of the Kuwaiti Commercial Code, (Law No. 68 of 1980), supplemented by provisions of Ordinance No. 36 of 1964. Only Kuwaiti nationals or Kuwaiti corporations may represent foreign principals. Appointment of a representative is compulsory to make sales in Kuwait. The agent must act within the scope of his contractual authority, otherwise he will be responsible for his acts. If the principal has not established a domicile in Kuwait, the representative's domicile shall be considered as the principal's domicile. Although an agent may not represent several principals handling competing products, distributors may, under local practices, represent several foreign principals manufacturing similar products. Agencies and distributorships may be exclusive or non-exclusive according to the representational agreement. Non-exclusive distributorships are not governed by Law No. 68, but by general contract law provisions.

Foreign principals must deal directly with the Kuwaiti representative, except in cases where the representative is connected with the official local representative of the foreign principal. Under the Code, the agent is always entitled to receive a remuneration for his services, even in cases where the principal makes direct sales in the agent's territory. The representative may exercise a lien on the principal's goods in his possession to safeguard his claims against the principal. This security right takes priority over the rights of other creditors, except for unpaid judicial fees, debts to the Kuwaiti government, and outstanding mortgages.

All representational contracts must be approved by the Ministry of Commerce. Definite term agreements must be in writing and contain provisions regulating at least the following particulars: (a) the nature of the representation, whether exclusive or not, (b) the territory of the agency, (c) the agent's remuneration, and (d) the duration of the representation. However, when the representative is obliged by the contract to incur substantial expenses, set-up storage and show rooms, maintenance services and repair facilities, the contract term of the agency may not be less than 5 years.

Indefinite term agreements may be terminated at any time provided a termination notice is given to the agent. On the other hand, a principal may not prematurely terminate or refuse to renew a definite term agreement without valid justification. Any of the following comprises just cause: a) a breach of contract by the agent, b) error or default during the execution of the agreement, or c) failure by the agent to develop or maintain goodwill and sales within the allotted territory. Termination without just cause makes a principal liable to compensate the agent for damages caused by the termination. The agent may not validly waive his right to compensation. If the agency contract is silent as to amounts of compensation payable, or the parties cannot agree on the amount to be paid, the injured party may sue for damages. All disputes occurring under the agency contact must be decided by the circuit court of the place of execution of the contract. The agency contract may include an arbitration clause. Law No. 68 is silent concerning the validity of choice of law and jurisdiction clauses.

Article 283 of the Law establishes the following statue of limitation rules. a) Claims for damage compensation based on unjust termination of the representation must be filed within 90 days following the expiration of the representation, and b) all other claims arising under the agency agreement must be filed within a term of 3 years after termination of the contractual relation.

Lebanon—Commercial agencies are regulated by Law No. 34 of August 10, 1967, as amended by Legislative Decree No. 9639 of February 6, 1975 (effective date: February 17, 1975).

Only Lebanese legal entities or nationals having a place of business in Lebanon may represent foreign principals. The agency contract must be in writing and registered with the Ministry of National Economy and Trade. All types of representational agreements are regulated by the law. Commercial representatives may not represent principals handling competing product lines, but may, on their own as principals, appoint subagents and subdistributors, except when prohibited by the representational agreement. Jurisdictional clauses are invalid and only Lebanese law applies to representational contract.

Except in cases where the agent is at fault, or for unlawful acts, a principal may not, without incurring liability for damage compensation to the agent, unilaterally terminate or refuse to renew an agency or distributorship agreement. The agent may not validly waive his right to obtain damage compensation for unjust termination of the principal-agent relationship. Damage claims may include loss of profits and damages suffered by the agent by reason of the agreement termination.

Customs authorities may suspend the principal's right to export goods into Lebanon until the agent's damage claim ward has been paid or settled.

Morocco—The Principal-agent relationship is governed by Dahir of May 21, 1943. This law applies when the agent is not a commercial enterprise. Code of Obligations and Contracts of August 12, 1913, as amended, applies to commercial representation enterprises. These are excluded from the scope of the Dahir of May 21, 1943. Under the code, a principal may, at any time, terminate an agreement. However, if the termination is premature or unjust, the agent may sue for compensation.

The Dahir of May 21, 1943, considers the principal-agent relation as a contract for "rendition of services." Therefore the agent is treated as an employee of the principal. This law does not recognize waiver of rights granted to the agent. The agreement will not be affected by any changes undergone by the principal employer. A new principal will be bound by the terms of the agreement. Termination of the business, except in cases of "force majeure" is no excuse for failure to observe the notice requirement. A definite term contract terminates at date of expiration. Even so, a principal may be held liable for refusing without just cause to renew an expired definite term agreement. An indefinite term agreement may be terminated for just cause and with service of notice of termination. The notice term varies in relation to the duration of the agency. Service of notice is only excused in cases of "force majeure".

Accordingly, an agent may claim the following compensation:

Definite term agreements. For premature termination and failure to renew without just cause.

(1) Any benefits that would have been earned before termination of the agreement.

(2) An indemnity for termination of the agreement, unless terminated for just cause.

Indefinite term agreements. For failure to serve notice of termination, or termination without just cause.

(1) Any benefits that would have been earned during the notice term.

(2) An indemnity established on the basis of nature of the service, duration of the service, and damages suffered.

If an indefinite or definite term agreement is terminated by death, accident, or disease, resulting in complete and permanent incapacity of the agent, he, his representative, or heirs, are entitled to compensation established on the basis of goodwill developed. Only Moroccan nationals, whether individual persons or legal entities, may represent foreign principals in the private sector. However, agents for sales to the military are prohibited. The parties are free to agree to the terms of the representational agreement, within the revisions of the Code of Obligations and Contracts.

Oman (Sultanate of)—Commercial agencies are regulated by Royal Decree No. 26/77 published in the Omani Official Gazette of January 6, 1977. The term commercial agencies, under the law, means agency, distributorship, and all representational contracts involving an intermediary relationship including contracts for the rendition of services to a foreign principal within the sultanate.

Only Omani nationals and firms, duly registered in the Commercial Register, and having a place of business within the Sultanate, may operate as representatives or agents for foreign companies. The agency contract must be in writing, duly registered with and certified by the Omani Chamber of Commerce and Industry. The contact must state the nationalities of the principals and agent, the name of the agency, a description of the goods to be sold, or services to be rendered, the agent's agreed remuneration, the rights and obligations of the contracting parties, and clearly describe the territory assigned to the agency.

Under the law the representation is exclusive. the agent is entitled to be paid a commission on any direct sales the principal may make within the assigned territory. Termination of an agency agreement without justification may make a principal liable to compensate the agent for damages. A similar situation obtains as a result of the premature termination of a definite term contract, or the refusal, without just cause, to renew a definite term agreement.

Qatar—The principal-agent relationship is regulated by articles 295-322 of the Commercial Law of 1971. The parties are free to convene the terms of their agreement including conditions and terms for termination of the relationship. Appointment of a representative is compulsory; only Qatar national or Qatar corporations may represent foreign principals. The representational agreement must be registered with the Ministry of Commerce and Economy.

The principal must reimburse the agent for expenses incurred in ordinary performance of the agency, plus interest from the date of the expenditure. The principal or the agent may terminate the agency by serving termination notice to the other party. The terminating party may be held liable to compensate the other for damages due to the termination of the agency at an inappropriate time or without just cause.

The agency also terminates by reason of the death or incapacity of the agent or the principal, completion of the enterprise or expiration of the contract terms. Arbitration of representational disputes is available under the supervision of the Ministry of Commerce and Industry.

Saudi Arabia—Commercial agencies and distributorships are governed by Saudi Decree of July 23, 1962, implemented by Ministry of Commerce Order No. 1897 of March 30, 1981. On the other hand the relationship between foreign contractors and their Saudi agents is governed by Decree No. 126 of January 17, 1978.

The agent or distributor may enter contacts with sub-agents or sub-distributors provided the original agent or distributor shall remain responsible concerning consumer regulations.

Only Saudi nationals, whether individuals or firms, many operate as agents or distributors. Legal entities or firms must have 100 percent Saudi capital and management. Only individuals or legal entities, registered and approved by the ministry of Commerce, may act as agents or distributors. Agency and distributorship contacts, translated into Arabic, must be filed by the agent with the Commercial register. Agency and distributorship contracts must comply with the following: (a) should be approved by the principal or its representative in its original country, (b) clearly state the duties and rights of the parties and their obligations towards the consumer, as to providing maintenance and spare parts, (c) identify the parties with indication of their respective nationalities, (d) give the scope of the agency, (e) specify duration of the agency and how renewed, and (f) state the conditions for termination of the agency. The Department of Interior Commerce of the Ministry of Commerce has issued a standard agency contract form which includes clauses regulating termination of the relationship and damages claimable by an injured party due to termination of the contract. A copy of this form is available from the Office of Trade Finance, Room 1211 U.S. Department of Commerce, Washington D.C.N.W. 20230.

Commercial disputes set up under the Ministry of Commerce and Industry are subject to strict religious-legal supervision. However, under the Arbitration Law, (Royal decree of April 25, 1983) purely commercial disputes may be settled through arbitration and out of the supervision of the Sharia Courts.

Decree 126 requires the foreign contractor to appoint, and be represented by a Saudi agent having a valid commercial register certification except in cases where the foreign principal is represented by a Saudi partner. Agents may not intervene in transactions involving the sale of weapons or related operation, nor in direct dealings between the Saudi Arabian and foreign governments.

The relationship between the foreign contractor and the Saudi agent is governed by the terms of the representational agreements. Principals must appoint at least one agent, but no more than ten, to represent them in the different operations. The agent's commission may not exceed 5 percent of the value of the contract entered by the foreign principal. Violations of the provisions of Decree 126 are punishable by exclusion from doing business in Saudi Arabia.

Syria—No special protective legislation has been enacted to regulate termination of agency and distributorship agreements. The principal-agent relationship is governed by Commercial Law of September 1949, supplemented by Decree No. 51 of September 30, 1979. The parties may agree as to the terms of their relationship, including provisions for termination or cancellation of the representation. In all cases, the law requires service of notice of termination to the agent. This notice varies in accordance with the agency's duration and type. Definite term agreements terminate on the date of expiration of the contract. Premature termination, without just cause, of a definite term agreement may make the principal liable to compensate the agent for damages caused by the termination. Upon actual termination of the agency, the law grants the agent a 60-to 90-day term to liquidate its obligations and notify the Directorate of the Foreign Companies Register. In this event a 2-month term is granted to the principal to appoint a new representative under penalty of being kept from doing business in the country until a new representative is duly appointed and registered with the Ministry.

All agency contracts must be registered with the Ministry of Economic and Foreign Trade. Representatives of foreign firms must register with and be approved by the Ministry. All agency representatives are considered exclusive. Only Syrian nationals or Syrian legal entities, residing in Syria, may engage in the business of representing foreign principals. In the case of corporations, at least 66 percent domestic stock ownership and 50 percent Syrian management are required. Only registered agents may import goods into the country. Syrian representatives must deal directly with the foreign principal.

Decree No. 51 of September 3, 1979 forbids all State circles, public establishments, and public and mixed sectors from accepting mediators or brokers in all kinds of foreign contracts concluded with natural persons or legal entities. The State deals with producers or distributors directly appointed by the producers in an official and established manner.

United Arab Emirates—(Abu Dhabi, Dubai, Sharja, Ajman, Umn-Al-Qaiwain, Ras-Al-Khaima, Fujaira).

New Federal Act No. 18 of August 11, 1981, in effect as of February 24, 1982, governs all representational agreements and the agency-distributorship profession within the above indicated United Arab Emirates. The representative must be a UAE national. If the representative is a firm or corporation, it must be 100 percent owned and managed by a UAE national. Only individuals or firms duly registered, approved, and licensed by the Ministry of Economy and Commerce and the Central Agencies Committee may operate as representatives of foreign firms. Violation of this provision may subject the representative to heavy fines and penalties. The UAE representative must be in direct contact with the foreign principal without intervening intermediaries or sub-agents of the principal. On the other hand, the foreign principal may be an export company, or wholly owned subsidiary of the principal. The representative must be appointed as an exclusive representative for the territory assigned to him, whether the appointment is for the whole Federation, a single, or a number of component counties. The exclusive representative is entitled to receive a commission on all sales and transactions occurring within this territory whether or not he has intervened in the operations.

The parties are free to convene the terms of their representational agreement. The agreement must be in writing, in the Arabic language, duly executed by the parties, legalized, notarized, registered and approved by the Ministry of Economy and Commerce. The agreement may be entered for a definite or an indefinite term.

Representational agreements may be terminated, without incurring liability to compensate the agent for damages suffered when terminated by mutual consent of the parties or for just cause accepted by the Commercial Agencies Committee. In cases when the contract is terminated prematurely, when the principal refuses to renew an expired definite term contract or when terminated by a reason beyond the agent's control, the agent may also be entitled to claim compensation upon proof that the agent has developed the principal's goodwill. This payment is not required when the relationship is terminated due to fault of the representative. Similarly, premature termination of a definite term agreement unilateral termination of the contract, or the principal's refusal to renew the agreement may make a principal liable to pay damage compensation to the representative for unjust termination of the contract. The law does not identify just causes for terminating or refusing to renew an expired agreement. The Central Agencies Committee is empowered by Law to intervene, settle, or decide disputes between the representative and the principal, and, accordingly, with powers to decide whether the termination was for just cause. The authorities may, at the request of the representative, place an attachment order on any imports made by others than the registered agent with regard to products originating from the agent's principal. Commercial agents under penalty of law, must keep available to the public necessary spare parts, components, materials, and accessories required for maintenance of goods imported and sold through the representative. A commercial agency may not be registered in the Commercial Agents Register in the name of a new agent, unless the previous agency contract has been terminated for just cause with the approval of the Commercial Agencies Committee, or by mutual consent of the parties.

AFRICA

Cameroon—No special law has been enacted to regulate the termination of agency and distributorship agreements. The principal-agent relationship is governed by the terms of the contract as covered by the parties, which may include provisions for the termination of the contractual relationship. Agency and distributorship contracts must be notarized, published in the Official Gazette, and the local press. To act as such, agents and distributors must be approved by and registered with the government.

Congo—The agent distributorship profession is not regulated by special laws. the parties are free to agree on the terms of their agreements, including the nature of the representation, whether exclusive or not, the representative's remuneration, as well as terms and conditions for terminating the relationship. All representatives of foreign firms must advise the Customs Bureau in advance regarding their representative standing the foreign products to be imported by them.

Central African Republic—An Ordinance of December 31, 1983 regulates agents and distributors. There are no legal provisions governing termination of agency and distributorship agreements. The parties are free to agree to the terms of their agreement including termination clauses. All representatives must be licensed, approved by, and registered with the Department of Commerce and Industry.

Gabon—There are no special laws governing agency and distributorship agreements. Basic principles of French law apply to the relationship. All representatives must be registered with the Gabon Chamber of Commerce and receive authorization from the Ministry of Commerce. The parties are free to agree to the terms of their agreement, including termination clauses. Usually, agents and distributors are appointed with exclusive representation rights.

Ivory Coast—Agency and distributorship agreements are governed by articles 1984 to 2010 of the Civil Code. Under the Code provisions, the parties may terminate their relationship at will giving a notice of termination to the other. Their parties may freely agree to the terms of the contract, within the legal limits of the Civil Code, and agree to terms and conditions involving termination of the contract. The legislation, following principles of French Jurisprudence, requires that upon termination of the relationship the agent or distributor should be compensated with an indemnity commensurate with his investments and efforts on behalf of the principal. The parties may by contract limit the extent of this liability.

Kenya—No special law has been enacted to regulate foreign agency and distributorship agreements. The principal-agent relationship is governed by the will of the parties as expressed in the agency or distributorship contract. The legal system follows British Common Law principles.

Madagascar—The conduct and termination of agency and distributor agreements between U.S. firms and their representatives in Madagascar are tied to the contractual terms agreed to by the parties involved. There are no state laws or regulations governing such agreements.

Nigeria—No special laws have been enacted to regulate foreign agency and distributorship agreements. The principal-agent relationship is governed by the will of the parties as expressed in the agency or distributorship agreement. Accordingly, the parties may agree on the territorial extent of the representation, remuneration of the representative, nature of the representation, whether exclusive or not, as well as terms and conditions governing the termination of the contract.

Senegal—No special legislation has been enacted to regulate the termination of agency agreements. The principal-agency relationship is governed by provisions of the Code des Obligations Civiles et Commerciales. Under the Code, the parties can draft termination of the relationship. Although Article 97 of the code provides: "contracts can only be revised or terminated by mutual consent of the parties, or for causes provided by law", an agency contract may provide for unilateral termination with or without just cause. Established custom requires that notice of termination, which include the reasons for termination, be sent to the agent at least 6 months before the expiration date of the contract.

Somalia—By Law No. 45 of July 10, 1975, the Supreme Revolutionary Council cancelled all commercial licenses issued to individuals and abolished all foreign agency representation in Somalia. A new Samali government office, set up within the Somalian Chamber of Commerce, shall be the sole authority that can carry out commercial transactions, monitor government purchases, and collect commission fee.

South Africa—No legislation has been enacted to regulate the termination of agency and distributorship agreements. The principal-agent relationship is governed by the agency contract which customarily includes reasons, terms, and conditions for termination of the relationship. The representative may be limited as to the territory of the agency. Representational contracts are customarily issued as definite term agreements regarding its duration and also include a clause providing for a review of the agent's performance.

Sudan—Sudan's import trade was nationalized by Decree of January 25, 1967 as part of a Sudanziation campaign initiated by the Revolutionary Government. Accordingly, only public sector corporations or companies officially set up may import coffee, cigarettes, rice, footwear, medicines, flour, cloth, insecticides, fertilizers, and jute. Agencies or distributorships engaged in the importation of consumer goods and construction equipment are also subject to Sudanisation plans.

Private-sector trading licenses are only issued to Sudanese nationals, although in rare cases non-Sudanese may obtain trading licenses provided they comply with the government Sudanisation plans.

Tanzania—No special law has been enacted to regulate foreign agency agreements. The relationship is governed by the will of the parties as expressed in the representation contract. The service of termination notice is supported by well established practices. Cancellation or termination of a definite term agreement before the expiration of its term may lead to a claim for damages.

The cancellations of all private trading licenses was announced on October, 1975 by Mr. Kawana. Tanzania's Prime Minister. Accordingly, all issued trading licenses had to be returned to the government. It seems that only legal persons may, if authorized by the government, carry out agency activities.

Tunisia—No special legislation has been enacted to regulate the termination of agency and distributorship agreements. The principal-agent relationship is governed by Articles 625 and 626 of the Commercial Code. On the other hand, Decree 61:14 of August 30, 1966 regulates the agency profession. Only Tunisian nationals, whether individuals or legal persons, may represent foreign principals.

The parties can draft their own agreement in its entirety, including providing for contract termination.

Indefinite term agreements may be terminated by the principal, without incurring liability to the agent, by giving a notice of contract termination. Definite term agreements terminate at the expiration of the contract term, but may be terminated earlier for "just cause".

Uganda—No special law has been enacted to regulate foreign agency agreements. The will of the parties as expressed in the agency contract shall govern the principal-agent relationship. Only registered and authorized autonomous agents having offices in Uganda may obtain the necessary import license for the importation of products.

Zaire—No special legislation has been enacted to regulate agency terminations. The principal-agent relationship is basically governed by the terms of the agency agreement. It is also governed by the Civil Code and by the Decree of January 1920. However, foreign trade is strictly regulated by Law 73/9 of January 5, 1973, and Departmental Decree 15 /CAB 4/73, which provides rules for the application of Law 73/9.

Only Zairian nationals or a 100 percent Zairian-owned corporations, organized under Zairian law may engage in commercial activity. However, the President of Zaire may by ordinance authorize foreigners, either individuals or legal entities, to conduct import operations.

Traders must be approved by the Ministry of Commerce and must be listed in the Commercial Register. Traders must deal directly with foreign principals and not use intermediaries, except when the foreign principal operates through export firms, or the Zairian agent has been granted exclusive representation, in which case imports must conform to the following: (1) the purchase order must be sent directly to the producer; (2) the supply contract must include a pro forma invoice; (3) the foreign invoice must be in the name of the Zairian importer, (4) the invoice should state net prices, commissions, or discounts involved; and (5) payment must be made directly to the producer. The parties may include contract clauses dealing with nature of the representation and conditions and terms for termination of the agency.

Zambia—No special law has been enacted to regulate the principal-agent relationship. The will of the parties as expressed in the agency contract will govern the relationship. Zambian laws on agency follow the general agency principles of British Common Law.

EUROPE

Austria—The principal-agent relationship is governed by the agency agreement within the provisions of the Mercantile Agents Law of 1921, as amended on June 15, 1978. This law also supplements agency contracts as to matters not covered by the agency agreement. Under the law the agent may not waive any right recognized in his favor, including his right to claim damages for termination of the agency and his right to continue working in the same line of business after termination.

Indefinite term agreements may be terminated by giving the agent a 6-week notice of termination, expiring at the end of the calendar quarter. A 3-month notice is required if the agency existed for more than 5 consecutive years. The parties to the agency contract may agree on longer or shorter termination notice terms. Definite term agreements may be terminated before their date of expiration based on "just cause" and service of termination notice. Both definite and indefinite term contracts may be terminated prematurely, or without service of notice of termination based on any of the following "just causes": (1) incapacity of the agent, (2) loss of the principal's trust, (3) breach by the agent of an essential clause of the agency contract (4) the agent's negligence in the performance of his duties, (5) default of the principal in paying provisions. Termination without just cause, or without observing terms or periods of notice of termination, may make a principal liable to compensate the agent for damages caused by the termination. In each case of termination by the principal, except in cases of breach by the agent, the principal has to pay a remuneration for goodwill developed by the agent. The amount of remuneration depends on the duration of the terminated agreement, but the principal has to pay the sum of provisions for 1 year at the most.

Belgium—In Belgium the representational relationship is governed by the Civil Code, supplemented by the Law of July 27, 1961, as amended on April 13, 1971, on "The Unilateral Termination of Certain Distributorships Granted for an Indefinite Term, and to the Notice To Be Given Prior to the Expiration Of a Distributorship Granted for a Fixed Term."

A Law of July 30, 1963 grants to commercial agents similar legal protection.

The parties to the representational agreement are free to stipulate whatever terms they mutually agree upon. However, they may not amend, revoke, or waive any of the rights to which the agent is entitled by law. Since only Belgian law is applicable to the contract, choice of law clauses are not recognized.

The termination of both exclusive and nonexclusive agreements which have no definite expiration date creates a liability for the severing party, unless there is mutual consent to the termination, or the other party has failed to meet its obligations under the agreement. To terminate any indefinite term agreement without liability, the severing party must give adequate notice to the other party and mutual agreement on the terms of severance must be reached. In the absence of such mutual agreement, the compensation due for termination by the principal may be determined by referring the matter to the courts.

If a principal terminates an agreement without justification, he, in addition to his liabilities under the contract, becomes liable to compensate the representative for (1) the value of any increase in goodwill for the principal's business due to the representative's actions, (2) the representative's expenses incurred in developing the business, and (3) the amount of any compensation claim discharged employees of the agent may have under Belgian law.

According to the Law, both exclusive and nonexclusive representational agreements which have a definite date of expiration may be terminated on such date without liability. However, these agreements may become indefinite term agreements if the parties agree to two further extensions of the termination date. Similarly, a definite term agreement may be considered extended for a further period if the terminating party thereto fails to give notice to the other, within a term ranging from 3 to 6 months anticipation, of his intention not to renew the contract upon the arrival of the expiration date.

The party responsible for terminating a definite term agreement before its expiration date is liable to the other party for damages, unless the severance is accomplished by mutual consent or is caused by a failure of the other party to meet its obligations under the agreement. In case of termination for a breach of obligation by the other party, notice of termination must be given by the terminating party, and failure to give such notice makes him liable for damages.

Exclusive representational agreements effective within the European Economic Community should be carefully worded to avoid violation of Articles 85-86 of the Treaty of Rome on antitrust and restrictive business practices.

Denmark—the principal-agent relationship is governed by Act No. 243 of May 8, 1971, as supplemented by a 1918 law, which gives the Chamber of Commerce the authority to render opinions concerning unjustified agency terminations. Under Act 243, the parties may terminate the relationship at any time without serving notice, except in cases where the parties have provided otherwise in their agreement. However, (1) an agency may not be terminated without compensation if the agent is entitled to a continuation and (2) any post-termination restriction on an agent's commercial activities may not exceed 2 years. The Chamber of Commerce recommended practice is to give agents 3 to 6 months' notice upon any termination. Subsequent to termination of the contract, the established practice is to give the agent an amount equal to 12 month's compensation for goodwill, based on the average of annual gross commissions for the last 3 to 5 years of the representation.

Finland—Law No. 389 of May 30, 1975, effective January 1st, 1976, regulates the principal-agent relationship. The word agent includes commercial agents, salesmen and traveling salesmen. Law 389 defines a commercial agent as an independent businessman having an established place of business.

The parties are free to include in their agency contract terms and conditions of their choice. This freedom is limited by the obligation to submit the principal-agent relationship to the jurisdiction of the laws and courts of Finland, and by the prohibition to waive the agent's right to remuneration and compensation established in the law.

Definite term agreements terminate on the expiration date of the contract. An expired agreement, however, is considered extended for a further period if the parties continue to operate under the contract beyond the expiration date, or if a party fails to give notice required by the contract of his intent to terminate the agreement on its expiration date. Unless the agency agreement otherwise provides, the termination notice should be given 3 months before the end of the calendar month in which the agreement will be terminated. If the contract has been in force for less than a year, a 1 month notice is sufficient. Agency agreements automatically terminate upon the declaration of bankruptcy of either party. Definite and indefinite term agreements may be terminated at any time for just cause, such as negligence, breach of the contract, or under circumstances that require the end of the contractual relationship. Either party may, without incurring liability, also terminate the agency agreement within a reasonable time after discovery of the following just causes: (1) fraud or deceit reflecting on the granting or acceptance of the agreement, (2) refusal to make a written agreement, (3) damage to the other party's interest under the contract or breach of confidence, and (4) failure to comply with the contract's obligations.

Except when otherwise provided in the agency contract, damages may include expenses incurred in the acquisition of buildings, inventories, stock, equipment and other business-related property.

An agent has a right to retain the principal's papers or property in his custody to exercise a privileged security interest until he receives payment.

France—Representational agreements may be classified in one of several categories, depending on the nature of the business relationships and the degree of mutual dependency of the parties. Therefore, representations may be governed by the Civil and Commercial Codes, a special regulatory decree or pertinent provisions of the social legislation or the French Labor Code.

The categories include: distributorship, statue-regulated commercial agencies, ordinary commercial agencies commission agencies or sales representatives; traveling salesmen and door-to-door salesmen (known as VRP or voyageur, representant, and placier). The distributorship is the most favored category because the parties are free to agree to the terms of the relationship, including clauses governing termination of the contract, the nature of the representation, and choice of law clauses.

European Economic community antitrust regulations, particularly those requiring registration of exclusive representation agreements, may be applicable. Commercial agents (nonstatutory) transact or negotiate business in the name of and for the account of their principal, and do not benefit from the French labor law, or employee-oriented social legislation. Agency agreements are subject to less strict regulations under the provisions of the EEC antitrust laws than exclusive agreements.

Commercial agents (statutory) operate professionally, free from direct control of the principal. The principal-agent relationship is governed by the agency contract, within the limits of regulatory provisions Decree No 58-1345 of December 23, 1958. Except when the agency agreement provides otherwise, the agent may sell the represented product for his own account, represent noncompeting lines, and employ and appoint under the responsibility subagents without obtaining specific authorization from the principal. However, these subagents, according to the circumstances under which they perform their work, may be subject to the provisions of articles 29K *et.seq.* of Volume I of the Labor Code, or to the provisions of Decree 58-1345.

The agency contract must be in writing and recorded on a special register at the Tribunal of Commerce. The contract duration at the election of the parties, may be for a definite or an indefinite term, may involve an exclusive representation, a "del credere" agency, and contain provisions for consignment of merchandise. Unless the statutory commercial agent is himself in breach of the agreement, he may claim damages from his principal for premature termination of the contract, for a major alteration of the terms of the agreement or for failure to renew a renewable agreement, notwithstanding any contract clause to the contrary.

Commission agents act in their own name for the account of the supplier, who remains the owner of the merchandise until its delivery to the ultimate purchaser. These agents are not protected by Decree No. 58-1345.

V.R.P.'s (voyageur, representant, and placier) comprise traveling salesmen, sales representatives, and door-to-door salesmen. They lack the capacity to transact business in their own name, to obligate the principal, and are subject to the supervision and control of the principal. Under the law, the V.R.P. is an employee, irrespective of what the contract calls him. V.R.P.'s are governed by French labor laws. (Laws of July 18, 1937 and March 7, 1957), which give a representative the right to obtain compensation from his employer for the number and value of accounts developed by the agent, if the relationship is terminated or the principal fails to renew the contract, notwithstanding any clause to the contrary.

Germany, Federal Republic—Sections 84-92 of the Commercial Code and Sections 663-665 and 672-675 of the Civil Code govern the principal-agent relationship. The law allows choice of law clauses as well as choice of jurisdiction; however, waivers of the agent's right to receive compensation for unjust termination of the agency agreement are not recognized as valid. The Commercial Code provides for minimum termination notice terms which vary in relation to the duration of the agreement; from a 6-week termination notice to become effective at the end of the calendar quarter for contracts of up to 3 years' duration, to a 3-month notice term when the contract has been in effect for more than 3 years. Otherwise, the parties are free to agree on the terms of their agreement.

Agency contracts terminate by operation of law in the event of death of the agent, bankruptcy of the principal, or termination of the business. Either party may terminate an indefinite term agreement by giving the other the adequate termination notice. Failure to serve notice may only be excused if termination is for just cause. Definite term agreements may also be terminated, before their date of expiration, for just cause.

The agent's right to receive compensation for unjust termination generally amounts to the value of the benefits that would have accrued to the agent during the omitted notice period. In cases where adequate termination notice is given to the agent, compensation may be claimed for the value of the goodwill developed by the agent. However, the agent's maximum compensation may not exceed an average commission for 1 year. Insurance agents on the other hand may be entitled to receive 3 years' commission upon termination of the representation, based on the average commissions for the preceding 5 years. If the contract was of less than 1-year duration, the agent's compensation will amount to the average commission for 1 year or to an amount corresponding to the contract's duration.

Upon termination of the relationship, the agent's commercial activities may be restricted up to 2 years following termination. The agent is entitled to compensation for the inactive term, except in cases of termination for just cause. A principal is under no obligation to compensate the agent if the agent fails to perform according to the requirements of the contract. Exclusive representational agreements effective within the European Economic Community should be carefully worded to avoid violation of Articles 85-86 of the Treaty of Rome on antitrust and restrictive business practices.

Greece—No special legislation has been enacted to regulate the termination of agency and distributorship agreements. The parties are free to agree on the terms and conditions of the agency contract, including such as exclusivity of the appointment, extent of the termination notice terms, conditions for termination of the agreement, choice of jurisdiction, and arbitration clauses. Agency contracts terminate by operation of law, upon bankruptcy, death of a contracting party, or interdiction of either the agent or the principal. However, a principal may be held liable to compensate the agent for damage caused by premature or unjustified termination of the relationship, including the value of goodwill and agency promotional expenses.

Italy—The principal-agent relationship is governed by Civil Code provisions (Royal Decree No. 262 of March 16, 1942), by a number of "Collective Economic Agreements" entered between (the representatives) of commercial agents and the association of agent employers, and by Law No. 613 of July 22, 1966, Law No. 316 of March 12, 1968, Presidential Decree No. 758 of April 30, 1968, and Ministerial Decrees of April 8, 1969, April 12, 1969, and Law No. 559 of July 29, 1971.

Commission agents selling the principal's goods within a given territory under a definite or indefinite term contract, are entitled to receive damage compensation, including social security charges and lost commissions, if the principal unilaterally terminates the agency without the agents, being at fault and without advance notice usually set forth in any contract.

No special law has been enacted to regulate the termination of distributorship agreements, nor do any legal provisions make the principal liable for termination of the relationship, so that termination of the agreement is governed by the terms of the contract. Exclusive representation agreements effective within the European Economic Community should be carefully worded to avoid violation of articles 85-86 of the Treaty of Rome, on antitrust and restrictive business practices.

Malta—No special protective legislation. The principal-agent relation is governed by provisions of the commercial Code and Civil Code. Definite term agreements terminate at the expiration of the agreement. Indefinite term agreements may be terminated at any time by giving notice of termination to the other party.

Upon termination of the agreement, the principal must safeguard the agent's rights to any earnings for business being transacted. No notice is required by either party when the agency is terminated due to bad faith.

Netherlands—The principal-commercial agent relationship is governed by Section 74-74r of the Commercial Code, as amended July 1, 1978. The Code provisions do not apply to distributorship contracts which are governed by general provisions of contract law. The Code incorporates pertinent provisions from the Benelux Commercial Agency Treaty.

The parties are free to agree to the terms of the agency agreement except that the agent may not validly waive any of the following rights: (1) the agent's right to remuneration, (2) the agent's right to receive compensation for undue or unjust termination of the relationship. (3) the right to receive goodwill compensation, (4) waivers of statue of limitation provisions. The agent may appoint sub-agents if not prohibited by the agency agreement. However, the agent shall be liable for the acts of the sub-agents appointed by him without the principal's authority. Choice of law clauses may be valid if not aimed at depriving the agent of any benefits granted to him by the law. If the contract is silent as to jurisdiction, Dutch Law governs the contract.

The law provides in all cases for a minimum 4 months' termination notice unless the parties have agreed on a different notice period. The law prohibits the parties from agreeing on a termination notice shorter than 1 month. These terms may be increased to 5 months for contracts of 5 or more years' duration and to 6 months for contracts of 6 or more years duration. A definite term agreement terminates on the contract's expiration date. It the parties continue operating under the contract, the agreement is considered extended for another period not to exceed 1 year. Service of termination notice is necessary for properly terminating definite term agreements. Unilateral termination of an agreement, either prematurely or without adequate notice, may make a principal liable for compensation to the agent. The agent may elect as compensation an amount equal to the commissions which would have accrued during the omitted notice term, commissions lost due to cutting short the definite term contract, or alternatively, the amount of actual damages suffered. In exceptional cases, and only for just cause or urgent reasons, the agency agreement may be terminated without service of notice provided that the other party is immediately advised of the reasons for termination. A party may also petition for judicial termination of the contract. Whatever the reasons or means for terminating an agency agreement, the agent is entitled to claim as compensation the value of the goodwill increased by his efforts. This compensation may not exceed 1 years' average commissions.

In cases where the agent satisfies the legal criteria of an employee of the principal labor law provisions that regulate employment contracts apply to the relationship.

Norway—According to the Norwegian Agent Law of June 30, 1916, as amended by the law of June 1. 1973, an agent is entitled to compensation should the principal give fewer than 3 months' notice of termination, regardless of whether a period of notice has been included in the agency agreement. If the appointment has lasted for less than 1 year, the notice of termination should be 1 month. The agent is also entitled to reasonable compensation for relevant investments he has made in agreement with the principal and to commission sales made by him or through his cooperation. This applies even though sales are concluded after the termination of the agency, provided the purchaser's orders have reached the principal or the agent prior to termination. The agent is also entitled to commission on orders considered to have resulted from his work while he held the agency. In the event of lack of proof of the size of the commission due and the agency having been in force more than 1 year, the commission shall be 3 months' commission based on the average monthly commission of the last year. This rule does not apply if 6 months' notice is given. However, if the principal terminates the agency for a valid reason (e.g. failure of the agent to fulfill his duties and obligations under his appointment), the agent will not be entitled to any of the compensations described above. It is deemed to be unfair competition to substitute one agent for another without giving the substituted agent prior notice of such change.

Portugal—No special law has been enacted to regulate termination of agency and distributorship agreements. The principal-agent relationship is governed by the Civil and Commercial Codes. Under the Codes the parties are free to agree on the terms of their representation agreement including contract termination provisions, service of contract termination notices, and damage compensation clause. The agency contract must be in writing and include clear reference to the agent's type of remuneration; otherwise it will be determined in accordance with local market custom. Agency contracts may terminate by revocation, resignation, incapacity, or death of the parties, insolvency, bankruptcy,, expiration of the contract, and completion of the business venture. Unjustified termination of the agency may make the terminating party liable to compensate the other for damages caused. Expect if otherwise agreed in the agency contract, damage compensation shall include reimbursement of profits the damaged party may have otherwise received had the contract been duly executed. In case of contract breach, damage compensation claim items are limited to those directly resulting a a consequence of the contract breach. Damage compensation claims are decided by Portuguese courts.

Spain—The principal-agent relationship is regulated by the Civil and Commercial Codes, complemented, in regard to commercial agents, by Decree of February 21, 1942, as amended by Decree of November 4, 1944, and resolution of January 20, 1950. On the other hand, commercial representatives are governed by the law of July 21, 1962, as amended by the "Law of Labor Relations," of April 8, 1976. This law placed individual commercial representatives under the scope of the labor laws. Commercial representatives are defined as natural persons that under a special labor relationship promote sales or purchases, whether on salary or commission, for one or more principals.

The principal and agent are free to stipulate whatever terms they agree upon, including provisions for the cancellation of the agency. In the absence of provision to the contrary in the agreement, the Commercial Code allows the principal to terminate the agency at any time after giving notice to the agent. However, the principal is obliged by law to pay the value of the agent's efforts to improve the goodwill of the principal's business, undertaken prior to the notice of termination.

The labor laws require any principal who terminates a commercial representation agreement with a natural person to make compensation to that person. Unless otherwise established by the terms of the representation contract, such compensation is to be determined by the courts. Such determination must fall within the following range: the equivalent of no fewer than 2 months' and no more than 2 years' earnings under the agreement. The indemnity is to be computed on the basis of the average income over the last 2 years or the entire term of the relationship, whichever has been shorter.

Sweden—The Act of April 18, 1914, as amended by Law 219 of May 1974, governs the principal-agent relationship to the extent that the agency agreement, commercial practice, or custom do not otherwise provide. Where specifically provided, however, the law will prevail over the agency agreement, commercial practice or custom. As supplemented by the Swedish Labor Code, this law also regulates the employer-employee relationship of traveling salesmen.

A notice of termination is required to terminate indefinite term agency agreements. The required notice term is 3 months for indefinite term agreements which have been in effect for 1 year or more. The period of notice for such agreements, which have been in effect for less than a year, must be at least 1 full calendar month after the month in which notice is given. The agent cannot waive such notice requirements. However, no notice is required when an indefinite term agency contact is terminated by the principal based on just cause.

Fixed term agreements, or contracts for specific business ventures, terminate at the expiration of the contract term or completion of the business venture. Fixed term agreements may be prematurely terminated by the principal only in the case where the principal has just cause for doing so. Law No. 219, which went into effect on July 1, 1974, is somewhat ambiguous on the question of whether or not there is a notice requirement for terminating fixed-term agreements. Therefore, prudence would suggest that notice be given even when the principal has just cause allowing him to prematurely terminate a fixed-term agreement without liability.

The principal has just cause, allowing him to prematurely terminate a fixed term agency agreement without incurring liability or an indefinite term agency without giving notice, when (1) the agent has been derelict in his duty to the principal, (2) the agent is in bankruptcy, or (3) the agent has breached the contract in such a manner that no reasonable cause exists for continuing the agreement.

In cases of unlawful termination by the principal of the relationship, the agent will normally be entitled to reasonable compensation for losses incurred. This includes the agent's costs for investments in buildings, stock, machinery, transportation facilities, and similar assets, which he has made in furtherance of the agency and with the consent of the principal. The agent can, with binding effect, waive his rights to such reimbursement only if the waiver is made when the investment is effected.

The agent has a right to receive commissions on sales completed after the agency has been terminated provided such sales resulted from the agent's efforts.

Switzerland—The principal-agent relationship is governed by the Swiss Code of Obligations. the Law of Agency Agreements, dated February 4, 1949, in force since January 1, 1950, has been included in the Code.

Choice of law clauses are not recognized if the agent is doing business in Switzerland. The agent may not waive the right to obtain compensation from the principal. If the agency contract does not include agency termination provisions, the law stipulates a 1-month minimum period forgiving notice of termination during the first year of the agreement. This period is extended to 2 months after the first year and the agreement may only be terminated at the end of each calendar quarter. Agreements providing for shorter notice terms must be in writing. Definite term agreements terminate on the termination date specified in the contract. If the parties continue to operate under a definite term agreement after its expiration, the contract is deemed to have been extended for another year.

The agent has an unwaiveable right to receive compensation for acts of the principal unduly preventing him from the free exercise of the agency, as well as for noncompetition clauses restricting the agent's future commercial activities after termination of the agency. Furthermore, the agent is entitled to compensation not to exceed 1 year's net profit for new clients gained for the principal, provided that the agreement was not terminated by the agent or terminated due to the agent's fault. The agent is also entitled to this compensation if the principal benefits substantially from the new clients after the agreement has been terminated.

Turkey—No special protective legislation has been enacted to regulate the termination of representational agreements. The principal-agent relationship is governed by Chapter VIII, Articles 116 to 134 of the Turkish Commercial Code. Except when otherwise provided in the contract, a principal may not appoint several agents in the same territory for the same line of products. The agent is precluded from carrying on the same line of business for two or more competing principals in the same geographical area.

Any party may terminate an indefinite term agreement by giving to the other party a 3-month termination notice. Definite term agreements may be terminated before expiration for just cause only. Failure to serve termination notice, or absence of just cause for terminating a definite term agreement, may make a party liable for damages. The principal-agent relationship may also terminate by operation of law in case of bankruptcy, death or interdiction of duties of principal or agent. In these cases the agent or his successors in the business are entitled to be compensated for estimated earnings that would have been earned if all outstanding business had been completed.

United Kingdom—No special legislation has been enacted to regulate the termination of representation agreements. The principal-agent relationship is regulated by the terms of the agency contract within Common Law principles derived from contract and agency law.

Agency representations may be terminated by agreement of the parties, by the principal revoking the agency contract, or renunciation of the agency by the agent. However, specific agreement to terminate the relationship is required if the agency is coupled with an interest, if the agent has assumed personal liability, or has become liable for personal losses. Termination may also occur due to expiration of the contract term, performance, frustration of the contractual purpose, or by operation of law in cases of death of the parties, bankruptcy of the principal, insolvency of the agent, war, or insanity of a party.

Either party may terminate the agency relationship by giving the other party a "reasonable" notice of termination, e.g., if the agent is under salary, 1 week's or 1 month's notice will suffice when the agent is paid by week or by monthly. When the agent is remunerated by commission, it has been estimated that a 6-month notice is adequate, although the parties to the agency contract may provide otherwise.

Penalty clauses in agency agreements are not enforceable. Damages may be awarded to the injured party following breach of the agency contract.

FAR EAST

Afghanistan—No official regulations restrict the activities of foreign traders to do business between the trader's country and Afghanistan. Appointment of Afghan nationals as agents is not compulsory, but is strongly recommended as Afghan purchasing practices are complex, confusing, and usually have a short lead time. Afghan national representatives of foreign firms must be licensed by the Ministry of Commerce, which requires disclosure from the foreign firm of contractual conditions including fees and commissions. The principal-agent relationship is governed by the terms of the agency contract, but the Ministry of Commerce may refuse to grant the agent's license if such terms are considered inappropriate.

Burma—The Burmese Trade Council in 1965 set up a government corporation called Myanma Export-Import Corporation (MEIC) to operate as sole "legal agency" for all foreign firms. No private individual or firm may be registered as a commission agent. On the other hand, foreign firms may appoint under salary a "technical representative" to perform nonsale promotional activities on behalf of a foreign principal. After the representative is approved and registered with MEIC, the corporation operates as intermediary with him and his foreign principal, handling correspondence and payment of salaries to the representative.

China, People's Republic of—All trade in China is State-controlled. All purchasing is done by State Trading Corporations and it is not possible to have an individual as sole agent or representative.

Hong Kong—No special laws have been enacted regulating the termination of agency agreements. The legislation follows English Common Law principles. The parties are to negotiate their contract conditions including provisions for termination of the relationship. Customarily the relationship is ended by serving a termination notice on the other party.

India—The principal-agent relationship is governed by Chapter X of the India Contract Act (sections 182-238). If the agency is for a fixed period, the principal must pay compensation to the agent for his revocation or termination of the agency without just cause. The agent is also liable for unjust termination. The principal may terminate an agreement prematurely if the agent is guilty of misconduct in the due discharge of his duties. Service of "reasonable" notice is required. The law does not define "reasonable" and each case is decided according to the facts. Indefinite term agreements may be terminated by the principal at any time. Service of reasonable notice of termination is advisable.

Agency agreements are also terminated by: (1) expiration of the contract terms, (2) death or incapacity of the principal, (3) death or incapacity of the agent, (4) completion of the business, or (5) impossibility of execution by reason of law or destruction of the subject matter.

Section 28 (1)a of the Foreign Exchange Regulation Act of 1973 forbids wholly or partially foreign-owned Indian companies to act as agents, or to accept appointment as agents, for any foreign individual or company without prior specific permission of the Reserve Bank of India. This approval is also required for agency agreements in effect before the date of the regulations.

Indonesia—The principal-agent relationship is regulated by Decree No. 295/M/SK/7/1982, issued by the Ministry of Industry, entitled: "Provisions Concerning sole-agency". Special implementing regulations were issued by Decree No. 446/M/SK/7/1982 for "Provisions concerning sub-agency of automotive products and heavy equipment".

Under Decree 195/1982, effective as of July 7, 1982, the sole-agency contract is exclusively governed by Indonesian law and must be approved by the Ministry of Industry. The agent must be a legal body organized under the laws of Indonesia. A national enterprise may operate as an agent and may deal with several lines of goods. A principal may freely select and appoint his agent, who shall be exclusive for the territory of Indonesia. The parties are free to agree to the terms of their agreement which must include: (a) name and full address of the contracting parties, (b) statement of the agreement's objectives, (c) description of the goods subject to the agreement, (d) provisions under which the agreement may be cancelled, and (e) determination of unsatisfactory conduct and non-performance by the agent. The contract duration may not be fewer than 3 years, extendable for identical periods, and no fewer than 5 years when the agent is engaged in the assembly or manufacture of products. The principal may not assign an agency to another national enterprise except for reasons established in the contract.

The agency agreement may only be terminated prior to its expiration, without incurring damage liability, by mutual consent of the parties, or when the sole agent is dissolved, goes bankrupt, or loses its business license. The principal may also terminate the contract unilaterally when the sub-agent engages in extremely unsatisfactory conduct or by reason of non-performance of the agreement. Unilateral termination makes the principal liable to compensate the agent for the costs or investments which the sole agent has made in the marketing distribution of the products, which may include: (a) stocks of goods in the agent's custody, (b) building or equipment for the goods, and (c) cost of training employees to handle the goods.

Korea—No special protective legislation has been enacted to regulate the termination of agency contracts. Although the principal-agent relationship is subject to the Commercial Code (Law No. 1000 of January 20, 1962), supplemented by the Civil Code, the parties are free to agree to nearly all the terms of their contract, including clauses regulating termination. Indefinite term agreements may be terminated at any time by giving the representative a 2-month termination notice. Definite term agreements expire on the date of expiration of the contract, but may also be terminated before expiration, for just cause following a 2-month termination notice.

The agency contract terminates by operation of law in the following cases: (1) assignment or termination of the business, (2) death or disability of any of the parties, or (3) bankruptcy or insolvency.

Only Korean nationals or Korean legal entities may act as representatives or agent for foreign exporters. Commercial representatives and agents must be registered with and approved by the Ministry of Industry and Trade. If an agent violates the law, the Minister may revoke his registration to do business.

Malaysia—No special legislation has been enacted to regulate the termination of agency and distributorship agreements. The relationship is governed by the contract terms as agreed by the parties within the provisions of articles 135-191 of the Malaysian Contract Law, supplemented by Law No. 136 of July 1, 1950 (1974 revision). Only Malaysian nationals, whether individuals or firms, may operate as agents or distributors. Legal entities must have 100 percent Malaysian capital and management. The local representative must be registered with the Ministry of Trade and Industry.

Revocation of the agency may be express or implied by reason of the conduct of the principal or agent. Reasonable termination notice must be given to the party being terminated. Failure to give notice may make a party liable to compensation for damages caused by the termination or the revocation. Definite term agreements may be prematurely terminated by the principal only based on just cause and giving the agent reasonable notice of termination. Otherwise, the terminating party may be liable to compensate the other for damages. Agencies may also be terminated by: (1) completion of the business, (2) death or incapacity of the principal or agent, (3) bankruptcy or insolvency of any of the parties.

Nepal—No special law has been enacted to regulate termination of agency contracts. All agencies must be government approved and registered. Nepalese nationals enjoy priority rights for registration as agents. The relationship of the parties is governed by the terms of their agreement. Indefinite term agreements may be terminated by serving termination notice on the other party. It is customary to also notify the Nepalese government of the expiration of the agency.

Pakistan—No special legislation has been enacted to regulate the termination of agency and distributorship agreements between local firms and their foreign principals. The principal-agent relationship is basically governed by the terms of the agency contract, subject to the provisions of Pakistani general contract law, much of which is modeled after British common law principles. If the contract is silent concerning termination, it is customary to give the agent at least a 3-month termination notice.

Philippines—There is no special legislation or provision in the Commercial Code relating to agency agreements between local firms and their foreign principals. The provisions concerning agencies may be found in Articles 1858 through 1932, inclusive, of the Civil Code. The only relevant provisions in the Civil Code provide that contracts are to be governed by the law of the country in which they are executed. When such contracts are executed before a diplomatic or consular official of the Republic of the Philippines in a foreign country, the requirements established by Philippine law will be observed in their execution.

In addition to contract termination, the parties agree to the contract termination as a matter of law on: (1) revocation by any of the parties; (2) withdrawal of the agent; (3) death, civil interdiction, insanity or insolvency of the principal or the agent; (4) dissolution of the firm or corporation; (5) accomplishment of the objective or purpose of the agency; and (6) expiration of the period for which the agency was established.

Singapore—There is no law applicable to the termination of agency or dealership agreements between firms and local agents. Customary practice allows the terms decided upon between two parties in the agreement or contract to govern the relationship.

Sri-Lanka—There is no special legislation governing termination of agency contracts either between local residents or between foreign and local residents. The agency contract is governed by the law of contracts and the provisions of the agreement. Reasonable notice of termination is customary.

Thailand—There is no specific law regulating the termination of agency agreements. Sections 797 to 848 of the Thai Commercial Code regulate the rights and duties of the parties to an agency agreement. These Code provisions prevail unless the parties, by private contract, agree otherwise. Such agreements cannot, on the other hand, override provisions of the Commercial Code on matters affecting public policy. Accordingly, except for the foregoing limitation, the parties may freely agree to the terms and conditions that shall govern their relationship, including clauses regulating the termination or cancellation of the representation. Thus the principal or the agent can terminate the agency at will, but under Section 827 of the Thai Commercial Code either party may be held liable to compensate the other for damages caused by the termination.

The principal-agent relationship may also terminate, unless otherwise provided in the contract, in case of death of either part, bankruptcy, insolvency, or by reason of the nature of the business.

Taiwan—No special law has been enacted to regulate the termination of agency agreements. The parties are free to agree to the terms of the agency contract. Either party may terminate an agency agreement without incurring liability, by giving termination notice to the other party, provided no contract breach occurs.

FOR MORE INFORMATION

Commercial Agency Guide for the Drawing up of Contracts Between Parties Residing in Different Countries, United States Council of the International Chamber of Commerce, 1212 Avenue of Americas, New York, N.Y. 10036.

Practical Aspects of Commercial Agency and Distribution Agreements in the European Community, by Robert T. Jones, January 1972, and **Overseas Distributorship Agreements,** by Marcellus R. Meek, April 1966, The Business Lawyer, American Bar Assn., 1155 East 60th St., Chicago, Ill. 60637.

Legal Considerations in Contracting with Foreign Agents and Distributors, by Michael Olson, Sorsey, Marquart, Windhorst, West and Halliday, 2400 First National Bank Bldg., Minneapolis, Minn 55402.

Protecting Local Distributors—A Growing Latin American Phenomenon, by Jonathan Russin, Kirkwood, Kaplan, Russin and Vecchi, 1218 16th St., N.W., Washington, D.C. 20036.

Signing Up Your Agent, by Colin McMillan and Sidney Paulden, International Trade Forum, October 1969, Volume V, No. 3, published by International Trade Centre UNCTAD/GATT, Palais des Nations 1211, Geneva 10, Switzerland.

Indemnities for Terminating Foreign Representatives, by Frederick O. Cowles, Boston University Press, Volume 53, No. 2, March 1973.

Appendix 12

Finding International Information

A. MARKET IDENTIFICATION AND ASSESSMENT

• Addresses to AID Missions Overseas, Office of Small and Disadvantaged Business Utilization/Minority Business Center, Agency for International Development, Washington, DC 20523. Free.

• AID Commodity Eligibility Listing, Office of Small and Disadvantaged Business Utilization/Minority Resource Center Agency for International Development, Washington, DC 20523, 1984 revised. This document lists groups of commodities, presents the Agency for International Development (AID) commodity eligibility list, gives eligibility requirements for certain commodities and describes commodities that are not eligible for financing by the agency. Free.

• AID Regulation 1, Office of Small Disadvantaged Business, Utilization/Minority Resource Center, Agency for International Development, Washing, DC 20523. This tells what transactions are eligible for financing by the Agency for International Development (AID), and the responsibilities of importers, as well as the bid procedures. Free.

Source: "A Basic Guide to Exporting," U. S. Department of Commerce, International Trade Administration, U. S. and Foreign Commercial Service, Washington, D. C., September, 1986.

- AID Financed Export Opportunities, Office of Small and Disadvantaged Business Utilization/ Minority Resource Center, Agency for International Development, Washington, DC 20523. These are fact sheets also referred to as "Small Business Circulars". They present procurement data about proposed foreign purchases. Free.

- American Bulletin of International Technology Transfer, International Advancement, P. O. Box 75537, Los Angeles, CA 90057. Bimonthly. This is a comprehensive listing of product and service opportunities offered and wanted for licensing and joint ventures agreements in the United States and overseas. $72 per year.

- Annual Worldwide Industry Reviews (AWIR), Export Promotion Services, U. S. Department of Commerce, P. O. Box, 14207, Washington, DC 20044; tel: (202) 377-2432. These reports provide a combination of country by country market assessments, export trends, and a 5-year statistical table of U. S. Exports for a single industry integrated into one report. They quickly show an industry's performance for the most recent year in most countries. Each report covers 8 to 18 countries. A single report is $200; two reports within the same industry are $350; and three reports within the same industry are $500.

- Big Business Blunders; Mistakes in Multinational Marketing, 1982, David A. Ricks, Doug Jones-Irwin, Homewood, IL 60430. 200 pp. $13.95.

- Business America, International Trade Administration, U. S. Department of Commerce. This magazine is the principle Commerce Department publication for presenting domestic and international business news and news of the application of technology to business and industrial problems. Available through the Superintendent of Documents, Government Printing Office Washington, DC 20402. Annual Subscription, $57.

- Catalogo de Publicaciones de la OPS, Pan American Health Organization/World Health Organization, 525 23rd Street, NW., Washington, DC 20037. A free guide of publications, many in of which are in English. This catalog is published in Spanish.

- Country Market Surveys (CMS), Export Promotion Services, U. S. Department of Commerce, P. O. Box 14207, Washington, DC 20044. Tel: (202) 377-2432. This report series offers short summaries of International Market Research (IMR) geared to the needs of the busy executive. They highlight market size, trends and prospects in an easy to read format. $10 per copy or $9 per copy for six or more.

- Country Trade Statistics (CTS), Export Promotion Services, U. S. Department of Commerce, P. O. Box 14207, Washington, DC 20044; tel: (202) 377-2432. This is a set of four key tables that indicate which U. S. products are in the greatest demands in a specific country over the most recent five-year period. They indicate which U. S. industries look best for export to a particular country and the export performance of single industries. Tables highlight the top U. S. exports, those with the largest market share, the fastest growing, and those which are the primary U. S. market. The CTS is $25 for the first country, and $10 for each additional country up to 25.

• Custom Statistical Service, Export Promotion Services, U. S. Department of Commerce, P. O. Box 14207, Washington, DC 20044; tel: (292) 377-2432. Individually tailored tables of U. S. exports or imports. The custom service provides data for specific products or countries of interest, or for one which may not appear in the standard ESP country and product rankings for a chosen industry. With Custom Statistics one can also obtain data in other formats such as quantity, unit quantity, unit value and percentages. Custom orders are priced by the number of products, countries, or other data desired, and range from $50 to $500.

• Developments in International Trade Policy, International Monetary Fund, Publications Unit, 700 19th Street, NW., Washington, DC 20431. This paper focuses on the main current issues in trade policies of the major trading nations. $5.

• Direction of Trade Statistics, International Monetary Fund, Publications Unit 700 19th Street, NW., Washington, DC 20431. This monthly publication provides data on the country and area distribution of countries' exports and imports as reported by themselves or their partners. A yearbook is published annually which gives seven years of data for 157 countries and two sets of world and area summaries. $36 for 12 monthly issues, including the yearbook, Single monthly issue is $14, the yearbook is $10.

• Directory of Leading U. S. Export Management Companies, 1984, Bergamo Book Co., 15 Ketchum Street, Westport, CT 06881. $37.50.

• Economic and Social Survey for Asia and the Pacific, UNIPUB, P. O. Box 1222, Ann Arbor, MI 48106. Tel: (800) 521-8110. This publication analyzes recent economic and social development in the region in the context of current trends. It examines agriculture, food industry, transport, public finance, wages and prices, and external trade sectors. $19.

• Element of Export Marketing, John Stapleton, 1984, Woodhead-Faulkner, Dover, NH, $11.25.

• Entry Strategies for Foreign Market—From Domestic to International Business, Franklin R. Root, American Management Association, 1977, 51 pp., $10.

• EXIM Bank Information Kit, Public Affairs Office, Export-Import Bank of United States, 811 Vermont Avenue, NW., Washington, DC 20571. This includes the Bank's annual report, which provides information on interest rates and the Foreign Credit Insurance Association.

• Export Development Strategies: U. S. Promotion Policy, Michael R. Czinkota and George Tasar, Praeger, New York, NY, 1982, $27.95.

• Export Directory, Foreign Agricultural Services, Department of Agriculture, 14th & Independence AVenues, SW., Room 5918-S, Washington, DC 20230. The directory describes the principle functions of the Foreign Agriculture Service and lists agricultural attaches. Free.

• Export Directory: Buying Guide, biennial, Journal of Commerce, 110 Wall Street, New York, NY 10005. $225.

• Export-Import Bank: Financing for American Exports—Support for American Jobs, Export-Import Bank of the United States, 1980. Free.

• Export/Import Operations; A Manager's "How to" and "Why" Guide, Robert M. Franko, 1979, Professional Business Services, Inc. $35.

• Export Statistics Profiles (ESP), Export Promotion Services, U. S. Department of Commerce, P. O. Box 14207, Washington, DC 20044; tel: (202) 377-2432. These tables of U. S. exports for a specific industry help identify the best export markets and analyze the industry's exports product-by-product, country-by-country over each of the last five years to date. Data is rank-ordered by dollar value. The price is $70.00 for each ESP.

• Export Strategies: Market and Competition, Nigel Percy, 1982, Allen & Unwin, Winchester, MA 01890, $30, (cloth), $13.95 (paper).

• Exporter's Encyclopedia, annual with semimonthly updates, Dun & Bradstreet International, One Exchange Plaza, Suite 715, Jersey City, NJ 07302. This provides a comprehensive, country-by-country coverage of 220 world markets. It contains an examination of each country's communications and transportation facilities, customs and trade regulations, documentation, key contacts, and unusual conditions that may affect operations. Financing and Credit abroad are also examined. $365 per year.

• Exporting: A Practical Manual for Developing Export Markets and Dealing with Foreign Customs, 2nd edition, Earnst Y. Maitland, 1982, 150 pp., Self-Counsel Press, $12.50.

• Exporting from the U.S.A.: How to Develop Export Markets and Cope with Foreign Customs, A. B. Marring, 1981, 114 pp., Self-Counsel Press, $12.95.

• Exporting to Japan, American Chamber of Commerce in Japan, 1982, A. M. Newman. $10.

• FAS Commodity Reports, U. S. Department of Agriculture, Foreign Agriculture Service, Room 5918, Washington, DC 20250. Tel: (202) 477-7937. These reports provide information on foreign agricultural production in 22 commodity areas. Reports are based on information submitted by Foreign Agricultural Service (FAS) personnel overseas. The publication frequency varies with the commodity. The price is $1 - $460 depending on commodity and whether the report is mailed or picked-up at USDA office.

- FATUS: Foreign Agricultural Trade of the United States, U. S. Department of Agriculture Service, Room 5918, Washington 20250. Tel: (202) 477-7937. This report of trends in and of events affecting this trade is published six times a year with two supplements. The price is $19 per year.

- Findex: The Directory of Market Research Reports, Studies and Surveys, FIND/SVP, The Information Clearinghouse, 500 Fifth Avenue, New York, NY 10036. Tel: (212) 354-2424. Over 10,000 listings. $245.

- Foreign Agriculture, U. S. Department of Agriculture, Foreign Agriculture Service, Room 5918, Washington, DC 20250. Tel: (202) 477-7937. A monthly publication containing information on overseas promotional activities. The price is $16 per year.

- Foreign Agriculture Circulars, U. S. Department of Agriculture, Foreign Agriculture Service, Room 5918, Washington, DC 20250; tel: (202) 477-7937. These individual circulars report on the supply and demand for commodities around the world. Products covered include: dairy, livestock, poultry, grains, coffee, and wood products. The frequency of publication varies with the commodity. The price is $3 to $66 depending on commodity.

- Foreign Commerce Handbook, Chamber of Commerce of the United States, 1615 H Street NW., Washington DC 20062. A publication containing organizations of assistance to U. S. exporters, as well as up-to-date published information on all important phases on international trade and investment. $10.

- Foreign Economic Trends (FET), Superintendent of Documents, U. S. Government Printing Office, Washington, DC 20402. Prepared by the U. S. and Foreign Commercial Service. This presents current business and economic developments and the latest economic indications in more than 100 countries. Annual subscription, $70; single copies are available for $1 from ITA Publications Distribution, Rm. 1617D, U. S. Department of Commerce, Washington, DC 20230.

- Foreign Market Entry Strategies, Franklin R. Root, 1982, AMACOM, New York, NY 10020, 304 pp. $24.95.

- General Economic Problems, OECD Publications and Information Center, Suite 1207, 1750 Pennsylvania Avenue, NW., Washington, DC 20006-4582. Tel: (202) 724-1859. This contains the latest monographs on: Economic policies and forecasts; growth; inflation, national accounts; international trade and payments; capital markets; interest rates; taxation; and energy, industrial and agricultural policies. $144.25.

- Glossary of International Terms, International Trade Institute, Inc., 5055 N. Main Street, Dayton, OH 45415; Tel (800) 543-2453, 68 pp, $17.50.

- A Guide to Export Marketing, International Trade Institute Inc., 5055 North Main Street, Suite 270, Dayton, OH 45415. Tel: (800) 453-2453. $50.

•   Handbook of International Statistic, UNIPUB, P. O. Box 1222, Ann Arbor, MI 48106. Tel: (800) 521-8110. The handbook examines structural trends in 70 developing and developed countries, including: Changes in the pattern of consumption for specific commodities; long-term patterns of growth; and the export performance of key industries. $22.

•   Highlights of U. S. Import and Export Trade, Superintendent of Documents, U. S. Government Printing Office Washington, DC 20402. Statistical book of U. S. imports and exports. Compiled monthly by the Bureau of the Census. $41 per year; single copies. $4.50.

•   How to Build an Export Business: An International Marketing Guide for Minority-Owned Businesses, Superintendent of Documents, U. S. Government Printing Office, Washington, DC 20402. $10.

•   International Development, OECD Publications and Information Center, Suite 1207, 1750 Pennsylvania Avenue, NW., Washington, DC 20006-4582. Tel: (202) 724-1857. This contains the latest monographs on: Financial Resources and aid policies, general problems of development, industrialization, transfer of technology, rural development, employment, human resources, immigration, and demography. $173.

•   International Financial Statistics, International Monetary Fund, Publications Unit, 700 19th Street, NW., Washington, DC 20431. This monthly publication is a standard source of international statistics on all aspects of international and domestic finance. It reports, for most countries of the world, current data needed in the analysis of problems of international payments, and of inflation and deflation, i.e., data on exchange rates, international liquidity, money and banking, international transactions, prices, production, government finance, interest rates, and other items. $10 per issue, or $100 per year, including a yearbook and two supplement series.

•   International Market Research (IMR) Reports, Export Promotion Services, U. S. Department of Commerce, P. O. Box 14207, Washington, DC 20044. Tel: (202) 377-2432. This is an in-depth industry sector analysis for those who want the complete data for one industry in one country. A report includes information such as behavior characteristics, trade barriers, market share figures, end user analysis, and trade contacts. $50 to $250.

•   International Market Information (IMI), Export Promotion Services, U. S. Department of Commerce, P. O. Box 14207, Washington, DC 20044. Tel: (202) 377-2432. These are special "bulletins" that point to unique market situations and new opportunities to U. S. exporters in specific markets. $15.00 to $100.

•   International Marketing, 5th edition, 1983, Phillip R. Cateora, Irwin, Homewood, IL 60430, $29.95.

• International Marketing, Raul Kahler, 1983, Southwestern Publishing Co., Cincinnati, OH 45227, 426 pp.

• International Marketing, 3rd edition, Vern Terpstra, 1983, Dryden Press, Hinsdale, IL 60521, 624 pp., $32.95.

• International Marketing, Revised Edition, Hans Thorelli & Helmut Becker, ed., 1980, Pergamon Press, Elmsford, NY 10523, 400 pp., $14.25.

• International Marketing, 2nd edition, 1981, L. S. Walsh International Ideas, Philadelphia, PA 19103, $15.95.

• International Marketing: An Annotated Bibliography, 1983 S. T. Cavusgil & John R. Nevin, ed., American Marketing Association, 139 pp., $8.

• International Marketing Handbook, 1985, 3 Vols., Frank S. Bair, ed., Gale Research Co., Detroit, MI 48226, 3,637 pp., $200.

• International Marketing Research, 1983, Susan P. Douglas & C. Samuel Craig, Prentice-Hall, Englewood Cliffs, NJ 07632, 384 pp., $27.95.

• International Monetary Fund: Publication Catalog, International Monetary Fund, Publications, Unit, 700 19th Street, NW., Washington, DC 20431. Free.

• International Trade Operations . . . A Managerial Approach, R. Duane Hall, Unz & Co., 190 Baldwin Ave., Jersey City NJ 07303, $42.50.

• Local Chamber of Commerce Which Maintain Foreign Trade Services, 1983. International Division, Chamber of Commerce of the United States, 1615 H Street, NW., Washington, DC 20062. This is a list of chambers of commerce that have programs to aid exporters. Free.

• Market Shares Reports, National Technical Information Services, U. S. Department of Commerce, Box 1553, Springfield, VA 22161. These are reports for over 88 countries. They provide basic data needed by exporters to evaluate overall trends in the size of markets for manufacturers. They also: Measure changes in the import demand for specific products; compare the competitive position of U. S. and foreign exporters, select distribution centers for U. S. products abroad, and identify existing and potential markets of U. S. components, parts, and accessories.

• Marketing Aspects of International Business, 1983, Gerald M. Hampton & Aart Van Gent, Klewer-Nijhoff Publishing, Bingham, MA $39.50.

• Marketing High-Technology, William L. Shanklin & John K. Ryans, Jr., DC Health & Co., 125 Spring Street, Lexington, MA 02173, $24.

• Marketing in Europe, Economic Intelligence Unit, Ltd., 10 Rockefeller Plaza, New York, NY 10020, monthly. This Journal provides detailed analysis of the European market for consumer goods. The issues are published in three subject groups: Food, drink and tobacco; clothing, furniture and consumer goods; and chemists; goods such as pharmaceuticals and toiletries. $380 for three groups per year.

• Marketing in the Third World, Erdener Kaynak, Praeger, New York, NY 10175, 302 pp., $29.95.

• Metric Laws and Practices, in International Trade—Handbook for U. S. Exports, U. S. Government Printing Office, Washington, DC 20402, 1982, 113 pp. $4.75.

• Monthly World Crop Production, U. S. Department of Agriculture, Foreign Agriculture Service, Room 5918, Washington, DC 20250. Tel: (202) 477-7937. This report provides estimates on the projection of wheat, rice, coarse grains, oilseeds, and cotton in selected regions and countries around the world.

• The Multinational Marketing and Employment Directory, 8th edition, World Trade Academy Press, Inc., 50 East 42nd Street, New York, NY 10017, 1982, two volumes. This directory lists more than 7,500 American corporations operating in the United States and overseas. The directory is recognized as an outstanding marketing source for products, skills and services in the United States and abroad. It is of particular value to manufacturers, distributors, international traders, investors, bankers, advertising agencies and libraries. It is also helpful for placement bureaus, executive recruiters, direct mail marketers, and technical and management consultants. The specialized arrangement of the information expedites sales in domestic and foreign markets. $90.

• Multinational Marketing Management, 3rd edition, 1984, Warren J. Keegan, Prentice Hall, Englewood Cliffs, NJ 07632, 720 pp., $31.95.

• OECD Publications, OECD Publications and Information Center, Suite 1207, 1750 Pennsylvania Avenue, NW., Washington, DC 20006-4582. Tel: (202) 724-4582. Free.

• Outlook for U. S. Agricultural Exports, U. S. Department of Agriculture, Foreign Agriculture Service, Room 5918, Washington, DC 20250. Tel: (202) 477-7937. The report analyzes current developments and forecasts U. S. Farm exports in coming months by commodity and region. Country and regional highlights discuss the reasons why sales of major commodities are likely to rise or fall in those areas. The price is $7 per year.

• Overseas Business Reports (OBR), Superintendent of Documents, U. S. Governments, U. S. Government Printing Office, Washington, DC 20402. These reports are prepared by the country specialists in the International Trade Administration (ITA). They include current marketing information, trade forecasts, statistics, regulations, and marketing profiles. Annual subscription, $26. Single copies are available from ITA Publications, Rm. 1617D, U. S. Department of Commerce, Washington, DC 20230.

- Product/Country Market Profiles, Export Promotion Services, U. S. Department of Commerce, P. O. Box 14702, Washington, DC 20044. Tel: (202) 377-2432. These products are tailor-made, single product/multi-country; or single country/multiproduct reports. They include trade contacts, specific opportunities, and statistical analyses. $300 to $500.

- Profitable Export Marketing: A Strategy for U. S. Business, Maria Ortiz-Buonafina, Prentice-Hall, Englewood Cliffs, NJ 07632, $9.95.

- Reference Book for World Traders, Annual, Croner Publications, Inc., 211 Jamaica Avenue, Queens Village, NY 11428. A loose-leaf reference book for traders. Gives information about export documentation, steamship lines and airlines, free trade zones, credit and similar matters. Supplemented monthly.

- Source Book ... The "How to" Guide for Exporters and Importers, Unz & Co., 190 Baldwin Avenue, Jersey City, NJ 07036.

- Trade and Development Report, UNIPUB, P. O. Box 1222, Ann Arbor, MI 48106. Tel: (800) 521-8110. This report reviews current economic issues and longer run development in international trade. $15.00.

- Trade Directories of the World, Annual, Croner Publication Inc., 211 Jamaica Avenue, Queens Village, NY 11428, $59.95 plus supplements.

- Trends in World Production and Trade, UNIPUB, Box 1222, Ann Arbor, MI 48106. Tel: (800) 521-8110. This report discusses the structural change in the world output, industrial growth patterns since 1960, changes in the pattern of trade in goods and services. Product groups and commodity groups are defined according to SITC criteria. $6.

- United Nations Publications, United Nations and Information Center, 1889 F. Street, NW., Washington, DC 2006. Free.

- U. S. Export Sales, U. S. Department of Agriculture, Foreign Agriculture Service, Room 5918, Washington, DC 20250. Tel: (202) 477-7937. A weekly report of agricultural export sales based on reports provided by private exporters. There is no cost for this publication.

- U. S. Export Weekly—International Trade Reporter, Bureau of National Affairs, Inc. $352. per year.

- U. S. Farmers Export Arm, U. S. Department of Agriculture, Foreign Agricultural Service, Room 5918 Washington, DC 20250 1980. Free.

- Weekly Roundup of World Production and Trade, U. S. Department of Agriculture Service, Room 5918, Washington, DC 20250. Tel: (202) 477-7937. This publication provides a summary of the week's important events in agricultural foreign trade and world production. Free.

• World Agriculture, U. S. Department of Agriculture, Foreign Agriculture Service, Room 5918, Washington, DC 20250. Tel: (202) 477-7937. Providers production information, data and analyses by commodity and country, along with a review of recent economic conditions and changes in food and trade policies. Price: $9 per year.

• World Agriculture Regional Supplements, U. S. Department of Agriculture, Foreign Agriculture Service, Room 5918, Washington, DC 20250. Tel: (202) 477-7937. Provides a look by region at agricultural developments during the previous year and the outlook for the year ahead. Reports are published on North America/ Oceania, Latin America, Eastern Europe, Western Europe, U.S.S.R., Middle East and North Africa, Subsaharan Africa, East Asia, China, South Asia, and Southeast Asia. Price: $18 per year.

• The World Bank Catalog of Publications, World Bank Publications, P. O. Box 37525, Washington, DC 200013 Free.

• World Economic Outlook: A Survey by the Staff of the International Monetary Fund, International Monetary Fund, Publications, Unit, 700 19th Street, NW., Washington, DC 20431. This report provides a comprehensive picture of the international situation and prospects. It highlights the imbalances that persist in the world economy and their effects on inflation, unemployment, real rates of interest and exchange rates. Published yearly. $8.

• World Economic Survey, UNIPUB, P. O. Box 1222, Ann Arbor, MI 48106. Tel: (800) 521-8110. This publication assesses the world economy. It provides an overview of developments in global economics for the past year and provides an outlook for the future. $12.

• Yearbook of International Trade Statistics, UNIPUB, P. O. Box 1222, Ann Arbor, MI 48106. Tel: (800) 521-8110. This yearbook offers international coverage of foreign trade statistics. Tables are provided for overall trade by regions and countries. Vol. I: Trade by Commodity. Vol. II Commodity Matrix Tables. Both Volumes $80.

B. SELLING & SALES CONTACTS

• American Export Register, Thomas Publishing Co., 1 Penn Plaza 250 No. 34th Street, New York, NY 10010, 1984. A listing of more than 25,000 firms, this book is designed for persons searching for U. S. suppliers, for foreign manufacturers seeking U. S. buyers or representatives for their products. It contains product lists in four languages, an advertiser's index, information about and a list of U. S. Chambers of Commerce abroad, and a list of banks with international services and shipping, financing and insurance information. $112.

- Background Notes, Superintendent of Documents, U. S. Government Printing Office, Washington, DC 20402. These are four to twelve page summaries on the economy, people, history, culture and government of about 160 countries. $42 per set; binders, $3.75.

- A Business Guide to the Near East and North Africa, 1981. Superintendent of Documents, U. S. Government Printing Office, Washington, DC 20402, 28 pp. This guide is designed to provide U. S. business with information on the nature of these markets, how do business in these areas, and how the Department of Commerce can help in penetrating these markets. $4.75.

- Commercial News (CN), Monthly export promotion magazine circulated only overseas, listing specific products and services of U. S. firms. Applications for participation in the magazine are available from the District Offices of the U. S. and Foreign Commercial Service, U. S. Department of Commerce.

- Directory of American Firms Operating in Foreign Countries, 10th Edition, 1984, World Trade Academy Press, 50 E. 42nd Street, New York, NY 10017, 1600 pp. This directory contains the most recent data on more than 4,200 American corporations controlling and operating more than 16,500 foreign business enterprises. It lists every American firm under the country in which it has subsidiaries or branches, together with their home office branch in the United States. It also gives the names and addresses of their subsidiaries or branches, products manufactured or distributed. $150.

- Export Mailing List Service (EMLS), Export Promotion Services, U. S. Department of Commerce, P. O. Box 14207, Washington, DC 20044. Tel: (202) 377-2432. These are targeted mailing lists of prospective overseas customers from the Commerce Department's automated worldwide file of foreign firms. EMLs identify manufacturers, agents, retailers, service firms, government agencies and other one-to-one contacts. Information includes name and address, cable and telephone numbers, name and title of a key official, product/service interests, and additional date. $35. and up.

- How to Get the Most from Overseas Exhibitions, International Trade Administration, Publications Distribution, Room 1617D, U. S. Department of Commerce, Washington, DC 20230. This eight-page booklet outlines the steps an exporter should take to participate in an overseas exhibition sponsored by the Department of Commerce. Free.

- Japan: Business Obstacles and Opportunities, 1983, McKinney & Co., John Wiley, NY $24.95.

- Management of International Advertising: A Marketing Approach, 1984, Dean M. Peeples & John K. Ryans. Allyn & Bacon, Boston, MA 02159, 600 pp., $48.

• Service Industries and Economic Development: Case Studies in Technology Transfer. Praeger Publishers, New York, NY 10175. 1984, 190 pp. $24.95.

• Top Bulletin, Export Promotion Services, U. S. Department of Commerce, P. O. Box 14207, Washington, DC 20044; tel: (202) 377-2432. A weekly publication of trade opportunities received each week from overseas embassies and consulates. $175 per year. Also available on computer tape.

• Trade Lists, Export Promotion Services, U. S. Department of Commerce, P. O. Box 14207, Washington, DC 20044. Tel: (202) 377-2432. Preprinted trade lists are comprehensive directories listing all the companies in a country across all product sectors, or all the companies in a single industry across all countries. Trade lists are priced from $12 to $40, depending on the age of publication.

• World Traders Data Reports (WTDRs), Export Promotion Services, U. S. Department of Commerce, P. O. Box 14207, Washington, DC 20044. Tel: (202) 377-2432. This service provides background reports on individual foreign firms. WTDRs are designed to help U. S. firms evaluate potential foreign customers before making a business commitment. $75 per report.

C. FINANCING EXPORTS

• Chase World Guide for Exporters, Export Credit Reports, Chase World Information Corporation, One World Trade Center, Suite 4533, New York, NY 10048. The **Guide**, covering 180 countries, contains current export financing methods, collection experiences and charges, foreign import and exchange regulations and related subjects. Supplementary bulletins keep the guide up to date throughout the year. The **Reports**, issued quarterly, specify credit terms granted for shipment to all the principal world markets. The reports show the credit terms offered by the industry groups as a whole, thereby enabling the reader to determine whether his or her terms are more liberal or conservative than the average for specific commodity groups. Annual subscription for both the **Guide** and **Reports**, $345.

• Commercial Export Financing: An Assist to Farm Products Sales, U. S. Department of Agriculture Foreign Agricultural Service Room 5918, Washington, DC 20250, 1980, brochure. Free.

• Export-Import Financing—A Practical Guide, Gerhart W. Schneider, Ronald Press, 1974. This book presents details of foreign trade financing and services available for making international payments. $59.95.

• FCIB International Bulletin, FCIB-NACM Corp., 475 Park Avenue South, New York, NY 10016, twice monthly. The Bulletin presents export information and review of conditions and regulations in overseas markets. $175 per year.

- Financing and Insuring Exports: A User's Guide to Eximbank and FCIA Programs, Export-Import Bank of the United States, User's Guide, 811 Vermont Avenue, NW., Washington, DC 20571. A 350 page guide which covers Eximbank's working capital guarantees, credit risk protection (guarantees and insurance), medium-term and long-term lending programs. Includes free updates during calendar year in which the guide is purchased. $50 (plus $5 postage and handling).

- Financial Institutions and Markets in the Far East, Morgan Guarantee Trust Company of New York, 23 Wall Street, New York, NY 10015. The book discusses export letters of credit, drafts, and other methods of payment and regulations of exports and imports.

- A Guide to Checking International Credit, International Trade Institute, Inc., 5055 North Main Street, Suite 270, Dayton, OH 45415.

- A Guide to Financing Exports, U. S. and Foreign Commercial Service, International Trade Administration Publications Distribution, Room 1617D, U. S. Department of Commerce, Washington, DC 20230, 1985. Brochure, 40 pp. Free.

- A Guide to Understanding Drafts, International Trade Institute, Inc., 5055 N. Main Street, Dayton, OH 45415. Tel: (800) 543-2455, 64 pp, $17.50.

- A Guide to Understanding Letters of Credit, International Trade Institute, Inc., 5055 N. Main Street, Dayton, OH 45415, 138 pp., $34.50.

- A Handbook of Financing U. S. Exports, Machinery and Allied Products Institute, 1200 18th Street, NW., Washington, DC 20036, $20.

- Official U. S. and International Financing Institutions: A Guide for Exporters and Investors, International Trade Administration, U. S. Department of Commerce. Available from the Superintendent of Documents, U. S. Government Printing Office, Washington, DC 20402, $2.75.

- Specifics on Commercial Letters of Credit and Bankers Acceptances, James A. Harrington, 1979 UNZ & Co., Division of Scott Printing Corp., 190 Baldwin Avenue, Jersey City, NJ 07036, 1979.

D. LAWS AND REGULATIONS

- Customs Regulations of the United States, Superintendent of Documents, Government Printing Office, Washington, DC 20402, 1971. Reprint includes amended text in revised page nos. 1 through 130 (includes subscription to revised pages). This contains regulations for carrying out customs, navigation and other laws administered by the Bureau of Customs.

• Distribution License, 1985 Office of Export Administration, Room 1620, U. S. Department of Commerce, Washington, DC 20230 free.

• Export Administration Regulations, Superintendent of Documents, Government Printing Office, Washington, DC 20402. Covers U. S. export control regulations and explanatory material. Last revised Oct 1, 1984. $65 plus supplements.

• Export Marketing of Capital Goods to the Socialist Countries of Eastern Europe, 1978, M. R. Hill, Gower Publishing Company, 200 pp., $50.75.

• Manual for the Handling of Applications for Patents, Designs and Trademarks Throughout the World, Ocrooibureau Los En Stigter B. V., Amsterdam, the Netherlands.

• Summary of U. S. Export Regulations, 1985, Office of Export Administration, Room 1620, Department of Commerce, Washington, DC 20230.

• Technology and East-West Trade, 1983, Summarizes the major provisions of the Export Administration Act of 1979 and its implications in East-West trade, Office of Technology Assessment, U. S. Department of Commerce, Washington, DC 20230 $4.75.

E. SHIPPING AND LOGISTICS

• Export Documentation Handbook, 1984 Edition, Dun & Bradstreet International, 49 Old Bloomfield Avenue, Mr. Lakes, NJ 07046. Compiled by Ruth E. Hurd, Dun's Marketing Services, 200 pp., $60.

• Export-Import Traffic Management and Forwarding, 6th edition, 1979. Alfred Murr, Cornell Maritime Press, Box 456, Centerville, MD 21617, 667 pp., $22.50. This publication presents the diverse functions and varied services concerned with the entire range of ocean traffic management.

• Export Shipping Manual, Indexed, looseleaf reference binder. Detailed current information on shipping and import regulations for all areas of the world. Bureau of National Affairs, 1231 25th Street, NW., Washington, DC 20037, $186 per year.

• Guide to Canadian Documentation, International Trade Institute, Inc., 5055 N. Main Street, Dayton, OH 45415, 68 pp., $24.50.

• Guide to Documentary Credit Operations, ICC Publishing Corporation, New York NY 1985, 52 pp. $10.95.

• Guide to Export Documentation, International Trade Institute Inc., 5055 N. Main Street, Dayton, OH 45415, 168 pp., $44.50.

• Guide to International Air Freight Shipping, International Trade Institute, 5055 N. Main Street, Dayton, OH 45415, $17.50

• Guide to International Ocean Freight Shipping, International Trade Institute, 5055 N. Main Street, Dayton, OH 45415, $34.50

Guide to Selecting the Freight Forwarder, International Trade Institute Inc., 5055 North Main Street, Suite 270, Dayton, OH 45415.

• Journal of Commerce Export Bulletin, 100 Wall Street, New York NY 10005, $200, per year. This is a weekly, newspaper that reports port and shipping developments. It lists products shipped from New York and ships and cargoes departing from 25 other U. S. ports. A "trade prospects" column lists merchandise offered and merchandise wanted.

• Shipping Digest, Geyer-McAllister Publications, Inc., 51 Madison Avenue, New York NY 10010. $26 per year. This is a weekly, which contains cargo sailing schedules from every U. S. port to every foreign port as well as international air and sea commerce news.

F. LICENSING

• Foreign Business Practices . . . Material on Practical Aspects of Exporting, International Licensing and Investment, 1981, International Trade Administration, U. S. Department of Commerce, Available from the Superintendent of Documents, U. S. Government Printing Office, Washington, DC 20402, 124 pp., $5.50.

• American Bulletin of International Technology Transfer, International Advancement, P. O. Box 75537, Los Angeles, CA 90057, $72 per year, bimonthly. This is a comprehensive listing of product and service opportunities offered and sought for licensing and joint ventures agreements in the United States and overseas.

• Forms and Agreements on Intellectual Property and International Licensing, 3rd edition, 1979, Leslie W. Melville, Clark Boardman Co., Ltd. New York, NY 10014, 800 pp. looseleaf, $210.

• International Technology Licensing: Competition, Costs, and Negotiation, 1981, J. Farok Contractor, Lexington Books Lexington, MA 02173, $23.95.

• Investing, Licensing, and Trading Conditions Abroad, Business International Corporation, base volume with monthly updates, $964.

• Licensing Guide for Developing Countries, 1978. UNIPUB, 345 Park Avenue South, New York NY 10010, $25. This book by the World Intelligence Property Organization covers the legal aspects of industrial property licensing and technology transfer agreements. It includes discussion of the negotiation process, the scope of licensing agreements, technical services and assistance, production, trademarks, management, compensation, default, and the expiration of agreements.

• Technology Licensing and Multinational Enterprises, 1979, Piero Telesio, Praeger Publishers, New York, NY 10175, 132 pp., $29.95.

G. CONSULATES AND OFFICIALS TRADE PROMOTION GROUPS

Foreign consulates in this country frequently publish periodicals for special reports of interest to the exporter. The Nigerian Consulate General in New York issues the *Nigerian Trade Journal*. The Belgian Industrial Information Service (New York) has prepared *Reaching New Markets from a Business Base in Belgium*, and the commercial office of the Italian Embassy sends out the monthly *Italian Trade Topics*. Although these publications are of a general nature, they provide a satisfactory introduction to the question of doing business in the foreign country.

H. CHAMBER OF COMMERCE

Many foreign chambers of commerce maintain offices in the United States, and the publications of this group often contain material of value to the exporter. The usual publications of this group are a monthly magazine, such as the *Belgian Trade Review* (The Belgian Chamber of Commerce in the United States) and the *German-American Trade News* (German-American Chamber of Commerce). In addition, these magazines may be supplemented with a newsletter published on a weekly or monthly basis.

Other publications from this group are also useful. For example, the membership directory of the French Chamber of Commerce in the United States contains material on the subject of doing business in France.

I. PERIODICALS ON MARKETING AND RELATED SUBJECTS

General periodicals on marketing and related subjects often contain valuable, particularly for exporters of consumer goods. Some of the magazines deal with specialized areas such as *South African Sales Promotion and Packaging* or the *New Zealand Retailer*. Other dealing with the general subject of marketing are *Det Danski Marked* (Denmark), *Studdi De Mercata* (Italy) and *Vendre* (France).

J. IMPORT/EXPORT MAGAZINES

Two distinct types of export publications originate from a number of different sources and may, therefore, be used for different purposes by the exporter. The first type of magazine is directed toward the exporter and seeks to help him or her by providing information about foreign markets, trade restrictions, and other important factors. Almost without exception these magazines are issued by governments and contain reports from the governments' overseas commercial representatives. As such, they are similar to *Business America*, published biweekly by the U. S. Department of Commerce. Outstanding examples of this type of export magazines include *Foreign Trade* (Canada), *Board of Trade Journal* (Great Britain), *Bulletin Commercial Belge* (Belgium), and *Overseas Trading* (Australia). The market reports appearing in these magazines are as useful to exporters in the United States as to exporters in the country publishing the magazine.

The other type of export magazine is directed primarily toward overseas customers and is prepared by private publishing firms, export associations, and government organizations. These magazines essentially contain advertisements and notices of products that the manufacturer would like to export. Export magazines of this type are sometimes useful for learning about the product offered by competitors in foreign markets. Firms advertising in these magazines may be expected to forward complete details about their product line upon request.

Among the magazines published by private firms are *Made in Europe* with an annual *Buyers' Guide, Overseas Post, Export Anzeiger, Export Market,* and *The German Exporter,* all of which are published in Germany. Others include *The Ambassador* (Great Britain), *The British Trade Journal and Export World, Oriental America, Japan Trade Monthly, Trade Channel Magazines, Asian Buyers Guide, Taiwan Buyers Guide,* and *Hong Kong Buyers Guide.*

Those issued by groups of exporters include *The South African Exporter, Featuring Sweden, The Finnish Trade Review,* and *The Israel Export and Trade Journal.*

The last group are those published by foreign governments and semiofficial organizations. These include *Italy Presents;* three from Japan, *Japan Commerce and Industry, Merchandise That Japan Offers,* and *Quality Goods on Parade; Polish Foreign Trade;* and *Canada Commerce.*

In addition to looking at sample copies of these magazines, the reader should consider corresponding with the editorial staff who is usually in a position to provide information for exporters to their country as well as importers from it.

Glossary 1

Revised American Foreign Trade Definitions—1941

Adopted July 30, 1941, by a Joint Committee representing the Chamber of Commerce of the United States of America, the National Council of American Importers, Inc., and the National Foreign Trade Council, Inc.

The following *Revised American Trade Definitions—1941* are recommended for general use by both exporters and importers. These revised definitions have no status at law unless there is specific legislation providing for them, or unless they are confirmed by court decisions. Hence, it is suggested that sellers and buyers agree to their acceptance as part of the contract of sale. These definitions will then become legally binding upon all parties.

Adoption by exporters and importers of these revised terms will impress on all parties concerned their respective responsibilities and rights.

GENERAL NOTES OF CAUTION

1. As foreign trade definitions have been issued by organizations in various parts of the world, and as the courts of countries have interpreted these definitions in different ways, it is important that sellers and buyers agree

that the contracts are subject to the *Revised American Foreign Trade Definitions—1941* and that the various points listed are accepted by both parties.

2. In addition to the foreign trade terms listed herein, there are terms that are at times used, such as Free Harbor, CIF. & C. (Cost, Insurance, Freight, and Commission), C.I.F.C. & I. (Cost, Insurance, Freight, Commission, and Interest), C.I.F. Landed (Cost, Insurance, Freight, Landed) and others. None of these should be used unless there has first been a definite understanding as to the exact meaning thereof. It is unwise to attempt to interpret other terms in the light of the terms given herein. Hence, whenever possible, one of the terms defined herein should be used.

3. It is unwise to use abbreviations in quotations or in contracts which might be subject to misunderstanding.

4. When making quotations, the familiar terms "hundredweight" or "ton" should be avoided. A hundredweight can be 100 pounds of the short ton, 112 pounds of the long ton. A ton can be a short ton of 2,000 pounds or a metric ton of 2,204.6 pounds, or a long ton of 2,240 pounds. Hence, the type of hundred-weight or ton should be clearly stated in quotations, and in sales confirmations. Also, all terms referring to quantity, weight, volume length or surface should be clearly defined and agreed upon.

5. If inspection, or certificate of inspection, is required, it should be agreed, in advance, whether the cost thereof is for account of seller or buyer.

6. Unless otherwise agreed upon, all expenses are for the account of seller up to the point at which the buyer must handle the subsequent movement of goods.

7 There are a number of elements in a contract that do not fall within the scope of these foreign trade definitions. Hence, no mention of these is made herein. Seller and buyer should agree to these separately when negotiating contracts. This particularly applies to so-called "customary" practices.

DEFINITIONS OF QUOTATIONS

(I) EX (Point of Origin)
"EX Factory," Ex Mill," "Ex Mine," "Ex Plantation," "Ex Warehouse," etc. (named point of origin)

Under this term, the price quoted applies only at the point of origin, and the seller agrees to place the goods at the disposal of the buyer at the agreed place on the date or within the period fixed.

Under this Quotation:

Seller must

(1) bear all costs and risks of the goods until such time as the buyer is obliged to take delivery thereof;

(2) render the buyer, at the buyer's request and expense, assistance in obtaining the documents issued in the country of origin, or of shipment, or of both, which the buyer may require either for purposes of exportation, or of importations at destination.

Buyer must

(1) take delivery of the goods as soon as they have been placed at this disposal at the agreed place on the date or within the period fixed;

(2) pay export taxes or other fees or charges, if any, levied because of exportation;

(3) bear all costs and risks of the goods from the time when he is obligated to take delivery thereof;

(4) pay all costs and charges incurred in obtaining the documents issued in the country of origin, or of shipment, or of both, which may be required either for purposes of exportation, or of importation at destination.

(II) F.O.B. (Free on Board)

Note: Seller and buyer should consider not only the definitions but also the "Comments on All F.O.B. Terms" given at end of this section in order to understand fully their respective responsibilities and rights under the several classes of "F.O.B." terms.

(II-A) "F.O.B. (named inland carrier at named inland point of departure)"

Under this term, the price quoted applied only at inland shipping point, and the seller arranges for loading of the goods on, or in, railway cars, trucks, lighters, barges, aircraft, or other conveyance furnished for transportation.

Under this quotation:

Seller must

(1) Place goods on, or in, conveyance, or deliver to inland carrier for loading;

(2) provide clean bill of lading or other transportation receipt, freight collect;

(3) be responsible for any loss or damage, or both, until goods have been placed in, or on, conveyance at loading point, and clean bill of lading at other transportation receipt has been furnished by the carrier;

(4) render the buyer, at the buyer's request and expense, assistance in obtaining the documents issued in the country of origin, or of shipment, or of both, which the buyer may require either for purposes of exportation, or of importation at destination.

Buyer must

(1) be responsible for all movement of the goods from inland point of loading, and pay all transportation costs;

(2) pay export taxes, or other fees or charges, if any, levied because of exportation;

(3) be responsible for any loss or damage, or both, incurred after loading at named inland point of departure;

(4) pay all costs and charges incurred in obtaining the documents issued in the country of origin, or of shipment, or of both, which may be required either for purposes of exportation, or of importation at destination.

(II-B) "F.O.B. (names inland carrier at named inland point of departure) Freight Prepaid to (named point of exportation)"

Under this term, the seller quotes a price including transportation charges to the named point of exportation and prepays freight to named point of exportation, without assuming responsibility for the goods after obtaining a clean bill of lading or other transportation receipt at named inland point of departure.

Under this quotation:

Seller must

(1) assume seller's obligations as under II-A, except that under (2) he must provide clean bill of lading or other transportation receipt, freight prepaid to named point of exportation.

Buyer must

(1) assume the same buyer's obligations as under II-A, except that he does not pay freight from loading point to named point of exportation.

(II-C) "F.O.B. (named inland carrier at named inland point of departure) Freight Allowed to (named point)"

Under this term, the seller quotes a price including the transportation charges to the named point, shipping freight collect and deducting the cost of transportation, without assuming responsibility for the goods after obtaining a clear bill of lading or other transportation receipt at named inland point of departure.

Under this quotation:

Seller must

(1) assume the same seller's obligations as under II-A, but deducts from his invoice the transportation cost to named point.

Buyer must

(1) assume the same buyer's obligations as under II-A, including payment of freight from inland loading point to name point, for which seller has made deduction.

(II-D) "F.O.B. (named inland carrier at named point of exportation)"

Under this term, the seller quotes a price including the cost of transportation of the goods to named point of exportation, bearing any loss or damage, or both, incurred up to that point.

Under this quotation:

Seller must

(1) place goods on, or in, conveyance, or deliver to inland carrier for loading;
(2) provide clean bill of lading or other transportation receipt, paying all transportation costs from loading point to named point of exportation;
(3) be responsible for any loss or damage, or both, until goods have arrived in, or on, inland conveyance at the named point of exportation;
(4) render the buyer, at the buyer's request and expense, assistance in obtaining the documents issued in the country of origin, or of shipment, or of both, which the buyer may either for purposes of exportation, or of importation at destination.

Buyer must

(1) be responsible for all movement of the goods from inland conveyance at named point of exportation;
(2) pay export taxes, or other fees or charges, if any, levied because of exportation;
(3) be responsible for any loss or damage, or both incurred after goods have arrived in, or on, inland conveyance at the named point of exportation;
(4) pay all costs and charges incurred in obtaining the documents issued in the country of origin, or of shipment, or of both which may be required either for purposes of exportation, or of importation at destination.

(II-E) "F.O.B. Vessel (named port of shipment)"

Under this term, the seller quotes a price covering all expenses up to, and including, delivery of the goods upon the overseas vessel provided by, or for, the buyer at the named port of shipment.

Under this quotation:

Seller must

(1) pay all charges incurred in placing goods, actually on board the vessel designated and provided by, or for, the buyer on the date or within the period fixed;

(2) provide clean ship's receipt or on-board bill of lading;

(3) be responsible for any loss or damage, or both, until goods have been placed on board the vessel on the date or within the period fixed;

(4) render the buyer, at the buyer's request and expense, assistance in obtaining the documents issued in the country of origin, or of shipment, or of both, which the buyer may require either for purposes of exportation, or of importation at destination.

Buyer must

(1) give seller adequate notice of name, sailing date, loading berth of, and delivery time to, the vessel;

(2) bear the additional costs incurred and all risks of the goods from the time when the seller has placed them at his disposal if the vessel named by him fails to arrive or to load within the designated time;

(3) handle all subsequent movement of the goods to destination;
    (a) provide and pay for insurance;
    (b) provide and pay for ocean and other transportation;

(4) pay export taxes, or other fees or charges if any, levied because of exportation;

(5) be responsible for any loss or damage, or both, after goods have been loaded on board the vessel;

(6) pay all costs and charges incurred in obtaining the documents, other than clean ship's receipt or bill of lading, issued in the country of origin, or of shipment, or of both, which may be required either for purposes of exportation, or of importation at destination.

(II-F) "F.O.B. (named inland point in country of importation)"

Under this term, the seller quotes a price including the cost of the merchandise and all costs of transportation to the named inland point in the country of importation.
    Under this quotation:

Seller must

(1) provide and pay for all transportation to the named inland point in the country of importation;

(2) pay export taxes, or other fees or charges, if any, levied because of exportation;

(3) provide and pay for marine insurance;

(4) provide and pay for war risk insurance, unless otherwise agreed upon between the seller and buyer;

(5) be responsible for any loss or damage, or both, until arrival of goods on conveyance at the named inland point in the country of importation;

(6) pay the costs of certificates of origin, consular invoices, or any other documents issued in the country of origin, or of shipment, or of both, which the buyer may require for the importation of goods into the country of destination and, where necessary, for their passage in transit through another country;

(7) pay all costs of landing, including wharfage, landing charges, and taxes, if any;

(8) pay all costs of customs entry in the country of importation;

(9) pay customs duties and all taxes applicable to imports, if any, in the country of importation.

Note: The seller under this quotation must realize that he is accepting important responsibilities, costs, and risks, and should therefore be certain to obtain adequate insurance. On the other hand, the importer or buyer may desire such quotations to relieve him of the risks of the voyage and to assure him of his landed costs at inland point of country of importation. When competition is keen, or the buyer is accustomed to such quotations from other sellers, seller may quote such terms, being careful to protect himself in an appropriate manner.

Buyer must

(1) take prompt delivery of goods from conveyance upon arrival at destination;

(2) bear any costs and be responsible for all loss or damage, or both after arrival at destination.

COMMENTS ON ALL F.O.B. TERMS

In connection with F.O.B. terms, the following points of caution are recommended:

1. The method of inland transportation, such as trucks, railroad cars, lighters, barges, or aircraft should be specified.

2. If any switching charges are involved during the inland transportation, it should be agreed, in advance, whether these charges are for account of the seller or the buyer.

3. The term "F.O.B. (named port)," without designating the exact point at which the liability of the seller terminates and the liability of the buyer begins, should be avoided. The use of this term gives rise to disputes as to the liability of the seller or the buyer in the event of loss or damage arising while the goods are in port, and before delivery to or on board the ocean carrier. Misunderstandings may be avoided by naming the specific point of delivery.

4. If lighterage or trucking is required in the transfer of goods from the inland conveyance to ship's side, and there is a cost therefore, it should be understood, in advance, whether the cost is for account of the seller or the buyer.

5. The seller should be certain to notify the buyer of the minimum quantity required to obtain a carload, a truckload, or a barge-load freight rate.

6. Under F.O.B. terms, excepting "F.O.B. (named inland point in country of importation)," the obligation to obtain ocean freight space, and marine and war risk insurance, rests with the buyer. Despite this obligation on the part of the buyer, in many trades the seller obtains the ocean freight space, and marine and war risk insurance, and provides for shipment on behalf of the buyer. Hence, seller and buyer must have an understanding as to whether the buyer will obtain the ocean freight space, and marine and war risk insurance, as is his obligation, or whether the seller agrees to do this for the buyer.

7. For the seller's protection, he should provide in his contract of sale that marine insurance obtained by the buyer include standard warehouse to warehouse coverage.

(III) F.A.S. (free along side)

Note: Seller and buyer should consider not only the definition but also the "Comments" given at the end of this section, in order to understand fully their respective responsibilities and rights under "F.A.S." terms.

"F.A.S. Vessel (named port of shipment)"

Under this term, the seller quotes a price including delivery of the goods along side overseas vessel and within reach of its loading tackle.

Under this quotation:

Seller must

(1) place goods along side vessel or on dock designated and provided by, or for, buyer on the date or within the period fixed; pay any heavy lift charges, where necessary, up to this point;

(2) provide clean dock or ship's receipt;

(3) be responsible for any loss or damage, or both, until goods have been delivered along side the vessel or on the dock;

(4) render the buyer, at the buyer's request and expense, assistance in obtaining the documents issued in the country of origin, or of shipment, or of both, which the buyer may require either for purposes of exportation, or of importation at destination.

Buyer must

(1) give seller adequate notice of name, sailing date, loading berth of, and delivery time to, the vessel;

(2) handle all subsequent movement of the goods from along side the vessel; (a) arrange and pay for demurrage of storage charges, or both, in warehouse or on wharf, where necessary;
(b) provide and pay for insurance;
(c) provide and pay for ocean and other transportation;

(3) pay export taxes, or other fees or charges, if any, levied because of exportation;

(4) be responsible for any loss or damage, or both, while the goods are on a lighter or other conveyance along side vessel within reach of its loading tackle, or on the dock awaiting loading, or until actually loading on board the vessel, and subsequent thereto;

(5) pay all costs and charges incurred in obtaining the documents, other than clean dock or ship's receipt, issued in the country of origin, or of shipment, or of both, which may be required either for purposes of exportation, or of importation at destination.

F.A.S. COMMENTS

1. Under F.A.S. terms, the obligation to obtain freight space, and marine and war risk insurance, rests with the buyer. Despite this obligation on the part of the buyer, in many trades the seller obtains ocean freight space, and marine and war risk insurance, and provides for shipment on behalf of the buyer. In others, the buyer notifies the seller to make delivery along side a vessel designated by the buyer and the buyer provides his own marine and war risk. Hence, seller and buyer must have an understanding as to

whether the buyer will obtain the ocean freight space, and marine and war risk insurance, as is his obligation, or whether the seller agrees to do this for the buyer.

2. For the seller's protection, he should provide in his contract of sale that marine insurance obtained by the buyer include standard warehouse to warehouse coverage.

(IV) C.&F. (cost and freight)

Note: Seller and buyer should consider not only the definitions but also the "C.&F. Comments" and the "C.&F. and C.I.F. Comments", in order to understand fully their respective responsibilities and rights under C.&F. terms.

"C.&F. (named point of destination)"

Under this term, the seller quotes a price including the cost of transportation to named point of destination.

Under this quotation:

Seller must

(1) provide and pay for transportation to named point of destination;

(2) pay export taxes, or other fees or charges, if any, levied because of exportation;

(3) obtain and dispatch promptly to buyer, or his agent, clean bill of lading to named point of destination;

(4) where received-for-shipment ocean bill of lading may be tendered, be responsible for any loss or damage, or both, until the goods have been delivered into the custody of the ocean carrier;

(5) where on-board ocean bill of lading is required, be responsible for any loss or damage, or both, until the goods have been delivered on board the vessel;

(6) provide, at the buyer's request and expense, certifies or origin, consular invoices, or any other documents issued in the country of origin, or of shipment, or of both, which the buyer may require for importation of goods into country of destination and, where necessary, for their passage in transit through another country.

Buyer must

(1) accept the documents when presented;

(2) receive goods upon arrival, handle and pay for all subsequent movement of the goods, including taking delivery from vessel in accordance with bill

of lading clauses and terms; pay all costs of handling, including any duties, taxes, and other expenses at named point of destination;

(3) provide any pay for insurance;

(4) be responsible for loss of or damage to goods, or both, from time and place at which seller's obligations under (4) and (5) above have ceased;

(5) pay the costs of certificates of origin, consular invoices, or any other documents issued in the country of origin, or of shipment, or of both, which may be required for the importation of goods into the country of destination and, where necessary, for the passage in transit through another country.

C. & F. COMMENTS

1. For the seller's protection, he should provide in his contract of sale that marine insurance obtained by the buyer include standard warehouse to warehouse coverage.

2. The comments listed under the following C.I.F. terms in many cases apply to C. & F. terms as well, and should be read and understood by the C. & F. seller and buyer.

(V) C.I.F. (cost, insurance, freight)

Note: Seller and buyer should consider not only the definitions but also the "Comments" at the end of this section, in order to understand fully their respective responsibilities and rights under "C.I.F." terms.

"C.I.F. (named point of destination)"

Under this term, the seller quotes a price including the cost of the goods, the marine insurance, and all transportation charges to the named point of destination.

Under this quotation:

Seller must

(1) provide and pay for transportation to named point of destination;

(2) pay export taxes, or other fees or charges, if any, levied because of exportation;

(3) provide and pay for marine insurance;

(4) provide war risk insurance as obtainable in seller's market at time of shipment at buyer's expense, unless seller has agreed that buyer provide for war risk coverage (See Comments 10(c));

(5) obtain and dispatch promptly to buyer, or his agent, clean bill of lading to named point of destination, and also insurance policy or negotiable insurance certificate;

(6) where received-for-shipment ocean bill of lading may be tendered, be responsible for any loss or damage, or both until the goods have been delivered into the custody of the ocean carrier;

(7) where on-board ocean bill of lading is required, be responsible for any loss or damage, or both, until the goods have been delivered on board the vessel;

(8) provide, at the buyer's request and expense, certificates of origin, consular invoices, or any other documents issued in the country of origin, or of shipment, or both, which the buyer may require for importation of goods into country of destination and, where necessary, for their passage in transit through another country.

Buyer must

(1) accept the documents when presented;

(2) receive the goods upon arrival, handle and pay for all subsequent movement of the goods, including taking delivery from vessel in accordance with bill of lading clauses and terms, pay all costs of lading, including any duties, taxes, and other expenses, at named point of destination;

(3) pay for war risk insurance provided by seller;

(4) be responsible for loss of or damage to goods, or both, from time and place at which seller's obligations under (6) or (7) above have ceased;

(5) pay the cost of certificates of origin, consular invoices, or any other documents issued in the country of origin, or of shipment, or both, which may be required for importation of the goods into the country of destination and, where necessary, for their passage in transit through another country.

C. & F. AND C.I.F. COMMENTS

Under the C. & F., and C.I.F. contracts there are the following points on which the seller and the buyer should be in complete agreement at the time that the contract is concluded:

1. It should be agreed upon, in advance, who is to pay for miscellaneous expenses, such as weighing or inspection charges.

2. The quantity to be shipped on any one vessel should be agreed upon, in advance, with a view to the buyer's capacity to take delivery upon arrival and discharge of the vessel, within the free time allowed at the port of importation.

3. Although the terms C. & F. and C.I.F. are generally interpreted to provide the charges for consular invoices and certificates of origin are for the account of the buyer, and are charged separately, in many trades these charges are included by the seller in his price. Hence, seller and buyer should agree, in advance, whether these charges are part of the selling price, or will be invoiced separately.

4. The point of final destination should be definitely known in the event the vessel discharges at a port other than the actual destination of the goods.

5. When ocean freight space is difficult to obtain, or forward freight contracts cannot be made at firm rates, it is advisable that sales contracts, as an exception to regular C. & F. or C.I.F. terms, should provide that shipment within the contract period be subject to ocean freight space being available to the seller, and should also provide that changes in the cost of ocean transportation between the time of sale and the time of shipment be for account of the buyer.

6. Normally, the seller is obligated to prepay the ocean freight. In some instances, shipments are made freight collect and the amount of the freight is deducted from the invoice rendered by the seller. It is necessary to be in agreement on this, in advance, in order to avoid misunderstanding which arises from foreign exchange fluctuations which might affect the actual cost of transportation, and from interest charges which might accrue under the letter of credit financing. Hence, the seller should always prepay the ocean freight unless he has a specific agreement with the buyer, in advance, that goods can be shipped freight collect.

7. The buyer should recognize that he does not have the right to insist on inspection of goods prior to accepting the documents. The buyer should not refuse to take delivery of goods on account of delay in the receipt of documents, provided the seller has used due diligence in their dispatch through the regular channels.

8. Sellers and buyers are advised against including a C.I.F. contract any indefinite clause at variance with the obligations of a C.I.F. contract as specified in these Definitions. There have been numerous court decisions in the United States and other countries invalidating C.I.F. contracts because of the inclusion of indefinite clauses.

9. Interest charges should be included in cost computations and should not be charged as a separate item in C.I.F. contracts, unless otherwise agreed upon, in advance, between the seller and buyer; in which case, however,

the term C.I.F. and I. (Cost, Insurance, Freight, and Interest) should be used.

10. In connection with insurance under C.I.F. sales, it is necessary that seller and buyer be definitely in accord upon the following points:

(a) The character of the marine insurance should be agreed upon in so far as being W.A. (With Average) or F.P.A. (Free of Particular Average), as well as any other special risks that are covered in specific trades, or against which the buyer may wish individual protection. Among the special risks that should be considered and agreed upon between seller and buyer are theft, pilferage, leakage, breakage, sweat, contact with other cargoes, and others peculiar to any particular trade. It is important that contingent or collect freight and customs duty should be insured to cover Particular Average losses, as well as total loss after arrival and entry but before delivery.

(b) The seller is obligated to exercise ordinary care and diligence in selecting an underwriter that is in good financial standing. However, the risk of obtaining settlement of insurance claims rests with the buyer.

(c) War risk insurance under this term is to be obtained by the seller at the expense and risk of the buyer. It is important that the seller be in definite accord with the buyer on this point, particularly as to the cost. It is desirable that the goods be insured against both marine and war risk with the same underwriter, so that there can be no difficulty arising from the determination of the cause of the loss.

(d) Seller should make certain that in his marine or war risk insurance, there be included the standard protection against strikes, riots and civil commotions.

(e) Seller and buyer should be in accord as to the insured valuations, bearing in mind that merchandise contributes in General Average on certain bases of valuation which differ in various trades. It is desirable that a competent insurance broker be consulted, in order that full value be covered and trouble avoided.

(VI) "Ex Dock (named port of importation)"

Note: Seller and buyer should consider not only the definitions but also the "Ex Dock Comments" at the end of this section, in order to understand fully their respective responsibilities and right under "Ex Dock" terms.

Under this term, seller quotes a price including the cost of the goods and all additional costs necessary to place the goods on the dock at the named port of importation, duty paid, if any.

Under this quotation:

Seller must

(1) provide and pay for transportation to named port of importation;

(2) pay export taxes, or other fees or charges, if any, levied because of exportation;

(3) provide and pay for marine insurance;

(4) provide and pay for war risk insurance, unless otherwise agreed upon between the buyer and seller;

(5) be responsible for any loss or damage, or both, until the expiration of the free time allowed on the dock at the named port of importation.

(6) pay the costs of certificates of origin, consular invoices, legalization of bill of lading, or any other documents issued in the country of origin, or of shipment, or of both, which the buyer may require for the importation of goods into the country of destination and, where necessary, for their passage in transit through another country;

(7) pay all costs of landing, including wharfage, landing charges, and taxes, if any;

(8) pay all costs of customs entry in the country of importation;

(9) pay customs duties and all taxes applicable to imports, if any, in the country of importation, unless otherwise agreed upon.

Buyer must

(1) take delivery of the goods on the dock at the named port of importation within the free time allowed;

(2) bear the cost and risk of the goods if delivery is not taken within the free time allowed.

EX DOCK COMMENTS

This term is used principally in United States import trade. It has various modifications, such as "Ex Quay," "Ex Pier," etc., but it is seldom, if ever, used in American export practice. Its use in quotations for export is not recommended.

Glossary 2

Commercial Terms

A.B. or AKtb: for Aktiebolager, a Swedish joint stock company.

A.G.: for Aktien-Gesellschaft, German joint stock company.

A/P—Authority to Pay: a letter, used primarily in the Far East, addressed by a bank to a seller of merchandise, authorizing the purchase, with or without recourse, of draft(s) and document(s) to a stipulated amount drawn on a foreign buyer in payment of specified merchandise shipment(s).

A.S. or AKts: Aktieselskabet, a Danish joint stock company (Aktieselskabet in Norway).

Acceptance: a draft, payable at a determinable future, date upon the face of which the drawee acknowledges his obligation to pay it at maturity.

    (a) **Banker's Acceptance:** a draft of which a bank is drawee; and acceptor;

    (b) **Trade Acceptance:** a draft, usually arising from the sales of merchandise, of which the drawee and acceptor is an individual or a mercantile concern.

Ad Valorem Duty: see Duty.

Advisory Capacity: a term designating the limited power of a shipper's agent or representative abroad not authorizing him to make definite decisions and adjustments without reference to his principals.

After Date: the time begins to run from the date of a draft bearing this phrase; fixed date of maturity does not depend upon the date of acceptance of the draft.

Source: Crocker National Bank, International Division, 44 Montgomery St., San Fransicso, CA 94104.

464

After Sight: time begins to run from the date of acceptance of a draft bearing this phrase.

Agio: the premium paid to exchange one currency for another.

Allenge: a slip of paper attached to a bill of exchange, acceptance or note, providing space for additional endorsements.

Arbitrage: the buying of foreign exchange, securities, or commodities in one market and the simultaneous selling in another market, in terms of a third market. By this manipulation a profit is made because of the difference in the rates of exchange or in the prices of securities or commodities involved.

Average: see Ocean Marine Insurance Policy.

Back-to-Back Credit: a term used to denote a letter of credit issued for the account of a buyer of merchandise already holding a letter of credit in his favor. The "back-to-back" letter of credit is issued in favor of the supplier of the merchandise to cover the same shipment stipulated in the credit already held by the buyer. The terms of both letters of credit, with the exception of the amount and expiration date, are so similar that the same documents presented under the "back-to-back" credit are subsequently applied against the credit in favor of the buyer. However, the buyer or beneficiary of the first credit, substitutes his draft and invoice for those presented by the supplier.

Barter: the exchange of commodities using merchandise as compensation, instead of money. Countries having blocked currencies often use this "method."

Beneficiary: the person in whose favor a draft is issued or a letter of credit opened.

Bill of Exchange (or Draft): an unconditional written order addressed by one person to another, signed by the donor and requiring the addressee to pay on demand or at a fixed date a certain sum in money to the order of a specified person.

Bill of Lading (Ocean): a document signed by the captain, agents, or owners of a vessel, furnishing written evidence for the conveyance and delivery of seaborne merchandise to a destination, it represents a receipt for merchandise and contract to deliver it as freight.

   (a) **Clean:** a term describing a bill of lading when the transportation company had not noted irregularities in the packing or general condition of the shipment.

   (b) **Straight:** a non-negotiable bill of lading that consigns the goods directly to a stipulated consignee.

   (c) **Order:** a bill of lading usually issued to the shipper, whose endorsement is required to effect its negotiation.

(d) **Order "Notify":** a bill of lading issued usually to the order of the shipper with the individual clause that the consignee is to be notified upon arrival of the merchandise, however, without giving the consignee title to the merchandise.

(e) **Through Bill of Lading:** a bill of lading used when several carriers, normally connecting, are involved.

Binder: a temporary insurance coverage pending the later issuance of an insurance policy or certificate.

Blocked Exchange: exchange not freely convertible into other currencies.

Bonded Warehouse: a building for storing goods authorized by customs officials until removal, without the payment of duties.

Both to Blame Collision Clause: see Ocean Marine Insurance Policy.

Carrier: freight company, air ocean, inland, truck, rail.

C. & F.—Cost & Freight: see revised American Foreign Definitions.

C.I.F.—Cost, Insurance & Freight: see revised American Foreign Definitions section.

Certificate of Inspection: a document often required with shipments of perishable or other goods, when certification notes the good condition of the merchandise immediately prior to shipment.

Certificate of Manufacture: a statement sometimes notarized by a producer, usually also the seller, or merchandiser that indicates the goods have been manufactured and are at the disposal of the buyer.

Certificate of Origin: a specified document certifying the country of origin of the merchandise required by certain foreign countries for tariff purposes, it sometimes requires the signature of the consul of the country to which it is destined.

Charges Forward: a banking term used when foreign and domestic bank commission charges, interest and government taxes in connection with the collection of a draft are for the drawee's account.

Charges Here: a banking term used when foreign and domestic bank commission charges, interest and government taxes in connection with the collection of a draft are for the drawer's account.

Charter Party: a written contract between the owner of a vessel and the one (the charterer) desiring to empty the vessel, setting forth the terms of the arrangement, i.e., freight rate and ports involved in the contemplated trip.

Clean Draft: a draft without attached documents.

Commercial Invoice: a statement of transaction between a seller and buyer prepared by the seller, and a description of the merchandise, price, terms, etc.

Consignee: the person, firm or representative to which a seller or shipper sends merchandise.

Consignment: merchandise shipped to a foreign agent or customer when an actual purchase has not been made, but under an agreement obliging the consignee to pay the consignor for the goods when sold.

Consignor: the seller or shipper of merchandise.

Consular Documents: bills of lading, certificates of origin or special invoice forms that are officially signed by the consul of the country of destination.

Consular Invoice: a detailed statement of goods shipped certified by the consul at the point of shipment.

Consular Visa: an official signature the consul of the country of destination affixes to certain shipping documents.

Cover Note: the British equivalent of the United States "Binder."

Customs Broker: licensed by U. S. Customs to clear shipments for clients, also can forward goods "In Bond" to your port.

D/A-Documents Against Acceptance: instructions from a shipper to his bank that the documents attached to a time draft for collection are deliverable to the drawee against his acceptance of the draft.

D/P-Documents Against Payment: instructions a shipper gives to his bank that the documents attached to a draft for collection are deliverable to the drawee only against his payment of the draft.

Date Draft: a draft drawn to mature on a fixed date, irrespective of its acceptance date.

Delivery Order: a delivery order issued to or by a warehouse, a railroad, a steamship company or airline, or anyone with the authority and legal right to claim or order delivery of merchandise.

Discount:

    (a) Commercial: an allowance from the quoted price of goods, made usually by the deduction of a certain percentage from the invoice price.

    (b) Financial: a deduction from the face value of commercial paper, such as bills of exchange and acceptances, in consideration of receipt by the seller of cash before maturity date.

Dishonor: refusal on the part of the drawee to accept a draft or to pay it when due.

Dock Receipt: receipt issued by an ocean carrier or its agent for merchandise delivered at its dock or warehouse awaiting shipment.

Documentary Credit: a commercial letter of credit providing for payment by a bank to the name beneficiary, usually the seller of merchandise, against delivery of documents specified in the credit.

Documents: papers customarily attached to foreign drafts, consisting of ocean bills of lading, marine insurance certificates, and commercial invoices, and where required, including certificates of origin and consular invoices.

Domicile: the place where a draft of acceptance is made payable.

Draft: see Bill of Exchange.

Drawback: see Duty.

Drawee: the address of a draft, i.e., the person on whom the draft is drawn.

Drawer: the issuer, or signer, of a draft.

Drop Ship: shipment by foreign shipper directly to your domestic customer. Price includes freight and postage.

Duty:

(a) **ad valorem** duty means an assessed amount at a certain percentage rate on the monetary value of an import.

(b) **Specific duty:** an assessment on the weight or quantity of an article without preference to its monetary value or market price.

(c) **Drawback:** a recovery in whole or in part of duty paid on imported merchandise at the time of exportation, in the same or different form.

E. & O.E.—Errors and Omissions Excepted: a phrase accompanying the shipper's signature on an invoice, by which he disclaims final responsibility for typographical errors or unintentional omissions.

Endorsement: a signature on the reverse of a negotiable instrument made primarily for the purpose of transferring the holder's rights to another person, it constitutes a contract between the holder and all parties to the instrument. Each endorser thus orders the prior parties to fulfill the contract to his endorsee and also agrees with the endorsees that, if they do not, he will.

English and Colonial Clause: a clause used in connection with drafts drawn in sterling on the British Commonwealth and Colonies, requiring the drawee of a draft to pay exchange (plus English and Colonial stamps) at the current London exchange rate for the negotiation of drafts on the colonies.

Expiration Date: the final date upon which draft(s) under a letter of credit may be presented for negotiation.

Extension: an additional period granted by the drawer for payment of a draft when the drawee is unable or unwilling to make payment on the maturity date.

F.A.S.—Free Alongside Vessel: see Revised Foreign Trade Definitions.

F.O.B.—Free on Board: (destination) (named point) (vessel)-see Revised Foreign Trade Definitions.

F.P.A.—Free of Particular Average: see Ocean Marine Insurance Policy.

First of Exchange: the original of a draft drawn in original and duplicate.

Foreign Exchange: a general term applied to transaction involving foreign currencies.

Future Exchange Contract: usually a contract between a bank and its customer to purchase or sell foreign exchange at a fixed rate with delivery at a specified time, generally used because the customer desires to preclude the risk of fluctuations in foreign exchange rates.

G.m.b.H.: the abbreviation for the German term "Gesellschaft mit beschraenkter Haftung," meaning a limited liability company. The equivalent of "incorporated."

Go-Down: a warehouse in the Far East where goods are stored and delivered when warranted.

In Bond: a term applied to the status of merchandise admitted provisionally to a country without payment of duties—either for storage in a bonded warehouse or for trans-shipment to another point, where duties will eventually be imposed.

In Case of Need: a term used of the agent of representative of a shipper abroad, to whom a bank may apply for instructions, when the shipper directs.

Inherent Vice: a condition causing damage to merchandise by reason of its own inherent defects.

Insurance Certificate: see Ocean Marine Insurance Policy.

Jettison: the throwing overboard of part of a craft's cargo or equipment in order to save the remainder.

Letter of Credit-Commercial: a letter addressed by a bank, at the insurance and responsibility of a buyer of merchandise, to a seller, authorizing him to draw drafts to a stipulated amount under specified terms and undertaking conditionally or unconditionally to provide eventual payment for drafts.

(a) Confirmed Irrevocable Letter of Credit: a letter to which has been added the responsibility of a bank other than the issuing bank.

(b) **Irrevocable Letter of Credit:** a letter of credit which can neither be modified not cancelled without the agreement of all concerned.

(c) **Revocable Letter of Credit:** a revocable credit may be modified or cancelled at any time without notice to the beneficiary. However, payment or acceptances made by the negotiating bank within the terms of the credit prior to receipt of cancellation notice from the issuing bank validly bind all concerned parties.

(d) **Revolving Credit:** a letter from the issuing bank notifying a seller of merchandise that the amount involved when utilized will again become available, usually under the same terms and without issuance of another letter.

Special Clauses:

(a) **Red Clause:** a clause authorizing the drawing of clean drafts without documents accompanied by a statement that pertinent shipping documents will be furnished later.

(b) **Telegraphic Transfer Clause:** a clause including an undertaking by the issuing bank to pay the draft amount to the negotiating bank upon receipt of an authenticated cablegram from the latter indicating it has received the required documents.

Letter of Credit—Traveler's (Circular): a letter addressed by a bank to its corresponding banks authorizing them to honor drafts of the holder to the amount of credit.

Lighterage: the cost of loading or unloading a vessel by barges.

Lloyd's Registry: an organization maintained for the classification of ships in order that interested parties may know the quality and condition of the vessels offered for insurance or employment.

Ltd.—Limited: originally a British abbreviation denoting a company that limits the owner's liability to the amount of invested or subscribed capital.

M/V: motor vessel.

Mate's Receipt: receipt by the mate of a vessel acknowledging receipt of cargo. This type of receipt is not usually encountered except in case of chartered vessels.

Maturity Date: the date when a note, draft, or acceptance becomes due for payment.

Ocean Marine Insurance Policy: an indemnity contract designed to reimburse an insured for the loss because of unforeseen circumstances or damage to merchandise shipped. The basic marine policy insures transportation perils but can be amended to cover additional hazards.

(a) **Open Policy:** a marine insurance contract in which the insurer agrees that all shipments moving at the insured's risk are automatically covered under the policy and the insured agrees to report the shipments and to pay premium thereon to the insurer.

(b) **Special Marine Policy:** sometimes referred to as a marine insurance certificate—this is a policy covering a specific shipment, most frequently used to provide evidence of insurance.

Marine Insurance Terms:

(a) **Average:** a term of marine insurance meaning loss or damage.

(b) **General Average:** a loss arising from a voluntary sacrifice made of any part of the vessel or cargo, or expenditure to prevent loss of the whole and for the benefit of all persons at interest. The loss is apportioned not only among all the shippers including those whose poverty is lost, but also to the vessel itself, Until the assessment is paid, a lien lies against the entire cargo.

(c **Particular Average:** a marine insurance term meaning a partial loss, or damage.

(d) **With Average (W.A.) or With Particular Average (W.P.A.):** provides protection for partial loss by perils of the sea it amounts to a certain percentage, usually 3 percent of the insured value. The 3 percent, a franchise, is not a deductible percentage, rather the minimum amount of claim. The franchise does not apply when a vessel is involved in a fire, stranding, sinking, burning, or a collision, or in General Average losses.

(e) **Free of Particular Average, American Conditions—(FPAAC):** covers only those losses directly resulting from fire, stranding, sinking or collision of the vessel.

(f) **Free of Particular Average, English Conditions—(FPAEC):** this resembles PFAAC except that partial loss resulting from any peril of the sea becomes recoverable when the vessel has been stranded, sunk, burned, on fire or in a collision with the insured cargo aboard. The actual damage need not directly result from these specified perils—only that one of them has occurred.

(g) **Average Irrespective of Percentage:** the broadest "with Average" clause permits full recovery, regardless of percentage, or of partial losses due to perils of the sea.

The foregoing clauses may be broadened by adding coverage for theft, pilferage, non-delivery, breakage, or leakage, for example.

(h) **All Risks:** the broadest marine insurance coverage insures merchandise against all risks of physical loss or damage from any external cause which may arise. Delay, deterioration, loss of market, inherent vice, capture and seizure, war, strikes, riots and civil commotion represent various exclusions.

(i) **Warehouse to Warehouse:** a common marine insurance term referring to coverage which attaches to the goods upon their leaving the shipper's warehouse. It continues during the ordinary course of transit until delivery of the merchandise at the consignee's warehouse, within specified time limits.

(j) **Both to Blame Collision Clause:** this constitutes protection against a disclaimer of liability and it appears in some bills of lading when damage results from negligence of both vessels that are parties to an accident.

(k) **Strikes, Riots, and Civil Commotion—(S.R. & C.C.):** the marine policy does not cover the risks of strikes, riots, and civil commotion, except on endorsement.

(l) **Free of Capture and Seizure—(F.C. & S.):** this clause excludes the risks of war and warlike operations from the marine policy.

(m) **War Risk:** although not covered under any of the foregoing terms of average, the risks of war may be covered under a separate open War Risk only Policy or by endorsement of the Special or Individual Marine Policy.

Open Policy: See Ocean Marine Insurance Policy.

Par of Exchange: the equivalent of the unit of money in one country expressed in the currency of another country, using gold as the standard value.

Parcel Post Receipt: a signed postal acknowledgment of delivery of a shipment made by parcel post.

Particular Average: see Ocean Marine Insurance.

Payee: the person to whom a draft or check is made payable.

Per Mille: per 1,000 a basis upon which quotations are frequently made in foreign countries, instead of fractional percentage, e.g., one per mille (1°/00) is equal to one tenth per cent (1/10%).

Per Pro (p.pl): an abbreviation for per procuration, applied to the signature of an authorized agent on behalf of his principal.

Perils of the Sea: a marine insurance policy phrase referring to accidents or casualties of the sea which a simple marine policy insures.

Protest: this represents a certificate of dishonor provided by a consul, vice consul, notary public, or other person so authorized when an instrument presented for acceptance or payment is refused.

Pty: "proprietary," signifying a privately owned company in Great Britain and the Commonwealth.

Rate of Exchange: an expression signifying the basis upon which the money of one country will be exchanged for that of another.

Rebate Rate: the rate per cent deductible if a bill of exchange or draft is paid before its maturity date.

Red Clause: see Letters of Credit.

S.A.: Sociedad Anonima, Societe Anonyme and for Societa Anomima, joint stock companies in Spanish-and-French-speaking countries and Italy, respectively.

S/S: steamship

S. en C.: Sociedad en Comandita, a silent partnership in Spanish-speaking countries.

Second of Exchange: the duplicate of a draft drawn in original and duplicate.

Security Agreement: an agreement that creates or provides for security interest.

Security Interest: indicates an interest in personal property or fixtures securing payment or performance of an obligation.

Ship's Manifest: a written instrument duly signed by the captain, containing a true list of the individual shipments comprising a vessel's cargo.

Sight Draft: a draft payable upon presentation to the drawee.

Specific Duty: see Duty.

Tare: the weight of the container or package holding merchandise.

Telegraphic Transfer Clause: see Letters of Credit.

Tenor: the term fixed for payment of a draft.

Time Draft: a draft maturing at a fixed or terminable future date.

Transit Shipment: a term designating a shipment destined for an interior point or a place best reached by reshipment from another port.

Trust Receipt: a written agreement, signed and delivered by the trustee in a trust receipt transaction, designating the goods, documents or instruments concerned and signifying that the entruster has a security interest therein.

Usance: the same as tenor.

W.A. (W.P.A.): With Average. (With Particular Average.)

Warehouse Receipt: a receipt supplied by a warehouseman for goods he has placed in storage.

  (a) Negotiable: transferable by endorsement and requiring surrender of an receipt to the warehouseman for delivery of the goods.

(b) **Non-Negotiable:** indicates the non-transferability of goods will be delivered only to the person named therein or to a third party only on written order, i.e., delivery order.

Weight:

(a) **Gross:** generally, the total weight of the shipped merchandise including all containers and packing material.

(b) **Legal:** generally, the weight of the merchandise plus the immediate container, a definition that varies somewhat by country.

(c) **Net:** generally, the weight of the merchandise unpacked, exclusive of containers. This definition also varies somewhat in other countries.

Wharfage: a charge assessed by docks for the handling of incoming or outgoing merchandise.

Without Recourse: a form of endorsement specifying that the endorser does not agree to pay a dishonored instrument, it does not otherwise affect the general warranties by an endorser.

Bibliography

PAMPHLETS

All of the following are introductory pamphlets that are either free or cost only a few dollars.

A Basic Guide to Exporting. September 1986. U. S. Department of Commerce, Washington, D. C.

A Business Guide to the Near East and North Africa. 1981. U. S. Department of Commerce, Washington, D. C.

Export Information Services for U. S. Business Firms. U. S. Department of Commerce, Washington, D. C.

Importing into the United States. June 1986. U. S. Customs Service, Washington, D. C.

International Countertrade: A Guide for Managers and Executives. Pompiliu Verzariu, November 1984. U. S. Department of Commerce, Washington, D. C.

Overseas Export Promotion Calendar. October 1986–December 1987. U. S. Department of Commerce, Washington, D. C.

Paying for Imports with Foreign Currencies. American Importers Association, 420 Lexington, Avenue, New York NY 10017.

Source Book: The "How To" Guide for Importers and Exporters. UNZ & Co., 190 Baldwin Avenue, Jersey City, NJ 08306.

A Summary of U. S. Export Administration Regulations, Revised June 1985. U. S. Department of Commerce, Washington, D. C.

U. S. Importing Requirements. U. S. Customs Service, Washington, D. C.

BOOKS

The following books provide the beginner with a solid nucleus for an import/export library.

Americans Abroad. 1984. John Z. Kysler, Praiger Publishers, New York, NY.

Building an Import Export Business. 1987. Kenneth D. Weiss, John Wiley & Sons, Inc., New York, NY.

Do's and Taboos Around the World. 1985. Roger E. Axtell, John Wiley & Sons, Inc., New York, NY.

Exportise. 1983. Edited by Peg Pollard, The Small Business Foundation of America, Inc., Boston, MA.

Going International. 1985. Lennie Copeland and Lewis Griggs, Random House, Inc., New York, NY.

High-Tech Exporters Sourcebook. 1986. Land Grant LGC Publishing, Brooklyn, NY.

DIRECTORIES AND BIBLIOGRAPHIES

The following are reference works with which the beginner should be familiar.

American Export Register. Thomas Publishing Co., One Penn Plaza, New York, NY 10010.
Lists over 155,000 exporters, along with the product each handles. Good reference for the beginner.

Business International Corporation Master Key Index. Quarterly with annual accumulations. One Dag Hammarskjold Plaza, New York, NY.
Contains research reports, management reports, and a periodicals list. Some of these reports are quite helpful because they contain surveys of product categories in numerous countries.

Custom House Guide. North American Publishing Company, 134 N. 13th, Philadelphia, PA 191907.
Most important references for the potential importer. Lists the text of the Tariff Schedules of the United States, plus complete information on Customs brokers, steamship lines, and agents. Monthly supplement entitled "American Import and Export Bulletin" contains important news and current customs regulations.

Exporter's Encyclopedia. Annual. Dun & Bradstreet International, One Diamond Hill Road, Murray Hill, NJ 07924.
Most comprehensive reference work for the potential exporter. Gives important marketing, shipping, banking, communications, and exchange regulations for most of the countries of the world. Has a semimonthly news sheet entitled "World Meeting" on current events related to international trade.

Foreign Commerce Hand Book. 17th Edition, 1981. Chamber of Commerce of the U. S., Washington, D. C.
Useful and inexpensive guide to foreign commerce sources. Very complete and easy to use for the beginner.

BOOKS—GENERAL

The following provides the beginner with assistance in establishing a business when he or she has never run one before.

JOSEPH MANCUSO, *How to Start, Finance and Manage Your Own Small Business*. 1986. Englewood Cliffs, NJ: Prentice-Hall.

JOHN R. TAYLOR, *How to Start and Succeed in a Business of Your Own*. 1978. Englewood Cliffs, NJ: Prentice-Hall.

BARBARA BRABEC, *Homemade Money: A Definitive Guide to Success in Home Business*. 1978. White Hall, VA: Betterway Publications.

BERNARD KAMOROFF, *Small-Time Operator—How to Start Your Own Small Business, Keep Your Books, Pay Your Taxes and Stay Out of Trouble*. Laytonville, CA: Bells Springs Publishing.

WILLIAM DELANY, *So You Want to Start a Business*. 1984. Englewood Cliffs, NJ: Prentice-Hall.

NEED FURTHER ASSISTANCE?

If, after reading this book, you need further help in developing an import or export operation, you may contact:

Mr. Howard Goldsmith
Intercontinental Trade Specialists
17340 Boswell Place
Granada Hills, CA 91344
(818) 368-8465

Consultations in person or by phone are available. Assistance is offered on a project, open account, or retainer basis. Fees charged are predetermined by mutual agreement.

Seminars are available to organizations on beginning and advanced aspects of international trade (e.g., marketing, operations, finance, and travel preparation). Contact Intercontinental Trade Specialists to discuss which program would be best for your organization.

Index